KEY INDICATORS
FOR ASIA AND THE PACIFIC
2017
48TH EDITION

ASIAN DEVELOPMENT BANK

6 ADB Avenue, Mandaluyong City, 1550 Metro Manila, Philippines
Tel +63 2 632 4444; Fax +63 2 636 2444
www.adb.org

ISBN 978-92-9257-911-1 (Print), 978-92-9257-912-8 (e-ISBN)
Publication Stock No. FLS178890-2
http://dx.doi.org/10.22617/FLS178890-2

Notes:
In this publication, "$" refers to US dollars.
Corrigenda to ADB publications may be found at http://www.adb.org/publications/corrigenda
ADB recognizes "China" as the People's Republic of China; "Hong Kong" as Hong Kong, China; "Korea" as the Republic of Korea; "Vietnam" as Viet Nam; and "United States of America" and "USA" as the United States.

Foreword

The *Key Indicators for Asia and the Pacific 2017* (*Key Indicators 2017*), the 48th edition of this series, provides statistics on a comprehensive set of economic, financial, social, environmental, and Sustainable Development Goal (SDG) indicators for the 48 regional members of the Asian Development Bank (ADB).

As the data in this publication demonstrates, Asia and the Pacific's development continues to be impressive on many fronts. Between 2002 and 2013, approximately 707 million people in the region moved out of extreme poverty, based on the $1.90 a day poverty line. The region's share of global GDP increased from 29% to 41%, in terms of purchasing power parity, between 2000 and 2016. Energy efficiency, measured as GDP per unit of energy use, improved 1.5% annually between 2000 and 2014. And the maternal mortality ratio was halved between 2000 and 2015. As statistics on participation in global value chains show, the region has cushioned the impact of the slowdown in global trade observed since 2011 by increasing the domestic content of its exports and relying more on domestic absorption as a driver of growth.

While the region has done remarkably well, several challenges remain. Around 330 million people in Asia and the Pacific still live in extreme poverty. Economic growth in the region has been accompanied by a rise in carbon dioxide emissions and a decline in renewable freshwater resources per capita. The region's population is gradually aging, and by 2050 it is estimated that for the first time in history there will be roughly as many people in the region over the age of 65 as under the age of 15.

Meeting the region's development challenges requires policy makers from across Asia and the Pacific to engage in partnerships and formulate policies that promote the common goal of continued socioeconomic progress. In turn, the effective monitoring of these policies requires the availability of timely, disaggregated, and reliable data, a particularly challenging task within the framework of the SDGs. Doing so entails the collection and compilation of data for 232 global indicators with disaggregation across several domains such as sex, age, race, ethnicity, income level, migratory status, disability, and geographic location. To fulfill these data needs, investments in statistical methodology, technological innovations in data collection methods, and a global commitment to strengthened statistical capacity in developing economies are needed.

One such effort is a recent ADB technical assistance project that supports the development of methodological guidelines for data collection on asset ownership from a gender perspective under the Evidence and Data for Gender Equality (EDGE) initiative of the United Nations Statistics Division. A summary of findings from EDGE pilot surveys in Georgia, Mongolia, and the Philippines is presented in this publication.

We appreciate the continued cooperation of our statistical partners in regional member economies who have provided the most recent data from their official sources, as well as international agencies from which the data in many of the publication's tables are sourced. We hope that *Key Indicators* will remain a valuable resource for information on key development issues across the region for a wide audience including policy makers, development practitioners, government officials, researchers, students, and the general public. As always, we welcome feedback from our users on both the content and structure of the publication.

Takehiko Nakao
President
Asian Development Bank

Acknowledgments

The *Key Indicators for Asia and the Pacific 2017* (*Key Indicators 2017*) was prepared by the Development Economics and Indicators Division (ERDI) of the Economic Research and Regional Cooperation Department (ERCD), Asian Development Bank (ADB) under the overall supervision of Rana Hasan.

Contributions from ERCD's statistical partners—regional members and international organizations—who shared their data for the statistical tables on the Sustainable Development Goals (SDG) indicators (Part I), regional tables (Part II), global value chains (Part III), and country tables are greatly appreciated. ADB resident missions in Afghanistan, Armenia, Azerbaijan, Bangladesh, Bhutan, Cambodia, the People's Republic of China, Georgia, India, Indonesia, Kazakhstan, the Kyrgyz Republic, the Lao People's Democratic Republic, Mongolia, Myanmar, Nepal, Pakistan, Papua New Guinea, Sri Lanka, Tajikistan, Thailand, Timor-Leste, Turkmenistan, Uzbekistan, and Viet Nam provided support in compiling the data from their respective countries. ADB's Pacific Liaison and Coordination Office, Philippines Country Office, and Pacific Subregional Office also provided help in data compilation. We also appreciate the continuing cooperation of the governments and other international agencies.

The statistical tables including the country tables were prepared by ERDI staff and consultants under the general guidance of Kaushal Joshi, Mahinthan Joseph Mariasingham, Arturo Martinez Jr., and Lakshman Nagraj Rao, with the technical assistance of Pamela Lapitan, Melissa Pascua, and Eric Suan. The research team included Raymond Adofina, Glenita Amoranto, Nalwino Billones, Eileen Capilit, Clemence Fatima Cruz, Ephraim Cuya, Criselda De Dios, Eduardo Dulay Jr., Josephine Ferre, Karen Firshan, Ma. Laarni Revilla, Lea Rotairo, Iva Sebastian, Christian Flora Mae Soco, Rea Jean Tabaco, Orlee Velarde, Priscille Villanueva, and Ma. Josefina Villena. Proofreading of statistical tables was done with the assistance of Ma. Roselia Babalo, Aileen Gatson, and Oth Marulou Gagni. The analysis of SDG indicators was prepared by Jose Ramon Albert and Lakshman Nagraj Rao, while the SDG data chapter on compilation of sex-disaggregated data on asset ownership was prepared by Hema Swaminathan in collaboration with Kaushal Joshi and Arturo Martinez Jr. The analysis of regional trends was done by Kevin Donahue, Kaushal Joshi, and Arturo Martinez Jr. The statistical tables and analytical reports for parts I and II were reviewed by Kaushal Joshi, Mahinthan Joseph Mariasingham, Arturo Martinez Jr., and Lakshman Nagraj Rao. Mahinthan Joseph Mariasingham and Julieta Magallanes, in collaboration with John Arvin Bernabe, Donald Jay Bertulfo, Carlos Vincent Chua, Nina Ashley Dela Cruz, Paul Neilmer Feliciano, Janine Elora Lazatin, and Dianne Lara Monis produced statistical tables on global value chains. Cherry Lynn Zafaralla edited the publication with the assistance of Lawrence Casiraya and Layla Amar as proofreaders.

Rhommell Rico designed the cover and graphics for the publication, led the typesetting process, and provided technical support for the preparation of all dissemination materials. Joe Mark Ganaban and Joseph Manglicmot assisted in typesetting. The publishing team of the ADB Department of External Relations (DER) performed an overall compliance check. The Office of Information Systems and Technology staff provided database management and technology support, while the Logistics Management Unit of the Office of Administrative Services facilitated the timely and smooth production of *Key Indicators 2017*. Erik William Churchill and Sean James Crowley, assisted by DER staff, organized the dissemination activities.

Yasuyuki Sawada
Chief Economist and
Director General

Contents

Sustainable Development Goals - Boxes and Figures

Social Indicators

Regional Trends and Tables - Boxes and Figures

PART III - Global Value Chains

Asia's Emerging Role in International Production Sharing Agreements: From Factories in Asia to Markets in Asia

Tables

Statistical Partners

The preparation and publication of the *Key Indicators for Asia and the Pacific 2017* would not have been possible without the support, assistance, and cooperation of partners in the regional members of the Asian Development Bank (ADB) and in international, private, and nongovernment organizations. These partners—who shared their data, knowledge, expertise, and other information—help provide ADB, policy makers, and other data users with a better understanding of the performance of countries in Asia and the Pacific, so that better policies can be formulated to improve the quality of life of people in the region.

REGIONAL MEMBERS

Afghanistan	Central Statistics Organization (http://cso.gov.af/en) Da Afghanistan Bank (http://www.centralbank.gov.af) Ministry of Finance (http://mof.gov.af/en)
Armenia	Central Bank of Armenia (https://www.cba.am/en) National Statistical Service of the Republic of Armenia (http://www.armstat.am/en)
Australia	Australian Bureau of Statistics (http://www.abs.gov.au) Department of Industry, Innovation and Science (http://www.industry.gov.au) Reserve Bank of Australia (http://www.rba.gov.au)
Azerbaijan	Central Bank of the Republic of Azerbaijan (http://en.cbar.az) State Statistical Committee of the Republic of Azerbaijan (http://www.stat.gov.az/?lang=en)
Bangladesh	Bangladesh Bank (http://www.bb.org.bd) Bangladesh Bureau of Statistics (http://www.bbs.gov.bd) Ministry of Finance (http://www.mof.gov.bd/en)
Bhutan	Ministry of Finance (http://www.mof.gov.bt) Ministry of Labor and Human Resources (http://www.molhr.gov.bt) National Statistics Bureau (http://www.nsb.gov.bt) Royal Monetary Authority of Bhutan (http://www.rma.org.bt)
Brunei Darussalam	Autoriti Monetari Brunei Darussalam (http://www.ambd.gov.bn) Department of Economic Planning and Development (http://www.depd.gov.bn) Ministry of Finance (http://www.mof.gov.bn/)
Cambodia	Ministry of Economy and Finance (http://www.mef.gov.kh) National Bank of Cambodia (http://www.nbc.org.kh) National Institute of Statistics (http://www.nis.gov.kh)

China, People's Republic of	National Bureau of Statistics of China (http://www.stats.gov.cn/english) The People's Bank of China (http://www.pbc.gov.cn) State Administration of Foreign Exchange (http://www.safe.gov.cn)
Cook Islands	Cook Islands Statistics Office (http://www.mfem.gov.ck/statistics) Ministry of Finance and Economic Management (http://www.mfem.gov.ck)
Fiji	Bureau of Statistics (http://www.statsfiji.gov.fj) Reserve Bank of Fiji (http://www.rbf.gov.fj/)
Georgia	Ministry of Finance of Georgia (http://mof.ge/en/) National Bank of Georgia (http://www.nbg.gov.ge) National Statistics Office of Georgia (http://www.geostat.ge)
Hong Kong, China	Census and Statistics Department (http://www.censtatd.gov.hk) Hong Kong Monetary Authority (http://www.hkma.gov.hk)
India	Central Statistics Office (http://mospi.nic.in) Ministry of Finance (http://finmin.nic.in) Reserve Bank of India (http://www.rbi.org.in)
Indonesia	Bank Indonesia (http://www.bi.go.id/web) Badan Pusat Statistik-Statistics Indonesia (http://www.bps.go.id) Ministry of Energy and Mineral Resources (http://www.esdm.go.id) PT Pertamina (Persero) (http://barata.com/en/)
Japan	Bank of Japan (http://www.boj.or.jp/en) Economic and Social Research Institute (http://www.esri.go.jp) Japan Customs (http://www.customs.go.jp/english/) Japan Statistics Bureau (http://www.stat.go.jp/english) Ministry of Economy, Trade and Industry (http://www.meti.go.jp) Ministry of Finance (http://www.mof.go.jp) The Institute of Energy Economics, Japan (http://oil-info.ieej.or.jp/)
Kazakhstan	Committee on Statistics, Ministry of National Economy of the Republic of Kazakhstan (formerly Agency of Statistics of the Republic of Kazakhstan) (http://www.stat.gov.kz) National Bank of Kazakhstan (http://www.nationalbank.kz)
Kiribati	Kiribati National Statistics Office (http://www.mfed.gov.ki/statistics/)

Korea, Republic of	Bank of Korea (http://bok.or.kr/eng/engMain.action) Ministry of Strategy and Finance (http://english.mosf.go.kr) Statistics Korea (http://kostat.go.kr)
Kyrgyz Republic	National Bank of the Kyrgyz Republic (http://www.nbkr.kg) National Statistical Committee of the Kyrgyz Republic (http://www.stat.kg)
Lao People's Democratic Republic	Bank of the Lao PDR (http://www.bol.gov.la) Lao Statistics Bureau (http://www.lsb.gov.la) Ministry of Finance (http://www.mof.gov.la)
Malaysia	Bank Negara Malaysia (http://www.bnm.gov.my) Department of Statistics, Malaysia (http://www.dosm.gov.my) Ministry of Finance Malaysia (http://www.treasury.gov.my)
Maldives	National Bureau of Statistics (http://statisticsmaldives.gov.mv/) Maldives Monetary Authority (http://www.mma.gov.mv) Ministry of Finance and Treasury (http://www.finance.gov.mv)
Marshall Islands	Economic Policy, Planning and Statistics Office (http://rmi.prism.spc.int/)
Micronesia, Federated States of	Division of Statistics (http://www.fsmstats.fm/) Department of Resources and Development (http://www.fsmrd.fm/)
Mongolia	Bank of Mongolia (http://www.mongolbank.mn/eng) National Statistics Office of Mongolia (http://en.nso.mn)
Myanmar	Central Bank of Myanmar (http://www.cbm.gov.mm/) Central Statistical Organization (https://www.csostat.gov.mm) Ministry of National Planning and Economic Development (https://www.mnped.gov.mm)
Nauru	Ministry of Finance and Economic Planning (http://www.naurugov.nr) Nauru Bureau of Statistics (http://www.spc.int/prism/country/nr/stats)
Nepal	Central Bureau of Statistics (http://cbs.gov.np) Ministry of Finance (http://www.mof.gov.np) Nepal Rastra Bank (http://www.nrb.org.np)
New Zealand	Ministry of Business, Innovation and Employment (www.mbie.govt.nz) Reserve Bank of New Zealand (http://www.rbnz.govt.nz) Statistics New Zealand (http://www.stats.govt.nz)

Pakistan	Ministry of Finance (http://www.finance.gov.pk) Pakistan Bureau of Statistics (http://www.pbs.gov.pk) State Bank of Pakistan (http://www.sbp.org.pk)
Palau	Bureau of Budget and Planning, Ministry of Finance (http://palaugov.pw/budgetandplanning/)
Papua New Guinea	Bank of Papua New Guinea (http://www.bankpng.gov.pg) Department of Treasury (http://www.treasury.gov.pg) National Statistical Office (http://www.nso.gov.pg)
Philippines	Bangko Sentral ng Pilipinas (http://www.bsp.gov.ph) Bureau of Local Government Finance (http://www.blgf.gov.ph) Bureau of the Treasury (http://www.treasury.gov.ph) Department of Budget and Management (http://www.dbm.gov.ph) Department of Energy (http://www.doe.gov.ph) Philippine Statistics Authority (http://www.psa.gov.ph)
Samoa	Samoa Bureau of Statistics (http://www.sbs.gov.ws) Central Bank of Samoa (http://www.cbs.gov.ws)
Singapore	Department of Statistics (http://www.singstat.gov.sg) International Enterprise Singapore (http://www.iesingapore.gov.sg) Ministry of Finance (http://www.mof.gov.sg) Ministry of Manpower (http://www.mom.gov.sg) Ministry of Trade and Industry (http://www.mti.gov.sg) Monetary Authority of Singapore (http://www.mas.gov.sg)
Solomon Islands	Central Bank of Solomon Islands (http://www.cbsi.com.sb) Solomon Islands National Statistics Office (http://www.statistics.gov.sb)
Sri Lanka	Central Bank of Sri Lanka (http://www.cbsl.gov.lk) Department of Census and Statistics (http://www.statistics.gov.lk)
Taipei,China	Central bank of Taipei,China (http://www.cbc.gov.tw) Directorate-General of Budget, Accounting and Statistics (http://eng.dgbas.gov.tw) Ministry of Finance (http://www.mof.gov.tw)
Tajikistan	National Bank of Tajikistan (http://www.nbt.tj) Agency on Statistics under President of the Republic of Tajikistan (http://www.stat.tj)

Thailand	Bank of Thailand (http://www.bot.or.th) Ministry of Finance (http://www2.mof.go.th) National Economic and Social Development Board (http://eng.nesdb.go.th/nesdb_en) National Statistical Office (http://web.nso.go.th)
Timor-Leste	Central Bank of Timor-Leste (http://www.bancocentral.tl) Ministry of Finance (http://www.mof.gov.tl) General Directorate of Statistics (http://www.statistics.gov.tl)
Tonga	Ministry of Finance and National Planning (http://www.finance.gov.to) National Reserve Bank of Tonga (http://www.reservebank.to) Department of Statistics (http://www.spc.int/prism/tonga)
Turkmenistan	Central Bank of Turkmenistan (www.cbt.tm/en) Ministry of Finance (http://www.minfin.gov.tm/) National Institute of State Statistics and Information State Statistics Committee of Turkmenistan (http://www.stat.gov.tm)
Tuvalu	Central Statistics Division (http://www.spc.int/prism/tuvalu)
Uzbekistan	Cabinet of Ministers (http://www.gov.uz/en/government) Central Bank of Uzbekistan (http://www.cbu.uz) Ministry of Finance of the Republic of Uzbekistan (http://www.mf.gov.uz) State Committee of the Republic of Uzbekistan on Statistics (http://www.stat.uz)
Vanuatu	Department of Finance and Treasury (https://doft.gov.vu) Reserve Bank of Vanuatu (http://www.rbv.gov.vu) Vanuatu National Statistics Office (http://www.vnso.gov.vu)
Viet Nam	General Statistics Office (http://www.gso.gov.vn) Ministry of Finance (http://www.mof.gov.vn) State Bank of Vietnam (http://www.sbv.gov.vn)

INTERNATIONAL, PRIVATE, AND NONGOVERNMENT ORGANIZATIONS

Association of Southeast Asian Nations
Australian Institute of Petroleum
CEIC Data
European Bank for Reconstruction and Development
Food and Agriculture Organization of the United Nations
Graduate School USA, Pacific Islands Training Initiative
The Institute of Energy Economics, Japan, The Oil Information Center
International Energy Agency
International Labour Organization
International Monetary Fund
International Telecommunication Union
Interstate Statistical Committee of the Commonwealth of Independent States
Joint United Nations Programme on HIV/AIDS
Organisation for Economic Co-operation and Development
Pacific and Virgin Islands Training Initiatives, Graduate School USA
Secretariat of the Pacific Community
Transparency International
UNESCO Institute for Statistics
United Nations Children's Fund
United Nations Conference on Trade and Development
United Nations Department of Economic and Social Affairs
United Nations Development Programme
United Nations Economic Commission for Europe
United Nations Economic and Social Commission for Asia and the Pacific
United Nations Educational, Scientific and Cultural Organization
United Nations Environment Programme
United Nations Human Settlements Programme
United Nations Population Division
United Nations Statistics Division
United Nations World Tourism Organization
United States Census Bureau
United States Bureau of Economic Analysis
World Bank
World Health Organization
WHO/UNICEF Joint Monitoring Programme (JMP) for Water Supply and Sanitation
World Trade Organization

Guide for Users

The *Key Indicators for Asia and the Pacific 2017 (Key Indicators 2017)* has the following structure. The Highlights section presents key messages from various parts of the publication. Part I comprises the data tables and brief analyses of trends of select indicators for the Sustainable Development Goals (SDGs) for which data are available. The indicators are presented according to the United Nations SDG global indicator framework. The last section of Part I discusses the challenges of compiling sex-disaggregated data on asset ownership and how this measurement issue can be addressed.

Part II consists of 98 statistical tables grouped into eight themes: People; Economy and Output; Money, Finance, and Prices; Globalization; Transport and Communications; Energy and Electricity; Environment; and Government and Governance. Each theme is further divided into subtopics. Accompanying tables in Part II contain indicators related to a subtopic.

The SDGs and themes in Parts I and II start with a short commentary including charts and followed by tables describing the status of economies with respect to selected targets and key trends of selected indicators.

The scales used in some figures and charts are adjusted to visually show relatively small numbers. In addition, figures and charts appearing in this publication are also provided with a digital object identifier to facilitate easier access to data.

The accompanying statistical tables are presented for 48 economies of the Asia and Pacific region that are members of the Asian Development Bank (ADB). The term country, used interchangeably with economy, is not intended to make any judgment as to the legal or other status of any territory or area. The 48 economies have been broadly grouped into developing member economies and developed member economies aligned with the operational effectiveness of ADB's regional departments. The latter refer exclusively to the three economies of Australia, Japan, and New Zealand. Based on ADB's regional operations, the remaining 45 developing member economies are further divided into five groups based on ADB's operational regions: Central and West Asia, East Asia, South Asia, Southeast Asia, and the Pacific. Economies are listed alphabetically per economy group. The term "regional members" used in some tables refers to all 48 regional members of ADB, both developing and developed. Indicators are shown for the most recent year (usually 2016) or period for which data are available and, in most tables, for an earlier year or period (usually 2000).

In addition to the discussion of trends with respect to select SDG indicators, Part I features a section that focuses on the challenges associated with collecting and compiling sex-disaggregated statistics on asset ownership, arising from the lack of standardized guidelines and methodologies. Furthermore, both Parts I and II present several discussion boxes on important measurement issues.

Part III contains select indicators for depicting Asia and the Pacific economies' participation in global value chains (GVCs), and their sector-specific comparative advantage in terms of exports. Typical indicators of international trade that mainly refer to the value of exports and imports of goods and services can be traced back to the traditional trading of final goods across borders. Today's globalization has made many economies more open to trade, which provides opportunities to scale up production among firms, and allocate their resources more efficiently by moving their production chains across borders where there is comparative advantage. GVC statistics provide detailed information on cross-border trading transactions of inputs used in different stages of production—from raw materials, to intermediate inputs, up to the final products purchased by the end consumers.

Data for the SDG indicators, regional tables, and country tables are mainly obtained from two sources: ADB's statistical partners in regional members, and international statistical agencies, particularly from the United Nations SDG Indicators Global Database. The indicators data presented in Part I are from either official country sources or the SDG Indicators Global Database, a master set of data prepared by the Department of Economic and Social Affairs of the United Nations Secretariat; and databases maintained by several international agencies that prepared one or more of the series of statistical indicators included in the SDG Indicators Global Database based on their area of expertise and as per their mandates. The data presented in Part III are mainly drawn from the ADB Multi Region Input–Output Tables Database.

Data produced and disseminated by international agencies are generally based on country data—data produced and disseminated by the country (including data adjusted by the country to meet international standards). However, it should be noted that national data may be compiled using national standards and practices and, as such, international agencies often adjust the data for international comparability. In such cases, data disseminated by the international agencies may differ from data from national sources. In other cases, when data for a specific year or set of years are not available; or they are available from multiple national sources (surveys, administrative data sources, and other sources); or when there are data quality issues, the relevant international agency may estimate the data. Some indicators are regularly produced for the purpose of global monitoring by the designated agency and there are no corresponding data at the country level (e.g., population below $1.90 at 2011 purchasing power parity). In other cases, the differences between data from national and international agencies may be because most recent and/or revised data available at the country level are not yet available with the relevant international agency. Some data gaps are filled by supplementing or deriving data collected through sample surveys financed and carried out by international agencies. For example, many of the health indicators are estimated using data from the Multiple Indicator Cluster Surveys and Demographic and Health Surveys.

ADB exercises due care and caution in collecting the data before publication. Nevertheless, data from international sources presented in this publication may differ from those available within countries. Thus, for a detailed description of how the indicators are compiled by the international agencies, readers may refer to the metadata available from databases of the individual international agencies; or the SDG Indicators Global Database website for metadata of SDG indicators. Comparable and standardized national data gathered through a robust data reporting mechanism of the international agencies should be the basis for all data in the global monitoring databases, and global indicators should be produced in full consultation with national statistical agencies.

Data obtained from the regional members are comparable to the extent that the regional members follow standard statistical concepts, definitions, and estimation methods recommended by the United Nations and other applicable international agencies. Nevertheless, regional members invariably develop and use their own concepts, definitions, and estimation methodologies to suit their individual circumstances, and these may not necessarily comply with recommended international standards. Thus, even though attempts are made to present the data in a comparable and uniform format, they are subject to variations in the statistical methods used by regional members, such that full comparability of data may not be possible. These variations are reflected in the footnotes of the statistical tables, or noted in the Data Issues and Comparability sections. Moreover, the aggregates for developing member economies and regional members shown in some tables are treated as approximations of the actual total or average, or growth rates, due to missing data from the primary source. No attempt has been made to impute the missing data.

The data published by ADB do not constitute any form of advice or recommendation. In case of any questions on the data, users of this publication are requested to make inquiries and seek advice from the appropriate data sources.

Fiscal Year

The data cutoff date for this issue is **August 2017**.

Twenty-three regional members have varying fiscal years not corresponding to the calendar year. Whenever the statistical series (for example, national accounts or government finance) are compiled on a fiscal year basis, these are presented under single-year captions corresponding to the period under which most of the fiscal year falls, as follows:

Regional Members	Fiscal Year	Year Caption
Afghanistan	21 December 2015 to 20 December 2016	2016
Cook Islands	1 July 2015 to 30 June 2016	2016
Brunei Darussalam (after 2002) Hong Kong, China India Japan Myanmar New Zealand Singapore	1 April 2016 to 31 March 2017	2016
Fiji	1 August 2015 to 31 July 2016	2016
Australia Bangladesh Bhutan Nauru Pakistan Samoa Tonga	1 July 2015 to 30 June 2016	2016
Nepal	16 July 2015 to 15 July 2016	2016
Lao People's Democratic Republic Marshall Islands Micronesia, Federated States of Palau Thailand	1 October 2015 to 30 September 2016	2016

Key Symbols

... data not available at cutoff date
– magnitude equals zero
0 or 0.0 magnitude is less than half of unit employed
* provisional, preliminary, estimate, budget figure
| marks break in series
> greater than
< less than
≥ greater than or equal to
≤ less than or equal to
na not applicable

Measurement Units

kg	kilogram
km	kilometer
kWh	kilowatt-hour
kt	kiloton
ktoe	kiloton of oil equivalent
m^3	cubic meter
mj	megajoule
teu	twenty-foot equivalent unit
$\mu g/m^3$	micrograms per cubic meter

Abbreviations

ABS	Australian Bureau of Statistics
ADB	Asian Development Bank
ADB SDBS	Asian Development Bank Statistical Database System
ASEAN	Association of Southeast Asian Nations
BBP	Bureau of Budget and Planning
BBS	Bangladesh Bureau of Statistics
BOJ	Bank of Japan
BOL	Bank of the the Lao People's Democratic Republic
BOP	balance of payments
BOT	Bank of Thailand
BPM5	Balance of Payments Manual, fifth edition
BPM6	Balance of Payments and International Investment Position Manual, sixth edition
BPNG	Bank of Papua New Guinea
BREE	Bureau of Resources and Energy Economics
CBA	Central Bank of the Republic of Azerbaijan
CBS	Central Bureau of Statistics

CBS	Central Bank of Samoa
CBSL	Central Bank of Sri Lanka
CIF	cost, insurance, and freight
CO_2	carbon dioxide
CPH	Census of Population and Housing
CPI	consumer price index
CSD	Central Statistics Division
CSO	Central Statistics Organization
CY	calendar year
DCS	Department of Census and Statistics
DGBAS	Directorate-General of Budget, Accounting and Statistics
DHS	Demographic and Health Survey
DMC	developing member country
DOS	Department of Statistics
DOTS	Direction of Trade Statistics
EDGE	Evidence and Data for Gender Equality
EPPSO	Economic Policy Planning and Statistics Office
ESCAP	Economic and Social Commission for Asia and the Pacific
ESY	Energy Statistics Yearbook
FAO	Food and Agriculture Organization of the United Nations
FDI	foreign direct investment
FOB	free on board; freight on board
FSM	Federated States of Micronesia
FVA	foreign value added
GCF	gross capital formation
GDP	gross domestic product
GDS	General Directorate Statistics
GEOSTAT	National Statistics Office of Georgia
GHG	greenhouse gas
GHO	Global Health Observatory
GNI	gross national income
GSO	General Statistics Office
GVC	global value chain
GWG	global working group
HDI	Human Development Index
HIV	human immunodeficiency virus
IAEG-SDGs	UN Inter-agency and Expert Group on SDG Indicators
IDA	International Development Association
IEA	International Energy Agency
ILO	International Labour Organization
IMF	International Monetary Fund
ISIC	International Standard Industrial Classification
ITU	International Telecommunication Union
J-REIT	Japan's real estate investment trust

JSB	Japan Statistics Bureau
KILM	Key Indicators of the Labour Market
Lao PDR	Lao People's Democratic Republic
LCU	local currency unit
LFS	Labor Force Survey
LFS-PUF	Labor Force Survey public use file
LSB	Lao Statistics Bureau
LVC	local value chain
MDG	Millennium Development Goal
MMA	Maldives Monetary Authority
MMFs	money market funds
MMR	maternal mortality ratio
MOF	Ministry of Finance
MOLAR	Ministry of Labor and Human Resources
MPI	multidimensional poverty index
NBC	National Bank of Cambodia
NBS	National Bureau of Statistics
NBS	Nauru Bureau of Statistics
NDCs	noncommunicable diseases
NESDB	National Economic and Social Development Board
NIS	National Institute of Statistics
NISSI	National Institute of State Statistics and Information
NPISH	nonprofit institutions serving households
NPL	nonperforming loan
NRB	Nepal Rastra Bank
NRBT	National Reserve Bank of Tonga
NSB	National Statistics Bureau
NSO	National Statistics Office; National Statistical Office
NSS	National Statistical Service
ODA	official development assistance
OECD	Organisation for Economic Co-operation and Development
PBS	Pakistan Bureau of Statistics
PITI-VITI	Pacific and Virgin Islands Training Initiatives
PLI	price level index
PPI	producer price index
PPP	purchasing power parity
PRISM	Pacific Regional Information System
PSA	Philippine Statistics Authority
R&D	research and development
RBV	Reserve Bank of Vanuatu
RMA	Royal Monetary Authority
RMI	Republic of the Marshall Islands
RMS	Results Measurement System
SBS	Samoa Bureau of Statistics

SCS	State Committee of the Republic of Uzbekistan on Statistics
SDG	Sustainable Development Goal
SDR	special drawing right
SDSN	Sustainable Development Solutions Network
SINSO	Solomon Islands National Statistical Office
SNA	System of National Accounts
SNZ	Statistics New Zealand
SPC	Secretariat of the Pacific Community
SSC	State Statistics Committee of Turkmenistan
SSC	State Statistical Committee of the Republic of Azerbaijan
SSIC	Singapore Standard Industrial Classification
TAJSTAT	Agency on Statistics under President of the Republic of Tajikistan
TDoS	Tonga Department of Statistics
TSIC	Thailand Standard Industrial Classification
UNAIDS	Joint United Nations Programme on HIV/AIDS
UNCTAD	United Nations Conference on Trade and Development
UNDESA	United Nations Department of Economic and Social Affairs
UNDP	United Nations Development Programme
UNEP	United Nations Environment Programme
UNESCO	United Nations Educational, Scientific and Cultural Organization
UNFPA	United Nations Population Fund
UNICEF	United Nations Children's Fund
UNIDO	United Nations Industrial Development Organization
UNODC	United Nations Office on Drugs and Crime
UNSD	United Nations Statistics Division
US	United States
VNSO	Vanuatu National Statistics Office
WDI	World Development Indicators
WHO	World Health Organization
WPP	World Population Prospects

Unless otherwise indicated, "$" refers to United States dollars.

HIGHLIGHTS

Part I. Sustainable Development Goals

The Sustainable Development Goals (SDGs), also known as the Global Goals, replaced the Millennium Development Goals (MDGs) in 2015. With 232 indicators embedded within 17 goals and 169 targets to be achieved by 2030, the SDGs are significantly more ambitious than the MDGs.

The discussion on SDGs is divided into two sections. The first section presents a snapshot of Asia and the Pacific for selected SDG indicators and is organized into five themes—People, Planet, Prosperity, Peace, and Partnership. The second section provides a summary of findings from pilot surveys conducted in Georgia, Mongolia, and the Philippines by ADB in collaboration with the national statistics offices of these countries, to support the development of standardized methods and guidelines for collecting sex-disaggregated data on asset ownership.

People

- Based on the latest data, an estimated 330 million people in Asia and the Pacific are still living on less than $1.90 a day (2011 purchasing power parity [PPP]), representing roughly 9% of the region's total population. This is a reduction from about 1.04 billion people that were living below the poverty line of $1.90 a day (2011 PPP) in 2002.

- The region has managed to significantly reduce the prevalence of undernourishment between 2000 and 2015. In 22 developing member economies, the prevalence of undernourishment is less than 10%.

- South Asia is the largest recipient of total official flows to the agriculture sector in the region, followed by Central and West Asia, Southeast Asia, East Asia, and the Pacific, respectively.

- Maternal mortality ratio declined in Asia and the Pacific from 264 deaths per 100,000 live births in 2000, to 123 deaths per 100,000 live births in 2015. Within the same time frame, under-five mortality declined from 70 deaths per 1,000 live births to 36 deaths per 1,000 live births. Neonatal mortality rate is estimated at 20 deaths per 1,000 live births in 2015, compared to 35 deaths per 1,000 live births in 2000.

- The proportion of teachers in primary education who have received at least the minimum organized teacher training exceeds 90% in 21 out of 32 economies of Asia and the Pacific with available data. For lower secondary education, the proportion exceeds 90% in 12 out of 20 regional economies. In upper secondary education, the proportion exceeds 90% in 10 out of 15 regional economies with available data.

- In Asia and the Pacific, significant gaps persist in ensuring women's full participation in political leadership. The share of women parliamentarians exceeded one-fifth in only one-third of economies, with Timor-Leste having the highest share at 38.5%.

Planet

- In 29 out of 44 economies of Asia and the Pacific with available data for 2015, at least 90% of the population are using safely managed drinking water services.

- In about half of the 43 economies of Asia and the Pacific with available data for 2015, at least 85% of the population are using safely managed sanitation services.
- The majority of the economies in Asia and the Pacific have experienced an increase in material footprint per capita since 2000.
- In more than half of the regional economies with available data, the annual urban mean concentration of fine suspended particles less than 2.5 microns in diameter (PM 2.5) is at least two-and-a-half times the maximum level set by the World Health Organization.
- Nearly three-fifths of all economies in Asia and the Pacific have strategies and regulatory mechanisms for disaster risk reduction and management, in line with the Sendai Framework.

Prosperity

- As of 2014, 20 out of 47 economies in Asia and the Pacific have universal access to electricity; in 11 regional economies, more than 20% of the population still do not have access to electricity.
- In 2014, 14 out of 46 economies reported at least 90% of their populations relying primarily on clean fuels and technology for cooking.
- Manufacturing value added per capita has grown by at least 50% between 2000 and 2016 in 25 out of 47 economies in the region.
- Based on latest available data over about a five year period, the bottom 40% of the population experienced faster growth in per capita income (or expenditure) than the national average in 13 out of 16 developing economies in the region.
- Based on latest data, less than 60% of adults in 19 out of 27 developing economies of Asia and the Pacific have an account at a bank or other financial institution.
- Research and development expenditures are rising in the Asia and Pacific economies; however, only four developing economies and three developed economies have research and development expenditures exceeding 1% of gross domestic product.

Peace

- The proportion of unsentenced detainees declined between 2005 and 2015 in 15 out of 31 regional economies with available data.
- In 17 out of 32 economies of Asia and the Pacific with available data, 25% or more of firms experienced at least one bribe payment request, while in Bhutan, Georgia, and the Federated States of Micronesia, the proportion of firms experiencing at least one bribe payment request was less than 5%.

Partnership

- In four-fifths of the 40 economies with available data in Asia and the Pacific, average financial and technical assistance through North–South, South–South, and triangular cooperation has risen between 2000–2007 and 2008–2015.
- More than 90% of regional economies have conducted a population census since 2007. Nearly half of the developing economies (23 out of 45) have prepared a national statistical plan to address the growing demand for statistics to monitor development.

Collecting Sex-Disaggregated Data on Asset Ownership—Evidence from Pilot Surveys

- There is empirical evidence suggesting that the ability of women to own and control assets is critical for securing gender equity and delivering on the sustainable development agenda. Despite this body of evidence, sex-disaggregated data needed for monitoring the progress on relevant targets in the 2030 Sustainable Development Agenda are scarce.

- The Evidence and Data for Gender Equality (EDGE) is a global initiative that seeks to develop methodological guidelines for collecting sex-disaggregated asset ownership and entrepreneurship data. The EDGE pilot surveys conducted by ADB in collaboration with the national statistics offices of Georgia, Mongolia, and the Philippines are powerful case studies as they have demonstrated that with the availability of standardized methods and guidelines, such data collection exercises are feasible.

- The pilot surveys have produced extremely rich data on asset ownership and control at the individual level, and have provided valuable lessons for the methodological guidelines for data collection. For the EDGE initiative to be sustainable in the long term, both data producers and data users must work together. There must be a conscious effort to ensure that such data is produced regularly, is of the highest quality, and is disseminated in a timely fashion. It is also incumbent on policy makers, researchers, and the larger development community to utilize this data to monitor the progress of and advocate for gender equality in the economic sphere.

Part II. Region at a Glance

The presentation of data on Regional Trends and Tables is grouped into eight themes—People; Economy and Output; Money, Finance, and Prices; Globalization; Transport and Communications; Energy and Electricity; Environment; and Government and Governance. Each of these themes includes a brief analysis of key trends of select indicators highlighting important recent developments in Asia and the Pacific.

People

- The combined populations of the 48 regional members of ADB exceeded 4 billion in 2016, accounting for nearly 55% of the global total. The two most populous economies in the world, the People's Republic of China and India, have populations of 1.4 billion and 1.3 billion, respectively. The list of most populous economies in the region also includes Indonesia (259 million), Pakistan (195 million), and Bangladesh (161 million).

- The annual population growth rate of Asia and the Pacific fell from 1.2% in 2000 to 1.0% in 2016, compared with a decline in the global average from 1.3% to 1.1%. The United Nations projects that Asia and the Pacific's share of the world population will fall to slightly less than half of the global total by 2050.

- The region's current population is relatively youthful, but it is aging. The most populous 5-year age cohort in Asia and the Pacific in 2000 comprised individuals aged 5–9 years; in 2016, it was individuals aged 25–29 years. By 2050, for the first time in history, there will be roughly as many people in Asia over the age of 65 as under the age of 15.

- While Asia and the Pacific's urbanization rate is increasing, fewer than half of all people in the region lived in urban areas in 2016, which is well below average urbanization rates of about 70%–80% in other regions of the world, excluding Africa.

- Measured by the Human Development Index (HDI), eight economies in Asia and the Pacific—Australia; Brunei Darussalam; Hong Kong, China; Japan; the Republic of Korea; New Zealand; Singapore; and Taipei,China—were among the "very high" tier of human development in 2015. At the same time, the region's economies that improved their HDI most significantly between 2000 and 2015 were those with relatively low HDI values initially, including Afghanistan, Cambodia, and Myanmar.

Economy and Output

- Asia and the Pacific accounted for 40.9% of global GDP in 2016, up from 29.4% in 2000. The People's Republic of China, India, and Japan accounted for about 70% of the region's total output in 2016.

- All but two of the 38 regional economies with available data experienced GDP growth between 2015 and 2016. During the review period, the most rapid average annual growth rates were in Nauru, Uzbekistan, Bangladesh, the Lao People's Democratic Republic, and Cambodia, respectively.

- Measured as a share of GDP at current prices, exports of goods and services declined across Asia and the Pacific from an (arithmetic) average of 47.1% in 2000 to 44.4% in 2016. Imports of goods and services also declined in Asia and the Pacific during the review period from an (arithmetic) average of 52.8% of GDP in 2000 to 48.6. % in 2016.

- Twenty-three of 36 regional economies for which data are available experienced an increase in gross capital formation as a percentage of GDP between 2000 and 2016. Capital formation comprises fixed investment in the form of buildings, civil engineering, machinery, and equipment.

Money, Finance, and Prices

- The (arithmetic) average of the region's consumer price inflation rose slightly in 2016 to 3.1% from 3.0% in 2015.

- The money supply expanded in 2016 in 36 of the 39 regional economies for which data are available.

- Domestic credit has expanded since 2000 in 32 of 36 regional economies for which data are available.

- The ratio of nonperforming loans to total gross loans increased in 2016 in 14 out of 22 regional economies compared with a year earlier.

Globalization

- The People's Republic of China and Hong Kong, China were the recipients of the largest net foreign direct investment inflows in nominal terms in 2016; Hong Kong, China and Singapore were the largest recipients of foreign direct investment as a share of GDP for economies with available data.

- While global trade growth remained sluggish in 2016, the total value of exports from Asia and the Pacific approached that of the world's export leader, Europe.

- The aggregate level of remittances in Asia and the Pacific has increased significantly from about $36 billion in 2000 to nearly $253 billion in 2016. India and the People's Republic of China received the most remittances in the region in nominal terms, followed, in order, by the Philippines, Pakistan, Bangladesh, and Viet Nam. As a share of GDP, remittances accounted for more than one-quarter of GDP in 2016 in the Kyrgyz Republic, Nepal, Tajikistan, and Tonga.

Transport and Communications

- Air carrier departures increased between 2000 and 2016 in 29 out of 39 Asia and the Pacific economies for which data are available.

- The People's Republic of China led the region in fixed broadband subscriptions in 2016 by a wide margin. Hong Kong, China; the Republic of Korea; and New Zealand had the highest subscription rates per 100 inhabitants.

Energy and Electricity

- The economies of Asia and the Pacific collectively accounted for 44% of the global energy use in 2014, surpassing all other regions by a wide margin. The People's Republic of China accounted for more than half of regional energy demand and exceeded a fifth of the world total in 2014. The next largest regional consumers of energy in 2014 were India and Japan. The region's global share of energy consumption is expected to increase in the decades ahead due to continued rapid gains in GDP per capita and increased use of energy-consuming goods.

- Asia and the Pacific also led the world by a wide margin in energy production in 2014, comprising 36% of the global total. The People's Republic of

China led all regional economies in production in 2014, accounting for more than half of the regional total and 18.8% of the global total.

- Since 2000, per capita electricity consumption increased in 38 out of 42 developing member economies for which data are available except Solomon Islands, Tajikistan, and Uzbekistan. All three developed member economies—Australia, Japan, and New Zealand—experienced declines in per capita electricity consumption during the review period.

- Energy efficiency—measured as the amount of GDP per unit of energy use—in Asia and the Pacific was $7.2 in 2014, which was below the global average of $7.7. Of the 40 regional economies for which data are available, 32 increased their level of energy efficiency between 2000 and 2014.

Environment

- Economic progress in Asia and the Pacific has been accompanied by rising carbon dioxide emissions. Based on latest data, the region was responsible for 47% of total annual global carbon dioxide emissions. The top five emitters—the People's Republic of China, India, Japan, the Republic of Korea, and Indonesia, respectively—were responsible for more than two-thirds of the regional total.

- Deforestation was reported in almost one-third of the Asia and Pacific region's economies but large economies like the People's Republic of China and India experienced an increase in total forested land in 2014.

- Between 2000 and 2014, 21 regional economies saw an increase in the percentage of land devoted to agriculture, 24 experienced a decline, and 3 had no change. The largest gains as a share of total land occurred in Armenia, Sri Lanka, and Viet Nam; the largest declines were observed in the Cook Islands, Mongolia, and New Zealand.

- Between 2002 and 2014, internal renewable freshwater resources of the Asia and Pacific region's economies declined on a per capita basis in all but two of the 37 economies for which data are available.

Government and Governance

- In 2016, three-quarters of the economies in Asia and the Pacific incurred fiscal deficits. In addition, fiscal deficits exceeded 2% of GDP in half of the region's economies. As a percentage of GDP, the largest deficits were in Mongolia, Myanmar, and Tajikistan; the largest surpluses were in the Federated States of Micronesia; Hong Kong, China; and Palau.

- Government expenditure as a share of GDP rose between 2015 and 2016 in more than half of the economies in the region. The largest gains were in Mongolia, Nauru, and Nepal; the largest declines were in Azerbaijan, Solomon Islands, and Turkmenistan.

- The (arithmetic) average number of days required to start a business in developing member economies for which data are available declined from 50 days in 2005 to 19 days in 2016, compared to the decline in the global average from 51 days to 21 days during the same period.

Part III. Global Value Chains

To discern the state and evolution of international production sharing arrangements associated with global value chains (GVCs) and illuminate relevant policy issues, ADB is producing and analyzing statistics on trade-in-value-added and economies' participation in globalized production processes.

- Between 2014 and 2016, economies in the Asia and Pacific region mitigated the local impact of the slowdown in global trade by increasing the domestic content in their exports and by catering to burgeoning domestic demand.

- Even though Japan; the Republic of Korea; and Taipei,China (the three largest advanced economies of the region) have been highly integrated into global production networks, the domestic content in the products of many of their sectors has increased markedly since 2014.

- In Southeast Asia, especially in countries like Indonesia, Malaysia, the Philippines, Thailand, and Viet Nam, strong economic growth despite stagnating trade in final and intermediate products propelled the development and maturation of local value chains. The contribution of the business support services sector to the Philippines' economic growth expanded significantly between 2014 and 2016.

- Many of the smaller economies in the region are yet to participate in global or regional value chains in any meaningful manner, given their relative factor endowment advantages. Although resource-rich countries such as Brunei Darussalam and Mongolia have been strongly linked to global supply chains, their participation in GVCs is quite likely at the extreme upstream, perhaps in the relatively lower value-adding segments of the chains.

- The value chain participation of the local textiles manufacturing sector continues to be critical to the economies of Bangladesh, Cambodia, and Sri Lanka even as the import content of the exports of the sector have decreased gradually over time due to localization of additional segments of the relevant global and regional value chains.

- Among the countries in Central and West Asia, the participation of Kazakhstan and the Kyrgyz Republic in value chains is largely confined to the primary resources sectors, the output levels of which are intrinsically linked to the global demand for fuels and minerals. In Pakistan, even though GDP has been posting healthy growth since 2012, the economy's production and supply chains remain largely localized.

- Expanding and deepening participation in tourism value chains has been contributing significantly to the economic growth of many economies in the Asia and Pacific region. These value chains are especially critical for countries like Fiji, Cambodia, Maldives, Nepal, and Sri Lanka.

PART I

Sustainable Development Goals Trends and Tables

Introduction to the Sustainable Development Goals Trends and Tables

The SDGs comprise 169 targets across 17 goals to be achieved by 2030. These goals and targets will be monitored and reviewed using a framework of 232 global indicators developed by the Inter-Agency Expert Group on SDG Indicators.[1] This makes the SDGs significantly more ambitious than the MDGs, with double the number of goals, triple the number of targets, and nearly quadruple the number of indicators.

The current set of statistical indicators are grouped into three tiers—Tier 1, Tier 2, and Tier 3. Indicators classified as Tier 1 have a clear and established methodology, and data are regularly collected by many countries. Tier 2 indicators are those that have an established methodology but are not regularly collected by many countries. Tier 3 indicators do not have established standards and/or estimation methodology. Of the 232 SDG indicators, 82 belong to Tier I, 61 are Tier II, and 84 are categorized under Tier III. Five indicators have multiple tiers since different components of these indicators are classified into different tiers.

The 2030 Development Agenda promises to leave no one behind; therefore, monitoring the progress on SDGs requires that the indicators be disaggregated, where relevant, by income, sex, age, race, ethnicity, migratory status, disability, geographic location, or other characteristics, in accordance with the *Fundamental Principles of Official Statistics* (UN 2013). However, such disaggregated data are scarce for many SDG and other development indicators. For example, there is a lack of sex-disaggregated data on ownership of assets in most parts of the world—including in many countries in Asia and the Pacific—despite evidence that women's asset ownership is associated with several positive outcomes such as better nutrition and education for their children, increased bargaining power within the household, and protection against domestic violence. Lack of standard guidelines for collection of data on ownership of assets is one of the reasons that such data are not currently produced by the national statistical systems.

Recognizing the need to addressing data and methodological issues, the Asian Development Bank (ADB), in collaboration with the United Nations Statistics Division (UNSD) and the national statistics offices of Georgia, Mongolia, and the Philippines piloted methodological surveys in support of the Evidence and Data for Gender Equality (EDGE) initiative of the UNSD and the United Nations Entity for Gender Equality and Empowerment of Women. The results from these surveys will provide comprehensive inputs into the development of standardized methods and guidelines for collecting sex-disaggregated on asset ownership.

Part I of *Key Indicators 2017* is divided into two sections. The first section examines the status of economies in Asia and the Pacific using selected indicators from the global indicator framework of the SDG agenda. The second section provides a summary of findings from the three pilot surveys conducted to support the EDGE initiative, alongside lessons learned from the survey operations and data analyses.

1 Inter-Agency and Expert Group on SDG Indicators (IAEG-SDGs) was established in March 2015 by the United Nations Statistical Commission comprising of UN member states with regional and international agencies as observers. IAEG-SDGs was mandated to develop and implement the global indicator framework for the SDGs.

Section 1. Sustainable Development Goal Indicators in Asia and the Pacific

The Sustainable Development Goals (SDGs) chart an ambitious plan of action across five broad themes—People, Prosperity, Planet, Peace, and Partnership (UN, 2015). Embedded within these five themes are the 17 goals of the SDGs (Figure 1.1).

Figure 1.1: Sustainable Development Goals

Source: Adapted from http://www.un.org/sustainabledevelopment/sustainable-development-goals/

In March 2016, the UNSC approved a list of 230 indicators proposed by the IAEG-SDGs for global monitoring of the goals and targets of the 2030 Agenda for Sustainable Development. Upon the recommendation of the IAEG-SDGs, a revised set of 232 indicators was approved by the UNSC in March 2017, with 226 of the original 230 indicators either retained, reworded, or modified; 1 deleted, 5 replaced by new indicators; and 2 new indicators added.[2]

Given that only a third of the SDG indicators have an established methodology and are being regularly collected and compiled for most countries, there is a massive task confronting national statistical systems to meet the data gap for the remaining indicators. This challenge is further complicated by the fact that resources for statistical data collection and compilation have not increased commensurate to demands for new and better data. The *Cape Town Global Action Plan for Sustainable Development Data*[3] appeals for a commitment from governments, policy leaders, and the international community to undertake key actions on six strategic areas: coordination and leadership, innovation and modernization of national statistical systems, strengthening of basic statistical activities and programs, dissemination of data on sustainable development, building partnerships, and mobilizing resources (UN DESA 2017).

Although clear inter-linkages within and across the goals, targets, and indicators of the SDGs exist and are critical to achieving the objectives of the 2030 Agenda for Sustainable Development, for the convenience of the reader, this section is grouped into the five broad themes mentioned above. Statistical tables with recent data on selected SDG indicators for ADB regional member countries are accompanied by short analyses and supporting information presented in figures and boxes. The data presented here are compiled mainly from the UN Department of Economic and Social Affairs, UN Statistics Division's SDG Indicators Global Database, and from international organizations and economy sources.

2 The revised list of 232 SDG indicators is available at https://unstats.un.org/sdgs/indicators/indicators-list/. See also the 2017 IAEG-SDGs report to the UNSC (https://unstats.un.org/unsd/statcom/48th-session/documents/2017-2-IAEG-SDGs-E.pdf).

3 The *Cape Town Action Plan for Global Action Plan for Sustainable Development* was prepared by the High-level Group for Partnership, Coordination and Capacity-Building for Statistics for the 2030 Agenda (HLG-PCCB) which was established by the UNSC and comprised of chief statisticians from 23 national statistics offices.

The SDG Indicators Global Database sources data either from international agencies based on their respective areas of expertise, data estimated from sample surveys that are financed and carried out by international agencies, unadjusted data compiled by international agencies based on what is directly produced by national statistical offices and other country sources, or data adjusted by international agencies based on what is directly produced by national statistical offices and other country sources. To allow for comparability across countries, international agencies often undertake statistical adjustments, imputations to account for data unavailable for certain years, and data harmonization when compiled from multiple sources. For these reasons, the data presented in this publication may differ from those compiled by national statistical agencies. An in-depth description of data compilation techniques implemented for each indicator are available on the SDG Indicators Global Database's website and in the metadata provided alongside the statistical databases of international organizations responsible for compiling global indicators for tracking the SDG progress.

Most of the statistics presented in the tables and charts are usually presented for two data points between 2000 and 2016. These are referred to as the initial year (usually a year between 2000 and 2007 that is closest to 2000) and latest year (usually a year between 2008 and 2016 that is closest to 2016) depending on available data, with some exceptions.

People

To end poverty and hunger, in all forms and dimensions, and to ensure that all human beings can fulfill their potential in dignity and equality and in a healthy environment.

Snapshot

- Between 2002 and 2013, extreme poverty as measured by \$1.90 a day (at 2011 purchasing power parity) significantly declined in developing Asia from 31.8% to around 9.0% of the total population. This implies a reduction from about 1.04 billion people living below \$1.90 a day (at 2011 PPP) in 2002 to about 330 million persons in 2013.
- Of 16 economies that have urban–rural disaggregation on poverty rates using national poverty lines, majority have reduced poverty rates much faster in rural than in urban areas. However, rural poverty remains higher than urban poverty in all 16 economies.
- Undernourishment is less than 10% in 22 economies. However, the prevalence of undernourishment remains at over 20% in six economies.
- While the prevalence of stunting among children under the age of five has fallen in 23 out of 29 economies, more than 40% of children under the age of five in five economies have stunted growth.
- Together with neonatal and under-five mortality rates, maternal mortality ratio has declined significantly in several economies of developing Asia between 2000 and 2015.
- The proportion of teachers in primary education who have received at least the minimum organized teacher training exceeds 90% in 21 out of 32 economies of Asia and the Pacific with available data. For lower secondary education, the proportion exceeds 90% in 12 out of 20 regional economies; in upper secondary education, the proportion exceeds 90% in 10 out of 15 regional economies with available data.
- In nine out of 24 reporting economies of Asia and the Pacific with available data, more than 20% of women aged 20–24 years were either married or in a union before the age of 18.
- In Asia and the Pacific, significant gaps persist in ensuring women's full participation in political leadership. The share of women parliamentarians exceeded one-fifth in only one-third of economies, with Timor-Leste having the highest share at 38.5%.

SDGs 1, 2, 3, 4, and 5 are people-focused and aim at establishing and maintaining conditions that ensure the protection of human dignity alongside assisting those who are farthest behind. The goals include eradicating extreme poverty and hunger, promoting health, well-being, quality education, and gender equality.

SDG 1: End Poverty in All Forms Everywhere

Poverty reduction is at the heart of the sustainable development agenda, and countries have committed to eradicating poverty in all its dimensions by 2030. The poor, who have limited opportunities and capabilities, ought to be provided with basic needs, amenities, and social protection benefits so that they can build resilience to withstand various shocks to livelihood and welfare such as food price crises, armed conflict, and natural hazards.

Rates of extreme poverty vary considerably across regions of developing Asia. For instance, extreme poverty rates are currently over 10.0% in the Pacific (26.6%) and in South Asia (16.1%), but less than 10.0% in Southeast Asia (7.2%) and Central and West Asia (8.5%), and less than 5.0% in East Asia (1.8%) (see Figure 2.1).

Proportion of working population below the international poverty line of $1.90 a day (2011 PPP). In three economies, the proportion of working poor is over two-fifths of the workforce in recent years—Afghanistan (82.9%), Bangladesh (63.9%), and the Lao People's Democratic Republic (46.0%) (Table 2.1). Gender disparities can also be observed among the working poor, where in 14 of 35 economies with available data, the rates of working poor are higher among females than among males.

Figure 2.1: Proportion and Number of People in Extreme Poverty by Subregion, 2002 and 2013

M = million.
Note: The numbers next to the bubbles represent the proportion of population in extreme poverty and the number of extreme poor in millions.
Source: ADB estimates using World Bank's PovcalNet Database: http://iresearch.worldbank.org/PovcalNet/home.aspx (accessed 4 October 2016).

Proportion of population below the international poverty line of $1.90 a day (2011 PPP). Between 2002 and 2013, extreme poverty, as measured by $1.90 a day (at 2011 purchasing power parity), significantly declined in developing Asia from 31.8% to around 9.0% of the total population. This implies a reduction from about 1.04 billion people living below $1.90 a day (2011 PPP) in 2002 to about 330 million persons in 2013.[4]

Proportion of population living below the national poverty line. Countries across the world monitor changes in poverty conditions using nationally defined poverty lines. Methodologies and definitions of national poverty lines vary across

[4] For poverty, the aggregates presented for Developing Asia and the subregions are based on World Bank's estimates using common reference years for regional aggregation. For SDG Table 2.1 and Regional Trends Table 1.7, the poverty estimates presented are based on the actual survey years.

countries. Hence poverty rates based on national definitions are not comparable.

In 27 out of 32 economies of developing Asia with available data for initial and latest years, the proportion of people living below the national poverty line has declined (Table 2.1). Across developing Asia, latest data on poverty using national poverty lines show that 12 out of 16 economies with data on urban–rural disaggregation have reduced poverty rates much faster in rural than in urban areas (Figure 2.2). However, poverty rates for the rural population have remained higher than those of the urban population in all 16 economies.

Monetary poverty, whether examined with international or national poverty lines, does not describe the various deprivations that people face across nonmonetary dimensions such as education, health, nutrition, access to safe water, asset ownership, time, etc. The United Nations Development Programme and Oxford Group have proposed a Multidimensional Poverty Index that uses 10 indicators from the three broad dimensions of education, health, and living standards, but its use is not without cost as pointed out in Box 2.1.

SDG 2: End Hunger, Achieve Food Security and Improved Nutrition, and Promote Sustainable Agriculture

Countries endorsing the Sustainable Development Agenda have also committed to promoting sustainable solutions to end hunger, malnutrition, and food insecurity by 2030. Attaining SDG 2 will require improved access to food for everyone and further support to the agricultural sector, including policies to improve the productivity, incomes, and agricultural practices of small-scale farmers.

Prevalence of undernourishment. In 22 economies of Asia and the Pacific with available data, the prevalence of undernourishment is less than 10.0%, with 13 of these economies reporting a prevalence of less than 5.0% (Table 2.2). However, a

Figure 2.2: Proportion of Population Living below the National Poverty Line, by Urban-Rural Location
(%)

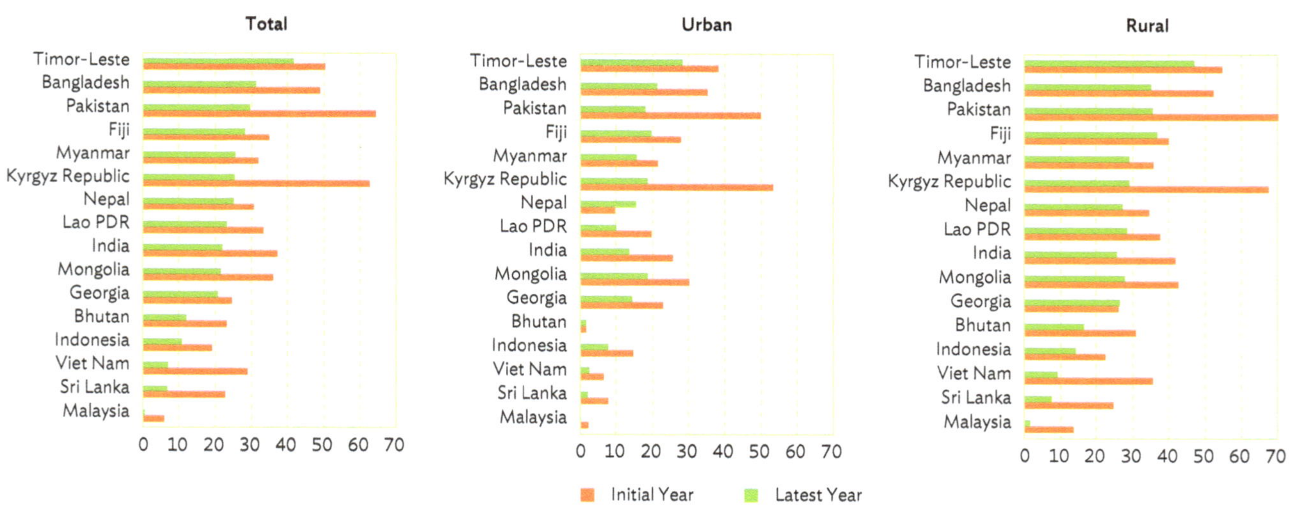

Lao PDR = Lao People's Democratic Republic.
Note: Initial year refers to 2000–2007 and latest year refers to 2010–2016.
Source: Table 2.1.

Box 2.1: Considerations on Using a Multidimensional Poverty Index

Poverty is traditionally associated with the lack of income or consumption. This has focused attention on the subsistence approach to measuring poverty: people with incomes (or its usual proxy, consumption) below a poverty threshold are poor. While people may be better off when they have higher incomes and other resources needed to lead a suitable life, conceptualizing disadvantage based exclusively on income overlooks the differing capacities of each person to access and to have command over these resources, as well as to improve their quality of life. Moreover, while income matters, rising incomes do not necessarily always translate into better health, better security, or improved community participation. Box Figure 2.1.1 enumerates several dimensions of poverty and disadvantage.

Box Figure 2.1.1: Select Dimensions of Poverty

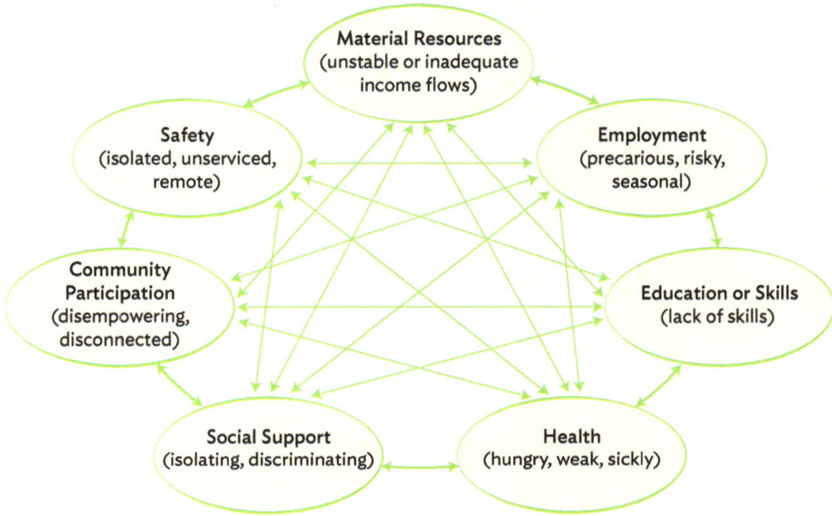

Source: Authors' rendering based on information from Martinez and Perales 2015.

Since the late 1970s, several schools of thought in measuring poverty have been proposed in the development literature as alternatives to the subsistence approach. One of the foremost alternatives is the relative deprivation approach pioneered by Peter Townsend. This approach covers a wide range of aspects of living standards other than income, such as the quality and quantity of familial, recreational, and other social activities. In his examination of living conditions in the United Kingdom, Townsend (1979) characterized poverty as the failure to achieve at least the minimum required living conditions. Where resources are so seriously below the resources commanded by the average person, those who are excluded from the ordinary standards of living, which society dictates as acceptable, are considered disadvantaged.

Another broad sense of disadvantage is the capability approach proposed by the Nobel Laureate Amartya Sen, who argues that well-being comes from a capability to function in society; thus, poverty arises when people lack key capabilities, and have inadequate income, low education, poor health, insecurity, low self-confidence, a sense of powerlessness, or the absence of rights such as freedom of speech (UNDP 2008, Sen 1999, Nussbaum and Sen 1993). This view signals a compelling shift from the traditional concept of disadvantage that is based solely on disposable means of living to the concept that is based on available basic needs, functionings, and opportunities that are necessary to live a valuable life.

The seminal ideas and concepts on relative deprivation introduced by Townsend and on capability introduced by Sen have led to the recognition for a need to move beyond the traditional subsistence approach for poverty assessment in terms of income, and to develop measures that would capture the multiple dimensions of poverty and welfare. In 2010, for instance, the Oxford Poverty and Human Development Initiative in collaboration with the UN Development Programme developed the Global Multidimensional Poverty Index or MPI (UNDP 2010). The Global MPI is an international measure of acute poverty that complements traditional income-based poverty measures by capturing a person's severe deprivation with respect to education, health, and living standards (OPHI 2017). Since then, several variants of MPI have been developed to accommodate various dimensions that are relevant for different country-specific contexts.

continued.

Box 2.1: *(continued)*

Box Figure 2.1.2 summarizes the relationship between unidimensional income and multidimensional poverty headcount rates in selected Asia and the Pacific economies. Although there seems to be a positive correlation between the two types of poverty measures (i.e., high (low) income poverty rates are generally accompanied by high (low) multidimensional poverty rates), there are countries where the relationship is not apparent. This suggests that multidimensional poverty measures provide additional information that unidimensional income-based measures are unable to capture.

Box Figure 2.1.2: Multidimensional and Income Poverty Rates in Selected Countries in Asia and the Pacific (%)

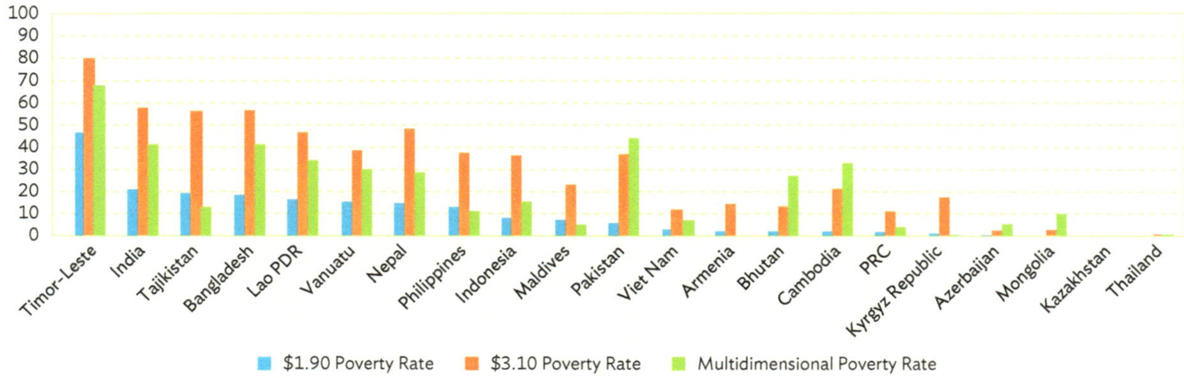

Lao PDR = Lao People's Democratic Republic, PRC = People's Republic of China.
Source: WDI and Global MPI Interactive Databank.

However, measuring poverty with a multidimensional lens is not without its challenges. A number of issues have been raised such as how to objectively identify the specific domains that should be taken into account in poverty analysis. Priority could be given to domains with high prevalence of disadvantage; growing trends in disadvantage; and significant contributions of disadvantage. In addition, poverty domains that are in line with the government's policy objectives should be given more attention.

Another contentious issue is the weights used for each domain to aggregate the different indicators for coming up with an overall multidimensional poverty index. The typical weights used lack the intrinsic meaning associated with relative prices, which are used to add the components of consumption or the incomes used for spending (Ravallion 2012). Further, these weights are not quite robust: slight changes in the weights have significant impact on multidimensional poverty rates (Martinez and Perales 2015). Given the complexity of these measurement issues, countries need to conduct a more thorough evaluation when working with and using multidimensional poverty indexes; and create dashboards on various poverty statistics to ensure that these measures contribute to better thinking about poverty, and better policies for reducing and eradicating poverty.

Sources:

A. Martinez and F. Perales. 2015.The Dynamics of Multidimensional Poverty in Australia. *Social Indicators Research*. 130 (2). pp. 479–496.

M. Nussbaum and A. Sen. 1993. *The Quality of Life*. Oxford: Oxford University Press.

Oxford Poverty and Human Development Initiative. 2017. Global Multidimensional Poverty Index Databank. OPHI. University of Oxford.

M. Ravallion. 2012. On Multidimensional Indices of Poverty. *Journal of Economic Inequality*. 9 (2). pp. 235–248.

A. Sen. 1999. *Development as Freedom*. Oxford: Oxford University Press.

P. Townsend. 1979. *Poverty in the United Kingdom: A Survey of Household Resources and Standards of Living*. Harmondsworth: Penguin Publishing.

United Nations Development Programme. 2008. *Human Development Report*. New York: United Nations.

United Nations Development Programme. 2010. *Human Development Report*. New York: United Nations.

considerable number of people in the region still lack regular access to adequate food, with the prevalence of undernourishment at over 20.0% in six economies: Tajikistan (33.2%), Timor-Leste (26.9%), Afghanistan (26.8%), Pakistan (22.0%), Sri Lanka (22.0%), and Mongolia (20.5%).

Prevalence of stunting among children under 5 years of age. Figure 2.3 shows that as of 2015, stunting affects more than two-fifths of children under 5 years of age in Timor-Leste (50.2%), Papua New Guinea (49.5%), Pakistan (45.0%), the Lao People's Democratic Republic (43.8%), and Afghanistan (40.9%). The prevalence of stunting among children below 5 years of age has fallen between the earliest and latest years for which data are available in 23 out of 29 economies with the steepest reductions in Nepal, Mongolia, Viet Nam, Afghanistan, and Cambodia. Developing economies where the prevalence of stunting among children under 5 years of age has increased between the earliest and latest years for which data are available include Malaysia, Pakistan, Thailand, and the Pacific economies of Papua New Guinea and Vanuatu (Table 2.2).

Prevalence of wasting among children under 5 years of age. Significantly fewer children aged 5 years and under are affected by wasting than stunting (Figure 2.3). Latest available data for developing member economies show that prevalence of wasting among children under 5 years of age is greater than 20% in Sri Lanka (21.4%) and India (21.0%). On the other hand, wasting prevalence is at most 2.5% in the PRC (2.3%), Georgia (1.6%), Japan (2.3%), the Republic of Korea (1.2%), and Mongolia (1.0%).

Figure 2.3: Prevalence of Stunting, Wasting and Overweight Among Children Aged 5 years and Under, Latest Years (%)

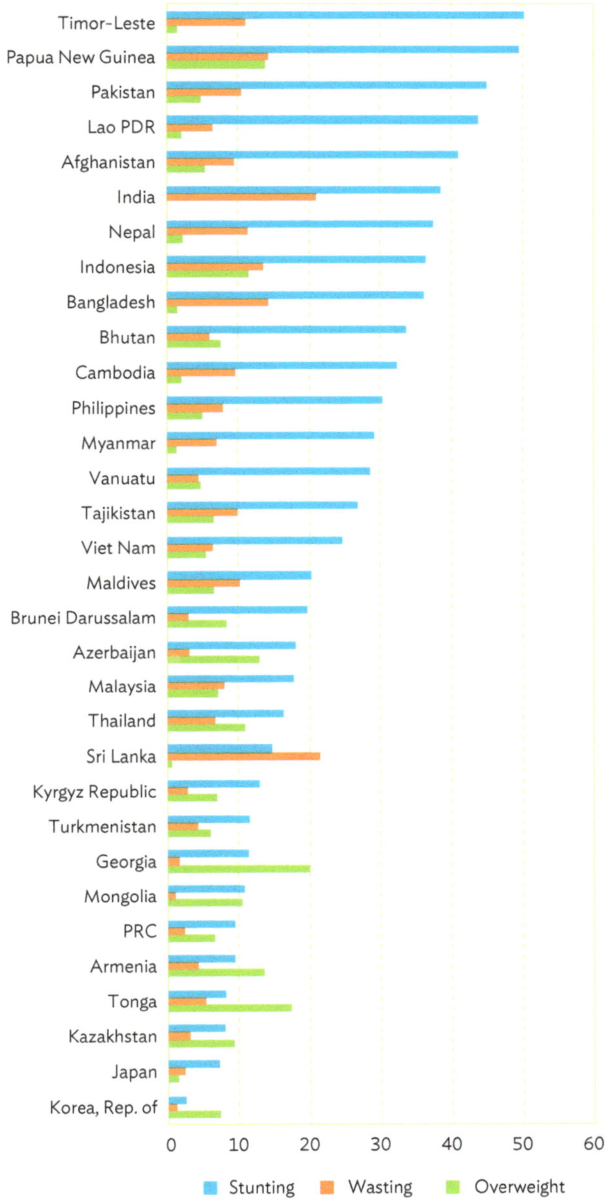

Lao PDR = Lao People's Democratic Republic, PRC = People's Republic of China.

Note: Only economies with recent estimates (2010 and later) are included.

Source: Table 2.2.

Prevalence of overweight among children under 5 years of age. Obesity among children under the age of five can result in severe health issues when they reach adulthood. Data show that the prevalence of overweight among children below 5 years of age is over 10% in eight regional economies: Armenia, Azerbaijan, Georgia, Indonesia, Mongolia, Papua New Guinea, Thailand, and Tonga. Many of these economies with high prevalence of overweight have prevalence rates of wasting among children under five below 5%. In almost half of 27 regional economies with data, the prevalence of overweight among children under 5 years of age has fallen or has stayed the same between the initial and final year of reporting.

Agriculture orientation index. The productive capacity of the agriculture sector depends on both public and private investments coming from domestic and foreign sources. Among 23 regional economies with available data, only the Republic of Korea and Singapore have a higher orientation toward the agriculture sector, with the agriculture share in government expenditures exceeding the sector's share in gross domestic product (GDP) (Table 2.3). Thirteen out of 23 economies have improved their agriculture orientation, with Singapore experiencing the steepest increase.

Gross disbursements of total official development assistance and other official flows from all donors to the agriculture sector. In the Asia and the Pacific region, South Asia has been the largest recipient of official development assistance (ODA) and other official flows to the agriculture sector, amounting to nearly $1.5 billion (in constant 2015 dollars) in 2015 (Figure 2.4). This is followed by Central and West Asia and Southeast Asia, which have about a billion each (in constant 2015 dollars) of official flows of disbursement to the agriculture sector. Across economies, India ($1.05 billion), the People's Republic of China ($386.4 million), Afghanistan ($328.1 million), and Pakistan ($291.7 million) were the four largest recipients of total official flows to the agriculture sector in 2015 (Table 2.3). On the other hand, declines of more than $40 million occurred in Bangladesh, Cambodia, the Kyrgyz Republic, and the Philippines between 2000 to 2015.

Figure 2.4: Total Official Flows (Official Development Assistance Plus Other Official Flows) to the Agriculture Sector
(constant 2015 $ million)

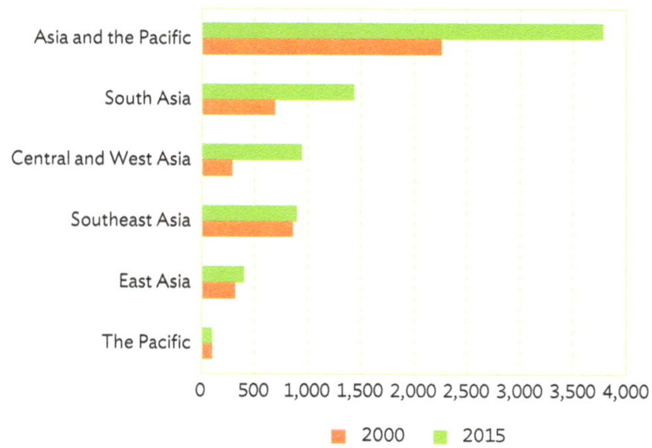

Source: Table 2.3.

SDG 3: Ensure Healthy Lives and Promote Well-Being for All at All Ages

SDG 3 aspires to healthy lives and well-being for everyone at every stage of life by 2030. Attaining this goal entails improving reproductive, maternal, and child health; ending the epidemics of HIV/AIDS, malaria, tuberculosis, and neglected tropical diseases; reducing noncommunicable and environmental diseases; achieving universal health coverage; and ensuring access to safe, affordable, and effective medicines and vaccines for all.

Maternal mortality ratio. Maternal deaths per 100,000 live births dropped significantly in Asia and the Pacific, with maternal mortality ratio (MMR) declining from 264 deaths per 100,000 live births in 2000 to 123 in 2015. South Asia led the reduction across regions of developing Asia with 203 fewer deaths per 100,000 live births from 377 in 2000. Maternal deaths decreased in 39 out of 43 economies in Asia and the Pacific, with Afghanistan displaying the largest decline from an MMR of 1,100 at the end of the last millennium, to an MMR of 396 in 2015. Next to Afghanistan, economies with the largest declines in maternal deaths between 2000 and 2015 include Cambodia, Nepal, the Lao People's Democratic Republic, and Timor-Leste. Despite this huge reduction, MMR exceeded 150 in nearly one-fourth of the economies (Table 2.4). Other economies with very high maternal deaths include Papua New Guinea (215), Pakistan (178), Myanmar (178), Bangladesh (176), and India (174). Economies with the lowest MMRs at 16 or fewer maternal deaths per 100,000 live births include Hong Kong, China; Kazakhstan; the Republic of Korea; Singapore; and Taipei,China; and the developed economies of Australia, Japan, and New Zealand.

Proportion of births attended by skilled health personnel. Accompanying a drop in maternal deaths is an increase in the proportion of births attended by skilled health personnel in many economies of Asia and the Pacific (Figure 2.5). Developing economies such as Afghanistan, Bangladesh, Bhutan, Cambodia, India, the Lao People's Democratic Republic, Nepal, and Pakistan, where less than half of births were attended by skilled health personnel in 2000, have made dramatic strides between 2000 and 2015 (Table 2.4.) Despite this progress, less than half of births are attended by doctors, nurses, and midwives in the Lao People's Democratic Republic (40.1%) and Bangladesh (42.1%). In these economies, MMR stands at 170 or more deaths per 100,000 live births.

Under-five mortality rate. Under-five mortality in Asia and the Pacific fell from 70 deaths per 1,000 live births in 2000 to 36 deaths per 1,000 live births in 2015. All regions have reduced their under-five mortality rates, with South Asia leading with a reduction of 44 deaths per 1,000 live births, followed by Central and West Asia with a drop of 35 deaths per 1,000 live births from 106 deaths per 1,000 live births (Figure 2.6). Nearly all economies, except Brunei Darussalam, reduced their under-five mortality rates, but at varying rates. Afghanistan, Azerbaijan, Bangladesh, Bhutan, Cambodia, India, the Lao People's Democratic Republic, Nepal, Tajikistan, and Timor-Leste reduced their under-five mortality rates by more than 40 deaths per 1,000 live births between 2000 and 2015 (Table 2.4).

Figure 2.5: Scatterplot of Maternal Mortality Ratio (maternal deaths per 100,000 live births) **and Proportion of Births Attended by Skilled Health Personnel** (%)

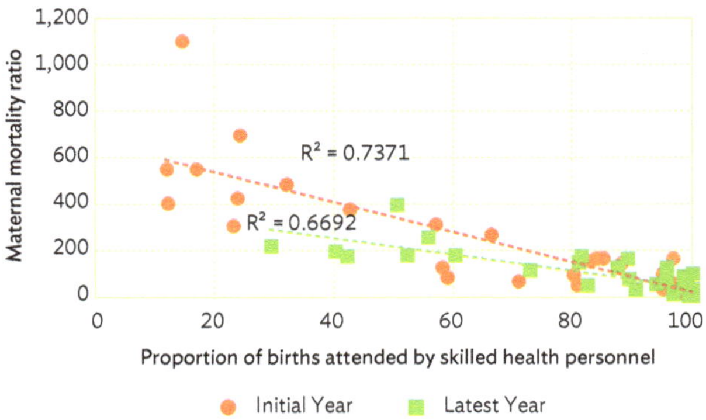

Note: Initial year refers to 2000–2007 and latest year refers to 2008–2015.
Source: Table 2.4.

Figure 2.6: Under-five Mortality Rate (per 1,000 live births)

Source: Table 2.4.

Neonatal mortality rate. Neonatal deaths decreased throughout Asia and the Pacific from 35 deaths to 20 deaths per 1,000 live births between 2000 and 2015. All regions reduced neonatal deaths, led by South Asia, and followed closely by East Asia, and Central and West Asia (Figure 2.7). Among regional economies, Cambodia and Maldives reported the largest reduction in neonatal deaths of 21 deaths per 1,000 live births, followed by Bangladesh (19), India (17), and Nepal (17).

Tuberculosis incidence rate. In the period 2000–2015, the incidence of tuberculosis has declined in 33 out of 48 regional economies, with Azerbaijan recording the largest decrease about 90%—from 681 per 100,000 people in 2000 to 69 in 2015—followed by Turkmenistan, Georgia, Samoa, and Tajikistan, respectively (Figure 2.8). The incidence of tuberculosis remains high at over 200 per 100,000 population in 13 economies, five of which are in the Pacific, with another four in Southeast Asia. In three Pacific economies—Kiribati, the Marshall Islands, and Tuvalu—tuberculosis incidence rate worsened by 20% or more between 2000 and 2015. The lowest incidence rates of less than 20 per 100,000 people are

Figure 2.7: Neonatal Mortality Rate
(per 1,000 live births)

Source: Table 2.4.

Figure 2.8: Tuberculosis Incidence
(per 100,000 population)

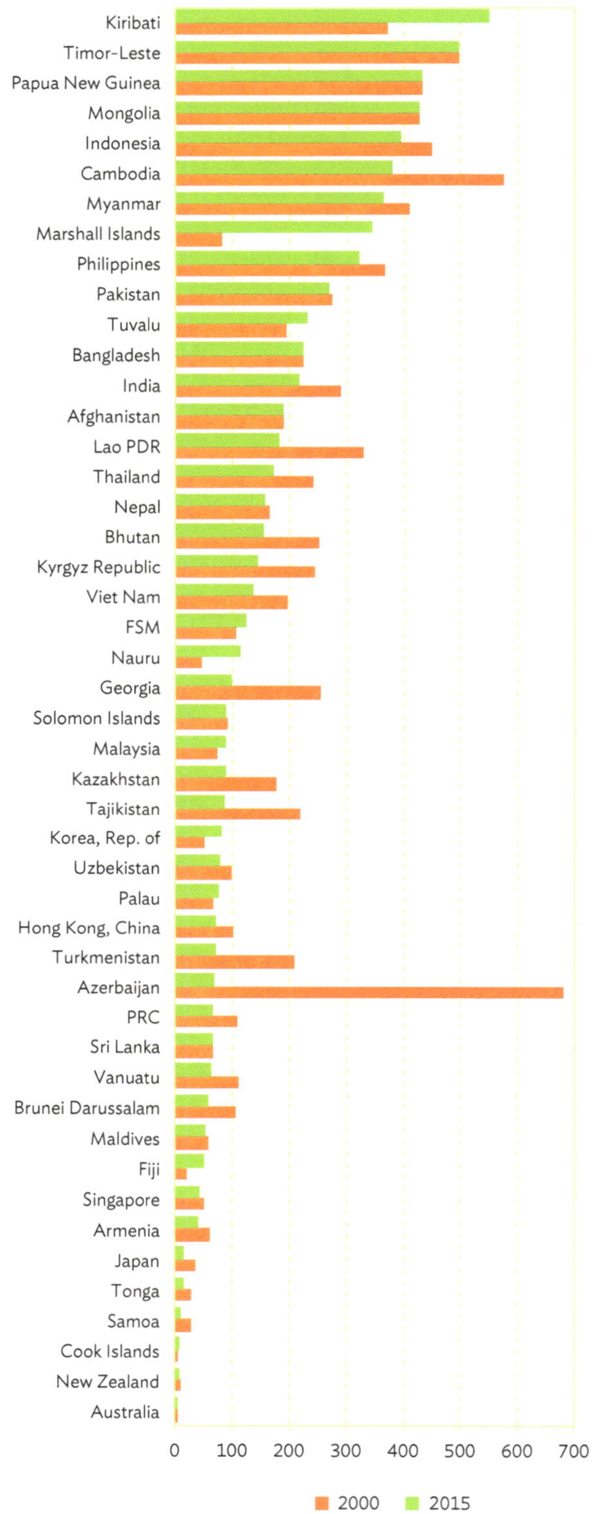

FSM = Federated States of Micronesia, Lao PDR = Lao People's Democratic Republic, PRC = People's Republic of China.
Source: Table 2.5.

in the developed economies of Australia, Japan, and New Zealand, as well as the Cook Islands, Samoa, and Tonga.

Malaria incidence rate. Malaria incidence in 2015 has declined in all 26 reporting developing economies from levels in 2000, but it persists as a problem in Asia and the Pacific, with incidence rate at over 60 per 100,000 people in Papua New Guinea (122) and Solomon Islands (67). Azerbaijan, the PRC, Georgia, the Kyrgyz Republic, Sri Lanka, Tajikistan, and Uzbekistan reported no new cases of malaria in 2015 (Table 2.5).

Mortality rate attributed to cardiovascular disease, cancer, diabetes, or chronic respiratory disease. The proportion of deaths attributed to the four main noncommunicable diseases (NCDs)—cardiovascular disease, cancer, diabetes, or chronic respiratory disease—has decreased across 39 out of 41 reporting economies between 2000 and 2015. Mortality rates from the four main NCDs between 2000 and 2015 fell in Kazakhstan, Maldives, Brunei Darussalam, Mongolia, and the Republic of Korea by at least 8 percentage points (Figure 2.9). Meanwhile, increases in the shares of deaths from NCDs have been reported in Myanmar and the Philippines from 2000 to 2015.

Death rate due to road traffic injuries. High incidence of death rates due to road traffic injuries per 100,000 persons was reported in Thailand (36.2), Viet Nam (24.5), the Cook Islands (24.2), Kazakhstan (24.2), and Malaysia (24.0) (Figure 2.10). Less than five deaths due to road traffic injuries per 100,000 persons was reported in the Federated States of Micronesia (1.9), Kiribati (2.9), Maldives (3.5), Singapore (3.6), and Japan (4.7). Reducing deaths and injuries from road traffic accidents by 2020 from half their 2013 levels is an ambitious SDG target especially given the continuing rise in the number of vehicles on the road.

Figure 2.9: Mortality Rate Attributed to Cardiovascular Disease, Cancer, Diabetes, or Chronic Respiratory Disease
(%)

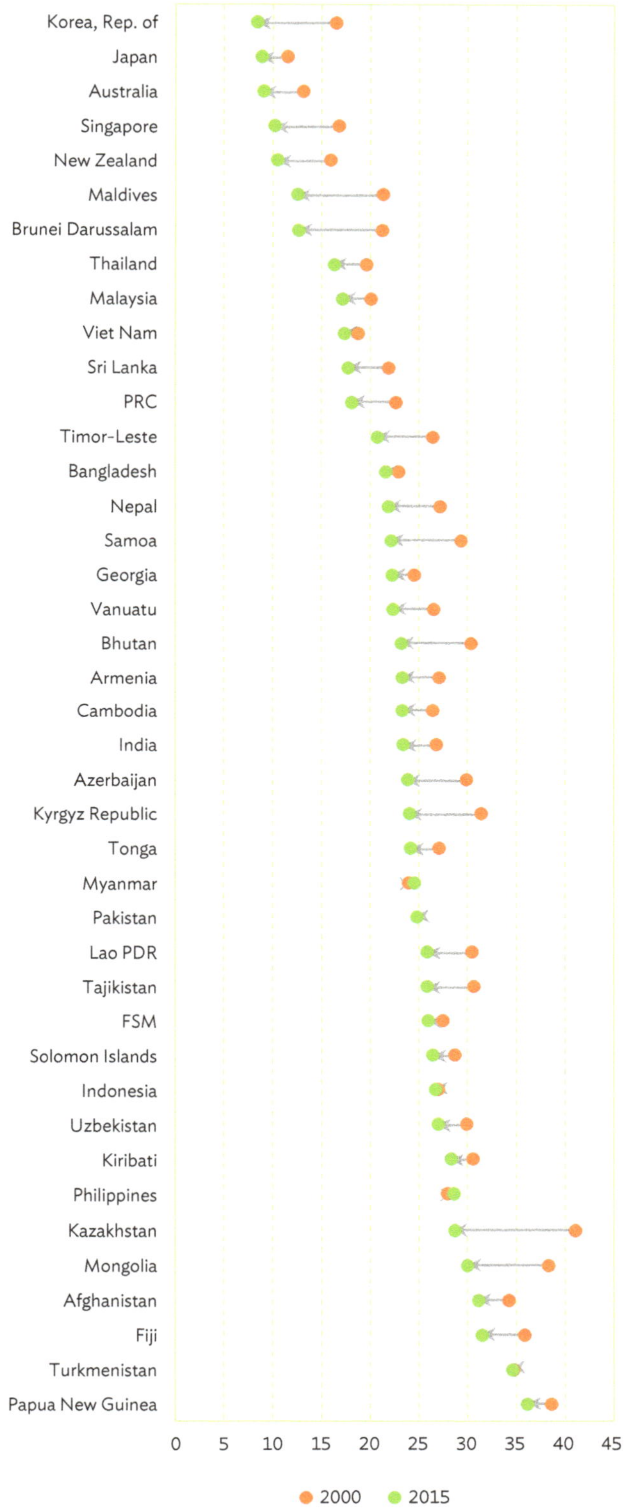

FSM = Federated States of Micronesia, Lao PDR = Lao People's Democratic Republic, PRC = People's Republic of China.
Source: Table 2.5.

Figure 2.10: Death Rate due to Road Traffic Injuries
(per 100,000 population)

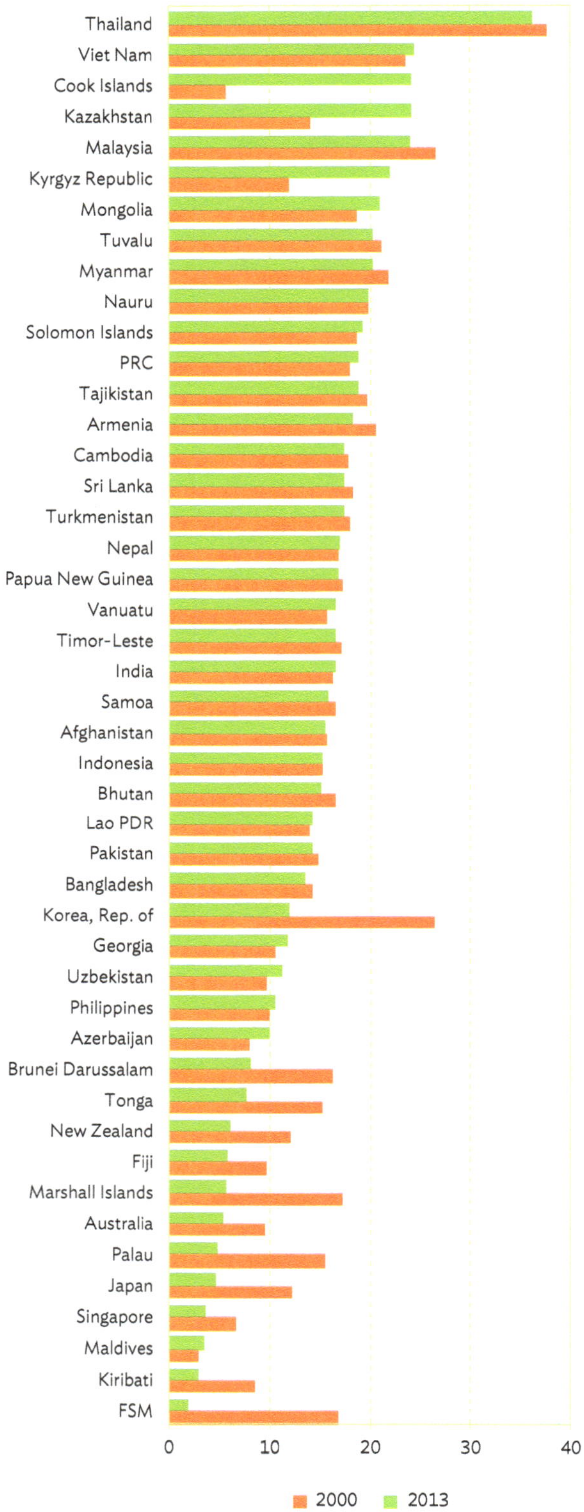

FSM = Federated States of Micronesia, Lao PDR = Lao People's Democratic Republic, PRC = People's Republic of China.
Source: Table 2.5.

Figure 2.11: Participation Rate in Organized Learning (1 Year Before the Official Primary Entry Age), by Sex
(%)

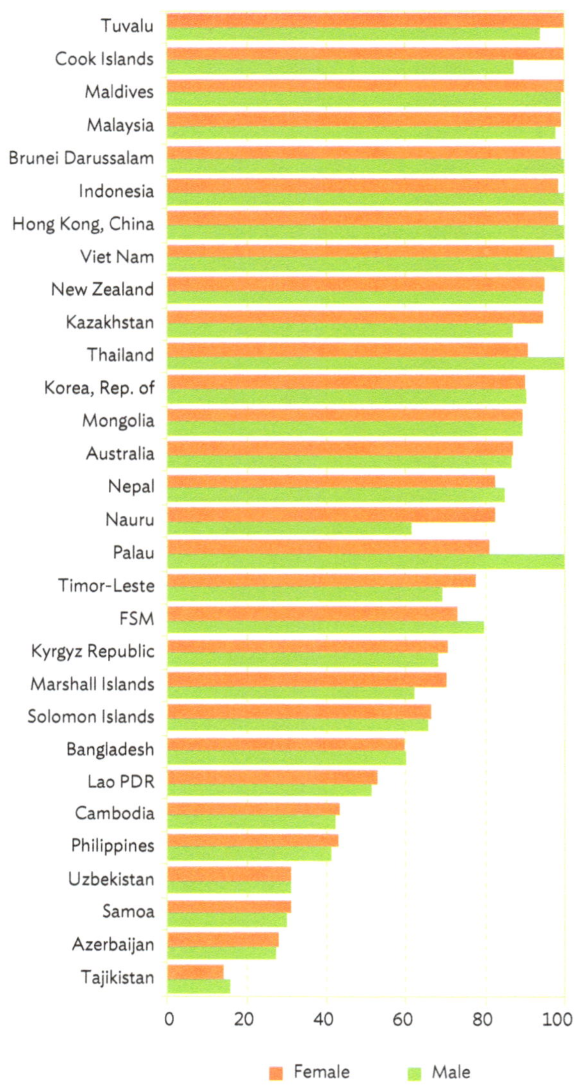

FSM = Federated States of Micronesia, Lao PDR = Lao People's Democratic Republic.
Note: Latest data available from 2009 to 2016.
Source: Table 2.7.

SDG 4: Ensure Inclusive and Equitable Quality Education and Promote Lifelong Learning Opportunities for All

Underlying the global commitment to realizing SDG4 is the recognition that universal attainment of quality education, relevant training, and opportunities for lifelong learning increases everyone's capacities to function well. This in turn, boosts sustained prosperity and inclusive growth.

Participation rate in organized learning (1 year before the official primary entry age), by sex. Seventeen out of 31 economies in Asia and the Pacific have achieved at least 80% participation rates in preschool programs a year before entering the official primary entry age for both sexes—Brunei Darussalam; the Cook Islands; Hong Kong, China; Indonesia; Kazakhstan; Malaysia; Mongolia; Nepal; Palau; the Republic of Korea; Thailand; Tuvalu; Viet Nam; and the developed economies of Australia, Japan, and New Zealand (Table 2.7). However, total participation rates are below 50% in 6 reporting economies—Cambodia, Georgia, the Philippines, Samoa, Tajikistan, and Turkmenistan. In 17 out of 30 economies that provide sex disaggregated information, participation rates in organized learning is greater than 80% for women.

Proportion of trained teachers in preprimary education. The proportion of teachers in preprimary education who have received at least the minimum organized teacher training exceeds 90% in 11 out of 22 member economies with available data. In three economies—the Kyrgyz Republic (46.2%), Myanmar (48.4%), and Vanuatu (46.0%)—the proportion of preprimary teachers who have received at least the minimum organized teacher training is below 50% (Figure 2.12a).

Proportion of trained teachers in primary education. The proportion of teachers in primary education who have received at least the minimum organized teacher training exceeds 90% in 21 out of 32 member economies with available data. In 11 of these economies, all teachers in primary education have received at least the minimum organized teacher training. These include Bhutan, Cambodia, the Cook Islands, Fiji, Kazakhstan, Mongolia, Papua New Guinea, the Philippines, Tajikistan, Thailand, and Uzbekistan. However, in Bangladesh (47.6%), the Kyrgyz Republic (72.0%), Palau (33.7%), Solomon Islands (59.2%), Sri Lanka (71.3%), and Vanuatu (27.9%), less than three-fourths of primary teachers have received at least the minimum organized teacher training (Figure 2.12b).

Proportion of trained teachers in lower secondary education. The proportion of teachers in lower secondary education who have received at least the minimum organized teacher training exceeds 90% in 12 out of 20 member economies with available data. All or nearly all lower secondary teachers in Bhutan, Fiji, Papua New Guinea, as well as the Southeast Asian economies of Cambodia, the Lao People's Democratic Republic, Thailand, and Viet Nam, have received at least the minimum organized teacher training. However, in Bangladesh (59.6%), Pakistan (61.2%), Palau (59.3%), Sri Lanka (57.3%), and Vanuatu (21.5%), less than three-fifths of lower secondary teachers have received at least the minimum organized teacher training (Figure 2.12c).

Proportion of trained teachers in upper secondary education. The proportion of teachers in upper secondary education who have received at least the minimum organized teacher training exceeds 90% in 10 out of 15 member economies with available data, including Brunei Darussalam (90.1%), Fiji (100.0%), Georgia (94.8%), the Lao People's Democratic Republic (99.0%), Myanmar (95.2%), Nepal (91.6%), Papua New Guinea (100.0%), Samoa (100.0%), Singapore (91.7%), and Thailand (100.0). However, in the Pacific economies of Kiribati (33.6%) and Vanuatu (20.5%), only a third of upper secondary teachers have received at least the minimum organized teacher training (Figure 2.12d).

Figure 2.12: Proportion of Trained Teachers in (a) Preprimary, (b) Primary, (c) Lower Secondary, and (d) Upper Secondary Education
(%)

Figure 2.12a: Proportion of Trained Teachers
in Preprimary Education

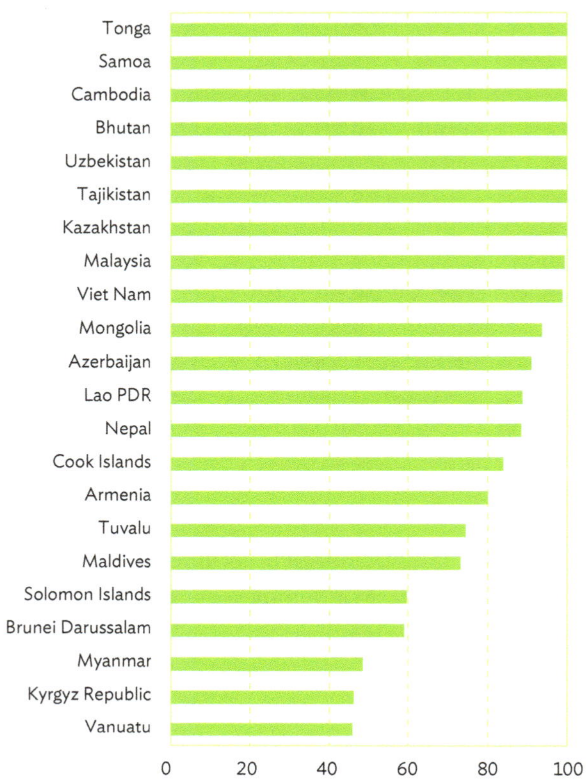

Figure 2.12b Proportion of Trained Teachers
in Primary Education

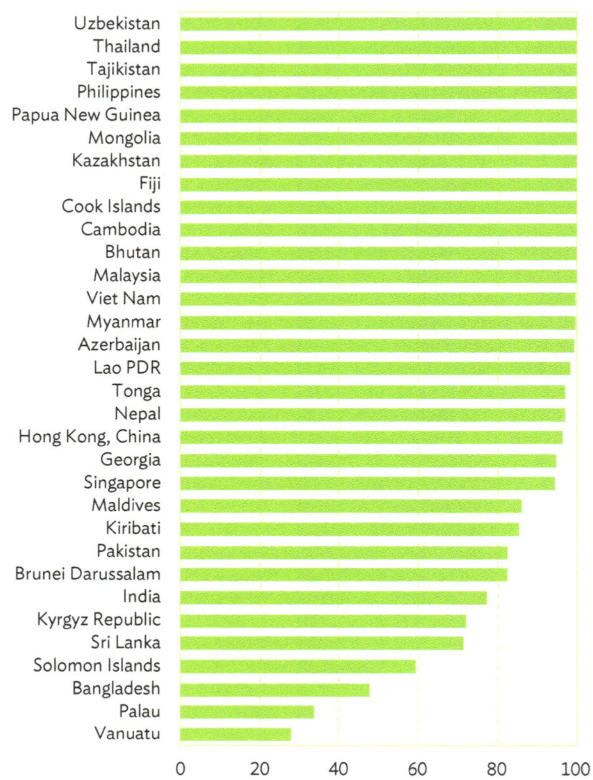

Figure 2.12c: Proportion of Trained Teachers
in Lower Secondary Education

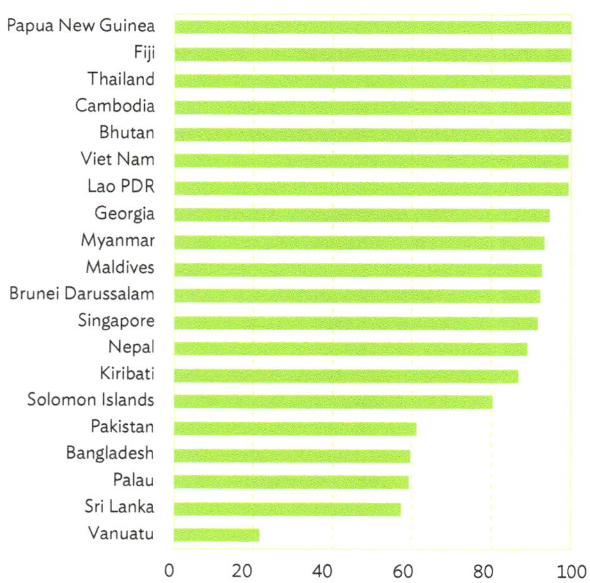

Figure 2.12d: Proportion of Trained Teachers
in Upper Secondary Education

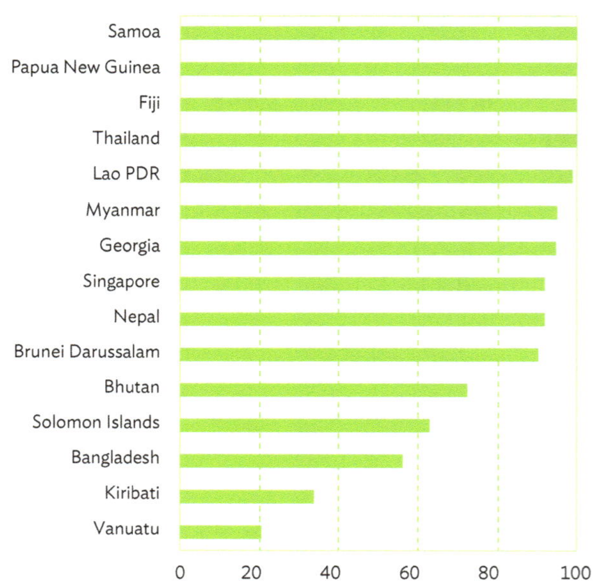

Lao PDR = Lao People's Democratic Republic.
Source: Table 2.8.

SDG 5: Achieve Gender Equality and Empower All Women and Girls

Ensuring that everyone is empowered to reach their full potential requires both men and women to be given equal opportunities in education, paid employment, and real decision-making power. SDG 5 focuses on gender equality, particularly the need to end all forms of discrimination against women and girls.

Proportion of women aged 20–24 years who were married or in a union before age 18. Article 16 of the *Universal Declaration of Human Rights* states that marriage before the age of 18 violates human rights. Early child marriage also directly impacts girls' education, health, psychological well-being, as well as the health of their offspring (Nour 2009). The latest data show that in 9 out of 24 economies in Asia and the Pacific, more than 20% of women aged 20–24 years were married or in a union before the age of 18. These include Bangladesh (58.6%), Nepal (36.6%), the Lao People's Democratic Republic (35.4%), Afghanistan (34.8%), Bhutan (25.8%), Pakistan (21.0%), Thailand (22.1%), Kiribati (20.3%), and Vanuatu (21.4%). In Armenia, Kazakhstan, Maldives, Mongolia, Tonga, and Turkmenistan, less than 10.0% of young women were married or in a union before the age of 18. In particular, across 12 economies in Asia and the Pacific for which data are available, the proportion of child marriages is moderately correlated with the proportion of females in vulnerable employment (Figure 2.13).

Figure 2.13: Scattterplot of Proportion of Women Aged 20–24 Years Who were Married or in a Union before Age 18 and Proportion of Females in Vulnerable Employment, Latest Year
(%)

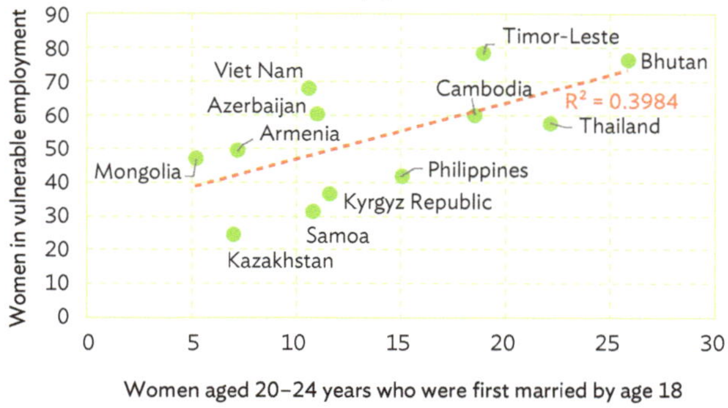

Sources: Table 2.9 and World Bank. World Development Indicators. http://databank.worldbank.org/data/reports.aspx?source=world-development-indicators (accessed 3 August 2017).

Proportion of seats held by women in national parliaments. An adequate representation of women in parliament increases the chances that interests of women and issues on gender equality will be served. In Asia and the Pacific, significant gaps persist, which do not lend to women's full and effective participation and equal opportunities for political leadership. Eighteen out of 46 economies in Asia and the Pacific have 10.0% or less representation of women in parliament (Figure 2.14). Of these economies, four Pacific economies—the Federated States of Micronesia, Palau, Tonga, and Vanuatu—reported no representation of women. Timor-Leste (38.5%) reported the highest percentage of female parliamentarians in 2016. Meanwhile, almost a third of the regional economies have at least one-fifth of parliamentary seats held by women, but this still stands well below parity, given that women represent roughly 49.0% of the total population in Asia and the Pacific.[5]

[5] Estimated based on available data from the 2017 Revision of World Population Prospects. http://esa.un.org/unpd/wpp/ (accessed on 1 August 2017).

Figure 2.14: Proportion of Seats Held by Women in National Parliaments, 2016
(%)

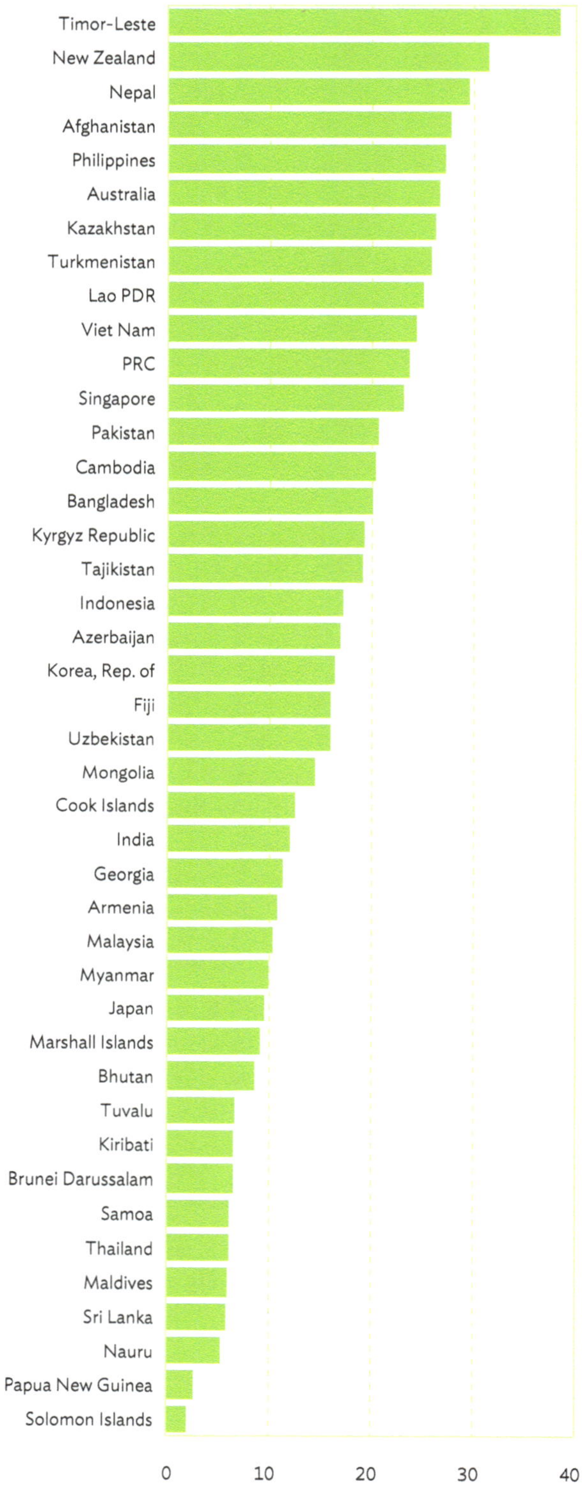

Lao PDR = Lao People's Democratic Republic, PRC= People's Republic of China.
Note: Data for the Cook Islands refer to 2014.
Source: Table 2.9.

Proportion of women in managerial positions. Greater involvement of women in managerial positions, both in public and private enterprises, translates into women's economic empowerment. Among the 29 economies in the region with available data, 12 economies have at least one-third of women in managerial positions (Figure 2.15). Women in the Cook Islands, the Philippines, and Samoa, accounted for almost half the managerial positions in their countries. Meanwhile, women in Bangladesh and the Kyrgyz Republic hold just 5% and 3%, respectively, of managerial jobs.

Figure 2.15: Proportion of Women in Managerial Positions, Latest Year
(%)

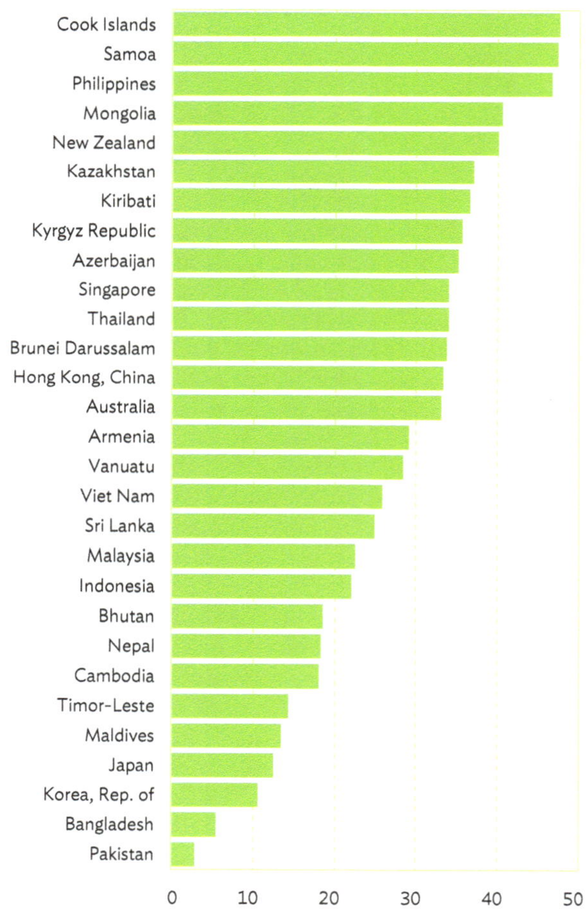

Source: Table 2.9.

Equity, Data Gaps, and Other Related Issues

While most countries achieved significant poverty reduction in rural compared to urban areas (based on national-level data), the rural population continues to be more at risk of being poor than the urban population. Sex disaggregation is not available for poverty rates using the international poverty line, except for the working population; neither is there any urban–rural breakdown. Poverty data, even based on national poverty lines, is not available for small segments of society, such as ethnic minorities and persons with disability, who may be at more risk of being poor than the average socioeconomic classes. For these cases, data should be collected from sources such as special surveys, administrative reporting systems, or crowdsourcing using innovative techniques. Furthermore, data on living conditions are typically sourced from household surveys that are usually conducted every 3–5 years, whereas more frequent poverty monitoring may be required to examine the effect of interventions, especially in economies that are very vulnerable to factors such as food price crises, armed conflict, and natural disasters.

Some developing economies have proxied sex-disaggregated poverty rates for the entire population through sex of the household head. However, the sex of the household head may not be a useful way of examining gender issues on poverty as the operational definition of the head of the household may be unclear and is often left either to the respondent or the field personnel collecting data to determine. There may be an inherent bias, both from the respondent and field personnel, toward reporting males as the head of the household, leading to lower estimates on the number of households headed by women, thereby rendering analysis on the difference in poverty rates between households headed by men and those headed by women challenging.

The methodology employed by the World Bank to establish the international poverty line and to generate comparable poverty rates with purchasing power parity (PPP) income and consumption data across countries and across time has been consistent. However, the measurement of household income or expenditure and the calculation of 2011 PPPs may have relatively high error margins in some countries as well as nonsampling errors. Even similar surveys may not be strictly comparable across countries due to differences in timing of survey, reference periods, sampling frames, and quality of data collected.

Poor people are exposed to various risks that make them vulnerable to income shocks and worsen their well-being. Conventional monitoring of poverty summarizes or provides a snapshot of people's welfare, but often does not examine movements of people across the socioeconomic ladder across time. Box 2.2 describes intergenerational mobility and why tracking it is important, but this will require longitudinal data on living conditions, which are not regularly conducted.

There are also conceptual challenges with measuring some indicators in SDG 2. For instance, a seemingly easy to measure indicator 2.3.2 (average income of small-scale food producer, disaggregated by sex and indigenous status), there are practical questions regarding its measurement. Should income of food producers be limited to agricultural sources, or also include other sources? Further, how do we define food producers? Should food producers include those engaged in farming, pastoral, and fishing activities, but exclude small industrial firms processing food? Finally, even if we are able to define food producers explicitly, will there be an internationally agreed cut-off for defining what is meant by "small-scale"?

Box 2.2: What is Intergenerational Mobility?

Poverty and inequality are usually presented in official headline statistics as cross-sectional measures. Nonetheless, leading researchers have argued that these measures are not to be regarded as one-off events because of the possibility for some people to either be consistently advantaged or disadvantaged and for others to move in and out of states of advantage and disadvantage over time, corresponding to the concept of socioeconomic mobility. Mobility is generally measured over a life cycle (intragenerational) or across generations (intergenerational).

Intergenerational mobility refers to the up and down movements along the socioeconomic ladder across generations. Higher rates of intergenerational mobility are usually found in fairer societies or those with lower levels of inequality (see Box Figure 2.2.1), as there exist more opportunities for everyone, regardless of family background, to move up and down the ladder. Meanwhile, in unfair societies, the poor tend to persist at the bottom and the rich stay on top because family background is still a major key to opportunities. There are a variety of ways to estimate intergenerational mobility, one of which is a calculation based on the relationship between parents' and children's educational attainment, occupation, or income.

Other than a benchmark for fairness, intergenerational mobility is also a valuable metric for assessing long-term international competitiveness, as it provides a glimpse of how today's younger generation will perform when they become adults. Moreover, there are many reasons why it is valuable to do international comparisons of intergenerational mobility. First, with the world becoming increasingly interconnected with globalization and international competitiveness becoming more vital, greater scrutiny has been made on the degree of intergenerational mobility among countries. Second, while it is important to reduce the intergenerational persistence of socioeconomic advantage, it is also generally recognized that having uncorrelated socioeconomic outcomes across generations is not a desired goal.

Box Figure 2.2.1: The Great Gatsby Curve

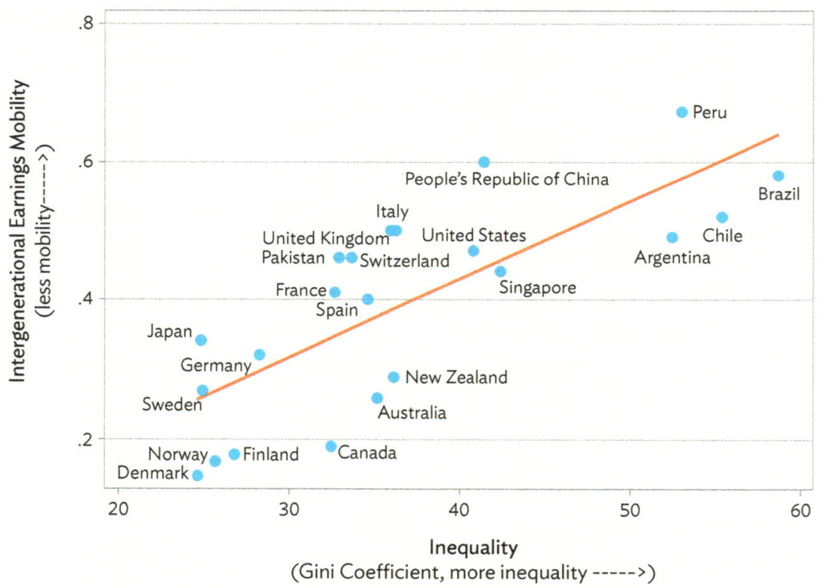

Source: Adapted from M. Corak. 2010. Inequality from Generation to Generation. The United States in Comparison. *IZA Discussion Paper*. No. 9929. http://ftp.iza.org/dp9929.pdf

Box 2.2: *(continued)*

If this were so, there would be no incentive and reason for parents to work hard for a better future for their children, as resources would not enhance their children's long-term prospects in this case. The comparison of intergenerational mobility levels across countries will help in identifying which mobility levels are relatively low and relatively high. As such, the common ground between countries sharing similar mobility regimes can be studied, which can then be fed into public discussion and policy planning.

However, finding the causal link between cross-country differences in intergenerational mobility and corresponding specific policy actions have proven to be tough, given the sparse comparable estimates of intergenerational mobility for many countries. Furthermore a lot of developing countries do not possess the data requirements for estimation, e.g., panel data or retrospective data with information on parent and adult child characteristics.

Nevertheless, initiatives have taken place to address this matter. First, increasingly, countries have begun regularly collecting the necessary and relevant panel data. Second, countries that have been collecting cross-sectional survey data are integrating retrospective data on the educational and occupational backgrounds of adult respondents' parents. Third, to address the lack of panel data, pseudo-panel estimation methods have been developed and are increasingly being used.

While progress in the region toward attaining universal primary education has been impressive, keeping children in primary school and transitioning them into upper levels of basic education continues to be challenging given supply-side and demand-side bottlenecks. Disparities in school participation and learning achievement between boys and girls, between children in rural and urban areas, and between children from poor and nonpoor families persist within economies. Specific interventions will be required to address these learning inequities.

Anthropometric measures of undernutrition (including stunted heights and wasting) as well as overnutrition (such as overweight) reflect the current nutritional status of persons being measured. These measures make use of objective methods of physical measurement of heights and weights with high specificity and sensitivity, in conjunction with ages. Basic measurement data are reproducible and inexpensive, requiring minimal training for observing measurement protocols. However, there are errors in measurement and issues about reference standards, i.e., local versus international standards. Further, there are arbitrary statistical cut-off levels for what are considered as anomalous values.

SDG indicators on mortality such as maternal mortality ratio, under-five mortality rate, neonatal mortality rate, mortality rate from the four main noncommunicable diseases, and suicide mortality rate—would ideally be sourced from vital registration systems. However, across many developing economies, these systems do not have full coverage. While there may be more incentives to have births registered, death registration may not be as incentivized. Aside from deaths being underreported, the causes of deaths, whether from death registration systems or medical certifications, may also be misreported. Data on mortality indicators for these economies are therefore usually based on household surveys, but sample surveys have varying reliability (based on sample size) and accuracy.

Data on under-five and neonatal mortality discussed in this report are produced by the United Nations Inter-Agency Group for Child Mortality Estimation based on a standardized methodology and data sourced nationally. These estimates are not necessarily the same as the official data from the countries.

Table 2.1: **Selected Indicators for SDG 1 - No Poverty**

By 2030,eradicate extreme poverty for all people everywhere, measured as people living below the international poverty line

By 2030, reduce at least by half the proportion of men, women, and children of all ages living in poverty in all its dimensions according to national definitions

Regional Member[a]	1.1.1a Proportion of Population below the International Poverty Line[b] (%)		1.1.1b Proportion of Employed Population below the International Poverty Line[b],by Sex (%) 2016		
	2000	2015	Total	Female	Male
Developing Member Economies					
Central and West Asia					
Afghanistan	...	...	82.9	87.2	82.0
Armenia	19.3 (2001)	2.3 (2014)	2.0	2.0	2.1
Azerbaijan	2.7 (2001)	0.5 (2008)	0.6	0.5	0.8
Georgia	21.0	9.8 (2014)	3.8	3.1	4.5
Kazakhstan	10.5 (2001)	0.0 (2013)	1.2	0.7	1.7
Kyrgyz Republic	42.2	1.3 (2014)	3.3	1.7	4.4
Pakistan	28.7 (2001)	6.1 (2013)	7.6	8.7	7.3
Tajikistan	30.8 (2003)	19.5 (2014)	3.0	2.7	3.2
Turkmenistan	...	...	2.9	1.6	3.7
Uzbekistan[d]	68.1	...	4.7	3.2	5.8
East Asia					
China, People's Rep. of	32.0[e] (2002)	1.9[e] (2013)	4.4	4.6	4.3
Hong Kong, China	...	...	–	–	–
Korea, Rep. of[f]	...	...	–	–	–
Mongolia	10.6 (2002)	0.2 (2014)	2.9	3.0	2.9
Taipei,China	...	...	3.1	3.2	3.0
South Asia					
Bangladesh	33.7	18.5 (2010)	63.9	66.2	62.7
Bhutan	35.2 (2003)	2.2 (2012)	4.0	4.3	3.8
India	38.2[e] (2004)	21.2[e] (2011)	12.1	13.3	11.7
Maldives	10.0 (2002)	7.3 (2009)	5.9	6.5	5.4
Nepal	46.1 (2003)	15.0 (2010)	7.7	7.8	7.6
Sri Lanka	8.3 (2002)	1.9 (2012)	4.0	3.8	4.1
Southeast Asia					
Brunei Darussalam	...	...	–	–	–
Cambodia	18.6 (2004)	2.2 (2012)	20.3	20.2	20.5
Indonesia	39.8[e]	8.3[e] (2014)	10.5	10.6	10.4
Lao PDR	26.1 (2002)	16.7 (2012)	46.0	45.6	46.4
Malaysia	0.4 (2004)	0.3 (2009)	2.9	3.1	2.8
Myanmar	...	...	9.7	9.0	10.3
Philippines	18.4	13.1 (2012)	8.6	6.6	9.8
Singapore	...	...	–	–	–
Thailand	2.6	0.0 (2013)	0.1	0.1	0.1
Viet Nam	38.8 (2002)	3.1 (2014)	3.8	4.0	3.7
The Pacific					
Cook Islands	...	...	...	...	...
Fiji	5.5 (2002)	4.1 (2008)	4.2	4.8	3.9
Kiribati	14.1 (2006)	...	...	...	...
Marshall Islands	...	...	...	...	...
Micronesia, Fed. States of	11.4 (2005)	17.4 (2013)	...	...	...
Nauru	...	...	...	...	...
Palau	...	...	...	...	...
Papua New Guinea	...	39.3 (2009)	14.6	13.8	15.4
Samoa	...	0.8 (2008)	...	...	...
Solomon Islands	45.6 (2005)	...	6.8	6.5	7.0
Timor-Leste[n]	44.2 (2001)	...	9.7	9.0	10.1
Tonga	2.8 (2001)	1.1 (2009)	...	...	...
Tuvalu	...	2.7 (2010)	...	...	...
Vanuatu	...	15.4 (2010)	...	...	...
Developed Member Economies					
Australia	...	...	...	...	...
Japan	...	...	...	...	...
New Zealand	...	...	...	...	...

(continued)

Goal 1. End poverty in all its forms everywhere

Table 2.1: **Selected Indicators for SDG 1 - No Poverty** *(continued)*

By 2030,eradicate extreme poverty for all people everywhere, measured as people living below the international poverty line

By 2030, reduce at least by half the proportion of men, women, and children of all ages living in poverty in all its dimensions according to national definitions

Regional Member[a]	1.2.1 Proportion of Population Living below the National Poverty Line, by Urban-Rural Location (%)					
	2000			2015		
	Total	Urban	Rural	Total	Urban	Rural
Developing Member Economies						
Central and West Asia						
Afghanistan	36.3 (2007)	28.9 (2007)	38.2 (2007)	39.1 (2013)	...	...
Armenia	53.5 (2004)	...	...	29.8	29.4	30.4
Azerbaijan	49.0 (2001)	...	...	4.9	...	...
Georgia	24.6[c] (2004)	23.0[c] (2004)	26.2[c] (2004)	20.6[c] (2016)	14.5[c] (2016)	26.5[c] (2016)
Kazakhstan	46.7 (2001)	36.0 (2001)	59.4 (2001)	2.6 (2016)	...	...
Kyrgyz Republic	62.6	53.3	67.6	25.4 (2016)	18.6 (2016)	29.0 (2016)
Pakistan	64.3 (2001)	50.0 (2001)	70.2 (2001)	29.5 (2013)	18.2 (2013)	35.6 (2013)
Tajikistan	72.4 (2003)	68.8 (2003)	73.8 (2003)	31.0	...	...
Turkmenistan	...	...	...	...	...	...
Uzbekistan[d]	...	...	...	12.8	...	...
East Asia						
China, People's Rep. of	...	...	49.8	...	...	5.7
Hong Kong, China	...	...	...	...	...	...
Korea, Rep. of[f]	...	...	...	16.0	...	...
Mongolia	36.1 (2002)	30.3 (2002)	42.7 (2002)	21.6 (2014)	18.8 (2014)	27.9 (2014)
Taipei,China	0.7[g]	...	...	1.5[g]	...	...
South Asia						
Bangladesh	48.9	35.2	52.3	31.5 (2010)	21.3 (2010)	35.2 (2010)
Bhutan	23.2 (2007)	1.7 (2007)	30.9 (2007)	12.0 (2012)	1.8 (2012)	16.7 (2012)
India	37.2[h] (2004)	25.7[h] (2004)	41.8[h] (2004)	21.9[h] (2011)	13.7[h] (2011)	25.7[h] (2011)
Maldives	21.0[i] (2002)	...	...	15.7 (2009)	18.2 (2009)	14.3 (2009)
Nepal	30.9 (2003)	9.6 (2003)	34.6 (2003)	25.2 (2010)	15.5 (2010)	27.4 (2010)
Sri Lanka	22.7 (2002)	7.9 (2002)	24.7 (2002)	6.7 (2012)	2.1 (2012)	7.6 (2012)
Southeast Asia						
Brunei Darussalam	...	...	...	...	...	...
Cambodia	47.8 (2007)	...	53.2 (2007)	14.0 (2014)	...	...
Indonesia	19.1[j]	14.6[j]	22.4[j]	10.9[k] (2016)	7.8[k] (2016)	14.1[k] (2016)
Lao PDR	33.5 (2003)	19.7 (2003)	37.6 (2003)	23.2 (2013)	10.0 (2013)	28.6 (2013)
Malaysia	6.0 (2002)	2.3 (2002)	13.5 (2002)	0.6 (2014)	0.3 (2014)	1.6 (2014)
Myanmar	32.1 (2005)	21.5 (2005)	35.8 (2005)	25.6 (2010)	15.7 (2010)	29.2 (2010)
Philippines	26.6 (2006)	...	...	21.6	...	...
Singapore	...	...	...	...	...	...
Thailand	42.3	22.2	51.4	7.2	...	...
Viet Nam	28.9 (2002)	6.6 (2002)	35.6 (2002)	7.0	2.5	9.2
The Pacific						
Cook Islands	28.4[l] (2006)	...	...	...	...	...
Fiji	35.0[l] (2002)	28.0[l] (2002)	40.0[l] (2002)	28.1[l] (2013)	19.8[l] (2013)	36.7[l] (2013)
Kiribati	21.8[l] (2006)	...	...	...	...	...
Marshall Islands	52.7[l] (2002)	...	...	...	...	...
Micronesia, Fed. States of	31.4[l] (2005)	...	...	41.2[l] (2013)	...	...
Nauru	25.1[l] (2006)	...	...	...	...	...
Palau	24.9[l] (2006)	...	...	...	...	...
Papua New Guinea	...	...	...	39.9[m] (2009)	29.3[m] (2009)	41.6[m] (2009)
Samoa	22.9[l] (2002)	...	...	18.8[l] (2013)	...	...
Solomon Islands	22.7[m] (2005)	...	...	12.7[m] (2012)	9.1[m] (2012)	13.6[m] (2012)
Timor-Leste[n]	50.4 (2007)	38.3 (2007)	54.7 (2007)	41.8 (2014)	28.3 (2014)	47.1 (2014)
Tonga	16.2[l] (2001)	...	...	22.1[l]	...	...
Tuvalu	21.2[l] (2004)	...	...	26.3[l] (2010)	24.8[l] (2010)	27.5[l] (2010)
Vanuatu	13.0[l] (2006)	...	11.5[l] (2006)	12.7[l] (2010)	...	10.0[l] (2010)
Developed Member Economies						
Australia	...	...	...	...	...	...
Japan	...	...	...	...	...	...
New Zealand	...	...	...	...	...	...

... = data not available at cutoff date, – = magnitude equals zero, 0.0 = magnitude is less than half of unit employed, Lao PDR = Lao People's Democratic Republic, SDG = Sustainable Development Goal.

a For indicators 1.1.1a and 1.2.1 and some economies, household income and expenditure surveys were conducted in overlapping years. The table adopts the approach of the World Bank's World Development Indicators of using the initial year of the survey as the reference period for the poverty estimates. This applies to Fiji, India, Maldives, Nepal, Pakistan, Papua New Guinea, and Sri Lanka for indicator 1.1.1a; and to Afghanistan, Fiji, India, Maldives, Pakistan, Samoa, Sri Lanka, Solomon Islands, and Tuvalu for indicator 1.2.1.
b For indicator 1.1.1a, data are consumption-based, except for Malaysia, which are income-based. For indicators 1.1.1a and 1.1.1b, the estimates are based on the international poverty line of $1.90 a day (2011 PPP).
c Refers to relative poverty or the share of population under 60% of the median consumption.
d For indicator 1.1.1a, the latest available data for Uzbekistan is for 2003: 66.8%.
e Weighted average of rural and urban estimates.
f For indicator 1.2.1, the earliest available data for the Republic of Korea is for 2012: 16.5%.
g Refers to percentage of low-income population to total population.
h Based on Tendulkar methodology, using mixed reference period.
i Based on half the median of Atoll expenditure per person per day equivalent to 22 rufiyaa.
j Reference period is February 2000.
k Reference period is March 2016.
l Data refer to percentage of population below the basic needs poverty line.
m Refers to poverty headcount ratio using the upper poverty line.
n For indicator 1.1.1a, the latest data for Timor-Leste is for 2007: 46.8%.

Sources: World Bank. PovcalNet Database. http://iresearch.worldbank.org/PovcalNet/povDuplicateWB.aspx (accessed 17 July 2017); economy sources; United Nations. Sustainable Development Goals Indicators Database. http://unstats.un.org/sdgs/indicators/database/ (accessed 18 July 2017); World Bank. World Development Indicators. http://databank.worldbank.org/data/reports.aspx?source=world-development-indicators (accessed 15 July 2017); International Labour Organization. ILOSTAT. http://www.ilo.org/ilostat (accessed 30 June 2017).

Table 2.2: **Selected Indicators for SDG 2 - Zero Hunger**

By 2030, end hunger and ensure access by all people, in particular the poor and people in vulnerable situations, including infants, to safe, nutritious and sufficient food all year round

By 2030, end all forms of malnutrition, including achieving, by 2025, the internationally agreed targets on stunting and wasting in children under 5 years of age, and address the nutritional needs of adolescent girls, pregnant and lactating women and older persons

Regional Member	2.1.1 Prevalence of Undernourishment (%)		2.2.1 Prevalence of Stunting among Children under 5 Years of Age[a] (%)	
	2000[b]	2015[c]	2000	2015
Developing Member Economies				
Central and West Asia				
Afghanistan	45.2	26.8	59.3 (2004)	40.9 (2013)
Armenia	21.4	5.8	17.7	9.4 (2016)
Azerbaijan	22.5	<5.0	24.1	18.0 (2013)
Georgia	14.8	7.4	14.7 (2005)	11.3 (2009)
Kazakhstan	<5.0	<5.0	17.5 (2006)	8.0
Kyrgyz Republic	15.2	6.0	18.1 (2006)	12.9 (2014)
Pakistan	22.4	22.0	41.5 (2001)	45.0 (2012)
Tajikistan	38.8	33.2	42.1	26.8 (2012)
Turkmenistan	9.0	<5.0	28.1	11.5
Uzbekistan	11.5	<5.0	25.3 (2002)	...
East Asia				
China, People's Rep. of	16.2	9.3	17.8	9.4 (2010)
Hong Kong, China	...	...	...	...
Korea, Rep. of	<5.0	<5.0	2.5 (2003)	2.5 (2010)
Mongolia	38.2	20.5	29.8	10.8 (2013)
Taipei,China	...	...	...	...
South Asia				
Bangladesh	23.1	16.4	50.8	36.1 (2014)
Bhutan	...	...	34.9 (2008)	33.6 (2010)
India	17.0	15.2	47.9 (2006)	38.4
Maldives	11.8	5.2	31.9 (2001)	20.3 (2009)
Nepal	22.2	7.8	57.1 (2001)	37.4 (2014)
Sri Lanka	29.9	22.0	18.4	14.7 (2012)
Southeast Asia				
Brunei Darussalam	<5.0	<5.0	...	19.7 (2009)
Cambodia	32.0	14.2	49.2	32.4 (2014)
Indonesia	17.2	7.6	42.4	36.4 (2013)
Lao PDR	39.2	18.5	48.2	43.8 (2011)
Malaysia	<5.0	<5.0	17.2 (2006)	17.7
Myanmar	52.4	14.2	40.8	29.2 (2016)
Philippines	21.3	13.5	33.8 (2003)	30.3 (2013)
Singapore	...	...	4.4	...
Thailand	19.0	7.4	15.7 (2006)	16.3 (2012)
Viet Nam	28.1	11.0	43.4	24.6
The Pacific				
Cook Islands	...	...	...	...
Fiji	<5.0	<5.0	7.5 (2004)	...
Kiribati	<5.0	<5.0	...	...
Marshall Islands	...	...	...	...
Micronesia, Fed. States of	...	...	...	...
Nauru	...	...	24.0 (2007)	...
Palau	...	...	...	...
Papua New Guinea	...	...	43.9 (2005)	49.5 (2010)
Samoa	6.6	<5.0	...	...
Solomon Islands	15.0	11.3	32.8 (2007)	...
Timor-Leste	43.9	26.9	55.7 (2002)	50.2 (2013)
Tonga	...	...	...	8.1 (2012)
Tuvalu	...	...	10.0 (2007)	...
Vanuatu	8.1	6.4	25.9 (2007)	28.5 (2013)
Developed Member Economies				
Australia	<5.0	<5.0	2.0 (2007)	...
Japan	<5.0	<5.0	...	7.1 (2010)
New Zealand	<5.0	<5.0	...	...

(continued)

Table 2.2: **Selected Indicators for SDG 2 - Zero Hunger** *(continued)*

Regional Member	2.2.2.a Prevalence of Malnutrition (Wasting) among Children under 5 Years of Age[a] (%)		2.2.2.b Prevalence of Malnutrition (Overweight) among Children under 5 Years of Age[a] (%)	
	2000	2015	2000	2015
Developing Member Economies				
Central and West Asia				
Afghanistan	8.6 (2004)	9.5 (2013)	4.6 (2004)	5.4 (2013)
Armenia	2.5	4.2 (2016)	16.0	13.6 (2016)
Azerbaijan	9.0	3.1 (2013)	6.2	13.0 (2013)
Georgia	3.0 (2005)	1.6 (2009)	21.0 (2005)	19.9 (2009)
Kazakhstan	4.9 (2006)	3.1	16.9 (2006)	9.3 (2016)
Kyrgyz Republic	3.4 (2006)	2.8 (2014)	10.7 (2006)	7.0 (2014)
Pakistan	14.2 (2001)	10.5 (2012)	4.8 (2001)	4.8 (2012)
Tajikistan	9.4	9.9 (2012)	6.7 (2005)	6.6 (2012)
Turkmenistan	7.1	4.2	4.5 (2006)	5.9
Uzbekistan	8.9 (2002)	...	11.1 (2002)	...
East Asia				
China, People's Rep. of	2.5	2.3 (2010)	3.4	6.6 (2010)
Hong Kong, China	...	...	...	...
Korea, Rep. of	0.9 (2003)	1.2 (2010)	6.2 (2003)	7.3 (2010)
Mongolia	7.1	1.0 (2013)	12.7	10.5 (2013)
Taipei,China	...	...	...	...
South Asia				
Bangladesh	12.5	14.3 (2014)	0.9	1.4 (2014)
Bhutan	4.7 (2008)	5.9 (2010)	4.4 (2008)	7.6 (2010)
India	20.0 (2006)	21.0	1.9 (2006)	...
Maldives	13.4 (2001)	10.2 (2009)	3.9 (2001)	6.5 (2009)
Nepal	11.3	11.3 (2014)	0.7 (2001)	2.1 (2014)
Sri Lanka	15.5	21.4 (2012)	1.0	0.6 (2012)
Southeast Asia				
Brunei Darussalam	...	2.9 (2009)	...	8.3 (2009)
Cambodia	16.9	9.6 (2014)	4.0	2.0 (2014)
Indonesia	5.5	13.5 (2013)	1.5	11.5 (2013)
Lao PDR	17.5	6.4 (2011)	2.7	2.0 (2011)
Malaysia	...	8.0	...	7.1
Myanmar	10.7	7.0 (2016)	2.4	1.3 (2016)
Philippines	6.0 (2003)	7.9 (2013)	2.4 (2003)	5.0 (2013)
Singapore	3.6	...	2.6	...
Thailand	4.7 (2006)	6.7 (2012)	8.0 (2006)	10.9 (2012)
Viet Nam	6.1	6.4	2.5	5.3
The Pacific				
Cook Islands	...	...	...	...
Fiji	6.3 (2004)	...	5.1 (2004)	...
Kiribati	...	...	...	...
Marshall Islands	...	...	...	...
Micronesia, Fed. States of	...	...	...	...
Nauru	1.0 (2007)	...	2.8 (2007)	...
Palau	...	...	...	...
Papua New Guinea	4.4 (2005)	14.3 (2010)	3.4 (2005)	13.8 (2010)
Samoa	...	...	...	...
Solomon Islands	4.3 (2007)	...	2.5 (2007)	...
Timor-Leste	13.7 (2002)	11.0 (2013)	5.7 (2002)	1.5 (2013)
Tonga	...	5.2 (2012)	...	17.3 (2012)
Tuvalu	3.3 (2007)	...	6.3 (2007)	...
Vanuatu	5.9 (2007)	4.4 (2013)	4.7 (2007)	4.6 (2013)
Developed Member Economies				
Australia	- (2007)	...	7.7 (2007)	...
Japan	...	2.3 (2010)	...	1.5 (2010)
New Zealand	...	...	...	...

... = data not available at cutoff date, – = magnitude equals zero, 0.0 = magnitude is less than half of unit employed, Lao PDR = Lao People's Democratic Republic, SDG = Sustainable Development Goal.

a According to the World Health Organization, for some economies, the estimates were adjusted where necessary to be nationally representative and to cover the age range 0–5 years, which might result in slight differences in prevalence from the survey results reported. Estimates for some economies are also "pending reanalysis." Details can be found in the "Notes" column of the *Joint Child Malnutrition Estimates - 2017 Edition.*
b Data refer to 3-year average for 1999–2001.
c Data refer to 3-year average for 2014–2016.

Sources: United Nations. Sustainable Development Goals Indicators Database. http://unstats.un.org/sdgs/indicators/database/ (accessed 18 July 2017); Food and Agriculture Organization of the United Nations. FAOSTAT. http://www.fao.org/economic/ess/ess-fs/ess-fadata/en/#.WXG4D2dlK71 (accessed 26 June 2017); UNICEF. *Joint Child Malnutrition Estimates - 2017 Edition.* http://data.unicef.org/resources/joint-child-malnutrition-estimates-2017-edition/ (accessed 26 June 2017).

Table 2.3: **Selected Indicators for SDG 2 - Improved Agricultural Investment**

Increase investment, including through enhanced international cooperation, in rural infrastructure, agricultural research and extension services, technology development and plant and livestock gene banks in order to enhance agricultural productive capacity in developing countries, in particular least developed countries

Regional Member	2.a.1 The Agriculture Orientation Index for Government Expenditures		2.a.2 Total Official Flows (Official Development Assistance Plus Other Official Flows) to the Agriculture Sector[a]	
	2001	2015	2000	2015
Developing Member Economies				
Central and West Asia				
Afghanistan	0.1 (2003)	0.2 (2013)	4.2	328.1
Armenia	...	0.1	14.5	36.6
Azerbaijan	...	0.5 (2014)	71.9	51.2
Georgia	0.1 (2003)	0.3	35.4	41.3
Kazakhstan	0.6 (2005)	0.6	3.7	65.2
Kyrgyz Republic	0.1	0.1 (2011)	79.0	24.0
Pakistan	0.0	0.0	60.0	291.7
Tajikistan	...	...	22.5	33.3
Turkmenistan	...	...	0.0	0.1
Uzbekistan	...	0.5 (2014)	0.2	68.8
East Asia				
China, People's Rep. of	0.3 (2007)	0.3 (2014)	310.1	386.4
Hong Kong, China	...	...	...	...
Korea, Rep. of	1.5	1.7 (2014)	...	...
Mongolia	0.2	0.1	4.1	17.5
Taipei,China	...	...	...	...
South Asia				
Bangladesh	0.2	0.7 (2013)	341.2	249.4
Bhutan	0.3	0.7	5.4	6.6
India	0.2	0.4 (2013)	221.9	1,048.5
Maldives	0.2	0.2 (2011)	0.0	0.6
Nepal	0.2 (2002)	0.4	74.7	101.0
Sri Lanka	0.2	0.6	50.0	33.6
Southeast Asia				
Brunei Darussalam	...	...	...	...
Cambodia	...	...	153.4	111.0
Indonesia	0.2 (2004)	0.1 (2013)	204.5	218.3
Lao PDR	...	...	26.8	66.1
Malaysia	0.4	0.3	8.1	4.6
Myanmar	...	...	1.9	142.3
Philippines	0.3	0.4	338.8	110.0
Singapore	1.9	7.6	...	...
Thailand	0.9	0.7	26.9	7.3
Viet Nam	0.1 (2006)	0.2 (2014)	102.0	236.7
The Pacific				
Cook Islands	...	...	0.0	0.3
Fiji	0.3 (2005)	0.3	1.0	19.7
Kiribati	...	...	7.1	2.5
Marshall Islands	...	0.1 (2014)	3.0	1.4
Micronesia, Fed. States of	...	0.2 (2014)	8.8	1.8
Nauru	...	...	0.2 (2003)	0.4
Palau	...	0.1 (2014)	0.2	0.7
Papua New Guinea	...	...	55.8	29.0
Samoa	...	0.4	2.5	3.8
Solomon Islands	...	0.1 (2014)	3.3	12.2
Timor-Leste	...	0.6	8.2	23.9
Tonga	...	...	0.2	1.8
Tuvalu	...	...	6.6 (2001)	2.1
Vanuatu	0.1 (2005)	0.2 (2012)	3.7	3.7
Developed Member Economies				
Australia	0.2	0.2	...	...
Japan	...	...	...	...
New Zealand	0.3 (2004)	...	...	...

... = data not available at cutoff date; 0.0 = magnitude is less than half of unit employed, Lao PDR = Lao People's Democratic Republic, SDG = Sustainable Development Goal.

a Data refer to gross disbursements (constant 2015 $ million).

Sources: Food and Agriculture Organization of the United Nations. http://www.fao.org/faostat/en/#data/EA (accessed 6 June 2017); United Nations. Sustainable Development Goals Indicators Database. http://unstats.un.org/sdgs/indicators/database/ (accessed 18 July 2017).

Goal 3. Ensure healthy lives and promote well-being for all at all ages

Table 2.4: **Selected Indicators for SDG 3 - Maternal and Child Health**

By 2030, reduce the global maternal mortality ratio to less than 70 per 100,000 live births

By 2030, end preventable deaths of newborns and children under 5 years of age, with all countries aiming to reduce neonatal mortality to at least as low as 12 per 1,000 live births and under-5 mortality to at least as low as 25 per 1,000 live births

Regional Member	3.1.1 Maternal Mortality Ratio (per 100,000 live births)[a]		3.1.2 Proportion of Births Attended by Skilled Health Personnel (%)[b]		3.2.1 Under-5 Mortality Rate (per 1,000 live births)[a]		3.2.2 Neonatal Mortality Rate (per 1,000 live births)[a]	
	2000	2015	2000	2015	2000	2015	2000	2015
Developing Member Economies								
Central and West Asia	**366**	**174**			**106**	**71**	**52**	**37**
Afghanistan	1100	396	14.3[c] (2003)	50.5[e]	137	91	45	36
Armenia	40	25	96.8[c]	99.8[e] (2016)	30	14	16	7
Azerbaijan	48	25	80.7[c]	99.9[e] (2014)	74	32	33	18
Georgia	37	36	95.5[e]	99.9[c] (2014)	36	12	21	7
Kazakhstan	65	12	98.3[e]	100.0[e] (2014)	44	14	20	7
Kyrgyz Republic	74	76	98.6[e]	98.4[c] (2014)	49	21	22	12
Pakistan	306	178	23.0[c] (2002)	52.1[d] (2013)	112	81	60	46
Tajikistan	68	32	70.7[c]	90.3[e] (2014)	93	45	30	21
Turkmenistan	59	42	97.2[c]	...	82	51	31	23
Uzbekistan	34	36	94.9[c]	100.0[e] (2014)	63	39	29	20
East Asia	**57**	**27**			**36**	**11**	**21**	**5**
China, People's Rep. of	58	27	96.6[e]	99.9[e] (2014)	37	11	21	6
Hong Kong, China	6	2	...	...	...	...	2[g]	1[g] (2012)
Korea, Rep. of	16	11	99.9[f]	100.0[f]	6	3	2	2
Mongolia	161	44	96.6[d]	98.9[c] (2013)	63	22	26	11
Taipei,China	8	12	...	...	...	...	...	...
South Asia	**377**	**174**			**90**	**46**	**44**	**27**
Bangladesh	399	176	12.1[d]	42.1[d] (2014)	88	38	43	23
Bhutan	423	148	23.7[e]	81.0[e] (2012)	80	33	33	18
India	374	174	42.5[c]	81.4[c] (2014)	91	48	45	28
Maldives	163	68	84.0[c] (2004)	95.5[c] (2012)	44	9	26	5
Nepal	548	258	11.9[e]	55.6[e] (2014)	81	36	39	22
Sri Lanka	57	30	96.0[e]	...	16	10	10	5
Southeast Asia	**200**	**110**			**49**	**27**	**21**	**13**
Brunei Darussalam	31	23	99.5[e]	100.0[e]	9	10	5	4
Cambodia	484	161	31.8[c]	89.0[d] (2014)	108	29	36	15
Indonesia	265	126	66.3[e] (2003)	87.4[c] (2013)	52	27	22	14
Lao PDR	546	197	16.7[c]	40.1[c] (2012)	118	67	43	30
Malaysia	58	40	96.6[e]	99.0[e] (2014)	10	7	5	4
Myanmar	308	178	57.0[c] (2001)	60.2[d] (2016)	82	50	37	26
Philippines	124	114	58.0[c]	72.8[c] (2013)	40	28	17	13
Singapore	18	10	99.7[f]	99.6[f]	4	3	2	1
Thailand	25	20	99.3[e]	99.6[d] (2012)	23	12	13	7
Viet Nam	81	54	58.8[c]	93.8[c] (2014)	34	22	16	11
The Pacific	**346**	**192**			**73**	**51**	**28**	**22**
Cook Islands	...	...	98.0[d]	100.0[e] (2009)	17	8	9	4
Fiji	42	30	96.9[c]	99.7[e] (2013)	25	22	14	10
Kiribati	166	90	85.0[d]	98.3[e] (2010)	71	56	29	24
Marshall Islands	...	...	86.2[c] (2007)	90.1[c] (2011)	41	36	19	17
Micronesia, Fed. States of	153	100	82.8[c]	100.0[e] (2009)	54	35	26	19
Nauru	...	...	97.4[d] (2007)	...	41	35	25	23
Palau	...	...	100.0[e]	100.0[c]	27	16	15	9
Papua New Guinea	342	215	39.0[e] (2004)	...	79	57	30	25
Samoa	93	51	80.0[d]	82.5[d] (2014)	22	18	12	10
Solomon Islands	214	114	85.5[d] (2007)	...	33	28	14	12
Timor-Leste	694	215	24.0[d] (2002)	29.3[c] (2010)	110	53	37	22
Tonga	97	124	95.0[d]	95.5[c] (2012)	18	17	8	7
Tuvalu	...	...	100.0[d]	...	43	27	25	18
Vanuatu	144	78	88.0[d]	89.4[d] (2013)	29	28	12	12
Developed Member Economies	**10**	**5**			**5**	**3**	**2**	**1**
Australia	9	6	99.3[f]	99.3[f] (2013)	6	4	4	2
Japan	10	5	99.8[f]	99.8[f] (2014)	5	3	2	1
New Zealand	12	11	97.3[f]	96.6[f] (2014)	7	6	4	3
DEVELOPING MEMBER ECONOMIES	**269**	**126**			**71**	**36**	**35**	**20**
REGIONAL MEMBERS	**264**	**123**			**70**	**36**	**35**	**20**
WORLD	**385**	**216**			**76**	**43**	**31**	**19**

... = data not available at cutoff date, Lao PDR = Lao People's Democratic Republic, SDG = Sustainable Development Goal.

a Regional aggregates are weighted averages estimated using population of annual live births for the respective year headings. The data for maternal, under-five, and neonatal deaths are from UNICEF Global databases. Aggregates are derived for reporting economies only. For maternal mortality ratio, aggregates for East Asia exclude Hong Kong, China and Taipei,China.
b Based on population-based national household survey data and routine health systems.
c Estimates are aligned with the standard definition of doctor, nurse, and/or midwife.
d Includes other health personnel not in alignment with the standard definition.
e No clear definition of health personnel.
f Institutional birth including all deliveries that occurred at a health facility.
g Calculated based on known births and deaths.

Sources: For indicator 3.1.1: World Health Organization. *Trends in Maternal Mortality: 1990 to 2015 Estimates by WHO, UNICEF, UNFPA, World Bank Group and the United Nations Population Division*; for Hong Kong, China: Centre for Health Protection. http://www.chp.gov.hk/en/data/4/10/27/110.html (accessed 30 June 2017), and Department of Health. *Annual Report 2012/2013*. Supplementary Tables. http://www.dh.gov.hk/english/pub_rec/pub_rec_ar/pub_rec_arpis_1213_html.html; for Taipei,China: Directorate-General of Budget, Accounting, and Statistics. http://eng.dgbas.gov.tw/public/data/dgbas03/bs2/yearbook_eng/y066.pdf (accessed 29 June 2017); for Indicator 3.1.2: UNICEF and WHO. Database 2016 of Skilled Health Personnel. https://data.unicef.org/topic/maternal-health/delivery-care/ (accessed 30 June 2017); for Indicators 3.2.1 and 3.2.2: United Nations International Children's Emergency Fund. Global Databases. http://www.data.unicef.org (accessed 30 June 2017); for Hong Kong, China: Department of Health. Annual Report 2012/2013. Supplementary Tables. http://www.dh.gov.hk/english/pub_rec/pub_rec_ar/pub_rec_arpis_1213_html.html (accessed 29 June 2017).

Table 2.5: **Selected Indicators for SDG 3 - Incidence of Communicable Diseases, Death Rate, and Adolescent Birth Rate**

By 2030, end the epidemics of AIDS, tuberculosis, malaria and neglected tropical diseases and combat hepatitis, water-borne diseases, and other communicable diseases

By 2030, reduce by one-third premature mortality from noncommunicable diseases through prevention and treatment and promote mental health and well-being

Strengthen the prevention and treatment of substance abuse, including narcotic drug abuse, and harmful use of alcohol

By 2020, halve the number of global deaths and injuries from road traffic accidents

By 2030, ensure universal access to sexual and reproductive health care services, including for family planning, information and education, and the integration of reproductive health into national strategies and programs

By 2030, substantially reduce the number of deaths and illnesses from hazardous chemicals and air, water and soil pollution and contamination

Substantially increase health financing and the recruitment, development, training and retention of the health workforce in developing countries, especially in least developed countries and small island developing states

Regional Member	3.3.1 Number of New HIV Infections (per 1,000 uninfected population)		3.3.2 Tuberculosis Incidence (per 100,000 population)		3.3.3 Malaria Incidence (per 1,000 population)		3.4.1 Mortality Rate Attributed to Cardiovascular Disease, Cancer, Diabetes, or Chronic Respiratory Disease (%)	
	2000	2015	2000	2015	2000	2015	2000	2015
Developing Member Economies								
Central and West Asia								
Afghanistan	0.02	0.03	190.0	189.0	107.1	23.6	34.2	31.0
Armenia	0.12	0.14	61.0	41.0	...	...	27.0	23.2
Azerbaijan	0.05	0.12	681.0	69.0	17.9	–	29.8	23.8
Georgia	0.07	0.28	254.0	99.0	11.3	–	24.4	22.2
Kazakhstan	0.06	0.21	177.0	89.0	...	...	40.9	28.6
Kyrgyz Republic	0.05	0.16	244.0	144.0	6.7	–	31.4	24.0
Pakistan	0.01	0.09	275.0	270.0	44.8	8.6	24.8	24.7
Tajikistan	0.17	0.19	219.0	87.0	18.3	–	30.6	25.8
Turkmenistan	...	...	208.0	70.0	...	...	34.7	34.5
Uzbekistan	0.32	0.01	99.0	79.0	5.6	–	29.8	26.9
East Asia								
China, People's Rep. of	...	...	109.0	67.0	0.1	–	22.6	18.1
Hong Kong, China	...	...	102.0	71.0	...	...	...	...
Korea, Rep. of	...	...	50.0	80.0	2.8	0.8	16.5	8.3
Mongolia	–	0.02	428.0	428.0	...	...	38.2	29.9
Taipei,China	...	...	...	...	...	...	...	...
South Asia								
Bangladesh	–	0.01	225.0	225.0	12.5	0.8	22.9	21.5
Bhutan	...	...	253.0	155.0	26.4	0.1	30.3	23.1
India	...	...	289.0	217.0	42.7	18.6	26.7	23.4
Maldives	...	...	59.0	53.0	...	...	21.2	12.4
Nepal	0.32	0.05	163.0	156.0	18.3	3.3	27.1	21.8
Sri Lanka	0.01	0.03	66.0	65.0	107.0	–	21.8	17.7
Southeast Asia								
Brunei Darussalam	...	...	107.0	58.0	...	...	21.1	12.6
Cambodia	0.82	0.05	575.0	380.0	207.0	13.0	26.3	23.3
Indonesia	0.07	0.29	449.0	395.0	99.1	26.1	26.9	26.6
Lao PDR	...	...	330.0	182.0	77.5	20.9	30.4	25.8
Malaysia	0.55	0.17	74.0	89.0	16.3	1.9	20.1	17.1
Myanmar	0.84	0.24	411.0	365.0	78.3	11.8	23.9	24.5
Philippines	0.01	0.06	368.0	322.0	4.3	0.4	27.9	28.6
Singapore	...	...	51.0	44.0	...	...	16.7	10.2
Thailand	0.52	0.11	241.0	172.0	11.9	2.7	19.5	16.2
Viet Nam	0.34	0.16	197.0	137.0	6.4	0.3	18.7	17.3
The Pacific								
Cook Islands	...	...	6.5	7.8	...	...	...	...
Fiji	...	...	22.0	51.0	...	...	35.8	31.4
Kiribati	...	...	373.0	551.0	...	...	30.5	28.2
Marshall Islands	...	...	81.0	344.0	...	...	...	...
Micronesia, Fed. States of	...	...	106.0	124.0	...	...	27.4	25.9
Nauru	...	...	46.0	113.0	...	...	...	...
Palau	...	...	65.0	76.0	...	...	...	...
Papua New Guinea	0.87	0.36	432.0	432.0	270.3	122.2	38.5	36.1
Samoa	...	...	28.0	11.0	...	...	29.2	22.1
Solomon Islands	...	...	92.0	89.0	475.7	67.0	28.6	26.4
Timor-Leste	...	...	498.0 (2002)	498.0	482.6	0.2	26.3	20.7
Tonga	...	...	28.0	15.0	...	...	27.0	24.1
Tuvalu	...	...	195.0	232.0	...	...	...	...
Vanuatu	...	...	110.0	63.0	135.0	3.3	26.5	22.3
Developed Member Economies								
Australia	0.05	0.05	6.3	6.0	...	...	13.0	8.9
Japan	...	...	36.0	17.0	...	...	11.4	8.8
New Zealand	...	...	10.0	7.4	...	...	15.9	10.4

(continued)

Goal 3. Ensure healthy lives and promote well-being for all at all ages

Table 2.5: **Selected Indicators for SDG 3 - Incidence of Communicable Diseases, Death Rate, and Adolescent Birth Rate** *(continued)*

Regional Member	3.6.1 Death Rate due to Road Traffic Injuries (per 100,000 population)		3.7.2 Adolescent Birthrate (Aged 15–19 Years) per 1,000 Women in That Age Group		3.9.1 Mortality Rate Attributed to Household and Ambient Air Pollution (per 100,000 population)	3.9.2 Mortality Rate Attributed to Unsafe Water, Unsafe Sanitation and Lack of Hygiene (exposure to unsafe Water, Sanitation and Hygiene for All (WASH) services) (per 100,000 population)
	2000	2013	2000	2014	2012	2012
Developing Member Economies						
Central and West Asia						
Afghanistan	15.7	15.5	...	...	114.8	34.6
Armenia	20.6	18.3	30.0 (2004)	22.7 (2013)	93.2	1.1
Azerbaijan	7.9	10.0	38.0	54.3 (2015)	47.0	2.1
Georgia	10.5	11.8	48.0 (2004)	46.5	204.9	0.2
Kazakhstan	14.1	24.2	33.0	31.0 (2015)	90.0	1.2
Kyrgyz Republic	12.0	22.0	34.7	65.0 (2013)	87.1	1.8
Pakistan	14.8	14.2	...	...	87.2	20.7
Tajikistan	19.7	18.8	37.3	54.0 (2011)	92.0	7.5
Turkmenistan	18.0	17.4	26.1	...	70.9	5.8
Uzbekistan	9.7	11.2	25.5 (2006)	29.5 (2010)	76.5	2.4
East Asia						
China, People's Rep. of	18.0	18.8	8.0	5.9 (2010)	161.1	0.4
Hong Kong, China	...	...	5.0	3.0	...	...
Korea, Rep. of	26.4	12.0	2.6	1.6	23.2	0.2
Mongolia	18.7	21.0	...	...	132.4	3.1
Taipei,China	...	...	...	...	...	...
South Asia						
Bangladesh	14.3	13.6	...	...	68.6	6.0
Bhutan	16.5	15.1	61.7	28.4 (2012)	58.9	7.1
India	16.3	16.6	...	...	133.7	27.4
Maldives	2.9	3.5	...	...	15.3	0.6
Nepal	16.9	17.0	...	...	103.2	12.9
Sri Lanka	18.3	17.4	...	...	125.4	3.3
Southeast Asia						
Brunei Darussalam	16.3	8.1	31.8	11.4	0.2	0.1
Cambodia	17.8	17.4	47.0 (2004)	57.0 (2013)	71.4	5.6
Indonesia	15.2	15.3	54.0	48.0 (2010)	85.0	3.6
Lao PDR	14.0	14.3	...	...	108.3	13.9
Malaysia	26.6	24.0	15.3 (2001)	12.7 (2012)	21.6	0.4
Myanmar	21.8	20.3	...	...	128.2	10.4
Philippines	9.9	10.5	55.0 (2001)	57.0 (2012)	88.7	5.1
Singapore	6.7	3.6	8.0 (2002)	2.7 (2015)	20.7	0.1
Thailand	37.7	36.2	...	...	64.0	1.9
Viet Nam	23.6	24.5	...	...	83.2	2.0
The Pacific						
Cook Islands	5.6	24.2	...	...	...	...
Fiji	9.6	5.8	34.8 (2002)	27.5 (2008)	95.1	3.0
Kiribati	8.5	2.9	42.0	49.9 (2010)	0.0	15.9
Marshall Islands	17.3	5.7	127.0 (2005)	82.2 (2011)	...	7.6
Micronesia, Fed. States of	16.8	1.9	57.9	...	0.1	9.7
Nauru	19.9	19.9	...	...	...	...
Palau	15.6	4.8	...	...	...	4.8
Papua New Guinea	17.3	16.8	...	...	46.3	12.4
Samoa	16.6	15.8	...	...	...	3.7
Solomon Islands	18.7	19.2	82.0	62.0 (2008)	54.3	10.4
Timor-Leste	17.1	16.6	78.3 (2001)	50.0 (2010)	91.6	10.3
Tonga	15.3	7.6	...	...	...	4.8
Tuvalu	21.2	20.3	...	...	...	...
Vanuatu	15.7	16.6	...	78.0 (2011)	0.9	7.3
Developed Member Economies						
Australia	9.5	5.4	17.8	12.6	0.4	0.0
Japan	12.3	4.7	5.1 (2005)	4.4	24.2	0.1
New Zealand	12.1	6.0	27.9	19.0 (2015)	0.5	0.6

... = data not available at cutoff date, – = magnitude equals zero, 0.0 = magnitude is less than half of unit employed, Lao PDR = Lao People's Democratic Republic, SDG = Sustainable Development Goal.

Sources: United Nations. Sustainable Development Goals Indicators Database. http://unstats.un.org/sdgs/indicators/database/ (accessed 18 July 2017); World Health Organization. http://www.who.int/tb/country/data/download/en/ (accessed 20 July 2017); http://www.who.int/violence_injury_prevention/road_safety_status/2015/GSRRS2015_data/en/ (accessed 21 July 2017); http://apps.who.int/gho/data/view.main.GSWCAH37v (accessed 22 July 2017); http://apps.who.int/gho/data/node.main.INADEQUATEWSH?lang=en (accessed 23 July 2017).

Table 2.6: **Selected Indicators for SDG 4 - Proficiency in Reading and Mathematics**
By 2030, ensure that all girls and boys complete free, equitable, and quality primary and secondary education leading to relevant and effective learning outcomes

Regional Member	4.1.1.a Proportion of Children and Young People at the End of Primary Achieving at Least a Minimum Proficiency Level in Mathematics (%)	4.1.1.b Proportion of Children and Young People at the End of Primary Achieving at Least a Minimum Proficiency Level in Reading (%)	4.1.1.c Proportion of Children and Young People at the End of Lower Secondary Achieving at Least a Minimum Proficiency Level in Mathematics (%)	4.1.1.d Proportion of Children and Young People at the End of Lower Secondary Achieving at Least a Minimum Proficiency Level in Reading (%)
	2011	2011	2015	2015
Developing Member Economies				
Central and West Asia				
Afghanistan	...	...	...	...
Armenia	71.5	...	76.4 (2011)	...
Azerbaijan	71.5	81.9	...	...
Georgia	72.8	86.5	42.9	48.3
Kazakhstan	88.0	...	90.8	42.9 (2012)
Kyrgyz Republic	...	...	...	...
Pakistan	...	...	...	...
Tajikistan	...	...	...	...
Turkmenistan	...	...	...	...
Uzbekistan	...	...	...	...
East Asia				
China, People's Rep. of	...	...	...	...
Hong Kong, China	99.2	99.2	91.0	90.7
Korea, Rep. of	99.6	...	84.5	86.3
Mongolia	...	...	...	...
Taipei,China	...	...	...	...
South Asia				
Bangladesh	...	...	...	...
Bhutan	...	...	...	...
India	...	...	...	...
Maldives	...	...	...	...
Nepal	...	...	...	...
Sri Lanka	...	...	...	...
Southeast Asia				
Brunei Darussalam	...	...	...	...
Cambodia	92.8	94.0	...	...
Indonesia	...	66.2	31.4	44.6
Lao PDR	...	...	...	...
Malaysia	...	...	75.8	47.3 (2012)
Myanmar	...	...	...	...
Philippines	...	...	...	...
Singapore	98.8	96.7	98.9	90.1 (2012)
Thailand	77.3	...	46.2	50.0
Viet Nam	100.0	100.0	80.9	86.2
The Pacific				
Cook Islands	...	...	...	...
Fiji	...	...	...	...
Kiribati	...	...	...	...
Marshall Islands	...	...	...	...
Micronesia, Fed. States of	...	...	...	...
Nauru	...	...	...	...
Palau	...	...	...	...
Papua New Guinea	...	...	...	...
Samoa	...	...	...	...
Solomon Islands	86.7 (2013)	62.2 (2013)	...	...
Timor-Leste	...	...	...	...
Tonga	...	...	...	...
Tuvalu	...	...	...	...
Vanuatu	...	...	...	...
Developed Member Economies				
Australia	95.2 (2014)	94.9 (2014)	78.0	81.9
Japan	99.0	...	89.3	87.1
New Zealand	85.2	91.7	78.4	82.7

... = data not available at cutoff date, Lao PDR = Lao People's Democratic Republic, SDG = Sustainable Development Goal.

Sources: United Nations. Sustainable Development Goals Indicators Database. https://unstats.un.org/sdgs/indicators/database/ (accessed 18 July 2017); United Nations Educational, Scientific and Cultural Organization Institute for Statistics. http://uis.unesco.org/ (accessed 27 July 2017).

Table 2.7: **Selected Indicators for SDG 4 - Early Childhood Education**
By 2030, ensure that all girls and boys have access to quality early childhood development, care, and preprimary education so that they are ready for primary education

Regional Member	4.2.2 Participation Rate in Organized Learning (1 year before the official primary entry age)[a,b] (%)					
	2000			2015		
	Total	Female	Male	Total	Female	Male
Developing Member Economies						
Central and West Asia						
Afghanistan	...	...	...	...	...	...
Armenia	...	...	...	...	...	...
Azerbaijan	15.8	16.1	15.6	27.6	28.0	27.3
Georgia	50.0 (2004)	53.3 (2004)	47.0 (2004)	...	...	...
Kazakhstan	...	...	...	90.7 (2016)	94.6 (2016)	87.1 (2016)
Kyrgyz Republic	42.1	42.9	41.3	69.2	70.5	68.0
Pakistan	...	...	...	...	...	...
Tajikistan	...	...	...	14.9 (2016)	14.0 (2016)	15.7 (2016)
Turkmenistan	...	...	...	...	...	...
Uzbekistan	...	...	...	31.1 (2016)	31.1 (2016)	31.2 (2016)
East Asia						
China, People's Rep. of	...	...	...	...	...	...
Hong Kong, China	99.9 (2007)	99.8 (2007)	100.0 (2007)	99.2 (2011)	98.3 (2011)	100.0 (2011)
Korea, Rep. of	50.3 (2005)	51.0 (2005)	49.8 (2005)	90.3	90.1	90.5
Mongolia	96.5 (2007)	100.0 (2007)	93.1 (2007)	89.4 (2012)	89.3 (2012)	89.4 (2012)
Taipei,China	...	...	...	...	...	...
South Asia						
Bangladesh	...	...	...	59.9 (2011)	59.6 (2011)	60.3 (2011)
Bhutan	...	...	...	...	...	...
India	...	...	...	...	...	...
Maldives	69.5	70.0	69.1	99.6 (2016)	100.0 (2016)	99.3 (2016)
Nepal	...	...	...	83.7 (2016)	82.5 (2016)	84.8 (2016)
Sri Lanka	...	...	...	...	...	...
Southeast Asia						
Brunei Darussalam	98.8 (2006)	97.4 (2006)	100.0 (2006)	99.6	99.1	100.0
Cambodia	26.5 (2006)	27.1 (2006)	25.9 (2006)	42.8 (2012)	43.4 (2012)	42.3 (2012)
Indonesia	...	...	...	99.3 (2014)	98.6 (2014)	100.0 (2014)
Lao PDR	...	...	...	52.2	52.9	51.5
Malaysia	76.9 (2002)	79.3 (2002)	74.7 (2002)	98.4	99.3	97.7
Myanmar	...	...	...	...	...	...
Philippines	24.0 (2001)	23.8 (2001)	24.1 (2001)	42.2 (2009)	43.0 (2009)	41.4 (2009)
Singapore	...	...	...	...	...	...
Thailand	99.1 (2006)	100.0 (2006)	98.2 (2006)	95.5	90.7	100.0
Viet Nam	78.8 (2006)	...	...	98.7	97.4	100.0
The Pacific						
Cook Islands	...	...	...	93.4	100.0	87.2
Fiji	48.6 (2004)	50.2 (2004)	47.1 (2004)	...	...	...
Kiribati	...	...	...	...	...	...
Marshall Islands	...	...	...	66.2	70.3	62.3
Micronesia, Fed. States of	...	...	...	76.4	72.9	79.7
Nauru	89.4 (2007)	78.5 (2007)	100.0 (2007)	71.2 (2014)	82.3 (2014)	61.6 (2014)
Palau	...	...	...	90.8 (2014)	81.1 (2014)	100.0 (2014)
Papua New Guinea	...	...	...	...	...	...
Samoa	...	...	...	30.5	31.0	30.1
Solomon Islands	...	...	...	66.0	66.3	65.8
Timor-Leste	...	...	...	73.2	77.4	69.2
Tonga	...	...	...	...	...	...
Tuvalu	...	...	...	96.9	100.0	94.0
Vanuatu	...	...	...	...	...	...
Developed Member Economies						
Australia	52.5 (2001)	53.2 (2001)	51.9 (2001)	86.8	86.9	86.7
Japan	97.3	...	...	95.7 (2013)	...	...
New Zealand	...	...	...	94.8	94.9	94.8

... = data not available at cutoff date, Lao PDR = Lao People's Democratic Republic, SDG = Sustainable Development Goal.

a Covers participation in early childhood education and preprimary education.
b The indicator measures the exposure of children to organized learning, but not the intensity of the learning programs.

Sources: United Nations Educational, Scientific and Cultural Organization Institute for Statistics. http://uis.unesco.org/ (accessed 28 June 2017); United Nations. Sustainable Development Goals Indicators Database. http://unstats.un.org/sdgs/indicators/database/ (accessed 18 July 2017).

Table 2.8: **Selected Indicators for SDG 4 - Teacher Training and Supply**
By 2030, substantially increase the supply of qualified teachers, including through international cooperation for teacher training in developing countries, especially least developed countries and small island developing states

Regional Member	4.c.1.a Proportion of Teachers in Preprimary Education Who Have Received at Least the Minimum Organized Teacher Training (% of total teachers)		4.c.1.b Proportion of Teachers in Primary Education Who Have Received at Least the Minimum Organized Teacher Training (% of total teachers)		4.c.1.c Proportion of Teachers in Lower Secondary Education Who Have Received at Least the Minimum Organized Teacher Training (% of total teachers)		4.c.1.d Proportion of Teachers in Upper Secondary Education Who Have Received at Least the Minimum Organized Teacher Training (% of total teachers)	
	2000	2016	2000	2016	2000	2016	2000	2016
Developing Member Economies								
Central and West Asia								
Afghanistan	...	...	...	...	...	...	...	...
Armenia	97.1(2002)	80.0 (2015)	66.7(2004)	...	...	...	...	...
Azerbaijan	79.2	91.2 (2015)	99.9	99.3 (2015)	...	...	...	...
Georgia	99.1	...	94.7	94.6 (2009)	76.8	94.6 (2009)	93.0	94.8 (2009)
Kazakhstan	...	100.0	...	100.0	...	...	...	...
Kyrgyz Republic	32.1	46.2 (2011)	46.4	72.0 (2012)	...	...	...	...
Pakistan	...	...	78.0(2004)	82.5 (2015)	...	61.2 (2015)	...	...
Tajikistan	91.3(2001)	100.0	81.6(2001)	100.0	94.0(2003)	...	94.4(2003)	...
Turkmenistan	...	...	...	...	...	...	...	...
Uzbekistan	100.0(2006)	100.0 (2011)	100.0(2006)	100.0 (2011)	...	...	...	...
East Asia								
China, People's Rep. of	...	...	...	...	...	...	...	...
Hong Kong, China	...	...	87.6	96.2 (2015)	...	...	...	...
Korea, Rep. of	...	...	...	...	...	...	...	...
Mongolia	100.0	93.6 (2012)	100.0	100.0 (2014)	100.0	...	100.0	...
Taipei,China	...	...	...	...	...	...	...	...
South Asia		...		...		...		...
Bangladesh	...	...	53.4(2005)	47.6 (2015)	36.8	59.6 (2013)	22.4	56.2 (2013)
Bhutan	93.8	100.0	94.8	100.0	93.5(2005)	100.0	...	72.2 (2008)
India	...	...	...	77.3 (2014)	...	...	...	...
Maldives	47.2	73.2 (2014)	66.5	86.1 (2014)	76.3	92.8 (2014)	54.4(2002)	...
Nepal	...	88.5	15.4(2001)	97.0	32.6	89.2	28.5(2002)	91.6
Sri Lanka	...	...	...	71.3 (2015)	...	57.3 (2015)	...	...
Southeast Asia								
Brunei Darussalam	64.4(2005)	58.9 (2015)	84.5(2005)	82.3 (2015)	...	92.3 (2015)	...	90.1 (2015)
Cambodia	98.1(2001)	100.0 (2015)	95.9(2001)	100.0 (2015)	99.7(2001)	100.0 (2015)	99.1(2001)	...
Indonesia	...	...	...	...	...	...	...	...
Lao PDR	83.1	88.9 (2015)	76.7	98.4 (2015)	98.5	99.5 (2015)	95.6	99.0 (2015)
Malaysia	...	99.6 (2015)	97.9	99.9 (2015)	...	...	...	...
Myanmar	50.3(2006)	48.4 (2014)	62.7	99.6 (2014)	62.1	93.3 (2014)	97.1	95.2 (2014)
Philippines	...	...	...	100.0 (2013)	...	...	...	...
Singapore	...	...	96.1(2007)	94.4 (2009)	94.4(2007)	91.6 (2009)	95.0(2007)	91.7 (2009)
Thailand	...	...	...	100.0 (2015)	...	100.0 (2015)	...	100.0 (2015)
Viet Nam	50.5	98.7 (2015)	80.1	99.6 (2015)	86.3	99.6 (2015)	...	...
The Pacific								
Cook Islands	60.9(2005)	83.9 (2015)	79.2(2007)	100.0 (2015)	...	...	...	...
Fiji	...	...	...	100.0 (2012)	...	100.0 (2012)	...	100.0 (2012)
Kiribati	...	...	93.9(2005)	85.4 (2008)	83.6(2005)	86.7 (2014)	43.1(2005)	33.6 (2008)
Marshall Islands	100.0(2002)	...	...	...	...	...	...	...
Micronesia, Fed. States of	...	...	...	...	...	...	...	...
Nauru	77.5(2006)	...	74.2(2007)	...	...	...	...	...
Palau	...	...	...	33.7	...	59.3	...	...
Papua New Guinea	...	...	...	100.0 (2012)	...	100.0 (2012)	...	100.0 (2012)
Samoa	...	100.0 (2015)	...	...	...	...	...	100.0 (2014)
Solomon Islands	...	59.5 (2014)	...	59.2 (2015)	...	80.3 (2015)	...	63.0 (2015)
Timor-Leste	...	...	...	...	...	...	...	...
Tonga	...	100.0 (2012)	...	97.1 (2014)	...	...	...	...
Tuvalu	...	74.6 (2014)	...	...	...	...	...	...
Vanuatu	100(2007)	46.0 (2015)	100.0(2007)	27.9 (2015)	...	21.5 (2015)	...	20.5 (2015)
Developed Member Economies								
Australia	...	...	...	...	...	...	...	...
Japan	...	...	...	...	...	...	...	...
New Zealand	...	...	...	...	...	...	...	...

... = data not available at cutoff date, Lao PDR = Lao People's Democratic Republic, SDG = Sustainable Development Goal.

Sources: United Nations. Sustainable Development Goals Indicators Global Database. http://unstats.un.org/sdgs/indicators/database/ (accessed 19 July 2017); United Nations Educational, Scientific and Cultural Organization. Institute for Statistics Data Centre Online. http://data.uis.unesco.org/ (accessed 26 June 2017).

Table 2.9: **Selected Indicators for SDG 5 - Early Marriage and Women in Leadership**

Eliminate all harmful practices, such as child, early and forced marriage, and female genital mutilation

Ensure women's full and effective participation and equal opportunities for leadership at all levels of decision making in political, economic, and public life

Regional Member	5.3.1 Proportion of Women Aged 20–24 Years Who Were Married or in a Union (%)				5.5.1 Proportion of Seats Held by Women in National Parliaments (%)	5.5.2 Proportion of Women in Managerial Positions (%)
	Before Age 15		Before Age 18			
	2000	2015	2000	2015	2016	2015
Developing Member Economies						
Central and West Asia						
Afghanistan	...	8.8	...	34.8	27.7	...
Armenia	...	– (2010)	...	7.2 (2010)	10.7	29.1
Azerbaijan	...	1.9 (2011)	...	11.0 (2011)	16.9	35.1
Georgia	...	...	...	...	11.3	...
Kazakhstan	...	0.2	...	7.0	26.2	37.1
Kyrgyz Republic	...	0.9 (2014)	...	11.6 (2014)	19.2	35.7
Pakistan	...	2.8 (2013)	...	21.0 (2013)	20.6	3.0 (2008)
Tajikistan	...	0.1 (2012)	...	11.6 (2012)	19.1	...
Turkmenistan	...	– (2016)	...	5.7 (2016)	25.8	...
Uzbekistan	0.3 (2006)	...	7.2 (2006)	...	16.0	...
East Asia						
China, People's Rep. of	...	...	...	...	23.6	...
Hong Kong, China	...	...	...	...	...	33.2
Korea, Rep. of	...	...	...	...	16.3	10.5
Mongolia	...	0.1 (2013)	...	5.2 (2013)	14.5	40.6
Taipei,China	...	...	...	...	...	...
South Asia						
Bangladesh	...	22.4 (2014)	...	58.6 (2014)	20.0	5.4 (2011)
Bhutan	...	6.2 (2010)	...	25.8 (2010)	8.5	18.5
India	18.2 (2006)	...	47.4 (2006)	...	12.0	...
Maldives	...	0.3 (2009)	...	3.9 (2009)	5.9	13.4 (2010)
Nepal	...	10.4 (2014)	...	36.6 (2014)	29.6	18.3 (2008)
Sri Lanka	1.7 (2007)	...	11.8 (2007)	...	5.8	24.8 (2014)
Southeast Asia						
Brunei Darussalam	...	...	...	...	6.5	33.8 (2014)
Cambodia	...	1.9 (2014)	...	18.5 (2014)	20.3	18.0 (2010)
Indonesia	...	1.1 (2013)	...	13.6 (2013)	17.1	22.0
Lao PDR	...	8.9 (2012)	...	35.4 (2012)	25.0	...
Malaysia	...	...	...	...	10.4	22.5
Myanmar	...	...	...	...	9.9	...
Philippines	...	2.0 (2013)	...	15.0 (2013)	27.2	46.6
Singapore	...	...	...	...	23.1	34.0
Thailand	...	3.8 (2012)	...	22.1 (2012)	6.1	33.9 (2014)
Viet Nam	...	0.9 (2014)	...	10.6 (2014)	24.3	25.8
The Pacific						
Cook Islands	...	...	...	...	12.5 (2014)	47.5 (2011)
Fiji	...	...	...	...	16.0	...
Kiribati	...	2.8 (2009)	...	20.3 (2009)	6.5	36.5 (2010)
Marshall Islands	5.5 (2007)	...	26.3 (2007)	...	9.1	...
Micronesia, Fed. States of	...	...	...	...	–	...
Nauru	1.9 (2007)	...	26.8 (2007)	...	5.26	...
Palau	...	...	...	...	–	...
Papua New Guinea	2.1 (2006)	...	21.3 (2006)	...	2.7	...
Samoa	...	0.7 (2014)	...	10.8 (2014)	6.1	47.3 (2014)
Solomon Islands	3.1 (2007)	...	22.4 (2007)	...	2.0	...
Timor-Leste	...	3.0 (2010)	...	18.9 (2010)	38.5	14.3 (2010)
Tonga	...	0.3 (2012)	...	5.6 (2012)	–	...
Tuvalu	0.0 (2007)	...	9.9 (2007)	...	6.7	...
Vanuatu	...	2.5 (2013)	...	21.4 (2013)	–	28.5 (2009)
Developed Member Economies						
Australia	...	...	...	...	26.7	33.1
Japan	...	...	...	...	9.5	12.5
New Zealand	...	...	...	...	31.4	40.0 (2008)

... = data not available at cutoff date, – = magnitude equals zero, Lao PDR = Lao People's Democratic Republic, SDG = Sustainable Development Goal.

Sources: United Nations. Sustainable Development Goals Indicators Database.https://unstats.un.org/sdgs/indicators/database (accessed 18 July 2017); for indicator 5.5.2 for Brunei Darussalam: Inter-Parliamentary Union. Women in National Parliaments. http://www.ipu.org/wmn-e/arc/classif011216.htm (accessed 4 August 2017); for the Cook Islands: Secretariat of the Pacific Community. http://www.spc.int/nmdi/mdg3 (accessed 30 June 2017).

Planet

To protect the planet from degradation, including through sustainable consumption and production, sustainably managing its natural resources and taking urgent action on climate change, so that it can support the needs of the present and future generations.

Snapshot

- In 29 out of 44 economies of Asia and the Pacific with available data for 2015, at least 90% of the population are using safely managed drinking water services.
- In about half of the 43 economies of Asia and the Pacific with available data for 2015, at least 85% of the population are using safely managed sanitation services.
- In more than half of the regional economies with available data, the annual urban mean concentration of fine suspended particles less than 2.5 microns in diameter (PM 2.5) is at least two-and-a-half times the maximum level set by the World Health Organization.
- The majority of the economies in Asia and the Pacific have experienced an increase in material footprint per capita since 2000.
- Between 2000 and 2015, Timor-Leste, Cambodia, the Lao People's Democratic Republic, the People's Republic of China, and Viet Nam more than doubled their domestic material consumption per capita, while in 9 out of 47 regional economies, including the three developed economies, negative growth in materials per person consumed was registered.
- Twenty eight out of 48 regional economies are known to have strategies and regulatory mechanisms for disaster risk reduction and management, in line with the Sendai Framework.
- Between 2000 and 2015, 17 out of 47 regional economies reported an increase in the proportion of forest area.
- More than half of regional economies scored at least 0.80 in the Red List Index in 2016. The Red List Index ranges between 0.0 (which means all species are "extinct") and 1.0 (which means all species are of "least concern").

Economic growth in many parts of the world has been accompanied by food and water insecurity, climate change, ocean acidification, and sea-level rise. SDGs 6, 11, 12, 13, 14, and 15 work toward ensuring availability and sustainable management of water and sanitation; building inclusive, safe, resilient, and sustainable cities; shifting production and consumption patterns; improving resilience and adaptive capacity to climate-related hazards and natural disasters; ensuring healthy coastal and marine resources for diversity; and using sustainable terrestrial ecosystems coupled with promoting resilience and quality of soil.

SDG 6: Ensure Availability and Sustainable Management of Water and Sanitation for All

Water supply, sanitation, hygiene, and management of water resources are linked to poverty reduction, good health, gender equality, as well as environmental sustainability. Contaminated water and poor sanitation are associated with the transmission of diseases such as cholera, diarrhea, dysentery, hepatitis A, typhoid, and polio; as well as protein-energy malnutrition, intestinal nematode infections, and schistosomiasis. Thus, the absence, inadequacy, or inappropriate management of water and sanitation services ultimately render people vulnerable to health risks. SDG 6 aims for universal access to water, sanitation, and hygiene under a broad framework.

Proportion of population using safely managed drinking water services. In Asia and the Pacific, 38 out of the 44 reporting economies have at least 90% access to safely managed drinking water services in urban areas, while 22 out of 42 reported a similar rate of access in rural areas (Figure 3.1). Universal access to safely managed drinking water services is available to all residents of Armenia, Bhutan, Georgia, Singapore; and developed economies of Australia, Japan, and New Zealand. On the other hand, Papua New Guinea is yet to provide three-fifths of its population access to safely managed drinking water services. Several South Asian economies have reported minimal urban–rural disparity in access to safe water. Rural areas in Bangladesh (87.0%) and Nepal (91.8%) report slightly greater access to safely managed drinking water services than urban areas (86.5% and 90.9%, respectively).

Figure 3.1: Proportion of Population Using Safely Managed Drinking Water Services, 2015
(%)

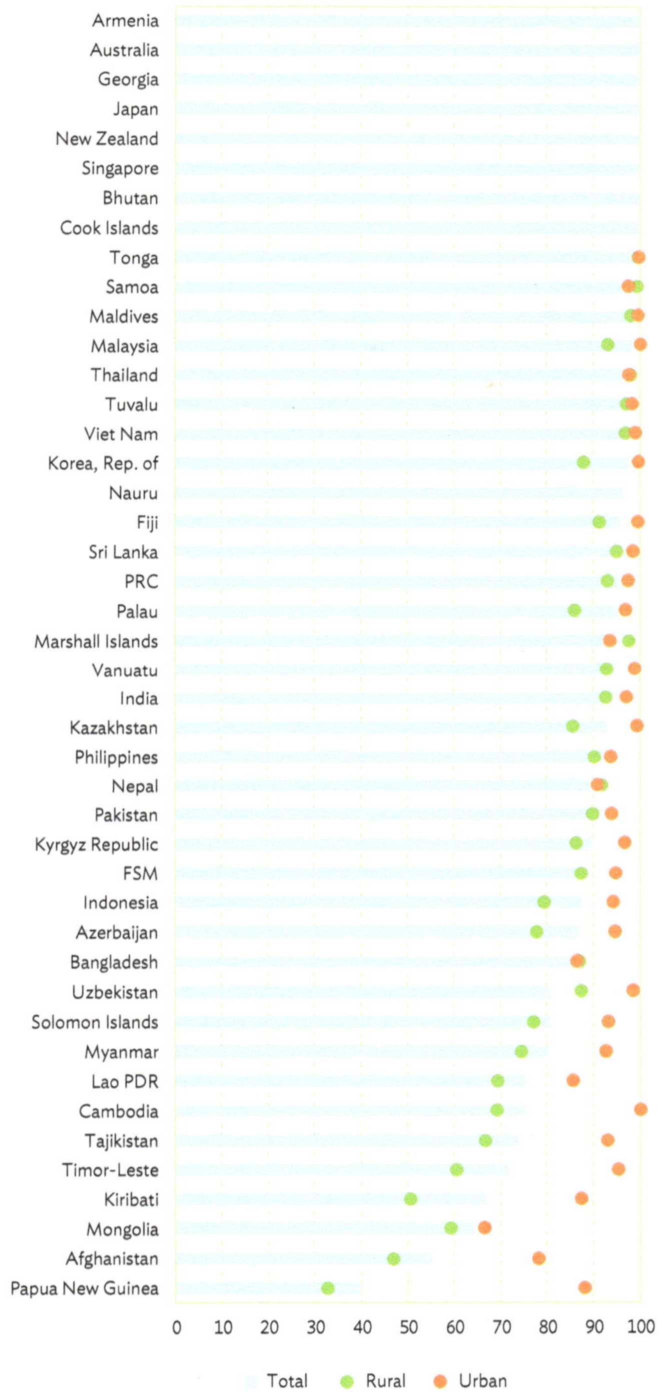

FSM = Federated States of Micronesia, Lao PDR = Lao People's Democratic Republic, PRC = People's Republic of China.

Note: For the Republic of Korea and Uzbekistan, total and rural refer to 2012 data (latest available data); for Palau, total and rural refer to 2011 data. The values for proportion of population using improved drinking water sources are the same for urban, rural, and total for Armenia, Australia, Bhutan, the Cook Islands, Georgia, Japan, New Zealand, and Tonga; and for urban and total for Nauru and Singapore.

Source: Table 3.1.

Proportion of population using safely managed sanitation services. While full access to safely managed sanitation services exists in the three developed economies of the region, namely, Australia, Japan, and New Zealand, significant efforts are still required to improve access in some developing member economies (Figure 3.2). In Afghanistan, less than half the population residing in urban areas use safely managed sanitation services, while only around a fourth do so in rural areas. In eight economies—Nepal (45.8%), Cambodia (42.4%), Timor-Leste (40.6%), Kiribati (39.7%), India (39.6%), Afghanistan (31.9%), Solomon Islands (29.8%), and Papua New Guinea (18.9%)—more than half of the total population lack access to safely managed sanitation facilities.

SDG 11: Make Cities and Human Settlements Inclusive, Safe, Resilient and Sustainable

The share of urban population to the total population in Asia and the Pacific has been rising at an average annual rate of 2.7% between 2005 and 2016, with the urban share of the region's population expected to be greater than 55% by 2030 (UN ESCAP 2016). This rapid pace of urbanization can be partly attributed to high labor demand in urban areas due to growth in industrial activities and services. Cities offer economies of scale in providing consumer services such as transport. However, faster economic growth and increased labor mobility also pose challenges for planning affordable housing, making cities inclusive, safe, resilient, and sustainable.

Figure 3.2: Proportion of Population Using Safely Managed Sanitation Services, 2015
(%)

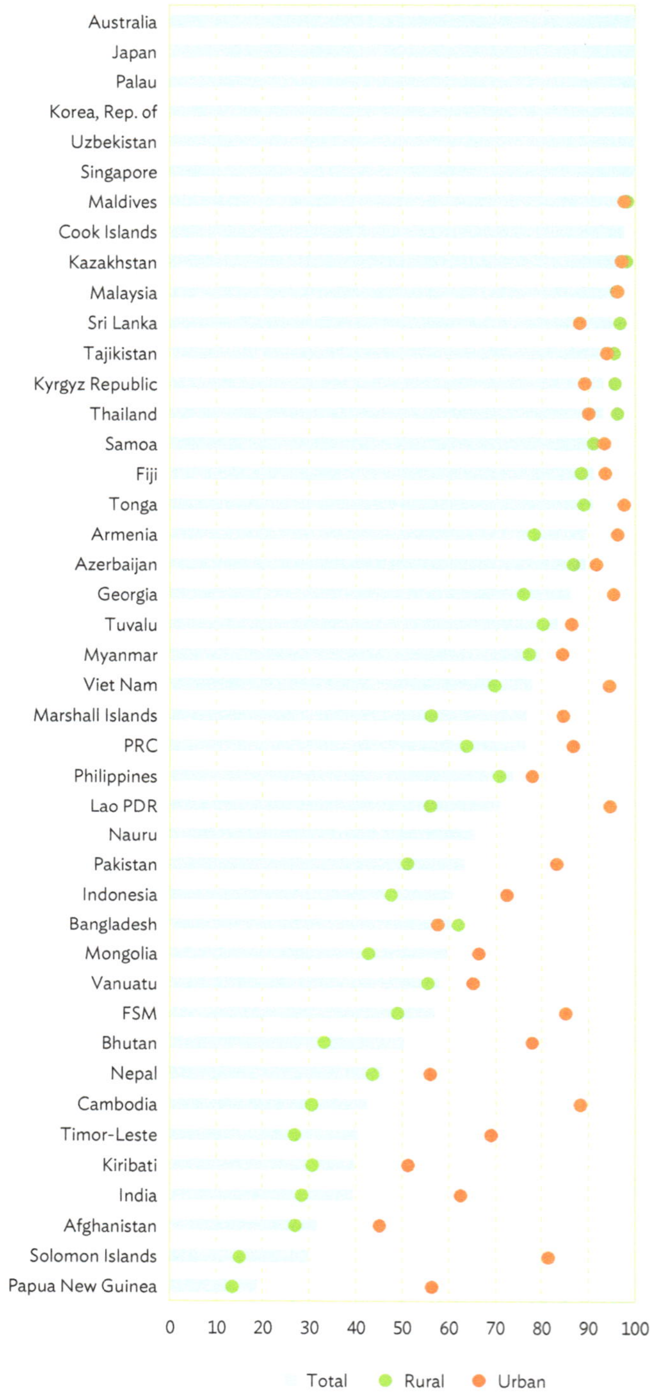

FSM = Federated States of Micronesia, Lao PDR = Lao People's Democratic Republic, PRC = People's Republic of China.

Note: For Tuvalu, total and rural refer to 2013 data (latest available data). The values for proportion of population using safely managed sanitation services is the same for urban, rural, and total for Australia, the Cook Islands, Japan, Palau, the Republic of Korea, and Uzbekistan; and for urban and total for Nauru and Singapore.

Source: Table 3.1.

Proportion of urban population living in slums, informal settlements, or inadequate housing. In all 13 economies in Asia and the Pacific for which data are available, the proportion of urban population living in slum areas has declined between 2000 and 2014 (Figure 3.3). The Lao People's Democratic Republic has seen the largest decline in latest years at 47.9 percentage points from its initial 2005 figure of 79.3%. Cambodia (23.8), Bangladesh (22.7), Mongolia (22.2), and Viet Nam (21.6), have done exceedingly well in reducing the share of their urban population living in slums by over 20 percentage points. Meanwhile, Myanmar (4.6), Pakistan (3.2), and Thailand (1.0) have reduced the proportion of urban population living in slum areas by less than 5 percentage points since 2000. Inadequate housing persists in several economies, with more than half of the urban population in Afghanistan (62.7%), Bangladesh (55.1%), Cambodia (55.1%), and Nepal (54.3%) still residing in slum areas or informal settlements as of 2014.

Average annual mean concentration levels of particulate matter 2.5 microns in diameter or smaller in urban areas. Air quality is usually measured by the levels of particulate matter equal to 2.5 microns in diameter or less (PM 2.5). The maximum level set by the World Health Organization (WHO) is 10 micrograms per cubic meter (μg/m³) as a standard for the average annual PM 2.5. In more than half of the regional economies, the concentration level in urban areas exceeds the WHO's threshold by 2.5 times (Figure 3.4). Out of the 37 economies in Asia and the Pacific that have data for recent years, Brunei Darussalam (5.4 μg/m³); Fiji (6.0 μg/m³), the Federated States of Micronesia (6.0 μg/m³), Solomon Islands (5.0 μg/m³), Vanuatu (7.0 μg/m³); Australia (5.8 μg/m³) and New Zealand (5.3 μg/m³)

Figure 3.3: Proportion of Urban Population Living in Slums in Selected Economies
(%)

Lao PDR = Lao People's Democratic Republic, PRC = People's Republic of China.
Note: For reference year 2000, data for Cambodia, the Lao PDR, Myanmar, and Thailand refer to 2005.
Source: Table 3.2.

are within the WHO standards. Bangladesh has the highest average annual mean concentration level of 88.8 μg/m³. Aside from Bangladesh, two South Asian economies—Nepal (74.3 μg/m³) and India (65.7 μg/m³); three Central and West Asian economies—Pakistan (67.7 μg/m³), Afghanistan (63.4 μg/m³), and Tajikistan (50.7 μg/m³); the People's Republic of China (59.5 μg/m³) and Myanmar (56.6 μg/m³) comprise the list of economies with concentration levels beyond 5 times the WHO standards.

Figure 3.4: Average Annual Mean Concentration Levels of Particulate Matter 2.5 Microns in Diameter or Smaller in Urban Areas, 2014
(μg/m³)

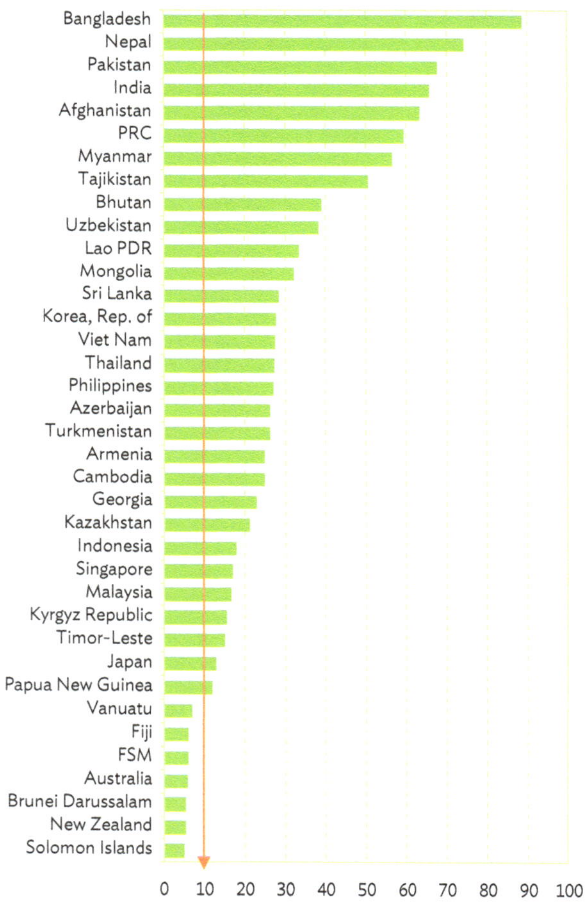

FSM = Federated States of Micronesia, Lao PDR = Lao People's Democratic Republic, PRC = People's Republic of China.
Source: Table 3.2.

SDG 12: Ensure Sustainable Consumption and Production Patterns

Consumption and production are fundamental to economic activities, but when unmanaged can contribute to depletion of natural resources. SDG 12 is designed to achieve sustainable consumption and production through minimal extraction of natural resources, reduction in the use of toxic materials, and reliance on production processes that result in less waste and fewer pollutants.

Material footprint per capita. Between 2000 and data available for latest year, 35 out of 37 economies in Asia and the Pacific have increased their material footprint per capita. Among economies, Hong Kong, China has the largest material footprint per capita at 120.1 million metric tons per capita (Table 3.2). Other economies with material footprint per capita greater than 20 million metric tons include Singapore (75.9), Australia (40.4), New Zealand (23.5), Japan (20.9), the People's Republic of China (20.8), and the Republic of Korea (26.4).

Domestic material consumption per capita. Between 2000 and the latest year for which data are available, a decline in domestic material consumption per person is observed in 12 out of 47 regional economies reporting data, including the developed economies of Australia, Japan, and New Zealand. For recent years, Australia had the highest domestic material consumption per person at 47.3 tons of materials per capita (Figure 3.5). Other economies with high domestic material consumption per capita at over 20 tons per person include Nauru (45.0), Mongolia (34.2), Singapore (39.0), Kazakhstan (27.3), the People's Republic of China (24.4), and New Zealand (21.9). Solomon Islands registered the lowest domestic material consumption per capita at 1.0 tons per person.

Figure 3.5: Domestic Material Consumption Per Capita, 2000 and Latest Year
(metric tons per capita)

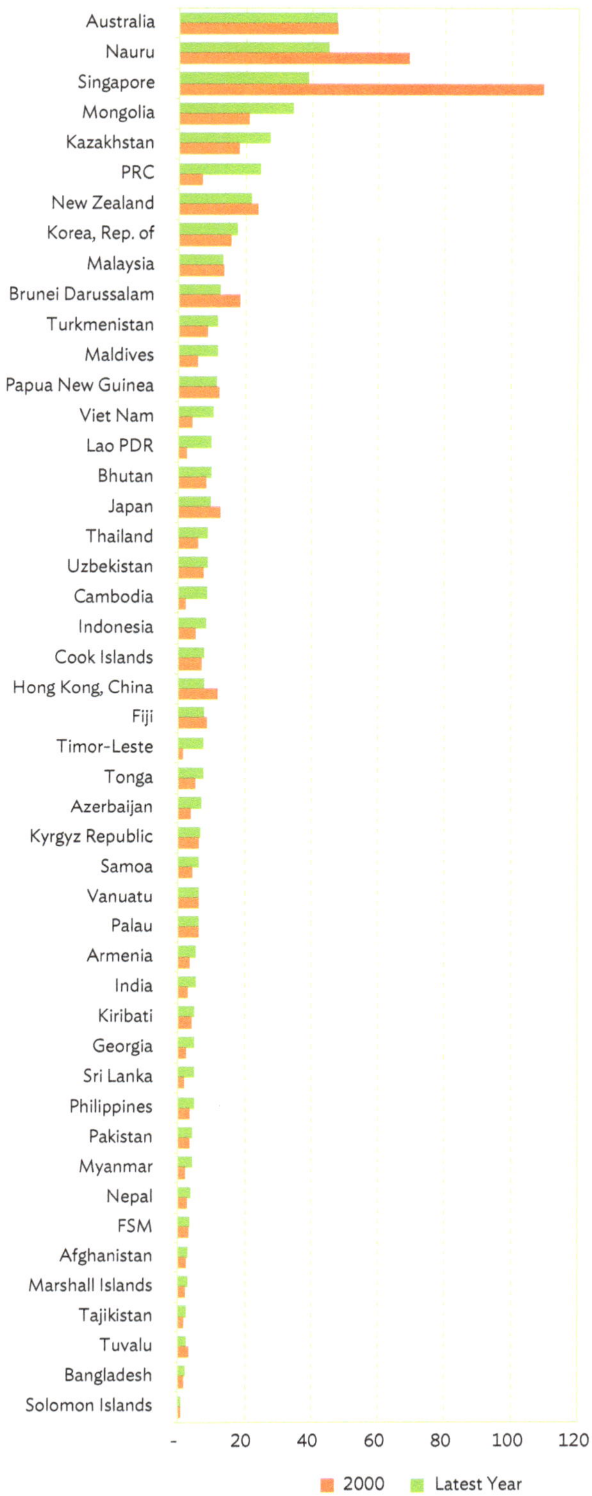

FSM = Federated States of Micronesia, Lao PDR = Lao People's Democratic Republic, PRC = People's Republic of China.

Note: Data refer to 2015 for all economies except Armenia; Azerbaijan; Brunei Darussalam; Georgia; Hong Kong, China; Kazakhstan; the Kyrgyz Republic; Pakistan; Samoa; Tajikistan; Turkmenistan; Uzbekistan; and Vanuatu, data for which are from 2010.

Source: Table 3.2.

SDG 13: Take Urgent Action to Combat Climate Change and Its Impacts

Various scientific studies have called attention to increasing occurrences of extreme weather events, rising sea levels, and drastic fluctuations in climatic variables. The impact of climate change on livelihoods, food production, and energy security are important concerns for the region. SDG 13 aims at development that builds resilience to climate-related hazards and natural disasters, especially among those who are most vulnerable to climate change and its impacts.

Countries adopting and implementing national disaster risk reduction strategies. The socioeconomic impact of a natural disaster depends on the extent, as well as their vulnerability and coping mechanism. Disaster prevention, which is seldom emphasized as much as disaster response, needs to be featured as an integral part of development strategies. The Sendai Framework for Disaster Risk Reduction 2015–2030, successor to the Hyogo Framework for Action 2005–2015, outlines seven targets and four priorities for action to build the resilience of nations and communities to disaster and climate risks. The Sendai Framework is a voluntary, nonbinding agreement among nations that recognizes that the state has the primary role to reduce disaster risk, but that responsibility should be shared with other stakeholders, including local governments and the private sector. The monitoring as well as implementation program for the Sendai Framework are meant to improve interventions aimed at disaster risk reduction, especially for several economies in the region that are extremely at risk from the harmful effects of climate-related disasters.

Twenty eight out of 48 regional economies are known to have strategies and regulatory mechanisms for disaster risk reduction and management, in line with the Sendai Framework. These are Afghanistan, Armenia, Australia, Bangladesh, Bhutan, Fiji, Georgia, India, Indonesia, Japan, Kazakhstan, the Republic of Korea, the Kyrgyz Republic, Malaysia, Mongolia, Nauru, Nepal, New Zealand, Pakistan, Papua New Guinea, the Philippines, the PRC, Samoa, Sri Lanka, Thailand, Tonga, Vanuatu, and Viet Nam (Table 3.2).

SDG 14: Conserve and Sustainably Use the Oceans, Seas, and Marine Resources for Sustainable Development

Oceans are facing various threats from resource depletion, marine pollution, as well as climate change, all of which can be partially attributed to human actions. Marine protected areas not only balance the ecological system, but also ensure the availability of more than enough fish and other aquatic resources for those who rely on fishing for a living. SDG 14 aims to conserve and sustainably use the world's oceans, seas, and marine resources.

Coverage of protected areas in relation to marine areas. Palau has registered 83.0% coverage of protected marine areas (Figure 3.6). Australia and New Zealand have managed to protect at least 30% of their marine areas, while Kiribati has managed to protect over 10% of its marine area. The remaining 31 countries have less than 6% coverage of protected marine areas. Twenty economies had less than 1% coverage of protected marine areas in 2016.

Figure 3.6: Coverage of Protected Areas in Relation to Marine Areas, 2016
(%)

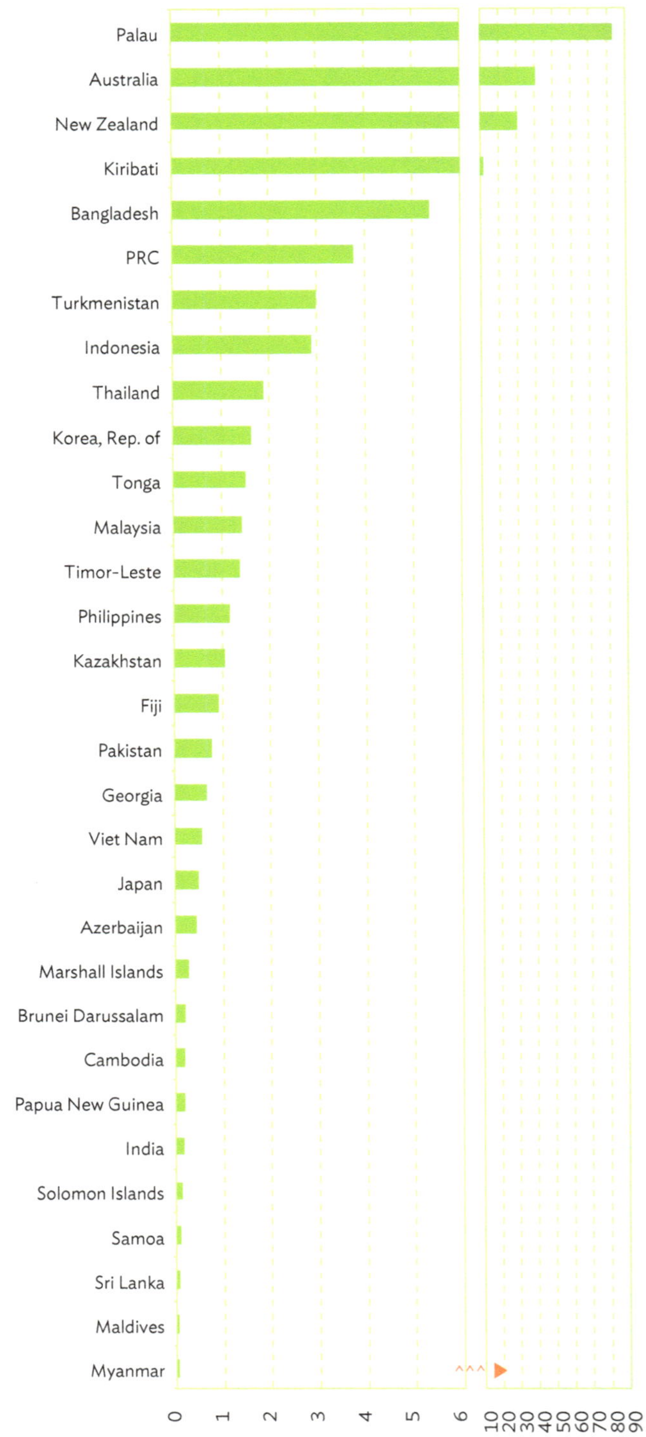

FSM = Federated States of Micronesia, PRC = People's Republic of China.
Note: Economies with values less than 0.05 are not presented in the chart. These include the Cook Islands, the Federated States of Micronesia, Tuvalu, and Vanuatu.
Source: Table 3.2.

SDG 15: Protect, Restore and Promote Sustainable Use of Terrestrial Ecosystems, Sustainably Manage Forests, Combat Desertification, and Halt and Reverse Land Degradation and Halt Biodiversity Loss

Forests sustain the air we breathe, the water we drink, and the food we eat. As the world's population grows, the demand for forest-related goods rises. Another major consequence of population growth is land-use change. Sustainable development involves protecting our forests, preventing desertification, and conserving biodiversity, all in sync with targets to mitigate the harmful impacts of climate change. SDG 15 seeks to ensure that present and future generations continue to benefit from the use of natural habitats and terrestrial ecosystems that are part of our common heritage.

Forest area as a proportion of total land area. Examining forest area over time helps with managing forests sustainably. Seventeen out of 47 reporting economies in the region have more than half of their land area covered with forests (Figure 3.7). Five of these economies are from the Pacific and registered a proportion of forest area to total land area not less than 70% in 2015—the Federated States of Micronesia, Palau, Solomon Islands, Papua New Guinea, and the Marshall Islands. Seven economies in Central and West Asia reported a forest cover of less than 10% in 2015—Turkmenistan (8.8%), Uzbekistan (7.3%), the Kyrgyz Republic (3.3%), Tajikistan (3.0%), Afghanistan (2.1%), Pakistan (1.9%), and Kazakhstan (1.2%). Viet Nam and the Lao People's Democratic Republic increased their forest cover by more than 10 percentage points between 2000 and 2015. Decline in forest cover of more than 10 percentage points was observed in Cambodia and Timor-Leste.

Figure 3.7: Proportion of Forest Area to Total Land Area (%)

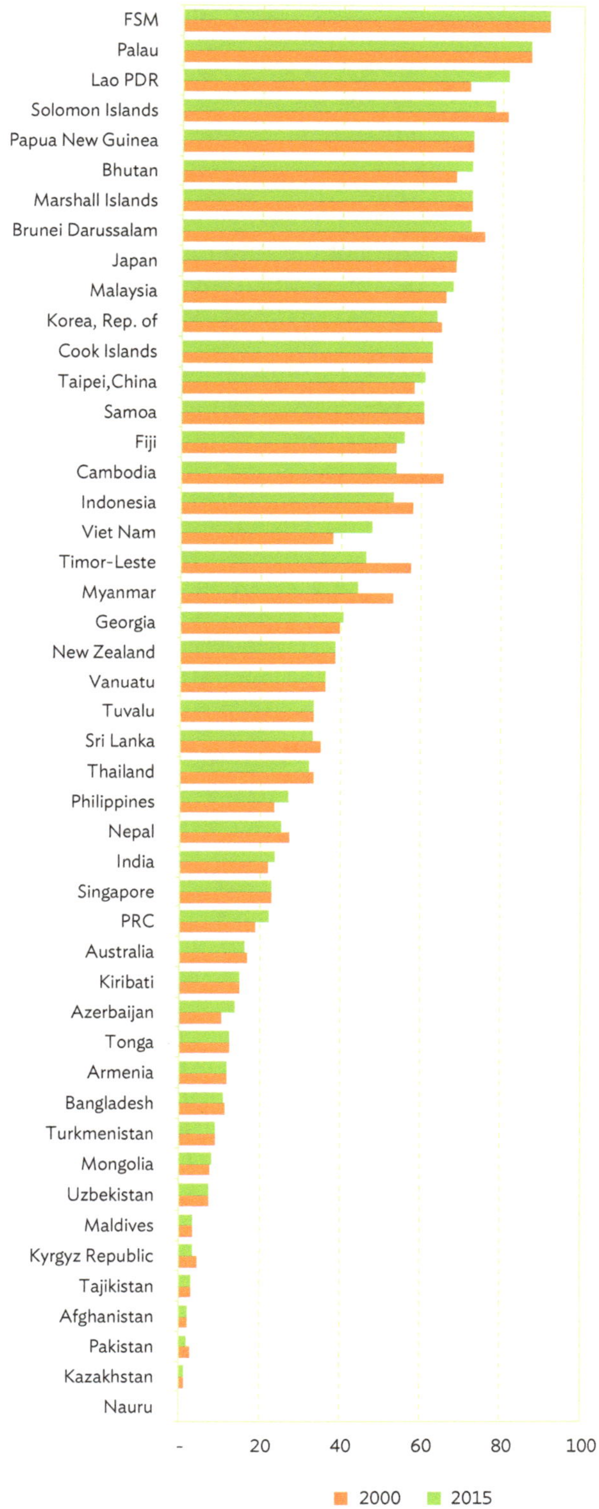

FSM = Federated States of Micronesia, Lao PDR = Lao People's Democratic Republic, PRC = People's Republic of China.
Note: 2000 data for Taipei,China refers to 2001.
Source: Table 3.2.

Red List Index. The International Union for the Conservation of Nature measures changes in aggregate extinction risk across groups of species using a Red List Index. The value of this index ranges from 0.0 (which means all species are categorized as "extinct") to 1.0 (which means all species are categorized as "least concern"). More than half of regional economies scored at least 0.80 in the index in 2016, but seven economies—Sri Lanka (0.57), New Zealand (0.64), the Philippines (0.64), Fiji (0.67), Vanuatu (0.67), India (0.69), and the Federated States of Micronesia (0.69)—scored below 0.7 (Figure 3.8). Sri Lanka experienced the biggest decline in the index of 0.09 points, (from 0.66 in 2000 to 0.57 in 2016). Five economies in Central and West Asia registered a score of at least 0.9 in the Red List Index in 2016: the Kyrgyz Republic (0.98), Tajikistan (0.98), Turkmenistan (0.97), Uzbekistan (0.97), and Azerbaijan (0.91). East Asia also performed relatively well, with Hong Kong, China being able to completely halt the extinction of its species for the past 16 years. Mongolia registered a Red List Index score of 0.95 in 2016, slightly lower than its score in 2000 of 0.96.

Figure 3.8: Red List Index

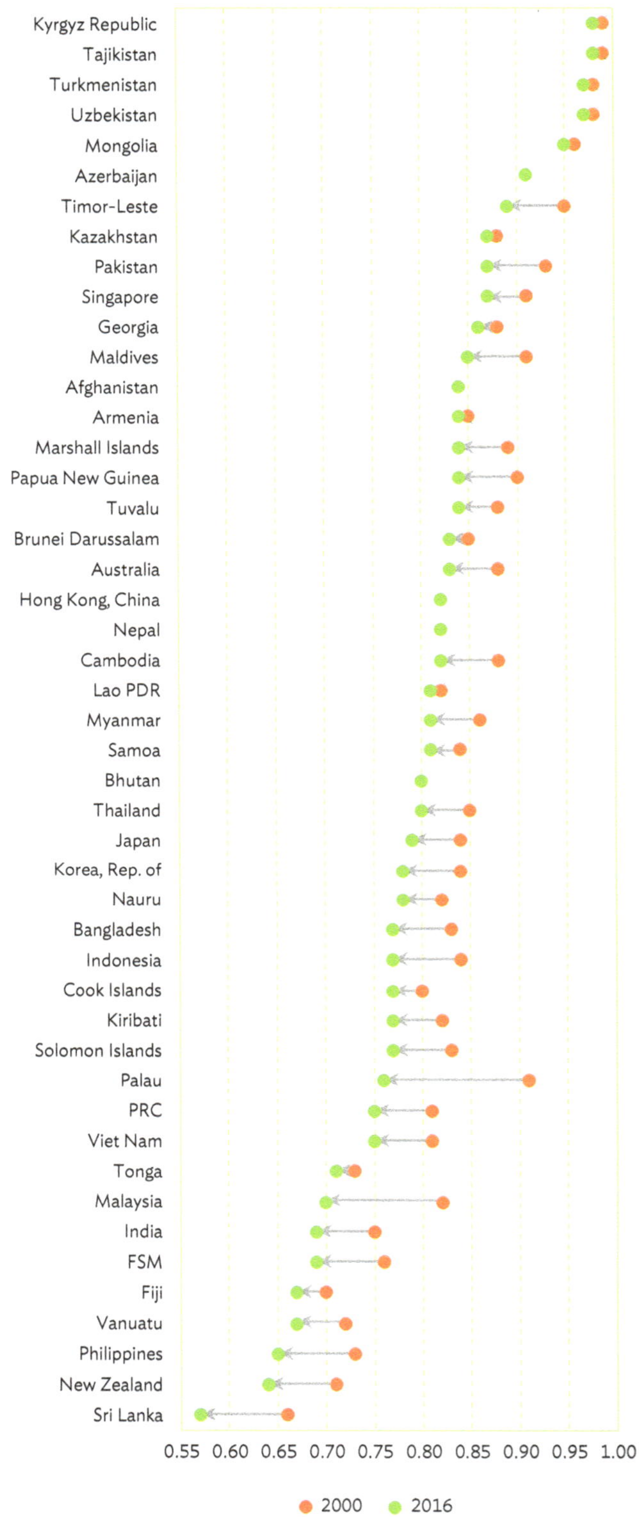

FSM = Federated States of Micronesia, Lao PDR = Lao People's Democratic Republic, PRC = People's Republic of China.
Source: Table 3.2.

Equity, Data Gaps, and Other Related Issues

In examining data and statistics on SDG indicators for Planet, one must be aware of issues on data comparability arising from conflicting definitions and lack of available data on sub-indicators. For instance, how countries define "urban" and "rural" varies considerably. According to the United Nations Department of Economic and Social Affairs (2014), to define an urban area, countries must use one or a combination of characteristics based on administrative criteria; a minimum population threshold; population density; economic activities (proxied by the number of establishments); physical characteristics (such as the presence of churches, markets, public buildings); infrastructure (such as paved roads, electricity, piped water, or sewers); and presence of education or health care services. Although many countries globally use minimum population thresholds to define an area as "urban," the thresholds vary across countries. The conflicting definitions on what is an urban area make it challenging to draw meaningful cross-country examinations on urbanization and the urban–rural divide.

In several regional economies, significant disparities on proportion of population using safely managed drinking water sources and sanitation services exist between rural and urban areas. These overall levels of access, and the relative levels of disparity, hold important consequences for sustainable human development.

The proportion of the urban population living in slums, informal settlements, or inadequate housing refers to the proportion of people living in urban households that lack at least one of the following five housing conditions: (i) access to safely managed drinking water services, (ii) access to safely managed sanitation services, (iii) sufficient living space (not overcrowded), (iv) durable housing, and (v) security of tenure (UN 2014). While data availability is generally good for safely managed drinking water and sanitation services, and sufficient living space, data on durable housing and security of tenure are unavailable in several countries.

While methodologies to calculate fish stocks are well established in developed economies, a substantial share of fish capture is in economies with inadequate mechanisms for systematic fisheries data collection. A concerted effort is required to collect and analyze high-quality fisheries data.

Although targets on pollution control are dependent on reliable data and statistics, pollution indicators are not regularly updated in many developing economies.

Climate change and its impact often hit the poor much harder than those in the upper segment of the income distribution. Disaggregation by sex and age groups on deaths from disasters would also be helpful as women and men, and people of varying age groups, are confronted with different challenges when facing disasters. Data on people affected by disasters in UNSD Global Database may have double counts in a year as some people may get affected by several disasters.

Table 3.1: **Selected Indicators for SDG 6 - Clean Water and Sanitation**

By 2030, achieve universal and equitable access to safe and affordable drinking water for all

By 2030, achieve access to adequate and equitable sanitation and hygiene for all and end open defecation, paying special attention to the needs of women and girls and those in vulnerable situations

By 2030, substantially increase water-use efficiency across all sectors, and ensure sustainable withdrawals and supply of freshwater to address water scarcity and substantially reduce the number of people suffering from water scarcity

By 2030, expand international cooperation and capacity-building support to developing countries in water- and sanitation-related activities and programmes, including water harvesting, desalination, water efficiency, wastewater treatment, recycling, and reuse technologies

Regional Member	6.1.1 Proportion of Population Using Safely Managed Drinking Water Services (%)					
	2000			2015		
	Total	Urban	Rural	Total	Urban	Rural
Developing Member Economies						
Central and West Asia						
Afghanistan	30.3	52.2	24.3	55.3	78.2	47.0
Armenia	92.6	98.5	81.7	100.0	100.0	100.0
Azerbaijan	74.1	88.3	59.0	87.0	94.7	77.8
Georgia	89.3	97.1	80.6	100.0	100.0	100.0
Kazakhstan	93.8	98.0	88.5	92.9	99.4	85.6
Kyrgyz Republic	78.4	96.2	68.8	90.0	96.7	86.2
Pakistan	88.5	95.4	85.0	91.4	93.9	89.9
Tajikistan	59.6	92.3	47.8	73.8	93.1	66.7
Turkmenistan	59.6	89.1	34.6	...	...	...
Uzbekistan	88.7	97.6	83.4	87.3 (2012)	98.5	80.9 (2012)
East Asia						
China, People's Rep. of	80.3	97.2	70.8	95.5	97.5	93.0
Hong Kong, China	...	...	...	...	...	...
Korea, Rep. of	93.4	98.1	75.3	97.6 (2012)	99.7	87.9 (2012)
Mongolia	56.3	74.2	32.4	64.4	66.4	59.2
Taipei,China	...	...	...	...	...	...
South Asia						
Bangladesh	76.0	83.2	73.7	86.9	86.5	87.0
Bhutan	83.9	98.2	79.0	100.0	100.0	100.0
India	80.6	92.3	76.1	94.1	97.1	92.6
Maldives	95.2	99.9	93.3	98.6	99.5	97.9
Nepal	77.1	94.3	74.5	91.6	90.9	91.8
Sri Lanka	79.7	94.8	76.3	95.6	98.5	95.0
Southeast Asia						
Brunei Darussalam	...	...	...	...	...	...
Cambodia	41.6	57.1	38.1	75.5	100.0	69.1
Indonesia	77.9	91.3	68.2	87.4	94.2	79.5
Lao PDR	45.5	72.2	37.9	75.7	85.6	69.4
Malaysia	94.1	97.4	88.6	98.2	100.0	93.0
Myanmar	66.6	84.6	59.9	80.6	92.7	74.4
Philippines	87.1	92.0	82.5	91.8	93.7	90.3
Singapore	100.0	100.0	...	100.0	100.0	...
Thailand	91.9	96.6	89.7	97.8	97.6	98.0
Viet Nam	77.4	93.6	72.2	97.6	99.1	96.9
The Pacific						
Cook Islands	99.9	99.9	99.9	99.9	99.9	99.9
Fiji	90.7	96.6	85.2	95.7	99.5	91.2
Kiribati	58.9	80.3	42.7	66.9	87.3	50.6
Marshall Islands	93.1	91.9	95.8	94.6	93.5	97.6
Micronesia, Fed. States of	90.1	94.1	89.0	89.0	94.8	87.4
Nauru	93.0	93.0	...	96.5	96.5	...
Palau	92.2	97.3	80.4	95.3 (2011)	97.0	86.0 (2011)
Papua New Guinea	35.1	87.5	27.1	40.0	88.0	32.8
Samoa	93.3	97.0	92.3	99.0	97.5	99.3
Solomon Islands	79.7	93.2	77.2	80.8	93.2	77.2
Timor-Leste	54.3	68.9	49.7	71.9	95.2	60.5
Tonga	98.6	97.4	99.0	99.6	99.7	99.6
Tuvalu	94.0	95.1	93.0	97.7	98.3	97.0
Vanuatu	75.8	95.7	70.3	94.5	98.9	92.9
Developed Member Economies						
Australia	100.0	100.0	100.0	100.0	100.0	100.0
Japan	100.0	100.0	100.0	100.0	100.0	100.0
New Zealand	100.0	100.0	100.0	100.0	100.0	100.0

(continued)

Table 3.1: **Selected Indicators for SDG 6 - Clean Water and Sanitation** *(continued)*

Regional Member	6.2.1 Proportion of Population Using Safely Managed Sanitation Services, Including a Hand-Washing Facility with Soap and Water (%)					
	2000			2015		
	Total	Urban	Rural	Total	Urban	Rural
Developing Member Economies						
Central and West Asia						
Afghanistan	23.4	31.2	21.3	31.9	45.1	27.0
Armenia	89.3	95.4	78.3	89.5	96.2	78.2
Azerbaijan	65.6	77.0	53.5	89.3	91.6	86.6
Georgia	95.7	96.4	94.9	86.3	95.2	75.9
Kazakhstan	96.8	96.5	97.1	97.5	97.0	98.1
Kyrgyz Republic	91.8	91.7	91.8	93.3	89.1	95.6
Pakistan	36.9	71.6	19.6	63.5	83.1	51.1
Tajikistan	90.4	92.4	89.7	95.0	93.8	95.5
Turkmenistan	62.3	76.9	49.9	...	...	...
Uzbekistan	90.9	97.5	86.9	100.0	100.0	100.0
East Asia						
China, People's Rep. of	58.8	75.3	49.6	76.5	86.6	63.7
Hong Kong, China	...	...	...	...	...	...
Korea, Rep. of	100.0	100.0	100.0	100.0	100.0	100.0
Mongolia	48.2	65.1	25.8	59.7	66.4	42.6
Taipei,China	...	...	...	...	...	...
South Asia						
Bangladesh	45.4	51.1	43.7	60.6	57.7	62.1
Bhutan	31.0	58.5	21.6	50.4	77.9	33.1
India	25.6	54.5	14.5	39.6	62.6	28.5
Maldives	79.4	97.7	72.5	97.9	97.5	98.3
Nepal	21.7	43.6	18.3	45.8	56.0	43.5
Sri Lanka	81.2	85.1	80.3	95.1	88.1	96.7
Southeast Asia						
Brunei Darussalam	...	...	...	...	...	...
Cambodia	16.3	43.3	10.2	42.4	88.1	30.5
Indonesia	47.1	65.8	33.6	60.8	72.3	47.5
Lao PDR	28.0	66.1	17.2	70.9	94.5	56.0
Malaysia	91.2	92.8	88.5	96.0	96.1	95.9
Myanmar	61.9	78.6	55.8	79.6	84.3	77.1
Philippines	63.8	72.5	55.9	73.9	77.9	70.8
Singapore	99.7	99.7	...	100.0	100.0	...
Thailand	91.3	89.4	92.2	93.0	89.9	96.1
Viet Nam	52.9	76.7	45.2	78.0	94.4	69.7
The Pacific						
Cook Islands	92.1	92.1	92.1	97.6	97.6	97.6
Fiji	74.6	89.1	61.3	91.1	93.4	88.4
Kiribati	34.2	46.9	24.7	39.7	51.2	30.6
Marshall Islands	70.1	80.4	47.6	76.9	84.5	56.2
Micronesia, Fed. States of	33.6	63.7	25.0	57.1	85.1	49.0
Nauru	65.7	65.7	...	65.6	65.6	...
Palau	81.0	88.6	63.4	100.0	100.0	100.0
Papua New Guinea	19.2	59.9	13.0	18.9	56.4	13.3
Samoa	92.2	93.9	91.8	91.5	93.3	91.1
Solomon Islands	25.5	81.4	15.0	29.8	81.4	15.0
Timor-Leste	37.4	52.7	32.5	40.6	69.0	26.8
Tonga	93.0	97.3	91.7	91.0	97.6	89.0
Tuvalu	78.4	81.1	76.0	83.3 (2013)	86.3	80.2 (2013)
Vanuatu	41.7	54.4	38.1	57.9	65.1	55.4
Developed Member Economies						
Australia	100.0	100.0	100.0	100.0	100.0	100.0
Japan	100.0	100.0	100.0	100.0	100.0	100.0
New Zealand	...	...	...	...	...	...

(continued)

Table 3.1: **Selected Indicators for SDG 6 - Clean Water and Sanitation** *(continued)*

Regional Member	6.4.2 Level of Water Stress: Freshwater Withdrawal as a Proportion of Available Freshwater Resources (%)		6.a.1 Amount of Water- and Sanitation-Related Official Development Assistance That is Part of a Government-Coordinated Spending Plan ($ million)	
	2000	2015	2000	2015
Developing Member Economies				
Central and West Asia				
Afghanistan	31.0	...	4.2	34.0
Armenia	22.3 (2002)	37.9 (2012)	10.3	36.3
Azerbaijan	29.0 (2002)	34.5 (2012)	20.3	55.7
Georgia	2.9 (2005)	2.9 (2008)	0.8	34.0
Kazakhstan	17.2 (2002)	18.4 (2010)	6.9	0.2
Kyrgyz Republic	42.7	...	0.5	17.5
Pakistan	69.9	74.4 (2008)	4.0	55.2
Tajikistan	53.2	...	3.8	36.1
Turkmenistan	100.6	...	0.0	0.2 (2011)
Uzbekistan	110.0 (2001)	...	2.0	96.1
East Asia				
China, People's Rep. of	19.5 (2005)	21.3 (2013)	516.4	183.2
Hong Kong, China	...	...	...	...
Korea, Rep. of	41.8 (2002)	...	...	...
Mongolia	1.6 (2006)	1.6 (2009)	0.3	6.4
Taipei,China	...	...	...	...
South Asia				
Bangladesh	...	2.9 (2008)	77.4	184.8
Bhutan	...	0.4 (2008)	0.2	0.9
India	31.9	33.9 (2010)	159.2	316.0
Maldives	...	15.7 (2008)	0.6 (2001)	7.2
Nepal	4.5	...	57.6	72.7
Sri Lanka	24.6	...	30.1	125.5
Southeast Asia				
Brunei Darussalam	...	1.9 (2014)	...	...
Cambodia	0.5 (2006)	...	1.6	52.0
Indonesia	5.6	...	81.5	72.3
Lao PDR	1.0 (2005)	...	36.3	38.2
Malaysia	1.6	...	352.2	63.7
Myanmar	2.8	...	1.4	35.2
Philippines	16.5 (2006)	17.0 (2009)	18.7	14.0
Singapore	...	31.7 (2014)	...	...
Thailand	13.1 (2007)	...	70.0	7.3
Viet Nam	9.3 (2005)	...	161.0	388.6
The Pacific				
Cook Islands	...	...	0.4	4.0
Fiji	0.3	...	0.4	1.9
Kiribati	...	...	0.6 (2001)	6.3
Marshall Islands	...	...	0.0 (2003)	1.0
Micronesia, Fed. States of	...	...	0.0 (2003)	1.7
Nauru	...	...	0.0 (2005)	0.0
Palau	...	...	0.0 (2003)	1.3
Papua New Guinea	0.0	...	11.9	4.4
Samoa	...	...	0.2	15.0
Solomon Islands	...	0.0 (2014)	2.0	7.2
Timor-Leste	14.3 (2004)	...	3.7	10.6
Tonga	...	...	9.3	1.6
Tuvalu	...	...	0.5 (2002)	2.7
Vanuatu	...	0.0 (2014)	0.5 (2003)	2.7
Developed Member Economies				
Australia	4.4 (2001)	3.9 (2013)	...	...
Japan	19.6 (2002)	18.9 (2009)	...	...
New Zealand	1.5 (2006)	1.6 (2010)	...	...

... = data not available at cutoff date, 0.0 = magnitude is less than half of unit employed, Lao PDR = Lao People's Democratic Republic, SDG = Sustainable Development Goal.

Sources: United Nations. Sustainable Development Goals Indicators Database. https://unstats.un.org/sdgs/indicators/database/ (accessed 18 July 2017); Food and Agriculture Organization of the United Nations. AQUASTAT. http://www.fao.org/nr/water/aquastat/data/query/index.html?lang=en (accessed 26 June 2017); World Health Organization and United Nations Children's Fund. Joint Monitoring Programme for Water and Supply Sanitation. https://www.wssinfo.org/data-estimates/tables/ (accessed 26 June 2017); Organisation for Economic Co-operation and Development. Credit Reporting System. http://stats.oecd.org/Index.aspx?DataSetCode=CRS1 (accessed 5 July 2017).

Goal 11. Make cities and human settlements inclusive, safe, resilient, and sustainable
Goal 12. Ensure sustainable consumption and production patterns
Goal 13: Take Urgent Action to Combat Climate Change and its Impacts
Goal 14. Conserve and sustainably use the oceans, seas, and marine resources for sustainable development
Goal 15. Protect, restore, and promote sustainable use of terrestrial ecosystems, sustainably manage forests, combat desertification, and halt and reverse land degradation, and halt biodiversity loss

Table 3.2: **Selected Indicators for SDGs 11, 12, 13, 14, and 15 - Sustainable Cities and the Environment, Responsible Consumption and Production, Life below Water, and Life on Land**

By 2030, ensure access for all to adequate, safe, and affordable housing, and basic services and upgrade slums

By 2030, reduce the adverse per capita environmental impact of cities, including by paying special attention to air quality and municipal and other waste management

By 2030, achieve the sustainable management and efficient use of natural resources

Strengthen resilience and adaptive capacity to climate-related hazards and natural disasters in all countries

By 2020, conserve at least 10 % of coastal and marine areas, consistent with national and international law and based on the best available scientific information

By 2020, ensure the conservation, restoration, and sustainable use of terrestrial and inland freshwater ecosystems and their services, in particular forests, wetlands, mountains, and drylands, in line with obligations under international agreements

Take urgent and significant action to reduce the degradation of natural habitats, halt the loss of biodiversity and, by 2020, protect and prevent the extinction of threatened species

Regional Member	11.1.1 Proportion of Urban Population Living in Slums, Informal Settlements or Inadequate Housing (%)		11.6.2 Average Annual Mean of Particulate Matter of 2.5 Microns in Diameter or Smaller (PM2.5) Concentration Levels in Urban Areas (µg/m³)	
			Total	Urban
	2000	2014	2014	2014
Developing Member Economies				
Central and West Asia				
Afghanistan	...	62.7	46.0	63.4
Armenia	...	14.4	20.7	25.0
Azerbaijan	...	...	23.8	26.3
Georgia	...	...	18.7	23.0
Kazakhstan	...	...	15.4	21.1
Kyrgyz Republic	...	...	15.0	15.4
Pakistan	48.7	45.5	59.8	67.7
Tajikistan	...	...	40.8	50.7
Turkmenistan	...	...	25.1	26.2
Uzbekistan	...	...	31.7	38.3
East Asia				
China, People's Rep. of	37.3	25.2	54.3	59.5
Hong Kong, China	...	...	...	...
Korea, Rep. of	...	...	26.8	27.8
Mongolia	64.9	42.7	20.1	32.1
Taipei,China	...	...	...	...
South Asia				
Bangladesh	77.8	55.1	83.5	88.8
Bhutan	...	...	48.3	39.0
India	41.5	24.0	62.4	65.7
Maldives	...	...	16.0	...
Nepal	64.0	54.3	64.0	74.3
Sri Lanka	...	...	26.7	28.5
Southeast Asia				
Brunei Darussalam	...	...	5.5	5.4
Cambodia	78.9 (2005)	55.1	23.0	25.0
Indonesia	34.4	21.8	14.4	17.8
Lao PDR	79.3 (2005)	31.4	26.8	33.5
Malaysia	...	...	14.8	16.6
Myanmar	45.6 (2005)	41.0	51.0	56.6
Philippines	47.2	38.3	22.2	27.1
Singapore	...	...	17.0	17.0
Thailand	26.0 (2005)	25.0	24.6	27.3
Viet Nam	48.8	27.2	25.7	27.6
The Pacific				
Cook Islands	...	...	...	...
Fiji	...	...	5.9	6.0
Kiribati	...	...	5.1	...
Marshall Islands	...	...	...	...
Micronesia, Fed. States of	...	...	6.0	6.0
Nauru	...	...	...	...
Palau	...	...	...	...
Papua New Guinea	...	...	10.4	12.0
Samoa	...	...	...	...
Solomon Islands	...	...	5.0	5.0
Timor-Leste	...	...	14.8	15.0
Tonga	...	...	...	...
Tuvalu	...	...	...	...
Vanuatu	...	...	6.3	7.0
Developed Member Economies				
Australia	...	...	5.7	5.8
Japan	...	...	12.5	12.9
New Zealand	...	...	5.2	5.3

(continued)

Goal 11. Make cities and human settlements inclusive, safe, resilient, and sustainable
Goal 12. Ensure sustainable consumption and production patterns
Goal 13: Take Urgent Action to Combat Climate Change and its Impacts
Goal 14. Conserve and sustainably use the oceans, seas, and marine resources for sustainable development
Goal 15. Protect, restore, and promote sustainable use of terrestrial ecosystems, sustainably manage forests, combat desertification, and halt and reverse land degradation, and halt biodiversity loss

Table 3.2: **Selected Indicators for SDGs 11, 12, 13, 14, and 15 - Sustainable Cities and the Environment, Responsible Consumption and Production, Life below Water, and Life on Land** *(continued)*

Regional Member	12.2.1 Material Footprint				12.2.2 Domestic Material Consumption			
	Million Metric Tons		Per Capita		Million Metric Tons		Per Capita	
	2000	2015	2000	2015	2000	2015	2000	2015
Developing Member Economies								
Central and West Asia								
Afghanistan	17.2	63.0	0.8	2.0	52.1	94.3	2.5	2.9
Armenia	7.8	14.3 (2010)	2.5	4.8 (2010)	10.4	16.0 (2010)	3.4	5.4 (2010)
Azerbaijan	16.9	40.7 (2010)	2.1	4.5 (2010)	29.5	63.2 (2010)	3.6	6.9 (2010)
Georgia	15.0	29.7 (2010)	3.2	6.8 (2010)	11.6	21.5 (2010)	2.4	4.9 (2010)
Kazakhstan	181.0	292.8 (2010)	12.4	18.4 (2010)	264.5	434.8 (2010)	18.1	27.3 (2010)
Kyrgyz Republic	29.8	37.8 (2010)	6.0	7.1 (2010)	30.3	35.2 (2010)	6.1	6.6 (2010)
Pakistan	325.9	577.2	2.3	3.1	488.1	813.7	3.4	4.3
Tajikistan	4.5	13.6 (2010)	0.7	1.8 (2010)	9.4	19.0 (2010)	1.5	2.5 (2010)
Turkmenistan	34.1	66.7 (2010)	7.6	13.2 (2010)	39.0	59.3 (2010)	8.7	11.8 (2010)
Uzbekistan	126.4	172.7 (2010)	5.1	6.2 (2010)	182.9	245.0 (2010)	7.4	8.8 (2010)
East Asia								
China, People's Rep. of	7,434.4	29,188.9	5.7	20.8	9,144.2	34,267.4	7.0	24.4
Hong Kong, China	597.0	847.0 (2010)	87.3	120.1 (2010)	81.0	54.6 (2010)	11.8	7.7 (2010)
Korea, Rep. of	1,013.3	1,311.6	22.0	26.4	727.7	872.3	15.8	17.5
Mongolia	8.9	46.0	3.7	15.7	50.2	100.0	20.9	34.2
Taipei,China	...	...	...	...	...	...	...	...
South Asia								
Bangladesh	196.9	306.3	1.5	1.9	230.1	346.8	1.7	2.2
Bhutan	3.2	9.2	5.7	11.9	4.6	7.6	8.2	9.8
India	2,575.2	5,783.2	2.5	4.5	3,133.0	6,766.5	3.0	5.3
Maldives	2.1	6.6	7.6	18.4	1.6	4.2	5.7	11.6
Nepal	29.8	71.2	1.3	2.5	59.8	105.4	2.6	3.7
Sri Lanka	27.3	71.9	1.4	3.3	36.0	105.4	1.9	4.9
Southeast Asia								
Brunei Darussalam	6.2	6.6 (2010)	18.5	16.5 (2010)	6.1	5.0 (2010)	18.3	12.4 (2010)
Cambodia	18.9	74.5	1.5	4.8	25.0	132.6	2.0	8.5
Indonesia	590.2	1,606.2	2.8	6.3	1,054.4	2,141.0	5.0	8.4
Lao PDR	7.8	44.4	1.4	6.3	13.5	70.0	2.5	10.0
Malaysia	382.0	632.7	16.3	20.6	318.4	409.1	13.6	13.3
Myanmar	29.9	116.8	0.6	2.2	106.5	226.4	2.2	4.2
Philippines	312.6	488.8	4.0	4.8	279.5	481.3	3.6	4.7
Singapore	261.7	426.5	66.8	75.9	429.2	219.0	109.6	39.0
Thailand	403.1	750.6	6.5	11.1	367.3	600.9	5.9	8.9
Viet Nam	272.5	832.3	3.4	8.9	327.2	965.9	4.0	10.3
The Pacific								
Cook Islands	...	...	...	...	0.1	0.2 (2010)	7.0	7.9 (2010)
Fiji	4.3	5.7	5.3	6.4	7.0	6.9	8.6	7.7
Kiribati	...	...	...	...	0.3	0.5 (2010)	4.1	5.0 (2010)
Marshall Islands	...	...	...	...	0.1	0.2 (2010)	2.2	2.9 (2010)
Micronesia, Fed. States of	...	...	...	...	0.3	0.4 (2010)	3.2	3.5 (2010)
Nauru	...	...	...	...	0.7	0.4 (2010)	69.0	45.0 (2010)
Palau	...	...	...	...	0.1	0.1 (2010)	6.2	6.1 (2010)
Papua New Guinea	13.0	28.8	2.4	3.8	66.1	86.7	12.3	11.4
Samoa	1.2	1.7 (2010)	7.1	9.1 (2010)	0.8	1.1 (2010)	4.3	6.2 (2010)
Solomon Islands	...	...	...	...	0.3	0.5 (2010)	0.8	1.0 (2010)
Timor-Leste	...	...	...	...	1.2	8.0 (2010)	1.4	7.4 (2010)
Tonga	...	...	...	...	0.5	0.8 (2010)	5.2	7.4 (2010)
Tuvalu	...	...	...	...	0.0	0.0 (2010)	3.2	2.3 (2010)
Vanuatu	1.2	2.2 (2010)	6.3	9.1 (2010)	1.1	1.4 (2010)	6.1	6.1 (2010)
Developed Member Economies								
Australia	633.2	967.0	32.9	40.4	917.4	1,132.2	47.6	47.3
Japan	3,138.1	2,651.5	25.0	20.9	1,564.1	1,231.3	12.4	9.7
New Zealand	85.3	107.8	22.1	23.5	91.8	100.6	23.8	21.9

(continued)

Goal 11. Make cities and human settlements inclusive, safe, resilient, and sustainable
Goal 12. Ensure sustainable consumption and production patterns
Goal 13: Take Urgent Action to Combat Climate Change and its Impacts
Goal 14. Conserve and sustainably use the oceans, seas, and marine resources for sustainable development
Goal 15. Protect, restore, and promote sustainable use of terrestrial ecosystems, sustainably manage forests, combat desertification, and halt and reverse land degradation, and halt biodiversity loss

Table 3.2: **Selected Indicators for SDGs 11, 12, 13, 14, and 15 - Sustainable Cities and the Environment, Responsible Consumption and Production, Life below Water, and Life on Land** *(continued)*

Regional Member	13.1.2 Number of countries that adopt and implement national disaster risk reduction strategies in line with the Sendai Framework for Disaster Risk Reduction 2015–2030[a]	14.5.1 Coverage of Protected Areas in Relation to Marine Areas (%)	15.1.1 Forest Area as a Proportion of Total Land Area (%)		15.5.1 Red List Index[b]	
	Latest Year	2016	2000	2015	2000	2016
Developing Member Economies						
Central and West Asia						
Afghanistan	2015	...	2.1	2.1	0.84	0.84
Armenia	2013	...	11.8	11.8	0.85	0.84
Azerbaijan		0.4	10.5	13.8	0.91	0.91
Georgia	2015	0.7	39.7	40.6	0.88	0.86
Kazakhstan	2013	1.1	1.2	1.2	0.88	0.87
Kyrgyz Republic	2015	...	4.5	3.3	0.99	0.98
Pakistan	2015	0.8	2.7	1.9	0.93	0.87
Tajikistan		...	3.0	3.0	0.99	0.98
Turkmenistan		3.0	8.8	8.8	0.98	0.97
Uzbekistan		...	7.3	7.3	0.98	0.97
East Asia						
China, People's Rep. of	2013	3.8	18.8	22.1	0.81	0.75
Hong Kong, China		...	...	...	0.82	0.82
Korea, Rep. of	2013	1.6	64.8	63.7	0.84	0.78
Mongolia	2015	...	7.5	8.1	0.96	0.95
Taipei,China		...	58.1(2001)	60.7	...	...
South Asia						
Bangladesh	2015	5.4	11.3	11.0	0.83	0.77
Bhutan	2015	...	68.4	72.3	0.80	0.80
India	2015	0.2	22.0	23.8	0.75	0.69
Maldives		0.1	3.3	3.3	0.91	0.85
Nepal	2015	...	27.2	25.4	0.82	0.82
Sri Lanka	2015	0.1	35.0	33.0	0.66	0.57
Southeast Asia						
Brunei Darussalam		0.2	75.3	72.1	0.85	0.83
Cambodia		0.2	65.4	53.6	0.88	0.82
Indonesia	2015	2.9	57.8	53.0	0.84	0.77
Lao PDR		...	71.6	81.3	0.82	0.81
Malaysia	2013	1.4	65.7	67.6	0.82	0.70
Myanmar		0.1	53.0	44.2	0.86	0.81
Philippines	2015	1.2	23.6	27.0	0.73	0.65
Singapore		...	22.9	22.9	0.91	0.87
Thailand	2015	1.9	33.3	32.1	0.85	0.80
Viet Nam	2015	0.6	37.8	47.6	0.81	0.75
The Pacific						
Cook Islands		–	62.5	62.5	0.80	0.77
Fiji	2015	0.9	53.6	55.7	0.70	0.67
Kiribati		11.8	14.8	14.8	0.82	0.77
Marshall Islands		0.3	72.2	72.2	0.89	0.84
Micronesia, Fed. States of		0.0	91.4	91.4	0.76	0.69
Nauru	2013	...	0.0	0.0	0.82	0.78
Palau		83.0	87.0	87.0	0.91	0.76
Papua New Guinea	2013	0.2	72.6	72.5	0.90	0.84
Samoa	2013	0.1	60.4	60.4	0.84	0.81
Solomon Islands		0.1	81.0	78.1	0.83	0.77
Timor-Leste		1.4	57.4	46.1	0.95	0.89
Tonga	2013	1.5	12.5	12.5	0.73	0.71
Tuvalu		0.0	33.3	33.3	0.88	0.84
Vanuatu	2013	0.0	36.1	36.1	0.72	0.67
Developed Member Economies						
Australia	2015	40.7	16.8	16.2	0.88	0.83
Japan	2015	0.5	68.2	68.5	0.84	0.79
New Zealand	2015	30.3	38.5	38.6	0.71	0.64

... = data not available at cutoff date, – = magnitude equals zero, Lao PDR = Lao People's Democratic Republic, SDG = Sustainable Development Goal.

a Refers to the most recent year when the economy adopted and implemented national disaster risk reduction strategies in line with the Sendai Framework for Disaster Risk Reduction 2015–2030.

b The Red List Index value ranges from 1, which means all species are categorized as "Least Concern" hence, that none are expected to go extinct in the near future; to 0, or all species are categorized as "Extinct," and so indicates how far the set of species has moved overall toward extinction.

Sources: United Nations. Sustainable Development Goals Indicators Database. https://unstats.un.org/sdgs/indicators/database/ (accessed 17 July 2017); United Nations Human Settlement Programme (UN-Habitat). World Cities Report. https://unhabitat.org/books/world-cities-report/. World Health Organization. Global Health Observatory data repository. http://apps.who.int/gho/data/view.main.SDGPM25116v?lang=en (accessed 28 June 2017). United Nations Environment Programme (UNEP), Natural Resources: Resource Efficiency Indicators https://uneplive.unep.org/material (accessed 30 June 2017) Food and Agriculture Organization of the United Nations. Global Forest Resources Assessment 2015. http://www.fao.org/3/a-i4808e.pdf (accessed 30 June 2015). For Taipei,China: economy source.

Prosperity

To ensure that all human beings can enjoy prosperous and fulfilling lives and that economic, social, and technological progress occurs in harmony with nature.

7 AFFORDABLE AND CLEAN ENERGY | 8 DECENT WORK AND ECONOMIC GROWTH | 9 INDUSTRY, INNOVATION AND INFRASTRUCTURE | 10 REDUCED INEQUALITIES

Snapshot

- As of 2014, 20 out of 47 economies in Asia and the Pacific have access to electricity, but in 11 regional economies, including Bangladesh and India, more than 20% of the population still do not have access to electricity.
- In 2014, 14 out of 46 economies reported at least 90% of their populations relying primarily on clean fuels and technology for cooking.
- The Lao People's Democratic Republic, Bhutan, and Nepal have over 80% of their respective final energy consumption based on renewable sources.
- Based on latest available data, unemployment rates for the age group of 15 years and above in 23 out of 41 reporting economies are below 5%.
- In 2014, less than 60% of adults in 19 out of 27 developing economies of Asia and the Pacific had an account at a bank or other financial institution.
- Manufacturing value added per capita in Asia and the Pacific has grown by at least 50% from 2000 to 2016 in more than half of 47 reporting economies, but negative growth has been observed in 13 economies.
- Research and development expenditures are rising in the Asia and Pacific economies; however, only four developing economies and three developed economies have research and development expenditures exceeding 1% percent of gross domestic product.
- Based on latest available data over about a five year period, the bottom 40% of the population experienced faster growth in per capita income (or expenditure) than the national average in 13 out of 16 developing economies in the region.

Ensuring sustainable development not only entails economic prosperity, but also requires growth to be inclusive, fair, and environmentally sustainable. SDGs 7 to 10 are focused on guaranteeing that everyone can enjoy prosperous and fulfilling lives, and that socioeconomic progress occurs in harmony with nature. The goals include universal access to affordable and clean energy; economic growth and decent work for all; resilient infrastructure, inclusive and sustainable industrialization, and fostered innovation; and reduced inequalities.

SDG 7: Ensure Access to Affordable, Reliable, Sustainable and Modern Energy for All

Energy is fundamental to almost every major human endeavor, and lack of access to affordable, reliable, sustainable, and modern energy can impede economic development. Emissions from inefficient energy usage may contribute to negative health outcomes, particularly among the poorest segments of society that rely on these unclean energy sources and have little or no access to health care. Expanding infrastructure and upgrading technology to provide affordable and clean energy to all can encourage growth as well as protect the environment.

Proportion of population with access to electricity. As of 2014, at least 95% of the population in 30 out of 47 economies with available data in Asia and the Pacific have access to electricity. Of these 30 economies, two-thirds enjoy universal access to electricity (Figure 4.1), an increase by 13 economies from seven economies in 2000. Across the region, 45 of 47 economies have increased or maintained the share of their populations with electricity access in the period 2000 to 2014. Despite this progress, a significant number of people still do not have access to electricity. Eleven economies are reported to provide electricity access to less than 80% of its population—Bangladesh (62.4%); Cambodia (56.1%) India (79.2%); the Lao People's Democratic Republic (78.1%); Myanmar (52.0%); and the Pacific economies of Kiribati (48.1%), the Federated States of Micronesia (71.7%), Papua New Guinea (20.3%), Solomon Islands (35.1%), Timor-Leste (45.4%), and Vanuatu (34.5%) (Table 4.1).

Figure 4.1: Proportion of Population with Access to Electricity, 2014
(%)

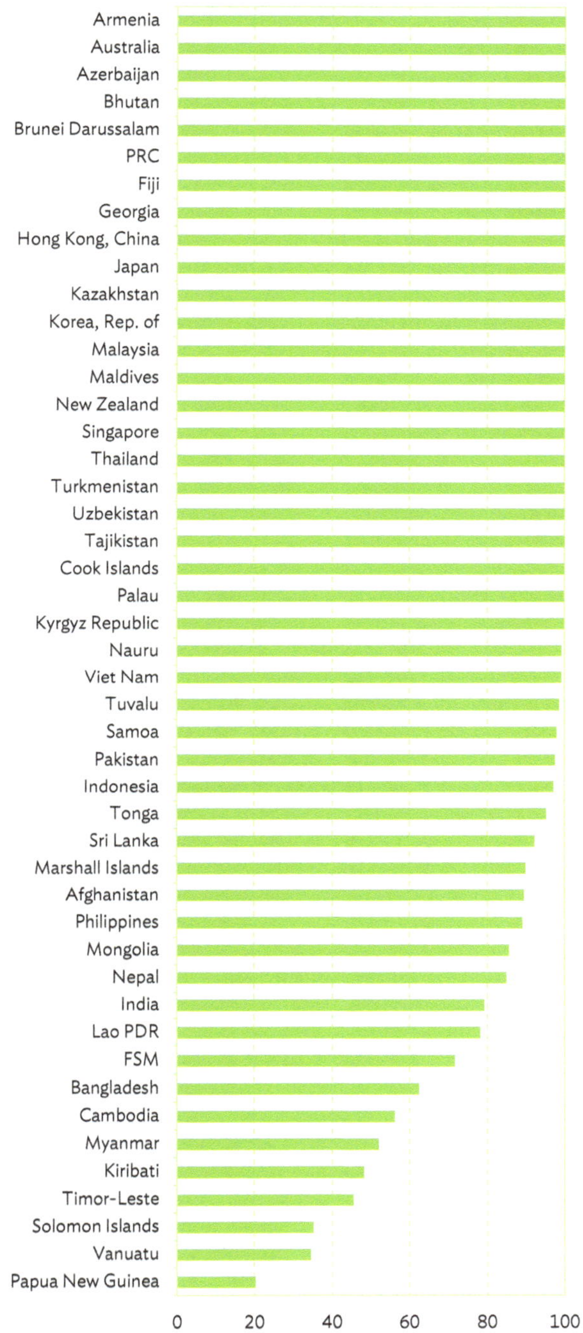

FSM = Federated States of Micronesia, Lao PDR = Lao People's Democratic Republic, PRC = People's Republic of China.
Source: Table 4.1.

Proportion of population with primary reliance on clean fuels and technology for cooking. Seven out of 46 reporting economies in 2000—Australia, Brunei Darussalam, Japan, the Republic of Korea, New Zealand, Singapore, and Turkmenistan—already had at least 95% of their respective populations relying on clean fuels and technology for cooking (Figure 4.2). Of the remaining 39 economies, 33 have reported an increase in reliance on clean fuels among their respective populations during 2000–2014, with Indonesia and Maldives reporting the biggest increases at over 50 percentage points (Table 4.1). By 2014, five other economies—Armenia, Azerbaijan, Malaysia, Maldives, Nauru—also had at least 95% of their populations relying on clean fuels and technology. On the other hand, the proportion of people relying on unclean fuels and technologies for cooking is over 80% in 10 economies—Afghanistan, Bangladesh, Cambodia, Kiribati, the Lao People's Democratic Republic, Myanmar, Solomon Islands, Sri Lanka, Timor-Leste, and Vanuatu.

Renewable energy share in total final energy consumption. Overall, 21 out of 47 economies reported at least one-fourth of their energy consumption coming from renewable resources (Figure 4.3). Over 80% of total final energy consumption in the Lao People's Democratic Republic (90.3%), Bhutan (86.7%), and Nepal (84.4%) is based on renewable sources (Table 4.1). The largest percentage point decline in the share of total final energy consumption coming from renewable resources was reported for Afghanistan (37.5 percentage points). Three other economies reported at least 20 percentage points decline in their renewable energy usage from 2000 to 2014: Bangladesh, Tajikistan, and Viet Nam.

Figure 4.2: Proportion of Population with Primary Reliance on Clean Fuels and Technology for Cooking
(%)

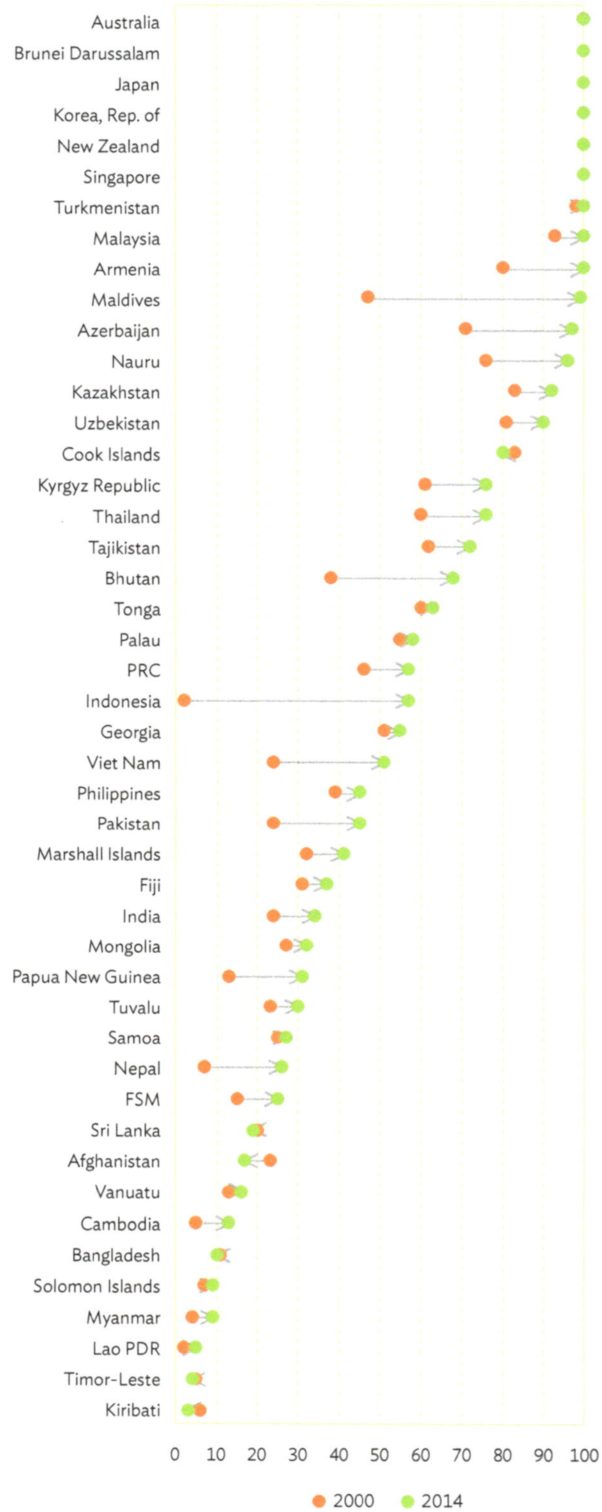

FSM = Federated States of Micronesia, Lao PDR = Lao People's Democratic Republic, PRC = People's Republic of China.
Source: Table 4.1.

Figure 4.3: Renewable Energy Share in the Total Final Energy Consumption, (%)

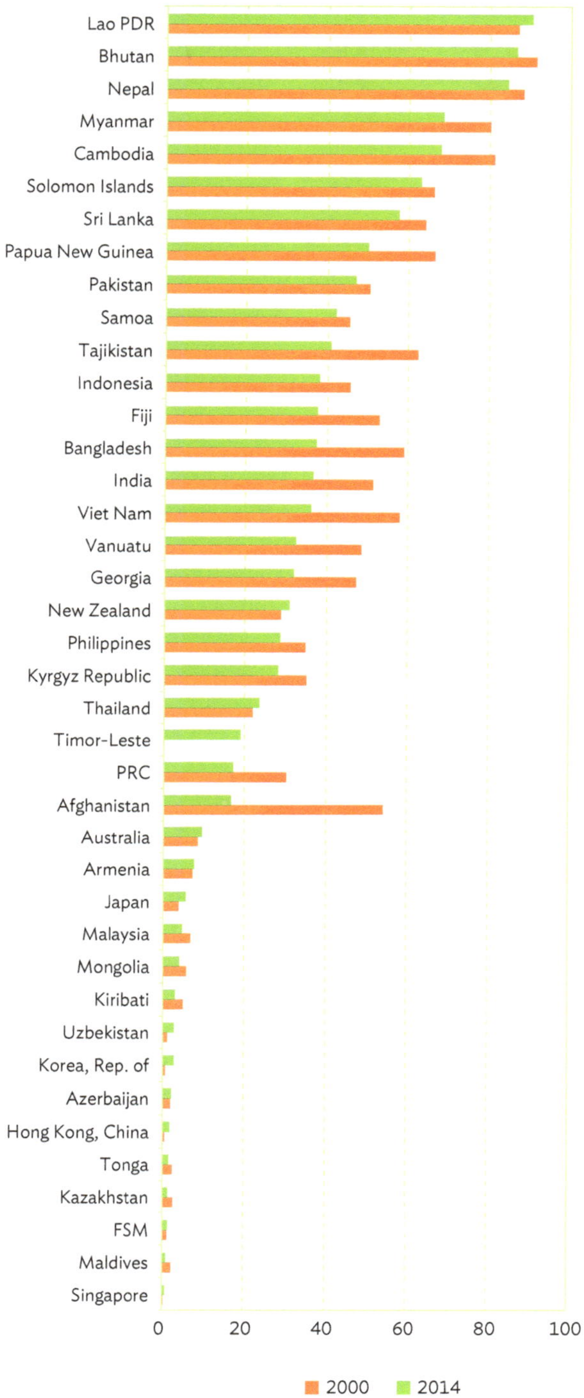

FSM = Federated States of Micronesia, Lao PDR = Lao People's Democratic Republic, PRC = People's Republic of China.

Note: Economies with values less than 0.5 are not presented in the chart. These include Brunei Darussalam, the Cook Islands, the Marshall Islands, Nauru, Palau, Turkmenistan, and Tuvalu.

Source: Table 4.1.

Energy intensity measured in terms of primary energy and GDP. Energy intensity is a proxy for energy efficiency, as it describes how much energy is used to produce one unit of economic output. Across most economies in Asia and the Pacific, energy intensity has improved. Latest data (Table 4.1) show that energy intensity levels are over 10 megajoules per US dollar (MJ/$) constant 2011 purchasing power parity (PPP) gross domestic product (GDP) in Turkmenistan (14.3), Palau (13.0), Uzbekistan (11.2), and Bhutan (11.1). In other economies in Asia and the Pacific, the energy intensity level ranges between 1.6 MJ/$ 2011 PPP GDP and 8.6 MJ/$ 2011 PPP GDP.

SDG 8: Promote Sustained, Inclusive and Sustainable Economic Growth, Full and Productive Employment and Decent Work for All

While economic growth is necessary for a country's progress, it is not sufficient to ensure increased access to opportunities and better living conditions for all segments of society. The pursuit of inclusive growth is therefore an important objective within the context of the SDGs. Promoting full and productive employment, and providing decent work for all plays a pivotal role in ensuring that growth is inclusive and sustainable.

Unemployment rate. Based on the latest available data, 23 out of 41 economies with data have registered unemployment rates for the age group of 15 years and above as 5% or below, while another five economies have over 10% unemployment rates (Table 4.3). Women registered a higher unemployment rate than men in 23 out of 38 economies with data available for the latest year. Figure 4.4 presents results for all reporting economies where total and sex-disaggregated unemployment rates for the age group of 15 years and above are greater than 1.

Figure 4.4: Unemployment Rate, 15 Years Old and Above, by Sex, Latest Year (%)

PRC = People's Republic of China.

Notes: Sex-disaggregated unemployment rates for population aged 15 years and above in the PRC and Fiji are not available. For Myanmar, total unemployment rate for population aged 15 years and above is less than 1. For Cambodia, the Lao PDR, and Thailand, total and sex-disaggregated unemployment rates for population 15 years and above are less than 1, which are not presented in this chart.

Source: Table 4.3.

Proportion of adults (15 years and older) with an account at a bank or other financial institution or with a mobile money service provider. While at least 97% of adult populations in developed member economies have accounts in banks, other financial institutions, or with mobile money service providers, only 8 out of 27 developing economies have reported at least 60% of people 15 years and older having access to the same (Table 4.5). East Asia is the only region where more than 80% of adults have an account at a bank, or other financial institution, or with a mobile money provider. For 17 out of 23 economies of Central and West Asia, Southeast Asia, and South Asia, less than 50% of adults reported having an account at a bank, financial institution or with a mobile money service provider.

SDG 9: Build Resilient Infrastructure, Promote Inclusive and Sustainable Industrialization, and Foster Innovation

Infrastructure provides basic physical facilities and services necessary to stimulate economic activity and growth. Inclusive and sustainable industrialization drives economic growth, creates jobs and wealth, and ultimately reduces poverty. Innovation leads to the development of new skills and competencies, and strengthens the productivity and competitiveness of industries. Amidst a rapidly changing global economic landscape, it is imperative that these three facets of SDG 9 work in tandem to ensure sustainable economic growth and adequate response to climate change.

Manufacturing value added per capita. Figure 4.5 shows that in 2016, Singapore posted the highest manufacturing value added per capita across all regional economies at $9,265.7 (at constant 2010 dollars). Manufacturing value added per capita was over $3,000 per person (at constant 2010 dollars) in six other regional economies, including Brunei Darussalam ($4,482.2); the Republic of

Korea ($7,556.8); Taipei,China ($4,586.1); and the developed member economies of Australia ($4,118.1), Japan ($8,514.2), and New Zealand ($3,719.1). Latest available year data for economies show that low manufacturing value added per capita (at constant 2010 dollars) has been registered in Timor-Leste ($7.3), Nepal ($38.8), and Tuvalu ($39.6). Meanwhile, negative growth in manufacturing value added per capita between 2000 and 2016 has been observed in Brunei Darussalam; Hong Kong, China; the Kyrgyz Republic; Tajikistan; in seven Pacific economies, the Cook Islands, Kiribati, Palau, Samoa, Timor-Leste, Tonga, Vanuatu; and in two developed economies, Australia and New Zealand.

Carbon dioxide emission per unit of value added. Three-fifths of 30 Asia and Pacific economies managed to lower carbon dioxide (CO_2) emissions per unit of gross domestic product (GDP) (2005 purchasing power parity) by at least a 20.0% between 2000 and 2014 (Table 4.8). Four of the five economies with the highest CO_2 emissions per unit of GDP in 2000 are in Central and West Asia: Uzbekistan, Turkmenistan, Kazakhstan, and Azerbaijan, respectively. Central and West Asia, however, has succeeded in reducing CO_2 emissions per value added, with half of 10 economies reducing CO_2 emissions by at least 28% between 2000 and 2014.

Figure 4.5: Manufacturing Value Added per Capita
(constant 2010 $)

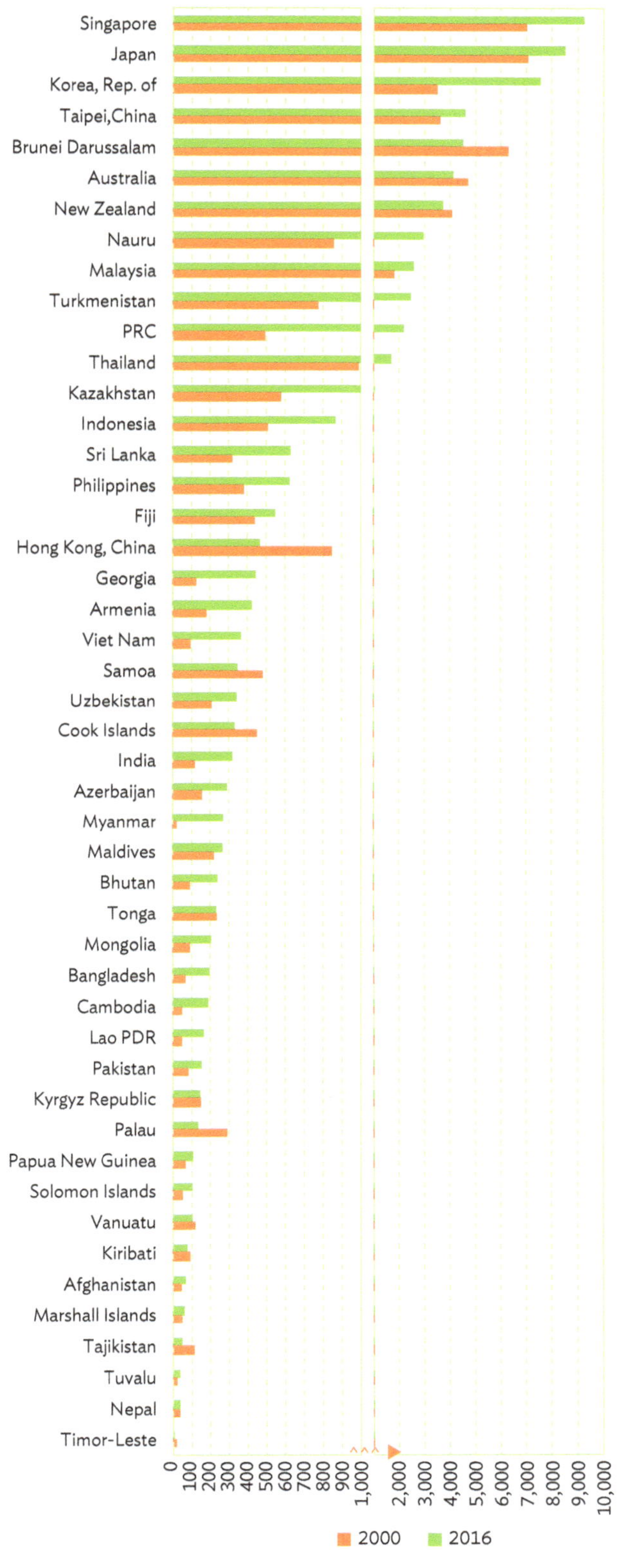

Lao PDR = Lao People's Democratic Republic, PRC = People's Republic of China.
Note: For the Cook Islands and Nauru, the latest available year is 2014.
Source: Table 4.7.

Research and development expenditure as a proportion of GDP. Research and development (R&D) spending as a proportion of GDP has risen between 2000 and 2015 in 16 economies in Asia and the Pacific (Table 4.9). However, in 2015, only seven economies fulfilled or surpassed the 1% R&D spending benchmark recommended by the United Nations Educational, Scientific and Cultural Organization. These are the Republic of Korea (4.2%), Japan (3.3%), Australia (2.2%), Singapore (2.2%), the People's Republic of China (2.1%), Malaysia (1.3%), and New Zealand (1.2%). Except for Hong Kong, China (0.8%); India (0.6%); and Thailand (0.6%), the rest of the regional economies had expenditures on R&D less than 0.5% of GDP.

SDG 10: Reduce Inequality Within and Among Countries

Stark, pervasive, and often mutually reinforcing economic inequalities are evident within and among economies in Asia and the Pacific. These income, wealth, and asset inequalities typically occur because of initial conditions that are beyond one's control, such as wealth, sex, residence, disability status, ethnicity, migrant status, and social marginalization. SDG 10 aims to reduce inequalities through the adoption of policies facilitating labor mobility and empowerment of the bottom group of income earners, alongside promoting socioeconomic inclusion regardless of one's sex, race, ethnicity, and other social constructs.

Growth rates of household expenditure or income per capita among the bottom 40% of the population and the total population. Available data for recent years show that in 13 out of 16 developing economies in the region with available data (Figure 4.6), the per capita income of the bottom 40% has grown faster than the national average, with the People's Republic of China (8.9%) and Mongolia (8.0%) reporting at least 8% growth rate for the poorest 40% of their respective households. The growth rate of per capita income among the bottom 40% of the population is lower than the average for the whole population in Armenia, India, and the Lao People's Democratic Republic.

Figure 4.6: Growth Rates of Expenditure (or Income per Capita) among the Bottom 40% and the Entire Population
(%)

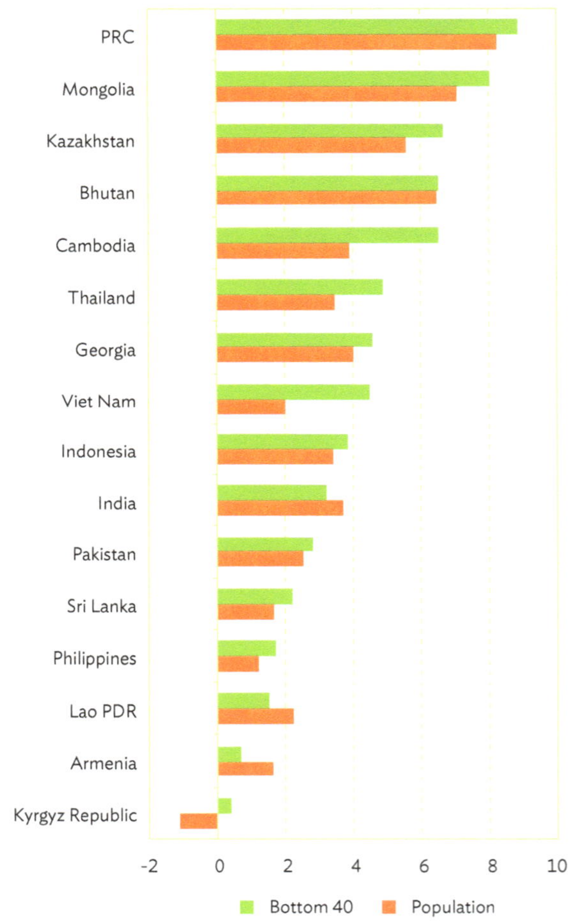

Lao PDR = Lao People's Democratic Republic,
PRC = People's Republic of China.
Source: Table 4.12.

Equity, Data Gaps, and Other Related Issues

In Asia and the Pacific, some segments of the population including the poor and those living in rural areas, do not have access to electricity, clean fuels, and technology for cooking. Closing this gap remains a challenge given the high costs of supplying electricity to rural households, limited capacity of rural households to pay for the service, and electricity generation shortages.

Employment generation is critical for inclusive economic growth, and the unemployment rate is an important indicator for understanding labor market dynamics. However, inequities in employment continue to persist, with unemployment rates being significantly higher for youth aged 15–24 years compared to adults aged 25 years and above. Data on unemployment for persons with disabilities is not available in most countries. Also, the sole use of the unemployment rate as a measure of success in job creation can be unsuitable for some developing economies in the region with a large informal sector. For these countries, examining underemployment and vulnerable employment is more suitable.

Labor share in GDP underestimates the proportion of GDP accrued to total employment, as it only covers the compensation of employees and does not include labor income for self-employed people. Moreover, data on income from self-employment are not always available for developing economies. Thus, labor share in GDP may be less relevant in developing economies within the region, where a large proportion of employment is in self-employment. However, an adjusted labor share may be estimated to account for labor income of self-employed workers.

Finally, while a positive correlation exists between poverty and inequality, the relative importance of growth and inequality to poverty varies across countries (ADB 2016). Some countries such as the PRC, India, Indonesia, and Viet Nam have reduced poverty significantly, even if the income of the bottom 40% has grown more slowly than that of the national average.

Table 4.1: **Selected Indicators for SDG 7 - Energy Efficiency and Access to Modern and Renewable Energy Sources**

By 2030, ensure universal access to affordable, reliable, and modern energy services

By 2030, increase substantially the share of renewable energy in the global energy mix

By 2030, double the global rate of improvement in energy efficiency

Regional Member	7.1.1 Proportion of Population with Access to Electricity (%)		7.1.2 Proportion of Population with Primary Reliance on Clean Fuels and Technology (%)		7.2.1 Renewable Energy Share in the Total Final Energy Consumption (%)		7.3.1 Energy Intensity Measured in Terms of Primary Energy and GDP (MJ/$ 2011 PPP GDP)	
	2000	2014	2000	2014	2000	2014	2000	2014
Developing Member Economies								
Central and West Asia								
Afghanistan	0.2	89.5	23.0	17.0	54.2	16.8	1.7	2.6
Armenia	98.9	100.0	80.0	100.0	7.2	7.7	9.4	5.4
Azerbaijan	98.0	100.0	71.0	97.0	2.1	2.1	13.2	3.8
Georgia	99.8	100.0	51.0	55.0	47.3	31.9	8.3	5.6
Kazakhstan	99.0	100.0	83.0	92.0	2.5	1.4	9.7	7.6
Kyrgyz Republic	99.8	99.8	61.0	76.0	35.2	28.3	9.6	8.6
Pakistan	75.2	97.5	24.0	45.0	50.4	47.2	5.5	4.4
Tajikistan	98.4	100.0	62.0	72.0	62.4	40.7	12.3	5.5
Turkmenistan	99.6	100.0	98.0	100.0	0.1	0.0	25.9	14.3
Uzbekistan	99.8	100.0	81.0	90.0	1.2	2.9	35.0	11.2
East Asia								
China, People's Rep. of	94.8	100.0	46.0	57.0	30.3	17.1	10.2	7.4
Hong Kong, China	100.0	100.0	...	...	0.6	1.8	2.5	1.6
Korea, Rep. of	100.0	100.0	100.0	100.0	0.7	2.8	8.1	6.6
Mongolia	67.3	85.6	27.0	32.0	5.7	4.0	9.0	6.8
Taipei,China	...	...	...	...	...	...	...	...
South Asia								
Bangladesh	32.0	62.4	11.0	10.0	59.0	37.5	3.5	3.1
Bhutan	32.1	100.0	38.0	68.0	91.4	86.7	21.8	11.1
India	59.6	79.2	24.0	34.0	51.6	36.5	7.0	4.9
Maldives	83.8	100.0	47.0	99.0	2.1	0.9	3.3	4.0
Nepal	27.2	84.9	7.0	26.0	88.3	84.4	9.3	7.7
Sri Lanka	69.4	92.2	20.0	19.0	64.2	57.6	3.4	2.0
Southeast Asia								
Brunei Darussalam	100.0	100.0	100.0	100.0	–	0.0	4.0	5.3
Cambodia	16.6	56.1	5.0	13.0	81.1	68.0	8.5	5.6
Indonesia	86.3	97.0	2.0	57.0	45.6	38.1	5.3	3.7
Lao PDR	43.1	78.1	2.0	5.0	87.1	90.3	5.4	2.3
Malaysia	96.7	100.0	93.0	100.0	6.7	4.8	5.4	5.1
Myanmar	45.9	52.0	4.0	9.0	80.2	68.5	9.0	3.2
Philippines	73.6	89.1	39.0	45.0	34.9	28.7	5.1	3.0
Singapore	100.0	100.0	100.0	100.0	0.3	0.6	3.8	2.7
Thailand	82.1	100.0	60.0	76.0	22.0	23.6	5.2	5.6
Viet Nam	86.1	99.2	24.0	51.0	58.0	36.2	5.9	5.7
The Pacific								
Cook Islands	97.5	99.9	83.0	80.0	–	–	...	...
Fiji	74.8	100.0	31.0	37.0	52.9	37.6	3.8	3.1
Kiribati	75.8	48.1	6.0	3.0	4.9	3.0	3.4	4.8
Marshall Islands	68.1	90.0	32.0	41.0	0.0	0.2	6.8	7.5
Micronesia, Fed. States of	46.0	71.7	15.0	25.0	1.2	1.3	5.5	6.8
Nauru	99.9	99.2	76.0	96.0	0.0	0.0	...	...
Palau	98.4	99.8	55.0	58.0	0.0	0.0	13.4	13.0
Papua New Guinea	12.3	20.3	13.0	31.0	66.4	50.0	9.9	7.9
Samoa	87.2	97.9	25.0	27.0	45.4	42.1	4.4	4.3
Solomon Islands	9.5	35.1	7.0	9.0	66.3	63.0	7.6	5.3
Timor-Leste	24.2	45.4	5.0	4.0	...	19.0	2.9	3.0
Tonga	85.4	95.3	60.0	63.0	2.5	1.6	3.3	3.1
Tuvalu	94.2	98.5	23.0	30.0	–	–	3.3	3.7
Vanuatu	22.2	34.5	13.0	16.0	48.7	32.4	4.0	4.3
Developed Member Economies								
Australia	100.0	100.0	100.0	100.0	8.4	9.5	6.7	5.2
Japan	100.0	100.0	100.0	100.0	3.9	5.5	5.3	4.1
New Zealand	100.0	100.0	100.0	100.0	28.9	30.9	6.6	5.6

... = data not available at cutoff date, – = magnitude equals zero, 0.0 = magnitude is less than half of unit employed, GDP = gross domestic product, Lao PDR = Lao People's Democratic Republic, MJ = megajoule, PPP = purchasing power parity, SDG = Sustainable Development Goal.

Sources: World Bank Energy Sector Management Assistance Program and International Energy Agency. Global Tracking Framework 2017. http://gtf.esmap.org/downloads (accessed 6 July 2017); United Nations. Sustainable Development Goals Indicators Database. http://unstats.un.org/sdgs/indicators/database/ (accessed 17 July 2017).

Table 4.2: **Selected Indicators for SDG 8 - Decent Work and Economic Growth**

Sustain per capita economic growth in accordance with national circumstances and, in particular, at least 7% gross domestic product per annum in the least developed countries

Achieve higher levels of economic productivity through diversification, technological upgrading, and innovation, including through a focus on high-value added and labor-intensive sectors

Regional Member	8.1.1 Annual Growth Rate of Real GDP per Capita at Constant 2005 $ (%)		8.2.1 Annual Growth Rate of Real GDP per Employed Person (%)	
	2000	2015	2000	2016
Developing Member Economies				
Central and West Asia				
Afghanistan	-8.7	-5.1	-8.1	-1.9
Armenia	6.5	2.6	7.3	2.5
Azerbaijan	10.1	-0.6	17.0	-2.9
Georgia	3.1	6.7	2.3	3.4
Kazakhstan	10.6	-0.3	8.8	-1.3
Kyrgyz Republic	4.1	1.8	3.0	1.2
Pakistan	1.9	3.4	1.8	2.0
Tajikistan	6.7	1.9	5.6	3.8
Turkmenistan	4.3	5.2	2.6	3.6
Uzbekistan	2.6	5.3	1.0	4.3
East Asia				
China, People's Rep. of	7.9	6.4	7.1	6.4
Hong Kong, China	6.2	1.6	4.3	1.8
Korea, Rep. of	8.2	2.2	4.8	2.0
Mongolia	0.2	0.6	-1.6	-2.2
Taipei,China	...	...	...	...
South Asia				
Bangladesh	3.9	5.3	1.2	4.7
Bhutan	5.7	3.9	1.8	3.4
India	2.2	6.3	2.0	5.6
Maldives	2.5	1.1	-4.0	0.1
Nepal	4.2	1.5	4.5	-1.7
Sri Lanka	5.3	4.3	5.1	4.7
Southeast Asia				
Brunei Darussalam	0.8	-1.9	-1.0	-0.8
Cambodia	6.4	5.3	3.1	5.0
Indonesia	3.5	3.5	2.7	3.1
Lao PDR	4.1	5.8	3.6	4.9
Malaysia	6.4	3.5	3.3	2.6
Myanmar	12.4	6.4	11.3	6.6
Philippines	2.2	4.3	6.0	3.8
Singapore	6.2	0.2	3.7	0.2
Thailand	3.3	2.5	1.1	2.8
Viet Nam	5.6	5.5	4.5	4.9
The Pacific				
Cook Islands	13.8	4.9	...	...
Fiji	-2.3	2.9	-2.5	1.5
Kiribati	10.1	1.9	...	...
Marshall Islands	5.7	0.5	...	...
Micronesia, Fed. States of	4.9	3.3	...	...
Nauru	-6.8	18.2	...	...
Palau	-1.3	4.7	...	...
Papua New Guinea	-4.9	4.4	-5.5	-0.2
Samoa	6.6	2.1	4.0	0.8
Solomon Islands	-16.5	1.2	-17.2	0.5
Timor-Leste	12.8	1.8	24.1	3.7
Tonga	2.6	3.2	2.4	1.2
Tuvalu	12.8	3.3	...	...
Vanuatu	3.1	-3.2	4.3	1.3
Developed Member Economies				
Australia	0.9	1.0	1.4	1.3
Japan	2.6	1.4	2.5	0.7
New Zealand	1.1	2.3	0.3	1.9

... = data not available at cutoff date, GDP = gross domestic product, Lao PDR = Lao People's Democratic Republic, SDG = Sustainable Development Goal.

Source: United Nations. Sustainable Development Goals Indicators Database. http://unstats.un.org/sdgs/indicators/database/ (accessed 17 July 2017).

Table 4.3: **Selected Indicators for SDG 8 - Unemployment**
By 2030, achieve full and productive employment and decent work for all women and men, including for young people and persons with disabilities, and equal pay for work of equal value

Regional Member	8.5.2.a Unemployment Rate for Age Group 15+, by Sex (%)					
	2000			2015		
	Total	Female	Male	Total	Female	Male
Developing Member Economies						
Central and West Asia						
Afghanistan	8.5 (2005)	9.5 (2005)	7.6 (2005)	8.2 (2011)	16.5 (2011)	6.4 (2011)
Armenia	35.8 (2001)	40.2 (2001)	31.9 (2001)	18.3	19.2	17.4
Azerbaijan	11.8	12.7	10.9	5.0	5.9	4.1
Georgia	10.8	10.5	11.1	12.0	10.2	13.5
Kazakhstan	10.4 (2001)	12.1 (2001)	8.9 (2001)	5.0	5.7	4.3
Kyrgyz Republic	12.6 (2002)	14.3 (2002)	11.2 (2002)	7.6	9.0	6.5
Pakistan	7.2	15.8	5.5	5.9	9.0	5.0
Tajikistan	...	...	...	11.5 (2009)	10.5 (2009)	12.3 (2009)
Turkmenistan	...	...	...	...	...	...
Uzbekistan	...	...	...	...	...	...
East Asia						
China, People's Rep. of	2.6	...	...	3.1 (2014)	...	...
Hong Kong, China	4.9	4.0	5.6	3.4 (2016)	3.0 (2016)	3.7 (2016)
Korea, Rep. of	4.4	3.7	5.0	3.7 (2016)	3.6 (2016)	3.8 (2016)
Mongolia	6.2 (2002)	6.2 (2002)	6.2 (2002)	4.9	4.3	5.4
Taipei,China	3.0	...	...	3.9 (2016)	3.6 (2016)	4.2 (2016)
South Asia						
Bangladesh	3.3	3.3	3.2	4.4 (2013)	7.4 (2013)	3.2 (2013)
Bhutan	1.9 (2001)	3.2 (2001)	1.3 (2001)	2.5 (2014)	3.5 (2014)	1.9 (2014)
India	4.3	4.3	4.3	4.9 (2014)	7.7 (2014)	4.1 (2014)
Maldives	2.0	2.7	1.6	5.2 (2014)	5.9 (2014)	4.8 (2014)
Nepal	8.8 (2001)	10.7 (2001)	7.4 (2001)	3.0 (2014)	3.4 (2014)	2.6 (2014)
Sri Lanka	7.7	11.4	5.9	4.7	7.6	3.0
Southeast Asia						
Brunei Darussalam	...	...	...	7.0 (2014)	7.9 (2014)	6.3 (2014)
Cambodia	2.5	2.8	2.1	0.2 (2014)	0.2 (2014)	0.2 (2014)
Indonesia	9.1 (2007)	10.8 (2007)	8.1 (2007)	5.6 (2016)	5.4 (2016)	5.7 (2016)
Lao PDR	1.4 (2005)	1.4 (2005)	1.4 (2005)	0.7 (2010)	0.7 (2010)	0.8 (2010)
Malaysia	3.0	3.1	3.0	3.1	3.4	2.9
Myanmar	...	...	...	0.8 (2016)	...	...
Philippines	11.2	11.5	11.0	6.3	5.8	6.6
Singapore	3.7	3.5	3.9	2.8 (2014)	3.0 (2014)	2.7 (2014)
Thailand	2.4	2.3	2.4	0.2	0.2	0.2
Viet Nam	2.3	2.1	2.4	2.1	2.0	2.3
The Pacific						
Cook Islands	13.1 (2001)	14.8 (2001)	11.7 (2001)	8.2 (2011)	8.1 (2011)	8.2 (2011)
Fiji	4.7 (2004)	6.0 (2004)	4.1 (2004)	9.0 (2012)	...	...
Kiribati	14.7 (2005)	18.2 (2005)	12.3 (2005)	30.6 (2010)	34.1 (2010)	27.6 (2010)
Marshall Islands	25.4 (2005)	...	...	4.7 (2011)	4.5 (2011)	4.9 (2011)
Micronesia, Fed. States of	...	...	...	...	...	...
Nauru	22.8 (2002)	29.7 (2002)	17.0 (2002)	23.0 (2011)	25.5 (2011)	21.4 (2011)
Palau	2.3	2.8	2.0	...	...	...
Papua New Guinea	2.9	...	...	2.6 (2011)	1.4 (2011)	3.7 (2011)
Samoa	5.0 (2001)	6.2 (2001)	4.4 (2001)	8.7 (2014)	10.3 (2014)	7.8 (2014)
Solomon Islands	...	...	...	...	...	...
Timor-Leste	...	...	...	3.1 (2010)	4.8 (2010)	2.8 (2010)
Tonga	5.2 (2003)	7.4 (2003)	3.6 (2003)	...	...	...
Tuvalu	6.5 (2002)	8.6 (2002)	5.0 (2002)	...	...	...
Vanuatu	...	...	...	5.5 (2009)	6.2 (2009)	4.9 (2009)
Developed Member Economies						
Australia	6.3	6.1	6.5	5.7 (2016)	5.8 (2016)	5.7 (2016)
Japan	4.7	4.5	4.9	3.1 (2016)	2.8 (2016)	3.4 (2016)
New Zealand	6.1	6.0	6.3	5.1 (2016)	5.5 (2016)	4.8 (2016)

(continued)

Goal 8. Promote sustained, inclusive and sustainable economic growth, full and productive employment and decent work for all

Table 4.3: **Selected Indicators for SDG 8 - Unemployment** *(continued)*
By 2030, achieve full and productive employment and decent work for all women and men, including for young people and persons with disabilities, and equal pay for work of equal value

Regional Member	8.5.2.b Unemployment Rate for Age Group 15-24, by Sex (%)					
	2000			2015		
	Total	Female	Male	Total	Female	Male
Developing Member Economies						
Central and West Asia						
Afghanistan	...	...	...	...	...	...
Armenia	48.2 (2001)	56.4 (2001)	41.9 (2001)	32.0	36.7	28.0
Azerbaijan	14.0 (2007)	10.5 (2007)	18.2 (2007)	13.4	15.8	11.4
Georgia	21.1	20.5	21.6	30.8	35.2	28.6
Kazakhstan	17.3 (2002)	19.3 (2002)	15.7 (2002)	3.9 (2013)	4.3 (2013)	3.6 (2013)
Kyrgyz Republic	20.1 (2002)	21.2 (2002)	19.3 (2002)	15.0	19.1	12.5
Pakistan	13.3	29.2	11.1	7.7 (2008)	10.5 (2008)	7.0 (2008)
Tajikistan	...	...	...	...	...	...
Turkmenistan	...	...	...	...	...	...
Uzbekistan	...	...	...	...	...	...
East Asia						
China, People's Rep. of	...	...	...	...	...	...
Hong Kong, China	11.2	10.4	11.9	9.9 (2016)	8.5 (2016)	10.9 (2016)
Korea, Rep. of	10.8	9.0	13.6	10.7 (2016)	10.5 (2016)	11.0 (2016)
Mongolia	...	...	...	13.1	14.4	12.2
Taipei,China	7.3	...	...	12.1 (2016)	12.5 (2016)	11.7 (2016)
South Asia						
Bangladesh	10.7	10.3	11.1	9.9 (2013)	9.6 (2013)	10.1 (2013)
Bhutan	6.2 (2005)	7.2 (2005)	5.5 (2005)	10.7	12.7	8.2
India	10.0 (2005)	10.4 (2005)	9.8 (2005)	10.1 (2012)	12.0 (2012)	9.5 (2012)
Maldives	4.4	5.1	4.0	25.4 (2010)	21.4 (2010)	29.1 (2010)
Nepal	...	...	...	2.2 (2008)	1.6 (2008)	2.9 (2008)
Sri Lanka	23.7	30.8	19.9	20.7	27.3	16.5
Southeast Asia						
Brunei Darussalam	...	...	...	25.4 (2014)	28.1 (2014)	23.5 (2014)
Cambodia	...	...	...	1.6 (2012)	1.4 (2012)	1.8 (2012)
Indonesia	25.1 (2007)	27.3 (2007)	23.8 (2007)	18.7 (2016)	18.8 (2016)	18.6 (2016)
Lao PDR	...	...	...	1.8 (2010)	1.7 (2010)	1.9 (2010)
Malaysia	10.9 (2007)	11.5 (2007)	10.5 (2007)	10.7	11.8	9.9
Myanmar	...	...	...	1.6	1.8	1.4
Philippines	25.3	29.5	22.9	15.0	16.0	14.3
Singapore	8.8	11.2	6.4	9.2 (2008)	12.2 (2008)	6.4 (2008)
Thailand	6.6	6.0	7.0	1.0	1.1	0.8
Viet Nam	4.6 (2004)	4.9 (2004)	4.4 (2004)	7.0	7.3	6.8
The Pacific						
Cook Islands	...	...	...	15.5 (2011)	15.3 (2011)	15.6 (2011)
Fiji	...	...	...	...	...	...
Kiribati	39.3 (2005)	41.6 (2005)	37.2 (2005)	54.0 (2010)	61.8 (2010)	47.6 (2010)
Marshall Islands	...	...	...	...	...	...
Micronesia, Fed. States of	...	...	...	...	...	...
Nauru	38.0 (2002)	46.1 (2002)	31.6 (2002)	...	...	...
Palau	...	...	...	...	...	...
Papua New Guinea	5.3	...	...	...	...	...
Samoa	12.2 (2001)	15.5 (2001)	10.6 (2001)	19.1 (2014)	25.3 (2014)	15.6 (2014)
Solomon Islands	...	...	...	...	...	...
Timor-Leste	...	...	...	11.1 (2010)	20.0 (2010)	11.1 (2010)
Tonga	...	...	...	...	...	...
Tuvalu	...	...	...	...	...	...
Vanuatu	...	...	...	10.6 (2009)	11.2 (2009)	10.2 (2009)
Developed Member Economies						
Australia	12.1	11.2	12.9	12.7 (2016)	11.4 (2016)	13.9 (2016)
Japan	9.1	7.9	10.2	5.1 (2016)	4.5 (2016)	5.7 (2016)
New Zealand	13.5	12.4	14.6	13.2 (2016)	13.4 (2016)	13.1 (2016)

(continued)

Table 4.3: **Selected Indicators for SDG 8 - Unemployment** *(continued)*
By 2030, achieve full and productive employment and decent work for all women and men, including for young people and persons with disabilities, and equal pay for work of equal value

Regional Member	8.5.2.c Unemployment Rate for Age Group 25+, by Sex (%)					
	2000			2015		
	Total	Female	Male	Total	Female	Male
Developing Member Economies						
Central and West Asia						
Afghanistan	...	...	...	...	...	...
Armenia	32.7 (2001)	36.5 (2001)	29.2 (2001)	16.4	17.0	15.8
Azerbaijan	5.2 (2007)	4.3 (2007)	6.1 (2007)	3.8	4.6	3.0
Georgia	9.7	9.5	9.8	10.2	8.5	11.6
Kazakhstan	7.9 (2002)	9.9 (2002)	6.0 (2002)	5.4 (2013)	6.1 (2013)	4.7 (2013)
Kyrgyz Republic	10.4 (2002)	12.4 (2002)	8.8 (2002)	5.9	7.0	5.1
Pakistan	4.9	12.3	3.4	3.8 (2008)	7.9 (2008)	2.8 (2008)
Tajikistan	...	...	...	...	...	...
Turkmenistan	...	...	...	...	...	...
Uzbekistan	...	...	...	...	...	...
East Asia						
China, People's Rep. of	...	...	...	...	...	...
Hong Kong, China	4.1	3.0	4.8	2.8 (2016)	2.5 (2016)	3.0 (2016)
Korea, Rep. of	3.7	2.7	4.3	3.2 (2016)	2.9 (2016)	3.4 (2016)
Mongolia	...	...	...	3.9	3.3	4.5
Taipei,China	2.3	...	...	3.2 (2016)	2.8 (2016)	3.6 (2016)
South Asia						
Bangladesh	0.9	0.7	1.0	2.9 (2013)	6.4 (2013)	1.6 (2013)
Bhutan	1.9 (2005)	1.7 (2005)	2.0 (2005)	1.3	1.6	1.1
India	2.8 (2005)	3.6 (2005)	2.5 (2005)	2.0 (2010)	2.8 (2010)	1.8 (2010)
Maldives	1.1	1.8	0.8	6.6 (2010)	9.9 (2010)	4.7 (2010)
Nepal	...	...	...	1.0 (2008)	0.9 (2008)	1.1 (2008)
Sri Lanka	3.5	6.2	2.2	2.6	4.8	1.3
Southeast Asia						
Brunei Darussalam	...	...	...	4.1 (2014)	4.9 (2014)	3.5 (2014)
Cambodia	...	...	...	1.2 (2012)	1.0 (2012)	1.3 (2012)
Indonesia	5.0 (2007)	6.3 (2007)	4.2 (2007)	3.0 (2016)	2.6 (2016)	3.2 (2016)
Lao PDR	...	...	...	0.4 (2010)	0.3 (2010)	0.4 (2010)
Malaysia	1.4 (2007)	1.3 (2007)	1.5 (2007)	1.5	1.6	1.4
Myanmar	...	...	...	0.5	0.6	0.5
Philippines	7.1	6.6	7.4	4.0	3.3	4.5
Singapore	5.6	5.9	5.5	3.4 (2008)	3.5 (2008)	3.4 (2008)
Thailand	1.5	1.5	1.4	0.3	0.3	0.3
Viet Nam	1.5 (2004)	1.8 (2004)	1.1 (2004)	1.3	1.1	1.4
The Pacific						
Cook Islands	...	...	...	6.5 (2011)	6.5 (2011)	6.4 (2011)
Fiji	...	...	...	...	...	...
Kiribati	7.9 (2005)	10.1 (2005)	6.5 (2005)	20.9 (2010)	22.8 (2010)	19.2 (2010)
Marshall Islands	...	...	...	...	...	...
Micronesia, Fed. States of	...	...	...	...	...	...
Nauru	14.1 (2002)	20.7 (2002)	8.6 (2002)	...	...	...
Palau	...	...	...	...	...	...
Papua New Guinea	2.1	...	...	...	...	...
Samoa	2.7 (2001)	3.0 (2001)	2.6 (2001)	6.4 (2014)	7.1 (2014)	6.0 (2014)
Solomon Islands	...	...	...	...	...	...
Timor-Leste	...	...	...	2.1 (2010)	2.7 (2010)	1.9 (2010)
Tonga	...	...	...	...	...	...
Tuvalu	...	...	...	...	...	...
Vanuatu	...	...	...	3.7 (2009)	4.5 (2009)	3.2 (2009)
Developed Member Economies						
Australia	4.9	4.7	5.1	4.3 (2016)	4.6 (2016)	4.1 (2016)
Japan	4.2	3.9	4.3	2.9 (2016)	2.7 (2016)	3.2 (2016)
New Zealand	4.6	4.6	4.6	3.6 (2016)	4.0 (2016)	3.1 (2016)

... = data not available at cutoff date, Lao PDR = Lao People's Democratic Republic, SDG = Sustainable Development Goal.

Sources: United Nations. Sustainable Development Goals Indicators Database. https://unstats.un.org/sdgs/indicators/database/ (accessed 18 July 2017); International Labour Organization. ILOSTAT. http://www.ilo.org/ilostat/ (accessed 26 June 2017).

Goal 8. Promote sustained, inclusive and sustainable economic growth, full and productive employment and decent work for all

Table 4.4: Selected Indicators for SDG 8 - Youth Participation in Education and Work, Child Labor

By 2020, substantially reduce the proportion of youth not in employment, education, or training

Take immediate and effective measures to eradicate forced labor, end modern slavery and human trafficking; and secure the prohibition and elimination of the worst forms of child labor, including recruitment and use of child soldiers; and by 2025 end child labor in all its forms

Regional Member	8.6.1 Proportion of Youth (Aged 15–24 Years) Not in Education, Employment, or Training (%)		8.7.1 Proportion of Children Aged 5–17 Years Engaged in Child Labour (%)	
	2000	2015	2000	2014
Developing Member Economies				
Central and West Asia				
Afghanistan	...	...	...	...
Armenia	...	35.6	...	...
Azerbaijan	19.5 (2005)	9.6 (2010)	6.1 (2005)	...
Georgia	...	...	...	...
Kazakhstan	18.6 (2001)	9.5 (2016)	...	...
Kyrgyz Republic	10.6 (2007)	21.4	36.3 (2007)	37.1
Pakistan	...	...	...	...
Tajikistan	38.2 (2007)	...	5.0 (2005)	...
Turkmenistan	...	...	...	...
Uzbekistan	...	...	...	...
East Asia				
China, People's Rep. of	...	...	...	...
Hong Kong, China	...	6.6	...	...
Korea, Rep. of[a]	...	18.0 (2013)	...	...
Mongolia	18.5 (2006)	16.8	6.2 (2002)	9.4 (2013)
Taipei,China	...	...	...	...
South Asia				
Bangladesh	31.5 (2002)	20.2 (2013)	15.1 (2003)	6.8 (2013)
Bhutan	...	...	...	...
India	26.1 (2004)	27.5 (2012)	4.1 (2004)	2.1 (2012)
Maldives	...	56.4 (2010)	...	...
Nepal	...	9.2 (2013)	...	19.1
Sri Lanka	...	27.7 (2014)	...	10.3 (2009)
Southeast Asia				
Brunei Darussalam	...	17.2 (2014)	...	...
Cambodia	...	7.8 (2012)	25.3 (2007)	16.3
Indonesia	...	24.8	...	5.2 (2009)
Lao PDR	...	5.1 (2010)	...	11.9 (2010)
Malaysia	...	1.2	...	...
Myanmar	...	18.6	...	...
Philippines	...	22.1 (2016)	11.4 (2001)	9.4 (2011)
Singapore	...	11.4 (2014)	...	...
Thailand	...	14.6 (2016)	...	...
Viet Nam	...	0.6	...	...
The Pacific				
Cook Islands	...	...	...	...
Fiji	...	...	...	...
Kiribati	...	...	...	...
Marshall Islands	...	...	...	...
Micronesia, Fed. States of	...	...	...	...
Nauru	...	...	...	...
Palau	...	...	...	...
Papua New Guinea	...	...	...	...
Samoa	...	38.2 (2012)	...	...
Solomon Islands	...	...	...	...
Timor-Leste	...	...	...	...
Tonga	...	...	...	...
Tuvalu	...	...	...	...
Vanuatu	...	...	...	...
Developed Member Economies				
Australia	...	11.1	...	...
Japan	...	3.6	...	...
New Zealand	10.8 (2004)	12.0 (2016)	...	...

... = data not available at cutoff date, Lao PDR = Lao People's Democratic Republic, SDG = Sustainable Development Goal.

a Refers to youth aged 15–29 years.

Sources: United Nations. Sustainable Development Goals Indicators Database. https://unstats.un.org/sdgs/indicators/database/ (accessed 18 July 2017); International Labour Organization. ILOSTAT. http://www.ilo.org/ilostat (accessed 21 July 2017); for the Republic of Korea (Indicator 8.6.1): The Organisation for Economic Co-operation and Development. OECD. https://data.oecd.org/ (accessed 7 July 2017).

Goal 8. Promote sustained, inclusive and sustainable economic growth, full and productive employment and decent work for all

Table 4.5: **Selected Indicators for SDG 8 - Access to Banking, Insurance and Financial Services, and Trade**

Strengthen the capacity of domestic financial institutions to encourage and expand access to banking, insurance, and financial services for all

Increase Aid for Trade support for developing countries, in particular least developed countries, including through the Enhanced Integrated Framework for Trade-related Technical Assistance to Least Developed Countries

Regional Member	8.10.1 Number of Commercial Bank Branches and ATMs per 100,000 Adults				8.10.2 Proportion of Adults (15 Years and Older) with an Account at a Bank or Other Financial Institution or with a Mobile Money Service Provider (%)	
	Commercial Bank Branches		ATMs			
	2004	2015	2004	2015	2011	2014
Developing Member Economies						
Central and West Asia						
Afghanistan	0.4	2.3	0.0	1.0	14.4	12.2
Armenia	10.8	22.2	3.0	57.5	18.6	21.8
Azerbaijan	6.5	10.5	17.0 (2006)	35.7	18.5	30.7
Georgia	9.4	32.4 (2016)	2.0	73.6 (2016)	39.8	47.5
Kazakhstan	3.7	3.0 (2016)	10.0	74.4 (2016)	47.5	59.0
Kyrgyz Republic	5.1	8.3	0.6	30.2	6.0	20.9
Pakistan	7.7	10.6 (2016)	0.8	10.1 (2016)	13.1	10.4
Tajikistan	5.0	6.5 (2013)	0.6 (2005)	10.4 (2013)	3.6	16.0
Turkmenistan	...	...	...	...	0.7	2.2
Uzbekistan	38.8	37.1 (2016)	0.9	22.1 (2016)	24.9	45.2
East Asia						
China, People's Rep. of	...	8.8 (2016)	9.6 (2006)	81.4 (2016)	75.6	83.6
Hong Kong, China	23.5	22.3	...	49.8	92.9	97.1
Korea, Rep. of	16.8	16.5 (2016)	208.3	278.7	94.8	95.7
Mongolia	40.0	70.4	...	72.7	81.2	93.7
Taipei,China	...	...	...	...	...	...
South Asia						
Bangladesh	6.9	8.4	0.1	6.8	39.8	34.5
Bhutan	14.4	15.7 (2016)	0.5	33.2 (2016)	...	38.9
India	9.0	13.5	2.3 (2005)	19.7	40.5	58.6
Maldives	10.3	15.2 (2016)	7.4	32.4 (2016)	...	...
Nepal	2.6	8.9	...	9.0	32.6	41.1
Sri Lanka	8.8	18.6	9.4 (2007)	17.2	76.5	85.4
Southeast Asia						
Brunei Darussalam	21.2	20.3	35.3	77.1	...	...
Cambodia	2.3 (2006)	6.1	0.0 (2005)	13.3	5.6	15.3
Indonesia	5.2	17.8	8.6	53.3	26.0	45.3
Lao PDR	...	2.9	...	23.2	31.2	...
Malaysia	14.1	10.6 (2016)	27.2	49.7 (2016)	77.1	84.1
Myanmar	1.8	3.4 (2016)	...	2.6 (2016)	...	27.0
Philippines	8.2	9.1 (2016)	10.3	27.8 (2016)	37.1	37.1
Singapore	11.7	9.1 (2016)	47.9	58.7 (2016)	99.3	96.5
Thailand	7.8	12.5 (2016)	19.9	114.6 (2016)	78.5	82.3
Viet Nam	...	3.8	1.4	24.0	29.5	39.5
The Pacific						
Cook Islands	...	...	...	...	...	...
Fiji	9.3	12.3	19.0	45.9	...	...
Kiribati	...	5.7 (2013)	...	14.3 (2013)	...	...
Marshall Islands	12.0	20.6	3.0 (2007)	5.9	...	...
Micronesia, Fed. States of	12.3	14.5 (2016)	3.1	14.5 (2016)	...	...
Nauru	...	...	...	...	...	...
Palau	31.2	47.1	...	...	...	...
Papua New Guinea	1.9	2.8	4.0	7.9	...	...
Samoa	17.6	21.5	12.1	41.3	...	...
Solomon Islands	7.5	4.2 (2016)	1.5	11.9 (2016)	...	...
Timor-Leste	1.2	5.0	...	6.7	...	...
Tonga	24.1	29.8	22.5	28.3	...	...
Tuvalu	...	...	...	...	...	...
Vanuatu	19.6	21.4	4.9	39.9	...	...
Developed Member Economies						
Australia	30.7	28.7	133.8	164.6	99.7	99.2
Japan	34.6	34.1 (2016)	124.3	127.7 (2016)	96.4	97.5
New Zealand	35.0	29.0	59.1	69.5	99.4	99.9

... = data not available at cutoff date, Lao PDR = Lao People's Democratic Republic, SDG = Sustainable Development Goal.

Sources: For indicator 8.10.1; International Monetary Fund. IMF Financial Access Survey database http://data.imf.org/?sk=E5DCAB7E-A5CA-4892-A6EA-598B5463A34C (accessed 11 July 2017); for Indicator 8.10.2. United Nations. Sustainable Development Goals Indicators Database. http://unstats.un.org/sdgs/indicators/database/ (accessed 9 June 2017).

Goal 9. Build resilient infrastructure, promote inclusive and sustainable industrialization and foster innovation

Table 4.6: **Selected Indicators for SDG 9 - Air Transport, Passenger, and Freight Volumes**
Develop quality, reliable, sustainable, and resilient infrastructure, including regional and transborder infrastructure, to support economic development and human well-being, with a focus on affordable and equitable access for all

Regional Member	9.1.2 Passenger Volume, by Road Transport (thousand passenger kilometers)	9.1.2 Passenger Volume, by Air Transport (thousand ton kilometers)	9.1.2 Passenger Volume, by Air Transport (thousand passenger kilometers)	9.1.2 Freight Volume, by Air Transport (metric tons)
	2015	2015	2015	2015
Developing Member Economies				
Central and West Asia				
Afghanistan	5,066.0	6,991.0	2,232,946,027	89,622.0
Armenia	3,129.0	559.0	...	...
Azerbaijan	45,708.0	12,157.0	3,318,010,600	11,535.5
Georgia	7,734.0	677.0	418,577,760	84.8
Kazakhstan	83,813.0	15,978.0	9,691,533,108	13,911.0
Kyrgyz Republic	1,531.0	1,316.0	1,007,497,593	50.2
Pakistan	59,933.0	168,186.0	19,263,161,478	66,605.4
Tajikistan	2,104.0	822.0	2,030,386,690	31.7
Turkmenistan	18,647.0	4,368.0	4,585,583	...
Uzbekistan	12,750.0	11,801.0	6,463,850,350	38,778.0
East Asia				
China, People's Rep. of	4,501,733.0	6,489,321.0	725,901,418,000	6,292,942.0
Hong Kong, China	363,014.0	43,782.0	136,155,721,870	2,272,888.3
Korea, Rep. of	378,372.0	104,812.0	119,739,105,696	2,312,236.2
Mongolia	5,164.0	12,215.0	1,091,997,741	3,535.6
Taipei,China	...	...	...	...
South Asia				
Bangladesh	53,793.0	16,972.0	6,928,356,170	53,733.2
Bhutan	1,828.0	956.0	381,111,389	406.6
India	10,526,770.0	1,508,550.0	140,474,446,040	832,258.0
Maldives	1,167.0	710.0	...	...
Nepal	6,552.0	16,225.0	681,332,822	10,821.0
Sri Lanka	41,475.0	11,903.0	14,103,822,000	118,456.0
Southeast Asia				
Brunei Darussalam	12,283.0	6,286.0	3,717,686,000	20,440.0
Cambodia	5,964.0	2,723.0	1,259,604,870	1,592.5
Indonesia	362,073.0	288,357.0	87,569,012,595	567,306.4
Lao PDR	3,467.0	547.0	789,902,283	1,275.5
Malaysia	348,913.0	27,398.0	93,691,664,990	524,070.5
Myanmar	16,492.0	4.0	1,058,121,849	22,937.7
Philippines	124,142.0	62,194.0	51,553,808,890	204,547.7
Singapore	229,617.0	...	123,329,081,529	1,113,826.4
Thailand	235,460.0	187,640.0	87,123,868,045	573,589.1
Viet Nam	58,208.0	38,597.0	39,401,803,730	239,759.3
The Pacific				
Cook Islands	...	...	29,100,984	3,658.0
Fiji	1,223.0	1,711.0	4,554,096,000	16,888.9
Kiribati	40.0	23.0	...	...
Marshall Islands	...	...	...	...
Micronesia, Fed. States of	63.0	54.0	...	...
Nauru	...	...	148,380,876	5,494.3
Palau	290.0	77.0	...	...
Papua New Guinea	3,604.0	3,671.0	1,295,451,023	17,296.4
Samoa	149.0	130.0	21,490,172	69.2
Solomon Islands	255.0	176.0	329,065,262	1,206.1
Timor-Leste	205.0	...	...	...
Tonga	140.0	88.0	...	...
Tuvalu	6.0	3.0	...	...
Vanuatu	204.0	118.0	286,179,430	1,155.7
Developed Member Economies				
Australia	296,201.0	212,848.0	144,361,100,926	291,033.4
Japan	1,027,902.0	255,394.0	167,906,000,000	2,321,511.0
New Zealand	44,728.0	17,836.0	31,776,294,127	181,885.7

... = data not available at cutoff date, Lao PDR = Lao People's Democratic Republic, SDG = Sustainable Development Goal.

Source: United Nations. Sustainable Development Goals Indicators Global Database. http://unstats.un.org/sdgs/indicators/database/ (accessed 27 June 2017).

Table 4.7: **Selected Indicators for SDG 9 - Growth in Manufacturing**
Promote inclusive and sustainable industrialization and, by 2030, significantly raise industry's share of employment and gross domestic product, in line with national circumstances, and double its share in least developed countries

Regional Member	9.2.1.a Manufacturing Value Added Share in GDP[a] (%)		9.2.1.b Manufacturing Value Added per Capita[a] (at constant 2010 $)		9.2.2 Manufacturing Employment as a Proportion of Total Employment (%)	
	2000	2016	2000	2016	2000	2015
Developing Member Economies						
Central and West Asia						
Afghanistan	17.2	10.4	47.2	67.6	...	...
Armenia	13.0	10.8	179.3	423.3	10.7 (2002)	8.0
Azerbaijan	9.6	5.0	158.2	289.9	4.6	4.9
Georgia	9.6	11.5	128.1	442.7	5.9	...
Kazakhstan	13.0	9.9	578.9	1,024.6	7.7 (2001)	6.4
Kyrgyz Republic	23.2	14.4	149.9	147.0	6.4	7.4
Pakistan	10.0	13.1	84.1	152.2	11.5	13.0 (2008)
Tajikistan	27.1	5.3	114.0	49.3	4.7 (2004)	5.5 (2009)
Turkmenistan	33.0	34.9	773.4	2,473.5	...	...
Uzbekistan	25.4	16.7	206.9	342.1	...	...
East Asia						
China, People's Rep. of	28.3	32.1	494.4	2,170.2	...	...
Hong Kong, China	3.7	1.3	847.4	467.5	10.4	3.0
Korea, Rep. of	22.9	29.5	3,499.1	7,556.8	20.3	17.1 (2016)
Mongolia	5.9	5.3	93.9	204.9	6.8	7.1
Taipei,China	24.6	22.5	3,613.1	4,586.1	...	...
South Asia						
Bangladesh	13.5	19.3	67.6	198.0	7.3	12.5 (2010)
Bhutan	7.6	8.6	92.2	238.0	2.0 (2005)	6.5
India	15.7	17.0	119.2	319.4	12.1 (2005)	11.4 (2010)
Maldives	5.2	2.9	219.9	266.2	12.9	11.2 (2014)
Nepal	8.1	5.6	37.5	38.8	8.8 (2001)	6.6 (2008)
Sri Lanka	20.1	18.1	319.1	628.6	16.5 (2002)	18.2 (2014)
Southeast Asia						
Brunei Darussalam	17.4	14.0	6,288.2	4,482.2	8.5 (2001)	3.8 (2014)
Cambodia	11.5	17.6	49.1	189.2	3.3 (2004)	10.9 (2010)
Indonesia	23.7	21.8	508.3	866.0	13.0	13.5
Lao PDR	8.1	10.8	51.3	164.2	...	...
Malaysia	27.0	23.9	1,817.9	2,595.7	22.8	16.5
Myanmar	8.5	22.7	23.7	267.6	...	...
Philippines	23.6	22.5	380.5	624.7	10.0	8.3
Singapore	20.5	18.2	7,011.3	9,265.7	20.7	11.1
Thailand	28.5	28.7	989.3	1,711.8	14.5	16.5 (2014)
Viet Nam	12.8	21.0	95.9	365.4	9.2	14.4 (2014)
The Pacific						
Cook Islands	3.5	2.5 (2014)	448.8	332.4 (2014)	...	3.9 (2011)
Fiji	12.8	12.5	439.8	548.5	...	...
Kiribati	5.1	4.9	91.8	78.3	1.6	13.2 (2010)
Marshall Islands	1.8	1.7	48.1	62.3	...	0.7 (2010)
Micronesia, Fed. States of	...	...	...	...	...	...
Nauru	15.1	24.6 (2014)	855.6	2,955.1 (2014)	...	...
Palau	2.9	1.3	290.5	133.7	0.7	3.2 (2008)
Papua New Guinea	5.8	5.7	70.2	105.8	1.1	...
Samoa	17.0	9.2	482.8	346.7	14.6 (2001)	6.8 (2014)
Solomon Islands	4.9	7.0	52.4	103.3	...	...
Timor-Leste	2.0	0.2	16.9	7.3	...	3.2 (2010)
Tonga	7.1	6.1	235.0	230.6	24.7 (2003)	...
Tuvalu	0.8	1.0	24.2	39.6	...	...
Vanuatu	4.3	3.5	117.2	102.7	...	1.9 (2009)
Developed Member Economies						
Australia	9.4	6.6	4,679.6	4,118.1	12.1	7.6 (2016)
Japan	17.4	18.8	7,050.1	8,514.2	20.5	16.2 (2016)
New Zealand	13.7	9.9	4,063.0	3,719.1	15.8	9.9 (2016)

... = data not available at cutoff date, GDP = gross domestic product, Lao PDR = Lao People's Democratic Republic, SDG = Sustainable Development Goal.

a United Nations Statistics Division data used for indicators 9.2.1.a and 9.2.1.b were computed from GDP, manufacturing value added, and population data.

Sources: United Nations. Sustainable Development Goals Indicators Database. https://unstats.un.org/sdgs/indicators/database/ (accessed 13 June 2017); United Nations Industrial Development Organization. MVA Database. https://stat.unido.org/database/MVA%202017 (accessed 30 June 2017).

Table 4.8: **Selected Indicators for SDG 9 - Carbon Dioxide Emissions**
By 2030, upgrade infrastructure and retrofit industries to make them sustainable, with increased resource-use efficiency and greater adoption of clean and environmentally sound technologies and industrial processes, with all countries taking action in accordance with their respective capabilities

Regional Member	9.4.1 Carbon Dioxide Emissions[a]			
	Per Unit of GDP (PPP) (kilograms CO_2 equivalent per $1 constant 2005 PPP GDP)		Per Unit of Manufacturing Value Added (kilograms per constant $)	
	2000	2014	2000	2014
Developing Member Economies				
Central and West Asia				
Afghanistan	...	...	...	...
Armenia	0.4	0.2	1.3	0.4
Azerbaijan	0.8	0.2	2.0	0.7
Georgia	0.3	0.2	1.0	0.8
Kazakhstan	0.8	0.6	2.1	1.9
Kyrgyz Republic	0.4	0.5	1.1	1.7
Pakistan	0.2	0.2	1.9	1.2
Tajikistan	0.3	0.2	-	0.2
Turkmenistan	1.6	0.9	0.2	0.2
Uzbekistan	1.9	0.6	3.0	1.4
East Asia				
China, People's Rep. of	0.7	0.5	1.4	1.1
Hong Kong, China	0.2	0.1	0.7	2.1
Korea, Rep. of	0.4	0.3	0.6	0.2
Mongolia	0.8	0.6	2.2	2.4
Taipei,China	0.4	0.3	...	...
South Asia				
Bangladesh	0.1	0.1	0.5	0.4
Bhutan	...	...	...	...
India	0.3	0.3	1.5	1.5
Maldives	...	...	...	...
Nepal	0.1	0.1	1.3	1.7
Sri Lanka	0.1	0.1	0.1	0.1
Southeast Asia				
Brunei Darussalam	0.2	0.2	0.1	0.2
Cambodia	0.1	0.1	0.1	0.1
Indonesia	0.2	0.2	0.5	0.4
Lao PDR	...	...	...	...
Malaysia	0.3	0.3	0.6	0.4
Myanmar	0.1	0.1	2.1	0.3
Philippines	0.2	0.1	0.4	0.2
Singapore	0.2	0.1	0.1	0.2
Thailand	0.3	0.2	0.5	0.5
Viet Nam	0.2	0.3	1.9	1.7
The Pacific				
Cook Islands	...	...	...	...
Fiji	...	...	...	...
Kiribati	...	...	...	...
Marshall Islands	...	...	...	...
Micronesia, Fed. States of	...	...	...	...
Nauru	...	...	...	...
Palau	...	...	...	...
Papua New Guinea	...	...	...	...
Samoa	...	...	...	...
Solomon Islands	...	...	...	...
Timor-Leste	...	...	...	...
Tonga	...	...	...	...
Tuvalu	...	...	...	...
Vanuatu	...	...	...	...
Developed Member Economies				
Australia	0.5	0.4	0.5	0.4
Japan	0.3	0.3	0.3	0.2
New Zealand	0.3	0.2	0.4	0.4

... = data not available at cutoff date, GDP = gross domestic product, Lao PDR = Lao People's Democratic Republic, PPP = purchasing power parity, SDG = Sustainable Development Goal.

a Refers to carbon dioxide emissions from fuel combustion.

Sources: United Nations. Sustainable Development Goals Indicators Database. http://unstats.un.org/sdgs/indicators/database/ (accessed 18 July 2017); for Taipei,China: International Energy Agency. http://www.iea.org/publications/freepublications/publication/CO2-emissions-from-fuel-combustion-highlights-2016.html (accessed 6 July 2017).

Table 4.9: **Selected Indicators for SDG 9 - Research and Development**
Enhance scientific research, upgrade the technological capabilities of industrial sectors in all countries, in particular developing countries, including, by 2030, encouraging innovation and substantially increasing the number of research and development workers per 1 million people and public and private research, and development spending

Regional Member	9.5.1 Research and Development Expenditure as a Proportion of GDP[a] (%)		9.5.2 Researchers (Full-Time Equivalent)[b] (per million inhabitants)	
	2000	2015	2000	2015
Developing Member Economies				
Central and West Asia				
Afghanistan	...	...	...	...
Armenia	0.19	0.25	...	...
Azerbaijan	0.34	0.22	...	...
Georgia	0.22	0.32	...	1,641
Kazakhstan	0.18	0.17	556 (2007)	1,028 (2013)
Kyrgyz Republic	0.16	0.12	...	...
Pakistan	0.13	0.25	347 (2005)	537
Tajikistan	0.09 (2001)	0.11	...	...
Turkmenistan	...	...	...	...
Uzbekistan	0.36	0.21	...	687
East Asia				
China, People's Rep. of	0.90	2.07	726	2,732
Hong Kong, China	0.46	0.76	1,445	3,788 (2014)
Korea, Rep. of	2.18	4.23	2,988	8,789
Mongolia	0.19	0.16	...	...
Taipei,China	...	...	...	...
South Asia				
Bangladesh	...	...	...	...
Bhutan	...	...	...	...
India	0.74	0.63	302	403
Maldives	...	...	...	...
Nepal	...	0.30 (2010)	265 (2002)	...
Sri Lanka	0.14	0.10 (2013)	283 (2004)	224 (2013)
Southeast Asia				
Brunei Darussalam	0.02 (2002)	...	408 (2002)	...
Cambodia	0.05 (2002)	0.12	39 (2002)	122
Indonesia	0.07	0.08 (2013)	213	90 (2009)
Lao PDR	0.04 (2002)	...	49 (2002)	...
Malaysia	0.47	1.30	430	2,666
Myanmar	0.11	...	91 (2001)	...
Philippines	0.14 (2002)	0.14 (2013)	113 (2003)	272 (2013)
Singapore	1.82	2.20 (2014)	4,942	7,726 (2014)
Thailand	0.24	0.63	505 (2001)	1,319
Viet Nam	0.18 (2002)	0.37 (2013)	139 (2002)	879 (2013)
The Pacific				
Cook Islands	...	...	...	...
Fiji	...	...	...	...
Kiribati	...	...	...	...
Marshall Islands	...	...	...	...
Micronesia, Fed. States of	...	...	...	...
Nauru	...	...	...	...
Palau	...	...	...	...
Papua New Guinea	...	...	...	...
Samoa	...	...	...	...
Solomon Islands	...	...	...	...
Timor-Leste	...	...	...	...
Tonga	...	...	...	...
Tuvalu	...	...	...	...
Vanuatu	...	...	...	...
Developed Member Economies				
Australia	1.58	2.20 (2013)	5,004	6,434 (2008)
Japan	2.90	3.28	7,134	6,913
New Zealand	1.10 (2001)	1.15 (2013)	3,830 (2001)	5,576 (2013)

... = data not available at cutoff date, 0.0 = magnitude is less than half of unit employed, Lao PDR = Lao People's Democratic Republic, R&D = research and development, SDG = Sustainable Development Goal.

a R&D expenditure as a proportion of gross domestic product is the amount of R&D expenditure divided by the total output of the economy.
b The researchers (in full-time equivalent) per million inhabitants is a direct measure of the number of R&D workers per 1 million people.

Sources: UNESCO Institute of Statistics, Organisation for Economic Co-operation and Development, Eurostat (Statistical Office of the European Union), and Network on Science and Technology Indicators – Ibero-American and Inter-American. African STI Indicators Initiative of AU/NEPAD. http://www.uis.unesco.org/ (accessed 27 June 2017).

Goal 9. Build resilient infrastructure, promote inclusive and sustainable industrialization and foster innovation

Table 4.10: **Selected Indicators for SDG 9 - Official International Support and Industry Value Added**
Facilitate sustainable and resilient infrastructure development in developing countries through enhanced financial, technological and technical support to African countries, least developed countries, landlocked developing countries and small island developing States

Support domestic technology development, research and innovation in developing countries, including by ensuring a conducive policy environment for, inter alia, industrial diversification and value addition to commodities

Regional Member	9.a.1 Total Official Flows for Infrastructure[a] (constant 2014 $ million)		9.b.1 Proportion of Medium and High-Tech Industry Value Added in Total Value Added (%)	
	2000	2015	2000	2014
Developing Member Economies				
Central and West Asia				
Afghanistan	0.4	521.5	13.6	9.5
Armenia	130.3	355.2	9.5	4.0
Azerbaijan	23.4	321.3	16.5	15.7
Georgia	137.7	432.4	21.4	17.8
Kazakhstan	224.2	588.4	5.2	16.5
Kyrgyz Republic	89.8	138.7	5.9	6.7
Pakistan	464.4	1,822.0	25.2	24.6
Tajikistan	16.1	191.6	2.7	2.5
Turkmenistan	1.8	12.4	...	...
Uzbekistan	45.7	525.8	...	...
East Asia				
China, People's Rep. of	2,178.8	2,322.1	42.9	41.4
Hong Kong, China	...	...	39.5	33.9
Korea, Rep. of	...	...	58.9	63.2
Mongolia	110.7	177.1	2.5	6.2
Taipei,China	...	...	...	...
South Asia				
Bangladesh	607.0	1,041.1	21.1	9.5
Bhutan	29.8	50.5	...	...
India	2,924.5	4,716.1	41.3	39.9
Maldives	11.2	5.4	...	...
Nepal	110.4	289.1	12.1	8.6
Sri Lanka	73.0	544.4	9.4	6.7
Southeast Asia				
Brunei Darussalam	...	...	3.3	3.3
Cambodia	42.4	192.8	0.3	0.3
Indonesia	104.9	5,051.2	35.7	35.1
Lao PDR	69.8	142.0	...	...
Malaysia	514.0	68.5	51.2	42.1
Myanmar	0.0	139.6	...	...
Philippines	722.9	738.1	38.1	55.2
Singapore	...	...	78.5	80.7
Thailand	628.2	150.4	37.9	40.7
Viet Nam	1,039.2	2,900.9	23.5	31.1
The Pacific				
Cook Islands	0.9	9.8	...	...
Fiji	0.2	8.0	8.5	6.8
Kiribati	1.4	23.3	...	...
Marshall Islands	3.1	253.7	...	...
Micronesia, Fed. States of	4.8	10.7	...	...
Nauru	0.0 (2002)	7.6	...	...
Palau	0.2	4.6	...	...
Papua New Guinea	205.8	220.7	12.6	12.6
Samoa	2.9	23.3	...	...
Solomon Islands	8.8	32.5	...	...
Timor-Leste	2.4	61.5	...	...
Tonga	4.7	23.6	1.6	1.6
Tuvalu	0.1 (2002)	22.6	...	...
Vanuatu	9.4	29.4	...	...
Developed Member Economies				
Australia	...	...	27.2	29.9
Japan	...	...	52.0	55.0
New Zealand	...	...	12.5	17.3

... = data not available at cutoff date, 0.0 = magnitude is less than half of unit employed, Lao PDR = Lao People's Democratic Republic, SDG = Sustainable Development Goal.

a Gross disbursements of total official development assistance and other official flows from all donors in support of infrastructure.

Source: United Nations. Sustainable Development Goals Indicators Database. http://unstats.un.org/sdgs/indicators/database/ (accessed 18 July 2017).

Goal 9. Build resilient infrastructure, promote inclusive and sustainable industrialization and foster innovation

Table 4.11: **Selected Indicators for SDG 9 - Coverage by Mobile Networks**

Significantly increase access to information and communications technology and strive to provide universal and affordable access to the internet in least developed countries by 2020

Regional Member	9.c.1.a Proportion of Population Covered by 2G Mobile Networks[a] (%)		9.c.1.b Proportion of Population Covered by 3G Mobile Networks[b] (%)	9.c.1.c Proportion of Population Covered by LTE/WiMAX Mobile Networks[c] (%)
	2000	2015	2015	2015
Developing Member Economies				
Central and West Asia				
Afghanistan	72.0 (2007)	89.2	40.0	...
Armenia	38.0 (2001)	100.0	99.9	46.5
Azerbaijan	93.5	100.0	97.3	50.0
Georgia	79.0 (2001)	99.0	99.0	82.0
Kazakhstan	94.0 (2001)	96.6	72.7	65.5
Kyrgyz Republic	5.2 (2004)	97.8	59.0	1.6
Pakistan	27.1 (2001)	86.0	46.0	16.0
Tajikistan	0.0 (2001)	...	...	60.0
Turkmenistan	12.4 (2001)	...	...	25.0
Uzbekistan	75.0 (2002)	98.0	32.0	10.0
East Asia				
China, People's Rep. of	50.0 (2001)	99.5	95.0	85.0
Hong Kong, China	100.0	100.0	99.0	99.0
Korea, Rep. of	99.0	99.9	99.0	99.0
Mongolia	58.0	99.0	95.0	90.0
Taipei,China	...	...	...	...
South Asia				
Bangladesh	40.0 (2001)	99.4	71.0	65.0
Bhutan	5.4 (2005)	98.0	80.0	40.0
India	21.1 (2001)	93.5 (2013)	0.1 (2009)	4.0
Maldives	40.0	100.0 (2013)	100.0	58.0
Nepal	10.0 (2006)	82.0	20.4 (2009)	0.0
Sri Lanka	57.9 (2001)	99.0	83.0	35.0
Southeast Asia				
Brunei Darussalam	...	97.0	91.0	80.0
Cambodia	80.0	99.0	70.0	30.0
Indonesia	89.0	95.0	60.0	5.0
Lao PDR	55.0 (2005)	98.0	65.0	5.0
Malaysia	95.0 (2001)	96.0	92.0	71.0
Myanmar	10.0 (2006)	95.0	79.3	0.0
Philippines	70.0	99.0 (2014)	78.0 (2014)	39.0
Singapore	100.0	100.0	100.0	100.0
Thailand	25.9 (2005)	97.0	97.0	21.0
Viet Nam	70.0 (2006)	94.0	...	0.0
The Pacific				
Cook Islands	...	...	...	...
Fiji	40.0	88.0	68.4	17.0
Kiribati	...	70.0	63.0	54.0
Marshall Islands	...	...	...	65.0
Micronesia, Fed. States of	0.0	80.0	15.0	...
Nauru	...	98.0	98.0	0.0
Palau	30.0 (2005)	98.0	88.0	...
Papua New Guinea	...	89.0	...	35.0
Samoa	...	97.0	86.0	0.0
Solomon Islands	35.0	91.0	11.5	...
Timor-Leste	38.0 (2003)	96.0	96.0	...
Tonga	70.0 (2001)	92.0	70.0	0.0
Tuvalu	15.0 (2004)	...	...	...
Vanuatu	20.0 (2002)	93.0	51.0	18.0
Developed Member Economies				
Australia	95.6	99.0	99.0	94.0
Japan	99.0	99.9	99.9	99.0
New Zealand	97.0	98.0	98.0	88.0

... = data not available at cutoff date, 0.00 = magnitude is less than half of unit employed, EV-DO = evolution-data optimized, HSPA = high speed packet access, Lao PDR = Lao People's Democratic Republic, LTE = long-term evolution, SDG = Sustainable Development Goal, UMTS = universal mobile telecommunications system, WiMAX = worldwide interoperability for microwave access.

a The original indicator refers to "Percentage of the population covered by a mobile-cellular network." This refers to the percentage of inhabitants within range of a mobile-cellular signal, irrespective whether or not they are subscribers or users. This is calculated by dividing the number of inhabitants within range of a mobile-cellular signal by the total population and multiplying by 100.

b The original indicator refers to "Percentage of the population covered by at least a 3G mobile network." This refers to the percentage of inhabitants within range of at least a 3G mobile-cellular signal, irrespective whether or not they are subscribers. This is calculated by dividing the number of inhabitants covered by at least a 3G mobile-cellular signal by the total population and multiplying by 100.

c The original indicator refers to "Percentage of the population covered by at least an LTE/WiMAX mobile network." This refers to the percentage of inhabitants within range of LTE/LTE-Advanced, mobile WiMAX/WirelessMAN, or other more advanced mobile-cellular networks, irrespective of whether or not they are subscribers. This is calculated by dividing the number of inhabitants covered by the previously mentioned mobile-cellular technologies by the total population and multiplying by 100. It excludes people covered only by HSPA, UMTS, EV-DO, and previous 3G technologies; and also excludes fixed WiMAX coverage.

Sources: International Telecommunication Union. Official communication, 30 March 2017; United Nations. Sustainable Development Goals Indicators Global Database. http://unstats.un.org/sdgs/indicators/database/ (accessed 18 July 2017).

Table 4.12: **Selected Indicators for SDG 10 - Household Income and Consumption Growth**
By 2030, progressively achieve and sustain income growth of the bottom 40% of the population at a rate higher than the national average

Regional Member	10.1.1.a Growth Rates of Household Expenditure or Income per Capita among the Bottom 40% of the Population[a] (%)	10.1.1.b Growth Rates of Household Expenditure or Income per Capita[a] (%)
Developing Member Economies		
Central and West Asia		
Afghanistan	...	...
Armenia	0.7 (2009–2014)	1.6 (2009–2014)
Azerbaijan	...	...
Georgia	4.6 (2009–2014)	4.0 (2009–2014)
Kazakhstan	6.7 (2008–2013)	5.6 (2008–2013)
Kyrgyz Republic	0.4 (2009–2014)	-1.1 (2009–2014)
Pakistan	2.8 (2007–2013)	2.5 (2007–2013)
Tajikistan	...	...
Turkmenistan	...	...
Uzbekistan	...	...
East Asia		
China, People's Rep. of	8.9 (2008–2012)	8.2 (2008–2012)
Hong Kong, China	...	...
Korea, Rep. of	...	...
Mongolia	8.0 (2010–2014)	7.1 (2010–2014)
Taipei,China	...	...
South Asia		
Bangladesh	...	...
Bhutan	6.5 (2007–2012)	6.5 (2007–2012)
India	3.2 (2004–2011)	3.7 (2004–2011)
Maldives	...	...
Nepal	...	...
Sri Lanka	2.2 (2006–2012)	1.7 (2006–2012)
Southeast Asia		
Brunei Darussalam	...	...
Cambodia	6.5 (2008–2012)	3.9 (2008–2012)
Indonesia	3.8 (2011–2014)	3.4 (2011–2014)
Lao PDR	1.5 (2007–2012)	2.2 (2007–2012)
Malaysia	...	...
Myanmar	...	...
Philippines	1.7 (2006–2012)	1.2 (2006–2012)
Singapore	...	...
Thailand	4.9 (2008–2013)	3.5 (2008–2013)
Viet Nam	4.5 (2010–2014)	2.0 (2010–2014)
The Pacific		
Cook Islands	...	...
Fiji	...	...
Kiribati	...	...
Marshall Islands	...	...
Micronesia, Fed. States of	...	...
Nauru	...	...
Palau	...	...
Papua New Guinea	...	...
Samoa	...	...
Solomon Islands	...	...
Timor-Leste	...	...
Tonga	...	...
Tuvalu	...	...
Vanuatu	...	...
Developed Member Economies		
Australia	...	...
Japan	...	...
New Zealand	...	...

... = data not available at cutoff date, Lao PDR = Lao People's Democratic Republic, SDG = Sustainable Development Goal.

a Based on real mean per capita consumption or income measured at 2011 purchasing power parity using the PovcalNet database (http://iresearch.worldbank.org/PovcalNet). Data reported are based on consumption, except for the Philippines, which collects income data.

Source: World Bank. Global Database of Shared Prosperity. http://www.worldbank.org/en/topic/poverty/brief/global-database-of-shared-prosperity (accessed 27 June 2017); International Labour Organization. Key Indicators of the Labour Market. http://www.ilo.org/ilostat (accessed 29 June 2017); United Nations. Sustainable Development Goals Indicators Global Database. http://unstats.un.org/sdgs/indicators/database/ (accessed 18 July 2017).

Peace

To foster peaceful, just, and inclusive societies which are free from fear and violence. There can be no sustainable development without peace and no peace without sustainable development.

Snapshot

- Intentional homicide rates were lower in 29 out of 39 economies between 2003 and 2015.
- The proportion of unsentenced detainees declined between 2005 and 2015 in 15 out of 31 regional economies with available data.
- In 17 out of 32 economies of Asia and the Pacific with available data, 25% or more of firms experienced at least one bribe payment request, while in Bhutan, Georgia, and the Federated States of Micronesia, the proportion of firms experiencing at least one bribe payment request was less than 5%.

The Sustainable Development Agenda aims to promote peaceful and inclusive societies by promoting access to justice for all, and building effective, transparent, and accountable institutions at all levels to uphold political stability, human rights, and the rule of law.

SDG 16: Promote Peaceful and Inclusive Societies for Sustainable Development, Provide Access to Justice for All and Build Effective, Accountable, and Inclusive Institutions at All Levels

Number of victims of intentional homicide per 100,000 population. While reported crime rates may underestimate incidence of crime, official crime rates, particularly reports on intentional homicide, provide a description of broad crime patterns and a sense of overall level of safety on the streets. Latest data show that three of the five economies with the highest rates of intentional homicide are in the Pacific, while 11 economies including the three economies of Developed Asia have intentional homicide rates of 1.0 or less for every 100,000 persons (Table 5.1). These rates have been decreasing in 29 economies, including the three most populous economies in the region—the PRC, India, and Indonesia. In the Pacific, rates have increased in four out of eight economies that have reported data from 2003 to latest year. Among 47 regional economies with data, Tuvalu, with 20.3 intentional homicides for every 100,000 persons, has the highest homicide rate, followed by Papua New Guinea (10.4). Other economies with homicide rates of at least 7.5 intentional homicides for every 100,000 persons include the Philippines (9.8), Pakistan (7.8), and Kiribati (7.5). Singapore has the lowest rate at 0.2 intentional homicides per 100,000 people. Aside from Singapore, economies with rates under 1.0 intentional homicides for every 100,000 persons include Australia (1.0); Brunei Darussalam (0.5); Hong Kong, China (0.3); Indonesia (0.5); Japan (0.3); Maldives (0.9); New Zealand (0.9); the PRC (0.7); Taipei,China (0.8); and Tonga (1.0).

Unsentenced detainees as a proportion of overall prison population. In 15 out of 31 regional economies with available data, the proportion of unsentenced detainees has decreased between 2005 and 2015 (Table 5.1), with Afghanistan having the largest reduction of 51.5 percentage points from 81.0% in 2005 to 29.5% in 2015. Timor-Leste (24.1%) and Georgia (15.2%) have also reduced the proportion of unsentenced detainees by over 30 percentage points. However, over 60% of the prison population are unsentenced detainees in Bangladesh (74.6%), Pakistan (69.3%), India (67.3%), and the Philippines (60.0%). The percentage of unsentenced detainees is less than 10% in Kiribati (9.8%), Brunei Darussalam (7.9%) and Tonga (7.4%). Figure 5.1 illustrates how unsentenced detainees as a proportion of overall prison population has changed between 2005 and 2015.

Figure 5.1: Unsentenced Detainees as a Proportion of Overall Prison Population (%)

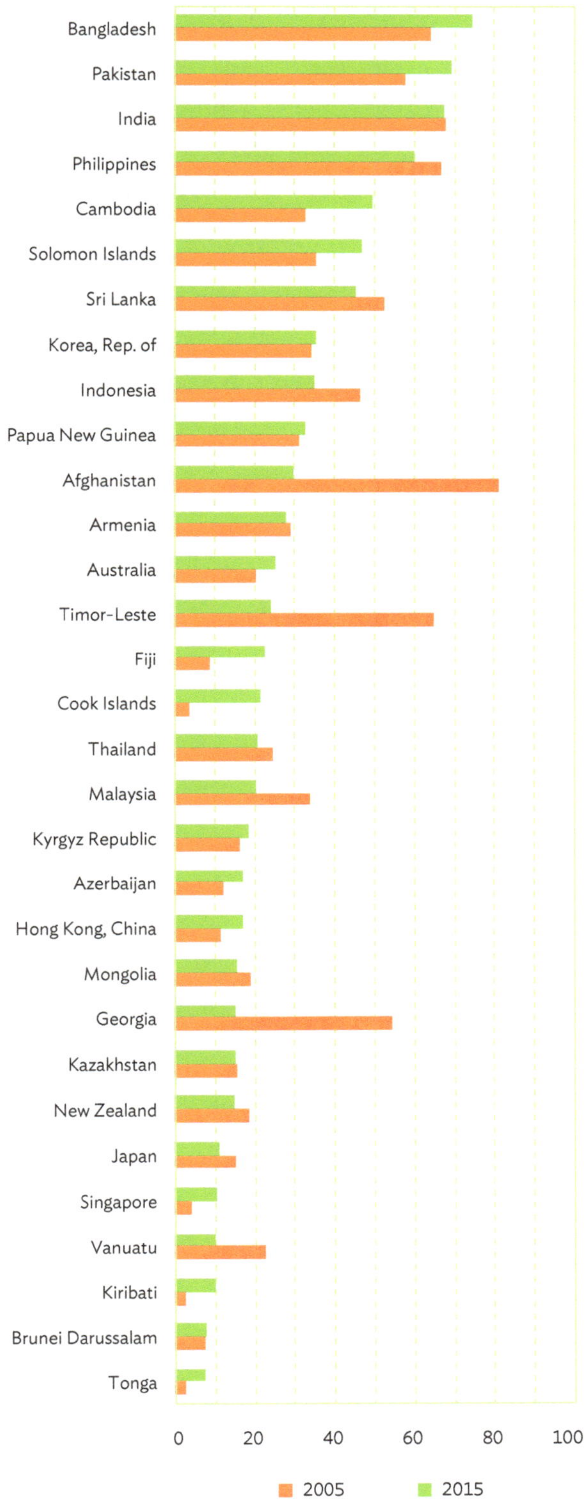

Source: Table 5.1.

Bribery incidence among firms in Asia and the Pacific. Corruption is an impediment to good governance, development, and prosperity. In its Enterprise Surveys, the World Bank obtains information on whether firms are solicited for gifts or informal payments while meeting public officials. Latest year data show that in 17 out of 32 reporting economies, the proportion of firms that have experienced at least one bribe payment request is 25% or more (Figure 5.2). Economies with the smallest proportion of firms experiencing at least one bribe payment request include Bhutan (0.9%), Georgia (2.2%), and the Federated States of Micronesia (4.5%).

Figure 5.2: Proportion of Firms Experiencing at Least One Bribe Payment Request, Latest Year
(%)

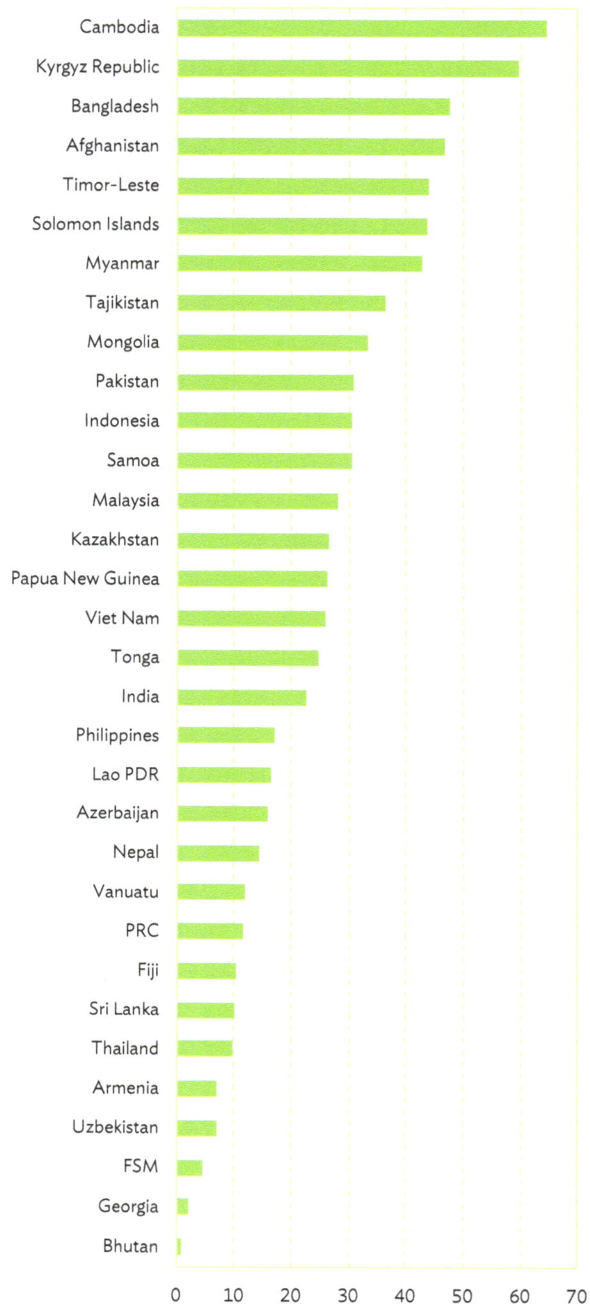

FSM = Federated States of Micronesia, Lao PDR = Lao People's Democratic Republic, PRC = People's Republic of China.

Note: Fiji, the Federated States of Micronesia, Samoa, Tonga, and Vanuatu use data for 2009. Sri Lanka uses data for 2011. The PRC uses data for 2012. Armenia, Azerbaijan, Bangladesh, Georgia, Kazakhstan, the Kyrgyz Republic, Mongolia, Nepal, Pakistan, Tajikistan, and Uzbekistan use data for 2013. Afghanistan, India, and Myanmar use data for 2014. Bhutan, Indonesia, Malaysia, Papua New Guinea, the Philippines, Solomon Islands, Timor-Leste, and Viet Nam use data for 2015. Cambodia, the Lao People's Democratic Republic, and Thailand use data for 2016.

Source: Table 5.1.

Equity, Data Gaps, and Other Related Issues

Data needed to monitor SDG 16 can be quite sparse, even for indicators that are available. Further, statistics on these indicators are not always collected regularly. Some indicators, such as conflict-related deaths by sex, age, and cause, are of clear relevance to monitoring peace, but the international standards for these indicators have not yet been established.

Indicators on intentional homicide, conflict-related deaths, and the proportion of children under 5 years of age whose births have been registered, should rely on information from vital registration systems. However, in many developing countries, vital registration systems are not fully functional. Producing reliable estimates of the number and causes of death, in both conflict and nonconflict situations, is challenging. The systematic recording of births in many developing countries is also a serious challenge. In the absence of reliable administrative data, household surveys such as the Demographic and Health Surveys, and the Multiple Indicator Cluster Survey have become a key source of data to monitor levels and trends in birth registration, as well as deaths.

As information and communication technology becomes an integral part of everyday life, new opportunities such as open data initiative and crowdsourced data can be explored to spread and access information. Civil society organizations and research institutions have a vast role to play in supplementing data and statistics collected by governments to monitor the extent to which peace, justice, and the rule of law are being sustained.

Goal 16. Promote peaceful and inclusive societies for sustainable development, provide access to justice for all and build effective, accountable and inclusive institutions at all levels

Table 5.1: **Selected Indicators for SDG 16 - Peace, Justice, and Strong Institutions**
Significantly reduce all forms of violence and related death rates everywhere
Promote the rule of law at the national and international levels and ensure equal access to justice for all
Substantially reduce corruption and bribery in all their forms
By 2030, provide legal identity for all, including birth registration

Regional Member	16.1.1 Number of Victims of Intentional Homicide (per 100,000 population)		16.3.2 Unsentenced Detainees as a Proportion of Overall Prison Population (%)	
	2003	2015	2005	2015
Developing Member Economies				
Central and West Asia				
Afghanistan	...	6.6 (2012)	81.0	29.5
Armenia	2.7 (2004)	2.5	29.0	27.9
Azerbaijan	2.2	2.5 (2014)	12.1	17.0
Georgia	6.6	2.7 (2014)	54.2	15.2
Kazakhstan[b]	13.2	4.8	15.6	15.0
Kyrgyz Republic	8.3	5.1	16.2	18.4
Pakistan	6.3	7.8 (2012)	57.8	69.3
Tajikistan	3.1 (2006)	1.4 (2013)	...	...
Turkmenistan	4.9 (2005)	4.2	...	...
Uzbekistan	3.6 (2005)	3.0	...	...
East Asia				
China, People's Rep. of	1.9	0.7 (2014)	...	...
Hong Kong, China	0.8	0.3	11.5	16.9
Korea, Rep. of	...	...	34.2	35.1
Mongolia	13.9	7.2	18.8	15.6
Taipei,China	1.0 (2006)	0.8	...	...
South Asia				
Bangladesh	2.5	2.5	64.0	74.6
Bhutan	...	2.7 (2014)	...	...
India	3.6	3.2 (2014)	67.9	67.3
Maldives	1.0 (2007)	0.9 (2013)	...	...
Nepal	3.0	2.3 (2014)	...	...
Sri Lanka[b]	6.8	2.9 (2013)	52.4	45.4
Southeast Asia				
Brunei Darussalam	0.9	0.5 (2013)	7.2	7.9
Cambodia	3.9	1.8 (2011)	32.6	49.3
Indonesia	0.7	0.5 (2014)	46.7	35.0
Lao PDR	9.6 (2005)	6.9	...	...
Malaysia	2.3	1.9 (2010)	33.8	20.4
Myanmar	1.7	2.4	...	...
Philippines[b]	7.8	9.8 (2014)	66.7	60.0
Singapore	0.6	0.2	4.1	10.2
Thailand	9.9	3.5	24.6	20.8
Viet Nam	1.3	1.5 (2011)	...	...
The Pacific				
Cook Islands	...	3.1 (2012)	3.7	21.6
Fiji	2.6 (2007)	3.0 (2012)	8.7	22.7
Kiribati	...	7.5 (2012)	2.6	9.8
Marshall Islands	...	4.7 (2012)	...	...
Micronesia, Fed. States of	4.6 (2005)	4.7	...	...
Nauru	...	1.3 (2012)	...	...
Palau	...	3.1 (2012)	...	...
Papua New Guinea	10.5	10.4 (2010)	31.3	32.5
Samoa	...	3.2 (2013)	...	...
Solomon Islands	4.4 (2004)	3.8 (2008)	35.4	46.7
Timor-Leste	2.4 (2004)	3.7 (2010)	64.7	24.1
Tonga	6.0	1.0 (2012)	2.6	7.4
Tuvalu	-	20.3 (2012)	...	...
Vanuatu	2.5 (2005)	2.1	22.5	10.0
Developed Member Economies				
Australia	1.7	1.0	20.4	25.3
Japan	0.6	0.3 (2014)	15.0	11.2
New Zealand[e]	1.1	0.9 (2014)	18.4	14.9

(continued)

Goal 16. Promote peaceful and inclusive societies for sustainable development, provide access to justice for all and build effective, accountable and inclusive institutions at all levels

Table 5.1: **Selected Indicators for SDG 16 - Peace, Justice, and Strong Institutions**
Significantly reduce all forms of violence and related death rates everywhere
Promote the rule of law at the national and international levels and ensure equal access to justice for all
Substantially reduce corruption and bribery in all their forms
By 2030, provide legal identity for all, including birth registration

Regional Member	16.5.2 Proportion of Firms Experiencing at Least One Bribe Payment Request (%)	16.9.1 Proportion of Children Under 5 Years of Age Whose Births have been Registered with a Civil Authority[a] (%)	
	2013	2006	2014
Developing Member Economies			
Central and West Asia			
Afghanistan	46.8 (2014)	6.0 (2003)	42.3 (2015)
Armenia	7.1	96.0 (2005)	99.6 (2010)
Azerbaijan	15.9	93.6	...
Georgia	2.2	92.0 (2005)	99.6 (2013)
Kazakhstan[b]	26.7	99.0	99.7 (2011)
Kyrgyz Republic	59.8	95.7	97.7
Pakistan	30.8	26.6 (2007)	33.6 (2013)
Tajikistan	36.3	88.0 (2005)	88.4 (2012)
Turkmenistan	...	95.5	...
Uzbekistan	7.0	99.9	...
East Asia			
China, People's Rep. of	11.6 (2012)	...	...
Hong Kong, China	...	...	...
Korea, Rep. of	...	...	...
Mongolia	33.4	98.0 (2005)	99.3 (2013)
Taipei,China	...	...	...
South Asia			
Bangladesh	47.7	10.0	20.2
Bhutan	0.9 (2015)	...	99.9 (2010)
India	22.7 (2014)	41.1	71.9
Maldives	...	73.0 (2000)	92.5 (2009)
Nepal	14.4	35.0	58.1
Sri Lanka[b]	10.0 (2011)	97.2 (2007)	...
Southeast Asia			
Brunei Darussalam	...	...	...
Cambodia	64.7 (2016)	66.4 (2005)	73.3
Indonesia	30.6 (2015)	55.0 (2002)	68.5[c] (2013)
Lao PDR	16.4 (2016)	72.0	74.8 (2012)
Malaysia	28.2 (2015)	...	...
Myanmar	42.9 (2014)	64.9 (2003)	72.4 (2010)
Philippines[b]	17.2 (2015)	83.0 (2000)	90.2 (2010)
Singapore	...	...	...
Thailand	9.9 (2016)	99.5	99.4[c] (2012)
Viet Nam	26.1 (2015)	92.7 (2005)	96.1
The Pacific			
Cook Islands	...	...	...
Fiji	10.5 (2009)	...	...
Kiribati	...	...	93.5 (2009)
Marshall Islands	...	95.9 (2007)	...
Micronesia, Fed. States of	4.5 (2009)	...	...
Nauru	...	82.6 (2007)	...
Palau	...	...	...
Papua New Guinea	26.4 (2015)	...	...
Samoa	30.5 (2009)	...	58.6
Solomon Islands	43.8 (2015)	80.0 (2007)	...
Timor-Leste	44.2 (2015)	53.0 (2003)	55.2 (2010)
Tonga	24.9 (2009)	...	93.4 (2012)
Tuvalu	...	49.9 (2007)	...
Vanuatu	11.9 (2009)	43.0 (2007)	43.4[c] (2013)
Developed Member Economies			
Australia	...	...	100.0[d] (2015)
Japan	...	...	100.0[d] (2015)
New Zealand[e]	...	...	100.0[d] (2015)

... = data not available at cutoff date, – = magnitude equals zero, Lao PDR = Lao People's Democratic Republic, MICS = Multiple Indicator Cluster Surveys, SDG = Sustainable Development Goal.

a Changes in the definition of birth registration were made from the second and third rounds of MICS2 and MICS3 to the fourth round (MICS4). In order to allow for comparability with later rounds, data from MICS2 and MICS3 on birth registration were recalculated according to the MICS4 indicator definition. Therefore, the recalculated data presented here may differ from estimates included in MICS2 and MICS3 national reports.

b For indicator 16.1.1, changes in definitions and/or counting rules are reported by the member state to indicate a break in the time series.

c Data differ from the standard definition or refer to only part of an economy.

d As indicated in the United Nations Office on Drugs and Crime data, estimates of 100% were assumed given that civil registration systems in these economies are complete and all vital events (including births) are registered.

e For indicator 16.1.1, data for 2000–2006 refer to offenses; data for 2007 onward refer to victims of intentional homicide.

Sources: For indicator 16.1.1: United Nations Office on Drugs and Crime. UNODC Statistics Online. https://data.unodc.org/ (accessed 29 June 2017); for indicator 16.3.2: United Nations. SDG Indicators Global Database. https://unstats.un.org/sdgs/indicators/database/ (accessed 13 June 2017); for indicator 16.5.2: World Bank. World Development Indicators. http://data.worldbank.org/ (accessed 29 June 2017); for indicator 16.9.1: United Nations Children's Fund: http://data.unicef.org/child-protection/birth-registration.html (accessed 29 June 2017); World Bank. World Development Indicators. http://databank.worldbank.org/data/reports.aspx?source=sustainable-development-goals-(sdgs)# (accessed 7 July 2017).

Partnership

To mobilize the means required to implement this agenda through a revitalized Global Partnership for Sustainable Development, based on a spirit of strengthened global solidarity, focused in particular on the needs of the poorest and most vulnerable and with the participation of all countries, all stakeholders, and all people.

Snapshot

- In four-fifths of 40 developing economies in Asia and the Pacific, the average financial and technical assistance (through North–South, South–South, and triangular cooperation) has risen between 2000–2007 and 2008–2015.
- More than 90% of regional economies have conducted a population census since 2007. Nearly half of the developing economies (23 out of 45) have prepared a national statistical plan to address the growing demand for statistics to monitor development.

The attainment of the Global Goals by 2030 requires strengthened partnerships and improved coordination across governments, the development community, and the private sector. This will not only ensure that financial and technical resources are mobilized strategically, but also increase transparency and accountability.

SDG 17: Strengthen the Means of Implementation and Revitalize the Global Partnership for Sustainable Development

Dollar value of financial and technical assistance (including through North–South, South–South and triangular cooperation) committed to developing countries. Since the value of financial and technical assistance can fluctuate annually, it is useful to examine averages over a longer period. Upon examining the periods 2000–2007 and 2008–2015, it is observed that in four-fifths of 40 developing economies, financial and technical assistance has, on average, risen between the two periods (Figure 6.1). The value of financial and technical assistance in Myanmar increased by more than 8.7 times, from $15.2 million in 2000–2007 to $131.7 million in 2008–2015. This was followed by Kazakhstan, Afghanistan, Uzbekistan, and the Philippines, respectively, which all experienced at least a two time increase in value of financial and technical assistance between 2000–2007 and 2008–2015. Afghanistan received the largest financial and technical assistance, averaging at $1.5 billion per year between 2008 and 2015. Other developing economies receiving over $500 million, on average, in 2008–2015 include Indonesia ($1,326.4 million), Pakistan ($744.0 million), Viet Nam ($658.4 million), India ($604.2 million), and the PRC ($533.2 million). Less than $5 million of financial and technical assistance were provided in 2008–2015 to the Pacific economies of Palau ($3.2 million), Tuvalu ($3.7 million), and the Cook Islands ($4.1 million).

Value of all resources made available to strengthen statistical capacity in developing countries. Data on value of resources made available to strengthen statistical capacity are available for 40 out of 45 developing economies in 2014. Viet Nam ($6,559,859.4), reported the highest value for this indicator, followed by Armenia ($3,696,148.0) and Afghanistan ($3,020,102.4) (Table 6.1).

Figure 6.1: Dollar Value of Financial and Technical Assistance Committed to Developing Countries
(constant 2015 $ million)

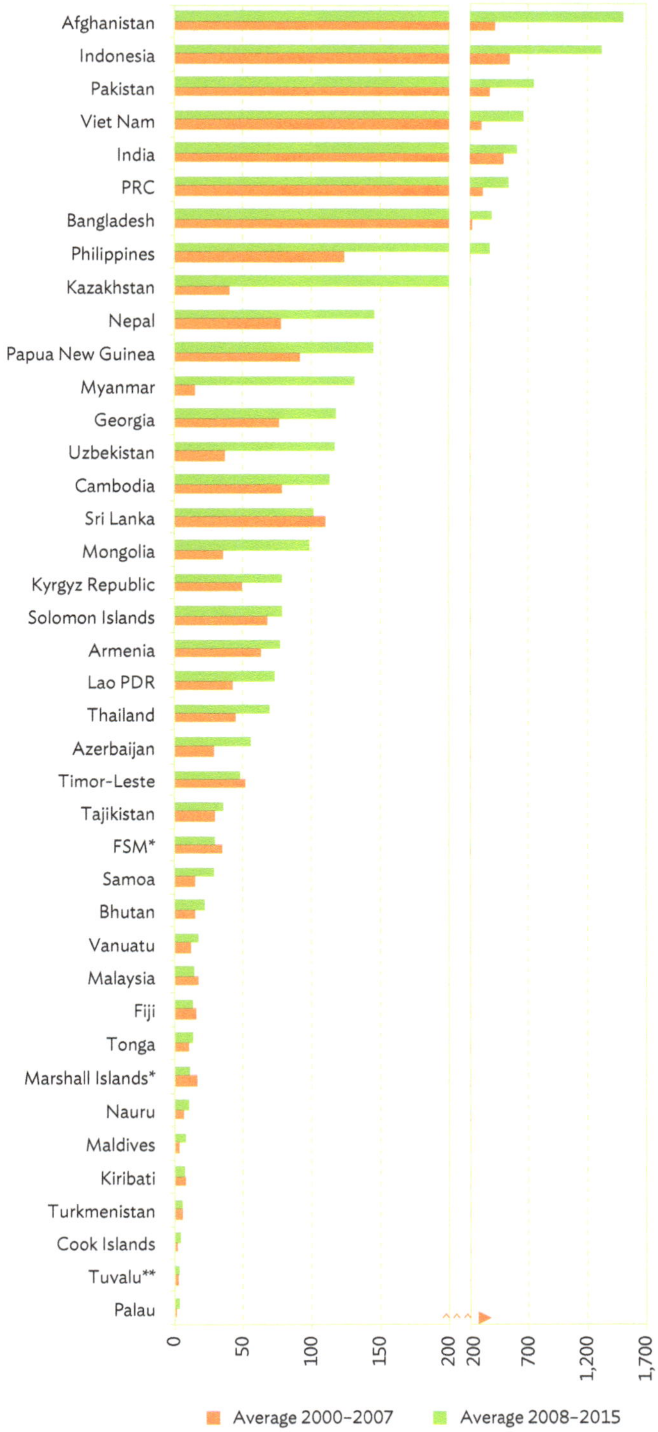

FSM = Federated States of Micronesia, Lao PDR = Lao People's Democratic Republic, PRC = People's Republic of China.
*Value for average 2000–2007 refers to average of 2001 to 2007, **Value for average 2000–2007 refers to average of 2000 and 2002 to 2007.
Source: Table 6.1.

Number of countries that have conducted at least one population and housing census in the last 10 years. While statistics production does not fully reflect statistical capacity, the non-conduct of key statistical activities such as population censuses that are considered vital suggest the lack of support from governments for national statistical systems. This indicator not only tracks countries that have conducted a population and housing census, but also those compiling detailed population and housing statistics from population registers, administrative records, sample surveys, and other sources. In the Asia and Pacific region, 42 out of 45 developing economies have conducted a population and housing census since 2007 (Table 6.1).

Equity, Data Gaps, and Other Related Issues

Indicators for various targets under the theme of partnership are not available, and when available, they are sparse and not regularly updated. Difficulty in monitoring progress with respect to SDG 17 may also arise due to the lack of quantitative targets in some areas.

In its *Statistical Yearbook for Asia and the Pacific (2015)*, the United Nations (UN) Economic and Social Commission for Asia and the Pacific (ESCAP) examined results of the World Bank's Statistical Capacity Index Dashboard, and suggested that countries in Asia and the Pacific have generally more adequate key data sources than in the Middle East, North Africa, and Sub-Saharan Africa, but adequacy is lower than in Latin America and the Caribbean. ESCAP also reports that while 50 out of 51 reporting countries in the Asia and Pacific region have statistical legislation specifying the responsibilities of statistics producers across government, only 44 of these countries have articles in these legislations protecting the independence of official statistics from political influence. Thus, countries will need to strengthen national statistical institutions so that they can improve existing data sources, as well as quickly adapt to the rapid increase in use of new data sources. This not only involves the provision of adequate resources and infrastructure for development of statistics, but also the establishment and/or maintenance of enabling environments and ecosystems to produce reliable data and statistics. Strong national statistical institutions will be required, not only to build, but also maintain partnerships for a data ecosystem that utilizes available information to attain sustainable development by 2030. Box 6.1. discusses measurement errors from using traditional recall-based methods to estimate total plot area, rice yield, and rice production in one province of the Lao People's Democratic Republic; and calls for an improvement in statistical capacity of government agencies tasked with providing such information.

Box 6.1: Bias in Plot Area, Yield, and Production Measurement: Evidence from Savannakhet Province, Lao People's Democratic Republic

Goal 2 of the Sustainable Development Agenda on zero hunger aims, among other targets, to "double the agricultural productivity and incomes of small scale food producers by 2030." To accurately monitor the progress made toward achieving this goal and target, timely, cost-effective, and high-quality estimates of agricultural land area, yield, and production are needed. Collecting such data in developing countries can, however, be time-consuming, costly, and methodologically challenging. Estimates of these agricultural statistics are also prone to measurement errors in the absence of a sound and well-designed methodology. Inaccurate agricultural statistics can lead to inappropriate policies, thereby impacting food security.

In the Lao People's Democratic Republic, the Asian Development Bank (ADB) in collaboration with the Center for Agricultural Statistics of the Ministry of Agriculture and Forestry conducted a methodological study in Savannakhet Province. This work was undertaken through a statistics capacity building technical assistance project piloted across four Southeast Asian countries.[a] Rice area and yield were estimated through the implementation of a farmer recall survey and compared with objective measures, such as plot areas[b] mapped using global positioning system (GPS), and rice yields[c] estimated by crop cutting for the same set of plots. A multistage stratified random sample utilizing an area frame was implemented to select the plots for this study. Fieldwork was implemented during the rainy season of 2015.

a ADB. 2013. *Innovative Data Collection Methods for Agricultural and Rural Statistics*. Manila (Regional Capacity Development Technical Assistance 8369). This technical assistance was implemented by ADB in partnership with government agricultural ministries and national statistical offices in the Lao People's Democratic Republic, the Philippines, Thailand, and Viet Nam.

b Although GPS measures are more objective than farmer estimates and are often referred to as the new "gold standard" (Carletto et al. 2015), measurement bias may arise due to satellite position, signal propagation, and receiver type, with overall position error ranging from 0.5 meters to 4 meters (Hofmann-Wellenhof et al. 2008). These errors are likely to be more prominent for smaller plots than larger plots.

c The crop-cutting technique relies on identifying a randomized spot on a plot (a square, circle, or triangle) of a certain dimension and harvesting the crop within this spot to calculate the quantity harvested. It is considered as the gold standard for estimating yield (FAO 1982).

continued.

Box 6.1: *(continued)*

Box Figure 6.1.1 shows the ratio of farmer-reported area, yield, and production versus values for the same variables objectively measured by GPS-based plot area quartile. For all three variables, a clear overestimation is observed. For the full sample, plot area, on average, is overreported by farmers roughly 2.9 times relative to GPS measurement; meanwhile, the average farmer-reported yield is roughly twice the yield estimate obtained through crop cutting. Consequently, rice production is overestimated roughly 3.9 times by farmers relative to objectively measured production.

Also, a clear downward trend exists for all three measures, whereby farmers significantly overestimate area, yield, and production on smaller plots, with the degree of overestimation decreasing with plot area. Such a systematic bias is likely to have direct consequences on the interpretation of results while estimating several policy-relevant agricultural relationships.

Box Figure 6.1.1: Ratio of Farmer Estimates to Objective Measures for Rice Area, Yield, and Production by Plot Area Quartile Based on Global Positioning System

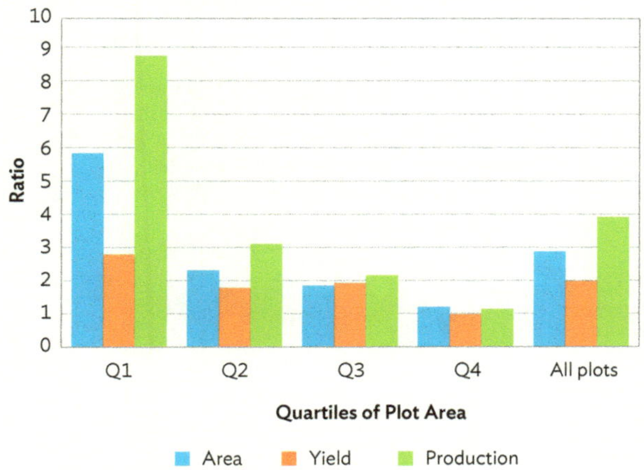

Finally, administrative data for the Lao People's Democratic Republic[d] point to a yield estimate of 4.3 tons per hectare for the rainy season of 2015 in Savannakhet, revealing an overestimation of roughly 2.2 tons per hectare relative to crop cutting estimates for the same season from this validation study.

The results from this study suggest that data users need to carefully consider existing agricultural statistics and survey methods. They also point toward the need to improve agricultural data quality through targeted investments in quality data, objective measurement approaches, as well as improvement in statistical capacity of government agencies tasked with providing such information.

d Department of Planning and Cooperation, Ministry of Agriculture and Forestry. 2016. *Agricultural Statistics Yearbook 2015*. Vientiane, Lao PDR: Ministry of Agriculture and Forestry.

Sources:

C. Carletto, S. Gourlay, and P. Winters. 2015. From Guesstimates to GPStimates: Land Area Measurement and Implications for Agricultural Analysis. *Journal of African Economies*. 24 (5). pp. 593–628

Food and Agriculture Organization of the United Nations. 1982. *Estimation of Crop Areas and Yields in Agricultural Statistics*. Rome

B. Hofmann-Wellenhof, H. Lichtenegger, and E. Wasle. 2008. GNSS—*Global Navigation Satellite Systems*. New York: Springer-Verlag.

Official development assistance and partnerships in the development community, including North–South and South–South cooperation, have provided mechanisms to assist those ravaged by conflict, natural disasters, and other risks factors, and have encouraged growth and trade across countries. Cross-thematic linkages in the Global Goals and targets point to the need for multistakeholder partnerships that go beyond a traditional sectoral approach to a more integrated approach. This requires strong coordination among various stakeholders in the development community, including cofinancing of partnership initiatives, as well as joint progress reporting on the extent of attainment of the SDGs.

Goal 17. Strengthen the means of implementation and revitalize the Global Partnership for Sustainable Development

Table 6.1: Selected Indicators for SDG 17 - Development Financing and Statistical Capacity Building

By 2020, enhance capacity-building support to developing countries, including for least developed countries and small island developing states, to increase significantly the availability of high-quality, timely, and reliable data disaggregated by income, gender, age, race, ethnicity, migratory status, disability, geographic location, and other characteristics relevant in national contexts

By 2030, build on existing initiatives to develop measurements of progress on sustainable development that complement gross domestic product, and support statistical capacity building in developing countries

Regional Member	17.9.1 Dollar Value of Financial and Technical Assistance (including through North-South, South-South and triangular cooperation) Committed to Developing Countries (constant 2015 $ million)		17.18.3 Availability of National Statistical Plan[a]	17.19.1 Value of All Resources Made Available to Strengthen Statistical Capacity in Developing Countries ($)		17.19.2 Number of Countries That Have Conducted at Least One Population and Housing Census in the Last 10 Years[b]
	Average, 2000-2007	Average, 2008-2015	2016	2006	2014	Latest Year
Developing Member Economies						
Central and West Asia						
Afghanistan	411.8	1,509.4	B	2,069,399.8	3,020,102.4	...
Armenia	63.2	77.1	B	56,731.6	3,696,148.0	2011
Azerbaijan	29.1	55.7	...	140,534.9	32,316.8	2009
Georgia	76.2	117.9	C, D	342,978.6	152,019.0	2014
Kazakhstan	40.3	204.8	...	372,625.0	1,600.0	2009
Kyrgyz Republic	49.3	78.4	B	260,060.6	87,885.0	2009
Pakistan	368.2	744.0	...	4,916,521.4	16,150.0	...
Tajikistan	29.2	36.0	B	2,411,705.4	2,500,000.0	2010
Turkmenistan	6.1	5.6	...	279,722.6	18,738.0	2012
Uzbekistan	37.5	117.3	...	272,261.8	161.2	...
East Asia						
China, People's Rep. of	306.2	533.2	A, B, C	1,568,187.0	418,083.5	2010
Hong Kong, China	...	...	B	...	...	2016
Korea, Rep. of	...	...	A, B, C, E	...	...	2015
Mongolia	35.9	98.2	...	2,994,147.0	94,714.7	2010
Taipei,China	...	...	...	...	...	2010
South Asia						
Bangladesh	216.3	389.8	B	1,245,957.6	357,903.0	2011
Bhutan	14.8	21.6	B	528,875.6	176,752.2	2017
India	483.7	604.2	B	1,171,518.6	1,717,187.1	2011
Maldives	3.6	8.0	B	136,444.6	200,000.0 (2013)	2014
Nepal	78.2	145.8	...	568,917.5	163,912.8	2011
Sri Lanka	110.1	101.8	...	361,402.2	469,210.3	2012
Southeast Asia						
Brunei Darussalam	...	...	...	...	...	2011
Cambodia	78.4	112.8	...	5,058,885.2	322,949.9	2008
Indonesia	539.2	1,326.4	B, D	795,895.3	1,500.0 (2013)	2010
Lao PDR	42.9	73.0	A, B, C, D	468,513.1	246,420.1	2015
Malaysia	17.4	13.9	...	274,242.8	92,130.2 (2012)	2010
Myanmar	15.2	131.7	...	1,187,054.1	1,314,445.9	2014
Philippines	124.2	371.8	B, C, D, E	773,000.7	186,702.0	2010
Singapore	...	...	B	...	...	2010
Thailand	45.2	69.2	...	510,883.2	24,017.1	2010
Viet Nam	298.0	658.4	B	1,698,915.4	6,559,859.4	2009
The Pacific						
Cook Islands	2.1	4.1	B	43,363.3	36,337.0	2016
Fiji	15.6	13.7	...	151,154.8	28,758.5	2017
Kiribati	7.7	7.6	...	34,046.4 (2007)	5,089.9 (2013)	2015
Marshall Islands	16.8	11.5	...	53,283.3	1,630.0	2011
Micronesia, Fed. States of	35.2	29.9	...	210,191.8	5,090.9 (2013)	2010
Nauru	6.6	10.7	...	34,046.4 (2007)	5,089.9 (2013)	2011
Palau	1.6	3.2	...	120,972.2	46,661.1	2015
Papua New Guinea	91.8	145.3	...	1,018,701.9	15,721.0	2011
Samoa	15.0	28.8	B	174,911.1	26,717.0	2016
Solomon Islands	67.9	78.3	...	66,377.7	25,543.0	2009
Timor-Leste	51.5	47.7	B	172,795.8	32,361.5	2015
Tonga	10.0	13.5	...	120,885.9	15,702.1	2016
Tuvalu	2.9	3.7	...	7,618.0 (2007)	5,089.9 (2013)	2012
Vanuatu	11.9	17.5	B	489,116.6	5,089.9 (2013)	2016
Developed Member Economies						
Australia	...	...	B	...	...	2016
Japan	...	...	A, B, C	...	...	2015
New Zealand	...	...	...	...	...	2013

... = data not available at cutoff date, Lao PDR = Lao People's Democratic Republic, SDG = Sustainable Development Goal.

a A - National statistical plan fully funded, B - National statistical plan under implementation, C - National statistical plan with funding from government, D - National statistical plan with funding from donors, E - National statistical plan with funding from others.

b Refers to the most recent year population and housing census was conducted.

c Value for average 2000–2007 refers to average of 2001–2007.

d Value for average 2000–2007 refers to average of 2000 and 2002–2007.

Sources: Partnership in Statistics for Development in the 21st Century (PARIS21) http://www.paris21.org/ (accessed 28 June 2017); United Nations. Sustainable Development Goals Indicators Global Database. http://unstats.un.org/sdgs/indicators/database/ (accessed 19 July 2017); national statistics office of Taipei,China. https://eng.stat.gov.tw/np.asp?ctNode=1549 (accessed 28 June 2017); Bhutan Trust Fund for Environmental Conservation. http://www.bhutantrustfund.bt/?p=925 (accessed 21 July 2017); and Fiji Bureau of Statistics. http://www.statsfiji.gov.fj/census (accessed 21 July 2017).

Section 2. Collecting Sex-Disaggregated Data on Asset Ownership: Evidence from Pilot Surveys

Introduction

The Beijing Platform for Action 1995, heralded as one of the most progressive frameworks for advocating gender equality, is more than 2 decades old. Since its inception, tremendous progress has been made in achieving gender equality globally, but significant gaps continue to exist. Bridging the inequalities with respect to women's access to productive resources is still a challenge in many parts of the world.

While the need to promote greater gender equality is recognized and addressed in both the Millennium Development Goals and Sustainable Development Goals (SDGs), the SDGs take on the issue by explicitly linking gender equality in economic resources to the sustainable development agenda. In particular, the importance of ensuring women's equal rights to economic resources, ownership, and control over land and other forms of property is mentioned under SDG targets 1.4, 2.3, and 5.a (Box 7.1).

The importance of asset ownership and wealth for individual and household welfare has been documented in recent decades. There is a greater appreciation for the complex interlinkages between asset ownership, sustainable livelihoods, and the ability to transition and stay out of poverty, with implications for current and intergenerational household well-being. Often, it is the ownership of certain kinds of assets (a house or land, for example) that determines if households are structurally poor (in poverty over a longer period) or have temporarily slipped into poverty due to a negative income shock. Assets can aid income diversification and can be used to access credit by serving as collateral.

The ability of women to own and control assets is critical for securing gender equity and delivering on the sustainable development agenda. Empirical evidence from the intrahousehold resource allocation literature across diverse contexts suggests that women's asset ownership is associated with better nutrition and education for their children (Quisumbing and Maluccio 2000, Doss 2006); increased bargaining power within the household as evinced by greater participation in household decision making and increased mobility (Garikipati 2009, Twyman et al. 2015, Swaminathan et al. 2011); and protection against the experience of domestic violence (Panda and Agarwal 2007, Oduro et al., 2016, Bonilla et al. 2017). Research from Sub-Saharan Africa suggests that strengthening women's land rights and tenure security has implications for agricultural productivity and soil conservation practices (Goldstein and Udry 2008; Ali, Deininger, and Goldstein 2014).

Despite this body of strong evidence linking women's asset ownership and development goals, such sex-disaggregated data needed for monitoring of the progress on relevant targets in the 2030 Agenda is scarce. Conventional surveys, including those conducted by national statistical agencies, use the household as the unit of data collection. Information is obtained on household asset ownership (land, dwelling, and so on) from a household member, usually the head of the household; but this information is of rather limited use as individuals own assets, not households. Any gender analysis (or for that matter, any analysis based on individual characteristics) gets limited to comparisons between households headed by males and households headed by females, categorized based on the sex of the household head. This approach does not shed any light on men in households headed by women or women in households headed by men. Data from Latin America and Caribbean show that for certain categories of assets, gender inequality is overestimated by headship analysis as it ignores women in male-headed households (Deere, Alvarado, and Twyman 2012). Similarly, Peterman et al. (2011) found in

Uganda that using the sex of the household head as a gender indicator underestimates the differences in agricultural productivity between male-owned and female-owned plots.

Sex-disaggregated asset data can also highlight the gendered experience of poverty, which is not captured using household-level data. A study on multidimensional poverty from Karnataka, India finds that gender differentials in poverty are significant based on individual poverty lines (a difference of 34 percentage points between male and female poverty rates), but are almost nonexistent when assigned the household poverty line (1 percentage point difference) (Vijaya, Lahoti, Swaminathan 2014). Among other attributes, individual-level asset ownership data was used to construct individual poverty scores. The study also finds that the poverty of poor women in nonpoor households was driven largely by lack of education and lack of asset ownership, even when the household was classified as an asset holder.

Recent numerous initiatives have embarked on collecting individual-level asset data. However, the data collection protocols including the questionnaire design, methodology, and sampling procedure, are not standardized across these initiatives, rendering cross-data comparisons difficult. Hence, despite these initiatives, there is still a lot of ground to cover in terms of providing methodological guidelines and building capacity of national statistical agencies for basic data collection.

The Evidence and Data for Gender Equality (EDGE) project is an attempt to systematically address the data and methodological lacuna in the domain of sex-disaggregated data. EDGE is a global initiative that seeks to accelerate the production of internationally comparable sex-disaggregated data on health, education, asset ownership, employment, and entrepreneurship through two related activities: creation of an online gender data portal to share existing data on education, health, and employment; and development of methodological guidelines for collecting sex-disaggregated asset ownership and entrepreneurship data.

The second objective of the EDGE initiative was achieved through a multistakeholder approach involving national statistical agencies, researchers with relevant expertise, and regional and international agencies: United Nations Statistics Division, UN Women, Asian Development Bank (ADB), Food and Agriculture Organization of the United Nations, Organisation for Economic Co-operation and Development, and the World Bank. The methodology developed under the EDGE initiative was piloted in seven countries: Georgia, Maldives, Mexico, Mongolia, the Philippines, South Africa, and Uganda, and the experience gained from the conduct of pilot household surveys is being used by the UN Statistics Division to develop methodological guidelines on the collection of data on asset ownership and control from a gender perspective.

ADB provided technical and financial support for the implementation of the household Pilot Surveys on Measuring Asset Ownership and Entrepreneurship from a Gender Perspective in Georgia, Mongolia, and the Philippines using methodology developed under the EDGE initiative and adapted to the country context.[6] The project partners are the National Statistics Office of Georgia (GeoStat), National Statistics Office of Mongolia, Philippine Statistics Authority, and UN Statistics Division.

This section summarizes some of the preliminary findings and valuable lessons from the pilot surveys conducted by ADB and collaborating national statistical agencies.[7]

6 ADB. 2012. *Statistical Capacity Development for Social Inclusion and Gender Equality*. Manila (R-CDTA 8243).

7 Detailed final results of the initiative will be disseminated in a forthcoming publication. Survey questionnaires are available online and can be accessed through https://unstats.un.org/edge/

Box 7.1: SDGs and Women's Rights to Ownership and Control of Economic Resources

In September 2015, the General Assembly of the United Nations adopted the 2030 Agenda for Sustainable Development to end poverty, protect the planet, and ensure prosperity for all by building upon the achievements of the Millennium Development Goals. The 2030 Agenda comprises 17 Sustainable Development Goals and 169 targets. The 2030 Agenda recognizes that empowerment of women and girls through gender equality in ownership and control of economic resources among other measures is critical to achieving the vision set out in the 2030 Agenda. Explicit targets relating of economic ownership of assets in the SDGs are as follows:

> *SDG Target 1.4: By 2030, ensure that all men and women, particularly the poor and the vulnerable, have equal rights to economic resources, as well as access to basic services, ownership and control over land and other forms of property, inheritance, natural resources, appropriate new technology, and financial services, including microfinance.*
>
> *SDG 2 Target 2.3: By 2030, double the agricultural productivity and the incomes of small-scale food producers, in particular women, indigenous peoples, family farmers, pastoralists and fishers, including through secure and equal access to land, other productive resources and inputs, knowledge, financial services, markets and opportunities for value addition, and non-farm employment.*

On the other hand, SDG 5 (achieve gender equality and empower women and girls) recognizes gender equality as an intrinsic human right, and target 5.a notes that countries should ***"undertake reforms to give women equal rights to economic resources, as well as access to ownership and control over land and other forms of property, financial services, inheritance and natural resources, in accordance with national laws."*** Asset ownership and control by women and their security of tenure is central to the indicators for monitoring progress in target 5.a:

> *SDG Indicator 5.a.1: (a) Proportion of total agricultural population with ownership or secure rights over agricultural land, by sex; and (b) share of women among owners or rights-bearers of agricultural land, by type of tenure.*
>
> *SDG Indicator 5.a.2: Proportion of countries where the legal framework (including customary law) guarantees women's equal rights to land ownership and/or control.*

Asset Ownership and Control: A Gender Perspective

Figure 7.1 presents the EDGE conceptual framework for measuring asset ownership and control from a gender perspective, which guided the implementation of the pilot surveys. The framework maps out the different domains of information needed to be collected through the survey so that it can facilitate a comprehensive gender analysis of asset ownership and control.

What sets this framework apart is that the notion of asset ownership is deconstructed so there is a clear recognition that assets are held by individual household members and not by a notional household unit. This framework forces us to think about the ways in which gender intersects with how assets are acquired, what ownership means, and how these assets are used.

The left panel of Figure 7.1 suggests that any exploration of the gendered ownership of assets must be located within the specific country context with respect to social norms, inheritance laws, and marital regimes as these determine how men and women acquire assets. Social norms that delineate roles and responsibilities between men and women are important contextual factors that can affect the implementation of such laws as well as the effective use of and control over assets by women. Furthermore, countries with pluralistic legal regimes determine acquisition of assets and offer a diverse meaning of ownership across customary and statutory law.

The center panel of the EDGE framework illustrated in Figure 7.1 implies that ownership can be conceptualized as a bundle of rights that can vary according to the context and type of asset. The most frequently collected information from household surveys is **reported ownership** and is based on the

Figure 7.1: Conceptual Framework for Measuring Asset Ownership and Control from a Gender Perspective

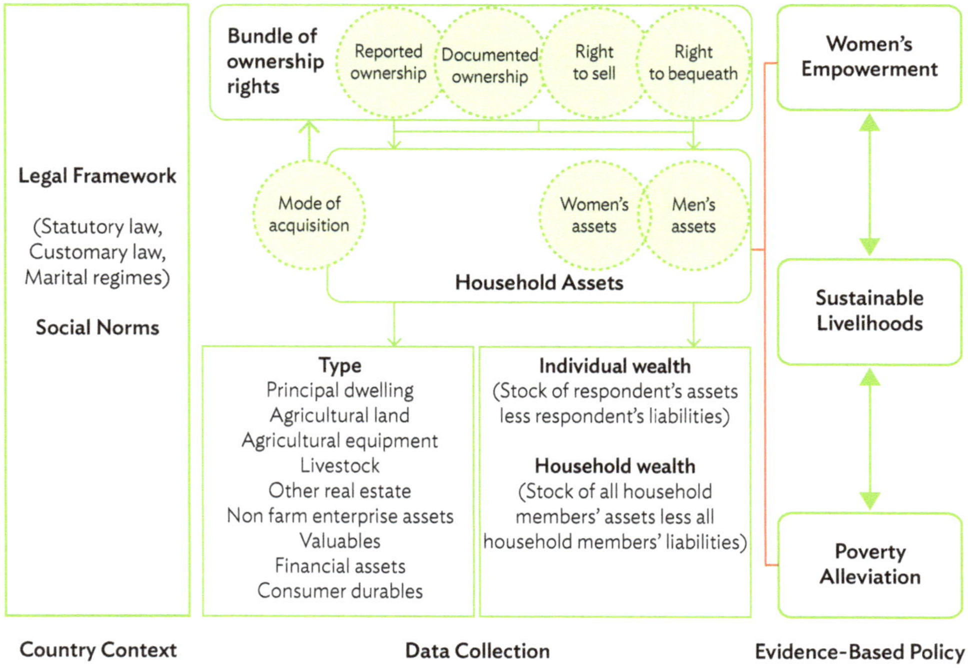

Source: United Nations. 2017. United Nations Methodological Guidelines on the Production of Statistics on Asset Ownership from a Gender Perspective. Draft presented to the Statistical Commission in its 48th Session, 7–10 March 2017.

respondent's assessment of who owns an asset. If individuals are asked only about the assets they own, then reported ownership reflects their self-perception of being owners or not. Reported ownership data can also be collected via proxy reporting (for example, when the head or most knowledgeable member of the household identifies all owners of a house or parcel of land). Both approaches are interesting from a bargaining power perspective, as a woman's bargaining power and empowerment may depend on whether she considers herself an owner of an asset and how she is perceived by other household members.

Documented ownership, on the other hand, is a more formalized concept where individuals can claim legal right over an asset by having their name listed on an ownership document. Examples of such documents include formal title deed, purchase agreement, and property tax records. The documentation requirements can vary across countries and sometimes, several supporting documents are necessary to prove ownership. Having one's name listed on a document can provide greater security of tenure in some situations.

The **right to alienate** an asset is also an important aspect of ownership. These are captured through the **right to sell** and the **right to bequeath**.

In many countries, particularly in Asia and Africa, the full bundle of rights may not be vested in one individual. Someone could be a reported owner, but not be listed on any ownership document. Gendered social norms could influence reporting of ownership; women may never be reported as owners even if the law allows them to own property. In some contexts, due to a tenure system where land is not owned but leased for 99 years or more, one may not possess the right to sell the property but can have the right to bequeath it to their children.

The framework also illustrates the diverse forms in which assets can be held, i.e., whether owned exclusively by an individual, or jointly with household or nonhousehold members. Joint ownership with spouses is the most typical, but joint ownership with parents, siblings, other family members, and nonfamily members is also possible. The form of ownership of an asset could be significant in explaining the bundle of rights. One would expect stronger alienation rights in individual ownership, whereas in joint ownership, the distribution of rights between the owners may be subject to negotiation or determined by the social context. This may have relevance in the context of gender analysis of asset ownership and rights.

Assets are acquired via the market, through state transfers, within marriage and/or consensual union, or through inheritance or gifts. A country's legal framework that governs inheritance and marital regimes interacts with prevalent social norms to promote or discriminate against women's asset ownership. Countries that do not legally discriminate between sons and daughters in terms of inheritance may still show a male bias in property transfer due to patriarchal traditions. The marital regime that regulates marital assets (or assets within a consensual union) affects how assets are owned, either individually or jointly. Three types of marital regimes are distinguished: separation of property, partial community property, and full community property.[8] Georgia and Mongolia follow the partial community property regime, while the Philippines follows the full community property regime. The main difference in these regimes is in the treatment of inherited property. In the full community property, inheritance is treated on par with marital assets; in partial community property, inheritance is kept separate from marital assets.

8 Under a separation of property regime, separate ownership of property brought into marriage and any property acquired and inherited during marriage is maintained. Under a partial community property regime, property acquired during marriage by either spouse is treated as joint property of both spouses. On the other hand, all individual property brought into, acquired, and inherited during marriage is treated as the joint property of both spouses under a full community property regime.

An asset in the EDGE framework is defined as "a store of value representing a benefit or a series of benefits accruing to the economic owner by holding or using the entity over a period of time," consistent with the 2008 System of National Accounts (SNA).

The EDGE surveys collected individual-level data on physical and financial assets, with a broader definition of physical assets than considered under the SNA approach. Data were collected on the following items: (i) dwelling, (ii) agricultural land, (iii) livestock, (iv) small and large agricultural equipment, (v) nonagricultural enterprise owned by household members and enterprise assets, (vi) other real estate, (vii) consumer durables, (viii) financial assets, (ix) liabilities, and (x) valuables. These items were chosen because they are important in crafting policies and programs that strengthen women's property rights and promote women's empowerment. Small agricultural equipment, and consumer durables are not considered assets under the 2008 SNA, but were included along with nonagricultural enterprises owned by household members in the EDGE pilots due to their importance for livelihoods, and overall individual and household well-being.

The surveys also collected valuation data on assets for two reasons. First, valuation data enables the calculation of individual wealth, an important component of well-being. It can enable an understanding of wealth inequality among individuals. Typically, wealth inequality is higher than consumption or income inequality as it represents accumulated assets over a period of time (OECD 2015). Second, valuation captures other attributes of an asset such as quality, size, location, and so on, which are missed by a numerical count of assets owned by men and women. Often, women own fewer assets relative to men. These assets may be of inferior quality. For example, women may own a few parcels of land with poorer soil quality. Since individual wealth is determined by quantity and quality of assets, these differences in ownership patterns may show a significant gender wealth gap that is not revealed when one compares data on men's and women's likelihood of owning assets. The respondents reported the value of their assets at current market price. Operationally, the collection of data on assets' values in the pilot survey posed severe challenges due to high levels of nonresponse to valuation-related questions.

Constructing Individual-Level Asset Ownership Estimates—Survey Methodology

The Georgia and Mongolia surveys (sample of 3,160 and 3,008 households, respectively) are nationally representative, while the Philippines survey (sample of 1,536 households) is representative for the province of Cavite only. The samples were selected following a two-stage stratified sampling design in Georgia and the Philippines, and a three-stage design in the case of Mongolia. Households within each selected primary sampling unit formed the succeeding sampling units.

A maximum of three adults 18 years of age or above were interviewed in each sampled household. A *primary respondent* was identified by the household members as the most knowledgeable member with respect to the household assets. The spouse or partner, if any, of the primary respondent formed the second respondent. The two together formed the principal couple. For households with three adult members or less, all adults were included in the sample. For households with more than three adult members, the two adults comprising the principal couple were selected with probability equal to one, and a third member was chosen randomly from the remaining adults. The total respondents interviewed were 5,937; 5,592, and 3,456 in Georgia, Mongolia, and Cavite, Philippines respectively. Table 7.1 summarizes the profile of the respondents based on the distribution of sex, marital status, and educational level.

Table 7.1: Percentage Distribution of Respondents by Sex, Marital Status, and Educational Level

Key sociodemographic variables	Georgia	Mongolia	Cavite, Philippines
Sex			
Male	42.1	44.5	46.4
Female	57.9	55.5	53.6
Marital Status			
Married	66.1	71.3	67.7
Widowed/Separated/Divorced	19.3	13.9	11.5
Never married	14.6	14.8	20.8
Educational level			
Primary or lower	3.2	26.9	17.2
Secondary	43.4	45.3	46.4
Post secondary nontertiary	24.5	n.a.	n.a.
Tertiary or above	29.0	27.7	36.4

n.a. = not applicable.

Source: Asian Development Bank estimates using Evidence and Data for Gender Equality pilot surveys.

A methodological innovation of the EDGE pilots was the construction of individual-level asset ownership estimates once such data were collected. Each respondent was asked to provide individual ownership information of all assets owned either exclusively or jointly with others by each adult member of the household, including those held by themselves. The interview protocol required interviews to be conducted separately and simultaneously to prevent any bias due to information sharing among the respondents. Based on this information, individual asset ownership was analyzed and estimated following two approaches: self-assigned ownership (SAO) and ownership assigned by any respondent (OAAR).

The SAO approach considers only those assets that are owned by the respondents themselves. Thus, the information provided by the respondent on assets owned by other members of the household and in which she or he does not have a stake is ignored. The SAO approach is premised on the notion that individuals have the most accurate knowledge about the assets they themselves own.

The OAAR method aggregates information from all respondents to arrive at a universe of asset owners for all household assets. It is the most inclusive approach to identifying owners. A household member is treated as an owner as long as he or she is reported as an owner by at least one respondent. This is closer to conventional household surveys that allow for proxy reporting by one respondent, but is different in that there is more than one respondent per household. Thus, the expectation would be that ownership information is more diffused across household members than what is obtained with one proxy respondent.

Another interesting perspective to the survey methodology was to collect information from self-assigned owners about "hidden assets," i.e., assets that the respondent owns, but has not been revealed to other household members. A large proportion of hidden assets can bias the estimates of asset ownership. It also reflects a fear of appropriation of assets or loss of control over assets, which provides insights into the larger institutional context of asset ownership.

Obviously, estimates of asset ownership will vary depending on the approach to data collection, and the data collected from the EDGE pilot surveys in the three countries also provide an opportunity to see a comparative picture or divergence in the estimates from these two approaches of calculating individual asset ownership estimates. These questions—how many people to interview in a household, whom to interview, should there be proxy reporting or self-reporting of information on asset ownership—are important considerations for survey design.

Key Results from the Surveys in Georgia, Mongolia, and Cavite, Philippines

This section presents the main findings from the EDGE pilots such as trends and patterns in asset ownership and control for men and women, and how these assets are acquired. These are examined using a gender lens, highlighting gender disparities in the asset domain.

Three sets of indicators summarized by sex and other sociodemographic characteristics—incidence of asset ownership, distribution of form of ownership, and the gender wealth gap—were generated to understand inequalities in asset ownership from a gender perspective. Indicators on incidence and distribution of asset ownership were calculated for all assets covered in the pilot surveys, while the gender wealth gap was computed only for the dwelling.

The EDGE surveys also obtained information on **forms of ownership** by sex (whether an asset is owned exclusively or jointly) and **modes of acquisition**, also by sex. These may impact the rights that owners, especially women, can wield over assets. The discussion below focuses on estimates based on the SAO approach and are calculated for individuals 18 years and above. However, a comparison of estimates for incidence of asset ownership using SAO and OAAR approaches is also presented.

Incidence of Asset Ownership: Reported and Documented

The incidence measure tells us what percentage of the total adult population, by sex, are asset owners. The incidence gap or the gender asset gap is the difference in ownership rates between men and women. Figure 7.2 presents the reported and documented incidence by sex for immovable property (these are high-valued and are also likely to be income-generating assets) across the three countries. The dwelling is an important asset and is widely owned as reflected in the reported ownership numbers: by 80% of men and 76% of women in Georgia, by 60% of men and 33% of women in Mongolia, and by 34% of men and equal proportion of women in Cavite. The incidence measure for dwellings shows the highest gender gap for Mongolia, almost no gap for Cavite, and only a 5 percentage points difference for Georgia. This ranking of countries is maintained for documented ownership as well, though the proportion of men and women with documents is significantly lower, suggesting that many reported owners do not have their names on documents. This is particularly stark for Georgia where documented owners are about half of reported owners.

Figure 7.2: Incidence of Ownership of Select Assets
(%)

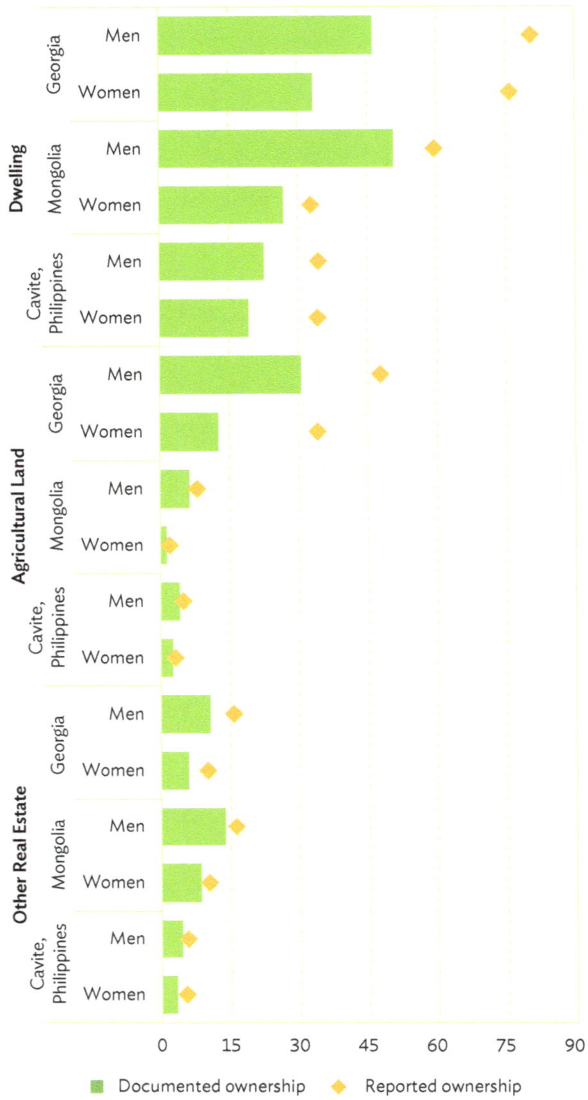

Source: Asian Development Bank estimates using Evidence and Data for Gender Equality pilot surveys.

The incidence of ownership of agricultural land is much lower in Mongolia and Cavite compared to Georgia. Landownership is less than 5% in Cavite and reflects the relatively urban nature of Cavite province. In Mongolia, landownership is only 8% and 2% for men and women, respectively, but much higher in Georgia at 48% and 34% for men and women, respectively. The relatively low proportion of land ownership in Mongolia is presumably due to the communal nature of land and the relatively high proportion of landownership in Georgia is mainly due to the receipt of private land by rural households after the collapse of the Soviet Union. The absolute gender gaps in incidence are of course smaller; however, the pattern of gender disparity in ownership is similar to that of the dwelling unit.

Among the immovable assets for which data are collected through the survey, the asset with the highest prevalence of ownership varies by sex and by country. The incidence of ownership is highest for the dwelling unit for men and women in Georgia (80% and 76%, respectively) but only for men in Mongolia (60%). At 36% for women in Mongolia and 51% and 44% for men and women, respectively, in Cavite, it is small agricultural equipment that has the highest ownership rate. Interestingly, livestock is held by almost 40% of men and women in Georgia, and is more commonly owned by men in the other two countries. Documented ownership rates are lower in all countries, with not much of a difference between reported and documented in Mongolia and Cavite, and ranging from 4 to 43 percentage points in Georgia.

Other real estate refers to residential and nonresidential buildings other than dwelling and nonagricultural land. Within the category of immovable property, real estate ownership is lowest in Georgia. In Mongolia and Cavite, it is higher than ownership of agricultural land, but lower than ownership of dwelling. Men and women are equally likely to own real estate in Cavite while in Georgia and Mongolia, there is a gender gap of less than 5 percentage points.

Figure 7.3 presents the incidence of assets other than immovable property summarized by sex. Ownership of large agricultural equipment is almost negligible in Mongolia and Cavite; but it is not uncommon to hold small agricultural equipment. Low ownership of large agricultural equipment could be due to low ownership of agricultural land, and often, farmers will rent the equipment due to their high costs of acquisition. The module on small agricultural equipment was not implemented in Georgia as small agricultural equipment tends

Figure 7.3: Incidence of Reported Ownership of Select Assets (%)

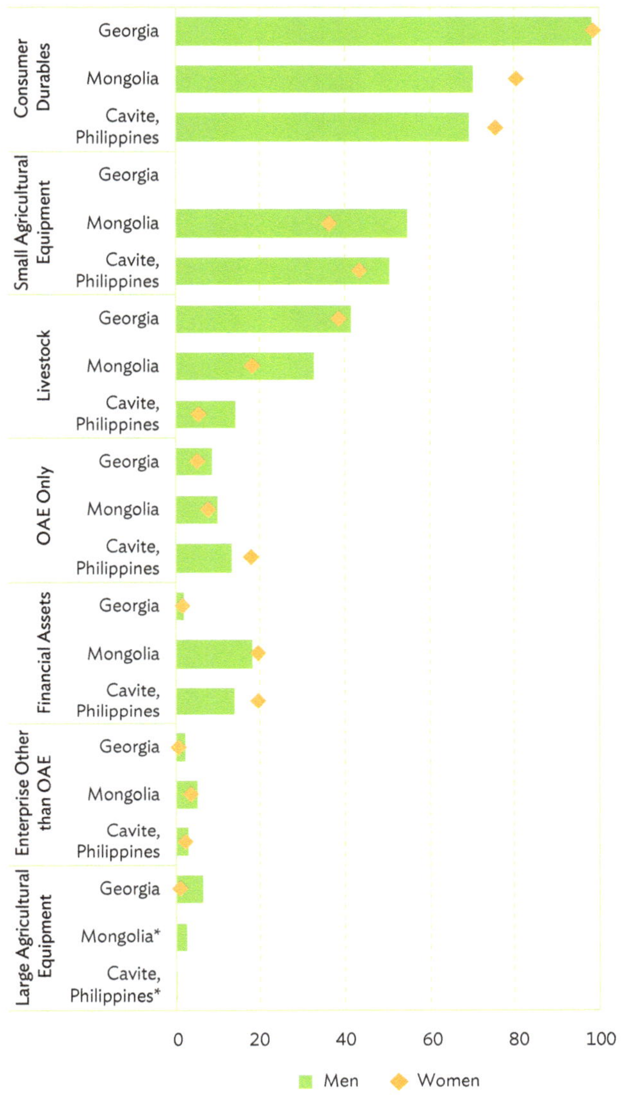

OAE = own-account enterprise.
Note: * Corresponds with fewer than 25 observations and thus may not be sufficient for data analysis.
Source: Asian Development Bank estimates using Evidence and Data for Gender Equality pilot surveys.

to be owned by all household members. However, ownership pattern among men and women seems more distinct for large agricultural equipment, with only 1% of Georgian women owning such equipment compared to 6% of Georgian men. Approximately 40% of both men and women adult population in Georgia own livestock; whereas at 33% for men and 18% for women, the gender gap in ownership is highest in Mongolia.

Overall, the incidence of ownership of nonagricultural enterprises is low for both men and women and concentrated in the own-account enterprises—defined as those with no paid workers but possibly employing (unpaid) contributing family workers—suggesting that these are fairly small operations. Interestingly, in Cavite, the gender gap is reversed in favor of women for own-account enterprises, but not for enterprises that employ at least one paid worker.

As expected, the incidence of ownership of consumer durables is highest among all assets in all the three countries, with overall incidence in favor of women. On the other hand, the results suggest that women are slightly more likely to own financial assets than men in Mongolia and Cavite.[9]

Comparing overall trends, men are more likely to be owners of assets than women in all three countries. On average, the gender gap in incidence is highest in Mongolia for most assets and lowest in Cavite. Focusing on immovable property, men in Mongolia are twice as likely as women to own their dwellings, four times as likely to own land, and a little more than one-and-a-half times as likely to own other real estate.

The incidence of hidden physical assets was observed to be less than 2% in all three countries with the exception of financial assets and liabilities. Mongolia shows the lowest proportion of hidden financial assets and liabilities; the highest incidence is in Georgia for financial assets; while Cavite is highest for liabilities, though still less than 5%. The gender gaps in the proportion of hidden assets are not substantive, with the maximum gap being 4 percentage points for financial assets in Mongolia.

[9] The estimates of incidence of ownership of financial asset are lower than expected. This finding could be attributed to the limitations on how the concept of financial assets was conceptualized in the survey instruments. Further investigation is needed to be able to understand this issue.

Lastly, comparing SAO and OAAR, the results suggest that the estimates of the incidence of reported and documented ownership are generally higher using the OAAR approach but there are variations across asset types, sex, and country. On average, these differences are small, less than 5 percentage points in most instances, barring a few. Georgia shows the largest difference for reported and documented ownership, where the self-assigned approach gives lower estimates for dwelling and agricultural land incidence rates for men and women (Figure 7.4). Rather surprisingly, reported and documented ownership for Mongolian men using the self-assigned approach is higher by 5 and 3 percentage points, respectively, suggesting a lack of information sharing within the household on such matters.

On the other hand, the trends in gender disparities in ownership do not change. A larger proportion of men are more likely to own dwelling and agricultural land compared to women, with the greatest disparities in Mongolia, and almost negligible in Cavite.

Figure 7.4: Comparison of Estimates of Incidence of Ownership of Select Assets Using Self-Assigned Ownership and Ownership Assigned by Any Respondent Approaches (%)

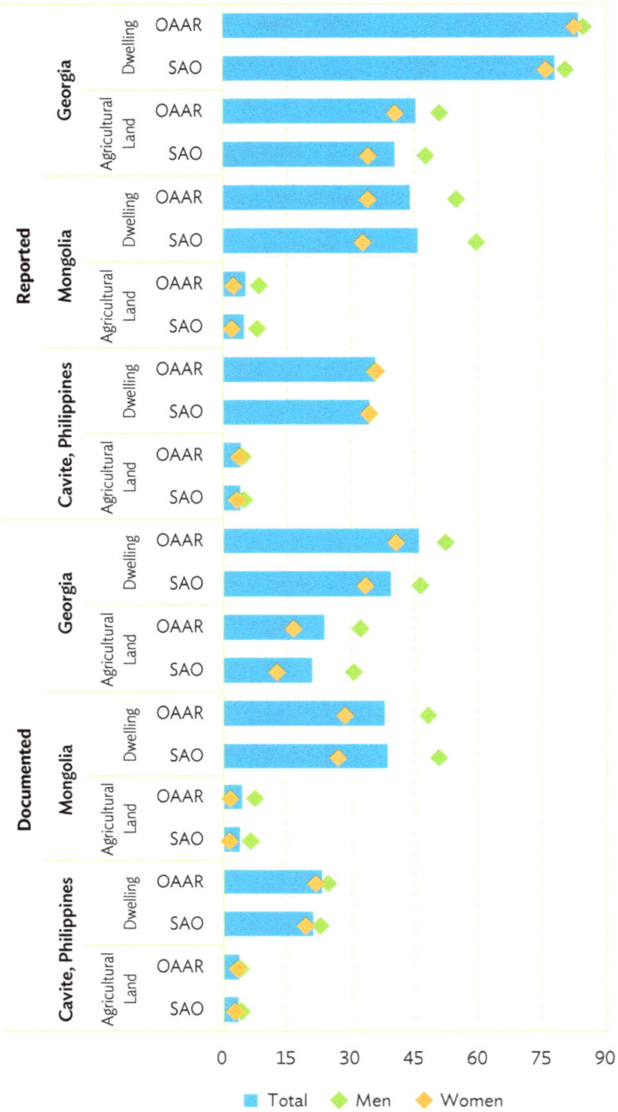

OAAR = ownership assigned by any respondent, SAO = self-assigned ownership.
Source: Asian Development Bank estimates using Evidence and Data for Gender Equality pilot surveys.

Gender Wealth Gap

There are a couple of advantages to the incidence indicator. For one, data for it are relatively easy to collect. For another, it lends itself to easy interpretation: what proportion of the population by sex are homeowners or owners of agricultural land? There is, however, information that incidence indicators cannot provide. For example, incidence indicators mask variations in the quantity owned, say, of agricultural land. In computing for proportions, an individual with 10 hectares of land is treated equally as an individual with 0.5 hectares of land. In addition, incidence indicators also do not reveal the quality of the asset in question. In such cases, the gender wealth gap complements the gender incidence gap. Following other surveys, valuation in the EDGE pilots was based on current sale price where respondents were asked to value the asset if it were to be sold on the date of the interview.

However, there are several challenges associated with the collection of valuation data and construction of wealth indicators. Depending on the asset and the context, it may be difficult to obtain valuation data due to missing markets, lack of awareness of the respondent regarding markets prices, or simply reluctance to share sensitive financial information.

These lead to a high proportion of missing values, which might render the data less reliable or unusable. Considering the dwelling example, the EDGE pilots show some variation in the proportion of missing values. On average, women are less likely than men to provide a value for their dwelling. At 15% for men and 18% for women, the nonresponse for dwelling valuation is lowest in Mongolia, followed by Cavite (48% for men and 60% for women); then Georgia (65% for men and 72% for women). Obviously, the nonresponse rates for valuation of dwelling in Cavite and Georgia are very high for both men and women and therefore any estimates using this data will be subject to limitations. Unsurprisingly, there are more missing values for agricultural land than dwelling. The trends for men and women's responses across the three countries are similar to that of valuation of the dwelling unit. Imputation of missing values is a possibility, but it requires information on asset characteristics that may be correlated with its value.

Figure 7.5: Share of Men and Women in Total Value of Dwellings (%)

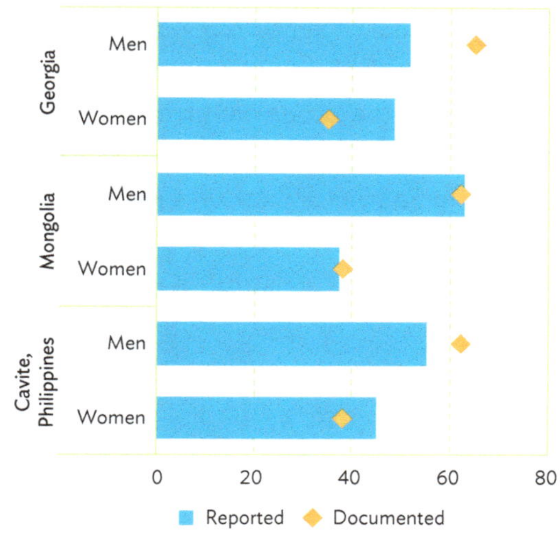

Notes: Estimates are weighted and calculated based on self-assigned ownership approach. The share of men and women owners in the population corresponds to owners who have reported and documented values of dwellings and excludes owners who are nonhousehold members. Philippines refers to the province of Cavite.

Source: Asian Development Bank estimates using Evidence and Data for Gender Equality pilot surveys.

Another aspect to valuation is that once data is obtained, it is important to ensure that there is no double counting of assets. For example, if an asset is jointly owned, the value of the asset must be apportioned among all the owners, equally or in the same ratio as indicated by the ownership share.

Keeping these caveats on data in mind, we now consider the gender wealth gap for the dwelling unit based on the self-assigned ownership of assets (Figure 7.5).[10] Looking at the wealth shares based on reported ownership of dwelling, in no country is women's share of dwelling wealth greater than 50%. At 49%, it is almost equal in Georgia, followed by Cavite at 45% and Mongolia at 37%. Contrasting women's share of wealth to their share of owners provides some insights. In Georgia and Cavite, women represent more than half of all reported dwelling owners (53% and 51%, respectively), but their share of dwelling wealth is lower than 50%, suggesting that the dwellings owned by women may be less valuable than those owned by men. Figure 7.5 also presents wealth shares calculated based on documented ownership. Compared with reported ownership, the gap becomes more pronounced for documented ownership in Georgia and Cavite, while it is more or less same in Mongolia.

Mode of Acquisition

As earlier illustrated in the conceptual framework (Figure 7.1), men and women acquire their assets in several ways, an understanding of which can help in addressing gender inequalities in asset ownership. For the dwelling unit, the market is the dominant means of asset acquisition for women in Mongolia (48%) and Cavite (50%), whereas women in Georgia are most likely to acquire it through marriage or custom (39%), followed by purchase (32%). The pattern is similar for men who are most likely to purchase their dwelling in Mongolia and Cavite, but about 45% of men owners receive it as a gift from a household member in Georgia. At 34%, purchase is the second most prevalent means of acquiring a dwelling

10 Although wealth gap between men and women can be calculated for other types of assets, there are technical issues associated with doing such calculations. Thus, we focus on dwelling only.

for male owners in Georgia. Inheritance, whether natal or marital, while not totally unimportant, is also not a typical means of acquiring a dwelling; at 15%, inheritance is relatively more important for women in Cavite than in the other countries. The patterns are largely similar for male inheritance. Between 10% to 15% of male and female owners are beneficiaries of government programs in Mongolia and Cavite. On the other hand, nonagricultural enterprises were mostly founded directly by the respondents and no substantial difference is observed between men and women (Figure 7.6).

In general, with regard to dwellings, EDGE results suggest that the modes of acquisition are not gender-biased in Cavite. On the contrary, in Mongolia, markets and marital custom are slightly biased toward women, while inheritance shows a slight male bias. In Georgia, one finds more significant gender biases. Women are less likely than men to inherit or receive a gift from household members, but more likely to acquire via marital law and custom.

The mode of acquisition of agricultural land shows greater variation between countries, but is more similar for men and women within countries. For both men and women, the dominant means to acquire land is through purchases in Georgia (43% and 36%, respectively); via government programs in Mongolia (57% and 45%, respectively); and through inheritance in the Philippines (39% and 42%, respectively), which is almost fully comprised of natal family inheritance. Among the three countries, purchase of land is least common in Mongolia, presumably due to the communal nature of land. Acquisition within marriage or custom is the second most prevalent means for Georgian women, while it is natal inheritance[11] for women in Mongolia, and purchasing for women in Cavite. It is worth noting that unlike Georgia and Mongolia, there is no gender bias in market participation in Cavite, with about 30% of men and women purchasing their agricultural land.

11 The ranking excludes acquisition classified under "others" category.

Figure 7.6: Distribution of Mode of Acquisition of Select Assets (%)

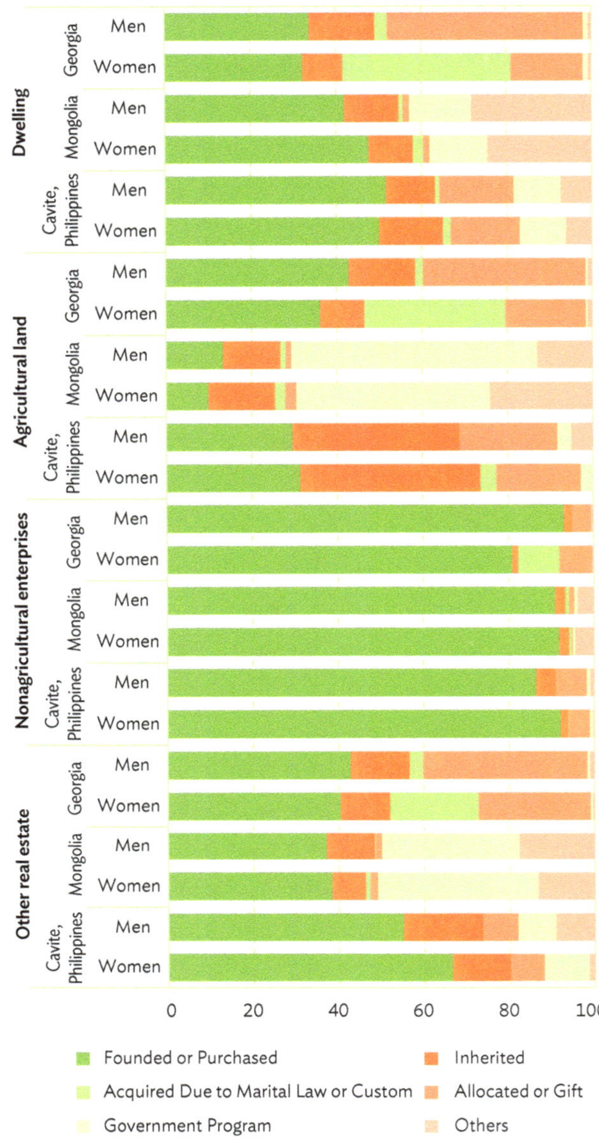

Note: Inherited combines natal and non-natal family members; allocated combines household and nonhousehold members; and others combines encroachment, "do not know", and other responses. "Founded" relates to nonagricultural enterprises only.

Source: Asian Development Bank estimates using Evidence and Data for Gender Equality pilot surveys.

Purchase is the dominant mode of acquisition for other real estate in all three countries, with similar levels between men and women within each country. Cavite is the exception, with a greater proportion of women purchasing property than men (67% versus 55%). In line with the patterns observed for other property (dwelling and agricultural land), the second most prevalent means of acquiring other real estate is marital law and custom for Georgian women (but not for men who acquire through allocation or gift from household members); government allocations for men and women in Mongolia (32% and 38%, respectively); and natal inheritance for men and women in the Philippines (18% and 11%, respectively).

There seems to be no male bias in inheritance in Cavite; in fact, for dwelling and agricultural land, women are more likely to inherit than men. In Georgia, women are purchasing immovable property, but there is also a substantive proportion of women who acquire their assets within the institution of marriage, reflecting the importance of the partial community of marriage regime followed in that country.

Figure 7.7: Distribution of Forms of Asset Ownership (%)

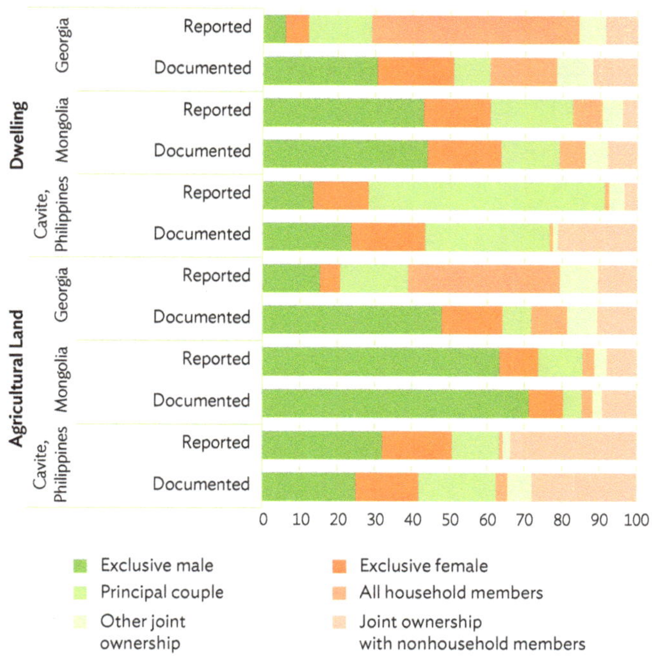

Source: Asian Development Bank estimates using Evidence and Data for Gender Equality pilot surveys.

Forms of Ownership and Alienation Rights over Assets

Asset incidence measures, while providing a sense of the prevalence of asset ownership by men and women, do not reveal any information on whether the asset is owned exclusively or jointly owned with one or more individuals. The forms of ownership are influenced by inheritance and marital regimes, which in turn impact the bundle of ownership rights (Figure 7.1). Figure 7.7 presents different forms of ownership by sex for dwelling and agricultural land in Georgia, Mongolia, and Cavite.

For dwelling owners, there is no variation in trend (except for Georgia) between reported and documented ownership. In Mongolia, exclusive male owners are dominant (43% and 44% for reported and documented, respectively), while in Cavite, ownership by the principal couple is the most prevalent 63% and 33% for reported and documented, respectively. This partly reflects the Philippines's full community of property marital regime whereby marital assets are treated as joint, whether inherited or acquired. In Georgia, all household members are the dominant category as reported owners (55%), but this moves to exclusive male owners for documented ownership (31%), suggesting that the perception of ownership is more inclusive than the documented reality (Figure 7.7).

Agricultural land shows more variation between reported and documented ownership. Reported ownership by all household members (40%) is most common in Georgia. In Mongolia and Cavite, men are most likely to be exclusive owners. Reported and documented ownership with nonhousehold members is also common in Cavite, reflecting the relatively urban nature of Cavite province, with urban households co-owning agricultural land in rural areas with extended family members. (Recall from Figure 7.2 that less than 5% of the adult population in Cavite owns any agricultural land.) Similar with Georgia, the proportion of exclusive male owners is higher for documented than reported dwelling owners in Mongolia, and mainly comes at the expense of women as exclusive owners, and principal couple owners. On average, the gender gap in exclusive ownership is highest in Mongolia for reported and documented owners of immovable property and is also high for documented ownership for agricultural land in Georgia.

Gender differences in alienation rights over assets, selling, or bequeathing as depicted in Figures 7.8 and 7.9 are quite stark across the three countries, and to a certain extent, mirror the forms of ownership. Male owners are more likely to have stronger alienation rights than female owners as to sale and bequeathing of assets. The dwelling is the most commonly held asset across countries, where the right of sale for men and women, respectively, are 90% versus 80% in Georgia, 97% versus 90% in Mongolia, and 93% versus 88% in Cavite (Figure 7.8).

A larger proportion of Mongolian men and women owners have exclusive alienation rights over sale and bequeathing compared to owners in the other countries. For example, nearly three-quarters of Mongolian male owners have exclusive rights to bequeath their dwelling compared to 25% and 38% for men in Georgia and Cavite, respectively. Similar trends are observed with women owners as well in Mongolia. About 52% have an exclusive right to

Figure 7.8: Distribution of Rights to Sell of Select Assets (%)

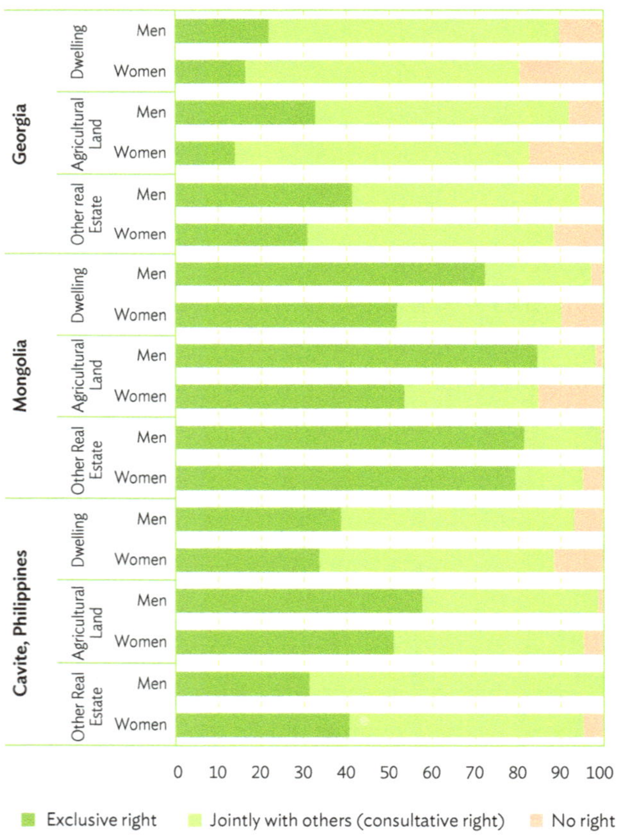

Note: The number of observation for large agricultural equipment is too small to facilitate comparison of categories of right to sell. Detailed information on the number of observations can be found at https://www.adb.org/sites/default/files/publication/357006/sdgedge-fig-7-8.xlsx

Source: Asian Development Bank estimates using Evidence and Data for Gender Equality pilot surveys.

Figure 7.9: Distribution of Rights to Bequeath of Select Assets (%)

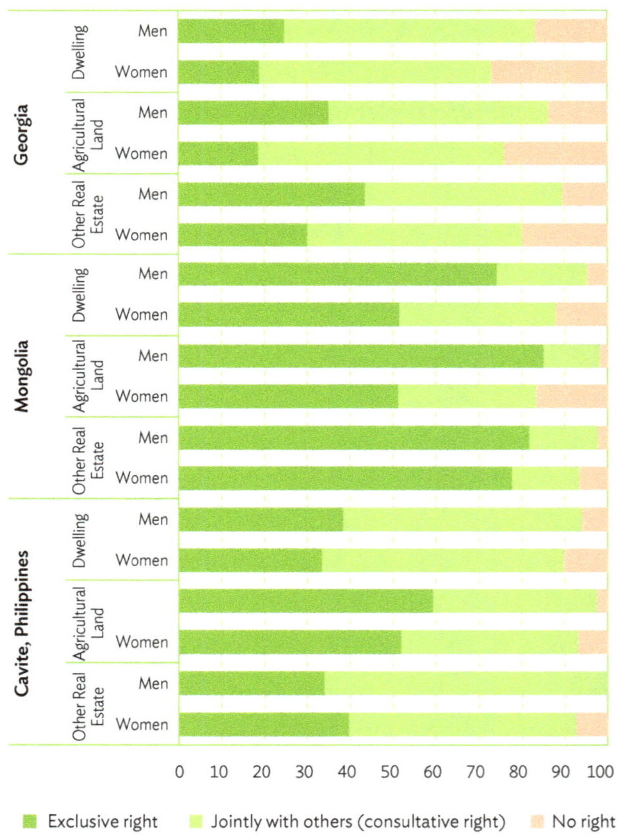

Note: The number of observation for large agricultural equipment is too small to facilitate comparison of categories of right to bequeath. Detailed information on the number of observations can be found at https://www.adb.org/sites/default/files/publication/357006/sdgedge-fig-7-9.xlsx

Source: Asian Development Bank estimates using EDGE pilot surveys.

bequeath their dwelling, compared to 19% and 34% in Georgia and Cavite, respectively (Figure 7.9). This can be related to the relatively strong individual ownership patterns that are evident among Mongolian men and women.

Within Mongolia however, the proportion of female owners with no rights of alienation is higher than the proportion of male owners with no rights, reflecting a gender bias against women owners. It is Georgian women though, who seem the most disadvantaged compared with Mongolian and Cavite women owners in terms of having no economic rights over their assets. Almost one-fifth of women owners do not have any right to sell their dwelling or land, while a quarter do not have any bequeathing rights over these assets. Further, the results suggest that consulting rights are more prevalent in Georgia for both men and women. This could presumably be due to how the asset was acquired. Allocation or gifts from household members is the dominant mode for men, while women acquire due to custom, or within the marriage, or from household members, which could possibly explain why economic decisions regarding these assets are either taken consultatively, or with women are excluded.

Women in Cavite, on the other hand, are more likely to have purchased their immoveable property or inherited it from their natal family, which ensures that they are not deprived of their economic rights over their assets. On average, the proportion of owners in Cavite with no rights to sell or bequeath their assets is largely smaller than those in the other countries. The survey results suggest that exploring how men and women acquire and own assets provides a perspective to the enjoyment of rights over these assets (Figures 7.8 and 7.9).

Summary

Collecting sex-disaggregated data on asset ownership is a critical step in building evidence toward bridging inequalities with respect to women's access to and control over productive resources. The lack of comparable national-level data on men and women's asset ownership using standard concepts is a serious constraint in shaping policy and programs that promote gender equality.

Even as absence of standardized methodological approaches for collecting individual-level asset data has been a constraint, these data are typically not collected by national statistical agencies for several reasons: time taken to administer the survey, financial and technical capacity constraints, cultural notions of how property or assets may be owned, and so on. The EDGE pilot surveys in Georgia, Mongolia, and the Philippines conducted by national statistics offices are powerful case studies as they have demonstrated that with the availability of standardized methods and guidelines, such data collection is feasible. The key contribution of the three pilot surveys is the development of methodological guidelines by the United Nations Statistics Division efforts under the global EDGE initiative for collecting such data. These guidelines are grounded in field experience, and with minimal adaptation can be applied across diverse geographies and social contexts. The methodological and practical experience through the three pilot surveys under ADB's project along with other methodological surveys and approaches piloted in Maldives, Mexico, South Africa, and Uganda also under EDGE initiative provide a solid basis for finalizing the United Nations methodological guidelines on the production of statistics on asset ownership from a gender perspective.

It is important to reiterate a few valuable lessons learned through these pilot surveys. First, one needs a basket of indicators (incidence, distribution, forms, wealth) to undertake a comprehensive gender analysis of asset ownership. Depending on what is being examined, the objectives of data collection can be defined while being cognizant of its strengths and limitations. Second, with clarity on survey objectives and information needs, it is possible to prioritize an indicator or set of indicators and decide data collection, i.e., the survey design, survey questionnaires, and sampling methodology. Third, collection of valuation data through household surveys is challenging. It may be necessary to supplement survey data with other administrative information, or to plan ahead for imputation of missing data.

The pilot surveys have produced an extremely rich data on asset ownership and control at the individual level and provided valuable lessons for the methodological guidelines for data collection. For this initiative to become part of statistical program of national statistics agencies and sustainable in the long term, both data producers and data users—have to work together. There has to be a conscious effort to ensure that such data is produced regularly, is of the highest quality, and is disseminated in a timely fashion. It is also incumbent on policy makers, researchers, and the larger development community to utilize such data to monitor the progress of and advocate for gender equality in the economic sphere.

References

D. Ali, K. Deininger, and M. Goldstein. 2011. Environmental and Gender Impacts of Land Tenure Regularization in Africa: Pilot evidence from Rwanda. *World Bank Policy Research Working Paper*. No. 5765. Washington, DC. https://openknowledge.worldbank.org/handle/10986/3527

Asian Development Bank (ADB). 2016. *Key Indicators for Asia and the Pacific 2016*. Manila. http://www.adb.org/sites/default/files/publication/204091/ki2016.pdf

J. Bonilla, et al. 2017. Cash for Women's Empowerment? A Mixed-Methods Evaluation of the Government of Zambia's Child Grant Program. *World Development*. 95 (C). pp. 55–72. http://www.sciencedirect.com/science/article/pii/S0305750X15311682

C. Deere, G. Alvarado, and J. Twyman. 2012. Gender Inequality in Asset Ownership in Latin America: Female Owners vs Household Heads. *Development and Change*. 43 (2). pp. 505–530. http://onlinelibrary.wiley.com/doi/10.1111/j.1467-7660.2012.01764.x/full

C. Doss. 2006. The Effects of Intrahousehold Property Ownership on Expenditure Patterns in Ghana. *Journal of African Economies*. 15(1). pp. 149–180. https://www.researchgate.net/publication/5212968_The_Effects_of_Intrahousehold_Property_Ownership_on_Expenditure_Patterns_in_Ghana

S. Garikipati. 2009. Landless But Not Assetless: Female Agricultural Labour on the Road to Better Status, Evidence from India. *Journal of Peasant Studies*. 36 (3). pp 517–545. https://www.researchgate.net/publication/248943632_Landless_But_Not_Assetless_Female_Agricultural_Labour_on_the_Road_to_Better_Status_Evidence_from_India

M. Goldstein and C. Udry. 2008. The Profits of Power: Land Rights and Agricultural Investment in Ghana. *Journal of Political Economy*. 116(6) pp. 981–1022. Chicago: University of Chicago Press. http://siteresources.worldbank.org/INTPUBSERV/Resources/477250118600763 4742/GoldsteinProfitsofPower.pdf

N. Nour. 2009. Child Marriage: A Silent Health and Human Rights Issue. *Reviews in Obstetrics and Gynecology*. 2 (1). pp. 51–56. https://www.ncbi.nlm.nih.gov/pmc/articles/PMC2672998/

A. Oduro and H.A. Seshie-Nasser. 2016. Delayed Primary School Enrolment among Boys and Girls in Ghana. *International Journal of Educational Development*. 49. pp. 107–114. http://www.sciencedirect.com/science/article/pii/S0738059315300304

Organisation for Economic Co-operation and Development. 2015. Household Wealth Inequality across OECD Countries: New OECD Evidence. *OECD Statistics Brief*. https://www.

oecd.org/std/householdwealth-inequality-across-OECD-countries-OECDSB21.pdf

P. Panda and B. Agarwal. 2007. Toward Freedom from Domestic Violence: The Neglected Obvious. *Journal of Human Development*. 8 (3). pp. 359–388. https://www.amherst.edu/media/view/92083/original/freedom%20from%20domestic%20violence.pdf

A. Peterman, et al. 2011. Understanding the Complexities Surrounding Gender Differences in Agricultural Productivity in Nigeria and Uganda. *The Journal of Development Studies*. 4(10). pp. 1482–1509. http://www.tandfonline.com/doi/abs/10.1080/00220388.2010.536222

A. Quisumbing and J. Maluccio. 2000. *Intrahousehold Allocation and Gender Relations*. FCND Briefs. No. 84. Washington, DC: International Food Policy Research Institute. http://ageconsearch.umn.edu/record/15932/files/dp00084b.pdf

H. Swaminathan, J. Suchitra, and R. Lahoti. 2011. *Karnataka Household Asset Survey: Measuring the Gender Asset Gap*. Bangalore. Indian Institute of Management Bangalore. http://genderassetgap.org/sites/default/files/KHAS.MeasuringGenderAssetGap.2011.pdf

J. Twyman, P. Useche, and C. Deere. 2015. Gendered Perceptions of Land Ownership and Agricultural Decision-Making in Ecuador: Who are the Farm Managers? *Land Economics*. 91 (3). pp. 479–500. http://le.uwpress.org/content/91/3/479.full.pdf+html

United Nations. 1948. *Universal Declaration of Human Rights*. http://www.ohchr.org/EN/UDHR/Documents/UDHR_Translations/eng.pdf

United Nations. 2013. *Fundamental Principles of Official Statistics*. https://unstats.un.org/unsd/dnss/gp/FP-Rev2013-E.pdf

United Nations. 2015. *Transforming Our World: The 2030 Agenda for Sustainable Development*. http://www.un.org/ga/search/view_doc.asp?symbol=A/RES/70/1&Lang=E

United Nations Economic and Social Commission for Asia and the Pacific (UN ESCAP). 2015. *Statistical Yearbook for Asia and the Pacific 2015*. United Nations: New York. http://www.unescap.org/sites/default/files/SYB2015_Full_Publication.pdf

United Nations Economic and Social Commission for Asia and the Pacific (UN ESCAP). 2016. *Statistical Yearbook for Asia and the Pacific 2016: SDG Baseline Report*. United Nations: New York. http://www.unescap.org/sites/default/files/publications/ESCAP_SYB2016_SDG_baseline_report.pdf

United Nations Department of Economic and Social Affairs (UN DESA). 2015. *World Urbanization Prospects 2014 Revision*. United Nations: New York. https://esa.un.org/unpd/wup/Publications/Files/WUP2014-Report.pdf

United Nations Department of Economic and Social Affairs (UN DESA). 2007. *Proportion of Urban Population Living in Slums*. http://www.un.org/esa/sustdev/natlinfo/indicators/methodology_sheets/poverty/urban_slums.pdf

United Nations Department of Economic and Social Affairs (UN DESA). 2017. *Cape Town Global Action Plan for Sustainable Development Data*. United Nations: New York. https://undataforum.org/WorldDataForum/wpcontent/uploads/2017/01/Cape-Town-Action-Plan-For-Data-Jan2017.pdf

R. Vijaya, R. Lahoti, and H. Swaminathan. 2014. Moving from the Household to the Individual: Multidimensional Poverty Analysis. *World Development*. 59. pp. 70–81. https://doi.org/10.1016/j.worlddev.2014.01.029

PART II

Regional Trends and Tables

Introduction to the Regional Tables and Trends

The 2017 issue of *Key Indicators for Asia and the Pacific* features 98 statistical tables summarizing regional trends in social, economic, and environmental developments in member economies of the Asian Development Bank (ADB) in Asia and the Pacific. The statistical tables and their commentaries are divided into eight themes: People; Economy and Output; Money, Finance, and Prices; Globalization; Transport and Communications; Energy and Electricity; Environment; and Government and Governance.

Each theme is accompanied by a brief description of trends highlighting important recent developments observed in select indicators. Visualizations of data patterns are summarized through charts and figures that compare indicators for ADB member economies for the latest year available (e.g., 2016). Often, indicators for the latest year are also compared with the previous year (e.g., 2015) or with an earlier year (e.g., 2000 or 2005) in order to identify regional, subregional, and economy-level trends.

People highlights demographic trends in terms of the size and growth of the population; age dependency ratios; urbanization, employment; health and education resources; and the Human Development Index. The section also contains statistics on birth, death, and fertility rates; poverty and inequality; and international migration.

Economy and Output presents tables and charts on gross domestic product (GDP) levels and growth; related statistics taken from the national accounts such as gross national income, value added, consumption expenditure, capital formation, exports and imports, and gross domestic saving; and production indicators. This theme compares the relative size of economies both within the region and in the world using data on GDP expressed in purchasing power parity (PPP) terms. This section also discusses trends in external trade and domestic consumption.

Money, Finance, and Prices summarizes the latest statistics on inflation and other monetary and financial statistics. These include data on money supply, interest rates, bank lending, official exchange rates, and stock markets.

Globalization focuses on external trade, balance of payments, international reserves, capital flows, external indebtedness, and tourism. This theme discusses trends in merchandise exports and imports; the increasing importance of services exports in some regional economies; remittances from migrant workers, which are significant sources of income for many economies in the region; net official loans and grants; and net private capital flows. More detailed statistical tables on global value chains are provided in Part III.

Transport and Communications features statistics on road and rail networks, air carrier departures, container port traffic, and motor vehicle injuries and fatalities. This theme also includes statistics on mobile and fixed telephone subscriptions, and broadband internet penetration rates. The discussion covers the upgrading of road networks and expansion of rail networks across the region, increases in both vehicle ownership and road fatalities, and the surge in mobile telephone and broadband internet subscriptions.

Energy and Electricity comprises statistics on energy productivity, supplies and uses of primary energy, and electricity consumption and generation. The discussion focuses on trends in demand for energy across Asia and the Pacific.

Environment includes indicators related to land use, forest resources, and air and water pollution. The discussion covers greenhouse gas emissions, particularly carbon dioxide emissions; deforestation; and freshwater resources.

Government and Governance presents statistics on governments' tax revenue; fiscal balances; and expenditure on health and education services, and on social security and welfare. It also includes statistics on the time and cost required to register a new business in each economy, as well as the economy's latest global rankings for Transparency International's Corruption Perceptions Index. The discussion focuses on regional trends in fiscal performance, government spending priorities, and the time and cost associated with starting a business.

Part II also presents several discussion boxes covering important measurement issues such as examination of the prices paid by the poor and the use of disaggregated data on gross fixed capital formation for estimating infrastructure investments.

I. People

Snapshot

- The total population of Asia and the Pacific has increased by nearly 652 million, from 3.4 billion people in 2000 to 4.1 billion people in 2016. The region now accounts for 55% of the global population.
- The dependency ratio decreased between 2000 and 2016 for most developing member economies as the number of youth reaching their working-age years more than compensated for those reaching retirement age.
- While Asia and the Pacific's urbanization rate is increasing, fewer than half of all people in the region lived in urban areas in 2016, which is well below average urbanization rates of about 70%–80% in other regions of the world, excluding Africa.
- The quality of life, as measured by the Human Development Index, improved most significantly between 2000 and 2015 in Afghanistan, Cambodia, and Myanmar.
- Primary and secondary educational attainment varies widely across the region, with a gender gap in favor of females being more common at the secondary level.

Key Trends

The total population of Asia and the Pacific increased by nearly 652 million, from 3.4 billion people in 2000 to 4.1 billion people in 2016. The region now accounts for 55% of the global population. The combined populations of the 48 regional members of the Asian Development Bank (ADB) reached 4.1 billion in 2016, or 54.8% of the world's total population (Figure 1.1a). This was more than three times the share of Africa, the region comprising the next largest share of the global population. Since 2000, the region's total population increased by nearly 652 million, which is even higher than the current total population of Southeast Asia of 635 million.

Among subregions in Asia and the Pacific, South Asia is the most populous, comprising 36.9% of the regional total in 2016. This was followed by East Asia (35.9%), Southeast Asia (15.5%), Central and West Asia (7.6%), and the Pacific (0.3%) (Figure 1.1b).

Figure 1.1a: Percentage Distribution of Population by Global Region, and by Economy in Asia and the Pacific, 2016

PRC = People's Republic of China.
Note: The aggregate for the West Asia region was adjusted to exclude Armenia, Azerbaijan, and Georgia, which are included in the total for Asia and the Pacific.
Source: Table 1.1.

Figure 1.1b: Percentage Distribution of Population in Asia and the Pacific, 2016

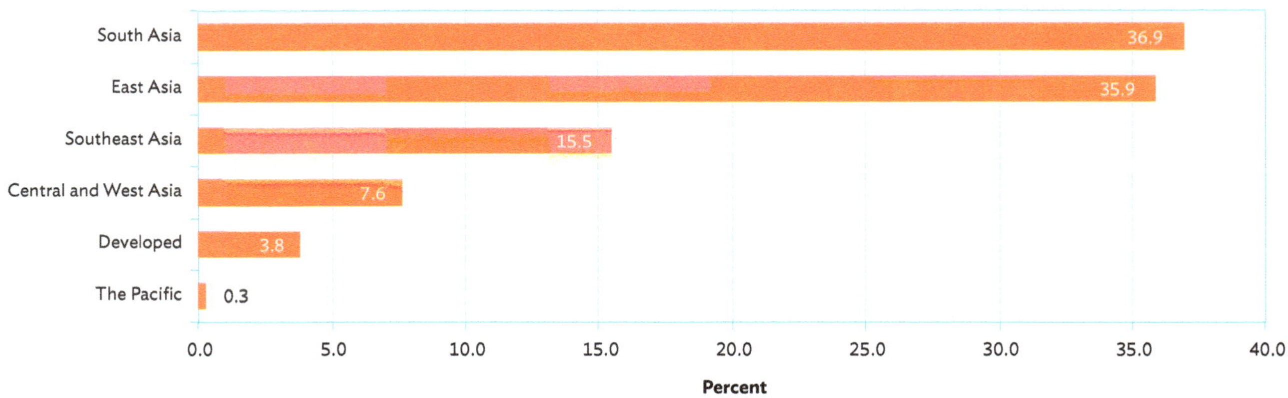

Source: Table 1.1.

In 2016, the two most populous economies in the world, the People's Republic of China (PRC) and India, had populations of 1.4 billion and 1.3 billion, respectively. The list of the most populous economies in the region also includes Indonesia (259 million), Pakistan (195 million), and Bangladesh (161 million). The economies with the smallest populations in the region were Tuvalu (11.3 thousand), Nauru (13 thousand), Palau (17.9 thousand), and the Cook Islands (19 thousand).

The region's population growth rate since 2000 has slowed more rapidly than the global average. The annual population growth rate of Asia and the Pacific fell from 1.2% in 2000 to 1.0% in 2016, compared with a decline in the global average from 1.3% to 1.1% (Table 1.1). The Asia and Pacific economies with the highest annual population growth rates between 2000 and 2016 were Papua New Guinea (3.1%), Maldives (3.0%), Vanuatu (2.5%), and Solomon Islands (2.3%). The economies with the lowest average growth rates include Armenia (–0.4%), Palau (–0.3%), the Federated States of Micronesia (–0.2%), and Japan (0.0%).

The United Nations projects that the world population will reach 9.8 billion in 2050, with Asia and the Pacific's share of the global total dipping only slightly to about 49.2%. (UN DESA 2017).

In 2050, there will be roughly as many people in Asia and the Pacific over the age of 65 years as under the age of 15 years. The region's current relatively youthful population is evident in Figure 1.2, which presents sex-disaggregated population pyramids for Asia and the Pacific for 2000, 2016, and 2050. The "youth bulge" moves its way up the pyramid in later years as increasing life expectancy (Table 1.9) and decreasing fertility rates (Table 1.10) alter the composition of the region's population. By 2050, for the first time in history, there will be roughly as many people in Asia over the age of 65 as under the age of 15 (Smith and Majmundar 2012). In the same year, the male population is projected to exceed the female population in every 5-year age group below 55–59 years old. At this age range, the impact of women's longer average life expectancy begins to outweigh the traditional imbalance in favor of male children (Hesketh and Xing 2006).

Figure 1.2: Population Pyramid in 5-year Age Groups in Asia and the Pacific, by Sex
(million)

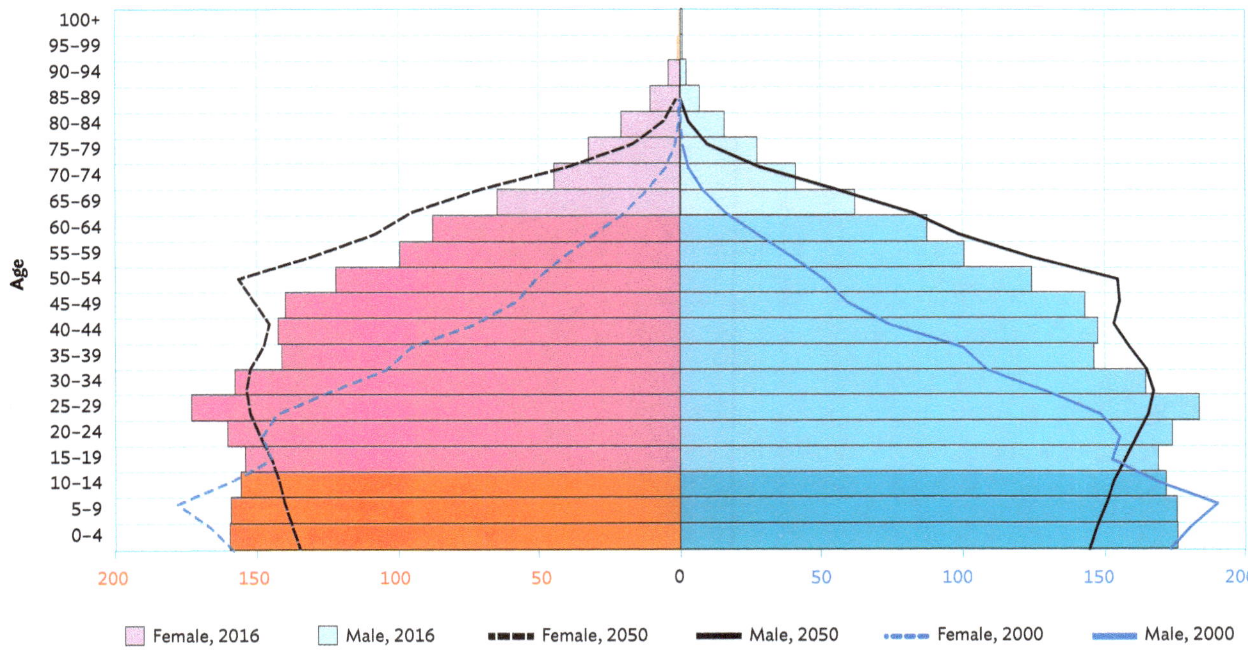

Source: United Nations, Department of Economic and Social Affairs, Population Division. 2017. World Population Prospects: The 2017 Revision. https://esa.un.org/unpd/wpp/

The dependency ratio decreased between 2000 and 2016 for most developing member economies as the number of youth reaching their working-age years more than compensated for those reaching retirement age. Figure 1.3 presents the dependency (age–population) ratio in 2000, 2016, and 2050 for each economy in Asia and the Pacific by distinguishing between those age groups that are typically not in the labor force (14 years and below, and 65 years and above) and those typically in the labor force (15–64 years). The dependency ratio decreases during the review period for every developing member economy except Sri Lanka and Palau. By 2050, the dependency ratio is expected to increase in those developing member economies with aging populations in which there are more retirements than new entrants into with the workforce, as was the case among all three developed members between 2000 and 2016.

In the decades ahead, many governments in the region will face fiscal challenges, reduced productive capacity, and lower long-term economic growth. The likely economic and social impacts of aging of the region's population in the decades ahead are discussed in Box 1.1.

Figure 1.3: Age Dependency Ratio

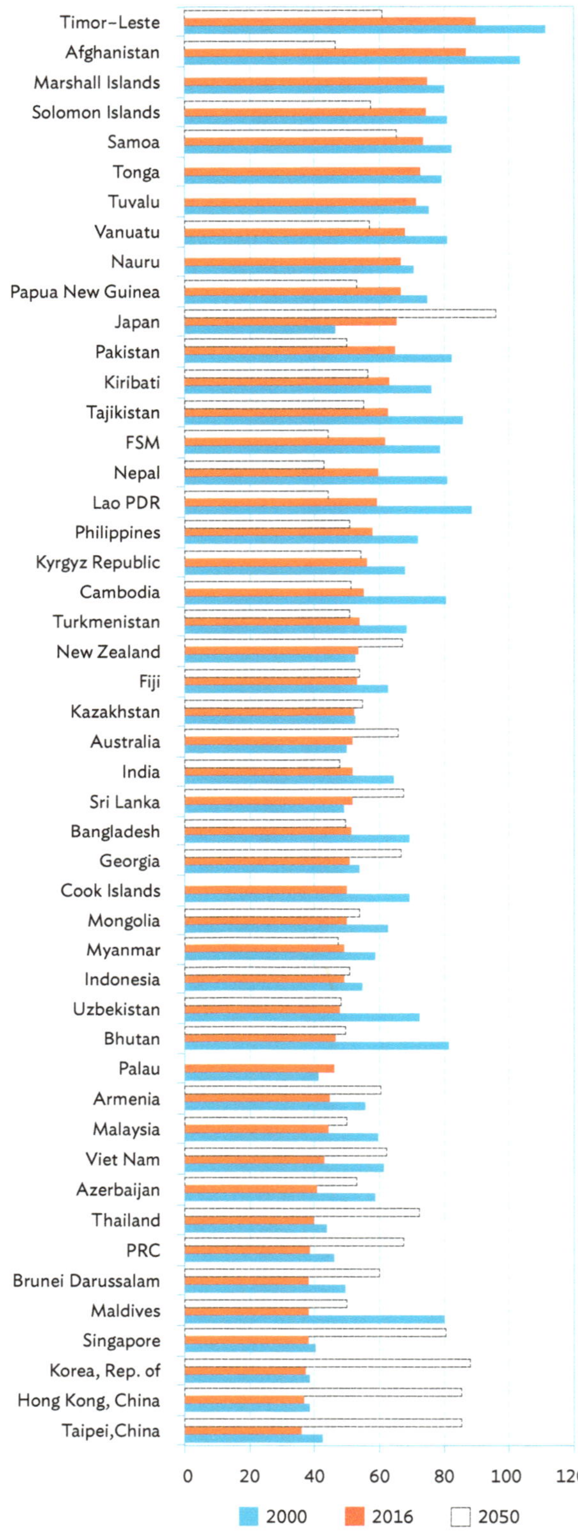

FSM = Federated States of Micronesia, Lao PDR = Lao People's Democratic Republic, PRC = People's Republic of China.
Source: Table 1.4.

Box 1: Population Aging in Asia and the Pacific: From Demographic Dividend to Demographic Tax

Asia and the Pacific has benefitted economically in recent decades from a demographic dividend triggered by declining fertility rates in economies with relatively youthful populations, leading to a subsequent decline in the dependency ratio and a burgeoning workforce. According to a World Bank estimate, the expansion of the labor force contributed about one-third of per capita income growth in East Asia between 1960 and 2000 (WB 2016). Today, Asia and the Pacific is experiencing another demographic transition as its population ages. The United Nations projects that the region's elderly population (aged 65 years and over) will grow from about 334 million in 2016 to about 870 million in 2050; during this period, the elderly's share of the total population will increase from 8.1% to 18.1% (UN 2017).The looming increase in the region's old-age dependency ratio—the number of people aged 65 years and over divided by the number of those of working age—will constrain future economic growth. Governments in the region will need to craft appropriate policies to address the impacts of this demographic tax.

The initial stage of the current demographic transition in Asia and the Pacific, which began as early as the 1950s in some parts of the region, altered the age distribution of the population as the proportion of the young in the total population increased in response to declining under-5 mortality rates. The age structure of an economy undergoing such a transition resembles a pyramid, with the base of the pyramid representing an expanding youth population. The median age in Asia subsequently began to rise as fertility rates declined precipitously amid improvements in public health, rising incomes, and urbanization. Increases in life expectancy across the region also contributed to a rise in the median age. Many economies reaped a demographic dividend as an expanding share of the working-age population helped accelerate economic growth. The rapid economic expansion in parts of Asia and the Pacific, particularly East Asia, was also facilitated by the presence of social, economic, and political institutions that capitalized on the growth potential offered by a demographic transition (Bloom, Canney, and Malaney 2000).

As part of the population aging process, the age structure in an economy gradually becomes uniform as the average number of births per woman falls to two. (Eventually, the age structure in an economy will resemble an inverse pyramid if fertility levels fall even further.) The decline in the working-age population as a share of the total population has an adverse effect on the labor supply, thereby negatively impacting potential growth as relatively fewer workers become responsible for supporting an increasing number of retirees. For example, by 2050, it is estimated that there will be about 198 million fewer working-age individuals in the People's Republic of China (PRC) than there are now. Furthermore, they will be responsible for supporting an elderly population that will have expanded by more than 217 million during that time.

A range of policies can be considered to address the economic impacts of population aging. In economies where family support systems are a critical component of caring for the elderly (e.g., the PRC; the Republic of Korea; Taipei,China; and Thailand), adult day care services and tax relief for multigenerational families can allow adult children to continue working in support of their aging parents. Mandatory retirement ages may need to be reevaluated in some cases, particularly in economies where there is a lower retirement age for women than men despite women living longer on average. Reforming labor laws to encourage firms to retain older workers by making employment conditions more flexible—by allowing part-time working hours or wage scales that are not automatically based on seniority—could also create more job opportunities for the elderly and delay retirement.

Personal savings are another key part of addressing population aging in Asia and the Pacific. Within the region, the elderly in South Asia (e.g., India) and Southeast Asia (e.g., Indonesia, the Philippines, and Thailand) are the most reliant upon personal savings for financing consumption after retirement. To facilitate saving, governments in the region should strive to effectively manage inflation and ensure that domestic financial markets offer secure, long-term investment opportunities. The governments of Malaysia and Singapore have gone even further by implementing mandatory personal savings accounts.

Public pension programs both provide an economic safety net for the elderly and allow for risk pooling. Such programs can meet the retirement needs of the poor and address challenges facing the poor and nonpoor alike, including long-term disability and outliving one's savings. At the same time, public pension programs can be difficult to administer, particularly in lower-income economies in

(continued on next page)

(Box 1 continued)

which the agricultural and/or informal sector accounts for a large share of total employment. Good governance is required to ensure effective payments collection and funds management. Furthermore, the experiences of developed economies have shown the risk of establishing potentially unsustainable pay-as-you-go systems. As the old-age dependency ratio in an economy increases, such systems can only be maintained by reducing benefits and/or raising payroll taxes.

Finally, the increased costs of providing health care for an expanding elderly population will place fiscal strain on many governments in the region. In Japan, health care spending per capita for the elderly is about four times higher than for the rest of the population (East-West Center 2002). Many governments will have to face such fiscal burdens from a lower level of economic development than was the case with Japan or other advanced economies. This will make it more difficult to balance a commitment to providing health care for the elderly with the ability and willingness of taxpayers to fund public health schemes.

There is, of course, variation in the status of population aging across Asia and Pacific economies, which will affect policy responses in individual economies. In Japan, the proportion of the population aged 65 years and older was 26.6% in 2016, while in the high-income developing economies of East Asia—such as Hong Kong, China; the Republic of Korea; and Taipei,China—the shares of the elderly population in 2016 were 15.8%, 13.4%, and 12.8%, respectively. By comparison, economies in South Asia and the Pacific generally still have young populations, with subregional averages of only 5.8% and 4.0% of the population aged 65 years and over, respectively. The populations of the economies of Central and West Asia and Southeast Asia are also relatively young, with a few notable exceptions. For example, the percentage of the total population aged 65 years and over in 2016 in Georgia and Armenia was 14.7% and 11.1%, respectively, while the corresponding figures for Singapore and Thailand were 12.3% and 11.0%, respectively (Table 1.4).

Despite these differences in age structure across the region, all economies in Asia and the Pacific will eventually face many of the same challenges over the long term given the prevalence of declining birth rates and extended life expectancies. Economies that are at a more advanced stage of population aging need to immediately address the challenges of transitioning from a demographic dividend to a demographic tax. Those at a relatively earlier stage should learn the lessons of how other economies have benefited from their demographic dynamism and how they are preparing for the future.

Sources:

Asian Development Bank. 2011. *Asian Development Outlook 2011*. Manila.

East-West Center. 2002. *The Future of Population in Asia*. Honolulu.

D. Bloom, D. Canney, and P. Malaney. 2000. *The Economic Consequences of Demographic Change in East Asia*. www.nber.org/chapters/c8148.pdf

L. Kihara. 2017. IMF Warns Asia to Act Early on Rapidly Aging Population. *Reuters*. 8 May 2017.

United Nations, Department of Economic and Social Affairs, Population Division. World Population Prospects, 2017 Revision. https://esa.un.org/unpd/wpp/DataQuery/ (accessed 31 July 2017).

World Bank. 2016. World Bank East Asia and Regional Reports. *Live Long and Prosper: Aging in East Asia and the Pacific*. Washington, DC.

While Asia and the Pacific's urbanization rate is increasing, fewer than half of all people in the region lived in urban areas in 2016, which is well below average urbanization rates of about 70%–80% in other regions of the world, excluding Africa. By global region, Asia's urbanization rate of 47.5% in 2014 exceeded only that of Africa at 40.0%. Urbanization rates in other regions of the world in 2014 were 81.5% for North America, 79.5% for Latin America and the Caribbean, 73.4% for Europe, and 70.8% for Oceania (UN DESA 2014).

Between 2000 (or the earliest year for which data are available) and 2016 (or the latest year for which data are available), the urban share of the total population increased in 7 of the 10 economies in Central and West Asia, 4 of the 5 economies in East Asia, 5 of the 6 economies in South Asia, 8 of the 10 economies in Southeast Asia, 10 of the 14 economies of the Pacific, and all 3 developed member economies (Figure 1.4, Table 1.2).[1]

The quality of life, as measured by the Human Development Index (HDI), improved most significantly between 2000 and 2015 in Afghanistan, Cambodia, and Myanmar. Figure 1.5a shows HDI values for each of the region's economies in 2015.[2] Some of the region's high income economies such as Brunei Darussalam; Hong Kong, China; the Republic of Korea; Singapore; and Taipei,China had an HDI value in 2015 exceeding 0.8. On the other hand, the economies with the lowest HDI values in 2015 include Afghanistan (0.48), Papua New Guinea (0.52), and Solomon Islands (0.52). Overall, 73% of the region's developing member economies had an HDI value equal to or exceeding 0.6, and about half had an HDI value equal to or exceeding 0.7.

Figure 1.4: Urbanization Rate
(%)

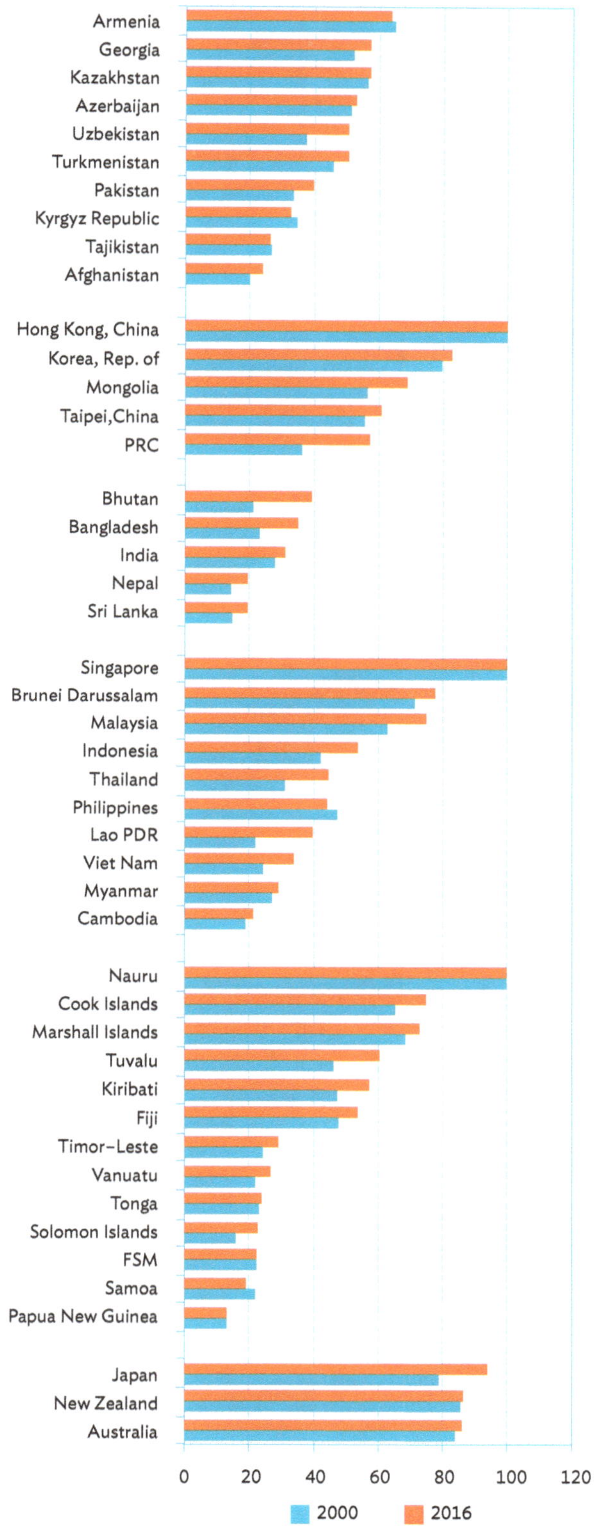

FSM = Federated States of Micronesia, Lao PDR = Lao People's Democratic Republic, PRC = People's Republic of China.
Source: Table 1.2.

1 No change in the urbanization rate was observed during the review period in three of the region's economies that were fully urbanized in 2000: Hong Kong, China; Nauru; and Singapore.

2 The HDI is calculated by the United Nations Development Programme for economies worldwide. It covers three important aspects of welfare: long and healthy life, access to education, and decent standards of living.

Figure 1.5b shows the average annual increase in HDI values between 2000 and 2015 in those economies for which comparable data are available. Average annual HDI growth rates were highest in some of the same economies that had low HDI values at the end of the review period, including Afghanistan, Cambodia, and Myanmar. Other economies posting notably high annual average growth rates in HDI between 2000 and 2015 are Timor-Leste, the Lao People's Democratic Republic, and India. Expectedly, the three developed economies of Asia and the Pacific whose HDI values exceeded 0.85 in 2000 and 0.90 based on latest data, had low annual growth rates.

Figure 1.5a: Human Development Index, 2015

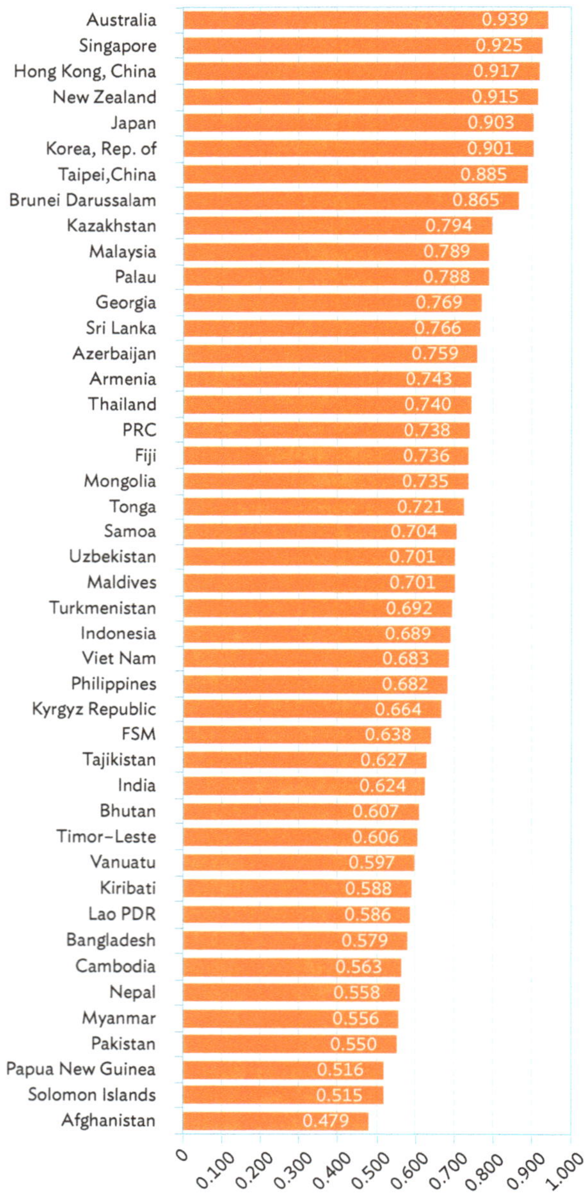

FSM = Federated States of Micronesia, Lao PDR = Lao People's Democratic Republic, PRC = People's Republic of China.
Note: For Taipei,China, data are obtained from DGBAS.
Source: Table 1.8.

Figure 1.5b: Human Development Index Average Annual Growth, 2000–2015
(%)

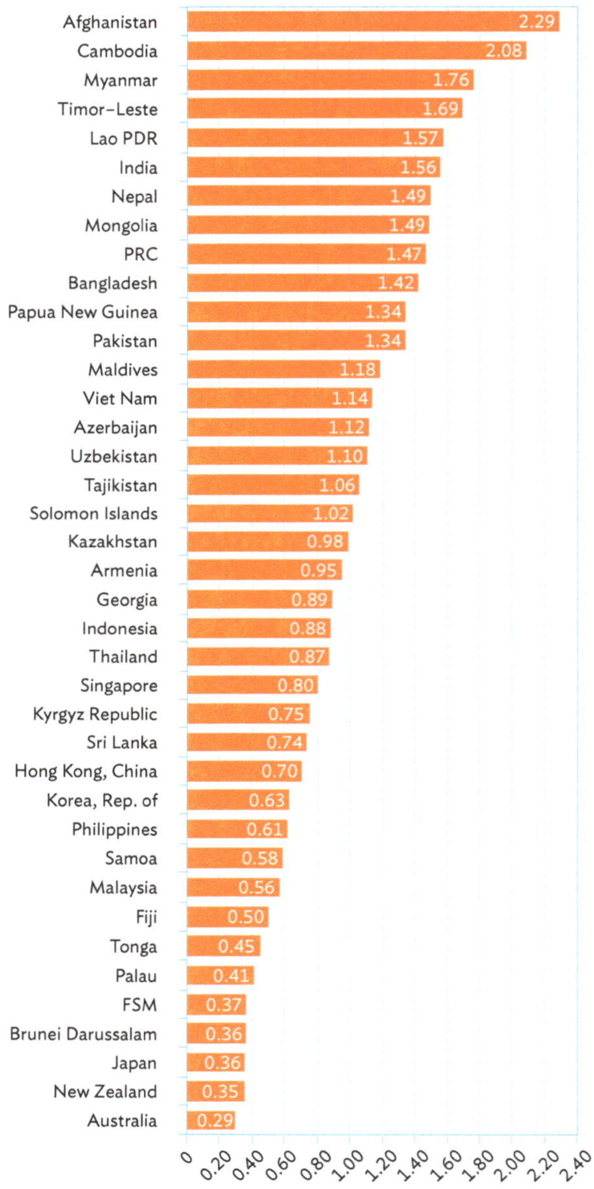

FSM = Federated States of Micronesia, Lao PDR = Lao People's Democratic Republic, PRC = People's Republic of China.
Source: Table 1.8.

Primary and secondary educational attainment varies widely across the region, with a gender gap in favor of females being more common at the secondary level. Education is a major driver of economic growth; lack of education can limit employment opportunities, increase the risk of social exclusion and poverty, and restrict participation in civic and political affairs (McMahon 1998). Figures 1.6a and 1.6b show the gross intake levels for the last grades of primary and secondary education, respectively, for both males and females. At the primary level, Nauru, Pakistan, and Papua New Guinea exhibit the largest gender gap in favor of males, while in Bangladesh, Kiribati, and Tuvalu the gender gap notably favors females at the primary level. The gender gap in favor of males persists in Pakistan and Tajikistan at the secondary level, and either persists or increases in favor of females in Bangladesh, the Cook Islands, Kiribati, and Tuvalu.

Figure 1.6a: Primary Education Completion Rate, Latest Year (%)

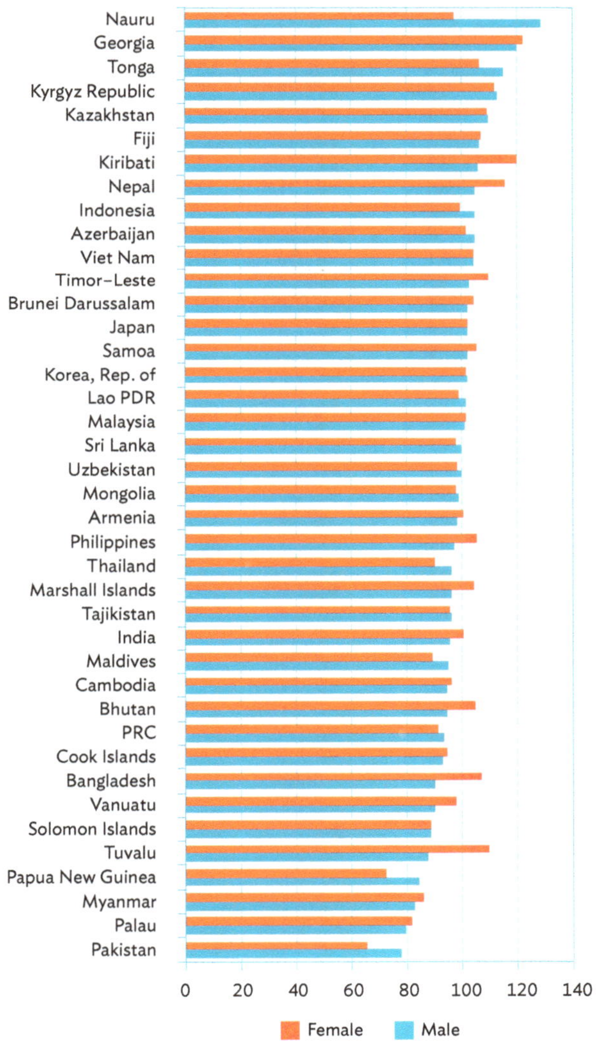

Lao PDR = Lao People's Democratic Republic, PRC = People's Republic of China.
Note: This chart includes economies with available data between 2011 and 2016.
Source: Table 1.11.

Figure 1.6b: Secondary Education Completion Rate, Latest Year (%)

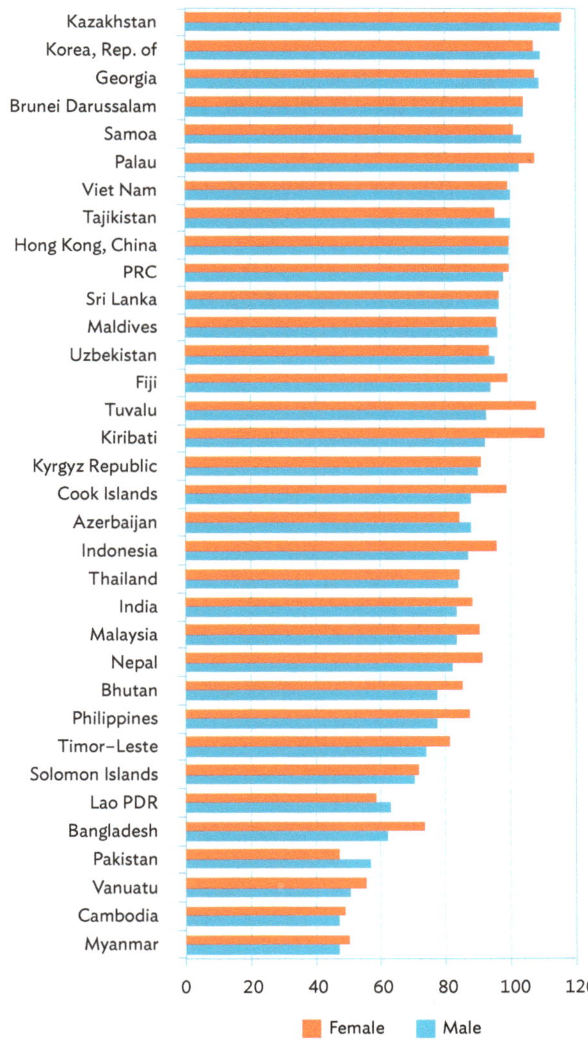

Lao PDR = Lao People's Democratic Republic, PRC = People's Republic of China.
Note: This chart includes economies with available data between 2011 and 2016.
Source: UNESCO Institute for Statistics Database. UIS.Stat. http://data.uis.unesco.org/ (accessed 30 June 2017).

Data Issues and Comparability

Demographic data are either based on vital registration records, or on censuses and surveys. In many developing member economies, vital registration records are incomplete and therefore cannot be used for statistical purposes. In most economies, population censuses are conducted every 10 years. For this reason, the growth rates are probably more reliable than the population levels. The United Nations Department of Economics and Social Affairs' Population Division used future trends on fertility, mortality, and international migration to project population numbers until 2100. The medium-fertility variant used in *World Population Prospects, 2017 Revision* assumes global fertility to fall from over 2.5 births per woman in 2010–2015 to around 2.4 in 2025–2030 and 2.0 in 2095–2100.

Statistics on urban population are compiled according to each economy's national definition, as there is no agreed international standard for defining an urban area. National estimates are used for urban ratios. If national estimates are not available, data from *World Urbanization Prospects* are used.

Data on numbers of physicians and health resources are compiled by the World Health Organization, while data on pupils, teachers, and educational resources are compiled by the UNESCO Institute of Statistics from country sources.

Household surveys are the best source for labor force data but these surveys are not carried out in all economies. Some rely on census data supplemented by enterprise surveys and unemployment registration records. Unemployment registration records are often incomplete and may refer only to formal employment, while a breakdown by economic activities also may not be available.

Table 1.1: **Midyear Population**

Regional Member	Population (million)				Annual Population Growth Rates[f] (%)			
	2000	2005	2010	2016	2000	2005	2010	2016
Developing Member Economies								
Central and West Asia	**231.7**	**253.7**	**279.0**	**310.8**	**1.8**	**1.8**	**2.0**	**1.8**
Afghanistan[a]	21.0	23.6	26.0	29.2	1.4	1.5	2.0	2.1
Armenia	3.2	3.1	3.0	3.0	-0.3	-0.6	-0.7	-0.4
Azerbaijan	8.1	8.5	9.1	9.8	1.1	1.2	1.2	1.1
Georgia[a]	4.4	4.3	4.4	3.7	-0.8	0.1	1.2	0.2
Kazakhstan	14.9	15.1	16.3	17.8	-0.3	0.9	1.4	1.5
Kyrgyz Republic[a]	4.9	5.1	5.4	6.0	1.4	1.2	0.3	2.1
Pakistan	140.0	156.0	173.5	195.4	2.4	2.2	2.1	1.9
Tajikistan	6.2	6.9	7.6	8.6	2.1	2.1	2.2	1.1
Turkmenistan	4.5	4.7	5.0	5.4	1.2	1.1	1.3	1.2
Uzbekistan	24.7	26.2	28.6	31.8	1.4	1.2	2.9	1.8
East Asia	**1,345.7**	**1,387.8**	**1,423.4**	**1,467.9**	**0.8**	**0.6**	**0.5**	**0.6**
China, People's Rep. of[a]	1,267.4	1,307.6	1,340.9	1,382.7	0.8	0.6	0.5	0.6
Hong Kong, China	6.7	6.8	7.0	7.3	0.9	0.4	0.7	0.6
Korea, Rep. of	47.0	48.2	49.6	51.2	0.8	0.2	0.5	0.5
Mongolia	2.4	2.5	2.7	3.1	1.3	1.1	1.8	2.0
Taipei,China	22.2	22.7	23.1	23.5	0.8	0.4	0.3	0.2
South Asia	**1,189.6**	**1,290.5**	**1,382.6**	**1,510.6**	**1.6**	**1.5**	**1.4**	**1.2**
Bangladesh	129.3	138.6	148.6	160.8	1.4	1.5	1.4	1.2
Bhutan	0.6	0.6	0.7	0.8	1.3	1.3	1.8	1.5
India[a]	1,019.0	1,106.0	1,186.0	1,299.0	1.8	1.5	1.4	1.2
Maldives[b, c]	0.3	0.3	0.4	0.5	1.5	3.3	2.3	3.7
Nepal	21.0	25.3	26.3	28.3	3.0	2.3	1.4	1.4
Sri Lanka	19.4	19.6	20.7	21.2	1.3	0.9	1.0	1.1
Southeast Asia	**515.4**	**550.1**	**590.5**	**634.5**	**1.5**	**1.3**	**2.0**	**1.2**
Brunei Darussalam	0.3	0.4	0.4	0.4	2.5	1.8	1.8	1.5
Cambodia	12.5	13.3	14.1	15.2	1.3	1.3	1.3	1.3
Indonesia	206.3	219.9	238.5	258.7	1.2	1.3	2.7	1.3
Lao PDR	5.1	5.6	6.0	6.6	2.0	2.0	1.5	1.4
Malaysia	23.5	26.0	28.6	31.7	2.5	2.1	1.8	1.5
Myanmar[a]	47.7	50.0	51.7	52.9	1.2	0.8	0.7	0.9
Philippines	76.8	84.7	93.1	103.2	2.3	1.9	2.3	1.7
Singapore	4.0	4.3	5.1	5.6	1.7	2.4	1.8	1.3
Thailand	62.2	64.1	65.9	67.5	1.1	0.6	0.6	0.4
Viet Nam	77.1	81.9	86.9	92.7	1.4	1.2	1.1	1.1
The Pacific[d]	**8.0**	**9.1**	**10.4**	**12.1**	**3.3**	**2.6**	**2.7**	**2.6**
Cook Islands	18.0	21.5	23.7	19.0	9.1	5.9	4.9	1.6
Fiji	802.0	827.0	850.7	871.0	0.6	0.7	0.6	0.4
Kiribati[a]	84.5	92.5	103.1	111.6	1.7	1.8	2.1	1.3
Marshall Islands	51.2	51.2	52.9	54.2	0.8	1.4	1.2	0.4
Micronesia, Fed. States of[a]	107.0	105.6	102.8	102.5	0.2	-0.3	-0.5	0.2
Nauru	10.1	9.5	9.7	13.0	1.0	-2.2	1.9	4.2
Palau	18.9	19.8	18.3	17.9	0.3	0.8	-1.9	1.6
Papua New Guinea	5,190.8	6,051.7	7,055.4	8,482.0	3.3	3.1	3.1	3.1
Samoa	175.1	179.9	186.4	192.1	0.9	0.5	0.8	0.5
Solomon Islands	418.6	470.1	528.0	606.8	2.3	2.3	2.3	2.3
Timor-Leste	779.0	945.4	1,066.4	1,208.6	1.2	1.8	2.7	2.1
Tonga[c]	99.1	101.2	102.8	104.0	0.4	0.4	0.2	0.2
Tuvalu	9.5	10.3	11.1	11.3	1.3	3.1	0.5	1.2
Vanuatu	191.7	217.8	245.4	283.4	2.7	2.6	2.7	2.2
Developed Member Economies	**149.7**	**152.1**	**154.5**	**155.8**	**0.2**	**0.2**	**0.3**	**0.3**
Australia	19.0	20.2	22.0	24.1	1.2	1.2	1.6	1.4
Japan	126.8	127.8	128.1	127.0	0.2	0.0	0.0	0.0
New Zealand	3.9	4.1	4.4	4.7	0.6	1.1	1.1	2.1
DEVELOPING MEMBER ECONOMIES[e]	**3,290.4**	**3,491.2**	**3,685.8**	**3,935.9**	**1.3**	**1.1**	**1.2**	**1.0**
REGIONAL MEMBERS[e]	**3,440.1**	**3,643.3**	**3,840.2**	**4,091.7**	**1.2**	**1.1**	**1.1**	**1.0**
WORLD	**6,145.0**	**6,542.2**	**6,958.2**	**7,467.0**	**1.3**	**1.3**	**1.2**	**1.1**

0.0 = magnitude is less than half of unit employed, Lao PDR = Lao People's Democratic Republic.

a Population figures are as of 1 January for Georgia and the Kyrgyz Republic, 1 May for Afghanistan, 30 September for the Federated States of Micronesia, 1 October for India and Myanmar, 7 November for Kiribati, and 31 December for the People's Republic of China.
b As of 1 March for 2000.
c For 2016, refers to 2015 population.
d Population figures for the Pacific developing member economies are in thousands while the regional total for the Pacific are in millions.
e For reporting economies only.
f The annual population growth rate is calculated as the percentage change of the population between the reference year and the year prior to the reference year. For example, the population growth rates under the column heading "2016" refers to the population growth between 2015 and 2016.

Sources: Economy sources; United Nations Population Division, Department of Economic and Social Affairs. 2017 Revision of World Population Prospects. https://esa.un.org/unpd/wpp/ (accessed 25 July 2017).

Table 1.2: **Migration and Urbanization**

Regional Member	Net International Migration Rate[a] (per 1,000 population)				Urban Population (as % of total population)			
	2000–2005	2005–2010	2010–2015	2015–2020	2000	2005	2010	2016
Developing Member Economies								
Central and West Asia								
Afghanistan	8.2	–5.8	2.9	–1.7	20.0	20.3	21.9	23.7
Armenia	–10.6	–12.5	–2.1	–1.7	64.8	64.0	63.5	63.6
Azerbaijan	0.9	1.2	0.0	0.0	51.1	52.5	53.0	53.0
Georgia	–12.1	–13.7	–14.9	–2.5	52.0	52.2	53.0	57.2
Kazakhstan	0.6	–0.4	1.9	–	56.5	57.1	54.5	57.2
Kyrgyz Republic	–6.9	–2.9	–4.9	–3.3	34.7	34.8	34.1	32.6
Pakistan	–0.9	–1.7	–1.3	–1.1	33.2	34.6	36.3	39.9
Tajikistan	–2.5	–2.0	–2.5	–2.2	26.6	26.4	26.4	26.4 (2015)
Turkmenistan	–5.4	–2.5	–1.9	–0.9	45.9	47.0	48.4	50.4
Uzbekistan	–1.9	–1.0	–0.4	–0.3	37.2	36.1	51.3	50.7
East Asia								
China, People's Rep. of	–0.3	–0.4	–0.2	–0.2	36.2	43.0	50.0	57.4
Hong Kong, China	1.9	2.6	2.1	4.0	100.0	100.0	100.0	100.0
Korea, Rep. of	0.3	–0.6	0.7	0.8	79.6	81.3	81.9	82.6
Mongolia	–1.2	–1.1	–1.1	–1.0	56.6	61.9	69.2	68.9
Taipei,China[b]	1.8	...	1.5	1.3	55.8	57.7	59.3	61.0
South Asia								
Bangladesh	–2.2	–4.8	–3.2	–2.8	23.1	24.2	25.9	34.9
Bhutan	9.4	4.9	2.6	0.0	21.0	30.9	34.8	39.5
India	–0.4	–0.5	–0.4	–0.4	27.7	28.8	29.9	31.0 (2015)
Maldives	9.2	10.5	11.2	4.4	27.0	35.0 (2006)	40.5	...
Nepal	–6.5	–7.8	–2.7	–2.4	14.1	14.6	17.1	19.6
Sri Lanka	–4.7	–5.2	–4.7	–4.3	14.6 (2001)	15.2	18.2 (2012)	19.3
Southeast Asia								
Brunei Darussalam	1.9	–1.1	1.0	0.8	71.2	73.5	75.5	77.5
Cambodia	–0.6	–4.3	–2.0	–1.9	18.6	19.5	20.0	20.9
Indonesia	–0.8	–0.6	–0.7	–0.6	42.0	45.9	49.9	53.7 (2015)
Lao PDR	–5.3	–3.7	–5.5	–2.1	22.0	27.4	33.1	39.7
Malaysia	5.3	5.3	5.3	1.6	62.9	66.5	71.0	74.8
Myanmar	–5.3	–5.9	–1.8	–0.4	27.0	28.9	31.4	29.2 (2015)
Philippines	–2.7	–3.3	–1.3	–1.2	47.1	46.6	45.3	44.3
Singapore	20.7	18.8	12.7	10.4	100.0	100.0	100.0	100.0
Thailand	1.2	0.2	0.5	0.3	31.1	32.5	42.0	44.5 (2013)
Viet Nam	–1.6	–2.0	–0.4	–0.4	24.2	27.1	30.5	33.9 (2015)
The Pacific								
Cook Islands	...	...	...	...	65.2	71.0	73.3	74.8
Fiji	–15.1	–6.8	–6.6	–4.4	47.9	49.9	51.8	53.7 (2015)
Kiribati	–4.6	–1.2	–4.0	–3.6	47.5	49.1	54.1	57.1 (2015)
Marshall Islands	...	...	...	...	68.4	69.9	71.3	72.7 (2015)
Micronesia, Fed. States of	–24.1	–23.1	–15.8	–11.3	22.3	22.3	22.3	22.4
Nauru	...	...	...	...	100.0	100.0	100.0	100.0
Palau	...	...	...	...	69.5	77.4	77.0	...
Papua New Guinea	–	–	–	–	13.2	13.1	13.0	13.0
Samoa	–17.7	–16.8	–13.4	–12.7	22.0	21.2	20.1	19.0
Solomon Islands	–2.2	–4.8	–4.3	–3.9	15.8	17.8	20.0	22.8
Timor-Leste	0.8	–17.6	–8.5	–7.6	24.3	26.3	29.5	28.9
Tonga	–16.3	–16.0	–15.4	–8.9	23.0	23.2	23.4	23.8
Tuvalu	...	...	...	...	46.0	49.7	54.8	60.6
Vanuatu	–0.5	1.0	0.5	0.4	21.7	23.5	24.4	26.4
Developed Member Economies								
Australia	5.9	10.6	8.0	6.9	84.1 (2001)	84.6	85.2	85.8
Japan	0.3	0.4	0.6	0.4	78.6	86.0	90.5	93.9
New Zealand	6.7	2.9	4.0	3.2	85.7	86.1	86.2	86.4

... = data not available at cutoff date, 0.0 = magnitude is less than half of unit employed, – = magnitude equals zero, Lao PDR = Lao People's Democratic Republic.

a Refers to annual average.
b For urban population, refers to localities of 100,000 or more inhabitants.

Sources: Economy sources; United Nations Population Division, Department of Economic and Social Affairs. 2014 Revision of World Urbanization Prospects—Data Query. https://esa.un.org/unpd/wup/DataQuery/ (accessed 14 July 2017).

Table 1.3: **Population Aged 0–14 Years and Aged 15–64 Years**[a]
(% of total population)

Regional Member	Aged 0–14 Years				Aged 15–64 Years			
	2000	2005	2010	2016	2000	2005	2010	2016
Developing Member Economies								
Central and West Asia	**39.3**	**36.5**	**34.8**	**33.9**	**56.2**	**58.8**	**60.6**	**61.5**
Afghanistan	48.6	47.6	47.8	43.9	49.2	50.2	49.9	53.6
Armenia	25.8	21.5	19.5	19.9	64.2	66.6	69.5	69.0
Azerbaijan	31.1	26.2	22.8	23.2	63.0	67.2	71.3	71.0
Georgia	22.6	19.5	18.0	18.9	65.0	66.2	67.7	66.3
Kazakhstan	27.6	24.5	24.0	27.4	65.6	67.8	69.1	65.8
Kyrgyz Republic	34.9	31.0	29.9	31.5	59.6	63.4	65.6	64.1
Pakistan	41.1	38.2	36.2	34.9	54.8	57.6	59.4	60.6
Tajikistan	42.5	38.1	35.7	35.2	53.9	58.0	60.8	61.4
Turkmenistan	36.3	32.6	29.5	30.8	59.5	62.8	66.3	65.0
Uzbekistan	37.3	32.6	29.1	28.0	58.1	62.6	66.4	67.7
East Asia	**24.4**	**19.8**	**17.7**	**17.5**	**68.6**	**72.4**	**73.7**	**72.2**
China, People's Rep. of	24.6	19.9	17.8	17.7	68.5	72.4	73.8	72.2
Hong Kong, China	16.9	14.4	11.9	11.2	72.1	73.4	75.1	73.0
Korea, Rep. of	20.6	18.8	16.1	13.7	72.2	72.3	73.2	72.9
Mongolia	34.8	28.9	27.0	29.3	61.5	67.3	69.2	66.7
Taipei,China	21.4	19.2	16.1	13.6	70.1	71.2	73.2	73.6
South Asia	**35.0**	**33.0**	**31.1**	**28.3**	**60.7**	**62.3**	**63.8**	**65.9**
Bangladesh	37.1	34.4	32.1	28.9	59.1	61.3	63.2	66.0
Bhutan	41.4	34.9	30.6	26.9	55.1	61.3	65.3	68.3
India	34.7	32.8	30.9	28.2	60.9	62.4	64.0	66.0
Maldives	40.7	31.6	25.5	23.4	55.6	64.2	70.1	72.5
Nepal	41.0	39.7	37.0	31.7	55.2	56.0	58.1	62.7
Sri Lanka	26.8	25.6	25.4	24.3	67.0	67.6	67.3	66.0
Southeast Asia	**31.8**	**29.9**	**28.0**	**26.5**	**63.3**	**64.9**	**66.6**	**67.4**
Brunei Darussalam	30.6	27.8	26.0	23.4	67.0	69.2	70.6	72.3
Cambodia	41.6	37.1	33.3	31.4	55.3	59.5	62.9	64.4
Indonesia	30.7	30.0	29.0	27.7	64.6	65.2	66.2	67.1
Lao PDR	43.4	40.3	36.3	33.3	53.1	56.1	60.0	62.8
Malaysia	33.4	30.5	27.9	24.6	62.7	65.1	67.1	69.3
Myanmar	32.1	30.9	30.0	27.4	63.0	64.3	65.1	67.1
Philippines	38.5	37.1	33.9	32.0	58.3	59.4	62.0	63.3
Singapore	21.5	19.1	17.3	15.2	71.2	72.6	73.6	72.5
Thailand	24.0	21.3	19.2	17.7	69.5	70.9	71.9	71.4
Viet Nam	31.7	27.2	23.7	23.1	61.9	66.3	69.8	70.0
The Pacific	**40.5**	**39.5**	**38.3**	**36.6**	**56.3**	**57.1**	**58.1**	**59.5**
Cook Islands	34.7	31.4	28.0	26.7	59.1	61.3	64.0	66.7
Fiji	35.0	30.5	29.0	28.6	61.5	65.4	66.2	65.4
Kiribati	40.0	36.9	36.1	34.8	56.7	59.5	60.4	61.4
Marshall Islands	42.3	41.3	41.8	39.3	55.5	56.5	55.9	57.1
Micronesia, Fed. States of	40.3	38.8	36.9	33.6	56.0	57.2	59.3	61.9
Nauru	40.1	37.1	35.6	40.0	58.6	61.2	63.1	60.0
Palau	23.9	24.1	20.5	21.1	70.7	70.2	73.7	68.4
Papua New Guinea	39.7	39.1	38.3	36.3	57.1	57.6	58.3	60.0
Samoa	40.7	39.6	38.3	36.9	54.8	55.6	56.7	57.7
Solomon Islands	41.9	41.3	40.8	39.2	55.2	55.7	55.9	57.3
Timor-Leste	50.4	49.2	45.6	43.7	47.4	48.3	51.3	52.7
Tonga	38.4	38.2	37.4	36.3	55.8	55.8	56.8	57.9
Tuvalu	37.1	34.3	32.0	33.3	57.0	60.1	62.7	58.3
Vanuatu	41.5	39.7	38.2	36.1	55.2	57.0	57.9	59.6
Developed Member Economies	**15.8**	**14.8**	**14.4**	**14.1**	**68.0**	**66.6**	**64.7**	**61.5**
Australia	20.9	19.8	19.0	18.9	66.8	67.3	67.5	65.8
Japan	14.8	13.8	13.4	12.9	68.2	66.5	64.1	60.5
New Zealand	22.7	21.5	20.5	19.8	65.5	66.4	66.4	65.2
DEVELOPING MEMBER ECONOMIES	**30.5**	**27.6**	**25.8**	**24.4**	**64.0**	**66.4**	**67.8**	**68.2**
REGIONAL MEMBERS	**29.9**	**27.1**	**25.3**	**24.0**	**64.2**	**66.4**	**67.7**	**67.9**
WORLD	**30.2**	**28.0**	**26.7**	**26.2**	**63.0**	**64.7**	**65.7**	**65.7**

Lao PDR = Lao People's Democratic Republic.

a For 2016, the United Nations Population Division projected the economies' population based on the medium-fertility variant where fertility is above 2.5 children per woman in 2010–2015 censuses.

Sources: United Nations Department of Economic and Social Affairs, Population Division. World Population Prospects, The 2017 Revision. https://esa.un.org/unpd/wpp/ (accessed 26 June 2017); for the Cook Islands, Kiribati, the Marshall Islands, Nauru, Palau, and Tuvalu: Statistics for Development Division: http://sdd.spc.int/en/ (accessed June 2015).

Table 1.4: **Population Aged 65 Years and Over and Age Dependency Ratio[a]**

Regional Member	Aged 65 Years and Over (% of total population)				Age Dependency Ratio			
	2000	2005	2010	2016	2000	2005	2010	2016
Developing Member Economies								
Central and West Asia	**4.5**	**4.7**	**4.6**	**4.6**	**78.0**	**70.0**	**65.0**	**62.6**
Afghanistan	2.2	2.2	2.3	2.5	103.3	99.0	100.4	86.6
Armenia	10.0	11.9	11.0	11.1	55.8	50.1	43.8	44.9
Azerbaijan	5.8	6.6	5.9	5.8	58.7	48.8	40.3	40.9
Georgia	12.4	14.3	14.3	14.7	53.9	51.1	47.8	50.8
Kazakhstan	6.8	7.7	6.8	6.8	52.4	47.4	44.6	52.1
Kyrgyz Republic	5.5	5.6	4.5	4.4	67.9	57.7	52.5	55.9
Pakistan	4.1	4.3	4.4	4.5	82.4	73.6	68.4	65.0
Tajikistan	3.6	3.9	3.4	3.4	85.6	72.3	64.4	62.7
Turkmenistan	4.3	4.6	4.1	4.2	68.2	59.2	50.7	53.8
Uzbekistan	4.6	4.8	4.5	4.3	72.1	59.8	50.7	47.7
East Asia	**7.0**	**7.8**	**8.5**	**10.3**	**45.7**	**38.1**	**35.6**	**38.5**
China, People's Rep. of	6.9	7.7	8.4	10.1	46.1	38.1	35.6	38.5
Hong Kong, China	11.0	12.3	13.0	15.8	38.6	36.2	33.2	36.9
Korea, Rep. of	7.2	8.9	10.7	13.4	38.5	38.3	36.6	37.1
Mongolia	3.7	3.7	3.8	3.9	62.5	48.5	44.4	49.8
Taipei,China	8.5	9.6	10.7	12.8	42.7	40.4	36.5	35.8
South Asia	**4.4**	**4.7**	**5.1**	**5.8**	**64.9**	**60.6**	**56.6**	**51.7**
Bangladesh	3.8	4.3	4.7	5.1	69.2	63.1	58.2	51.5
Bhutan	3.5	3.8	4.2	4.8	81.4	63.2	53.2	46.5
India	4.4	4.8	5.1	5.8	64.3	60.1	56.3	51.5
Maldives	3.7	4.3	4.5	4.1	79.9	55.9	42.7	38.0
Nepal	3.8	4.3	4.9	5.6	81.0	78.4	72.2	59.5
Sri Lanka	6.2	6.8	7.3	9.7	49.2	48.0	48.7	51.5
Southeast Asia	**4.9**	**5.2**	**5.5**	**6.1**	**57.9**	**54.1**	**50.2**	**48.3**
Brunei Darussalam	2.4	3.0	3.4	4.3	49.4	44.5	41.6	38.3
Cambodia	3.1	3.4	3.7	4.3	80.7	67.9	58.9	55.4
Indonesia	4.7	4.8	4.8	5.2	54.8	53.5	51.1	48.9
Lao PDR	3.6	3.7	3.7	4.0	88.5	78.4	66.6	59.3
Malaysia	3.9	4.4	4.9	6.1	59.4	53.5	49.0	44.3
Myanmar	4.8	4.8	4.9	5.5	58.6	55.6	53.6	49.0
Philippines	3.3	3.5	4.1	4.7	71.6	68.2	61.4	57.9
Singapore	7.3	8.2	9.0	12.3	40.5	37.7	35.8	38.0
Thailand	6.5	7.8	8.9	11.0	43.9	41.0	39.1	40.1
Viet Nam	6.4	6.6	6.6	6.9	61.5	50.9	43.3	42.9
The Pacific	**3.1**	**3.3**	**3.6**	**4.0**	**77.5**	**75.0**	**72.1**	**68.2**
Cook Islands	6.2	7.3	8.0	6.7	69.3	63.1	56.2	50.0
Fiji	3.4	4.1	4.8	6.0	62.5	53.0	51.1	53.0
Kiribati	3.3	3.6	3.5	3.8	76.3	68.0	65.6	62.9
Marshall Islands	2.1	2.2	2.3	3.6	80.0	76.9	78.8	75.0
Micronesia, Fed. States of	3.7	4.0	3.8	4.6	78.7	74.8	68.8	61.6
Nauru	1.3	1.7	1.3	0.0	70.7	63.4	58.5	66.7
Palau	5.4	5.7	5.8	10.5	41.4	42.5	35.7	46.2
Papua New Guinea	3.2	3.3	3.4	3.7	75.1	73.7	71.5	66.7
Samoa	4.5	4.8	5.1	5.5	82.5	79.9	76.5	73.4
Solomon Islands	2.8	3.0	3.3	3.5	81.0	79.6	78.8	74.5
Timor-Leste	2.2	2.6	3.1	3.5	111.1	107.1	94.9	89.6
Tonga	5.7	6.0	5.9	5.8	79.1	79.2	76.1	72.8
Tuvalu	5.9	5.6	5.3	8.3	75.4	66.5	59.5	71.4
Vanuatu	3.3	3.3	3.9	4.3	81.2	75.4	72.9	67.8
Developed Member Economies	**16.3**	**18.6**	**20.9**	**24.5**	**47.1**	**50.1**	**54.6**	**62.7**
Australia	12.3	12.9	13.4	15.3	49.7	48.6	48.1	51.9
Japan	17.0	19.7	22.5	26.6	46.6	50.3	55.9	65.3
New Zealand	11.8	12.1	13.1	15.0	52.7	50.6	50.5	53.4
DEVELOPING MEMBER ECONOMIES	**5.5**	**6.0**	**6.4**	**7.4**	**56.3**	**50.6**	**47.5**	**46.7**
REGIONAL MEMBERS	**6.0**	**6.5**	**7.0**	**8.1**	**55.8**	**50.6**	**47.7**	**47.3**
WORLD	**6.8**	**7.3**	**7.6**	**8.1**	**58.7**	**54.6**	**52.3**	**52.2**

Lao PDR = Lao People's Democratic Republic.

a For 2016, the United Nations Population Division projected the economies' population based on the medium-fertility variant where fertility is above 2.5 children per woman in 2010–2015 censuses.

Sources: United Nations Department of Economic and Social Affairs, Population Division. World Population Prospects, The 2017 Revision. https://esa.un.org/unpd/wpp/ (accessed 26 June 2017); for the Cook Islands, Kiribati, the Marshall Islands, Nauru, Palau, and Tuvalu: Statistics for Development Division. http://sdd.spc.int/en/ (accessed June 2015).

Table 1.5: **Labor Force Participation Rate**[a]
(%)

Regional Member	2000	2005	2010	2011	2012	2013	2014	2015	2016
Developing Member Economies									
Central and West Asia									
Afghanistan	50.6	51.7	51.3	51.5	51.7	52.1	52.4	52.5	52.5
Armenia	61.4	57.7	61.2	63.0	62.7	63.4	63.1	62.5	61.0
Azerbaijan	77.6	68.4	64.8	64.5	64.5	64.7	65.1	65.4	66.0
Georgia	65.2	64.0	64.2	65.2	66.9	66.2	66.5	67.8	67.5
Kazakhstan	66.0	69.4	71.2	71.6	71.7	71.7	70.7	71.1	70.0
Kyrgyz Republic	64.9	64.9	64.1	64.8	64.2	62.5	62.7	62.9	63.1
Pakistan	29.0	30.4	33.0	33.0	32.8	32.9	32.3	32.3	...
Tajikistan	56.3	55.0	50.3	49.4	48.9	48.6	47.8	48.0	...
Turkmenistan	60.5	60.5	60.6	60.9	61.2	61.5	61.8	62.0	62.1
Uzbekistan	59.0	59.2	60.6	60.9	61.1	61.4	61.6	61.8	62.0
East Asia									
China, People's Rep. of	77.5	73.5	70.9	70.9	70.9	71.0	71.0	70.9	70.8
Hong Kong, China	61.4	60.9	59.6	60.1	60.5	61.2	61.1	61.1	61.1
Korea, Rep. of	61.2	62.0	61.0	61.1	61.3	61.5	62.4	62.6	62.8
Mongolia	62.9	63.5	61.6	62.5	63.5	61.9	62.1	61.5	60.5
Taipei,China	57.7	57.8	58.1	58.2	58.4	58.4	58.5	58.7	58.8
South Asia									
Bangladesh	54.9	58.5 (2006)	59.3	...	...	57.1	...	...	58.5
Bhutan	56.5 (2001)	60.4	68.6	67.4	64.4	65.3	62.6	63.1	...
India	37.6	39.2	37.4 (2009)	36.4	...	...	...	...	...
Maldives	54.3	62.4	65.7	66.2	66.6	67.1	67.6	68.0	68.3
Nepal	85.8	84.6	83.4	83.3	83.2	83.1	83.0	83.0	83.0
Sri Lanka	50.3	49.3	48.6	52.9	52.5	53.7	53.2	53.8	53.8
Southeast Asia									
Brunei Darussalam	67.9 (2001)	...	...	68.9	...	...	65.6	...	...
Cambodia	65.2	74.6 (2004)	87.0	87.5	84.2	83.0	82.6	...	...
Indonesia	67.8	66.8	67.7	66.8	67.8	66.8	66.6	65.8	...
Lao PDR	79.9 (2001)	66.6	79.2	...	...	...	...	...	...
Malaysia	65.4	63.3	63.7	64.5	65.6	67.3	67.6	67.9	67.7
Myanmar	...	...	...	...	...	...	63.4	64.7	...
Philippines	64.9	65.1	64.1	64.6	64.2	63.9	64.4	63.7	63.5
Singapore[b]	63.2	63.0	66.2	66.1	66.6	66.7	67.0	68.3	68.0
Thailand[c]	71.5	72.5	72.3	72.1	71.8	71.1	70.3	69.8	68.8
Viet Nam	49.6	52.5	77.4	77.0	76.8	77.5	77.7	77.8	77.3
The Pacific									
Cook Islands[d]	69.0 (2001)	70.2 (2006)	...	71.0	...	...	...	...	...
Fiji	57.4	56.2	54.9	54.8	54.7	54.6	54.4	54.3	54.3
Kiribati	80.9	63.6	59.3	...	...	...	...	66.0	...
Marshall Islands	51.1	51.1	...	41.7	...	...	...	...	...
Micronesia, Fed. States of	58.6	...	57.3	...	...	...	...	...	...
Nauru	...	75.8 (2006)	...	64.0	...	...	...	...	...
Palau[e]	67.5	69.1	...	...	68.1	...	...	77.4	...
Papua New Guinea	72.2	72.9	71.7	71.3	70.8	70.6	70.3	70.3	70.4
Samoa	50.6 (2001)	49.8 (2006)	...	41.3	...	...	...	...	...
Solomon Islands	...	...	62.7 (2009)	...	...	...	...	...	...
Timor-Leste	56.0 (2001)	60.2 (2004)	41.7	...	...	30.6	...	...	...
Tonga	...	94.8 (2003)	...	...	...	...	...	...	...
Tuvalu	58.2 (2002)	...	...	...	59.4	...	...	...	...
Vanuatu	77.0	73.6	71.0	71.1	71.1	71.1	71.0	71.0	71.0
Developed Member Economies									
Australia	63.1	64.4	65.4	65.4	65.1	64.9	64.7	64.9	64.7
Japan	62.4	60.4	59.6	59.3	59.1	59.3	59.4	59.6	60.0
New Zealand	65.2	67.7	68.0	68.3	68.0	68.2	68.9	69.0	70.6

... = data not available at cutoff date, Lao PDR = Lao People's Democratic Republic.

a Based on labor force concepts and definitions of the economy, and thus may vary.
b Refers to Singapore residents only.
c Includes seasonally inactive labor force.
d Covers all wage and salary earners from all islands.
e Includes members of the armed forces on active duty.

Sources: Economy sources; for Afghanistan, the People's Republic of China, Fiji, the Kyrgyz Republic, Maldives, Nepal, Papua New Guinea, Turkmenistan, Uzbekistan, and Vanuatu: International Labour Organization. ILOSTAT. http://www.ilo.org/ilostat/ (accessed 21 June 2017); for Nauru and Tuvalu: Secretariat of the Pacific Community. National Minimum Development Indicator Database. http://www.spc.int/nmdi/ (accessed 21 June 2017).

Table 1.6: **Employment in Agriculture, Industry, and Services**[a]
(% of total employment)

Regional Member	Agriculture 2000	Agriculture 2005	Agriculture 2010	Agriculture 2016
Developing Member Economies				
Central and West Asia				
Afghanistan	69.6 (2001)	69.6 (2004)	...	39.5
Armenia	44.4	46.2	38.6	33.6
Azerbaijan	39.1	38.7	38.2	36.3
Georgia	52.8 (2001)	54.3	52.2	49.1
Kazakhstan	31.4	31.9	28.3	16.2
Kyrgyz Republic	53.1	38.5	31.2	29.3 (2015)
Pakistan	48.4	43.0	45.0	42.3 (2015)
Tajikistan	65.0	67.5	65.9	64.9 (2015)
Turkmenistan[b]	47.6	48.2 (2004)	...	...
Uzbekistan	34.4	29.1	26.8	27.7
East Asia				
China, People's Rep. of[c]	50.0	44.8	36.7	27.7
Hong Kong, China	0.3	0.3	0.0	0.0
Korea, Rep. of	10.6	7.9	6.6	4.9
Mongolia	48.6	39.9	33.5	30.4
Taipei,China	7.8	5.9	5.2	4.9
South Asia				
Bangladesh	50.8	48.1 (2006)	47.5	42.7
Bhutan	46.5 (2001)	43.6	59.4	58.0 (2015)
India	59.9	56.1	53.2 (2009)	...
Maldives[d]	13.7	15.9 (2007)	4.3	10.4 (2014)
Nepal	...	...	65.6 (2011)	...
Sri Lanka[e]	36.0	32.8	32.5	28.7 (2015)
Southeast Asia				
Brunei Darussalam	...	...	...	...
Cambodia	73.7	60.3	72.3	64.3 (2014)
Indonesia	45.3	44.0	38.3	32.9 (2015)
Lao PDR	82.7 (2001)	76.3	72.2	...
Malaysia	16.7	14.6	13.6	11.4
Myanmar	...	...	...	53.2 (2015)
Philippines	37.1	35.7	33.2	27.0
Singapore[f]	0.1	0.1	0.2	0.1
Thailand	44.2	38.6	38.2	31.2
Viet Nam[g]	65.1	55.1	49.5	41.8
The Pacific				
Cook Islands[h]	7.2 (2001)	4.9 (2006)	4.3 (2011)	...
Fiji[i]	1.5	1.1	1.7	40.8 (2014)
Kiribati[j]	...	2.7	22.1	24.3 (2015)
Marshall Islands	20.5	...	11.0	...
Micronesia, Fed. States of	52.2	...	...	...
Nauru	...	...	...	...
Palau	7.1	7.8	...	6.4 (2015)
Papua New Guinea	...	...	...	...
Samoa	39.9 (2001)	35.4 (2006)	37.0 (2011)	...
Solomon Islands[k]	...	...	41.5 (2009)	...
Timor-Leste	...	...	51.0	40.5 (2013)
Tonga	...	27.9 (2006)	...	...
Tuvalu	...	...	...	...
Vanuatu	...	...	...	...
Developed Member Economies				
Australia	4.8	3.6	3.2	2.6
Japan	5.1	4.4	4.0	3.4
New Zealand	8.8	6.9	6.7	6.3

Table 1.6: **Employment in Agriculture, Industry, and Services**[a] *(continued)*
(% of total employment)

Regional Member	Industry			
	2000	2005	2010	2016
Developing Member Economies				
Central and West Asia				
Afghanistan	6.2 (2001)	6.2 (2004)	...	14.8
Armenia	20.6	15.9	17.4	15.8
Azerbaijan	12.1	12.4	13.7	14.3
Georgia	5.8 (2001)	3.8	6.5	6.7
Kazakhstan	18.2	17.9	18.7	20.6
Kyrgyz Republic	10.5	17.6	21.1	20.9 (2015)
Pakistan	11.5	20.3	20.9	23.6 (2015)
Tajikistan	9.1	8.7	7.9	6.7 (2015)
Turkmenistan[b]	13.0	13.8 (2004)	...	...
Uzbekistan	12.7	13.2	22.7	23.0
East Asia				
China, People's Rep. of[c]	22.5	23.8	28.7	28.8
Hong Kong, China	19.6	14.4	11.2	11.9
Korea, Rep. of	20.4	26.6	24.9	24.9
Mongolia	14.1	16.8	16.2	19.0
Taipei,China	28.1	36.4	35.9	35.9
South Asia				
Bangladesh	13.1	14.6 (2006)	17.6	20.5
Bhutan	5.6 (2001)	17.2	6.6	9.6 (2015)
India	16.3	18.8	21.5 (2009)	...
Maldives[d]	19.0	27.9 (2007)	9.4	18.8 (2014)
Nepal	...	...	9.8 (2011)	...
Sri Lanka[e]	23.6	25.4	24.6	25.8 (2015)
Southeast Asia				
Brunei Darussalam	...	...	...	...
Cambodia	7.0	9.7	9.2	9.0 (2014)
Indonesia	17.4	18.8	19.3	21.8 (2015)
Lao PDR	8.7 (2001)	...	8.1	...
Malaysia	32.5	29.7	27.8	27.5
Myanmar	...	...	...	15.5 (2015)
Philippines	16.2	15.4	15.0	17.5
Singapore[f]	25.7	21.7	21.8	16.0
Thailand	20.2	22.4	20.8	23.7
Viet Nam[g]	13.1	17.6	21.0	24.8
The Pacific				
Cook Islands[h]	6.0 (2001)	14.2 (2006)	11.7 (2011)	...
Fiji[i]	30.8	30.8	23.9	12.5 (2014)
Kiribati[j]	...	3.2	16.1	18.2 (2015)
Marshall Islands	7.8	...	0.7	...
Micronesia, Fed. States of	...	...	...	...
Nauru	...	...	...	...
Palau	0.7	2.6	...	11.7 (2015)
Papua New Guinea	...	...	...	...
Samoa	19.7 (2001)	21.8 (2006)	12.2 (2011)	...
Solomon Islands[k]	...	...	13.0 (2009)	...
Timor-Leste	...	...	8.8	12.7 (2013)
Tonga	...	27.8 (2006)	...	...
Tuvalu	...	...	...	...
Vanuatu	...	...	...	...
Developed Member Economies				
Australia	21.5	21.1	21.0	19.5
Japan	31.2	27.5	25.4	24.3
New Zealand	12.6	22.4	20.6	20.9

Table 1.6: **Employment in Agriculture, Industry, and Services**[a] *(continued)*
(% of total employment)

Regional Member	Services			
	2000	2005	2010	2016
Developing Member Economies				
Central and West Asia				
Afghanistan	24.2 (2001)	24.2 (2004)	...	45.7
Armenia	35.0	37.8	44.0	50.6
Azerbaijan	48.7	48.8	48.1	49.3
Georgia	41.4 (2001)	41.9	41.3	44.2
Kazakhstan	50.5	50.2	53.0	63.2
Kyrgyz Republic	36.5	43.9	47.7	49.8 (2015)
Pakistan	40.0	36.7	34.2	34.2 (2015)
Tajikistan	26.0	23.9	26.3	28.4 (2015)
Turkmenistan[b]	39.4	38.0 (2004)	...	...
Uzbekistan	52.8	57.7	50.5	49.3
East Asia				
China, People's Rep. of[c]	27.5	31.4	34.6	43.5
Hong Kong, China	79.8	85.1	88.9	88.2
Korea, Rep. of	69.0	65.4	68.5	70.2
Mongolia	37.2	43.3	50.2	50.7
Taipei,China	64.1	57.7	58.8	59.2
South Asia				
Bangladesh	36.2	37.6 (2006)	35.3	36.9
Bhutan	47.9 (2001)	39.2	33.7	32.4 (2015)
India	23.7	25.1	25.3 (2009)	...
Maldives[d]	67.3	56.2 (2007)	...	70.8 (2014)
Nepal	...	...	24.6 (2011)	...
Sri Lanka[e]	40.3	41.8	42.9	45.6 (2015)
Southeast Asia				
Brunei Darussalam	...	...	...	...
Cambodia	19.3	30.0	18.6	26.6 (2014)
Indonesia	37.3	37.3	42.3	45.3 (2015)
Lao PDR	8.6 (2001)	...	19.7	...
Malaysia	50.8	55.6	58.7	61.1
Myanmar	...	...	...	31.3 (2015)
Philippines	46.7	48.1	51.8	55.6
Singapore[f]	74.2	78.2	77.9	83.9
Thailand	35.6	39.0	41.0	45.2
Viet Nam[g]	21.8	27.3	29.5	33.4
The Pacific				
Cook Islands[h]	86.7 (2001)	80.9 (2006)	84.0 (2011)	...
Fiji[i]	67.7	68.1	74.4	46.3 (2014)
Kiribati[j]	...	30.7	61.7	57.5 (2015)
Marshall Islands	72.3	...	88.2	...
Micronesia, Fed. States of	...	...	...	...
Nauru	...	...	...	...
Palau	92.2	89.6	...	82.0 (2015)
Papua New Guinea	...	...	...	...
Samoa	40.4 (2001)	42.8 (2006)	50.9 (2011)	...
Solomon Islands[k]	...	...	44.8 (2009)	...
Timor-Leste	...	...	39.8	46.7 (2013)
Tonga	...	44.3 (2006)	...	...
Tuvalu	...	...	...	...
Vanuatu	...	...	...	...
Developed Member Economies				
Australia	73.7	75.3	75.9	77.9
Japan	63.7	68.1	70.5	72.2
New Zealand	...	70.7	72.6	72.8

... = data not available at cutoff date, Lao PDR = Lao People's Democratic Republic.

a Data are based on labor force concepts and definitions adopted by economies. Some values may not sum to 100 due to limitations on data availability.
b The labor force data series includes individuals who are not registered.
c Refers to persons engaged in social labor and receiving remuneration payment or earning business income.
d Data for 2000 refer to persons 12 years old and over, and for 2006 onward, 15 years old and over. Figures include local population only.
e Some data may not add up because (i) data for 2005 and 2011–2013 cover all islands; (ii) data for 2003 exclude northern provinces; (iii) data for 2004 exclude Mullaitivu and Kilinochchi districts; and (iv) data for 2006–2010 and years before 2003 exclude northern and eastern provinces.
f Refers to Singapore residents only.
g Refers to total number of persons engaged in any activity regardless of age.
h Covers all wage and salary earners from all islands.
i Refers to paid employment as of end of June, except for 2000 and 2005, which refer to end of December.
j Refers to cash work and unpaid village work. For 2005, employment figures by industry include only paid (cash work) workers.
k Figure for 2009 refers to paid employment.

Source: Economy sources.

Table 1.7: **Poverty and Inequality**[a]

Regional Member	Proportion of Population below $1.90 a Day (2011 PPP) (%)		Proportion of Population Living below $3.10 a Day (2011 PPP) (%)		Income Ratio of Highest 20% to Lowest 20%[b]		Gini Coefficient	
	2000	Latest year	2000	Latest year	2000	Latest year	2000	Latest year
Developing Member Economies								
Central and West Asia								
Afghanistan	...	...	...	...	...	...	...	...
Armenia	19.3 (2001)	2.3 (2014)	53.1 (2001)	14.6 (2014)	5.7 (2001)	4.7 (2014)	0.354 (2001)	0.315 (2014)
Azerbaijan	2.7 (2001)	0.5 (2008)	16.3 (2001)	2.5 (2008)	6.0 (2001)	4.8 (2008)	0.365 (2001)	0.318 (2008)
Georgia	21.0	9.8 (2014)	45.1	25.3 (2014)	8.6	8.2 (2014)	0.405	0.401 (2014)
Kazakhstan	10.5 (2001)	0.0 (2013)	31.2 (2001)	0.3 (2013)	6.2 (2001)	3.6 (2013)	0.354 (2001)	0.263 (2013)
Kyrgyz Republic	42.2	1.3 (2014)	75.7	17.5 (2014)	4.7	3.7 (2014)	0.310	0.268 (2014)
Pakistan[c]	28.7 (2001)	6.1 (2013)	70.0 (2001)	36.9 (2013)	4.3 (2001)	4.4 (2013)	0.304 (2001)	0.307 (2013)
Tajikistan	30.8 (2003)	19.5 (2014)	64.8 (2003)	56.7 (2014)	5.2 (2003)	4.5 (2014)	0.327 (2003)	0.308 (2014)
Turkmenistan	...	...	...	...	...	...	...	...
Uzbekistan[d]	68.1	...	88.7	...	6.1	...	0.361	...
East Asia								
China, People's Rep. of[e]	32.0[f] (2002)	1.9[f] (2013)	56.4[f] (2002)	11.1[f] (2013)	...	9.2 (2012)	...	0.422 (2012)
Hong Kong, China	...	...	...	...	...	...	...	...
Korea, Rep. of[g]	...	...	...	...	...	...	...	0.302 (2014)
Mongolia	10.6 (2002)	0.2 (2014)	33.6 (2002)	2.7 (2014)	5.4 (2002)	5.0 (2014)	0.329 (2002)	0.320 (2014)
Taipei,China[h]	...	...	...	...	4.2	3.9 (2015)	0.294	0.279 (2015)
South Asia								
Bangladesh	33.7	18.5 (2010)	70.1	56.8 (2010)	4.9	4.7 (2010)	0.334	0.321 (2010)
Bhutan	35.2 (2003)	2.2 (2012)	60.9 (2003)	13.3 (2012)	9.9 (2003)	6.8 (2012)	0.468 (2003)	0.388 (2012)
India[c]	38.2[f] (2004)	21.2[f] (2011)	73.5[f] (2004)	58.0[f] (2011)	...	5.3 (2011)	...	0.352 (2011)
Maldives[c]	10.0 (2002)	7.3 (2009)	36.5 (2002)	23.3 (2009)	7.2 (2002)	7.1 (2009)	0.413 (2002)	0.384 (2009)
Nepal[c]	46.1 (2003)	15.0 (2010)	73.8 (2003)	48.4 (2010)	7.9 (2003)	5.0 (2010)	0.438 (2003)	0.328 (2010)
Sri Lanka[c]	8.3 (2002)	1.9 (2012)	33.9 (2002)	14.6 (2012)	7.1 (2002)	6.6 (2012)	0.410 (2002)	0.392 (2012)
Southeast Asia								
Brunei Darussalam	...	...	...	...	...	...	...	...
Cambodia	18.6 (2004)	2.2 (2012)	53.3 (2004)	21.6 (2012)	5.6 (2004)	4.4 (2012)	0.355 (2004)	0.308 (2012)
Indonesia	39.8[f]	8.3[f] (2014)	78.5[f]	36.4[f] (2014)	...	6.6 (2013)	...	0.395 (2013)
Lao PDR[c]	26.1 (2002)	16.7 (2012)	61.7 (2002)	46.9 (2012)	5.4 (2002)	6.3 (2012)	0.347 (2002)	0.379 (2012)
Malaysia	0.4 (2004)	0.3 (2009)	2.3 (2004)	2.7 (2009)	11.0 (2004)	11.3 (2009)	0.461 (2004)	0.463 (2009)
Myanmar	...	...	...	...	...	...	...	...
Philippines	18.4	13.1 (2012)	43.1	37.6 (2012)	9.7	8.4 (2012)	0.462	0.430 (2012)
Singapore	...	...	...	...	...	...	...	...
Thailand	2.6	0.0 (2013)	17.0	0.9 (2013)	8.1	6.5 (2013)	0.428	0.379 (2013)
Viet Nam	38.8 (2002)	3.1 (2014)	69.3 (2002)	12.0 (2014)	6.1 (2002)	6.8 (2014)	0.373 (2002)	0.376 (2014)
The Pacific								
Cook Islands	...	...	...	...	...	...	...	...
Fiji[c]	5.5 (2002)	4.1 (2008)	21.9 (2002)	18.5 (2008)	7.4 (2002)	8.2 (2008)	0.396 (2002)	0.428 (2008)
Kiribati	14.1 (2006)	...	34.7 (2006)	...	7.2 (2006)	...	0.376 (2006)	...
Marshall Islands	...	...	...	...	...	...	...	...
Micronesia, Fed. States of	11.4 (2005)	17.4 (2013)	28.5 (2005)	39.4 (2013)	9.1 (2005)	9.6 (2013)	0.431 (2005)	0.425 (2013)
Nauru	...	...	...	...	...	...	...	...
Palau	...	...	...	...	...	...	...	...
Papua New Guinea[c]	...	39.3 (2009)	...	64.7 (2009)	...	10.4 (2009)	...	0.439 (2009)
Samoa	...	0.8 (2008)	...	8.4 (2008)	...	7.9 (2008)	...	0.427 (2008)
Solomon Islands	45.6 (2005)	...	69.3 (2005)	...	10.5 (2005)	...	0.461 (2005)	...
Timor-Leste[i]	44.2 (2001)	...	72.8 (2001)	...	6.4 (2001)	...	0.376 (2001)	...
Tonga	2.8 (2001)	1.1 (2009)	7.6 (2001)	8.2 (2009)	7.1 (2001)	6.9 (2009)	0.378 (2001)	0.381 (2009)
Tuvalu	...	2.7 (2010)	...	16.3 (2010)	...	7.7 (2010)	...	0.411 (2010)
Vanuatu	...	15.4 (2010)	...	38.8 (2010)	...	6.6 (2010)	...	0.372 (2010)
Developed Member Economies								
Australia	...	...	...	...	5.9 (2001)	5.9 (2010)	0.341 (2001)	0.349 (2010)
Japan	...	...	...	...	...	5.4 (2008)	...	0.321 (2008)
New Zealand	...	...	...	...	...	...	...	0.333 (2012)

... = data not available at cutoff date, Lao PDR = Lao People's Democratic Republic, PPP = purchasing power parity.

a Data are consumption-based except for Malaysia, which is income-based. For the Gini coefficient, the data for the Republic of Korea and New Zealand are based on disposable income post taxes and transfers. The estimates for the Gini coefficient for Taipei,China are based on disposable income per capita.
b Derived from income or expenditure share of the highest 20% and lowest 20% groups.
c Household income and expenditure surveys for these economies were conducted in overlapping years. The table adopts the approach of the World Bank's World Development Indicators of using the initial year of the survey as the reference period for the poverty estimates.
d The latest available data for Uzbekistan is for 2003: 66.8% for proportion of population below $1.90 a day (2011 PPP); 87.8% for proportion of population below $3.10 a day (2011 PPP); 5.8 for income ratio of highest 20% to lowest 20%; and 0.353 for Gini coefficient.
e The earliest available data for the People's Republic of China is for 2008: 9.4 for income ratio of highest 20% to lowest 20%; and 0.428 for Gini coefficient.
f Values are weighted average of urban and rural populations.
g The earliest available data for the Gini coefficient using the new income definition for the Republic of Korea is 0.307 for 2012, and for New Zealand, 0.323 for 2011.
h The Gini coefficient for Taipei,China reflected in the table refers to Gini coefficient using per capita disposable income. The estimates using disposable income of households are 0.326 for 2000 and 0.338 for 2015.
i The latest data for Timor-Leste is for 2007: 46.8% for proportion of population below $1.90 a day (2011 PPP); 80.0% for proportion of population below $3.10 a day (2011 PPP); 4.6 for income ratio of highest 20% to lowest 20%; and 0.316 for Gini coefficient.

Sources: World Bank. PovcalNet Database. http://iresearch.worldbank.org/PovcalNet/index.htm (accessed 14 July 2017); World Bank. World Development Indicators. http://data.worldbank.org/data-catalog/world-development-indicators (accessed 12 July 2017); Organisation for Economic Co-operation and Development. Income Distribution and Poverty. http://stats.oecd.org/index.aspx?queryid=66670 (accessed 7 July 2017); for Taipei,China: Directorate-General of Budget, Accounting and Statistics. http://eng.dgbas.gov.tw/mp.asp?mp=2 (accessed 5 July 2017); Asian Development Bank estimates.

Table 1.8: **Human Development Index**

Regional Member	2000	2005	2010	2011	2012	2013	2014	2015	Rank in 2015[a]
Developing Member Economies									
Central and West Asia	**0.573**	**0.618**	**0.653**	**0.659**	**0.665**	**0.671**	**0.676**	**0.678**	
Afghanistan	0.340	0.405	0.454	0.463	0.470	0.476	0.479	0.479	169
Armenia	0.644	0.692	0.729	0.732	0.736	0.739	0.741	0.743	84
Azerbaijan	0.642	0.682	0.741	0.742	0.745	0.752	0.758	0.759	78
Georgia	0.673	0.714	0.742	0.749	0.755	0.759	0.768	0.769	70
Kazakhstan	0.685	0.747	0.766	0.774	0.782	0.789	0.793	0.794	56
Kyrgyz Republic	0.593	0.613	0.632	0.638	0.647	0.656	0.662	0.664	120
Pakistan	0.450	0.501	0.525	0.529	0.538	0.542	0.548	0.550	147
Tajikistan	0.535	0.579	0.608	0.613	0.617	0.622	0.625	0.627	129
Turkmenistan	...	...	0.665	0.672	0.678	0.683	0.688	0.692	111
Uzbekistan	0.594	0.626	0.664	0.673	0.681	0.690	0.697	0.701	105
East Asia	**0.706**	**0.774**	**0.811**	**0.817**	**0.822**	**0.829**	**0.833**	**0.835**	
China, People's Rep. of	0.592	0.646	0.700	0.703	0.713	0.723	0.734	0.738	90
Hong Kong, China	0.825	0.870	0.898	0.905	0.907	0.913	0.916	0.917	12
Korea, Rep. of	0.820	0.860	0.884	0.889	0.891	0.896	0.899	0.901	18
Mongolia	0.588	0.649	0.701	0.712	0.720	0.729	0.733	0.735	92
Taipei,China[b]	...	0.846	0.873	0.874	0.879	0.882	0.882	0.885	...
South Asia	**0.536**	**0.572**	**0.606**	**0.616**	**0.623**	**0.630**	**0.636**	**0.639**	
Bangladesh	0.468	0.506	0.545	0.557	0.565	0.570	0.575	0.579	139
Bhutan	...	...	0.572	0.581	0.589	0.596	0.604	0.607	132
India	0.494	0.536	0.580	0.590	0.599	0.607	0.615	0.624	131
Maldives	0.587	0.622	0.663	0.675	0.683	0.693	0.701	0.701	105
Nepal	0.446	0.476	0.529	0.538	0.545	0.551	0.555	0.558	144
Sri Lanka	0.686	0.718	0.746	0.752	0.757	0.760	0.764	0.766	73
Southeast Asia	**0.612**	**0.645**	**0.684**	**0.690**	**0.696**	**0.701**	**0.705**	**0.708**	
Brunei Darussalam	0.819	0.837	0.846	0.852	0.860	0.863	0.864	0.865	30
Cambodia	0.412	0.483	0.533	0.540	0.546	0.553	0.558	0.563	143
Indonesia	0.604	0.632	0.662	0.669	0.677	0.682	0.686	0.689	113
Lao PDR	0.463	0.503	0.542	0.554	0.563	0.573	0.582	0.586	138
Malaysia	0.725	0.732	0.774	0.776	0.779	0.783	0.787	0.789	59
Myanmar	0.427	0.474	0.526	0.533	0.540	0.547	0.552	0.556	145
Philippines	0.622	0.646	0.669	0.666	0.671	0.676	0.679	0.682	116
Singapore	0.820	0.839	0.911	0.917	0.920	0.922	0.924	0.925	5
Thailand	0.649	0.686	0.720	0.729	0.733	0.737	0.738	0.740	87
Viet Nam	0.576	0.618	0.655	0.662	0.668	0.675	0.678	0.683	115
The Pacific	**0.585**	**0.603**	**0.630**	**0.634**	**0.637**	**0.639**	**0.639**	**0.641**	
Cook Islands	...	...	...	...	...	...	...	...	...
Fiji	0.683	0.695	0.709	0.714	0.719	0.727	0.734	0.736	91
Kiribati	...	0.576	0.585	0.581	0.589	0.597	0.586	0.588	137
Marshall Islands	...	...	...	...	...	...	...	...	...
Micronesia, Fed. States of	0.604	0.622	0.638	0.640	0.641	0.639	0.637	0.638	127
Nauru	...	...	...	...	...	...	...	...	...
Palau	0.741	0.758	0.770	0.775	0.779	0.782	0.783	0.788	60
Papua New Guinea	0.422	0.454	0.494	0.501	0.506	0.511	0.515	0.516	154
Samoa	0.645	0.677	0.693	0.698	0.700	0.701	0.702	0.704	104
Solomon Islands	0.442	0.470	0.497	0.505	0.509	0.512	0.514	0.515	156
Timor-Leste	0.470	0.511	0.607	0.618	0.620	0.612	0.603	0.606	133
Tonga	0.674	0.695	0.712	0.717	0.718	0.716	0.718	0.721	101
Tuvalu	...	...	...	...	...	...	...	...	...
Vanuatu	...	0.572	0.591	0.592	0.591	0.596	0.598	0.597	134
Developed Member Economies	**0.874**	**0.892**	**0.904**	**0.908**	**0.912**	**0.915**	**0.917**	**0.919**	
Australia	0.899	0.915	0.927	0.930	0.933	0.936	0.937	0.939	2
Japan	0.856	0.873	0.884	0.889	0.894	0.899	0.902	0.903	17
New Zealand	0.868	0.888	0.901	0.904	0.908	0.910	0.913	0.915	13

... = data not available at cutoff date, Lao PDR = Lao People's Democratic Republic.

a Rank among the 188 economies classified in United Nations Development Programme. *Human Development Report 2016*. New York.
b Obtained from statistics bureau of Taipei,China.

Sources: United Nations Development Programme. Human Development Data (1990–2015). http://hdr.undp.org/en/data# (accessed 8 July 2017); for Taipei,China: Directorate General of Budget, Accounting and Statistics. http://eng.stat.gov.tw/ct.asp?xItem=25280&ctNode=6032&mp=5 (accessed 8 July 2017).

Table 1.9: **Life Expectancy at Birth**
(years)

Regional Member	Both Sexes		Female		Male	
	2000	2015	2000	2015	2000	2015
Developing Member Economies						
Central and West Asia						
Afghanistan	55.1	60.7	56.3	62.0	54.0	59.5
Armenia	71.3	74.8	74.7	78.7	68.0	71.1
Azerbaijan	66.8	70.8	69.9	74.1	63.8	67.8
Georgia	71.6	74.8	75.4	78.5	68.0	71.3
Kazakhstan	65.5	72.0	71.1	76.9	60.2	67.5
Kyrgyz Republic	68.6	70.7	72.4	74.8	64.9	66.7
Pakistan	62.8	66.4	63.6	67.4	62.0	65.4
Tajikistan	63.7	69.8	67.7	73.4	59.9	66.3
Turkmenistan	63.9	65.7	67.9	70.0	60.1	61.6
Uzbekistan	66.9	68.5	70.3	71.9	63.8	65.1
East Asia						
China, People's Rep. of	71.7	76.0	73.5	77.5	70.1	74.5
Hong Kong, China	80.9	84.3	83.9	87.3	78.0	81.4
Korea, Rep. of	75.8	82.2	79.6	85.5	72.3	79.0
Mongolia	62.9	69.8	65.9	74.2	60.1	65.6
Taipei,China	76.5	80.2	79.6	83.6	73.8	77.0
South Asia						
Bangladesh	65.3	72.0	65.7	73.3	65.0	70.7
Bhutan	60.7	69.8	60.7	70.1	60.6	69.6
India	62.6	68.3	63.5	69.9	61.8	66.9
Maldives	70.1	77.0	71.0	78.0	69.2	76.0
Nepal	62.3	70.0	63.4	71.5	61.3	68.6
Sri Lanka	71.1	75.0	74.9	78.4	67.5	71.7
Southeast Asia						
Brunei Darussalam	75.3	79.0	76.9	80.9	73.7	77.2
Cambodia	58.4	68.7	60.6	70.8	56.2	66.7
Indonesia	66.2	69.1	68.0	71.2	64.6	67.0
Lao PDR	58.9	66.5	60.3	68.0	57.5	65.2
Malaysia	72.9	74.9	75.0	77.3	70.9	72.6
Myanmar	62.1	66.0	64.2	68.2	60.1	64.0
Philippines	66.7	68.4	69.8	71.9	63.7	65.0
Singapore	78.0	82.6	80.0	84.9	76.0	80.4
Thailand	70.6	74.6	74.5	78.0	66.9	71.3
Viet Nam	73.1	75.8	78.1	80.6	68.4	71.2
The Pacific						
Cook Islands	71.9	75.8 (2016)	74.7	78.8 (2016)	69.2	73.0 (2016)
Fiji	67.6	70.3	70.2	73.4	65.2	67.3
Kiribati	64.0	66.1	67.0	69.5	61.1	63.0
Marshall Islands	68.4	73.1 (2016)	70.4	75.4 (2016)	66.6	70.9 (2016)
Micronesia, Fed. States of	67.3	69.2	67.9	70.3	66.7	68.2
Nauru	60.9	67.1 (2016)	64.5	70.5 (2016)	57.4	63.0 (2016)
Palau	68.5	73.1 (2016)	71.7	76.5 (2016)	65.4	69.9 (2016)
Papua New Guinea	58.8	62.8	61.0	65.0	56.7	60.7
Samoa	69.5	73.8	72.8	77.0	66.3	70.7
Solomon Islands	62.8	68.1	64.1	69.6	61.6	66.7
Timor-Leste	59.3	68.5	60.6	70.4	58.1	66.8
Tonga	70.8	72.9	72.8	76.0	68.8	70.1
Tuvalu	61.6	66.5 (2016)	63.6	68.8 (2016)	59.7	64.3 (2016)
Vanuatu	67.6	72.2	69.3	74.3	65.9	70.2
Developed Member Economies						
Australia	79.2	82.5	82.0	84.5	76.6	80.5
Japan	81.1	83.8	84.6	87.1	77.7	80.8
New Zealand	78.6	81.5	81.3	83.3	76.1	79.7
WORLD	**67.6**	**71.7**	**69.8**	**73.8**	**65.5**	**69.6**

Lao PDR = Lao People's Democratic Republic.

Sources: World Bank. World Development Indicators. http://data.worldbank.org/data-catalog/world-development-indicators (accessed 12 July 2017); for the Cook Islands, the Marshall Islands, Nauru, Palau, and Tuvalu: US Census Bureau Online. http://www.census.gov/ (accessed 22 June 2017); for Taipei,China: Directorate-General of Budget, Accounting and Statistics. Social Indicators. http://eng.dgbas.gov.tw/mp.asp?mp=2 (accessed 4 July 2017).

Table 1.10: **Births, Deaths, and Fertility Rates**

Regional Member	Crude Birth Rate (per 1,000 people)		Crude Death Rate (per 1,000 people)		Total Fertility Rate (births per woman)	
	2000	2015	2000	2015	2000	2015
Developing Member Economies						
Central and West Asia						
Afghanistan	48.3	33.3	12.1	8.0	7.5	4.7
Armenia	13.2	13.0	8.5	9.3	1.7	1.5
Azerbaijan	14.5	17.2	5.8	5.7	2.0	2.0
Georgia	12.0	13.4	10.0	11.5	1.6	1.8
Kazakhstan	14.9	22.7	10.1	7.5	1.8	2.7
Kyrgyz Republic	19.8	27.4	7.0	5.8	2.4	3.2
Pakistan	32.0	28.8	8.7	7.3	4.6	3.6
Tajikistan	30.6	30.2	7.8	5.6	4.0	3.5
Turkmenistan	23.7	20.8	7.7	7.8	2.8	2.3
Uzbekistan	21.4	23.5	5.5	4.9	2.6	2.5
East Asia						
China, People's Rep. of	14.0	12.1	6.5	7.1	1.4	1.6
Hong Kong, China	8.1	8.2	5.1	6.3	1.0	1.2
Korea, Rep. of	13.3	8.6	5.2	5.4	1.5	1.2
Mongolia	19.3	23.4	7.7	6.1	2.1	2.6
Taipei,China	13.8	8.9 (2016)	5.7	7.3 (2016)	1.7	1.2 (2016)
South Asia						
Bangladesh	27.6	19.5	6.9	5.4	3.2	2.1
Bhutan	27.6	17.4	8.8	6.2	3.6	2.0
India	26.5	19.7	8.7	7.3	3.3	2.4
Maldives	22.8	20.8	4.7	3.8	2.9	2.1
Nepal	32.1	20.2	8.5	6.3	4.0	2.2
Sri Lanka	18.5	15.6	7.0	6.8	2.2	2.1
Southeast Asia						
Brunei Darussalam	21.9	15.7	3.0	3.0	2.3	1.9
Cambodia	28.1	23.8	9.4	6.0	3.8	2.6
Indonesia	21.5	19.6	7.3	7.2	2.5	2.4
Lao PDR	31.9	26.3	9.8	6.6	4.3	2.9
Malaysia	22.5	16.8	4.4	5.0	2.8	1.9
Myanmar	24.3	17.5	9.1	8.3	2.9	2.2
Philippines	29.6	23.3	6.2	6.8	3.8	2.9
Singapore	13.7	9.7	4.5	4.8	1.6	1.2
Thailand	14.4	10.5	6.9	8.0	1.7	1.5
Viet Nam	17.5	16.9	5.5	5.8	2.0	2.0
The Pacific						
Cook Islands	23.1	14.1 (2016)	6.3	8.3 (2016)	3.2	2.2 (2016)
Fiji	24.7	19.7	6.1	7.0	3.1	2.5
Kiribati	30.6	28.5	7.6	7.0	4.1	3.7
Marshall Islands	35.0	25.0 (2016)	5.3	4.2 (2016)	4.4	3.1 (2016)
Micronesia, Fed. States of	29.9	23.6	6.3	6.1	4.3	3.2
Nauru	27.9	24.4 (2016)	7.2	5.9 (2016)	3.5	2.8 (2016)
Palau	14.5	13.4 (2014)	6.5	9.3 (2014)	2.0 (2005)	2.2
Papua New Guinea	34.8	28.2	9.1	7.6	4.5	3.7
Samoa	30.6	25.1	6.1	5.3	4.5	4.0
Solomon Islands	35.6	29.3	7.7	5.7	4.7	3.9
Timor-Leste	42.6	37.1	9.8	6.8	7.1	5.6
Tonga	28.3	24.3	6.3	6.0	4.3	3.7
Tuvalu	24.6	23.8 (2016)	10.8	8.6 (2016)	3.6	3.0 (2016)
Vanuatu	32.4	26.2	6.2	4.7	4.4	3.3
Developed Member Economies						
Australia	13.0	12.7	6.7	6.6	1.8	1.8
Japan	9.4	7.9	7.7	10.2	1.4	1.5
New Zealand	14.7	13.3	6.9	6.9	2.0	2.0
WORLD	**21.6**	**19.1**	**8.5**	**7.7**	**2.7**	**2.4**

Lao PDR = Lao People's Democratic Republic.

Sources: World Bank. World Development Indicators. http://data.worldbank.org/data-catalog/world-development-indicators (accessed 23 June 2017); for the Cook Islands, the Marshall Islands, Nauru, and Tuvalu: US Census Bureau Online. http://www.census.gov/ (accessed 23 June 2017); for Taipei,China: Directorate-General of Budget, Accounting and Statistics. Social Indicators. http://eng.dgbas.gov.tw/mp.asp?mp=2 (accessed 23 June 2017).

Table 1.11: **Primary Education Completion Rate**[a]
(%)

Regional Member	Both Sexes		Female		Male	
	2000	2015	2000	2015	2000	2015
Developing Member Economies						
Central and West Asia						
Afghanistan	...	...	...	...	...	...
Armenia	93.7 (2002)	99.1	94.7 (2002)	100.2	92.8 (2002)	98.1
Azerbaijan	89.5	103.3	85.5	101.6	93.8	104.7
Georgia	98.1	120.7	97.9	121.7	98.4	119.8
Kazakhstan	92.7	109.2 (2016)	92.8	108.8 (2016)	92.7	109.5 (2016)
Kyrgyz Republic	93.5	112.0	92.9	111.4	94.1	112.6
Pakistan	64.5 (2005)	71.9	53.7 (2005)	65.3	74.7 (2005)	77.9
Tajikistan	91.3	95.8 (2016)	...	95.8 (2016)	...	95.8 (2016)
Turkmenistan	...	...	...	...	...	...
Uzbekistan	101.3 (2001)	98.9 (2016)	101.2 (2001)	98.2 (2016)	101.3 (2001)	99.7 (2016)
East Asia						
China, People's Rep. of	84.4 (2006)	92.5	84.2 (2006)	91.4	84.6 (2006)	93.4
Hong Kong, China	...	...	...	...	...	...
Korea, Rep. of	103.6	101.6	104.1	101.2	103.1	101.9
Mongolia	87.0	98.3	89.3	97.8	84.6	98.8
Taipei,China	...	...	...	...	...	...
South Asia						
Bangladesh	64.4 (2005)	98.5	66.9 (2005)	107.0	62.0 (2005)	90.3
Bhutan	51.0	99.2 (2016)	47.3	104.4 (2016)	54.5	94.2 (2016)
India	71.8	97.5 (2014)	63.5	100.1 (2014)	79.3	95.2 (2014)
Maldives	177.7 (2001)	92.1 (2016)	183.6 (2001)	89.0 (2016)	172.0 (2001)	95.1 (2016)
Nepal	67.2	110.2 (2016)	57.2	115.7 (2016)	77.0	104.9 (2016)
Sri Lanka	107.3 (2001)	98.7	106.6 (2001)	97.7	107.9 (2001)	99.7
Southeast Asia						
Brunei Darussalam	116.0	103.2	113.0	104.2	118.7	102.2
Cambodia	51.1 (2001)	95.2	45.9 (2001)	95.9	56.1 (2001)	94.5
Indonesia	93.8 (2001)	102.0	94.2 (2001)	99.1	93.4 (2001)	104.8
Lao PDR	67.5	100.2	61.6	98.9	73.2	101.4
Malaysia	100.6	101.2	100.7	101.6	100.5	100.7
Myanmar	76.5	85.1 (2014)	74.2	...	78.7	...
Philippines	100.4 (2001)	101.0 (2013)	105.4 (2001)	105.0 (2013)	95.5 (2001)	97.3 (2013)
Singapore	...	...	...	...	...	...
Thailand	84.9	93.3	84.3	90.2	85.5	96.2
Viet Nam	99.0	104.1	96.6	103.9	101.3	104.3
The Pacific						
Cook Islands	112.0 (2007)	93.8	...	94.5	...	93.0
Fiji	95.0	106.4	93.9	106.7	96.0	106.1
Kiribati	99.0	112.4 (2014)	95.1	119.8 (2014)	102.7	105.5 (2014)
Marshall Islands	114.3 (2002)	99.8 (2011)	118.1 (2002)	103.9 (2011)	110.8 (2002)	95.9 (2011)
Micronesia, Fed. States of	...	...	...	...	...	...
Nauru	87.0 (2001)	112.4 (2014)	90.1 (2001)	97.3 (2014)	84.3 (2001)	128.3 (2014)
Palau	104.5 (2004)	80.3 (2016)	...	81.4 (2016)	...	79.4 (2016)
Papua New Guinea	55.1	78.6 (2012)	50.5	72.4 (2012)	59.5	84.4 (2012)
Samoa	94.0	103.5	95.5	105.1	92.7	102.0
Solomon Islands	...	88.6	...	88.5	...	88.7
Timor-Leste	...	106.1	...	109.7	...	102.7
Tonga	106.8 (2001)	110.9 (2013)	105.2 (2001)	106.4 (2013)	108.2 (2001)	115.1 (2013)
Tuvalu	101.7 (2001)	97.8	108.3 (2001)	109.4	96.1 (2001)	87.5
Vanuatu	92.1	93.8 (2013)	94.4	97.8 (2013)	89.9	90.2 (2013)
Developed Member Economies						
Australia	...	...	...	...	...	...
Japan	102.4	102.1 (2012)	102.3	102.0 (2012)	102.5	102.2 (2012)
New Zealand	...	...	...	...	...	...

... = data not available at cutoff date, Lao PDR = Lao People's Democratic Republic.

a The total number of new entrants in the last grade of primary education, irrespective of age, expressed as a percentage of the total population of the theoretical entrance age to the last grade of primary education.

Source: United Nations Educational, Scientific and Cultural Organization, Institute for Statistics Database. UIS.Stat. http://data.uis.unesco.org/ (accessed 30 June 2017).

Table 1.12: **Adult Literacy Rate**
(15 years and over, %)

Regional Member	Both Sexes		Female		Male	
	2000	2011	2000	2011	2000	2011
Developing Member Economies						
Central and West Asia						
Afghanistan	...	31.7	...	17.6	...	45.4
Armenia	99.4 (2001)	99.7	99.2 (2001)	99.7	99.7 (2001)	99.8
Azerbaijan	99.6 (2007)	99.8 (2016)	99.4 (2007)	99.7 (2016)	99.8 (2007)	99.9 (2016)
Georgia	99.7 (2002)	99.6 (2014)	99.6 (2002)	99.5 (2014)	99.8 (2002)	99.7 (2014)
Kazakhstan	...	99.8 (2010)	...	99.7 (2010)	...	99.8 (2010)
Kyrgyz Republic	...	99.2 (2009)	...	99.0 (2009)	...	99.5 (2009)
Pakistan	49.9 (2005)	57.0 (2014)	35.4 (2005)	44.3 (2014)	64.1 (2005)	69.1 (2014)
Tajikistan	99.5	...	99.2	...	99.7	...
Turkmenistan	...	...	...	...	...	...
Uzbekistan	98.6	100.0 (2015)	98.1	100.0 (2015)	99.2	100.0 (2015)
East Asia						
China, People's Rep. of	90.9	95.1 (2010)	86.5	92.7 (2010)	95.1	97.5 (2010)
Hong Kong, China	...	...	...	...	...	...
Korea, Rep. of	...	...	...	...	...	...
Mongolia	97.8	98.3 (2010)	97.5	98.3 (2010)	98.0	98.2 (2010)
Taipei,China	...	...	...	...	...	...
South Asia						
Bangladesh	47.5 (2001)	72.8 (2016)	40.8 (2001)	69.9 (2016)	53.9 (2001)	75.6 (2016)
Bhutan	52.8 (2005)	57.0 (2012)	38.7 (2005)	48.0 (2012)	65.0 (2005)	66.0 (2012)
India	61.0 (2001)	69.3	47.8 (2001)	59.3	73.4 (2001)	78.9
Maldives	98.4 (2006)	98.6 (2014)	98.4 (2006)	98.7 (2014)	98.4 (2006)	98.5 (2014)
Nepal	48.6 (2001)	59.6	34.9 (2001)	48.8	62.7 (2001)	71.7
Sri Lanka	90.7 (2001)	91.2 (2010)	89.1 (2001)	90.0 (2010)	92.3 (2001)	92.6 (2010)
Southeast Asia						
Brunei Darussalam	92.7 (2001)	96.1	90.2 (2001)	94.7	95.2 (2001)	97.4
Cambodia	73.6 (2004)	73.9 (2009)	64.1 (2004)	65.9 (2009)	84.7 (2004)	82.8 (2009)
Indonesia	90.4 (2004)	95.4 (2016)	86.8 (2004)	93.6 (2016)	94.0 (2004)	97.2 (2016)
Lao PDR	69.6	58.3	58.5	49.7	81.4	67.4
Malaysia	88.7	93.1 (2010)	85.4	90.7 (2010)	92.0	95.4 (2010)
Myanmar	89.9	75.6 (2016)	86.4	71.8 (2016)	93.9	80.0 (2016)
Philippines	92.6	96.4 (2013)	92.7	96.8 (2013)	92.5	96.0 (2013)
Singapore	92.5	97.0 (2016)	88.6	95.4 (2016)	96.6	98.7 (2016)
Thailand	92.6	92.9 (2015)	90.5	91.2 (2015)	94.9	94.7 (2015)
Viet Nam	90.2	93.5 (2009)	86.6	91.4 (2009)	93.9	95.8 (2009)
The Pacific						
Cook Islands	...	...	...	...	...	...
Fiji	...	...	...	...	...	...
Kiribati	...	...	...	...	...	...
Marshall Islands	...	98.3	...	98.2	...	98.3
Micronesia, Fed. States of	...	...	...	...	...	...
Nauru	...	...	...	...	...	...
Palau	...	96.6 (2015)	...	96.3 (2015)	...	96.8 (2015)
Papua New Guinea	57.3	...	50.9	...	63.4	...
Samoa	...	99.0	...	99.1	...	98.9
Solomon Islands	...	...	...	...	...	...
Timor-Leste	37.6 (2001)	58.3 (2010)	30.0 (2001)	53.0 (2010)	45.3 (2001)	63.6 (2010)
Tonga	99.0 (2006)	99.4	99.1 (2006)	99.4	99.0 (2006)	99.3
Tuvalu	...	...	...	...	...	...
Vanuatu	...	...	...	...	...	...
Developed Member Economies						
Australia	...	...	...	...	...	...
Japan	...	...	...	...	...	...
New Zealand	...	...	...	...	...	...

... = data not available at cutoff date, Lao PDR = Lao People's Democratic Republic.

Source: United Nations Educational, Scientific and Cultural Organization, Institute for Statistics Database. UIS.Stat. http://data.uis.unesco.org/ (accessed 28 July 2017).

Table 1.13: **Education Resources**

Regional Member	Primary Pupil-Teacher Ratio		Secondary Pupil-Teacher Ratio	
	2000	2015	2000	2015
Developing Member Economies				
Central and West Asia				
Afghanistan	42.3 (2006)	44.3	31.6 (2007)	37.7
Armenia	20.3 (2001)	...	...	...
Azerbaijan	18.7	13.5	...	...
Georgia	16.8	9.0	7.5	7.2
Kazakhstan	18.7 (2001)	18.6 (2016)	...	6.8 (2016)
Kyrgyz Republic	24.1	26.2	13.3	12.5
Pakistan	33.0	46.3	24.2 (2003)	21.1
Tajikistan	21.8	22.2 (2016)	16.4	15.4 (2011)
Turkmenistan	...	...	...	...
Uzbekistan	21.4	20.4 (2016)	11.5	10.4 (2016)
East Asia				
China, People's Rep. of	22.2 (2001)	16.3	17.1	13.8
Hong Kong, China	21.5	13.7	18.8 (2001)	13.0
Korea, Rep. of	32.1	16.5 (2014)	21.0	14.9 (2014)
Mongolia	32.6	28.2	19.9	14.5 (2010)
Taipei,China[a]	19.0	12.3 (2016)	17.6	13.7 (2016)
South Asia				
Bangladesh	47.0 (2005)	36.1	38.4	35.2 (2013)
Bhutan	41.1	38.0 (2016)	28.1 (2005)	14.3 (2014)
India	40.0	31.5	33.6	31.7
Maldives	22.7	10.3 (2016)	15.3	...
Nepal	38.0	22.4 (2016)	30.2	28.9 (2016)
Sri Lanka	26.3 (2001)	23.2	...	17.3 (2012)
Southeast Asia				
Brunei Darussalam	13.7	10.0	10.9	8.8
Cambodia	50.1	45.5	18.5	...
Indonesia	22.1	16.6 (2014)	14.6	15.5 (2014)
Lao PDR	30.1	24.2	21.3	18.7
Malaysia	19.6	11.5	18.4	12.0
Myanmar	32.8	27.6 (2014)	31.9	31.8 (2014)
Philippines	35.3	31.4 (2013)	36.4 (2001)	27.0 (2013)
Singapore	20.4 (2007)	17.4 (2009)	17.0 (2007)	14.9 (2009)
Thailand	20.8	16.9	24.0 (2001)	28.2
Viet Nam	29.5	19.2	...	...
The Pacific				
Cook Islands	17.8	17.2	13.9	13.9
Fiji	28.1	28.0 (2012)	20.2	19.3 (2012)
Kiribati	31.7	26.4 (2014)	21.0 (2001)	17.4 (2008)
Marshall Islands	16.9 (2002)	...	16.7 (2002)	...
Micronesia, Fed. States of	...	19.7	...	...
Nauru	21.5	39.5 (2014)	17.4	22.8 (2014)
Palau	15.7	14.2 (2016)	15.1	18.8 (2016)
Papua New Guinea	35.4	45.2 (2012)	...	27.4 (2012)
Samoa	24.0	30.2 (2010)	21.2	21.5 (2010)
Solomon Islands	...	25.7	10.1	25.9 (2012)
Timor-Leste	61.9 (2001)	31.4 (2011)	28.0 (2001)	24.3 (2011)
Tonga	22.1	21.9 (2014)	14.6	13.4 (2014)
Tuvalu	19.7	12.7	...	6.2
Vanuatu	22.5	26.6	24.7	20.6
Developed Member Economies				
Australia	...	...	...	...
Japan	20.7	16.4 (2014)	14.0	11.7 (2012)
New Zealand	18.4	14.4 (2014)	15.5	14.0 (2014)

... = data not available at cutoff date, Lao PDR = Lao People's Democratic Republic.

a Data for 2016 secondary pupil-teacher ratio include those for vocational secondary schools.

Sources: United Nations Educational, Scientific and Cultural Organization, Institute for Statistics Database. UIS.Stat. http://data.uis.unesco.org/ (accessed 1 July 2017); for Taipei,China: Directorate-General of Budget, Accounting and Statistics. Social Indicators. http://eng.dgbas.gov.tw/mp.asp?mp=2 (accessed 1 July 2017).

Table 1.14: **Health Care Resources**
(per 1,000 population)

Regional Member	Physicians		Hospital Beds	
	Initial year	Latest year	Initial year	Latest year
Developing Member Economies				
Central and West Asia				
Afghanistan	0.20 (2001)	0.30 (2014)	0.40 (2001)	0.50 (2012)
Armenia	...	2.80 (2014)	5.47 (2000)	3.90 (2012)
Azerbaijan	...	3.40 (2014)	8.68 (2000)	4.70 (2012)
Georgia	...	4.78 (2014)	4.77 (2000)	2.60 (2012)
Kazakhstan	...	3.27 (2014)	7.19 (2000)	7.20 (2012)
Kyrgyz Republic	...	1.85 (2014)	7.40 (2000)	4.80 (2012)
Pakistan	0.66 (2000)	0.81 (2014)	0.70 (2003)	0.60 (2012)
Tajikistan	2.18 (2000)	1.71 (2014)	6.54 (2000)	5.50 (2011)
Turkmenistan	4.36 (2002)	2.29 (2014)	4.90 (2004)	4.00 (2012)
Uzbekistan	...	2.45 (2014)	5.33 (2000)	4.40 (2010)
East Asia				
China, People's Rep. of	1.26 (2000)	1.49 (2011)	2.52 (2000)	3.80 (2011)
Hong Kong, China	...	...	...	...
Korea, Rep. of	1.73 (2004)	2.23 (2014)	6.10 (2000)	10.30 (2009)
Mongolia	2.76 (2002)	2.88 (2011)	7.50 (2002)	6.80 (2012)
Taipei,China	1.50 (2000)	2.14 (2015)	5.68 (2000)	6.90 (2015)
South Asia				
Bangladesh	0.24 (2001)	0.39 (2012)	0.30 (2001)	0.60 (2011)
Bhutan	0.19 (2004)	0.26 (2014)	1.60 (2001)	1.80 (2012)
India	0.53 (2000)	0.73 (2014)	0.69 (2002)	0.70 (2011)
Maldives	1.01 (2004)	1.58 (2010)	1.70 (2000)	4.30 (2009)
Nepal	0.21 (2004)	...	0.20 (2001)	...
Sri Lanka	0.42 (2000)	0.73 (2010)	2.90 (2000)	3.60 (2012)
Southeast Asia				
Brunei Darussalam	1.02 (2000)	1.47 (2012)	2.60 (2000)	2.80 (2012)
Cambodia	0.17 (2000)	0.17 (2013)	0.60 (2001)	0.70 (2011)
Indonesia	0.13 (2003)	0.20 (2012)	0.60 (2002)	0.90 (2012)
Lao PDR	0.28 (2000)	0.18 (2012)	0.90 (2002)	1.50 (2012)
Malaysia	0.69 (2000)	1.28 (2011)	1.80 (2001)	1.90 (2012)
Myanmar	0.36 (2004)	0.57 (2012)	0.70 (2000)	...
Philippines	0.57 (2000)	...	1.00 (2001)	1.00 (2011)
Singapore	1.43 (2001)	1.91 (2013)	2.90 (2001)	2.00 (2011)
Thailand	0.30 (2001)	0.39 (2010)	2.20 (2000)	2.10 (2010)
Viet Nam	0.52 (2001)	1.18 (2013)	2.40 (2001)	2.00 (2010)
The Pacific				
Cook Islands	0.78 (2001)	1.19 (2009)	...	...
Fiji	0.47 (2003)	0.44 (2009)	2.10 (2004)	2.10 (2009)
Kiribati	...	0.20 (2013)	1.50 (2004)	1.30 (2011)
Marshall Islands	0.60 (2007)	0.46 (2012)	...	2.70 (2010)
Micronesia, Fed. States of	0.60 (2000)	0.19 (2009)	2.80 (2000)	3.20 (2009)
Nauru	0.99 (2004)	1.00 (2010)	3.50 (2004)	5.00 (2010)
Palau	1.30 (2006)	1.42 (2010)	5.90 (2006)	4.80 (2010)
Papua New Guinea	0.05 (2000)	0.06 (2010)	...	...
Samoa	0.28 (2003)	0.46 (2008)	3.30 (2000)	...
Solomon Islands	0.13 (2003)	0.20 (2011)	2.20 (2003)	1.30 (2012)
Timor-Leste	0.00 (2001)	0.08 (2011)	...	5.90 (2010)
Tonga	0.36 (2001)	0.56 (2010)	3.20 (2001)	2.60 (2010)
Tuvalu	0.63 (2002)	1.22 (2009)	5.60 (2001)	...
Vanuatu	0.15 (2004)	0.19 (2012)	3.10 (2001)	1.70 (2008)
Developed Member Economies				
Australia	2.48 (2001)	3.37 (2013)	7.80 (2000)	3.90 (2010)
Japan	2.04 (2000)	2.30 (2012)	14.70 (2000)	13.70 (2009)
New Zealand	2.31 (2001)	2.85 (2014)	6.20 (2002)	2.30 (2011)

... = data not available at cutoff date, 0.00 = magnitude is less than half of unit employed, Lao PDR = Lao People's Democratic Republic.

Sources: For physicians (per 1,000 population): World Health Organization. Global Health Observatory. http://apps.who.int/gho/data/node.imr.HRH_26?lang=en (accessed 17 July 2017); for hospital beds (per 1,000 people): World Bank. World Development Indicators. http://data.worldbank.org (accessed 12 July 2017); for Taipei,China: Directorate-General of Budget, Accounting and Statistics. Monthly Bulletin of Statistics Online and Statistical Yearbook. http://eng.dgbas.gov.tw/mp.asp?mp=2 (accessed 28 June 2017).

Table 1.15: **Estimated Number of Adults Living with HIV**[a]
(aged 15 years and over, thousands)

Regional Member	Adults		Women	
	2000	2015	2000	2015
Developing Member Economies				
Central and West Asia				
Afghanistan	1.8	6.7	0.5	1.9
Armenia	1.0	3.6	0.2	0.7
Azerbaijan	1.4	10.6	0.4	3.1
Georgia	1.9	9.6	0.7	2.1
Kazakhstan	4.0	22.9	0.6	7.1
Kyrgyz Republic	0.8	8.0	0.2	2.6
Pakistan	8.6	99.5	2.3	29.6
Tajikistan	5.0	15.8	2.1	5.4
Turkmenistan	...	...	...	...
Uzbekistan	20.3	32.1	4.5	9.7
East Asia				
China, People's Rep. of	...	...	...	...
Hong Kong, China	...	...	...	...
Korea, Rep. of	...	...	...	...
Mongolia	0.0	0.4	0.0	0.1
Taipei,China	...	...	...	...
South Asia				
Bangladesh	1.0	9.3	0.2	3.2
Bhutan	...	...	...	...
India	1,949.2	1,979.1	674.8	794.0
Maldives	...	...	...	...
Nepal	22.6	37.8	6.7	14.2
Sri Lanka	0.6	4.1	0.2	1.3
Southeast Asia				
Brunei Darussalam	...	...	...	...
Cambodia	114.5	70.1	45.1	37.0
Indonesia	41.5	675.5	9.3	246.9
Lao PDR	...	...	...	...
Malaysia	99.4	91.1	3.7	12.7
Myanmar	187.1	215.3	44.5	77.2
Philippines	2.6	42.1	0.9	4.5
Singapore	...	...	...	...
Thailand	616.0	434.0	176.5	179.7
Viet Nam	101.1	250.2	15.3	76.5
The Pacific				
Cook Islands	...	...	...	...
Fiji	...	...	...	...
Kiribati	...	...	...	...
Marshall Islands	...	...	...	...
Micronesia, Fed. States of	...	...	...	...
Nauru	...	...	...	...
Palau	...	...	...	...
Papua New Guinea	23.2	36.9	12.6	21.3
Samoa	...	...	...	...
Solomon Islands	...	...	...	...
Timor-Leste	...	...	...	...
Tonga	...	...	...	...
Tuvalu	...	...	...	...
Vanuatu	...	...	...	...
Developed Member Economies				
Australia	15.3	26.8	1.2	2.8
Japan	...	...	...	...
New Zealand	...	...	...	...

... = data not available at cutoff date, 0.0 = magnitude is less than half of unit employed, Lao PDR = Lao People's Democratic Republic.

a The modeled HIV estimates are calculated by UNAIDS using the Spectrum developed by the Futures Institute, and the Estimates and Projections Package (www.futuresinstitute.org).

Source: UNAIDS. AidsInfo Online Database. http://www.aidsinfoonline.org/devinfo/libraries/aspx/home.aspx (accessed 17 July 2017).

II. Economy and Output

Snapshot

- Asia and the Pacific accounted for 40.9% of global gross domestic product (GDP) at purchasing power parity (PPP) in 2016, up from 29.4% in 2000; three economies—the People's Republic of China, India, and Japan—accounted for about 70% of the region's total output in 2016.
- All but two of the 38 regional economies with available data experienced real GDP growth between 2015 and 2016; the most rapid growth rates were in Nauru, Uzbekistan, Bangladesh, the Lao People's Democratic Republic, and Cambodia, respectively.
- Economies in Asia and the Pacific experienced a decline in external trade between 2000 and 2016.
- Twenty-three of 36 regional economies for which data are available experienced an increase in gross domestic capital formation between 2000 and 2016.
- Household consumption's share of GDP declined between 2000 and 2016 in nearly 70% of regional economies.

Key Trends

Asia and the Pacific accounted for 40.9% of global gross domestic product at purchasing power parity in 2016, up from 29.4% in 2000. Figure 2.1 presents global gross domestic product (GDP) shares by region at purchasing power parity (PPP) in 2000 and 2016. Asia and the Pacific's share of global GDP increased by 11.5 percentage points during the review period (Table 2.1), while the shares of Europe, North America, and South America dropped by 4.5 percentage points, 6.5 percentage points, and 1.2 percentage points, respectively. The rest of the world's share of global GDP increased by half of a percentage point.

Figure 2.1: Distribution of Gross Domestic Product at Purchasing Power Parity—Asia and Pacific Region in the World Economy
(%)

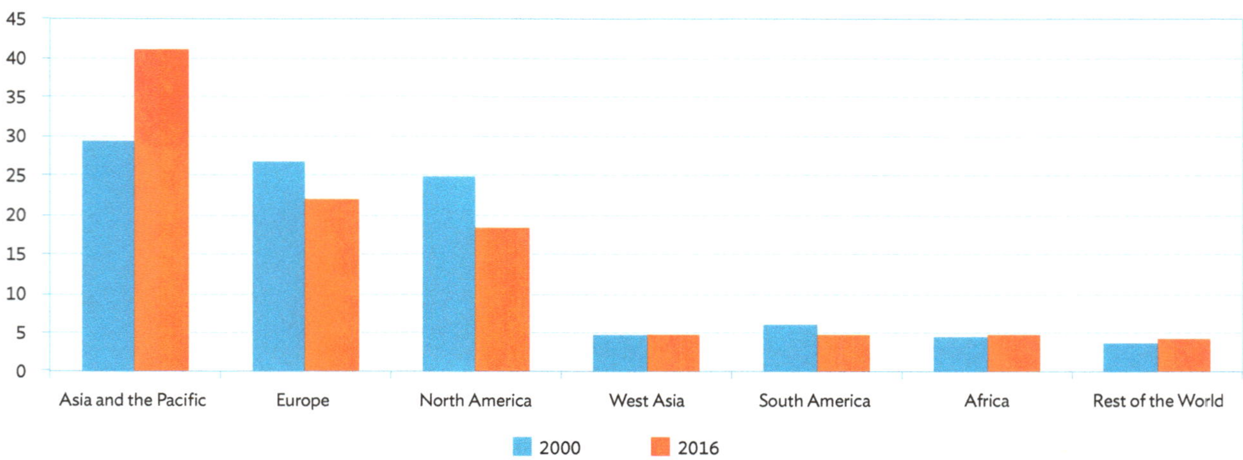

Sources: : Table 2.1 and World Bank. World Development Indicators. http://data.worldbank.org/ (accessed August 2017).

All but two of the 38 regional economies with available data experienced real GDP growth between 2015 and 2016; the most rapid growth rates were in Nauru, Uzbekistan, Bangladesh, the Lao People's Democratic Republic, and Cambodia, respectively. Between 2015 and 2016, every economy in Asia and the Pacific except Brunei Darussalam and Azerbaijan recorded GDP growth (Figure 2.2). The (arithmetic) average of Asia and the Pacific economies annual GDP growth during the review period was 3.9% (Table 2.9).

The region's most rapidly growing economy since 2015 is Nauru with real GDP growth of 10.4%. Revised national account estimates found that growth in recent years has been much higher than previously estimated, driven by a booming services sector and increased public spending (ADB 2017). The next highest growth rates in the region were observed in Uzbekistan (7.3%), Bangladesh (7.1%), the Lao People's Democratic Republic (7.0%), and Cambodia (7.0%).

Just three economies—the People's Republic of China, India, and Japan—accounted for about 70% of the region's total output in 2016, compared with about 63% in 2000 at purchasing power parity. Figure 2.3 shows the distribution of GDP at PPP within the region in 2000 and 2016. The People's Republic of China accounted for nearly half of the region's total (42.4%), followed by India (17.2%), and Japan (10.4%). Outside of the 10 largest economies, the region's remaining 38 economies together contribute 30% to the region's GDP at PPP.

Figure 2.2: Growth Rates of Real Gross Domestic Product, 2016
(%)

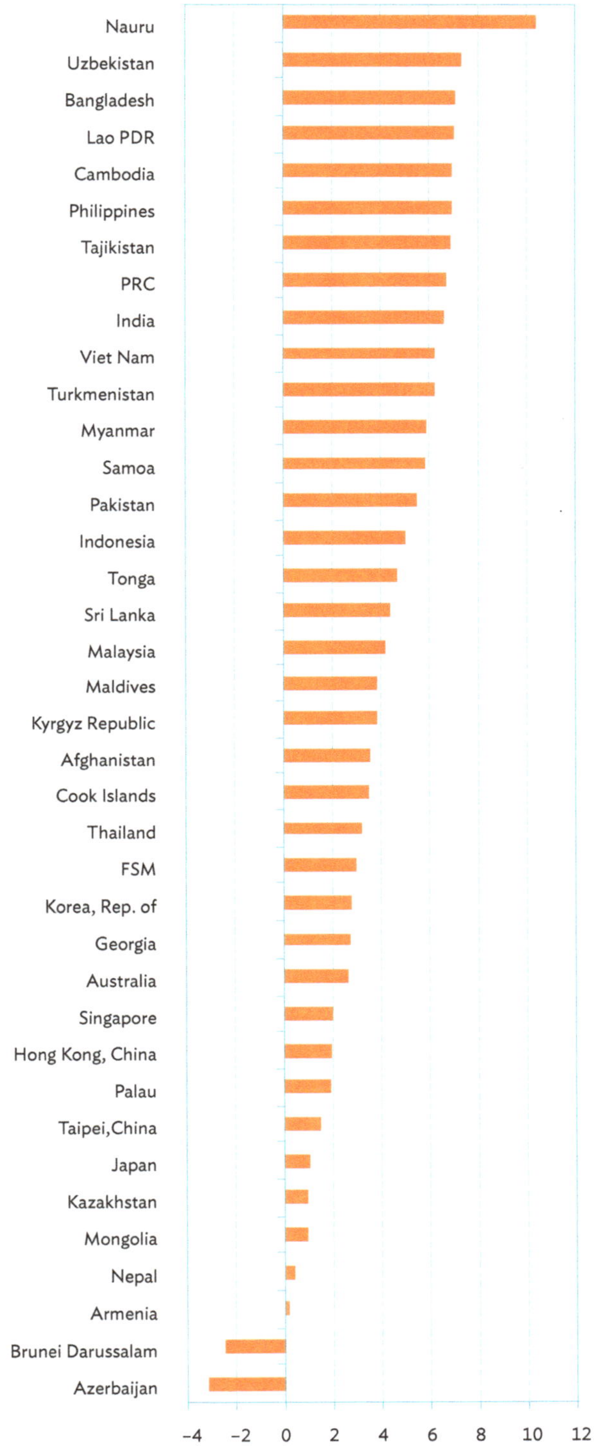

FSM = Federated States of Micronesia, Lao PDR = Lao People's Democratic Republic, PRC = People's Republic of China.
Source: Table 2.9.

Figure 2.3: Distribution of Gross Domestic Product at Purchasing Power Parity—Asia and Pacific Region
(%)

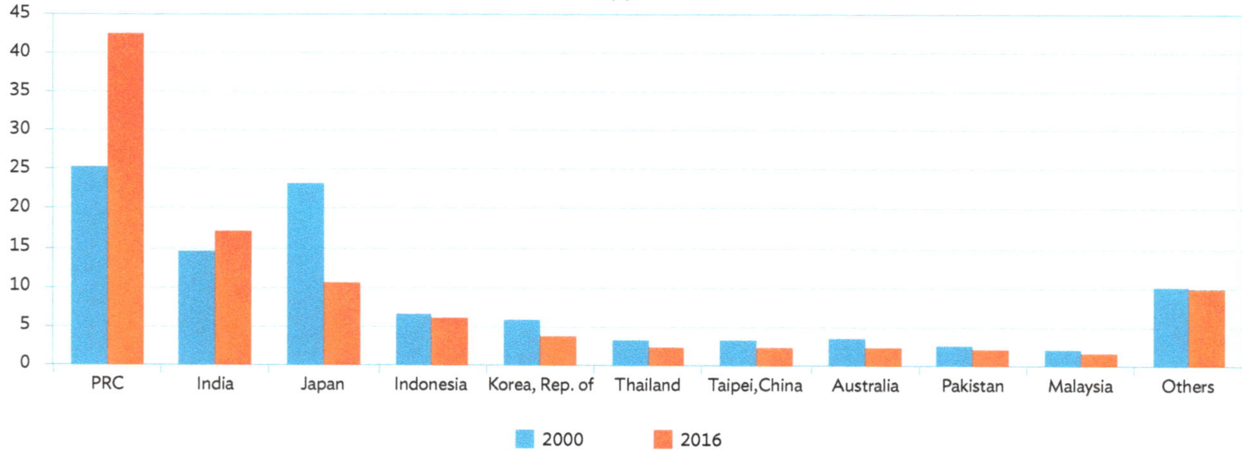

PRC = People's Republic of China.
Sources: Table 2.1 and World Bank. World Development Indicators. http://data.worldbank.org/ (accessed August 2017).

Economies in Asia and the Pacific experienced a decline in external trade between 2000 and 2016. Measured as a share of GDP at current prices, exports of goods and services declined across Asia and the Pacific from an (arithmetic) average of 47.1% in 2000 to 44.4% in 2016 (Table 2.7). The largest annual average percentage point declines in exports as a share of GDP during the review period occurred in Tajikistan (–5.5 percentage points), Malaysia (–3.3 percentage points), Turkmenistan (–1.6 percentage points), and Afghanistan (–1.6 percentage points) (Figure 2.4). The largest percentage gain occurred in Hong Kong, China, where the base effect of exports accounting for 126.0% of GDP in 2000 resulted in an increase of 3.8 percentage points per year during the review period. The next largest annual average percentage point increases in exports as a share of GDP between 2000 and 2016 were in Timor-Leste (3.1 percentage points) and Viet Nam (2.4 percentage points).

Imports of goods and services, measured as a share of GDP at current prices, also declined in Asia and the Pacific during the review period from an (arithmetic) average of 52.8% of GDP in 2000 to 48.6% in 2016. The largest annual average percentage point declines in imports during the review period occurred in Timor-Leste (–5.7 percentage points), Tajikistan (–3.9 percentage points), Turkmenistan (–2.7 percentage points), and Malaysia (–2.5 percentage points) (Figure 2.5). The largest annual average percentage point increase was again in Hong Kong, China (4.0 percentage points), where imports accounted for 121.6% of GDP in 2000 before jumping to 185.4% in 2016. The next largest annual average percentage point gains were in Viet Nam (2.1 percentage points) and the Kyrgyz Republic (1.9 percentage points).

Figure 2.4: Share of Exports of Goods and Services to Gross Domestic Product
(%)

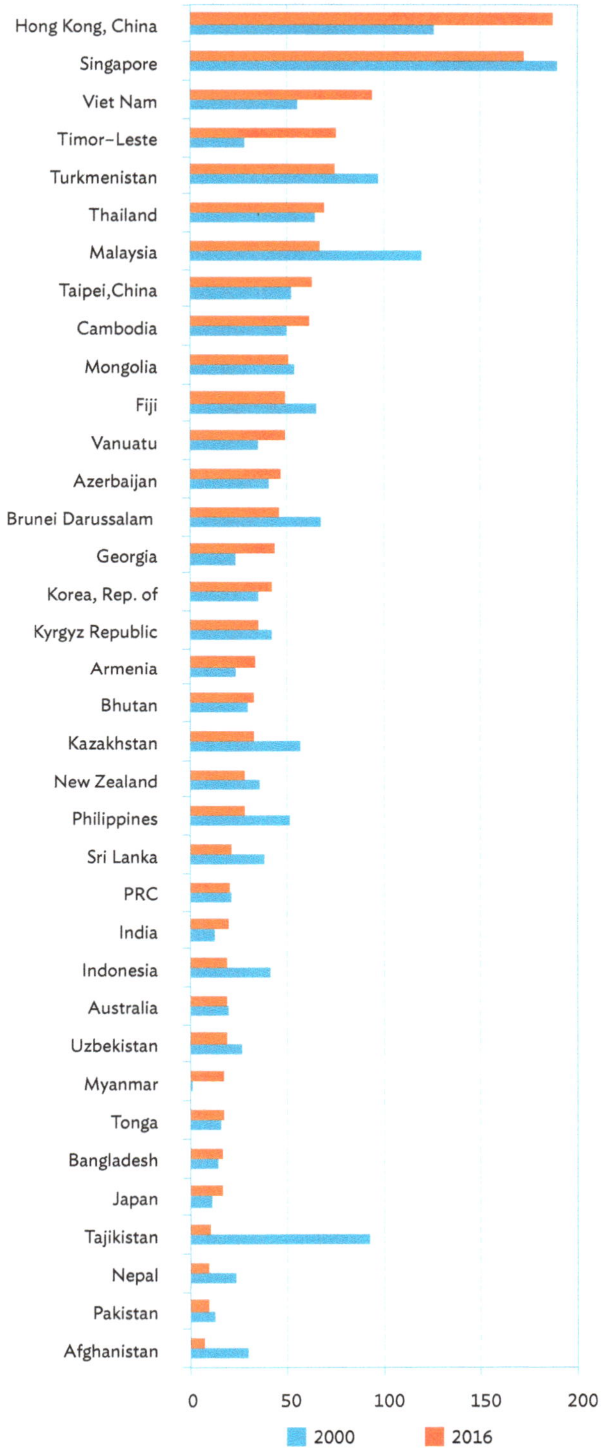

PRC = People's Republic of China.
Note: This chart includes economies with available data between 2000 and 2016. For Myanmar, data for 2000 is 0.5%.
Source: Table 2.7.

Figure 2.5: Share of Imports of Goods and Services to Gross Domestic Product
(%)

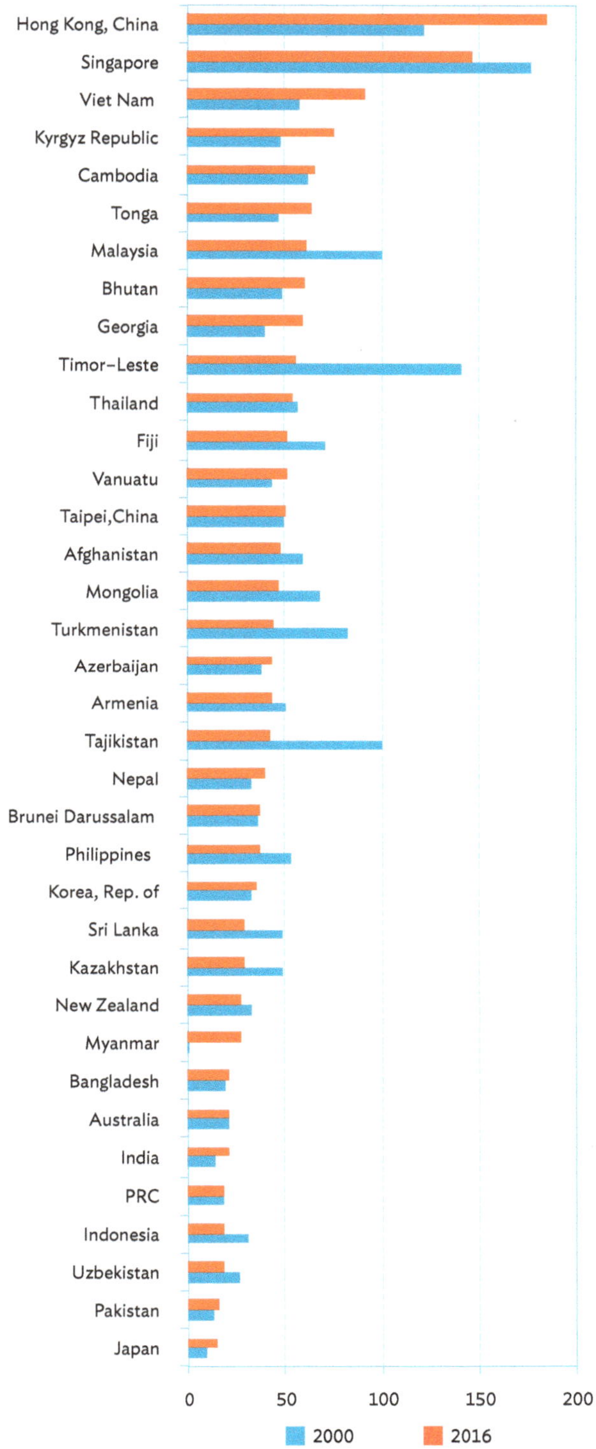

PRC = People's Republic of China.
Note: This chart includes economies with available data between 2000 and 2016. For Myanmar, data for 2000 is 0.6%.
Source: Table 2.7.

More than half of 36 regional economies for which data are available experienced an increase in gross capital formation as a percentage of GDP between 2000 and 2016. Figure 2.6 shows gross capital formation as a percentage of GDP in 2000 and 2016 for 36 regional economies for which data are available. Capital formation comprises fixed investment in the form of buildings, civil engineering, machinery, and equipment. Developed economies tend to have a larger and more modern stock of capital assets than developing economies. At the same time, rapidly developing economies often attempt to narrow this gap with increased investments and the incorporation of new technology.

More than half of regional economies reported a higher gross capital formation as a percentage of GDP in 2016 as compared with 2000; the rest a decline. The largest average annual gains were seen in Myanmar (1.4 percentage points), Brunei Darussalam (1.3 percentage points), and Tajikistan (1.2 percentage points). The largest decreases during the review period were observed in Timor-Leste (–0.8 percentage points); Singapore (–0.6 percentage points); and Taipei,China (–0.4 percentage points).

In 2016 (or the most recent year for which data are available), gross capital formation as a percentage of GDP ranged from a low of 15.6% in Pakistan to a high of 54.0% in Bhutan where the construction of hydropower projects is driving expanded investment and accelerating economic growth (ADB 2017). Turkmenistan had the next highest level of capital formation at 49.8%. Foreign direct investment in Turkmenistan is boosting value-added in oil, gas, and chemical production. The third highest level of capital formation was recorded in the People's Republic of China with gross domestic capital equivalent to 44.3% of GDP in 2016.

Figure 2.6: Share of Gross Capital Formation to Gross Domestic Product
(%)

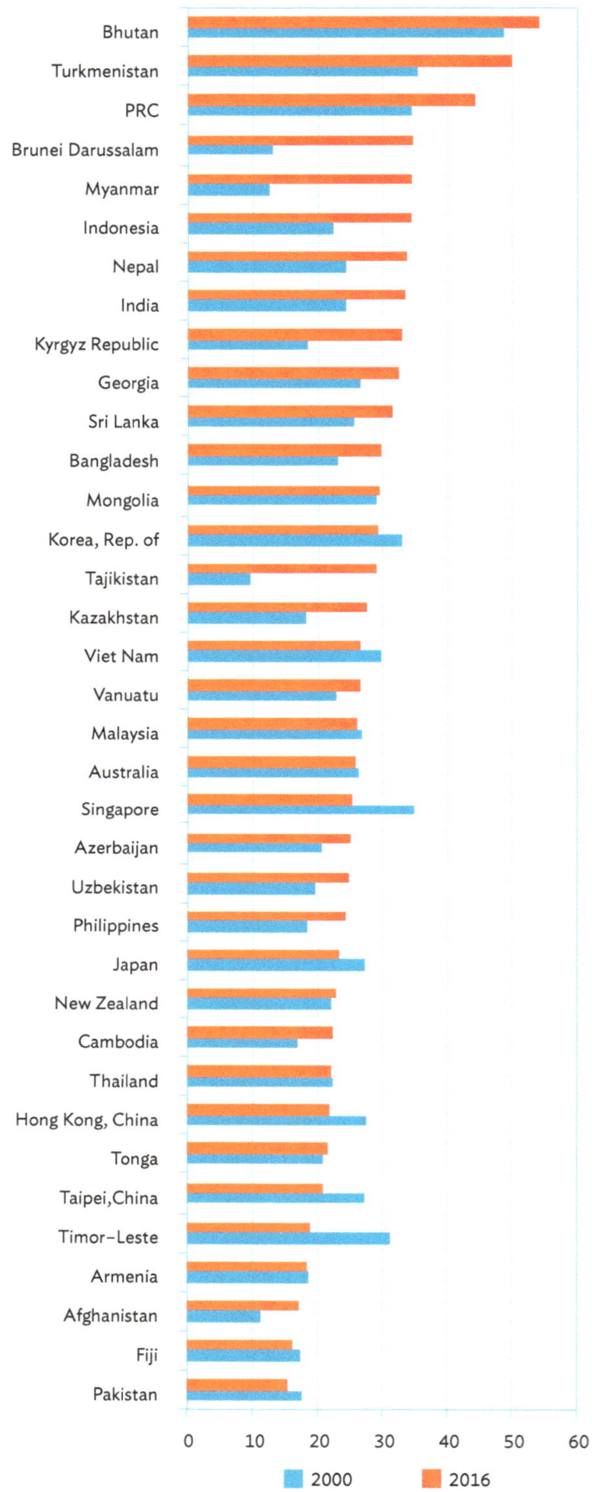

PRC = People's Republic of China.
Note: This chart includes economies with available data between 2000 and 2016.
Source: Table 2.6.

Data on gross fixed capital formation are also useful to better understand how much countries have been investing in infrastructure. Box 2.1 discusses how availability of disaggregated data on gross fixed capital formation can enhance estimates of infrastructure investments.

Box 2.1: How can Disaggregated Data on Gross Fixed Capital Formation Enhance Estimates of Infrastructure Investments?[a]

Given the key role that infrastructure plays in fostering growth and development, it is important for policymakers to have access to reliable and comparable statistics on how much is currently being invested in infrastructure, in which sectors, and by whom. Yet, as the recent Asian Development Bank (ADB) report, *Meeting Asia's Infrastructure Needs*, points out this information is surprisingly scarce. This is because many economies do not typically compile and publish data on infrastructure investments—whether by the government, state owned enterprises (SOEs), and/or the private sector—and there is no single way or international best practice to measure it (ADB 2017).

National accounts data on gross fixed capital formation (GFCF) is a rich source of information on how much the government, SOEs, and the private sector invest in physical assets in an economy. But not all components of GFCF are related to infrastructure. Consider the practice of using GFCF expenditures of the general government, or GFCF (GG), as a proxy measure of public infrastructure investment. GFCF (GG) captures investments in fixed assets by the government, including national and subnational governments, and social security funds and is readily available from the International Monetary Fund's Investment and Capital Stock Database for 170 countries from 1960 to 2015, which makes it suitable to analyze long-term public investment trends.

However, there are two major pitfalls of using the indicator GFCF (GG) to estimate general government infrastructure investment. First, it includes government investments in fixed assets in all economic sectors, but in some cases such as ADB's report, infrastructure is defined as including only transport, energy, water supply and sanitation, and telecommunications. Second, GFCF (GG) reflects the total investment made by a government on fixed assets of all types, which also includes investments that are not necessarily infrastructure-related. Thus GFCF (GG) includes all types of residential and non-residential buildings, civil engineering works, machinery and equipment, weapons systems, cultivated biological resources, and intellectual property products. Again, this is different from the definition followed in ADB's report which features investments in civil engineering works and infrastructure related to non-residential buildings and machinery and equipment.

Nevertheless, to illustrate the usefulness of GFCF data, the ADB report uses national accounts statistics for 2011 from Fiji and Pakistan to decompose GFCF into its infrastructure and noninfrastructure components. The data show that in 2011, in Fiji, noninfrastructure investment accounted for about 23% of GFCF (GG), while the noninfrastructure share of GFCF (GG) in Pakistan is 63% (Box Figure 2.1.1).

Box Figure 2.1.1: Decomposition of Gross Fixed Capital Formation for General Government into Infrastructure and Noninfrastructure Items, 2011 (%)

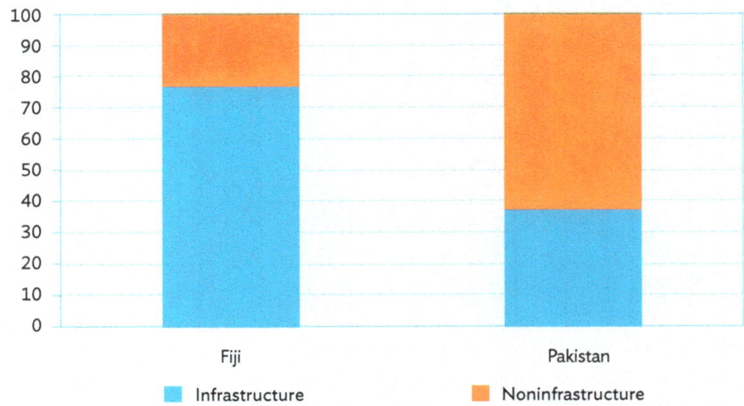

Sources: Bureau of Statistics of Fiji and Pakistan Bureau of Statistics.

(continued on next page)

[a] An earlier version of this box story appeared in K. Joshi, J. E. Lazatin, and J. P. Flaminiano. 2017. Can We Measure Infrastructure Investments More Accurately? https://blogs.adb.org/blog/can-we-measure-infrastructure-investments-more-accurately

(Box 2 continued)

One of the challenges with using the GFCF approach is the lack of a standardized classification mapping from economic sectors in national accounts to infrastructure sectors considered above. For instance, national statistics offices often classify investments in roads as GFCF (GG) under public works (or public administration) instead of under transport. In that case, GFCF (GG) classification by economic sectors in national accounts would underestimate the actual investment level. While on one side GFCF (GG) may overestimate general government investment in infrastructure, on the other side information about investments undertaken by the state-owned enterprises (SOEs) are still missing. This indicator may therefore underestimate public infrastructure investment if SOEs in an economy are heavily acquiring infrastructure assets through investments. However, it is difficult to infer the direction of the bias, without additional data.

To come up with a more accurate measure, disaggregated data used to estimate GFCF (GG) in national accounts can be extended to provide a standardized framework for satellite tabulations from national accounts. Had sufficient information been available, this method would result in data that complies with common statistical standards and allows more precise comparisons across regions, economies, sectors, and institutions.

More generally, improving infrastructure investment measures through analyzing disaggregated GFCF data would require additional tabulations by national accounts statisticians to compile infrastructure investment data by economic sector, asset type, and institutional sector. The feasibility of doing this would largely depend on the availability and level of details on acquired assets in the basic sources of data, such as government budget statements and financial statements of SOEs and private corporations. Aside from being able to correctly classify assets into infrastructure investments, there is also the bigger task of standardizing the methodology across economies.

Despite the mammoth task ahead, coming up with satellite tabulations for infrastructure investments using standardized data for GFCF will provide a complete measure of infrastructure investment for the entire economy. This will provide a much clearer understanding of actual investment flows in each period, and be able to segregate infrastructure investment from noninfrastructure investment. A more precise and accurate measure of infrastructure investment can better inform policy making to help realize our development goals.

Source:

ADB. 2017. *Meeting Asia's Infrastructure Needs*. Manila. https://www.adb.org/sites/default/files/publication/227496/special-report-infrastructure.pdf

Household consumption's share of GDP declined between 2000 and 2016 in nearly 70% of regional economies. As a percentage of GDP, household consumption fell in 25 of 36 regional economies for which data are available between 2000 and 2016 (Figure 2.7). The largest average annual declines during the review period occurred in Timor-Leste (–2.7 percentage points), Turkmenistan (–1.9 percentage points), and Afghanistan (–1.8 percentage points). The largest average annual gains were in the Kyrgyz Republic (1.7 percentage points), Malaysia (0.7 percentage points), and Nepal (0.5 percentage points).

As a share of the GDP, the (arithmetic) average household consumption expenditure of 36 Asia and the Pacific economies for which data are available was 65.4% in 2016 (Table 2.5). This compares with the 2015 global average of 58.0% (WB 2017). In 2016 (or the most recent year for which data are available), the highest levels of private household consumption were recorded in Tonga (96.6%), the Kyrgyz Republic (90.5%), and Nepal (84.6%); the lowest levels were observed in Turkmenistan (10.7%), Brunei Darussalam (21.2%), and Timor-Leste (29.0%).

Low rates of household consumer spending in some economies of Asia and the Pacific often reflect high rates of household saving, much of which is precautionary saving in the absence of sufficient social protection schemes (ADB 2010). Increased consumer spending can potentially reduce export dependence in large industrializing economies with existing high rates of saving (Loudiyi 2010).

Figure 2.7: Share of Household Consumption Expenditure to Gross Domestic Product
(%)

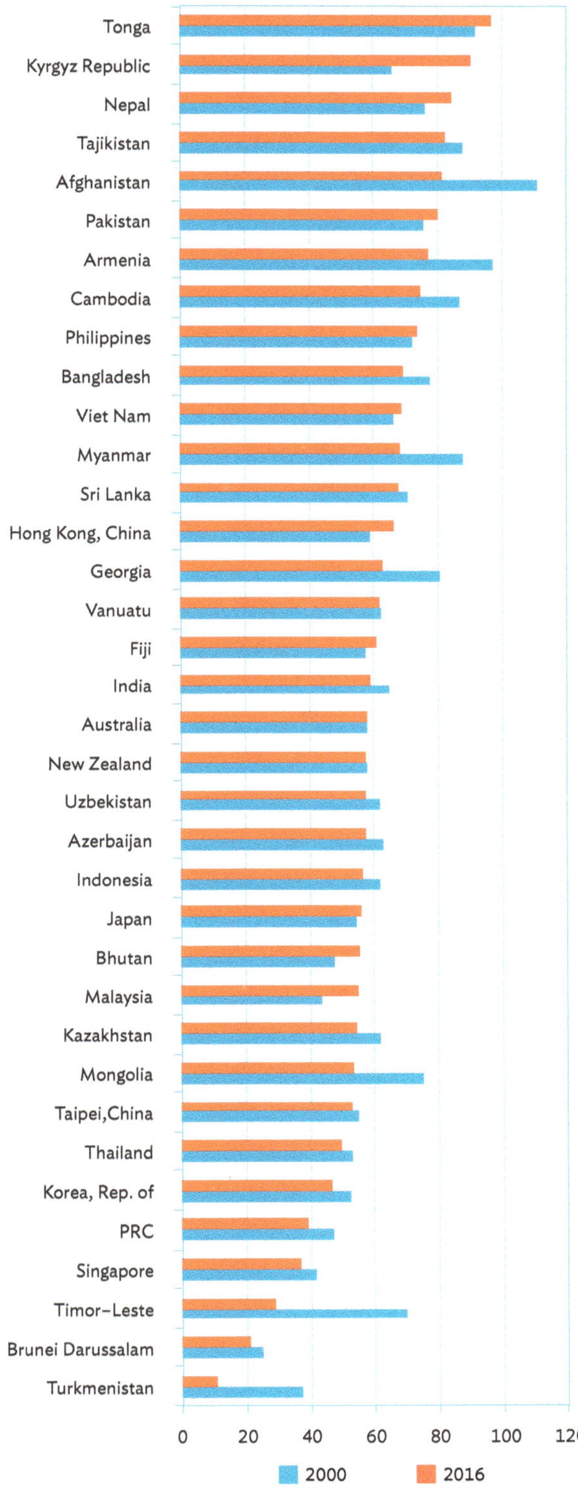

PRC = People's Republic of China.
Note: This chart includes economies with available data between 2000 and 2016.
Source: Table 2.5.

Data Issues and Comparability

Indicators in this theme are derived from national accounts compiled in accordance with the United Nations System of National Accounts (SNA). These indicators may not be fully consistent across economies because of differences in their data compilation frameworks, coverage of production boundaries, and changes in methodologies as national statistical offices gradually adopt the 2008 SNA framework. Furthermore, economies also have varying reference periods and price valuation methods. Some use the calendar year to compile national accounts while others use their fiscal year. Some economies with small statistical offices were not able to provide timely estimates.

Table 2.1: **Gross Domestic Product at Purchasing Power Parity**
(current international dollars, million)

Regional Member	2000	2005	2010	2011	2012	2013	2014	2015	2016
Developing Member Economies									
Central and West Asia									
Afghanistan	20,470 (2002)	26,954	46,549	51,634	58,333	63,113	66,224	65,735	69,013
Armenia	7,116	14,219	18,896	20,193	22,045	23,141	24,403	25,464	25,852
Azerbaijan	28,446	60,162	141,499	144,514	150,413	161,703	167,890	171,563	168,431
Georgia	11,430	18,288	25,902	28,346	30,701	32,254	34,349	35,719	37,182
Kazakhstan	117,400	215,982	321,378	352,286	375,997	404,994	429,559	439,390	454,156
Kyrgyz Republic	8,054	10,895	14,893	16,106	16,388	18,471	19,558	20,534	21,601
Pakistan	381,636	551,447	715,834	750,693	791,333	839,466	894,440	946,836	1,011,778
Tajikistan	6,163	10,990	16,539	17,287	18,934	20,672	22,445	24,033	26,032
Turkmenistan	18,749	27,498	49,556	58,014	65,641	73,505	82,454	88,974	95,586
Uzbekistan	48,918	71,507	118,646	131,147	144,515	158,597	174,016	189,960	207,470
East Asia									
China, People's Rep. of	3,703,736	6,639,273	12,484,968	13,957,940	15,331,824	16,788,030	18,335,663	19,811,754	21,417,150
Hong Kong, China	179,706	248,256	331,083	354,188	366,845	384,332	402,019	416,069	429,842
Korea, Rep. of	850,052	1,165,894	1,505,299	1,559,447	1,611,273	1,644,777	1,706,689	1,756,015	1,832,073
Mongolia	8,846	13,603	20,488	24,526	28,055	31,829	34,954	36,188	36,996
Taipei,China	480,625	657,933	893,930	947,053	984,435	1,022,324	1,082,429	1,101,878	1,132,964
South Asia									
Bangladesh	151,207	213,938	364,141	395,684	429,253	462,416	499,224	537,659	583,480
Bhutan	1,608	2,644	4,577	5,040	5,393	5,597	6,025	6,485	7,063
India	2,147,732	3,339,659	5,478,661	5,781,844	6,211,483	6,714,967	7,346,149	8,019,949	8,702,900
Maldives	1,495 (2001)	2,275	3,781	4,195	4,379	4,659	5,026	5,225	5,798
Nepal	28,486	38,000	52,654	55,504	59,274	63,008	68,194	71,108	72,416
Sri Lanka	84,448	112,586	168,798	186,763	207,597	218,113	233,031	246,935	261,140
Southeast Asia									
Brunei Darussalam	21,672	26,975	30,674	32,480	33,380	33,198	32,951	33,165	32,773
Cambodia	13,260	23,268	35,370	38,652	42,243	45,573	50,340	54,463	58,880
Indonesia	973,477	1,377,638	2,003,952	2,171,519	2,344,875	2,515,160	2,688,371	2,849,798	3,032,090
Lao PDR	9,388	14,966	23,065	26,229	29,575	32,464	35,562	38,558	41,807
Malaysia	299,738	424,427	581,371	624,786	671,129	713,972	770,448	817,434	863,286
Myanmar	47,733	98,203	182,865	197,077	215,424	237,348	260,903	282,688	287,201
Philippines	261,128	367,111	513,961	543,771	590,801	642,751	694,465	744,520	806,539
Singapore	165,055	235,355	358,655	388,845	411,339	438,886	462,703	476,720	492,631
Thailand	458,555	671,404	888,079	914,030	998,289	1,042,129	1,070,488	1,113,829	1,164,928
Viet Nam	151,084	255,657	382,113	414,339	444,114	475,755	513,249	553,422	595,524
The Pacific									
Cook Islands	...	...	...	...	...	...	...	...	...
Fiji	3,994	5,387	6,195	6,493	6,738	7,263	7,795	8,318	8,593
Kiribati	135	162	174	178	189	201	205	234	244
Marshall Islands	119	149	177	184	194	202	204	207	216
Micronesia, Fed. States of	270	313	342	354	362	355	348	365	379
Nauru	...	...	79	84	96	113	157	163	182
Palau	205	260	248	267	282	277	290	338	350
Papua New Guinea	7,912	9,891	21,319	22,938	25,006	26,736	29,096	...	...
Samoa	532	797	1,020	1,099	1,082	1,096	1,149	1,166	1,271
Solomon Islands	371	500	802	867	918	1,030	1,034	1,178	1,229
Timor-Leste	1,167	4,608	8,541	10,986	11,662	10,764	7,790	6,116	...
Tonga	358	449	508	534	547	540	561	588	626
Tuvalu	23	26	31	34	33	35	38	42	44
Vanuatu	416	486	683	705	731	757	789	791	833
Developed Member Economies									
Australia	505,757	664,703	863,447	933,417	968,591	1,055,739	1,089,656	1,105,632	1,128,909
Japan	3,398,784	4,045,734	4,481,979	4,573,187	4,746,699	4,967,052	5,013,008	5,167,094	5,262,479
New Zealand	82,978	106,148	136,022	143,508	145,406	160,669	167,681	174,410	183,299
DEVELOPING MEMBER ECONOMIES[a]	**10,702,916**	**16,960,036**	**27,818,296**	**30,238,854**	**32,743,121**	**35,362,570**	**38,263,678**	**41,001,575**	**43,988,550**
REGIONAL MEMBERS[a]	**14,690,435**	**21,776,622**	**33,299,745**	**35,888,967**	**38,603,817**	**41,546,030**	**44,534,024**	**47,448,711**	**50,563,237**

... = data not available at cutoff date, Lao PDR = Lao People's Democratic Republic.

a For reporting economies only.

Source: Asian Development Bank estimates.

Table 2.2: **Gross Domestic Product per Capita at Purchasing Power Parity**
(current international dollars)

Regional Member	2000	2005	2010	2011	2012	2013	2014	2015	2016
Developing Member Economies									
Central and West Asia									
Afghanistan	939 (2002)	1,142	1,790	1,948	2,160	2,295	2,357	2,298	2,363
Armenia	2,209	4,519	6,206	6,669	7,290	7,657	8,097	8,475	8,639
Azerbaijan	3,523	7,078	15,628	15,754	16,191	17,166	17,611	17,779	17,261
Georgia	2,577	4,232	5,839	6,343	6,826	7,193	7,649	9,618	9,994
Kazakhstan	7,888	14,259	19,690	21,278	22,392	23,774	24,845	25,051	25,514
Kyrgyz Republic	1,648	2,117	2,749	2,940	2,952	3,262	3,386	3,483	3,588
Pakistan	2,727	3,534	4,126	4,239	4,379	4,554	4,757	4,939	5,178
Tajikistan	996	1,604	2,171	2,216	2,370	2,533	2,688	2,811	3,011
Turkmenistan	4,165	5,792	9,829	11,361	12,689	14,027	15,536	16,558	17,574
Uzbekistan	1,984	2,733	4,154	4,470	4,854	5,244	5,658	6,069	6,515
East Asia									
China, People's Rep. of	2,941	5,103	9,348	10,401	11,323	12,338	13,405	14,413	15,489
Hong Kong, China	26,963	36,437	47,135	50,086	51,306	53,536	55,608	57,064	58,589
Korea, Rep. of	18,083	24,196	30,377	31,229	32,097	32,616	33,632	34,422	35,751
Mongolia	3,704	5,363	7,481	8,802	9,880	10,979	11,796	11,956	11,977
Taipei,China	21,665	28,946	38,630	40,833	42,304	43,793	46,250	46,963	48,179
South Asia									
Bangladesh	1,169	1,544	2,450	2,643	2,811	2,989	3,184	3,384	3,629
Bhutan	2,702	4,164	6,577	7,116	7,483	7,636	8,086	8,566	9,190
India	2,108	3,020	4,619	4,739	5,030	5,368	5,798	6,251	6,700
Maldives	4,900 (2001)	6,720	9,606	10,323	10,426	10,722	11,171	11,201	12,429
Nepal	1,354	1,502	2,006	2,095	2,207	2,315	2,472	2,544	2,556
Sri Lanka	4,362	5,731	8,173	8,949	10,164	10,599	11,219	11,778	12,316
Southeast Asia									
Brunei Darussalam	66,725	75,245	79,302	82,568	83,491	81,729	79,998	79,494	77,404
Cambodia	1,064	1,746	2,504	2,702	2,915	3,105	3,387	3,617	3,861
Indonesia	4,720	6,266	8,402	8,974	9,554	10,108	10,661	11,155	11,720
Lao PDR	1,845	2,662	3,818	4,279	4,756	5,146	5,557	5,939	6,348
Malaysia	12,760	16,295	20,336	21,498	22,742	23,867	25,178	26,200	27,267
Myanmar	1,001	1,965	3,535	3,781	4,100	4,480	5,018	5,390	5,429
Philippines	3,401	4,335	5,518	5,735	6,122	6,546	6,953	7,331	7,812
Singapore	40,978	55,172	70,647	75,013	77,430	81,287	84,594	86,128	87,855
Thailand	7,368	10,482	13,472	13,804	15,014	15,611	15,977	16,566	17,270
Viet Nam	1,959	3,121	4,396	4,717	5,003	5,300	5,657	6,034	6,424
The Pacific									
Cook Islands	...	...	...	...	...	...	...	...	...
Fiji	4,980	6,514	7,282	7,601	7,852	8,425	9,005	9,566	9,865
Kiribati	1,595	1,756	1,690	1,702	1,790	1,874	1,887	2,126	2,191
Marshall Islands	2,318	2,903	3,350	3,461	3,641	3,774	3,791	3,841	3,991
Micronesia, Fed. States of	2,526	2,967	3,327	3,452	3,543	3,475	3,410	3,571	3,697
Nauru	...	...	8,178	8,327	9,483	10,451	13,184	13,059	14,023
Palau	10,834	13,099	13,573	14,879	15,989	15,833	16,558	19,124	19,508
Papua New Guinea	1,524	1,634	3,022	3,153	3,333	3,456	3,648	...	...
Samoa	3,038	4,431	5,474	5,849	5,734	5,781	6,037	6,099	6,616
Solomon Islands	887	1,064	1,520	1,605	1,660	1,819	1,785	1,987	2,026
Timor-Leste	1,498	4,874	8,009	10,089	10,489	9,481	6,720	5,167	...
Tonga	3,616	4,436	4,945	5,178	5,297	5,211	5,401	5,648	6,018
Tuvalu	2,414	2,495	2,767	3,195	3,069	3,235	3,401	3,784	3,893
Vanuatu	2,171	2,234	2,782	2,801	2,830	2,861	2,909	2,852	2,940
Developed Member Economies									
Australia	26,578	32,944	39,191	41,782	42,616	45,669	46,446	46,472	46,787
Japan	26,795	31,663	34,996	35,779	37,211	39,007	39,432	40,699	41,438
New Zealand	21,509	25,677	31,264	32,735	32,986	36,170	37,182	37,951	39,061
DEVELOPING MEMBER ECONOMIES[a]	**3,261**	**4,867**	**7,558**	**8,093**	**13,497**	**14,387**	**15,371**	**16,264**	**17,233**
REGIONAL MEMBERS[a]	**4,280**	**5,988**	**8,683**	**9,224**	**14,959**	**15,900**	**16,841**	**17,728**	**18,669**

... = data not available at cutoff date, Lao PDR = Lao People's Democratic Republic.

a For reporting economies only.

Source: Asian Development Bank estimates.

Table 2.3: **Gross National Income per Capita, Atlas Method**
(current $)

Regional Member	2000	2005	2010	2011	2012	2013	2014	2015	2016
Developing Member Economies									
Central and West Asia									
Afghanistan	...	250	500	560	670	670	630	590	580
Armenia	660	1,540	3,470	3,530	3,880	4,120	4,150	4,020	3,760
Azerbaijan	610	1,270	5,410	5,560	6,480	7,450	7,700	6,550	4,760
Georgia	750	1,410	3,000	3,300	3,870	4,240	4,490	4,120	3,810
Kazakhstan	1,260	2,950	7,440	8,280	9,940	11,840	12,090	11,390	8,710
Kyrgyz Republic	280	450	850	880	1,040	1,190	1,250	1,180	1,100
Pakistan	490	730	1,080	1,150	1,260	1,360	1,390	1,430	1,510
Tajikistan	170	320	910	1,000	1,140	1,310	1,340	1,240	1,110
Turkmenistan	600	1,590	4,070	4,730	5,560	6,530	7,310	7,120	6,670
Uzbekistan	630	530	1,340	1,530	1,740	1,970	2,110	2,170	2,220
East Asia									
China, People's Rep. of	940	1,760	4,340	5,060	5,940	6,800	7,520	7,940	8,260
Hong Kong, China	26,930	28,890	33,620	35,690	36,320	38,530	40,170	41,100	43,240
Korea, Rep. of	10,740	17,790	21,260	22,540	24,550	25,760	26,800	27,250	27,600
Mongolia	470	900	2,000	2,600	3,660	4,350	4,240	3,850	3,550
Taipei,China	13,921	17,644	20,034	20,909	21,901	22,620	23,369	23,094	23,047
South Asia									
Bangladesh	420	530	780	870	940	1,010	1,070	1,190	1,330
Bhutan	770	1,210	1,970	2,150	2,290	2,300	2,340	2,350	2,510
India	440	700	1,220	1,380	1,480	1,520	1,560	1,600	1,680
Maldives	...	3,570	5,380	5,890	5,960	6,000	6,520	7,010	7,430
Nepal	230	310	540	600	690	720	730	730	730
Sri Lanka	880	1,220	2,430	2,860	3,360	3,490	3,670	3,750	3,780
Southeast Asia									
Brunei Darussalam	14,680	23,080	33,300	35,490	42,290	45,180	42,890	38,520	...
Cambodia	300	460	750	810	880	960	1,020	1,070	1,140
Indonesia	580	1,220	2,520	3,000	3,570	3,730	3,620	3,440	3,400
Lao PDR	280	460	1,000	1,120	1,350	1,590	1,840	2,000	2,150
Malaysia	3,460	5,280	8,240	9,040	10,150	10,760	11,000	10,440	9,850
Myanmar	170 (2002)	270	860	1,020	1,160	1,230	1,240	1,190	...
Philippines	1,220	1,520	2,730	2,620	2,980	3,300	3,470	3,520	3,580
Singapore	23,670	28,370	44,790	48,150	51,110	54,700	55,720	52,740	51,880
Thailand	1,980	2,790	4,580	4,950	5,520	5,730	5,750	5,690	5,640
Viet Nam	400	680	1,270	1,390	1,550	1,740	1,900	1,990	2,050
The Pacific									
Cook Islands	6,129	8,475	9,790	12,997	15,060	16,207	16,918	16,651	15,886
Fiji	2,230	3,590	3,650	3,760	4,120	4,700	4,850	4,810	4,840
Kiribati	1,330	1,730	1,990	2,010	2,450	2,840	3,250	3,390	2,380
Marshall Islands	2,850	3,570	3,790	3,960	3,990	4,270	4,390	4,550	4,450
Micronesia, Fed. States of	2,210	2,550	2,870	3,050	3,220	3,280	3,210	3,560	3,680
Nauru	...	...	5,800	6,760	9,190	13,330	14,730	11,850	10,750
Palau	5,890	9,250	8,910	9,310	9,670	9,760	10,650	12,180	12,450
Papua New Guinea	600	670	1,230	1,460	1,750	1,970	2,160	...	...
Samoa	1,600	2,370	3,200	3,470	3,780	3,920	4,040	4,070	4,100
Solomon Islands	1,010	890	910	1,120	1,510	1,820	1,820	1,910	1,880
Timor-Leste	780 (2002)	860	2,890	3,760	4,150	3,910	2,920	2,180	...
Tonga	2,050	2,470	3,560	3,770	4,200	4,310	4,370	4,240	4,020
Tuvalu	2,700 (2001)	3,620	4,400	4,700	4,420	5,590	4,800	5,620	5,090
Vanuatu	1,430	1,780	2,690	2,860	2,950	3,200	3,170	...	...
Developed Member Economies									
Australia	21,130	30,340	46,560	50,150	59,840	65,640	64,860	60,330	54,420
Japan	36,230	40,560	43,440	46,880	49,480	48,280	43,940	38,780	38,000
New Zealand	14,080	25,430	29,680	32,250	36,720	39,850	41,530	40,020	39,070

... = data not available at cutoff date, Lao PDR = Lao People's Democratic Republic.

Sources: World Bank. World Development Indicators Online. http://data.worldbank.org (accessed 25 July 2017); Asian Development Bank estimates using Atlas method based on economy sources for the Cook Islands and Taipei,China.

Table 2.4: **Agriculture, Industry, and Services Value Added**
(% of GDP)[a]

Regional Member	Agriculture				Industry				Services			
	2000	2005	2010	2016	2000	2005	2010	2016	2000	2005	2010	2016
Developing Member Economies												
Central and West Asia												
Afghanistan	43.7 (2002)	35.2	28.8	24.1	21.7 (2002)	26.0	21.3	22.0	34.6 (2002)	38.8	49.8	53.9
Armenia	25.1	20.6	18.8	17.4	38.3	44.7	36.3	26.9	36.5	34.6	45.0	55.7
Azerbaijan	17.1	9.8	5.9	6.0	45.3	63.3	64.3	51.7	37.5	26.9	29.8	42.3
Georgia	21.9	16.7	8.4	9.3	22.4	26.8	22.2	25.4	55.7	56.5	69.4	65.4
Kazakhstan	8.6	6.6	4.7	4.9	40.1	39.2	41.9	33.6	51.3	54.2	53.4	61.5
Kyrgyz Republic	36.6	31.3	18.7	14.4	31.3	22.0	28.2	28.3	32.1	46.7	53.1	57.3
Pakistan	27.4	24.4	24.3	24.6	18.8	21.1	20.6	19.4	53.8	54.5	55.1	56.0
Tajikistan	27.3	23.8	21.8	23.3	38.4	30.7	27.9	29.6	34.3	45.6	50.3	47.1
Turkmenistan	22.9	18.8	14.5	9.3 (2015)	41.8	37.6	48.4	56.9 (2015)	35.2	43.6	37.0	33.8 (2015)
Uzbekistan	34.4	29.5	19.8	17.6	23.1	29.1	33.3	32.9	42.5	41.4	46.9	49.5
East Asia												
China, People's Rep. of	14.9	12.0	9.8	8.9	45.7	47.2	46.6	40.0	39.4	40.9	43.6	51.2
Hong Kong, China	0.1	0.1	0.1	0.1 (2015)	12.6	8.7	7.0	7.4 (2015)	87.3	91.3	93.0	92.6 (2015)
Korea, Rep. of	4.4	3.1	2.5	2.2	38.1	37.5	38.3	38.6	57.5	59.4	59.3	59.2
Mongolia	30.9	22.1	13.1	13.3	25.0	36.2	37.0	35.3	44.1	41.7	50.0	51.4
Taipei,China	2.0	1.6	1.6	1.8	31.3	32.3	33.8	35.1	66.7	66.1	64.6	63.1
South Asia												
Bangladesh	25.5	20.1	17.8	14.8	25.3	27.2	26.1	28.8	49.2	52.6	56.0	56.5
Bhutan	27.4	23.2	17.5	17.4 (2015)	36.0	37.3	44.6	43.2 (2015)	36.6	39.5	37.9	39.4 (2015)
India	23.0	18.8	18.2	17.4	26.0	28.1	27.2	28.8	51.0	53.1	54.6	53.8
Maldives	6.9 (2001)	7.5	4.1	3.1 (2015)	13.2 (2001)	14.8	14.9	22.0 (2015)	79.9 (2001)	77.7	81.0	74.9 (2015)
Nepal	39.6	35.2	35.4	31.6	21.5	17.1	15.1	14.2	38.9	47.7	49.5	54.2
Sri Lanka	17.6	11.8	9.5	8.2	29.9	30.2	29.7	29.6	52.5	58.0	60.9	62.2
Southeast Asia												
Brunei Darussalam	1.0	0.9	0.7	1.2	63.7	71.6	67.4	56.5	35.3	27.5	31.9	42.4
Cambodia	37.9	32.4	36.1	26.3	23.0	26.4	23.2	31.3	39.1	41.2	40.8	42.4
Indonesia	15.6	13.1	14.3	14.0	45.9	46.5	43.9	40.8	38.5	40.3	41.8	45.3
Lao PDR	48.5	36.7	30.6	19.5	19.1	23.5	29.8	32.5	32.4	39.8	39.6	48.0
Malaysia	8.3	8.4	10.2	8.8	46.8	46.9	40.9	38.9	44.9	44.7	48.9	52.4
Myanmar	57.2	46.7	36.8	25.5	9.7	17.5	26.5	35.0	33.1	35.8	36.7	39.5
Philippines	14.0	12.7	12.3	9.7	34.5	33.8	32.6	30.9	51.5	53.5	55.1	59.5
Singapore	0.1	0.1	0.0	0.0	34.8	32.4	27.6	26.1	65.1	67.6	72.3	73.8
Thailand	8.5	9.2	10.5	8.3	36.8	38.6	39.9	35.8	54.7	52.2	49.6	55.8
Viet Nam	24.5	19.3	21.0	18.1	36.7	38.1	36.7	36.4	38.7	42.6	42.2	45.5
The Pacific												
Cook Islands	10.3	6.9	4.9	7.9	8.3	9.6	8.5	7.6	81.4	83.5	86.6	84.5
Fiji	16.5	14.1	11.0	11.3 (2015)	21.6	19.2	20.9	18.1 (2015)	61.9	66.8	68.1	70.7 (2015)
Kiribati	20.0	21.8	24.6	22.6 (2015)	12.2	9.3	10.3	14.4 (2015)	67.8	68.9	65.1	63.0 (2015)
Marshall Islands	10.4	9.2	15.6	14.3 (2015)	11.4	9.2	11.6	10.6 (2015)	78.2	81.6	72.9	75.1 (2015)
Micronesia, Fed. States of	25.3	24.2	26.7	27.8 (2015)	8.7	5.7	7.8	6.5 (2015)	66.1	70.2	65.5	65.8 (2015)
Nauru	...	7.8	4.3	...	...	-6.5	47.8	...	...	98.7	47.9	...
Palau	4.8	4.4	4.5	3.4	17.5	16.6	10.7	8.4	77.7	79.1	84.8	88.3
Papua New Guinea	35.2	34.0	20.2	18.8 (2014)	40.7	44.3	34.2	33.7 (2014)	24.1	21.7	45.5	47.5 (2014)
Samoa	16.7	12.3	9.1	10.4	26.8	30.6	25.9	22.7	56.6	57.2	65.0	66.9
Solomon Islands	...	32.8	30.4	28.0 (2014)	...	9.6	13.3	15.0 (2014)	...	57.6	56.3	57.0 (2014)
Timor-Leste[b]	23.3	7.4	4.8	9.2 (2015)	31.1	76.6	79.9	57.8 (2015)	45.7	16.0	15.3	33.1 (2015)
Tonga	22.2	20.0	18.2	19.3	20.7	19.0	20.0	19.4	57.1	61.0	61.8	61.3
Tuvalu	20.2	22.2	27.6	21.1 (2015)	7.3	8.3	4.7	13.4 (2015)	72.6	69.4	67.7	65.5 (2015)
Vanuatu	25.4	24.1	21.9	26.8 (2014)	12.2	8.5	13.0	8.7 (2014)	62.3	67.4	65.0	64.5 (2014)
Developed Member Economies												
Australia	3.4	3.2	2.4	2.6	26.7	26.8	27.1	24.4	69.9	70.1	70.6	73.3
Japan	1.5	1.1	1.1	1.1 (2015)	32.7	30.1	28.5	28.9 (2015)	65.8	68.8	70.4	70.0 (2015)
New Zealand	8.3	4.9	7.1	5.2 (2014)	25.3	25.8	23.0	23.4 (2014)	66.4	69.3	69.9	71.4 (2014)

... = data not available at cutoff date, 0.0 = magnitude is less than half of the unit employed, GDP = gross domestic product, Lao PDR = Lao People's Democratic Republic.

a Computed as a share of GDP at current prices.

b The treatment of oil production from 2004 onward reflects the 2008 System of National Accounts concepts on resident units. Prior to 2004, oil production was based on proportion of revenues between Timor-Leste and the licensee or lessee.

Source: Economy sources.

Table 2.5: **Household and Government Consumption Expenditure**
(% of GDP)[a]

Regional Member	Household Consumption				Government Consumption			
	2000	2005	2010	2016	2000	2005	2010	2016
Developing Member Economies								
Central and West Asia								
Afghanistan	111.2 (2002)	115.7	97.4	81.6	7.7 (2002)	10.0	14.0	12.0
Armenia[b]	97.1	75.5	82.0	77.0	11.8	10.6	13.1	13.9
Azerbaijan	63.0	41.6	38.9	57.4	15.2	10.4	10.9	13.1
Georgia	80.5	64.6	72.3	62.7	8.5	17.3	21.1	18.4
Kazakhstan[b]	61.9	49.9	45.4	54.3	12.1	11.2	10.8	11.8
Kyrgyz Republic[b]	65.7	84.5	84.6	90.5 (2015)	20.0	17.5	18.1	17.8 (2015)
Pakistan[b]	75.5	78.4	79.7	80.0	8.1	7.5	10.3	11.3
Tajikistan[b]	87.7	81.1	84.7	82.5 (2015)	11.6	14.6	11.3	15.0 (2015)
Turkmenistan[b]	37.1	46.6	5.0	10.7 (2014)	14.5	13.2	9.3	9.0 (2014)
Uzbekistan	61.9	46.7	47.9	57.5	18.7	17.6	15.8	16.1
East Asia								
China, People's Rep. of	46.9	40.2	35.4	39.3	16.6	14.0	12.8	14.4
Hong Kong, China[b]	58.6	57.5	61.4	66.1	9.4	9.2	8.9	10.0
Korea, Rep. of	52.5	50.7	48.6	46.4	11.3	13.3	14.5	15.2
Mongolia	75.1	55.2	55.2	53.3	15.3	12.1	12.7	14.5
Taipei,China	55.1	56.1	53.1	52.7	15.7	15.3	14.9	14.3
South Asia								
Bangladesh	77.5	74.4	74.1	69.1	4.6	5.5	5.1	5.9
Bhutan[b]	47.7	40.4	46.6	55.3 (2015)	21.9	21.9	20.0	17.8 (2015)
India[b]	64.6	58.3	56.0	58.8	12.6	10.9	11.4	11.7
Maldives	...	...	...	...	...	...	...	...
Nepal[b]	75.9	79.5	78.6	84.6	8.9	8.9	10.0	11.6
Sri Lanka	70.9	69.0	68.5	67.6	13.7	13.1	8.5	8.6
Southeast Asia								
Brunei Darussalam[b]	24.8	22.5	14.7	21.2	25.8	18.4	22.2	26.2
Cambodia[b]	86.7	84.3	81.3	74.4	5.2	5.8	6.3	5.2
Indonesia[c]	61.7	64.4	55.2	56.5	6.5	8.1	9.0	9.4
Lao PDR	...	...	...	...	...	...	...	...
Malaysia[c]	43.8	44.2	48.1	54.9	10.2	11.5	12.6	12.6
Myanmar[d]	87.7	86.9	67.3	68.2 (2015)	...	...	...	...
Philippines[b]	72.2	75.0	71.6	73.6	11.4	9.0	9.7	11.1
Singapore	41.5	39.1	35.5	36.5	10.7	10.2	10.2	11.3
Thailand	53.1	54.9	51.2	49.7	13.6	13.7	15.8	17.1
Viet Nam	66.5	65.5	66.6	68.5	6.4	5.5	6.0	6.5
The Pacific								
Cook Islands	...	...	...	...	...	...	...	...
Fiji[b]	57.2	77.0	72.3	60.9 (2015)	17.3	15.9	15.0	20.7 (2015)
Kiribati	...	...	...	...	...	...	...	...
Marshall Islands	...	79.0	81.0	81.4 (2015)	...	56.1	50.9	53.9 (2015)
Micronesia, Fed. States of	...	...	...	...	...	...	...	...
Nauru	...	...	...	...	...	...	...	...
Palau	...	63.8 (2007)	67.0	58.8	...	32.3 (2007)	36.6	27.2
Papua New Guinea[b]	44.6	48.0	...	...	16.6	16.1	...	...
Samoa	...	...	...	...	...	...	...	...
Solomon Islands	...	63.2	60.2	58.0 (2014)	...	45.7	40.8	33.2 (2014)
Timor-Leste[e]	69.9	22.1	15.1	29.0 (2015)	109.6	13.3	22.8	30.1 (2015)
Tonga	91.9	100.9	98.1	96.6 (2015)	18.2	15.5	18.1	19.9 (2015)
Tuvalu	...	...	...	...	...	...	...	...
Vanuatu	62.4	65.8	60.6	61.6 (2014)	16.4	13.2	17.5	13.2 (2014)
Developed Member Economies								
Australia	58.0	57.8	55.4	57.7	17.8	17.5	18.0	18.9
Japan	54.4	55.6	57.8	55.9	16.9	18.1	19.5	19.8
New Zealand	58.0	58.2	58.1	57.6 (2015)	17.0	17.9	19.5	18.7 (2015)

... = data not available at cutoff date, GDP = gross domestic product, Lao PDR = Lao People's Democratic Republic.

a Computed as a share of GDP at current prices.
b Data for household consumption includes nonprofit institution serving households.
c Data for household consumption before 2010 includes nonprofit institution serving households.
d Data for household consumption includes government consumption.
e The treatment of oil production from 2000 onward reflects the 2008 System of National Accounts concepts on resident units. Prior to 2000, oil production was based on proportion of revenues between Timor-Leste and the licensee or lessee.

Source: Economy sources.

Table 2.6: **Gross Capital Formation and Changes in Inventories**
(% of GDP)[a]

Regional Member	Gross Capital Formation				Change in Inventories			
	2000	2005	2010	2016	2000	2005	2010	2016
Developing Member Economies								
Central and West Asia								
Afghanistan	11.3 (2002)	21.8	17.5	17.2	...	...	5.3	30.1
Armenia	18.6	30.5	32.9	18.4	0.2	0.7	-0.6	0.7
Azerbaijan	20.7	41.5	18.1	24.9	-2.5	0.2	-0.1	0.1
Georgia	26.6	33.5	21.6	32.4	1.1	5.4	2.3	2.0
Kazakhstan	18.1	31.0	25.4	27.5	0.8	3.0	1.0	5.2
Kyrgyz Republic[b]	18.3	16.2	28.1	33.0 (2015)	1.7	0.2	-0.7	1.7 (2015)
Pakistan	17.6	17.7	15.8	15.6	1.6	1.6	1.6	1.6
Tajikistan	9.4	11.6	23.8	28.9 (2015)	2.0	0.5	-0.6	0.6 (2015)
Turkmenistan	35.4	22.9	51.9	49.8 (2014)	...	...	...	...
Uzbekistan	19.6	26.5	26.6	24.9	-4.4	4.5	-0.8	-2.9
East Asia								
China, People's Rep. of	34.4	41.4	47.6	44.3	1.0	0.9	2.6	1.5
Hong Kong, China	27.6	21.1	23.9	21.9	1.1	-0.3	2.1	0.4
Korea, Rep. of	32.9	32.2	32.0	29.2	1.3	1.3	1.5	-0.5
Mongolia	29.0	37.5	42.1	29.5	3.8	9.6	7.6	9.4
Taipei,China	27.2	24.5	25.0	20.8	0.9	0.3	1.3	-0.1
South Asia								
Bangladesh[c]	23.0	24.5	26.2	29.7	...	...	...	...
Bhutan	48.7	52.0	61.7	54.0 (2015)	-1.8	0.0	0.5	-0.3 (2015)
India	24.3	34.7	36.5	33.3 (2015)	0.7	2.8	3.5	2.2
Maldives	...	...	...	...	...	...	...	...
Nepal	24.3	26.5	38.3	33.7	5.0	6.5	16.1	4.9
Sri Lanka	25.4	26.1	30.4	31.5	0.6	2.8	5.9	3.2
Southeast Asia								
Brunei Darussalam	13.1	11.4	23.7	34.6	0.1	0.0	0.2	0.3
Cambodia	16.9	18.5	17.4	22.4 (2015)	-1.4	-0.4	1.2	1.0 (2015)
Indonesia	22.2	25.1	32.9	34.3	2.4	1.4	1.9	1.7
Lao PDR	...	...	...	...	...	...	...	...
Malaysia	26.9	22.4	23.4	26.1	1.6	0.1	1.0	0.3
Myanmar	12.4	13.2	23.2	34.4	0.7	0.5	0.3	1.3
Philippines	18.4	21.6	20.5	24.3	-3.7	1.6	0.0	-0.3
Singapore	34.9	21.4	28.2	25.3	2.9	-1.7	2.1	0.5
Thailand	22.3	30.4	25.4	22.0	0.7	2.7	1.4	-2.3
Viet Nam	29.6	33.8	35.7	26.6	2.0	2.5	3.0	2.9
The Pacific								
Cook Islands	...	...	...	...	...	...	...	...
Fiji	17.3	21.0	18.7	16.3 (2015)	1.9	1.4	2.9	0.0 (2015)
Kiribati	...	...	...	...	...	...	...	...
Marshall Islands	...	13.7	36.7	16.0 (2015)	...	0.2	0.1	-0.3 (2015)
Micronesia, Fed. States of	...	...	...	...	...	...	...	...
Nauru	...	...	...	...	...	...	...	...
Palau	...	29.0 (2007)	21.9	24.6	...	0.2 (2007)	0.7	1.9
Papua New Guinea	21.9	17.5	...	...	1.5	1.0	...	...
Samoa	...	...	...	...	...	...	...	...
Solomon Islands	...	...	...	...	...	...	...	...
Timor-Leste[d]	31.3	5.0	12.0	18.9 (2015)	-3.7	-	0.0	0.5 (2015)
Tonga	20.7	22.3	30.1	21.5 (2015)	0.5	0.3	0.5	0.4 (2015)
Tuvalu	...	...	...	...	...	...	...	...
Vanuatu	22.9	24.1	34.7	26.4 (2014)	0.5	0.7	0.8	0.7 (2014)
Developed Member Economies								
Australia	26.3	27.4	27.6	25.7	0.3	0.4	-0.2	-0.0
Japan	27.3	24.7	21.3	23.3	-0.1	0.1	0.0	0.2
New Zealand	22.0	25.4	20.1	22.9 (2015)	1.2	0.7	0.4	0.3 (2015)

... = data not available at cutoff date, 0.0 or -0.0= magnitude is less than half of unit employed, - = magnitude equals zero, GDP = gross domestic product, Lao PDR = Lao People's Democratic Republic.

a Computed as a share of GDP at current prices.
b Change in inventories is not included in gross capital formation.
c Change in inventories is included in gross capital formation.
d The treatment of oil production from 2000 onward reflects the 2008 System of National Accounts concepts on resident units. Prior to 2000, oil production was based on proportion of revenues between Timor-Leste and the licensee or lessee.

Source: Economy sources.

Table 2.7: **Exports and Imports of Goods and Services**
(% of GDP)[a]

Regional Member	Exports of Goods and Services				Imports of Goods and Services			
	2000	2005	2010	2016	2000	2005	2010	2016
Developing Member Economies								
Central and West Asia								
Afghanistan	29.7 (2002)	26.0	9.8	6.7	59.8 (2002)	73.6	43.9	47.6
Armenia	23.4	28.8	20.8	33.1	50.5	43.2	45.3	43.2
Azerbaijan	40.2	62.9	54.3	46.5	38.4	52.9	20.7	43.7
Georgia	23.0	33.7	35.0	43.5	39.7	51.6	52.8	59.1
Kazakhstan	56.6	53.2	44.2	32.4	49.1	44.6	29.9	28.8
Kyrgyz Republic	41.8	38.3	51.6	35.2 (2015)	47.6	56.8	81.7	75.8 (2015)
Pakistan	12.1	14.3	13.5	9.1	13.2	17.8	19.4	16.0
Tajikistan	92.4	54.3	26.8	10.3 (2015)	100.2	72.8	59.0	42.3 (2015)
Turkmenistan	97.2	65.0	76.3	74.2 (2014)	82.4	47.8	44.5	44.0 (2014)
Uzbekistan	26.5	37.9	33.1	18.8	26.7	28.7	24.5	18.1
East Asia								
China, People's Rep. of	20.9	33.8	26.3	20.6	18.5	28.4	22.6	18.4
Hong Kong, China	126.0	177.5	205.3	187.4	121.6	165.3	199.5	185.4
Korea, Rep. of	35.0	36.8	49.4	42.2	32.9	34.4	46.2	35.4
Mongolia	54.0	58.8	46.7	50.8	67.9	63.6	56.7	46.8
Taipei,China	51.9	60.6	70.9	62.9	49.9	56.4	63.9	50.7
South Asia								
Bangladesh	14.0	16.6	16.0	16.7	19.2	23.0	21.8	21.3
Bhutan	29.4	38.2	42.5	32.9 (2015)	48.3	64.4	70.7	60.0 (2015)
India	12.8	19.3	22.0	19.2	13.7	22.0	26.3	20.6
Maldives	...	...	...	...	...	...	...	...
Nepal	23.3	14.6	9.6	9.5	32.4	29.5	36.4	39.4
Sri Lanka	38.2	32.3	19.6	21.4	48.4	41.3	26.8	29.1
Southeast Asia								
Brunei Darussalam	67.4	70.2	67.4	46.0	35.8	27.3	28.0	37.4
Cambodia	49.9	64.1	54.1	61.3	61.7	72.7	59.5	65.7
Indonesia	41.0	34.1	24.3	19.1	30.5	29.9	22.4	18.3
Lao PDR	...	...	...	...	...	...	...	...
Malaysia	119.8	112.9	86.9	67.2	100.6	91.0	71.0	60.8
Myanmar	0.5	0.2	19.6	17.4	0.6	0.1	15.1	27.1
Philippines	51.4	46.1	34.8	28.0	53.4	51.7	36.6	36.9
Singapore	189.2	226.2	199.7	172.1	176.9	196.4	173.7	146.3
Thailand	64.8	68.4	66.5	68.9	56.5	69.5	60.8	54.2
Viet Nam	55.0	63.7	72.0	93.6	57.5	67.0	80.2	91.1
The Pacific								
Cook Islands	...	...	...	...	...	...	...	...
Fiji	65.4	51.0	57.8	48.8 (2015)	70.5	63.9	63.9	51.7 (2015)
Kiribati	...	...	...	...	...	...	...	...
Marshall Islands	...	36.6	44.2	46.8 (2015)	...	96.5	113.7	96.0 (2015)
Micronesia, Fed. States of	...	...	...	...	...	...	...	...
Nauru	...	...	...	...	...	...	...	...
Palau	...	48.1 (2007)	53.6	55.2	...	75.7 (2007)	76.5	67.6
Papua New Guinea	66.2	74.5	...	...	49.2	56.1	...	...
Samoa	...	...	...	...	...	...	...	...
Solomon Islands	...	33.3	47.6	54.4 (2014)	...	52.7	79.0	66.2 (2014)
Timor-Leste[b]	28.4	81.5	100.2	75.6 (2015)	141.5	22.7	50.7	55.4 (2015)
Tonga	15.4	17.7	13.2	17.0 (2015)	46.8	57.8	57.9	63.4 (2015)
Tuvalu	...	...	...	...	...	...	...	...
Vanuatu	34.7	45.4	46.6	48.7 (2014)	43.7	54.8	52.7	51.1 (2014)
Developed Member Economies								
Australia	19.4	18.1	19.4	18.9	21.4	20.8	20.4	21.1
Japan	10.6	14.0	15.0	16.2	9.2	12.5	13.6	15.2
New Zealand	35.7	28.3	30.3	28.0 (2015)	32.8	29.7	28.0	27.3 (2015)

... = data not available at cutoff date, GDP = gross domestic product, Lao PDR = Lao People's Democratic Republic.

a Computed as a share of GDP at current prices.
b The treatment of oil production from 2000 onward reflects the 2008 System of National Accounts concepts on resident units. Prior to 2000, oil production was based on proportion of revenues between Timor-Leste and the licensee or lessee.

Source: Economy sources.

Table 2.8: **Gross Domestic Saving**
(% of GDP)[a]

Regional Member	2000	2005	2010	2011	2012	2013	2014	2015	2016
Developing Member Economies									
Central and West Asia									
Afghanistan	-18.8 (2002)	-25.8	-11.4	-3.7	3.8	7.8	8.0	5.1	6.4
Armenia	-8.9	14.0	4.9	3.4	1.9	0.9	2.4	8.8	9.1
Azerbaijan	20.4	47.5	49.8	52.6	50.0	47.8	43.7	30.9	29.0
Georgia	9.9	15.7	3.8	7.6	9.3	11.8	12.3	14.0	16.8
Kazakhstan	26.0	38.9	43.8	47.3	43.5	39.9	40.8	34.6	33.9
Kyrgyz Republic	14.3	-2.1	-2.7	-1.6	-15.9	-15.6	-13.5	-8.3	...
Pakistan	16.5	14.2	10.0	9.1	7.1	8.2	8.2	9.3	8.7
Tajikistan	0.6	4.3	4.0	-10.8	-13.5	-13.9	-12.7	2.5	...
Turkmenistan	48.4	40.2	85.6	83.1	76.1	81.6	80.3	...	...
Uzbekistan	19.4	35.7	35.2	34.3	32.6	31.0	29.5	27.1	25.6
East Asia									
China, People's Rep. of	36.5	45.8	51.8	50.7	49.8	49.5	49.0	47.4	46.2
Hong Kong, China	32.0	33.3	29.8	28.0	26.4	24.6	24.0	23.9	23.9
Korea, Rep. of	34.9	34.5	35.2	34.5	33.8	34.1	34.5	35.7	36.0
Mongolia	9.6	32.7	32.1	36.3	33.5	30.7	30.4	27.4	32.3
Taipei,China	29.4	29.1	31.7	30.4	28.8	30.7	32.2	33.2	32.3
South Asia									
Bangladesh	17.9	20.0	20.8	20.6	21.2	22.0	22.1	22.2	25.0
Bhutan	29.7	25.9	33.4	38.4	43.6	24.1	30.7	26.9	...
India	...	...	...	...	...	...	...	...	...
Maldives	...	...	...	...	...	...	...	...	...
Nepal	15.2	11.6	11.5	14.0	11.0	10.6	11.9	8.8	5.3
Sri Lanka	15.4	17.9	23.1	20.2	27.2	24.6	24.2	20.9	23.8
Southeast Asia									
Brunei Darussalam	49.4	59.1	39.4	42.5	34.9	25.0	35.7	19.9	...
Cambodia	8.1	9.9	12.4	11.1	16.0	17.9	19.4	19.8	20.4
Indonesia	31.8	27.5	34.8	35.5	34.4	33.7	33.4	32.9	32.9
Lao PDR	...	...	...	...	...	...	...	...	...
Malaysia	46.1	44.3	39.3	38.8	36.5	34.5	34.3	32.7	32.5
Myanmar	12.3	13.1	32.7	37.0	36.6	33.8	32.6	31.8	26.7
Philippines	16.4	15.9	18.7	16.8	14.9	15.8	17.0	15.2	15.3
Singapore	47.2	51.2	54.3	54.1	53.3	52.8	53.2	52.7	51.2
Thailand	31.7	30.3	32.0	29.8	30.1	31.3	31.8	34.9	37.7
Viet Nam	27.1	29.0	27.4	27.7	29.6	28.4	27.9	25.7	24.9
The Pacific									
Cook Islands	...	...	...	...	...	...	...	...	...
Fiji	25.6	7.1	12.7	15.1	14.2	15.5	16.6	...	...
Kiribati	...	...	...	...	...	...	...	...	...
Marshall Islands	...	-36.5	-33.0	-31.8	-28.4	-24.3	-28.7	-36.6	...
Micronesia, Fed. States of	...	...	...	...	...	...	...	...	...
Nauru	...	...	...	...	...	...	...	...	...
Palau	...	7.4 (2007)	9.5	16.5	20.6	24.2	27.8	37.7	37.8
Papua New Guinea	38.8	35.9	...	...	...	...	...	...	...
Samoa	...	...	...	...	...	...	...	...	...
Solomon Islands	...	...	...	...	...	...	...	...	...
Timor-Leste[b]	31.8	18.3	60.8	71.5	74.2	68.5	53.6	39.2	...
Tonga	-10.0	-16.3	-16.1	-9.6	-12.8	-19.8	-21.3	...	...
Tuvalu	...	...	...	...	...	...	...	...	...
Vanuatu	21.2	13.9	27.0	21.5	20.9	23.3	24.0	...	...
Developed Member Economies									
Australia	24.2	24.7	26.6	28.2	28.2	27.3	26.9	25.3	23.5
Japan	29.0	26.8	22.9	21.6	21.1	20.9	21.3	23.2	...
New Zealand	19.7	17.6	26.8	17.7	17.3	19.5	19.6	20.3	...

... = data not available at cutoff date, GDP = gross domestic product, Lao PDR = Lao People's Democratic Republic.

a Computed as a share of GDP at current prices.

b The treatment of oil production from 2000 onward reflects the 2008 System of National Accounts concepts on resident units. Prior to 2000, oil production was based on proportion of revenues between Timor-Leste and the licensee or lessee.

Source: Economy sources.

Table 2.9: **Growth Rates of Real Gross Domestic Product**
(%)

Regional Member	2000	2005	2010	2011	2012	2013	2014	2015	2016
Developing Member Economies									
Central and West Asia									
Afghanistan	...	9.9	3.2	8.7	10.9	6.4	3.1	-1.8	3.6
Armenia	5.9	13.9	2.2	4.7	7.2	3.3	3.6	3.2	0.2
Azerbaijan	11.1	26.4	5.0	0.1	2.2	5.8	2.8	1.1	-3.1
Georgia	1.8	9.6	6.2	7.2	6.4	3.4	4.6	2.9	2.7
Kazakhstan	9.8	9.7	7.3	8.9	4.8	6.0	4.2	1.2	1.0
Kyrgyz Republic	5.4	-0.2	-0.5	6.0	-0.1	10.9	4.0	3.9	3.8
Pakistan	3.6 (2001)	6.5	1.6	2.7	3.5	4.4	4.7	4.7	5.5
Tajikistan	8.3	6.7	6.5	2.4	7.5	7.4	6.7	6.0	6.9
Turkmenistan	5.5	13.0	9.2	14.7	11.1	10.2	10.3	6.5	6.2
Uzbekistan	4.0	7.0	8.5	8.3	8.2	8.0	8.0	7.9	7.3
East Asia									
China, People's Rep. of	8.5	11.4	10.6	9.5	7.9	7.8	7.3	6.9	6.7
Hong Kong, China	7.7	7.4	6.8	4.8	1.7	3.1	2.8	2.4	1.9
Korea, Rep. of	8.9	3.9	6.5	3.7	2.3	2.9	3.3	2.8	2.8
Mongolia	1.1	7.3	-1.3 (2009)	17.3	12.3	11.6	7.9	2.4	1.0
Taipei,China	6.4	5.4	10.6	3.8	2.1	2.2	4.0	0.7	1.5
South Asia									
Bangladesh	6.0	6.0	5.6	6.5	6.5	6.0	6.1	6.6	7.1
Bhutan	6.9	7.1	11.7	7.9	5.1	2.1	5.7	6.5	...
India	3.8	9.3	10.3	...	5.4	6.1	7.2	7.9	6.6
Maldives	4.0	-8.1	7.2	8.7	2.5	4.7	6.0	2.8	3.9
Nepal	6.0	3.5	4.8	3.4	4.8	4.1	6.0	3.3	0.4
Sri Lanka	6.0	6.2	3.5 (2009)	8.4	9.1	3.4	5.0	4.8	4.4
Southeast Asia									
Brunei Darussalam	2.8	0.4	-1.8 (2009)	3.7	0.9	-2.1	-2.5	-0.4	-2.5
Cambodia	8.4	13.3	6.0	7.1	7.3	7.6	7.1	6.9	7.0
Indonesia	4.9	5.7	6.2	6.2	6.0	5.6	5.0	4.9	5.0
Lao PDR	6.3	6.8	8.1	8.0	...	8.0	7.6	7.3	7.0
Malaysia	8.9	5.3	7.4	5.3	5.5	4.7	6.0	5.0	4.2
Myanmar	13.7	13.6	9.6	5.6	7.3	8.4	8.0	7.0	5.9
Philippines	4.4	4.8	7.6	3.7	6.7	7.1	6.1	6.1	6.9
Singapore	8.9	7.5	15.2	6.2	3.9	5.0	3.6	1.9	2.0
Thailand	4.5	4.2	7.5	0.8	7.2	2.7	0.9	2.9	3.2
Viet Nam	6.8	7.5	6.4	6.2	5.2	5.4	6.0	6.7	6.2
The Pacific									
Cook Islands	13.9	-1.1	-3.0	1.0	4.7	-1.4	4.5	5.7	3.5
Fiji	-1.7	...	3.0	...	1.4	4.7	5.6	3.6	...
Kiribati	5.3	5.0	-1.6	0.6	5.1	5.0	0.4	7.5	...
Marshall Islands	5.9	2.9	6.4	1.7	3.7	2.4	-0.9	0.6	...
Micronesia, Fed. States of	4.8	2.1	3.3	1.0	-1.7	-3.0	-2.4	3.7	3.0
Nauru	...	-9.8	20.1	14.2	20.2	34.2	36.5	2.8	10.4
Palau	4.2 (2001)	1.3	3.0	5.1	3.9	-2.1	5.4	11.4	1.9
Papua New Guinea	-2.5	3.9	10.1	1.1	4.7	3.8	12.5	...	...
Samoa	8.6	4.7	4.4	3.5	-2.3	0.5	1.9	2.9	5.8
Solomon Islands	-14.2	9.2	9.7	7.4	2.3	2.8	2.0	...	...
Timor-Leste[a]	2.3 (2001)	52.7	-1.3	13.8	4.3	-11.3	-26.0	21.0	...
Tonga	-0.8	1.6	3.3	2.9	0.8	-3.1	2.0	2.5	4.7
Tuvalu	1.5 (2001)	-4.1	-3.1	7.9	-3.8	4.6	1.3	9.1	...
Vanuatu	5.9	5.3	1.6	1.2	1.8	2.0	2.3	...	...
Developed Member Economies									
Australia	3.9	3.2	2.0	2.4	3.6	2.6	2.6	2.4	2.6
Japan	2.8	1.7	4.2	-0.1	1.5	2.0	0.3	1.1	1.0
New Zealand	2.9	3.3	1.5	2.3	2.2	2.4	3.4	2.4	...

... = data not available at cutoff date, Lao PDR = Lao People's Democratic Republic.

a The treatment of oil production from 2000 onward reflects the 2008 System of National Accounts concepts on resident units. Prior to 2000, oil production was based on proportion of revenues between Timor-Leste and the licensee or lessee.

Source: Economy sources.

Table 2.10: **Growth Rates of Real Gross Domestic Product per Capita**
(%)

Regional Member	2000	2005	2010	2011	2012	2013	2014	2015	2016
Developing Member Economies									
Central and West Asia									
Afghanistan	...	8.2	1.3	6.6	8.9	4.5	0.9	-3.5	1.4
Armenia	6.2	14.5	2.9	5.2	7.3	3.3	3.9	3.6	0.6
Azerbaijan	9.9	24.9	3.8	-1.2	0.9	4.5	1.4	-0.1	-4.2
Georgia	2.6	9.4	5.0	6.4	5.7	3.7	4.5	...	2.6
Kazakhstan	10.2	8.7	5.7	7.4	3.3	4.4	2.7	-0.3	-0.5
Kyrgyz Republic	4.0	-1.4	-0.8	4.8	-1.4	8.7	2.0	1.8	1.7
Pakistan	1.5 (2001)	4.2	-0.5	0.7	1.4	2.3	2.6	2.7	3.5
Tajikistan	6.1	4.5	4.2	-0.0	5.0	5.2	4.3	3.5	5.7
Turkmenistan	4.3	11.8	7.8	13.2	9.7	8.8	8.9	5.2	4.9
Uzbekistan	2.6	5.7	5.5	5.4	6.6	6.3	6.2	6.0	5.5
East Asia									
China, People's Rep. of	7.7	10.7	10.1	9.0	7.4	7.3	6.7	6.4	6.1
Hong Kong, China	6.7	6.9	6.0	4.1	0.6	2.7	2.0	1.5	1.3
Korea, Rep. of	8.0	3.7	6.0	2.9	1.8	2.4	2.7	2.3	2.3
Mongolia	-0.2	6.1	-3.0 (2009)	15.3	10.2	9.4	5.6	0.2	-1.1
Taipei,China	5.6	5.0	10.3	3.6	1.7	2.0	3.8	0.5	1.3
South Asia									
Bangladesh	4.5	4.4	4.2	5.7	5.2	4.6	4.6	5.1	5.8
Bhutan	5.6	5.7	9.7	6.0	3.3	0.4	4.0	4.8	...
India	2.0	7.7	8.8	...	4.1	4.7	5.9	6.7	5.4
Maldives	2.4	-11.0	4.8	5.3	-0.8	1.2	2.4	-0.8	...
Nepal	2.9	1.2	3.4	2.5	3.4	2.7	4.5	1.9	-0.9
Sri Lanka	4.6	5.3	2.4 (2009)	7.3	11.5	2.6	4.0	3.9	3.2
Southeast Asia									
Brunei Darussalam	0.3	-1.3	-3.1 (2009)	2.0	-0.7	-3.7	-3.9	-1.7	-3.9
Cambodia	7.0	11.7	4.6	5.7	6.0	6.2	5.7	5.5	5.6
Indonesia	3.7	4.3	3.4	4.6	4.5	4.1	3.6	3.5	3.7
Lao PDR	4.2	4.7	6.6	6.5	...	6.5	6.1	5.7	5.5
Malaysia	6.2	3.2	5.5	3.6	3.9	3.3	3.6	2.9	2.7
Myanmar	12.4	12.7	8.9	4.8	6.4	7.5	7.1	6.1	5.0
Philippines	2.0	2.8	5.2	1.8	4.8	5.3	4.4	4.3	5.2
Singapore	7.1	5.0	13.2	4.0	1.4	3.3	2.3	0.7	0.7
Thailand	3.3	3.6	6.9	0.4	6.8	2.3	0.5	2.6	2.8
Viet Nam	5.3	6.3	5.3	5.1	4.1	4.3	4.9	5.5	5.1
The Pacific									
Cook Islands	4.4	-6.7	-7.5	24.0	3.6	3.4	4.5	5.1	1.9
Fiji	-2.3	...	2.3	...	1.0	4.2	5.2	3.1	...
Kiribati	3.5	3.1	-3.6	-0.6	3.8	3.7	-0.8	6.1	...
Marshall Islands	5.1	1.5	5.1	1.2	3.3	2.0	-1.3	0.3	...
Micronesia, Fed. States of	4.6	2.3	3.8	1.4	-1.4	-2.9	-2.4	3.5	2.8
Nauru	...	-7.8	17.9	10.1	17.7	28.0	23.9	-1.9	5.9
Palau	2.7 (2001)	0.5	5.0	7.1	5.8	-0.8	5.5	10.4	0.3
Papua New Guinea	-5.5	0.8	6.8	-1.9	1.5	0.7	9.1	...	...
Samoa	7.6	4.2	3.6	2.7	-2.7	0.1	1.4	2.5	5.3
Solomon Islands	-16.2	6.8	7.2	4.9	-0.0	0.5	-0.3	...	...
Timor-Leste[a]	1.0 (2001)	50.0	-3.9	11.4	2.2	-13.2	-27.6	18.5	...
Tonga	-1.2	1.1	3.1	2.6	0.6	-3.3	1.8	2.2	...
Tuvalu	1.1 (2001)	-7.0	-3.6	13.7	-5.3	3.3	0.1	7.8	...
Vanuatu	3.1	2.6	-1.0	-1.4	-0.8	-0.5	-0.1	...	...
Developed Member Economies									
Australia	2.7	2.0	0.4	1.0	1.9	0.8	1.1	1.0	1.2
Japan	2.6	1.7	4.2	0.1	1.7	2.2	0.5	1.2	1.0
New Zealand	2.3	2.2	0.4	1.5	1.7	1.7	1.9	0.5	...

... = data not available at cutoff date, -0.0 = magnitude is less than half of unit employed, GDP = gross domestic product, Lao PDR = Lao People's Democratic Republic.

a The treatment of oil production from 2004 onward reflects the 2008 System of National Accounts concepts on resident units. Prior to 2004, oil production was based on proportion of revenues between Timor-Leste and the licensee or lessee.

Source: Asian Development Bank estimates using economy sources.

Table 2.11: **Growth Rates of Agriculture Real Value Added**
(%)

Regional Member	2000	2005	2010	2011	2012	2013	2014	2015	2016
Developing Member Economies									
Central and West Asia									
Afghanistan	...	12.2	-18.0	4.7	3.3	8.3	3.7	-16.9	12.4
Armenia	-1.0	11.2	-16.0	14.0	9.5	7.6	6.1	13.2	-5.8
Azerbaijan	12.1	6.7	-4.7	5.8	6.6	4.9	-2.6	6.6	2.6
Georgia	-12.0	11.7	-4.2	8.5	-3.8	11.3	1.6	1.5	0.0
Kazakhstan	-3.2	7.1	-12.9	22.5	-17.4	11.2	1.3	3.5	5.2
Kyrgyz Republic	2.6	-4.2	-2.6	1.8	1.2	2.7	-0.5	6.2	3.0
Pakistan	-0.7 (2001)	7.0	0.2	2.0	3.6	2.7	2.5	2.1	0.3
Tajikistan	8.0 (2001)	2.8	6.8	0.4	9.5	7.7	9.2	3.4	5.9
Turkmenistan	-2.6	14.1	27.3	...	8.1	9.9	1.7	...	...
Uzbekistan	3.2	5.9	6.4	6.9	7.2	6.8	6.9	6.8	6.0
East Asia									
China, People's Rep. of	2.3	5.1	4.3	4.2	4.5	3.8	4.1	3.9	3.3
Hong Kong, China	0.3 (2001)	-0.2	3.9	0.8	-3.2	4.9	-6.0	-6.8	-3.2
Korea, Rep. of	1.1	1.4	-4.3	-2.0	-0.9	3.1	3.6	-0.4	-2.9
Mongolia	-16.3	11.3	3.6 (2009)	-0.3	21.1	19.2	13.7	10.7	4.8
Taipei,China	1.8	-3.9	2.3	4.5	-3.2	1.4	1.6	-8.3	-6.9
South Asia									
Bangladesh	7.4	2.2	6.2	4.5	3.0	2.5	4.4	3.3	2.8
Bhutan	5.4	1.1	0.9	2.4	2.3	2.4	2.4	4.6	...
India	-0.0	5.1	8.6	...	1.5	5.6	-0.2	0.7	4.9
Maldives	0.2	5.9	-0.9	1.1	0.0	5.1	0.2	-0.5	...
Nepal	4.9	3.5	2.0	4.5	4.6	1.1	4.5	1.1	0.0
Sri Lanka	2.3	1.8	3.2 (2009)	4.6	3.9	3.2	4.6	4.8	-4.2
Southeast Asia									
Brunei Darussalam	6.6	1.3	5.7 (2009)	-2.6	8.1	-1.2	4.7	6.4	-3.6
Cambodia	-1.2	15.7	4.0	3.1	4.3	1.6	0.3	0.2	1.4
Indonesia	1.9	2.7	3.0	3.9	4.6	4.2	4.2	3.8	3.3
Lao PDR	4.2	0.7	3.2	2.7	...	2.8	4.1	3.6	2.8
Malaysia	6.1	2.6	2.4	6.8	1.0	2.0	2.1	1.2	-5.1
Myanmar	11.0	12.1	4.7	-0.7	1.7	3.6	2.8	3.4	-0.4
Philippines	3.4	2.2	-0.2	2.6	2.8	1.2	1.7	0.1	-1.3
Singapore	-4.8	7.1	2.4	2.0	3.7	4.5	13.4	-3.6	-1.4
Thailand	6.8	-0.1	-0.5	6.3	2.7	0.7	-0.6	-5.4	0.6
Viet Nam	4.6	4.2	0.5	4.2	2.9	2.6	3.4	2.4	1.4
The Pacific									
Cook Islands	0.1	-3.5	1.9	-6.7	14.9	3.9	7.5	-0.6	3.4
Fiji	-1.2	...	-2.6	...	-1.9	6.7	1.9	6.3	...
Kiribati	-7.2	-7.4	-3.9	8.3	2.1	-0.7	5.9	-0.8	...
Marshall Islands	22.6	-9.1	27.7	5.8	10.5	0.7	-1.1	-0.2	...
Micronesia, Fed. States of	7.1	4.4	1.2	1.3	-0.2	-3.0	5.0	6.2	...
Nauru	...	...	...	...	...	...	...	...	...
Palau	-1.6 (2001)	6.7	-5.0	10.7	1.1	-8.6	-5.1	-4.4	3.7
Papua New Guinea	2.1	5.6	2.8	0.9	6.0	4.7	3.3	...	...
Samoa	8.1	2.4	-6.1	10.1	-12.6	8.9	1.1	5.6	6.4
Solomon Islands	-17.1	-1.8	14.8	2.3	-0.5	-0.8	7.1	...	...
Timor-Leste[a]	-0.1 (2001)	4.1	-2.9	-14.7	8.9	7.1	-0.5	0.3	...
Tonga	-2.5	-2.1	0.5	2.0	0.5	3.7	3.1	-2.7	2.1
Tuvalu	-2.2 (2001)	-1.1	12.4	-0.9	-3.6	-2.7	-0.6	-1.8	...
Vanuatu	4.3	2.3	4.8	6.1	2.2	4.8	4.2	...	...
Developed Member Economies									
Australia	6.5	4.2	-0.8	3.6	1.4	-0.6	0.7	0.8	-6.4
Japan	7.3	0.0	-5.8	1.1	0.6	0.3	-3.3	-8.8	...
New Zealand	3.6	5.2	-7.9	12.3	5.0	-2.6	6.2	2.3	...

... = data not available at cutoff date, -0.0 = magnitude is less than half of unit employed, Lao PDR = Lao People's Democratic Republic.

a The treatment of oil production from 2004 onward reflects the 2008 System of National Accounts concepts on resident units. Prior to 2004, oil production was based on proportion of revenues between Timor-Leste and the licensee or lessee.

Source: Economy sources.

Table 2.12: **Growth Rates of Industry Real Value Added**
(%)

Regional Member	2000	2005	2010	2011	2012	2013	2014	2015	2016
Developing Member Economies									
Central and West Asia									
Afghanistan	...	13.0	6.3	9.8	7.8	4.5	2.4	4.5	-1.9
Armenia	12.8	14.8	5.7	-0.0	5.7	0.5	-2.3	2.8	-0.9
Azerbaijan	5.7	43.6	3.7	-4.7	-1.0	4.3	0.4	-1.9	-5.9
Georgia	4.9	9.6	8.2	9.2	9.6	2.4	4.7	4.1	5.5
Kazakhstan	15.3	10.7	9.5	2.9	1.8	3.1	1.5	-0.4	0.6
Kyrgyz Republic	8.8	-9.8	2.5	7.3	-11.4	30.2	5.7	2.9	5.9
Pakistan	5.8 (2001)	6.5	3.4	4.5	2.5	0.8	4.5	5.2	5.8
Tajikistan	15.6 (2001)	7.7	5.6	-15.1	-2.6	4.0	14.9	16.3	15.7
Turkmenistan	1.0	10.6	-2.9	...	10.7	8.0	11.6	...	...
Uzbekistan	1.8	5.3	6.5	4.8	7.0	9.2	7.9	8.2	6.7
East Asia									
China, People's Rep. of	9.5	12.1	12.7	10.7	8.4	8.0	7.4	6.2	6.1
Hong Kong, China	-3.8 (2001)	-1.4	7.7	8.9	4.4	1.5	7.4	2.4	1.5
Korea, Rep. of[b]	...	...	...	...	...	...	...	...	...
Mongolia	1.5	4.2	-0.4 (2009)	8.8	14.8	14.6	12.7	9.9	-1.5
Taipei,China	7.1	7.6	20.8	6.0	3.3	1.7	7.2	-1.1	2.0
South Asia									
Bangladesh	6.2	8.3	7.0	9.0	9.4	9.6	8.2	9.7	11.1
Bhutan	7.3	3.8	12.5	4.1	6.8	3.9	3.7	8.1	...
India	6.0	9.7	7.6	...	3.3	3.8	7.5	8.8	5.6
Maldives	-3.3	10.3	4.3	12.1	0.8	-7.6	12.9	18.3	...
Nepal	8.6	3.0	4.0	4.3	3.0	2.7	7.1	1.4	-6.3
Sri Lanka	9.0	8.0	4.2 (2009)	9.3	9.0	4.1	4.9	1.8	6.7
Southeast Asia									
Brunei Darussalam	3.0	-1.8	-5.0 (2009)	3.2	-1.4	-5.6	-4.4	-0.0	-2.9
Cambodia	31.2	12.7	13.0	13.4	10.4	11.5	9.8	11.7	10.5
Indonesia	5.9	4.7	4.9	6.3	5.3	4.3	4.2	3.0	3.9
Lao PDR	9.3	10.6	17.5	14.6	...	7.7	7.3	7.0	12.0
Malaysia	13.6	3.6	8.4	2.5	4.9	3.6	6.0	5.1	4.4
Myanmar	21.3	19.9	18.6	10.2	8.0	11.4	12.1	8.3	8.9
Philippines	6.5	4.2	11.6	1.9	7.3	9.2	7.8	6.4	8.4
Singapore	11.6	8.2	25.3	7.0	2.3	2.0	3.4	-3.1	2.8
Thailand	2.6	5.3	10.5	-4.1	7.3	1.6	-0.1	2.8	2.3
Viet Nam	10.1	8.4	7.2	6.7	5.7	5.4	7.1	9.6	8.3
The Pacific									
Cook Islands	18.2	-6.3	-8.4	11.6	11.0	-6.3	-23.8	1.8	-22.0
Fiji	-5.5	...	6.5	...	-2.2	4.4	1.2	2.2	...
Kiribati	-6.4	6.7	2.4	-4.3	30.0	25.9	5.6	13.7	...
Marshall Islands	-14.5	4.6	-4.8	0.8	2.8	7.9	-16.7	-1.6	...
Micronesia, Fed. States of	6.6	-3.0	17.9	11.8	-1.3	-19.5	-28.5	-7.5	...
Nauru	...	...	...	...	...	...	...	...	...
Palau	26.1 (2001)	9.2	3.6	5.4	-5.3	-15.4	7.3	22.3	5.0
Papua New Guinea	-0.8	4.1	12.0	-8.4	-2.2	2.0	36.7	...	...
Samoa	14.4	4.7	10.1	2.4	-1.1	0.1	-1.9	1.5	2.4
Solomon Islands	-29.7	-3.1	15.4	38.2	-1.4	-2.0	-13.2	...	...
Timor-Leste[a]	-24.0 (2001)	73.4	-3.7	19.2	3.4	-17.5	-44.4	41.9	...
Tonga	-0.4	-2.8	11.6	5.5	1.2	-14.3	1.3	11.2	7.8
Tuvalu	5.0 (2001)	-18.2	-36.4	34.8	-23.0	35.0	-5.0	33.1	...
Vanuatu	46.4	5.3	12.6	-19.4	-22.1	9.8	3.2	...	...
Developed Member Economies									
Australia[b]	...	...	...	...	...	...	...	...	...
Japan[b]	...	...	...	...	...	...	...	...	...
New Zealand[b]	...	...	...	...	...	...	...	...	...

... = data not available at cutoff date, -0.0 = magnitude is less than half of unit employed, Lao PDR = Lao People's Democratic Republic.

a The treatment of oil production from 2000 onward reflects the 2008 System of National Accounts concepts on resident units. Prior to 2000, oil production was based on proportion of revenues between Timor-Leste and the licensee or lessee.

b National accounts are compiled using chain volume measures.

Source: Economy sources.

Table 2.13: **Growth Rates of Services Real Value Added**
(%)

Regional Member	2000	2005	2010	2011	2012	2013	2014	2015	2016
Developing Member Economies									
Central and West Asia									
Afghanistan	...	5.4	18.1	10.3	16.0	6.4	4.0	1.4	2.4
Armenia	3.1	14.7	4.7	6.1	6.9	2.8	6.7	1.0	4.0
Azerbaijan	9.6	9.6	8.8	7.2	7.6	8.6	7.6	4.4	-0.7
Georgia	5.5	6.5	8.2	5.8	5.9	3.6	4.5	3.0	2.3
Kazakhstan	8.4	10.4	6.0	4.8	10.4	6.9	5.7	3.1	0.9
Kyrgyz Republic	5.8	8.4	-1.3	6.7	6.3	4.8	4.6	3.5	2.9
Pakistan	5.1(2001)	8.1	3.2	3.9	4.4	5.1	4.5	4.4	5.5
Tajikistan	3.9(2001)	7.7	7.1	11.4	11.9	9.4	1.7	1.9	-0.2
Turkmenistan	18.0	27.1	16.1	...	-10.9	-9.2	-13.2	...	...
Uzbekistan	5.4	7.6	10.4	11.4	9.3	7.8	8.5	8.4	8.5
East Asia									
China, People's Rep. of	9.8	12.4	9.7	9.5	8.0	8.3	7.8	8.2	7.8
Hong Kong, China	1.8(2001)	7.8	6.9	5.2	1.8	2.7	2.5	1.7	2.3
Korea, Rep. of	7.3	3.9	4.4	3.1	2.8	2.9	3.3	2.8	2.3
Mongolia	10.5	9.7	0.8(2009)	17.8	10.3	7.8	7.8	0.6	2.1
Taipei,China	6.5	4.1	6.3	3.1	1.3	2.3	3.3	1.1	1.4
South Asia									
Bangladesh	5.5	6.4	5.5	6.2	6.6	5.5	5.6	5.8	6.3
Bhutan	8.7	14.8	12.1	13.3	0.7	1.6	8.2	8.3	...
India	5.1	10.9	9.7	...	8.3	7.7	9.7	9.7	7.7
Maldives	5.4	-13.8	8.0	5.8	1.5	6.4	4.6	1.6	...
Nepal	5.9	3.3	5.8	3.4	5.0	5.7	6.2	4.6	2.1
Sri Lanka	6.1	6.4	3.3(2009)	8.9	11.2	3.8	4.8	5.7	4.2
Southeast Asia									
Brunei Darussalam	2.5	4.1	2.1(2009)	4.9	5.5	4.7	0.6	-1.2	-1.6
Cambodia	8.9	13.1	3.3	5.7	7.4	8.7	8.7	7.1	6.8
Indonesia	5.2	7.9	8.4	8.4	6.8	6.4	6.0	5.5	5.6
Lao PDR	6.9	10.8	7.6	8.4	...	9.7	8.1	8.0	4.7
Malaysia	6.0	7.3	7.4	7.2	6.5	6.0	6.7	5.2	5.6
Myanmar	13.4	13.1	9.5	8.5	12.0	10.3	9.1	8.7	8.0
Philippines	3.3	5.8	7.2	4.9	7.1	7.0	6.0	6.9	7.4
Singapore	7.5	7.4	11.3	6.6	4.6	7.0	3.9	3.3	1.2
Thailand	4.8	12.1	7.0	-1.6	7.7	2.2	-1.6	2.2	-0.4
Viet Nam	5.3	8.6	-7.7	7.5	6.7	6.7	6.2	6.3	7.0
The Pacific									
Cook Islands	15.4	-0.3	-2.6	0.1	2.3	-0.6	7.4	5.3	7.0
Fiji	0.8	...	2.9	...	3.0	4.5	7.4	3.6	...
Kiribati	1.7	4.6	-0.1	-1.1	2.3	2.6	-0.2	6.5	...
Marshall Islands	6.3	3.2	3.5	1.5	1.8	1.4	2.5	2.3	...
Micronesia, Fed. States of	3.2	0.8	2.3	0.3	-1.7	-0.8	-1.2	2.7	...
Nauru	...	...	...	...	...	...	...	...	...
Palau	1.1(2001)	-1.2	3.1	4.4	3.5	-0.7	6.3	10.3	1.4
Papua New Guinea	-12.7	3.6	12.4	9.3	6.0	4.3	0.2	...	...
Samoa	6.2	5.2	4.0	2.5	-0.9	-0.2	3.3	3.1	7.1
Solomon Islands	-5.7	23.8	6.4	2.5	5.3	7.2	3.6	...	...
Timor-Leste[a]	31.3(2001)	8.5	11.0	11.9	7.2	1.6	10.3	3.1	...
Tonga	0.0	3.6	1.0	1.8	0.5	-0.5	1.6	2.7	3.7
Tuvalu	-0.5(2001)	-4.9	2.0	6.4	0.2	0.3	2.5	7.2	...
Vanuatu	2.2	6.6	3.0	3.2	4.4	0.1	2.4	...	...
Developed Member Economies									
Australia[b]	...	...	...	...	...	...	...	...	...
Japan[b]	...	...	...	...	...	...	...	...	...
New Zealand[b]	...	...	...	...	...	...	...	...	...

... = data not available at cutoff date, 0.0 = magnitude is less than half of unit employed, Lao PDR = Lao People's Democratic Republic.

a The treatment of oil production from 2000 onward reflects the 2008 System of National Accounts concepts on resident units. Prior to 2000, oil production was based on proportion of revenues between Timor-Leste and the licensee or lessee.

b National accounts are compiled using chain volume measures.

Source: Economy sources.

Table 2.14: **Growth Rates of Real Household Final Consumption**
(%)

Regional Member	2000	2005	2010	2011	2012	2013	2014	2015	2016
Developing Member Economies									
Central and West Asia									
Afghanistan	...	...	...	...	...	...	...	...	...
Armenia[a]	8.3	8.8	3.8	2.4	9.1	0.9	1.0	-7.7	1.0
Azerbaijan[a]	10.0	13.2	10.8	8.4	8.4	8.6	8.1	8.5	0.9
Georgia[a]	...	...	...	6.7	4.5	-0.1	3.2	0.1	...
Kazakhstan[a]	1.2	10.7	11.5	12.0	10.1	18.7	1.4	1.8	1.1
Kyrgyz Republic[a]	-5.0	8.3	2.7	9.3	11.2	8.0	3.0	-0.9	...
Pakistan[a]	3.5 (2001)	10.8	2.2	4.6	5.0	2.1	5.6	2.9	6.9
Tajikistan[a]	8.6 (2001)	20.6	10.5	24.2	15.0	9.3	1.8	-15.0	...
Turkmenistan[a]	-48.3	-15.2	-61.3	...	...	...	...	...	...
Uzbekistan	...	...	...	...	...	...	...	...	...
East Asia									
China, People's Rep. of	...	...	...	...	...	...	...	...	...
Hong Kong, China[a]	4.5	3.5	6.1	8.4	4.1	4.6	3.3	4.8	1.6
Korea, Rep. of	9.1	4.4	4.4	2.7	1.2	1.4	1.7	2.2	2.5
Mongolia	...	12.4 (2006)	-2.5 (2009)	15.8	13.3	15.6	6.3	8.2	-9.8
Taipei,China	5.1	3.3	3.8	3.3	1.8	2.4	3.2	2.9	...
South Asia									
Bangladesh	4.1	3.9	4.6	6.5	4.1	5.1	4.0	5.8	3.0
Bhutan[a]	0.4	1.3	5.5	5.9	-2.4	58.0	-6.4	7.2	...
India[a]	3.4	8.6	8.7	...	5.5	7.3	6.2	6.1	8.7
Maldives	...	...	...	...	...	...	...	...	...
Nepal[a]	3.5 (2002)	4.7	6.2	0.6	15.9	2.7	4.2	2.9	-0.9
Sri Lanka	4.0	1.7	0.9 (2009)	9.9	2.3	7.8	3.7	8.6	0.7
Southeast Asia									
Brunei Darussalam[a]	-7.0	-0.6	5.0 (2009)	5.4	8.7	6.0	-3.7	5.2	-1.3
Cambodia[a]	4.9	12.3	9.7	10.4	6.4	4.0	4.5	2.6	6.8
Indonesia[b]	1.6	4.0	4.7	5.1	5.5	5.4	5.1	5.0	5.0
Lao PDR	...	...	...	...	...	...	...	...	...
Malaysia[b]	13.0	9.1	6.9	6.9	8.4	7.3	7.0	6.0	6.1
Myanmar[c]	4.3	14.6	2.6	6.1	8.1	13.7	11.1	4.4	2.1
Philippines[a]	5.2	4.4	3.4	5.6	6.6	5.6	5.6	6.3	7.0
Singapore	14.7	3.4	5.9	4.2	3.7	3.3	2.4	4.6	0.6
Thailand	7.0	4.2	5.5	1.8	6.7	0.9	0.9	2.2	3.1
Viet Nam	3.1	5.8	8.2	4.1	4.9	5.2	6.1	9.3	7.3
The Pacific									
Cook Islands	...	...	...	...	...	...	...	...	...
Fiji	...	...	...	...	...	...	...	...	...
Kiribati	...	...	...	...	...	...	...	...	...
Marshall Islands	...	-1.4	1.8	0.4	-1.5	-2.9	1.5	0.4	...
Micronesia, Fed. States of	...	...	...	...	...	...	...	...	...
Nauru	...	...	...	...	...	...	...	...	...
Palau	...	...	0.2	3.4	4.6	0.7	2.0	6.7	5.6
Papua New Guinea[a]	-28.5	9.8	...	...	...	...	...	...	...
Samoa	...	...	...	...	...	...	...	...	...
Solomon Islands	...	9.3	8.7	3.9	3.8	4.2	4.6	...	...
Timor-Leste[d]	16.3 (2001)	-2.2	9.6 (2009)	-5.3	7.2	3.1	6.2	4.0	...
Tonga	3.5	2.2	-1.3	-3.5	1.6	...	...	...	...
Tuvalu	...	...	...	...	...	...	...	...	...
Vanuatu	...	2.4	2.6	3.0	3.0	3.5	3.9	...	...
Developed Member Economies									
Australia	4.1	4.5	2.3	3.8	2.6	1.5	2.7	2.6	2.9
Japan[a]	1.6	1.2	2.4	-0.4	2.0	2.4	-0.9	-0.4	0.4
New Zealand	1.4	4.8	2.6	3.3	2.5	3.5	3.0	2.8	...

... = data not available at cutoff date, Lao PDR = Lao People's Democratic Republic.

a Includes expenditure of nonprofit institutions serving households.
b Figures before 2010 include expenditures of nonprofit institutions serving households.
c Includes government consumption expenditure.
d The treatment of oil production from 2000 onward reflects the 2008 System of National Accounts concepts on resident units.

Source: Economy sources.

Table 2.15: **Growth Rates of Real Government Consumption Expenditure**
(%)

Regional Member	2000	2005	2010	2011	2012	2013	2014	2015	2016
Developing Member Economies									
Central and West Asia									
Afghanistan	...	...	...	...	...	...	...	...	...
Armenia	2.8	19.0	3.9	1.9	-1.4	7.6	-1.2	4.7	4.2
Azerbaijan	2.3	3.4	3.4	3.4	3.1	3.6	3.7	1.1	1.6
Georgia	...	...	...	1.0	7.3	4.3	11.2	22.1	...
Kazakhstan	15.0	10.8	2.7	11.9	13.5	1.7	9.8	2.4	2.4
Kyrgyz Republic	5.9	-2.7	-1.1	2.2	2.1	-0.4	-0.5	0.9	...
Pakistan	-6.7 (2001)	3.4	-0.6	0.0	7.3	10.1	1.5	8.1	8.2
Tajikistan	10.8 (2001)	0.4	0.9	7.8	2.1	2.3	7.6	3.3	...
Turkmenistan	28.0	17.9	3.8	...	...	...	...	...	...
Uzbekistan	...	...	...	...	...	...	...	...	...
East Asia									
China, People's Rep. of	...	...	...	...	...	...	...	...	...
Hong Kong, China	2.4	-2.6	3.4	2.5	3.6	2.7	3.1	3.5	3.3
Korea, Rep. of	0.9	4.5	3.8	2.2	3.4	3.3	3.0	3.0	4.3
Mongolia	...	5.5 (2006)	-6.0 (2009)	15.3	19.9	15.8	12.2	-4.7	8.9
Taipei,China	0.6	0.4	1.1	2.0	2.2	-0.8	3.7	-0.3	3.1
South Asia									
Bangladesh	0.9	7.7	6.8	6.7	3.1	5.8	7.9	8.8	8.4
Bhutan	–	2.8	7.5	3.6	-0.8	-10.1	2.4	10.8	...
India	1.4	8.9	5.8	...	0.6	0.6	9.6	3.3	20.8
Maldives	...	...	...	...	...	...	...	...	...
Nepal	7.8 (2002)	1.2	1.3	13.1	15.9	-6.7	10.0	7.4	-0.4
Sri Lanka	5.3	12.0	16.0 (2009)	-2.1	6.0	0.1	6.0	10.2	2.3
Southeast Asia									
Brunei Darussalam	7.7	-1.0	5.0 (2009)	5.3	0.4	3.6	1.9	-3.6	-6.5
Cambodia	12.4	3.9	-6.2	7.8	4.7	6.3	2.4	4.4	5.7
Indonesia	-0.9	6.6	0.3	5.5	4.5	6.7	1.2	5.3	-0.1
Lao PDR	...	...	...	...	...	...	...	...	...
Malaysia	1.6	6.5	3.4	14.2	5.4	5.8	4.3	4.4	1.0
Myanmar	...	...	...	...	...	...	...	...	...
Philippines	-1.0	2.1	4.0	2.1	15.5	5.0	3.3	7.6	8.4
Singapore	20.9	5.0	10.7	-2.3	-1.5	11.5	0.1	8.0	6.3
Thailand	2.8	8.0	8.9	3.7	7.2	1.8	2.8	3.0	1.6
Viet Nam	5.0	8.2	12.3	7.1	7.2	7.3	7.0	7.0	7.5
The Pacific									
Cook Islands	...	...	...	...	...	...	...	...	...
Fiji	...	...	...	...	...	...	...	...	...
Kiribati	...	...	...	...	...	...	...	...	...
Marshall Islands	...	1.5	0.3	1.1	7.2	1.1	-4.6	3.5	...
Micronesia, Fed. States of	...	...	...	...	...	...	...	...	...
Nauru	...	...	...	...	...	...	...	...	...
Palau	...	...	-0.6	-3.8	-2.1	2.3	3.9	-0.8	0.8
Papua New Guinea	3.7	1.1	...	...	...	...	...	...	...
Samoa	...	...	...	...	...	...	...	...	...
Solomon Islands	...	80.6	10.0	-17.2	-9.0	14.7	8.7	...	...
Timor-Leste[a]	33.5 (2001)	-30.2	18.9 (2009)	-8.3	-1.7	-14.7	12.4	3.7	...
Tonga	-2.8	-1.5	-8.6	-0.2	10.7	...	...	...	...
Tuvalu	...	...	...	...	...	...	...	...	...
Vanuatu	...	-0.1	4.3	-0.8	-1.3	2.2	-3.7	...	...
Developed Member Economies									
Australia	3.2	3.1	1.8	3.4	3.9	0.6	1.4	2.3	3.7
Japan	3.9	0.8	1.9	1.9	1.7	1.5	0.5	1.7	1.5
New Zealand	1.3	7.2	1.9	1.8	-0.2	1.9	3.1	2.7	...

... = data not available at cutoff date, 0.0 = magnitude is less than half of unit employed, – = magnitude equals zero, Lao PDR = Lao People's Democratic Republic.

a The treatment of oil production from 2000 onward reflects 2008 System of National Accounts concepts on resident units.

Source: Economy sources.

Table 2.16: **Growth Rates of Real Gross Capital Formation**
(%)

Regional Member	2000	2005	2010	2011	2012	2013	2014	2015	2016
Developing Member Economies									
Central and West Asia									
Afghanistan	...	...	...	...	...	...	...	...	...
Armenia	5.2	26.9	0.5	-5.2	0.5	-9.1	-3.0	-1.2	-8.7
Azerbaijan	2.6	5.8	2.0	1.0	4.0	4.5	-1.7	-11.1	-22.2
Georgia	...	...	...	28.0	19.1	-11.7	26.9	9.3	...
Kazakhstan	10.7	35.0	2.0	11.0	12.7	6.7	8.6	5.5	2.5
Kyrgyz Republic	22.1	13.7	-5.2	6.3	42.4	5.1	15.7	-2.3	...
Pakistan	2.5 (2001)	13.2	-6.5	-6.7	2.5	2.8	2.8	14.6	6.6
Tajikistan	39.2 (2001)	2.6	7.5	13.3	-21.9	15.1	17.6	25.3	...
Turkmenistan	-6.0	12.4	21.6	...	...	...	...	...	...
Uzbekistan	...	...	...	...	...	...	...	...	...
East Asia									
China, People's Rep. of	...	...	...	...	...	...	...	...	...
Hong Kong, China	16.1	0.0	11.3	3.1	3.5	3.1	1.6	-8.1	5.1
Korea, Rep. of	14.5	2.4	17.8	3.5	-2.3	-0.1	5.3	7.3	5.3
Mongolia	...	15.0 (2006)	-29.8 (2009)	62.8	17.4	1.4	-30.1	-26.5	13.2
Taipei,China	9.0	1.3	35.8	-5.7	-2.6	5.3	2.1	1.6	2.5
South Asia									
Bangladesh	7.3	10.7	8.6	9.6	10.6	5.4	9.9	7.1	8.9
Bhutan	26.5	-12.2	46.1	11.8	3.5	-35.7	24.4	16.5	...
India	-5.5	16.2	14.1	...	6.9	-5.2	8.5	7.5	...
Maldives	...	...	...	...	...	...	...	...	...
Nepal	-14.0 (2002)	9.5	34.4	0.3	-21.6	23.5	22.8	9.4	10.4
Sri Lanka	8.7	9.4	2.0 (2009)	20.2	21.7	-8.8	11.5	1.2	18.1
Southeast Asia									
Brunei Darussalam	6.7 (2001)	0.5	-0.3 (2009)	37.0	28.8	11.9	-31.2	6.6	-11.1
Cambodia	8.6	29.9	-18.6	9.8	6.2	25.0	8.8	9.9	10.0
Indonesia	12.9	12.4	8.8	7.9	11.0	2.8	5.7	3.0	5.2
Lao PDR	...	...	...	...	...	...	...	...	...
Malaysia	29.2	-2.5	25.3	4.5	19.0	4.9	2.6	6.4	4.2
Myanmar	11.3	29.8	34.6	33.1	13.6	12.3	7.5	16.1	4.3
Philippines	1.1	3.0	31.6	2.8	-4.3	27.9	4.2	18.4	23.7
Singapore	26.3	-0.4	24.2	3.2	13.6	4.6	-3.6	-3.0	-3.3
Thailand	8.0	21.7	32.0	2.6	11.1	3.2	-12.4	4.3	...
Viet Nam	10.1	11.2	10.4	-6.8	2.4	5.5	8.9	9.0	9.7
The Pacific									
Cook Islands	...	...	...	...	...	...	...	...	...
Fiji	...	...	...	...	...	...	...	...	...
Kiribati	...	...	...	...	...	...	...	...	...
Marshall Islands	...	4.2	18.5	-51.7	-49.0	146.3	-22.8	-0.3	...
Micronesia, Fed. States of	...	...	...	...	...	...	...	...	...
Nauru	...	...	...	...	...	...	...	...	...
Palau	...	...	14.8	15.5	-1.0	-11.4	51.7	-10.8	23.0
Papua New Guinea	36.8	-9.8	...	...	...	...	...	...	...
Samoa	...	...	...	...	...	...	...	...	...
Solomon Islands	...	71.1	88.7	-34.6	3.6	1.9	2.9	...	...
Timor-Leste[a]	6.1 (2001)	-2.5	139.2 (2009)	54.7	-12.5	-20.1	1.9	-10.0	...
Tonga	1.3	4.7	11.7	28.1	-3.7	...	...	...	...
Tuvalu	...	...	...	...	...	...	...	...	...
Vanuatu	...	7.8	-5.2	-15.2	-16.6	17.0	9.0	...	...
Developed Member Economies									
Australia	...	...	...	...	...	...	...	...	...
Japan	2.6	2.1	3.1	2.6	3.7	3.2	3.3	2.6	-0.4
New Zealand	-3.9	4.0	7.3	8.0	3.3	8.1	6.9	1.2	...

... = data not available at cutoff date, 0.0 = magnitude is less than half of unit employed, Lao PDR = Lao People's Democratic Republic.

a The treatment of oil production from 2000 onward reflects 2008 System of National Accounts concepts on resident units.

Source: Economy sources.

Table 2.17: **Growth Rates of Real Exports of Goods and Services**
(%)

Regional Member	2000	2005	2010	2011	2012	2013	2014	2015	2016
Developing Member Economies									
Central and West Asia									
Afghanistan	...	...	...	...	...	...	...	...	...
Armenia	19.0	15.9	26.5	14.7	8.4	8.6	6.4	4.9	19.2
Azerbaijan	15.4	52.8	9.1	2.0	-4.9	2.1	-1.9	-0.1	-5.5
Georgia	...	...	...	15.5	14.4	20.3	0.4	6.0	...
Kazakhstan	27.9	0.4	3.1	0.4	4.8	2.7	-2.5	-4.1	-4.4
Kyrgyz Republic	10.5	-11.0	-11.7	15.7	-19.2	12.3	-6.2	-5.6	...
Pakistan	12.2 (2001)	11.7	15.7	2.4	-15.0	13.6	-1.5	-6.3	-1.6
Tajikistan	-20.8 (2001)	2.9	23.0	1.0	1.0	-10.0	–	–	...
Turkmenistan	82.7	19.2	11.7	...	...	...	...	...	...
Uzbekistan	...	...	...	...	...	...	...	...	...
East Asia									
China, People's Rep. of	...	...	...	...	...	...	...	...	...
Hong Kong, China	16.9	12.2	17.6	4.8	3.2	7.8	1.0	-1.4	0.9
Korea, Rep. of	17.2	7.8	12.7	15.1	5.1	4.3	2.0	-0.1	2.1
Mongolia	...	6.1 (2006)	19.7 (2009)	18.2	8.3	12.8	53.2	0.1	15.9
Taipei,China	18.0	7.6	25.7	4.2	0.4	3.5	5.9	-0.3	2.1
South Asia									
Bangladesh	14.4	15.6	0.9	29.3	12.5	2.5	3.2	-2.8	2.2
Bhutan	3.3	34.3	7.5	3.2	-2.4	3.9	-5.8	-4.6	...
India	18.2	26.1	19.6	...	6.8	7.8	1.8	-5.3	4.5
Maldives	...	...	...	...	...	...	...	...	...
Nepal	-23.2 (2002)	-3.0	-10.4	-2.1	1.9	10.3	18.8	6.8	-13.7
Sri Lanka	17.1	6.6	-12.3 (2009)	10.2	-0.2	6.6	4.3	4.7	-0.7
Southeast Asia									
Brunei Darussalam	11.9	-1.3	-5.3 (2009)	-3.0	1.2	-5.7	0.9	-10.8	-9.2
Cambodia	39.4	16.4	16.0	18.9	7.9	20.9	11.3	7.2	8.6
Indonesia	26.5	16.6	15.3	14.8	1.6	4.2	1.1	-2.1	-1.7
Lao PDR	...	...	...	...	...	...	...	...	...
Malaysia	16.1	8.3	11.1	4.2	-1.7	0.3	5.0	0.6	0.1
Myanmar	79.3	3.6	10.9	-13.7	6.5	12.9	18.7	15.1	-0.4
Philippines	13.7	5.0	21.0	-2.5	8.6	-1.0	12.6	8.5	10.7
Singapore	14.6	12.5	17.4	6.4	1.4	5.8	4.0	2.6	1.6
Thailand	15.8	7.8	14.2	9.5	4.9	2.7	0.2	0.7	2.1
Viet Nam	11.0 (2002)	7.8	14.6	10.8	15.7	17.4	11.6	12.6	13.9
The Pacific									
Cook Islands	...	...	...	...	...	...	...	...	...
Fiji	...	...	...	...	...	...	...	...	...
Kiribati	...	...	...	...	...	...	...	...	...
Marshall Islands	...	7.6	24.1	2.4	2.7	10.7	1.7	-0.1	...
Micronesia, Fed. States of	...	...	...	...	...	...	...	...	...
Nauru	...	...	...	...	...	...	...	...	...
Palau	...	...	9.6	14.3	9.1	-6.6	12.4	16.8	-5.9
Papua New Guinea	7.1	6.8	...	...	...	...	...	...	...
Samoa	...	...	...	...	...	...	...	...	...
Solomon Islands	...	10.5	34.8	35.3	8.8	-6.8	-9.6	...	...
Timor-Leste	-23.7 (2001)	76.4	-3.5 (2009)	7.2	11.0	-13.2	-26.3	13.5	...
Tonga	-14.7	-2.8	-8.8	24.1	-0.8	...	...	...	...
Tuvalu	...	...	...	...	...	...	...	...	...
Vanuatu	...	7.1	0.4	10.4	-1.2	3.9	-0.5	...	...
Developed Member Economies									
Australia	9.7	3.3	5.1	0.9	5.0	5.4	6.0	6.7	6.7
Japan	12.7	7.2	24.9	-0.2	-0.1	0.8	9.3	2.9	1.2
New Zealand	6.1	-0.4	2.8	2.3	3.0	0.0	4.3	5.5	...

... = data not available at cutoff date, 0.0 = magnitude is less than half of unit employed, – = magnitude equals zero, Lao PDR = Lao People's Democratic Republic.

Source: Economy sources.

Table 2.18: **Growth Rates of Real Imports of Goods and Services**
(%)

Regional Member	2000	2005	2010	2011	2012	2013	2014	2015	2016
Developing Member Economies									
Central and West Asia									
Afghanistan	...	...	...	...	...	...	...	...	...
Armenia	7.2	14.3	12.8	-1.4	-2.8	-2.1	-1.0	-15.1	8.8
Azerbaijan	17.3	19.8	12.4	1.5	-3.1	1.1	-2.1	-0.5	-9.9
Georgia	...	...	...	17.9	15.6	2.9	11.1	10.4	...
Kazakhstan	28.0	12.1	2.9	2.8	24.8	7.8	-4.0	-0.1	-2.2
Kyrgyz Republic	0.4	6.5	-6.9	14.9	12.4	4.1	1.6	-13.2	...
Pakistan	2.2 (2001)	39.5	4.3	-0.1	-3.1	1.8	0.3	-1.6	11.7
Tajikistan	-14.5 (2001)	16.5	8.0	1.2	1.2	1.1	1.0	-	...
Turkmenistan	4.1	-9.3	7.4	...	...	...	...	...	...
Uzbekistan	...	...	...	...	...	...	...	...	...
East Asia									
China, People's Rep. of	...	...	...	...	...	...	...	...	...
Hong Kong, China	17.1	9.3	18.2	5.6	4.2	8.3	1.0	-1.8	1.2
Korea, Rep. of	21.8	7.8	17.3	14.3	2.4	1.7	1.5	2.1	4.5
Mongolia	...	6.7 (2006)	-4.7 (2009)	49.5	15.4	7.6	6.8	-11.4	13.3
Taipei,China	14.9	2.9	28.0	-0.5	-1.8	3.4	5.7	1.2	3.4
South Asia									
Bangladesh	10.2	19.1	0.7	29.2	10.5	1.2	1.2	3.2	-7.1
Bhutan	4.2	13.0	28.7	6.0	-7.1	-1.8	-3.2	10.1	...
India	4.6	32.6	15.6	...	6.0	-8.1	0.9	-5.9	2.3
Maldives	...	...	...	...	...	...	...	...	...
Nepal	-15.1 (2002)	6.9	28.3	-4.7	3.4	14.1	21.0	9.6	2.8
Sri Lanka	14.8	2.7	-9.6 (2009)	23.6	0.5	-1.5	9.6	10.6	7.9
Southeast Asia									
Brunei Darussalam	-6.2	10.2	-0.8 (2009)	33.7	20.6	14.5	-30.9	-11.7	1.8
Cambodia	30.6	17.3	10.3	16.3	8.1	24.5	10.1	6.5	8.6
Indonesia	25.9	17.8	17.3	15.0	8.0	1.9	2.1	-6.4	-2.3
Lao PDR	...	...	...	...	...	...	...	...	...
Malaysia	24.4	8.9	15.6	6.3	2.9	1.7	4.0	1.2	0.4
Myanmar	-8.0	2.2	51.9	1.2	3.7	54.4	22.3	21.6	-11.4
Philippines	11.8	3.3	22.5	-0.6	5.6	4.4	9.9	14.6	18.5
Singapore	20.5	11.5	16.3	5.0	2.5	5.9	3.0	2.9	0.3
Thailand	26.0	16.2	23.0	12.4	5.6	1.7	-5.3	0.0	-1.4
Viet Nam	15.8 (2002)	5.9	13.7	4.1	9.1	17.3	12.8	18.1	15.3
The Pacific									
Cook Islands	...	...	...	...	...	...	...	...	...
Fiji	...	...	...	...	...	...	...	...	...
Kiribati	...	...	...	...	...	...	...	...	...
Marshall Islands	...	7.1	8.7	-23.7	0.6	16.5	-7.1	8.2	...
Micronesia, Fed. States of	...	...	...	...	...	...	...	...	...
Nauru	...	...	...	...	...	...	...	...	...
Palau	...	...	3.7	5.4	7.6	2.3	15.8	1.1	5.4
Papua New Guinea	-4.7	4.7	...	...	...	...	...	...	...
Samoa	...	...	...	...	...	...	...	...	...
Solomon Islands	...	26.4	51.7	-6.4	3.8	-0.5	-0.6	...	...
Timor-Leste	25.5 (2001)	-14.1	48.8 (2009)	2.5	2.1	-13.4	19.6	-13.8	...
Tonga	-0.6	1.8	-4.5	5.5	2.6	...	...	...	...
Tuvalu	...	...	...	...	...	...	...	...	...
Vanuatu	...	2.9	-2.2	-1.9	0.8	6.5	0.2	...	...
Developed Member Economies									
Australia	12.1	12.4	6.4	10.3	11.5	0.1	-2.2	1.2	-0.3
Japan	9.3	6.1	11.2	5.8	5.4	3.3	8.3	0.8	-2.3
New Zealand	-1.1	4.9	11.5	6.6	1.3	8.1	7.4	2.1	...

... = data not available at cutoff date, 0.0 = magnitude is less than half of unit employed, Lao PDR = Lao People's Democratic Republic.

Source: Economy sources.

Table 2.19: **Growth Rates of Agriculture Production Index**
(%)

Regional Member	2000	2005	2010	2011	2012	2013	2014
Developing Member Economies							
Central and West Asia							
Afghanistan	-16.1	10.9	-0.8	-4.3	10.0	-2.2	3.8
Armenia	-1.5	17.4	-8.2	11.2	9.8	4.7	2.6
Azerbaijan	9.1	15.7	-0.7	7.1	4.1	1.6	-4.3
Georgia	-13.7	17.0	-6.5	9.2	-6.1	18.5	-4.5
Kazakhstan	-8.3	7.7	-13.7	31.9	-22.7	13.9	1.1
Kyrgyz Republic	4.8	-3.1	0.4	2.2	-1.4	1.2	-1.2
Pakistan	1.2	3.1	-2.1	5.0	-0.4	5.0	1.2
Tajikistan	12.6	-6.8	1.1	3.4	11.2	10.5	-3.3
Turkmenistan	6.8	3.3	-1.5	4.1	2.5	6.1	-5.9
Uzbekistan	3.2	5.3	4.6	5.3	3.6	5.7	-2.9
East Asia							
China, People's Rep. of	5.0	3.8	2.4	3.0	3.6	1.2	0.9
Hong Kong, China	2.4	13.5	–	6.7	6.3	–	-5.9
Korea, Rep. of	0.9	0.6	-5.9	-3.2	1.3	4.2	0.4
Mongolia	-1.8	-7.2	-20.4	7.4	5.6	9.4	1.7
Taipei,China	2.2	-5.7	2.1	3.7	-1.7	-1.2	1.3
South Asia							
Bangladesh	6.1	12.9	6.6	2.9	0.6	1.9	4.0
Bhutan	-11.8	27.1	6.0	16.7	-7.2	-6.6	2.4
India	-1.1	5.7	8.6	6.4	2.0	3.7	2.5
Maldives	5.9	-20.9	-4.0	-7.6	-6.5	-3.2	3.2
Nepal	5.1	2.0	1.0	7.2	15.2	-6.6	4.7
Sri Lanka	2.3	8.7	10.5	-3.8	3.8	9.5	-11.2
Southeast Asia							
Brunei Darussalam	13.1	-26.6	4.9	7.4	3.0	8.5	-6.3
Cambodia	1.9	27.2	8.9	14.1	2.7	0.7	0.7
Indonesia	3.4	2.7	2.6	2.5	7.3	0.9	1.9
Lao PDR	14.3	4.0	7.0	9.4	10.7	4.4	16.7
Malaysia	3.5	4.6	0.6	8.2	-0.2	2.0	-0.1
Myanmar	9.4	6.4	2.2	0.3	-8.2	3.7	2.2
Philippines	3.6	2.4	-0.8	3.1	3.7	2.0	0.2
Singapore	-59.2	-22.8	0.5	9.6	3.8	6.7	-0.2
Thailand	8.1	-2.1	-1.1	7.3	11.0	-0.9	-1.4
Viet Nam	3.3	3.8	2.7	4.4	6.5	0.5	2.2
The Pacific							
Cook Islands	-5.7	4.6	-3.4	-2.3	-1.8	3.6	-0.5
Fiji	-0.1	1.7	-6.1	14.0	-8.3	0.5	2.5
Kiribati	-5.5	1.2	-48.4	0.8	0.0	0.0	0.1
Marshall Islands	-74.9	15.2	-39.2	-13.2	11.9	6.1	–
Micronesia, Fed. States of	–	2.8	-18.8	-0.4	-1.4	6.1	12.6
Nauru	0.6	1.2	0.9	-3.0	5.1	2.1	0.9
Palau	...	...	...	...	...	...	...
Papua New Guinea	3.2	1.7	-1.4	4.2	-0.7	1.8	-29.4
Samoa	3.1	1.8	0.2	0.6	-0.7	-0.8	1.9
Solomon Islands	2.9	12.3	2.8	1.2	0.2	2.9	2.1
Timor-Leste	7.0	-2.3	-1.5	-13.2	7.9	-0.6	0.3
Tonga	-3.4	-0.2	-1.4	1.3	-1.3	-1.1	0.8
Tuvalu	6.2	2.1	-0.8	1.0	1.4	2.5	-0.0
Vanuatu	-4.7	1.8	24.0	-2.8	1.4	6.0	-8.9
Developed Member Economies							
Australia	-1.4	8.5	-2.9	10.3	7.4	-0.7	-2.8
Japan	-0.5	1.0	-2.4	-1.7	1.7	-0.4	-0.5
New Zealand	6.8	-2.2	1.4	0.6	4.6	0.5	6.1

... = data not available at cutoff date, – = magnitude is equal to zero, 0.0 = magnitude is less than half of unit employed, Lao PDR = Lao People's Democratic Republic.

Sources: Food and Agriculture Organization of the United Nations. FAOSTAT. http://foastat3.fao.org (accessed 20 June 2017); for Hong Kong, China and Taipei,China: economy sources.

Table 2.20: **Growth Rates of Manufacturing Production Index**
(%)

Regional Member	2000	2005	2010	2011	2012	2013	2014	2015	2016
Developing Member Economies									
Central and West Asia									
Afghanistan	...	...	...	...	...	...	...	...	...
Armenia	...	...	...	...	...	...	...	...	...
Azerbaijan	...	...	...	...	...	...	...	...	...
Georgia	...	...	...	...	...	...	...	...	...
Kazakhstan	17.3	15.9	15.1	...	-6.0	0.7	-0.8	-0.9	0.5
Kyrgyz Republic	...	...	...	...	...	...	...	...	...
Pakistan	...	18.2	4.7	...	1.2	4.3	5.5	3.3	3.3
Tajikistan	12.0	10.5	...	...	...	...	...	...	...
Turkmenistan	13.4	...	...	...	...	...	...	...	...
Uzbekistan	–	...	...	...	...	...	...	...	...
East Asia									
China, People's Rep. of	...	...	16.6	14.3	10.5	10.5	9.4	7.0	6.8
Hong Kong, China	-0.5	3.0	3.6	0.7	-0.8	0.1	-0.4	-1.5	-0.5
Korea, Rep. of	17.2	6.3	16.7	6.0	1.4	0.7	0.3	-0.3	1.0
Mongolia	...	...	...	...	...	...	...	...	...
Taipei,China	-17.4	3.2	26.5	4.7	-0.3	0.6	6.6	-1.5	2.0
South Asia									
Bangladesh	4.9	8.5	6.3	16.9	10.8	11.6	9.2	10.7	13.5
Bhutan	...	...	...	...	...	...	...	...	...
India	5.3	10.3	9.0	...	4.8	3.6	3.8	3.0	4.9
Maldives	...	...	...	...	...	...	...	...	...
Nepal	6.5	...	...	4.8	3.8	4.0	7.0	0.3	...
Sri Lanka	...	...	...	...	...	...	...	...	...
Southeast Asia									
Brunei Darussalam	...	...	...	...	...	...	...	...	...
Cambodia	48.8	...	...	...	...	...	...	...	...
Indonesia	3.6	1.3	4.8	4.1	4.1	6.0	4.8	4.8	...
Lao PDR	...	...	...	...	...	...	...	...	...
Malaysia	24.9	5.1	11.0	5.7	5.3	4.2	6.0	4.8	4.3
Myanmar	...	...	...	10.1	6.8	8.8	9.2	...	9.1
Philippines	...	1.1	23.3	1.0	7.7	14.0	7.4	2.3	14.3
Singapore	15.3	9.5	29.8	8.4	0.4	1.7	2.7	-5.1	3.7
Thailand	6.9	5.0	14.2	...	10.6	2.4	-5.2	0.3	2.6
Viet Nam	...	...	...	...	...	2.0	1.0	1.8	0.5
The Pacific									
Cook Islands	...	...	...	...	...	...	...	...	...
Fiji	-5.6	...	7.6	...	-25.7	5.2	2.9	4.0	...
Kiribati	...	...	...	...	...	...	...	...	...
Marshall Islands	...	...	...	...	...	...	...	...	...
Micronesia, Fed. States of	...	...	...	...	...	...	...	...	...
Nauru	...	...	...	...	...	...	...	...	...
Palau	...	...	...	...	...	...	...	...	...
Papua New Guinea	...	...	...	...	...	...	...	...	...
Samoa[a]	2.8	–	15.2	3.6	7.7	3.2	...	...	...
Solomon Islands	...	...	...	...	...	...	...	...	...
Timor-Leste	...	...	...	...	...	...	...	...	...
Tonga	...	...	...	...	...	...	...	...	...
Tuvalu	...	...	...	...	...	...	...	...	...
Vanuatu	...	...	...	...	...	...	...	...	...
Developed Member Economies									
Australia	1.2	-0.8	0.5	-0.1	0.7	-3.4	-1.5	-1.5	-2.8
Japan	5.7	1.3	15.6	-2.8	0.6	-0.8	2.1	-1.2	-0.1
New Zealand	4.3	0.6	4.3	-0.7	1.3	0.8	1.9	1.5	2.2

... = data not available at cutoff date, – = magnitude equals zero, Lao PDR = Lao People's Democratic Republic.

a Refers to volume indices of industrial production.

Source: Economy sources.

III. Money, Finance, and Prices

Snapshot

- The (arithmetic) average of the region's consumer price inflation rose slightly in 2016 to 3.1% from 3.0% in 2015.
- The money supply expanded in 2016 in 36 of the 39 regional economies for which data are available.
- Domestic credit has expanded since 2000 in 32 of 36 Asia and the Pacific economies for which data are available.
- The ratio of nonperforming loans to total gross loans increased in 2016 in 14 out of 22 regional economies compared with a year earlier.

Key Trends

The (arithmetic) average of the region's consumer price inflation slightly rose in 2016 to 3.1% from 3.0% in 2015. Falling oil prices, which dragged down consumer price index (CPI) in most economies in 2015, have since stabilized, resulting in a slight uptick in the region's (arithmetic) average rate of inflation from 3.0% in 2015 to 3.1% in 2016 (Table 3.1). Regional inflation is projected to accelerate further in 2017 and 2018, while remaining below the 10-year average of 3.9%.

The most rapid rates of inflation in 2016 were observed in Kazakhstan (14.6%) and Azerbaijan (12.4%), both of which underwent a currency devaluation in 2015; and in Nepal (9.9%), which continued to experience the disruptive economic and trade impacts of the earthquakes it suffered in 2015 (Figure 3.1) (ADB 2017).

Negative rates of inflation were recorded in Armenia (–1.4%), Palau (–1.0%), Brunei Darussalam (–0.7%), Singapore (–0.5%), the Cook Islands (–0.3%), the Federated States of Micronesia (–0.3%), and Japan (–0.1%).

Finally, the region's (arithmetic) average of food inflation decreased slightly to 3.4% in 2016 from 3.5% in 2015, while the (arithmetic) average of nonfood inflation rose to 2.8% from 2.4% during the same period (Tables 3.2 and 3.3).

Figure 3.1: Inflation Rate
(annual % change)

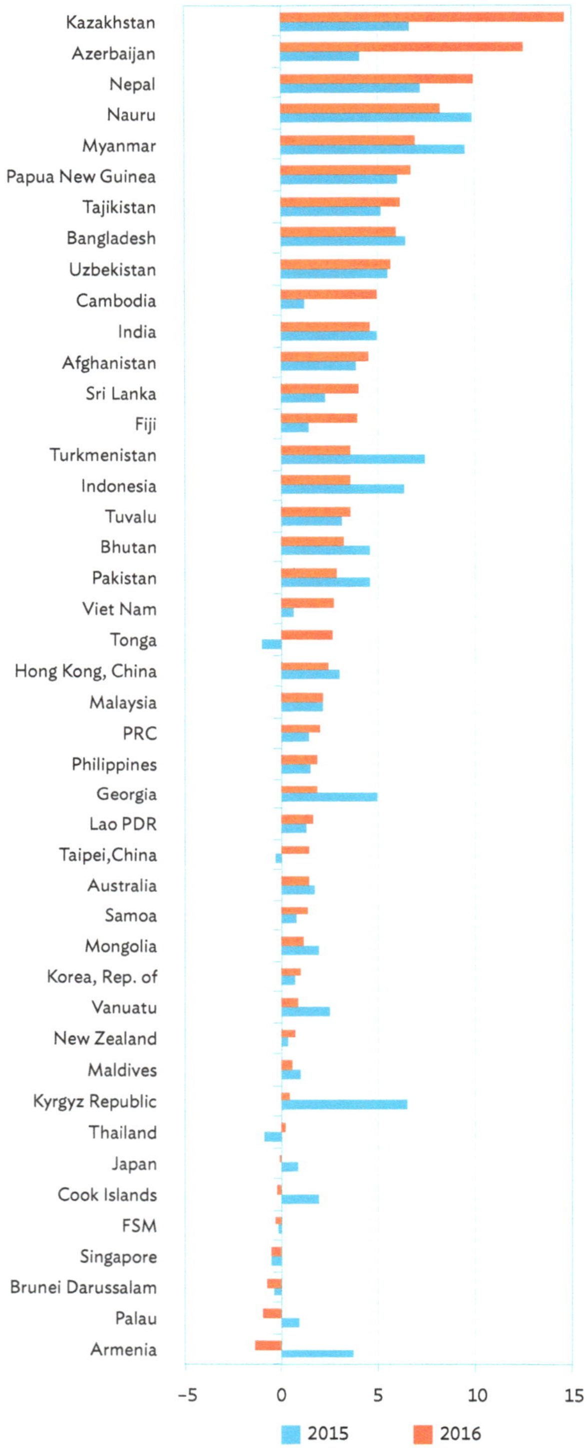

FSM = Federated States of Micronesia, Lao PDR = Lao People's Democratic Republic, PRC = People's Republic of China.
Note: This chart includes economies with available data for both 2015 and 2016.
Source: Table 3.1.

However, conventional measures of inflation do not necessarily reflect the movements in prices of items commonly consumed by the poor. Box 3 discusses the limitations of conventional price indices when examining the levels and movements of prices paid by the poor.

The money supply expanded in 2016 in all 39 regional economies for which data are available except in Azerbaijan, the Cook Islands, and Maldives. The money supply comprises the total currency in circulation and the value of deposits held in banks. Growth in the money supply that exceeds nominal gross domestic product (GDP) growth can lead to higher inflation; money supply growth below that of the nominal GDP growth rate can constrain real GDP growth. Governments can influence the money supply through borrowing and by setting interest rates (IMF 2016).

Figure 3.2 presents the expansion in the money supply in 2016 for the 39 regional economies for which data are available. The average rate of expansion was 11.8%. The largest increase in 2016 was recorded in Tajikistan (56.7%), where growing international reserves and increased demand for local currency raised reserve money (currency in circulation plus banks' reserves) (ADB 2017). The list of economies with large increase in money supply also includes Bhutan (23.0%), Georgia (20.2%), and Mongolia (20.2%).

Contractions in the money supply in 2016 were observed in Maldives (–0.2%), Azerbaijan (–1.9%), and the Cook Islands (–2.7%).

Box 3.1: Compiling Statistics on Prices Paid by the Poor

Monitoring the number of poor people in a country is an important component of any poverty reduction strategy. Conventionally, this is done by establishing a national poverty line that sets a minimum income threshold for a decent standard of living. Since national poverty lines vary from one country to another due to differences in the prices of basic commodities and services, and cost of living, in general, there is a need to develop a comparable measure, such as an international poverty line (IPL) for global poverty measurement and monitoring. In the early 1990s, the most widely accepted IPL, established by the World Bank, was roughly $1 per day based on 1985 prices. Today, internationally comparable poverty statistics are calculated based on poverty thresholds of $1.90 and $3.10 per day, which are both expressed in 2011 purchasing power parity (PPP) terms.

Converting an IPL into local currency units is a crucial step in estimating internationally-comparable poverty statistics. Instead of using market exchange rates, IPLs are converted into local currencies based on (consumption) PPPs, which allows for more meaningful cross-country comparisons without distortions induced by differences in price levels between countries. The PPPs are compiled through the International Comparison Program (ICP) and conducted under the charter of the United Nations Statistical Commission. This effort is coordinated by the World Bank and implemented by regional agencies such as the Asian Development Bank (ADB). The most recently concluded benchmark round of ICP was in 2011, hence, the current IPLs are based on the results of this round.

Over the last 15 years, there has been an increasing realization of the conceptual shortcomings of using conventional PPPs calculated from the ICP, as conversion factors for global poverty measurement. The PPPs reflect differences in national average prices between country X and country Y. Since the prices paid by the poor are not necessarily reflected in national average prices, the PPPs do not represent the purchasing power of the poor. A meaningful PPP for expressing IPLs in local currency would be a PPP that reflects the prices of goods and services that comprise the consumption basket of the poor. Furthermore, the expenditure weights used in the aggregation of conventional PPPs are based on national average expenditure shares. Given that income distributions in poorer countries are highly skewed, the average shares may differ significantly from the expenditure patterns associated with poorer sections of the population.

Having recognized the limitations of the typical (consumption) PPPs and the need for more accurate, focused, and meaningful currency converters for global poverty measurement, ADB conducted a pioneering study on poverty and PPP during implementation of the 2005 ICP for Asia and the Pacific (ADB 2008). The study developed a product list, or a basket of items, which are commonly used by the poor, and conducted surveys to collect price data on these products from the outlets and markets most accessible to the poor in Asia and the Pacific. The study also followed the recommended methodology of using expenditure weights for the poor as proposed by the Poverty Advisory Group of the Global Office at the World Bank. The results revealed that the use of poverty-specific price surveys and the adoption of the Poverty Advisory Group methodology led to significant changes in poverty PPPs, thereby affecting global and regional poverty measurements.

ADB conducted another study under the 2011 ICP for Asia and the Pacific as a contribution to ongoing research on global poverty measurement. Compared to the previous study, which required preparing a separate product list, or basket of items, of final consumption of poor households and conducting separate price surveys, the main objective of the subsequent study was to examine the feasibility of developing a poverty basket that is a subset of items already included in the final household consumption basket and directly using the price data collected under the 2011 ICP for Asia and the Pacific. The study identified a list of 186 products belonging to 45 basic headings deemed to be relevant for the poor. Using prices collected for the 186 selected items as a part of the 2011 ICP for Asia and the Pacific, poverty-specific PPPs were computed at the basic heading level as well as at the household consumption expenditure level using standard aggregation procedures. If it is feasible to find a good approximation of poverty-specific PPPs using data from the ICP, then it would no longer be necessary to conduct resource-intensive, poverty-specific price surveys.

(continued on next page)

(Box 3.1 continued)

While the latest study again found differences between the poverty-specific PPPs and conventional PPPs calculated for household final consumption expenditure, these differences were less pronounced than those found in the previous study. This may suggest that there are gains from conducting dedicated poverty-specific price surveys.[a]

The poverty-specific PPPs are just one piece of the puzzle in understanding how prices paid by the poor are different from prices paid by the nonpoor. In principle, the poverty PPPs capture the prices paid by the poor only at a specific point in time. For policy planning, price movements over time for items commonly consumed by the poor are also worth examining because even a slight rise in prices for these items can cause significant disruption in the well-being of the poor. Box Figure 3.1.1 shows how the prices of items commonly consumed by the poor in the Philippines increased at a different pace than the prices of other items.

Box Figure 3.1.1: Price Changes in Selected Commodity Items in the Philippines, 2012–2015

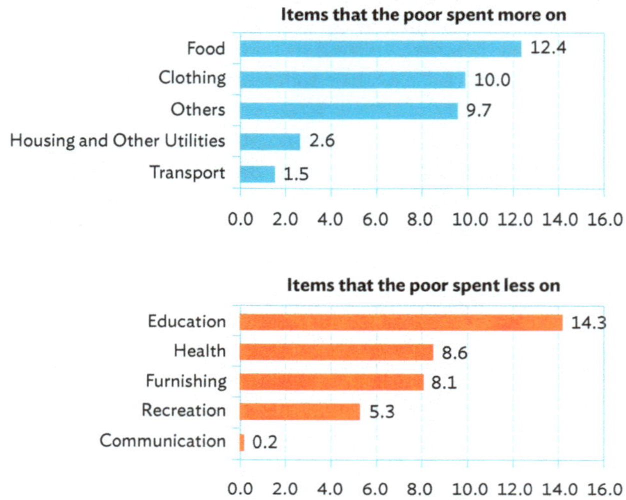

Source: Asian Development Bank estimates using data from the Philippine Statistics Authority.

Such price movements can be captured in consumer price index (CPI) for the poor; however, in many countries, a CPI for low-income people is not calculated separately. Compiling a CPI for the poor follows the same principle as that for poverty-specific PPPs. First, items that are commonly consumed by the poor need to be identified. However, unlike with poverty-specific PPPs in which the prices of items included in the basket for the poor are collected at a specific point in time, prices are tracked over time in compiling a CPI for the poor.

Compiling statistics on prices paid by the poor is important for measuring and examining poverty. Thus, continued research on how to improve and institutionalize the methods used to compile such statistics is necessary.

Source:

ADB. 2008. *Research Study on Poverty-Specific Purchasing Power Parities for Selected Countries in Asia and the Pacific*. Manila.

[a] Detailed results of the poverty-specific PPPs for the 2011 ICP in Asia and the Pacific will be provided in ADB. *Research Study on 2011 Poverty-Specific Purchasing Power Parities for Selected Countries in Asia and the Pacific*. Manila. Forthcoming.

Figure 3.2: Growth in Money, 2015–2016
(%)

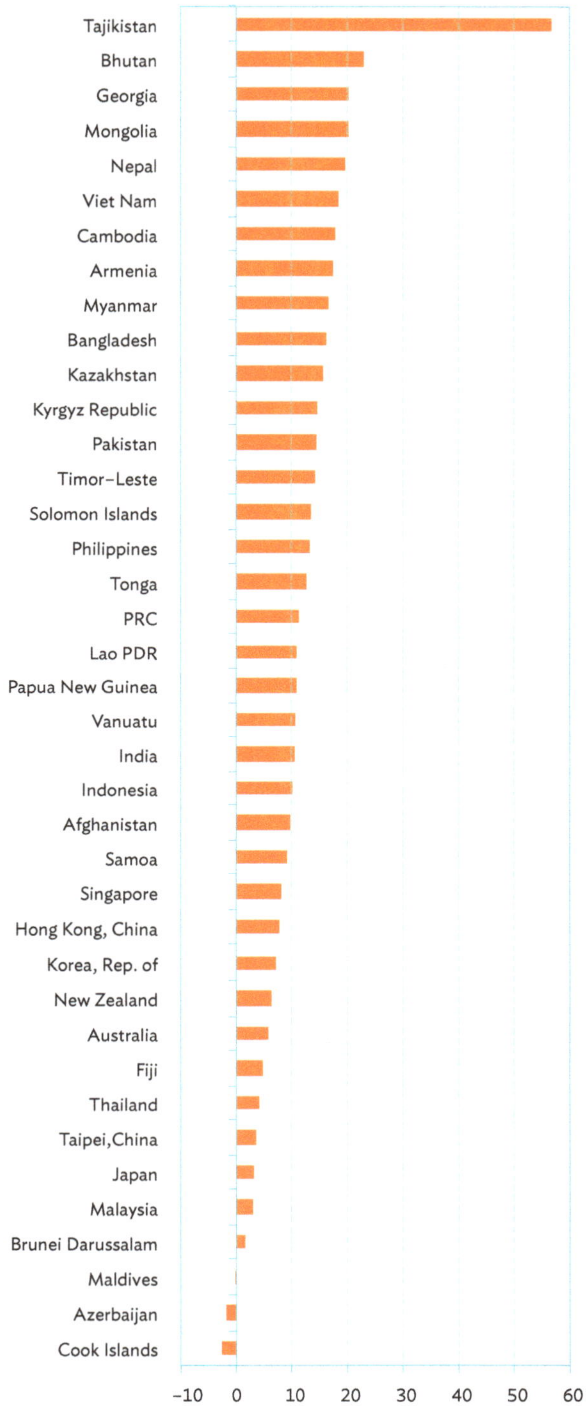

Lao PDR = Lao People's Democratic Republic, PRC = People's Republic of China.
Note: Australia, Azerbaijan, Fiji, Georgia, India, Japan, Kazakhstan, Malaysia, New Zealand, Papua New Guinea, Solomon Islands, and Turkmenistan use M3 while the rest use M2.
Source: Table 3.6.

It is important to note, however, that the money supply measures used in growth calculations vary from one economy to another.

Domestic credit has expanded since 2000 in 32 of 36 economies in Asia and the Pacific for which data are available. The amount of credit available in the banking sector increased in 32 of 36 regional economies between 2000 and 2016 (or the latest year for which data are available) (Figure 3.3). Viet Nam had the highest increase during the review period with average annual credit growth of 6.4 percentage points, followed by the Republic of Korea (6.2 percentage points), and the People's Republic of China (6.0 percentage points) (Table 3.10). The amount of domestic credit provided by the banking sector contracted during the review period on an average annual basis in Indonesia (–0.8 percentage point), Tonga (–0.3 percentage point), and Brunei Darussalam (–0.2 percentage point).

In 2016 (or the latest year for which data are available), Japan had the highest domestic credit-to-GDP ratio among all regional economies at 352.5%, followed by the People's Republic of China (215.0%) and Hong Kong, China (211.9%) (Figure 3.3). While the gap between credit growth and GDP growth in Japan remains large, it narrowed in 2016 (Standard Chartered Bank 2016). In Hong Kong, China, domestic credit growth accelerated ahead of the Hong Kong Monetary Authority adjusting its benchmark base rate in December in tandem with an increase in the United States' federal funds rate (ADB 2017).

Figure 3.3: Domestic Credit Provided by the Banking Sector
(% of GDP)

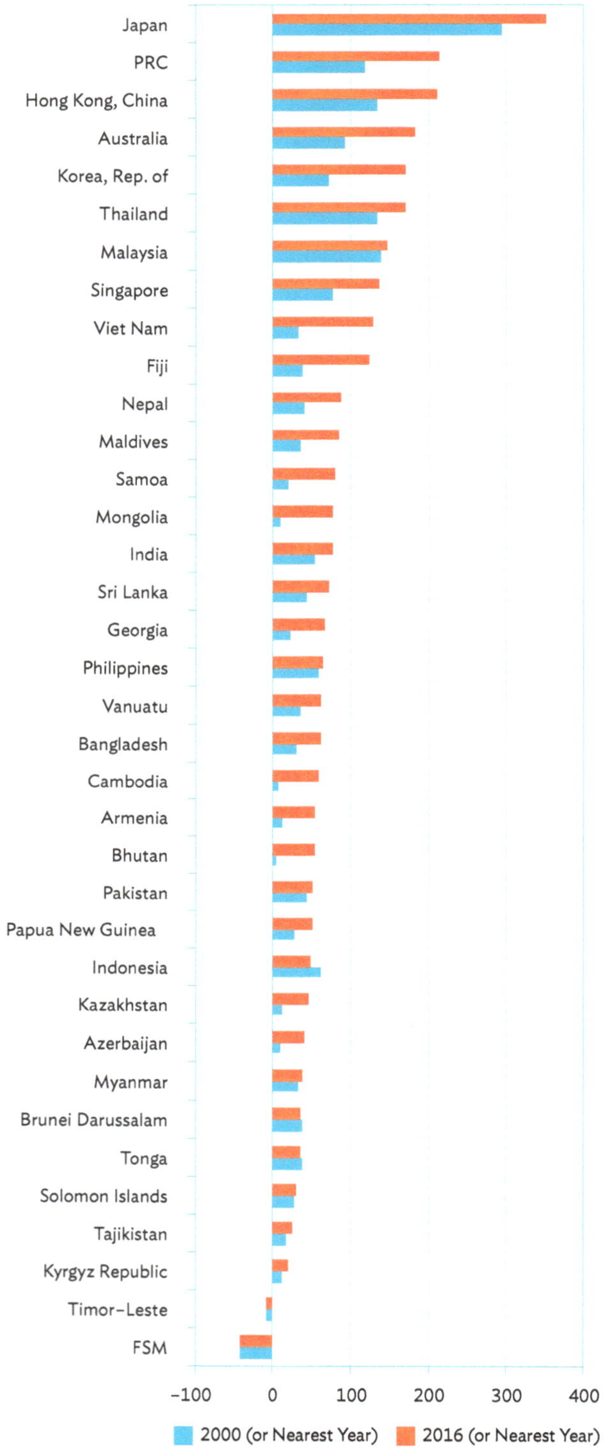

FSM = Federated States of Micronesia, GDP = gross domestic product, PRC = People's Republic of China.
Note: This chart includes economies with available data between 2000 and 2016.
Source: Table 3.10.

The Federated States of Micronesia (–42.2%), Timor-Leste (–8.8%), and Afghanistan (–1.2%) had negative domestic credit-to-GDP ratios in 2016 (or the latest year for which data are available), a reflection that claims on the central government exceeded central government deposits.

The ratio of nonperforming loans to total gross loans increased in 14 out of 22 regional economies in 2016 compared with a year earlier (Figure 3.4). The largest average annual increase in the ratio of nonperforming loans (NPLs) to total gross loans between 2015 and 2016 occurred in Brunei Darussalam (4.2 percentage points), India (3.3 percentage points), and the Kyrgyz Republic (1.8 percentage points). The largest average annual declines were observed in Maldives (–3.4 percentage points), Pakistan (–1.3 percentage points), Kazakhstan and Armenia (–1.2 percentage points).

The ratio of NPLs to total gross loans decreased between 2010 and 2016 in 20 of 31 regional economies for which data are available (Table 3.10). The most significant declines were observed in Afghanistan (–6.5 percentage points), Maldives (–2.6 percentage points), and Kazakhstan (–2.4 percentage points). The largest increases occurred in Tajikistan (3.2 percentage points), Vanuatu (1.5 percentage points), and India (1.3 percentage points).

Stock markets in Fiji, New Zealand, and Pakistan were the region's top performers in 2016. Fiji's stock market index gained 22.9% in 2016 despite the severe economic damage inflicted by Cyclone Winston (Figure 3.5). International relief and rehabilitation assistance and ambitious domestic public works helped the economy recover. In Pakistan, an improved growth outlook—supported by better security, macroeconomic stability, and strengthened economic fundamentals—was reflected in a sovereign rating upgrade from Standard & Poor's and significant gains in share prices of 13.2% on an annual basis. In Viet Nam, surging investment and

Figure 3.4: Nonperforming Bank Loans
(% of total gross loans)

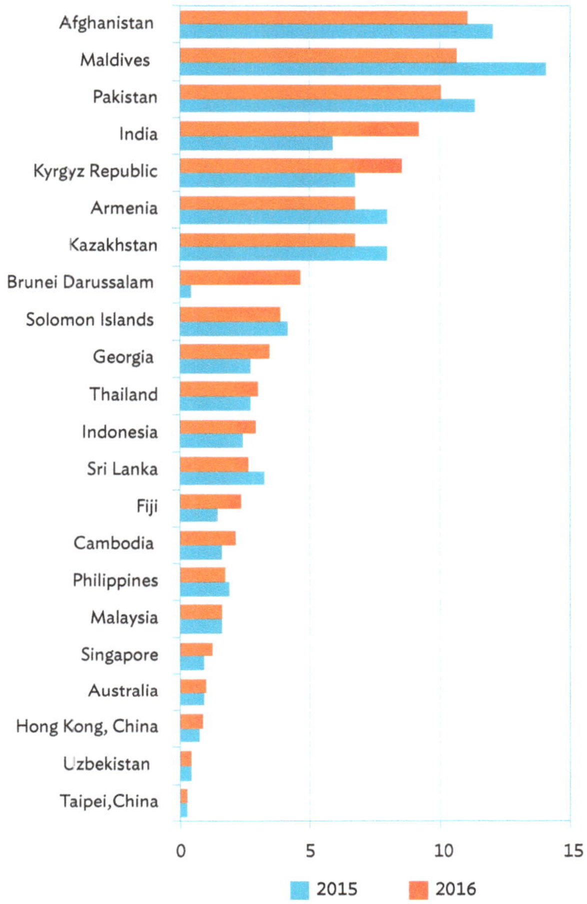

Note: This chart includes economies with available data for both 2015 and 2016.
Source: World Bank. World Development Indicators. http://data.worldbank.org/ (accessed 27 July 2017)

Figure 3.5: Top Performers in Asia and the Pacific Stock Market, 2016
(annual % change)

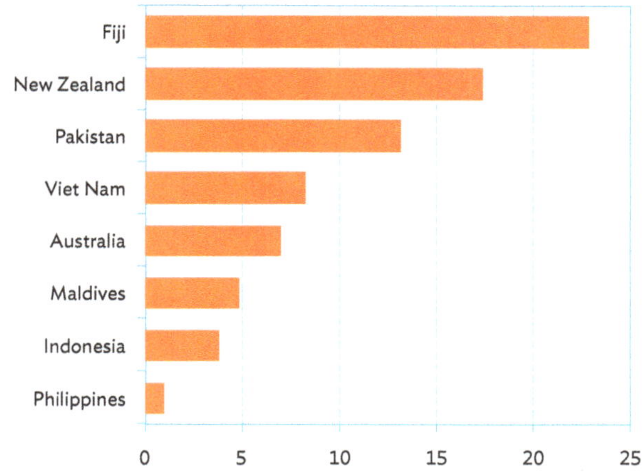

Source: Table 3.11.

consumption led to GDP growth of 6.0% or more for the third straight year in 2016 and an 8.2% annual increase in the stock market index (ADB 2017).

Data Issues and Comparability

The CPI coverage differs from country to country. Sometimes the basket of goods and services in the index is outdated or represents only urban areas or the capital city. Other price measurements, such as the wholesale price index and the producer price index, are not available in the Pacific countries, and it is recommended that an attempt is made to compile these indexes.

Some economies need to meet international reporting standards and classifications on the compilation of monetary and financial statistics, as detailed by the IMF on its Dissemination Standards Bulletin Board.

Broad money supply in most economies relates to M2. However, 12 of the 43 reporting economies report M3, which is broader than M2 as it also includes less liquid financial assets, thereby posing limits to comparability.

The methodology in compiling or measuring banks' average deposit and lending rates also varies for each economy. Some countries use the central bank policy rate while others use commercial bank rates.

Table 3.1: **Growth Rates of Consumer Price Index**[a]
(%)

Regional Member	2000	2005	2010	2011	2012	2013	2014	2015	2016
Developing Member Economies									
Central and West Asia									
Afghanistan	...	11.9	-4.5	13.7	8.4	6.4	5.7	3.8	4.5
Armenia	-0.8	0.6	8.2	7.7	2.6	5.8	3.0	3.7	-1.4
Azerbaijan	1.5 (2001)	8.3 (2006)	1.5 (2009)	7.9	1.1	2.4	1.4	4.0	12.4
Georgia	4.6	6.2	11.2	2.0	-1.4	2.4	2.0	4.9	1.8
Kazakhstan	13.2	7.6	7.1	8.3	5.1	5.8	6.7	6.6	14.6
Kyrgyz Republic	18.8	4.3	8.0	16.6	2.8	6.6	7.5	6.5	0.4
Pakistan	3.6	9.2	10.1	13.7	11.0	7.4	8.6	4.5	2.9
Tajikistan	60.6	7.1	9.8	9.3	6.4	3.7	7.4	5.1	6.1
Turkmenistan	8.0	10.7	4.4	5.3	5.3	6.8	6.0	7.4	3.5
Uzbekistan	24.9	7.8	7.6	7.3	7.2	7.0	6.4	5.5	5.6
East Asia									
China, People's Rep. of	0.4	1.8	3.3	5.4	2.6	2.6	2.0	1.4	2.0
Hong Kong, China	-3.7	0.8	2.3	5.3	4.1	4.4	4.5	3.0	2.4
Korea, Rep. of[b]	2.3	2.8	2.9	4.0	2.2	1.3	1.3	0.7	1.0
Mongolia	8.0 (2001)	9.5	12.9	8.9	14.0	12.5	10.4	1.9	1.1
Taipei,China	1.3	2.3	1.0	1.4	1.9	0.8	1.2	-0.3	1.4
South Asia									
Bangladesh	2.8	6.5	7.3	10.9	8.7	6.8	7.3	6.4	5.9
Bhutan	4.0	5.3	7.0	8.8	10.9	8.8	8.3	4.5	3.2
India	3.7	4.2	10.4	...	9.9	9.4	5.9	4.9	4.5
Maldives	-1.2	1.3	6.2	11.3	12.5	2.3	2.1	1.0	0.5
Nepal	3.3	4.5	9.6	9.6	8.3	9.9	9.1	7.2	9.9
Sri Lanka[c]	6.2	11.0	6.2	6.7	7.5	...	5.1	2.2	4.0
Southeast Asia									
Brunei Darussalam	1.2	1.1	0.4	0.1	0.1	0.4	-0.2	-0.4	-0.7
Cambodia[c]	-0.8	5.8	4.0	5.5	2.9	2.9	3.9	1.2	4.9
Indonesia[d]	9.3	10.5	5.1	5.4	4.3	7.0	6.4	6.4	3.5
Lao PDR	23.2	7.2	6.0	7.6	4.3	6.4	4.1	1.3	1.6
Malaysia	1.5	2.9	1.7	3.2	1.6	2.1	3.2	2.1	2.1
Myanmar	-0.2	9.4	7.7	5.0	1.5	8.9	5.0	9.5	6.9
Philippines	6.7	6.5	3.8	4.6	3.2	3.0	4.1	1.4	1.8
Singapore	1.3	0.5	2.8	5.2	4.6	2.4	1.0	-0.5	-0.5
Thailand	1.6	4.5	3.3	3.8	3.0	2.2	1.9	-0.9	0.2
Viet Nam	-1.6	8.3	10.0	18.6	9.2	6.6	4.1	0.6	2.7
The Pacific									
Cook Islands	3.2	2.5	-0.3	2.2	3.0	1.9	2.1	1.9	-0.3
Fiji	1.1	...	3.7	...	3.4	2.9	0.6	1.4	3.9
Kiribati[c]	0.4	-0.3	-3.9	1.5	-3.0	-1.5	2.1	0.6	...
Marshall Islands[c]	0.9	3.5	1.8	5.4	4.3	1.9	1.1	-2.2	...
Micronesia, Fed. States of	1.8	4.1	3.7	4.1	6.3	2.2	0.7	-0.2	-0.3
Nauru	2.3	9.8	-4.6	-0.8	-0.8	-2.0	0.3	9.8	8.2
Palau	-1.7 (2001)	3.9	1.4	4.7	3.6	3.4	4.2	0.9	-1.0
Papua New Guinea	15.6	1.8	6.0	4.4	4.6	5.0	5.2	6.0	6.7
Samoa	0.9	1.9	0.8	5.2	2.1	0.6	-0.5	0.7	1.3
Solomon Islands[c]	7.1	7.2	1.0	7.4	5.9	5.4	5.2	-0.6	...
Timor-Leste	...	1.5	9.2	15.4	4.4	...	0.7	0.6	...
Tonga	6.3	8.7	3.6	6.3	1.1	0.8	2.5	-1.0	2.6
Tuvalu	1.5 (2001)	3.2	-1.9	0.5	1.4	2.0	1.1	3.1	3.5
Vanuatu	2.5	0.8	2.9	1.0	1.5	7.2	0.9	2.5	0.8
Developed Member Economies									
Australia	2.4	2.4	2.3	3.1	2.3	2.3	2.7	1.7	1.4
Japan	-0.7	-0.3	-0.7	-0.2	-0.1	0.4	2.7	0.8	-0.1
New Zealand	2.6	3.0	2.3	4.0	1.1	1.1	1.2	0.3	0.6

... = data not available at cutoff date, CPI = consumer price index, Lao PDR = Lao People's Democratic Republic.

a Unless otherwise indicated, data refer to the whole economy.
b Data refer to all cities.
c Data refer to capital city.
d CPI data of Indonesia for 2000–2002 refer to CPI for 43 cities; for 2003–2007, 45 cities; for 2008–2013, 66 cities; and for 2014–2016, 82 cities.

Source: Economy sources.

Table 3.2: **Growth Rates of Food Consumer Price Index**[a]
(%)

Regional Member	2000	2005	2010	2011	2012	2013	2014	2015	2016
Developing Member Economies									
Central and West Asia									
Afghanistan	...	9.1	-9.1	13.9	7.0	5.3	9.9	4.0	5.6
Armenia	-2.2	0.7	8.6	11.2	2.3	5.8	2.2	3.0	-3.0
Azerbaijan	2.7 (2001)	11.9 (2006)	-1.5 (2009)	10.4	0.8	2.2	1.0	6.1	14.7
Georgia	7.5	8.3	23.1	0.6	-4.1	6.3	2.7	3.6	1.3
Kazakhstan	16.0	8.1	6.2	11.9	4.5	4.3	6.6	6.4	12.7
Kyrgyz Republic	...	7.0	6.5	25.0	-4.1	5.3	8.2	3.7	-6.5
Pakistan	2.2	12.5	13.0	18.0	11.0	7.1	9.0	3.5	2.1
Tajikistan	66.3	8.3	13.4	10.3	5.6	3.2	9.7	4.3	6.8
Turkmenistan	...	...	...	...	...	...	...	...	...
Uzbekistan	18.9	6.7	4.8	3.5	5.1	4.9	3.9	2.8	-0.4
East Asia									
China, People's Rep. of	1.7	-6.4	6.5	4.3	-6.2	-0.2	-1.5	-0.7	2.2
Hong Kong, China	-2.2	1.7	2.3	7.1	5.8	4.4	4.2	3.9	3.4
Korea, Rep. of[b]	1.1	3.1	6.6	8.2	3.9	0.7	0.2	1.6	2.5
Mongolia	...	12.8 (2007)	1.7 (2009)	...	...	...	...	...	...
Taipei,China	0.4	7.3	0.6	2.3	4.2	1.3	3.7	3.1	5.2
South Asia									
Bangladesh	2.6	7.9	8.5	14.1	7.7	5.2	8.6	6.7	4.9
Bhutan	...	5.7	8.8	10.2	13.9	8.7	10.4	3.2	3.9
India	1.6	4.2	10.0	...	11.2	12.1	6.4	4.9	4.2
Maldives	-4.7	8.0	7.5	19.9	20.9	4.3	0.7	0.5	0.8
Nepal	0.5	4.0	15.1	14.7	7.7	9.6	11.6	9.6	10.9
Sri Lanka[c]	4.5	11.4	6.9	8.8	4.7	...	4.3	5.5	6.1
Southeast Asia									
Brunei Darussalam	–	0.5	1.0	0.0	0.0	0.1	-0.2	0.8	-0.9
Cambodia[c]	-3.4	8.4	4.4	6.6	3.2	3.0	4.9	4.0	8.2
Indonesia[d]	2.7	10.0	9.4	6.9	5.7	9.3	...	7.6	6.6
Lao PDR	18.0	7.7	7.7	9.7	5.9	12.1	6.9	4.4	3.9
Malaysia	2.1	3.7	2.5	4.8	2.7	3.6	3.4	3.6	3.9
Myanmar	-2.6	9.3	7.2	3.9	-1.5	5.4	6.9	13.1	9.2
Philippines	3.0	6.4	4.1	5.7	2.4	2.8	6.3	3.3	1.3
Singapore	0.5	1.3	1.4	3.0	2.3	2.1	2.9	1.9	2.1
Thailand	-1.1	5.0	5.3	8.0	4.9	3.4	3.9	1.1	1.6
Viet Nam	-3.9	11.3	10.7	26.5	8.1	2.7	4.0	1.5	2.5
The Pacific									
Cook Islands	3.4	1.1	2.9	2.3	3.1	2.6	3.1	0.0	1.3
Fiji	-3.2	...	4.1	...	4.3	3.5	1.9	4.7	6.0
Kiribati[c]	0.7	-4.8	-11.1	-0.8	-2.4	-0.6	0.0	-0.5	1.2
Marshall Islands[c]	-0.8	0.3	-1.5	4.7	4.9	2.6	2.0	2.5	...
Micronesia, Fed. States of	1.1	3.4	2.2	2.6	4.5	2.6	0.8	0.5	...
Nauru	...	...	...	...	...	...	...	...	...
Palau	-2.4 (2001)	-1.5	1.8	4.8	4.4	3.2	1.5	1.7	-3.0
Papua New Guinea	13.6	3.5	5.4	-1.0	-1.4	-0.9	4.9	4.9	5.1
Samoa	-0.1	0.3	-6.6	5.3	1.9	0.7	-3.4	3.3	5.9
Solomon Islands[c]	6.6	5.6	-2.6	4.8	4.4	2.6	3.1	-2.9	...
Timor-Leste	...	0.4	12.0	18.7	4.7	...	0.7	0.5	...
Tonga	0.4	6.0	3.0	6.6	1.5	1.8	3.6	-1.3	1.3
Tuvalu	5.3 (2001)	5.5	-5.9	0.8	0.2	0.1	0.6	4.0	3.4
Vanuatu	2.0	0.5	5.2	1.0	2.3	1.5	1.7	3.6	2.3
Developed Member Economies									
Australia	2.1	1.6	1.6	3.7	0.7	0.5	1.3	2.1	0.1
Japan	-2.0	-0.9	-0.2	-0.4	0.1	-0.2	3.9	3.1	1.7
New Zealand	1.4	1.5	1.3	4.9	-0.3	0.6	0.7	0.4	0.0

... = data not available at cutoff date, – = magnitude equals zero, 0.0 = magnitude is less than half of unit employed, CPI = consumer price index, Lao PDR = Lao People's Democratic Republic.

a Coverage of food varies by economy. Unless otherwise indicated, data refer to the whole economy.
b Refers to all cities.
c Refers to capital city.
d CPI data of Indonesia for 2000–2002 refer to CPI for 43 cities; for 2003–2007, 45 cities; for 2008–2013, 66 cities; and for 2014–2016, 82 cities.

Source: Economy sources.

Table 3.3: **Growth Rates of Nonfood Consumer Price Index**[a]
(%)

Regional Member	2000	2005	2010	2011	2012	2013	2014	2015	2016
Developing Member Economies									
Central and West Asia									
Afghanistan	...	16.3	3.8	13.3	10.4	7.8	1.0	3.9	3.5
Armenia	3.0	0.5	9.6	3.4	4.6	4.6	1.7	5.6	-2.5
Azerbaijan	0.2 (2001)	5.3 (2006)	3.4 (2009)	2.6	1.0	0.8	3.2	3.8	16.7
Georgia	-0.8	3.6	5.0	1.0	-1.7	-1.6	0.7	6.4	2.0
Kazakhstan	11.5	6.3	6.4	5.4	4.3	3.1	6.9	8.1	22.4
Kyrgyz Republic	...	3.7	11.4	10.7	10.1	7.4	6.9	10.1	5.9
Pakistan	4.3	7.5	8.3	11.0	11.0	7.5	8.3	5.3	3.4
Tajikistan	44.2	2.7	5.5	7.2	6.7	6.1	2.9	7.8	5.7
Turkmenistan	...	...	...	...	...	...	...	...	...
Uzbekistan	36.6	6.9	5.3	8.3	4.9	5.5	7.6	6.3	10.2
East Asia									
China, People's Rep. of	...	...	...	...	...	...	...	...	...
Hong Kong, China	-4.1	0.5	2.2	4.6	3.4	4.3	4.6	2.6	2.0
Korea, Rep. of[b]	2.4	2.7	2.4	3.4	1.9	1.4	1.4	0.6	0.7
Mongolia	...	7.4 (2007)	12.5 (2009)	...	...	...	...	...	...
Taipei,China	1.6	0.5	1.1	1.1	1.1	0.6	0.3	-1.5	-0.1
South Asia									
Bangladesh	3.0	4.3	5.4	4.2	10.2	9.2	5.5	6.0	7.4
Bhutan	...	5.1	6.1	8.1	9.3	8.7	6.9	5.4	2.8
India	7.2	4.6	11.2	...	8.8	7.4	5.6	5.0	4.8
Maldives	-0.2	-0.8	3.8	8.5	10.0	1.4	2.7	1.1	0.5
Nepal	6.9	5.1	4.9	5.4	9.0	10.0	6.8	5.2	9.2
Sri Lanka[c]	10.1	10.7	5.4	4.5	13.2	...	5.4	1.0	-4.7
Southeast Asia									
Brunei Darussalam	...	...	...	0.1	0.3	0.4	-0.2	-0.7	-0.7
Cambodia[c]	1.2	3.9	3.8	4.5	2.7	2.0	2.7	-2.7	-3.0
Indonesia[d]	7.3	9.8	4.0	4.7	3.9	4.3	...	5.3	2.5
Lao PDR	30.4	6.7	4.2	6.1	3.1	2.0	1.8	-1.4	-0.7
Malaysia	1.3	2.7	1.4	2.5	1.3	1.6	3.0	1.2	1.3
Myanmar	...	9.4	8.8	7.3	7.4	12.9	2.1	3.8	3.1
Philippines	9.3	6.8	3.7	4.1	3.7	2.1	2.3	0.4	2.5
Singapore	1.7	0.2	3.2	5.9	5.2	2.4	0.5	-1.2	-1.3
Thailand	3.2	4.3	2.1	1.3	1.9	1.5	0.8	-2.0	-0.6
Viet Nam	-0.3 (2002)	5.6	9.1	13.3	8.4	4.6	2.9	-2.2	-1.3
The Pacific									
Cook Islands	3.1	3.0	-1.6	2.1	2.9	1.5	1.7	2.7	-0.9
Fiji	3.7	...	3.5	...	3.0	2.7	-0.3	0.3	...
Kiribati[c]	1.6	-1.9	2.8	4.8	22.8	-13.4	3.0	-1.1	3.7
Marshall Islands[c]	3.1	5.4	3.7	5.7	4.0	1.4	0.6	-4.9	...
Micronesia, Fed. States of	2.5	4.7	3.0	5.1	8.0	2.5	0.9	-0.3	...
Nauru	...	...	...	...	...	...	...	...	...
Palau	-1.6 (2001)	5.9	1.2	4.7	3.3	3.5	5.3	0.6	-0.2
Papua New Guinea	17.0	0.6	6.5	7.8	8.0	8.0	5.4	6.5	7.4
Samoa	1.6	3.3	3.4	3.4	2.1	0.6	2.7	-2.8	-3.2
Solomon Islands[c]	8.1	8.4	4.1	9.6	6.2	6.3	6.8	1.0	...
Timor-Leste	...	3.4	3.5	8.2	3.6	...	-0.1	1.5	...
Tonga	11.5	10.9	4.0	6.0	0.9	-0.1	1.5	-3.6	3.7
Tuvalu	...	...	...	0.3	2.3	3.4	1.4	2.5	3.6
Vanuatu	...	...	...	...	...	...	...	...	...
Developed Member Economies									
Australia	0.6	2.1	2.1	2.6	2.6	2.6	2.8	1.6	1.6
Japan	-0.3	-0.1	-0.9	-0.1	-0.2	0.6	2.3	0.0	-0.7
New Zealand	2.9	3.4	2.5	3.9	1.3	1.3	1.4	0.3	0.8

... = data not available at cutoff date, 0.0 = magnitude is less than half of unit employed, CPI = consumer price index, Lao PDR = Lao People's Democratic Republic.

a Coverage of nonfood varies by economy. Unless otherwise indicated, data refer to the whole economy.
b Refers to all cities.
c Refers to capital city.
d CPI data of Indonesia for 2000–2002 refer to CPI for 43 cities; for 2003–2007, 45 cities; for 2008–2013, 66 cities; and for 2014–2016, 82 cities.

Sources: Economy sources; Asian Development Bank estimates based on CPI weights from official sources.

Table 3.4: **Growth Rates of Wholesale and/or Producer Price Index**
(%)

Regional Member	2000	2005	2010	2011	2012	2013	2014	2015	2016
Developing Member Economies									
Central and West Asia									
Afghanistan	...	...	...	...	...	...	...	...	...
Armenia	0.8	7.7	22.6	9.1	7.0	4.7	8.5	-0.8	1.5
Azerbaijan	3.3 (2001)	17.3	30.5	33.5	4.5	-3.9	-5.1	-30.6	27.5
Georgia	5.8	7.5	11.3	12.8	1.6	-2.0	2.9	7.5	-0.1
Kazakhstan	38.0	23.7	25.2	27.2	3.5	-0.3	9.5	-20.5	16.8
Kyrgyz Republic	...	...	22.8	22.0	5.3	-2.1	1.4	8.7	6.4
Pakistan	1.8	6.7	13.8	21.2	10.4	7.4	8.2	-0.3	-1.1
Tajikistan	39.2	10.4	27.2	15.5	6.1	2.1	4.7	3.0	14.7
Turkmenistan	...	...	...	...	...	...	...	...	...
Uzbekistan	60.9	25.6	15.6	19.6	14.5	11.7	13.6	13.5	14.8
East Asia									
China, People's Rep. of	2.8	4.9	5.5	6.0	-1.7	-1.9	-1.9	-5.2	-2.0
Hong Kong, China	0.2	0.8	6.0	8.3	0.1	-3.1	-1.7	-2.7	1.3
Korea, Rep. of	2.1	2.1	3.8	6.7	0.7	-1.6	-0.5	-4.0	-1.8
Mongolia	...	...	...	...	...	...	...	...	...
Taipei,China	1.8	0.6	5.5	4.3	-1.2	-2.4	-0.6	-8.8	-3.0
South Asia									
Bangladesh[a]	-0.4	3.4	...	...	...	...	...	...	...
Bhutan	...	...	...	...	...	...	...	...	...
India	7.2	4.5	9.6	...	6.9	5.2	1.3	-3.7	1.7
Maldives	-2.4 (2002)	4.6	3.9	...	...	0.3	2.1	-2.4	...
Nepal	1.4 (2001)	7.3	12.6	9.9	6.4	9.0	8.3	6.1	6.3
Sri Lanka	1.7	11.5	2.6	19.9	3.5	9.2	3.2	1.0	4.2
Southeast Asia									
Brunei Darussalam	...	...	...	...	...	...	...	...	...
Cambodia	...	...	...	...	...	...	...	...	...
Indonesia[b]	12.5	15.3	4.9	7.5	3.8	5.0	5.4	4.4	7.9
Lao PDR	...	...	...	...	...	...	...	...	...
Malaysia	-1.8 (2001)	3.8 (2006)	-10.8 (2009)	12.3	-0.4	-2.7	1.5	-7.4	-1.1
Myanmar	...	...	...	...	...	...	...	...	...
Philippines	5.8	11.4	5.9	8.7	1.1	1.6	2.7	-3.9	1.2
Singapore	10.1	9.6	4.7	8.4	0.5	-2.7	-3.3	-15.3	-6.9
Thailand	3.8	9.2	9.4	5.5	1.0	0.3	0.1	-4.1	-1.2
Viet Nam	-0.2	4.4	12.6	18.4	3.4	5.3	3.3	-0.6	-0.5
The Pacific									
Cook Islands	...	...	...	...	...	...	...	...	...
Fiji	...	...	...	...	...	...	...	...	...
Kiribati	...	...	...	...	...	...	...	...	...
Marshall Islands	...	...	...	...	...	...	...	...	...
Micronesia, Fed. States of	...	...	...	...	...	...	...	...	...
Nauru	...	...	...	...	...	...	...	...	...
Palau	...	...	...	...	...	...	...	...	...
Papua New Guinea	...	...	...	...	...	...	...	...	...
Samoa	...	...	...	...	...	...	...	...	...
Solomon Islands	...	...	...	...	...	...	...	...	...
Timor-Leste	...	...	...	...	...	...	...	...	...
Tonga	...	...	...	...	...	...	...	...	...
Tuvalu	...	...	...	...	...	...	...	...	...
Vanuatu	...	...	...	...	...	...	...	...	...
Developed Member Economies									
Australia	2.6	3.6	-0.1	2.8	2.0	1.2	2.1	1.0	1.5
Japan	0.0	1.6	-0.1	1.5	-0.9	1.3	1.1	-3.0	-3.5
New Zealand	5.2	3.4	2.7	4.7	1.0	0.9	1.1	-1.3	0.8

... = data not available at cutoff date, 0.0 = magnitude is less than half of unit employed, Lao PDR = Lao People's Democratic Republic.

a For agricultural and industrial products only.
b Change of the wholesale price index for 2013 was estimated by rebasing January–October 2013 and 2012 data to 2005.

Source: Economy sources.

Prices

Table 3.5: **Growth Rates of Gross Domestic Product Deflator**
(%)

Regional Member	2000	2005	2010	2011	2012	2013	2014	2015	2016
Developing Member Economies									
Central and West Asia									
Afghanistan	...	11.6	14.3	10.4	9.3	3.5	-1.0	5.1	5.2
Armenia	-1.4	3.2	7.8	4.3	5.4	3.4	2.3	1.2	0.5
Azerbaijan	12.5	16.1	13.6	22.5	2.9	0.4	-1.3	-8.9	14.7
Georgia	4.7	7.9	8.5	9.5	1.1	-0.8	3.8	5.9	4.0
Kazakhstan	17.4	17.9	19.6	18.9	4.8	9.5	5.8	1.9	11.9
Kyrgyz Republic	27.2	7.1	10.0	22.5	8.7	3.2	8.4	3.4	2.5
Pakistan	5.3 (2001)	7.8	10.9	19.6	6.0	7.0	7.4	4.1	0.5
Tajikistan	22.7	9.5	12.4	18.8	11.8	4.3	5.5	0.2	5.2
Turkmenistan	21.3	7.0	2.3	12.8	8.3	1.2	0.6	-4.9	-5.0
Uzbekistan	47.1	21.4	16.5	16.6	15.0	14.3	11.7	9.2	8.1
East Asia									
China, People's Rep. of	2.0	3.9	6.9	8.1	2.4	2.2	0.8	...	...
Hong Kong, China	-3.4	-0.1	0.3	3.8	3.6	1.8	2.9	3.7	1.7
Korea, Rep. of	1.1	1.0	3.2	1.6	1.0	0.9	0.6	2.4	1.8
Mongolia	12.0	20.1	...	15.1	12.8	2.9	7.4	1.9	2.2
Taipei,China	7.6	-1.5	-1.5	-2.3	0.5	1.5	1.7	3.3	0.7
South Asia									
Bangladesh	1.9	5.1	7.1	7.9	8.2	7.2	5.7	5.9	6.7
Bhutan	3.7	5.9	6.0	8.6	9.2	5.9	7.6	3.4	...
India	3.6	4.2	9.0	...	7.9	6.2	3.2	1.8	3.6
Maldives	2.1	1.4	0.9	10.6	5.5	6.0	4.5	7.9	5.9
Nepal	4.7	5.8	14.4	11.0	6.6	6.1	9.0	5.1	5.0
Sri Lanka	6.7	10.4	5.9 (2009)	3.8	10.8	6.2	2.9	0.8	3.6
Southeast Asia									
Brunei Darussalam	29.0	18.8	5.3	20.2	1.2	-2.8	-1.8	-17.6	-9.2
Cambodia	-3.1	6.1	3.1	3.4	1.3	1.0	3.1	1.2	3.5
Indonesia	9.6	14.3	8.2	7.5	3.8	5.0	5.4	4.0	2.5
Lao PDR	21.8	7.8	3.1	7.6	...	6.5	5.7	2.3	3.0
Malaysia	-1.6 (2001)	4.0 (2006)	-6.0 (2009)	5.4	1.0	0.2	2.5	-0.4	1.9
Myanmar	2.5	19.2	7.0	10.3	3.1	4.4	4.2	4.1	3.6
Philippines	5.7	5.8	4.2	4.0	2.0	2.0	3.2	-0.6	1.6
Singapore	3.7	2.2	0.0	1.2	0.4	-0.2	-0.4	2.5	-1.4
Thailand	1.3	4.8	4.7	3.7	1.9	1.6	1.0	0.3	1.7
Viet Nam	3.4	9.0	12.1	21.3	10.9	4.8	3.7	-0.2	1.1
The Pacific									
Cook Islands	2.2	-2.6	6.2	1.4	-1.7	0.0	-1.0	1.9	-2.4
Fiji	-2.4	...	2.5	...	3.3	2.3	3.5	3.4	...
Kiribati	3.2	5.5	1.5	1.6	0.2	0.3	3.8	4.8	...
Marshall Islands	-3.0	2.0	1.4	3.1	3.3	0.8	-3.2	-2.6	...
Micronesia, Fed. States of	1.1	2.1	2.5	3.7	6.7	-0.1	3.1	-4.5	-0.3
Nauru	...	1.6	-18.4	7.0	16.4	-30.8	-23.5	-8.4	5.7
Palau	2.7 (2001)	8.9	-4.8	3.8	3.5	8.2	2.5	8.5	2.3
Papua New Guinea	13.1	7.9	9.9	8.8	-0.6	3.6	5.4	...	...
Samoa	1.1	5.1	2.0	4.4	2.9	0.8	1.5	0.4	0.4
Solomon Islands	6.9	8.8	1.8	4.8	4.2	6.8	1.9	4.0	...
Timor-Leste	-40.1	9.6	53.4	26.9	12.1	-4.9	-3.2	-36.5	...
Tonga	7.4	6.7	3.7	5.8	2.2	0.6	1.1	-0.1	0.4
Tuvalu	6.1 (2001)	0.7	2.5	0.8	0.8	2.1	5.1	4.6	...
Vanuatu	2.4	0.4	2.6	3.1	0.4	2.7	2.0	...	...
Developed Member Economies									
Australia	2.4	3.7	1.1	6.1	2.1	-0.1	1.4	-0.7	-0.3
Japan	-1.4	-1.0	-1.9	-1.7	-0.8	-0.3	1.7	2.1	0.3
New Zealand	2.5	2.4	3.0	2.8	-0.3	3.3	2.2	0.2	1.5

... = data not available at cutoff date; 0.0 = magnitude is less than half of unit employed, Lao PDR = Lao People's Democratic Republic.

Source: Economy sources.

Table 3.6: **Growth Rates of Money Supply**[a]
(%)

Regional Member	2000	2005	2010	2011	2012	2013	2014	2015	2016
Developing Member Economies									
Central and West Asia									
Afghanistan	...	44.6	26.9	21.3	8.7	9.9	8.1	3.1	9.7
Armenia	36.5	27.8	11.8	23.7	19.5	14.8	8.3	10.8	17.5
Azerbaijan[b]	21.8	22.3	24.3	32.1	20.7	15.0	11.8	–1.3	–1.9
Georgia[b]	39.2	27.9	30.1	14.5	11.4	24.5	13.8	19.3	20.2
Kazakhstan[b]	45.0	25.2	13.3	15.0	7.9	10.2	10.5	34.3	15.7
Kyrgyz Republic	12.1	9.9	21.1	14.9	23.8	22.8	3.0	14.9	14.6
Pakistan	9.4	19.8	13.0	16.8	13.4	16.9	12.6	12.8	14.5
Tajikistan	57.3	36.3	17.6	29.9	22.8	18.6	3.5	12.2	56.7
Turkmenistan[b]	94.6	5.6	74.2	52.1	37.4	26.0	10.0	18.0	...
Uzbekistan	37.1	54.4	52.4	32.3	29.2	22.5	15.8	17.5	...
East Asia									
China, People's Rep. of	12.3	16.5	19.7	17.3	14.4	13.6	11.0	13.3	11.3
Hong Kong, China	7.8	5.1	8.1	12.9	11.1	12.4	9.5	5.5	7.7
Korea, Rep. of	5.2	7.0	6.0	5.5	4.8	4.6	8.1	8.2	7.1
Mongolia	17.6	34.6	62.5	37.0	18.7	24.2	12.5	–5.5	20.2
Taipei,China	6.5	6.6	5.5	4.8	3.5	5.8	6.1	5.8	3.6
South Asia									
Bangladesh	18.6	16.7	22.4	21.3	17.4	16.7	16.1	12.4	16.3
Bhutan	16.1	13.2	16.5	4.1	5.9	3.3	26.0	3.8	23.0
India[b]	16.8	21.1	16.1	13.5	13.6	13.4	10.9	10.1	10.6
Maldives	4.2	10.6	14.6	20.0	4.9	18.4	14.7	12.3	–0.2
Nepal	21.8	8.3	14.1	28.0	22.7	16.4	19.1	19.9	19.5
Sri Lanka	12.9	19.1	18.0	20.9	18.3	18.0	13.1	17.2	...
Southeast Asia									
Brunei Darussalam	1.9 (2002)	–4.5	4.8	10.1	0.9	1.5	3.2	–1.8	1.5
Cambodia	26.9	16.1	20.0	21.4	20.9	14.6	29.9	14.7	17.9
Indonesia	14.3	16.3	15.4	16.4	15.0	12.8	11.9	9.0	10.0
Lao PDR	45.9	8.2	39.5	28.7	31.0	17.0	25.2	14.7	10.9
Malaysia[b]	5.1	8.3	6.8	14.3	9.0	7.3	7.0	2.6	3.0
Myanmar	42.2	27.3	42.6	42.5	16.2	24.8	26.2	32.9	16.6
Philippines	4.8	16.4	10.4	7.0	9.4	33.5	10.5	9.1	13.3
Singapore	–2.0	6.2	8.6	10.0	7.2	4.3	3.3	1.5	8.0
Thailand	4.0	6.1	10.9	15.1	10.4	7.3	4.7	4.4	4.2
Viet Nam	56.2	29.7	33.3	12.1	18.5	18.8	17.7	16.2	18.4
The Pacific									
Cook Islands	4.8	–5.2	–2.8	–13.4	19.2	–25.6	3.0	9.6	–2.7
Fiji[b]	–2.1	15.2	3.5	11.0	6.3	19.0	10.4	14.0	4.7
Kiribati	...	...	...	...	...	...	...	...	...
Marshall Islands	16.6	–0.8	9.4	–3.8	–13.4	...	31.0	30.8	...
Micronesia, Fed. States of	...	...	...	...	...	...	...	...	...
Nauru	...	...	...	...	...	...	...	...	...
Palau	...	...	...	...	...	...	...	...	...
Papua New Guinea[b]	5.4	29.5	11.4	16.1	11.0	6.7	3.4	8.0	10.9
Samoa	16.4	15.6	6.4	–6.1	–1.6	6.4	9.6	6.0	9.2
Solomon Islands[b]	0.4	46.1	13.3	25.8	17.4	12.4	5.1	15.5	13.4
Timor-Leste	155.5 (2001)	17.6	18.2	9.3	26.2	22.9	19.9	7.1	14.2
Tonga	8.3	12.1	5.1	2.7	–1.6	7.0	8.0	2.4	12.6
Tuvalu	...	...	...	...	...	...	...	...	...
Vanuatu	5.5	11.6	–6.0	1.3	–0.6	–5.6	8.6	11.4	10.6
Developed Member Economies									
Australia[b]	7.3	8.9	4.5	9.1	9.1	6.5	7.0	6.7	5.8
Japan[c]	1.9	0.4	1.9	2.6	2.2	3.4	2.8	2.5	3.2
New Zealand[b]	6.6	7.8	3.2	6.5	6.0	5.0	6.3	8.1	6.4

... = data not available at cutoff date, Lao PDR = Lao People's Democratic Republic.

a Data are based on M2 unless stated otherwise.
b Refers to M3.
c Refers to M3 except for 2000 (M2).

Source: Economy sources.

Table 3.7: **Money Supply**[a]
(% of GDP)

Regional Member	2000	2005	2010	2011	2012	2013	2014	2015	2016
Developing Member Economies									
Central and West Asia									
Afghanistan	11.0 (2002)	17.9	34.4	34.8	31.2	31.1	33.0	32.9	33.1
Armenia	14.7	16.3	26.3	29.8	31.6	33.9	34.7	36.8	42.9
Azerbaijan[b]	10.8	14.7	24.8	26.7	30.6	33.2	36.5	39.2	34.6
Georgia[b]	10.1	16.9	29.9	29.2	30.2	36.6	38.4	42.0	47.3
Kazakhstan[b]	15.3	27.2	38.9	34.5	33.9	32.2	32.3	42.1	43.1
Kyrgyz Republic	11.3	21.1	31.4	27.8	31.7	34.0	31.1	33.3	35.8
Pakistan	33.0	41.6	37.7	35.8	37.0	38.8	38.8	40.2	43.4
Tajikistan	8.2	15.5	12.0	12.8	13.1	13.9	12.8	13.5	18.8
Turkmenistan[b]	19.4	10.5	17.6	32.3	36.9	41.7	41.4	48.2	...
Uzbekistan	12.2	14.4	22.4	23.5	24.4	24.2	23.2	23.2	...
East Asia									
China, People's Rep. of	134.2	158.0	175.7	174.0	180.3	185.9	190.7	202.1	208.3
Hong Kong, China	272.9	310.1	401.7	416.5	439.4	470.3	487.2	484.4	502.1
Korea, Rep. of	111.4	111.1	131.2	131.4	133.3	134.4	139.8	144.2	147.0
Mongolia	21.1	37.5	48.0	48.7	45.6	49.3	47.8	43.4	50.6
Taipei,China	182.6	201.9	219.2	226.7	228.6	233.2	234.0	238.0	241.4
South Asia									
Bangladesh	31.5	40.9	45.5	48.1	49.0	50.3	52.1	52.0	52.9
Bhutan	50.8	57.8	70.5	62.7	57.8	55.2	61.4	57.7	61.6
India[b]	60.3	73.6	83.6	84.5	84.3	84.7	84.9	85.0	84.2
Maldives	41.1	47.0	53.4	53.3	51.7	55.1	57.1	57.8	52.4
Nepal	49.0	51.0	60.3	67.4	74.0	77.6	79.7	88.2	99.8
Sri Lanka	37.6	41.7	28.3	30.4	29.7	31.9	33.1	36.3	...
Southeast Asia									
Brunei Darussalam	77.8 (2001)	57.8	67.3	59.4	58.7	62.6	67.5	80.8	92.6
Cambodia	13.0	19.5	41.4	45.4	50.5	53.3	62.7	66.5	70.9
Indonesia	53.2	43.4	36.0	36.7	38.4	39.1	39.5	39.4	40.3
Lao PDR	17.4	18.7	38.0	42.1	43.8	44.5	49.0	51.2	51.5
Malaysia[b]	128.6	123.8	132.2	136.2	139.3	142.6	140.4	137.8	133.6
Myanmar	32.7	21.6	23.6	28.9	30.3	33.4	37.5	44.7	47.6
Philippines	39.7	41.2	47.6	47.2	47.5	58.0	58.5	60.6	63.1
Singapore	103.4	103.6	125.0	128.1	131.6	131.0	131.2	127.5	137.0
Thailand	122.4	104.1	109.0	119.9	121.1	124.3	127.3	128.4	127.4
Viet Nam	50.5	75.6	129.3	112.4	114.1	122.8	131.5	143.6	158.3
The Pacific									
Cook Islands	42.0	44.0	62.6	53.0	61.4	46.3	45.8	46.0	45.3
Fiji[b]	42.4	58.9	67.6	66.9	67.7	74.2	74.9	78.2	76.5
Kiribati	...	...	...	...	...	...	...	...	...
Marshall Islands	55.4	53.8	62.0	56.9	45.9	47.5	64.9	86.6	...
Micronesia, Fed. States of	...	...	...	...	...	...	...	...	...
Nauru	...	...	...	...	...	...	...	...	...
Palau	...	...	...	...	...	...	...	...	...
Papua New Guinea[b]	31.2	33.6	34.0	35.9	38.2	37.9	33.1	...	...
Samoa	38.2	41.1	45.0	39.1	38.3	40.2	42.6	43.8	44.9
Solomon Islands[b]	31.7	40.5	44.0	47.2	50.1	51.0	50.5	50.7	55.8
Timor-Leste	4.5	4.1	7.4	5.7	6.1	8.9	14.8	20.7	...
Tonga	29.2	39.0	40.9	38.6	36.8	40.4	42.3	41.1	44.0
Tuvalu	...	...	...	...	...	...	...	...	...
Vanuatu	89.7	98.6	83.3	80.8	78.6	70.9	73.8	...	...
Developed Member Economies									
Australia[b]	65.4	73.5	94.8	95.1	98.1	102.1	104.9	110.1	113.8
Japan[c]	123.4	198.7	218.8	228.6	232.1	236.0	237.7	236.3	240.8
New Zealand[b]	86.3	98.7	110.5	112.2	116.6	114.7	117.0	121.5	124.6

... = data not available at cutoff date, GDP = gross domestic product, Lao PDR = Lao People's Democratic Republic.

a Refers to M2, unless stated otherwise.
b Refers to M3.
c Refers to M3 except for 2002 (M2).

Source: Economy sources.

Table 3.8: **Interest Rate on Savings and Time Deposits**
(% per annum, period averages)

Regional Member	Savings Deposits				Time Deposits[a]			
	2000	2005	2010	2016	2000	2005	2010	2016
Developing Member Economies								
Central and West Asia								
Afghanistan	...	4.26 (2006)	5.10	1.49	...	4.72 (2006)	8.94	4.34
Armenia	...	...	...	...	20.72	6.66	10.70	12.50
Azerbaijan	...	...	...	...	10.40	9.38	10.96	5.53
Georgia[b]	10.98	6.79	8.71	4.47	9.85	10.23	11.60	6.71
Kazakhstan[b]	...	...	...	...	7.53	10.29	9.84	11.45
Kyrgyz Republic[c]	...	...	...	...	28.07	9.78	11.47	13.33
Pakistan[b]	5.71	1.24	5.02	3.73	7.37	4.21	7.21	4.70
Tajikistan	5.28 (2002)	3.63	3.83	0.94 (2015)	14.84 (2002)	20.16	17.78	15.57 (2015)
Turkmenistan	...	...	...	...	...	...	...	...
Uzbekistan	...	...	...	...	...	...	...	...
East Asia								
China, People's Rep. of	0.99	0.72	0.36	0.35	2.25	2.25	2.33	1.50
Hong Kong, China	4.50	0.97	0.01	0.01	5.40	1.73	0.16	0.15
Korea, Rep. of	7.08	3.57	3.18	1.47	7.94	3.72	3.86	1.56
Mongolia	13.80	12.60	10.70	13.07	...	...	...	...
Taipei,China	3.50	0.55	0.24	0.25	4.98	1.77	1.03	0.83
South Asia								
Bangladesh	5.81	4.19	4.88	3.60	8.97	8.31	9.00	7.30
Bhutan[d]	6.00	4.50	4.75	5.30	9.50	6.50	6.75	7.00
India	4.00	3.50	3.50	4.00	7.10	5.32	7.50	7.10
Maldives[e]	5.50	2.25	2.25	1.65	6.50	4.50	3.75	2.50
Nepal	5.25	3.38	7.00	2.24	6.88	3.63	8.13	5.76
Sri Lanka	8.40	5.00	5.00	5.00 (2015)	15.00	9.00	8.50	7.25 (2015)
Southeast Asia								
Brunei Darussalam	...	1.01	0.47	0.33	...	1.61	0.75	0.72
Cambodia	6.13	2.08	1.18	1.56	7.20	6.83	6.58	6.91
Indonesia	8.86	4.32	3.92	1.48	12.17	10.95	7.88	7.31
Lao PDR	...	...	...	...	...	...	...	...
Malaysia	2.72	1.41	0.94	1.00	4.24	3.70	2.81	3.18
Myanmar	...	...	...	...	...	...	...	...
Philippines[f]	7.40	3.80	1.60	0.72	10.50	6.00	2.07	3.03
Singapore	1.30	0.24	0.14	0.14	2.45	0.76	0.48	0.33
Thailand	2.50	1.88	0.50	0.47	3.50	3.00	1.55	1.40
Viet Nam	0.20	3.00	3.00	0.67 (2015)	6.24	8.40	11.50	6.32 (2015)
The Pacific								
Cook Islands	...	...	...	...	...	...	...	...
Fiji	...	...	...	...	...	...	...	...
Kiribati	...	...	...	...	...	...	...	...
Marshall Islands	...	...	...	...	...	...	...	...
Micronesia, Fed. States of	...	...	...	...	...	...	...	...
Nauru	...	...	...	...	...	...	...	...
Palau	...	...	...	...	...	...	...	...
Papua New Guinea	3.88	1.80	1.00	...	9.38	1.30	4.80	...
Samoa	3.00	2.75	0.88	1.00	7.35	6.38	2.25	2.90
Solomon Islands	...	...	...	...	...	...	...	...
Timor-Leste	0.20 (2002)	0.75	0.75	0.75	-	1.28	1.33	1.25
Tonga	3.15	3.36	1.51	2.46 (2015)	5.13	5.93	3.45	4.90 (2015)
Tuvalu	...	...	...	...	...	...	...	...
Vanuatu	...	...	...	...	...	...	...	...
Developed Member Economies								
Australia	...	5.40	4.50	1.55	5.90	4.55	6.00	2.35
Japan[g]	0.09	0.01	0.04	0.01	0.24	0.03	0.10	0.04
New Zealand[h]	...	...	...	...	6.49	6.90	4.72	3.30

... = data not available at cutoff date, – = magnitude equals zero, Lao PDR = Lao People's Democratic Republic.

a Refers to interest rate on time deposits of 12 months, unless otherwise indicated.
b Refers to interest rate on time deposits of over 12 months.
c Rates for time deposits refer to interest rates of commercial banks in national currency for 6–12 months.
d Rates for time deposits refer to rates on fixed deposits of 1 year to less than 3 years.
e Refers to interest rate on time deposits of 2–3 years.
f Rates for time deposits refer to rates charged on interest-bearing deposits with maturities of over 1 year.
g Refers to time deposits from 12 months to less than 2 years, computed as the arithmetic average of the monthly figures.
h Refers to interest rate on time deposits of 6 months.

Sources: Economy sources; for the People's Republic of China: CEIC database (accessed 18 July 2017).

Table 3.9: **Yield on Short-Term Treasury Bills and Lending Interest Rate**
(% per annum, period averages)

Regional Member	Yield on Short-Term Treasury Bills[a]				Lending Interest Rate			
	2000	2005	2010	2016	2000	2005	2010	2016
Developing Member Economies								
Central and West Asia								
Afghanistan	...	...	...	...	...	18.0 (2006)	15.7	15.0
Armenia[b]	24.4	4.1	10.6	9.8	31.6	18.0	19.2	17.4
Azerbaijan	16.7	7.5	1.8	13.0	19.7	17.0	20.7	16.4
Georgia	29.9 (2001)	11.6	9.6	8.4	24.7	17.6	15.8	12.6
Kazakhstan	6.6	3.3	...	...	...	...	...	...
Kyrgyz Republic	70.7	6.8	11.1	13.5 (2015)	51.9	26.6	23.1	22.2
Pakistan[c]	8.4	7.2	12.5	6.0	...	...	...	...
Tajikistan[d]	...	...	6.7	0.4 (2014)	25.6	23.3	23.4	25.8 (2015)
Turkmenistan	...	...	...	...	...	...	...	...
Uzbekistan	...	...	...	...	...	...	...	...
East Asia								
China, People's Rep. of[e]	2.6	1.9	2.6	4.8 (2014)	5.9	5.6	5.8	4.4
Hong Kong, China	5.7	3.7	0.3	0.7	9.5	7.8	5.0	5.0
Korea, Rep. of[f]	7.1	3.6	2.7	1.5	8.5	5.6	5.5	3.4
Mongolia[g]	...	13.7	12.9 (2012)	17.1	37.0	30.6	20.1	19.7
Taipei,China[h]	...	1.3	0.3	0.3	7.7	3.8	2.7	2.6
South Asia								
Bangladesh[d]	6.3	6.7	2.2	3.9	12.8	10.6	12.2	10.4
Bhutan[d]	7.3	3.5	2.0	5.5	16.0	14.0	14.0	14.2
India[d, i]	9.0	5.7	6.2	6.4	12.3	10.8	8.3	9.7
Maldives[j]	...	5.5 (2007)	4.9	3.5	13.0	13.0	10.4	10.8
Nepal[d]	5.3	2.2	6.8	2.3	9.5	8.1	8.0	...
Sri Lanka[k]	13.7 (2001)	10.4	7.6	10.2	14.3 (2001)	12.1	9.3	11.7
Southeast Asia								
Brunei Darussalam	...	...	...	...	5.5	5.5	5.5	5.5
Cambodia	...	...	...	...	...	...	...	...
Indonesia	...	...	...	...	18.5	14.1	13.3	11.9
Lao PDR[l]	29.9	18.6	8.0	...	32.0	26.8	22.6	...
Malaysia	2.9	2.5	2.6	2.8	7.7	6.0	5.0	4.5
Myanmar	...	...	...	...	15.3	15.0	17.0	13.0
Philippines[d]	9.9	6.1	3.5	1.5	10.9	10.2	7.7	5.6
Singapore	2.2	2.1	0.3	...	5.8	5.3	5.4	5.4
Thailand[d]	1.9 (2002)	2.7	1.4	1.4	7.8	5.8	5.9	6.3
Viet Nam[m]	5.4	6.1	11.1	4.2 (2015)	10.6	11.0	13.1	7.0
The Pacific								
Cook Islands	...	...	...	...	...	...	...	...
Fiji	3.5	1.9	3.4	1.4	8.4	6.8	7.5	5.9
Kiribati	...	...	...	...	...	...	...	...
Marshall Islands	...	...	...	...	...	...	...	...
Micronesia, Fed. States of	...	...	...	...	15.3	16.4	15.1	15.7
Nauru	...	...	...	...	...	...	...	...
Palau	...	...	...	...	...	...	...	...
Papua New Guinea[n]	17.0	3.8	4.6	4.6	17.5	11.5	10.4	8.4
Samoa	...	...	...	...	11.4 (2002)	11.4	10.7	9.1
Solomon Islands	7.0	4.5	3.7	0.5	14.6	14.1	14.4	10.1
Timor-Leste	...	...	...	...	...	16.7	11.0	14.2
Tonga	...	...	...	...	11.3	11.4	11.5	7.9
Tuvalu	...	...	...	...	...	...	...	...
Vanuatu	...	...	...	...	9.9	7.5	5.5	3.0
Developed Member Economies								
Australia[o]	6.0	...	4.4	...	7.7	7.3	7.3	5.4
Japan	0.7	0.0	0.1	-0.4	2.1	1.7	1.6	1.0
New Zealand	6.4	6.5	2.8	2.0	7.8	7.8	6.3	5.0

... = data not available at cutoff date, 0.0 = magnitude is less than half of unit employed, Lao PDR = Lao People's Democratic Republic.

a Refers to 3-month Treasury bills, unless otherwise indicated.
b Refers to average yield on 9–12-month Treasury bills since March 2001.
c Refers to weighted average yield on 6-month Treasury securities.
d Refers to 91-day Treasury bills.
e Refers to the monthly yield of 3-month Treasury bonds.
f Refers to 91-day certificates of deposit.
g Refers to weighted average rate on Treasury bills of all maturities. Beginning December 2012, refers to yield on 12-week Treasury bills.
h Refers to prime lending rates.
i Figures are for fiscal year ending March.
j Refers to rate on 28-day Treasury bills.
k Refers to weighted average rate on the last monthly issuance of 364-day Treasury bills since December 2001.
l Refers to weighted average auction rate for 12-month Treasury bills.
m Refers to average monthly yield on 360-day Treasury bills sold at auction.
n Refers to rate on 182-day Treasury bills.
o Refers to estimated closing yield in the secondary market on 13-week Treasury notes.

Sources: International Monetary Fund. International Financial Statistics. http://data.imf.org/ (accessed 27 July 2017); Organisation for Economic Co-operation and Development. Main Economic Indicators. http://dx.doi.org/10.1787/data-00043-en (accessed 27 July 2017); economy sources.

Table 3.10: **Domestic Credit Provided by Banking Sector and Bank Nonperfoming Loans**

Regional Member	Domestic Credit Provided by Banking Sector[a] (% of GDP)				Bank Nonperfoming Loans (% of total gross loans)	
	2000	2005	2010	2016	2010	2016
Developing Member Economies						
Central and West Asia						
Afghanistan	...	−4.8 (2006)	4.8	−1.2	49.9	11.1
Armenia[b]	11.5	8.8	27.8	54.4	3.0	6.7
Azerbaijan	9.6	11.2	23.0	40.0	...	...
Georgia	21.5	21.6	33.4	65.6	5.9	3.4
Kazakhstan[c]	12.3	39.0	45.4	44.8	20.9	6.7
Kyrgyz Republic[d]	12.2	13.8	12.5	19.3	14.8	8.5
Pakistan	41.6	46.5	46.2	51.4	14.7	10.1
Tajikistan[e]	17.9	13.0	7.6	25.2	7.4	20.4 (2014)
Turkmenistan	...	...	...	...	...	...
Uzbekistan[f]	...	...	...	...	1.0	0.4
East Asia						
China, People's Rep. of[g]	118.4	132.6	142.2	215.0	1.1	1.7 (2015)
Hong Kong, China[h]	134.0	139.8	195.4	211.9 (2015)	0.8	0.9
Korea, Rep. of[e]	70.9	125.5	151.0	170.1	0.6	0.5 (2014)
Mongolia	9.0	26.6	25.9	76.4	...	...
Taipei,China	1.8	1.9	0.9	...	0.6	0.3
South Asia						
Bangladesh[e]	30.2	47.7	57.4	60.6	5.8 (2011)	8.4 (2015)
Bhutan[e]	2.9	21.8	45.6	52.9	5.2	6.6 (2015)
India[e,i]	52.8	60.2	74.2	76.1 (2015)	2.7 (2011)	9.2
Maldives[e]	34.8	48.8	85.6	83.9	20.9 (2012)	10.6
Nepal	40.8	42.2	67.4	86.1	...	...
Sri Lanka	43.7	43.5	35.5	72.3	3.8 (2011)	2.6
Southeast Asia						
Brunei Darussalam	38.6	10.4	22.7	35.5	6.9	4.6
Cambodia[j]	6.4	7.2	22.7	58.8	3.1	2.1
Indonesia[k]	60.7	46.2	34.2	47.9	2.5	2.9
Lao PDR	9.0	8.1	26.7	...	...	...
Malaysia[l]	138.4	117.7	123.3	145.3	3.4	1.6
Myanmar	31.2	23.1	25.2	37.0	...	...
Philippines[m]	58.3	47.2	49.2	63.5	3.4	1.7
Singapore[n]	76.7	61.2	80.8	135.1	1.4	1.2
Thailand[e]	134.3	111.0	133.4	169.4	3.9	3.0
Viet Nam[e]	32.6	65.4	124.7	128.3 (2015)	2.1	2.3 (2015)
The Pacific						
Cook Islands	...	...	...	...	...	...
Fiji	37.9	111.6	132.3	122.1	4.4	2.3
Kiribati	...	...	...	...	...	...
Marshall Islands	...	...	...	...	...	...
Micronesia, Fed. States of[e]	−42.3	−24.6	−14.9	−42.2	...	...
Nauru	...	...	...	...	...	...
Palau	...	...	...	...	...	...
Papua New Guinea	28.2	22.2	34.8	51.0 (2014)	1.9	3.1 (2015)
Samoa[e]	18.3	31.8	63.4	79.1	...	3.7
Solomon Islands[e]	26.5	29.4	27.2	29.7	9.3	3.8
Timor-Leste	−8.7 (2002)	−9.2	−23.5	−8.8 (2015)	...	...
Tonga	38.8	48.3	39.9	34.7	14.4 (2012)	7.6 (2015)
Tuvalu	...	...	...	...	...	...
Vanuatu[o]	35.6	44.5	63.7	60.9	4.8	12.3 (2015)
Developed Member Economies						
Australia[p]	93.3	113.3	154.2	183.4	2.1	1.0
Japan	295.0	308.0	320.2	352.5 (2015)	...	...
New Zealand	108.0	126.4	150.7	...	...	...

... = data not available at cutoff date, BSP = Bangko Sentral ng Pilipinas, GDP = gross domestic product, Lao PDR = Lao People's Democratic Republic.

a Since the claims on the central government are a net item (claims on the central government minus central government deposits), this net figure may be negative, resulting in a negative figure of domestic credit provided by the banking sector.

b Nonperforming loans exclude financial leases and repurchase agreements that are not classified as deposits. A loan is classified as nonperforming if (i) full or partial repayment of principal amount or its interest is past due, e.g., 1 day in Armenia; (ii) interest payments have been recapitalized; and (iii) payment terms have been adjusted (refinanced) toward more favorable conditions for the borrower, or rolled over.

c A nonperforming loan is defined as the sum of loans classified as doubtful of fifth category and loss loans (excluding homogeneous loans classified as doubtful of fifth category and loss loans) plus provisions for homogenous loans.

d Nonperforming loans are all loans that are part of the "classified" category according to the National Bank of the Kyrgyz Republic.

e Loans are considered to be nonperforming if principal and/or interest is overdue for 90 days or more.

f Nonperforming loans include doubtful and bad loans based on the Central Bank of Uzbekistan regulation on classifying assets by their quality. Also includes provisions by commercial banks for covering possible losses in commercial banks. Data also include finanical leasing, interbank loans, and factoring.

g Loans are classified as nonperforming based on the repayment ability of borrowers; credit records of borrowers; willingness of borrowers to repay; guarantee of loans; legal obligations of loans repayment; and credit management of banks.

h Classification of loans is largely based on the assessment of the borrower's ability to repay and on the degree of doubt about the recoverability of the principal and interest of the loan.

i Nonperforming loans exclude financial leases and repurchase agreements that are not classified as deposits.

j Nonperforming loans are loans that no longer generate income and are classified as substandard, doubtful, or loss.

k Nonperforming loans are loans with arrears for 90 days or more. Rural banks that meet the definition of deposit takers are not included due to their relatively small asset size (not more than 2% of commercial banks' total assets).

l Data on nonperforming loans exclude repos that are not classified as deposits.

m Loans payable in lump sum and payable in quarterly, semiannual, and annual installments are considered as nonperforming if they remain unpaid 30 days after due date or after they have become past due. Loans payable in monthly installments are considered as nonperforming when three or more installments are in arrears. Loans payable in daily, weekly, or semimonthly installments are considered as nonperforming at the same time they become past due. Excluded from nonperforming loans starting 1 January 2013 are loans previously classified as "loss" by the BSP fully covered by allowance for probable losses; and outstanding credit card receivables classified as "loss" in the latest BSP examination; plus credit card receivables classified as "loss" by the bank but not to exceed the total amount classified as "loss" in the latest BSP examination.

n In addition to the past due for 90 days or more criterion, other characteristics that banks in Singapore consider when determining whether loans are nonperforming include (i) unfavorable economic and market conditions or operating problems that would affect the profitability and business of the borrower in future; (ii) weak financial condition, or inability of the borrower to generate sufficient cash flow to service the payments; (iii) difficulties experienced by the borrower in repaying other credit facilities granted by the same bank, or by other financial institutions; or (iv) breach of any key financial covenants by the borrower.

o Nonperforming loans are loans classified as substandard, doubtful, and loss.

p Nonperforming loans exclude repurchase agreements that are not classified as deposits. Includes both "past due" loans and "nonaccrual" loans.

Sources: World Bank. World Development Indicators. http://data.worldbank.org/ (accessed 27 July 2017); International Monetary Fund. http://fsi.imf.org/ (accessed 3 July 2017); for Taipei,China: economy source.

Table 3.11: **Growth Rates of Stock Market Price Index[a]**
(%)

Regional Member	2000	2005	2010	2011	2012	2013	2014	2015	2016
Developing Member Economies									
Central and West Asia									
Afghanistan	...	...	...	...	...	...	...	...	...
Armenia	...	...	...	...	...	...	...	...	...
Azerbaijan	...	...	...	...	...	...	...	...	...
Georgia	...	...	...	...	...	...	...	...	...
Kazakhstan	...	...	...	...	...	...	...	...	...
Kyrgyz Republic	...	...	...	...	...	...	...	...	...
Pakistan[b]	42.1	47.3	32.3	15.2	23.2	45.8	37.4	14.6	13.2
Tajikistan	...	...	...	...	...	...	...	...	...
Turkmenistan	...	...	...	...	...	...	...	...	...
Uzbekistan	...	...	...	...	...	...	...	...	...
East Asia									
China, People's Rep. of	37.3	-22.1	3.4	-5.7	-16.8	-1.1	1.5	66.0	-19.0
Hong Kong, China	26.5	11.1	19.3	-0.3	-4.4	10.4	2.7	4.8	-12.0
Korea, Rep. of	-8.7	28.5	23.6	12.6	-2.6	1.5	1.1	1.4	-1.2
Mongolia	...	68.5	138.5	38.5	-15.2	-5.7	-6.6	-17.2	-5.5
Taipei,China	5.7	1.0	23.1	2.6	-8.3	8.2	11.1	-0.4	-2.2
South Asia									
Bangladesh[b]	12.2	23.4	114.4	-10.4	-23.6	-9.8	15.0	-1.6	-1.7
Bhutan	...	...	...	...	...	...	...	...	...
India	11.2	32.6	29.8	-2.6	-2.5	11.4	25.2	10.9	-3.6
Maldives	...	51.8	-20.4	-22.9	-6.9	-5.3	-4.8	8.9	4.8
Nepal	...	...	...	...	...	...	...	...	...
Sri Lanka[b]	...	27.6	96.0	-8.5	-7.1	4.8	23.4	-5.5	...
Southeast Asia									
Brunei Darussalam	...	...	...	...	...	...	...	...	...
Cambodia	...	...	...	...	...	...	...	...	...
Indonesia[b]	-9.1	35.0	53.9	21.0	10.0	11.8	7.2	-1.3	3.8
Lao PDR	...	...	...	...	...	...	...	...	...
Malaysia	21.4	6.4	27.1	9.7	6.5	8.7	5.5	-6.1	-3.8
Myanmar	...	...	...	...	...	...	...	...	...
Philippines	-6.3	17.5	43.1	32.8	14.7	16.0	1.8	5.5	0.9
Singapore	8.6	16.7	30.3	0.3	0.7	7.6	1.2	-2.5	-11.6
Thailand	-18.7	4.2	45.6	21.3	17.3	21.3	-0.2	0.2	-2.1
Viet Nam[b]	...	8.3	12.2	-11.1	-4.2	18.7	18.9	-0.6	8.2
The Pacific									
Cook Islands	...	...	...	...	...	...	...	...	...
Fiji	...	14.9	-15.8	-5.3	8.6	-10.3	–	46.4	22.9
Kiribati	...	...	...	...	...	...	...	...	...
Marshall Islands	...	...	...	...	...	...	...	...	...
Micronesia, Fed. States of	...	...	...	...	...	...	...	...	...
Nauru	...	...	...	...	...	...	...	...	...
Palau	...	...	...	...	...	...	...	...	...
Papua New Guinea	...	52.5	26.2	3.2	-28.0	-15.3	-12.3	-6.3	...
Samoa	...	...	...	...	...	...	...	...	...
Solomon Islands	...	...	...	...	...	...	...	...	...
Timor-Leste	...	...	...	...	...	...	...	...	...
Tonga	...	...	...	...	...	...	...	...	...
Tuvalu	...	...	...	...	...	...	...	...	...
Vanuatu	...	...	...	...	...	...	...	...	...
Developed Member Economies									
Australia[b]	1.7	17.6	-2.6	-14.5	14.6	15.1	1.1	-2.1	7.0
Japan	11.6	13.5	2.0	-7.2	-6.5	46.0	12.6	22.7	-12.6
New Zealand	2.3	19.4	9.7	6.2	6.9	25.5	14.1	12.7	17.4

... = data not available at cutoff date, – = magnitude equals zero, Lao PDR = Lao People's Democratic Republic.

a Refers to growth rates of stock market prices (period average), unless otherwise indicated.
b Refers to growth rates of stock market prices as of end of period.

Sources: International Monetary Fund. 2017. International Financial Statistics. http://data.imf.org/ (accessed 10 July 2017); for Taipei,China: economy source.

Table 3.12: **Stock Market Capitalization**

Regional Member	Stock Market Capitalization ($ million)				Stock Market Capitalization (% of GDP)			
	2000	2005	2010	2016	2000	2005	2010	2016
Developing Member Economies								
Central and West Asia								
Afghanistan	...	...	...	...	...	...	...	...
Armenia	2 (2001)	43	145	...	0.1 (2001)	0.9	1.6	...
Azerbaijan	...	...	...	...	...	...	...	...
Georgia	24	355	1,060	...	0.8	5.5	9.1	...
Kazakhstan	1,289 (2002)	10,529	26,673	40,161	5.2 (2002)	18.4	18.0	30.0
Kyrgyz Republic	4	42	79	...	0.3	1.7	1.6	...
Pakistan	6,625	45,317	38,007	...	9.0	41.4	21.4	...
Tajikistan	...	...	...	...	...	...	...	...
Turkmenistan	...	...	...	...	...	...	...	...
Uzbekistan	32	37	...	...	0.2	0.3	...	...
East Asia								
China, People's Rep. of	...	401,852	4,027,840	7,320,738	...	17.6	66.0	65.4
Hong Kong, China	623,398	1,054,999	2,711,316	3,193,236	363.1	581.0	1,185.9	995.0
Korea, Rep. of	171,262	718,011	1,091,911	1,254,541	30.5	79.9	99.8	88.9
Mongolia	37	46	1,093	...	3.2	1.8	15.2	...
Taipei,China	262,295	485,825	752,335	842,806	79.1	129.3	168.6	159.2
South Asia								
Bangladesh	2,192	3,300	41,617	...	4.1	4.8	36.1	...
Bhutan	54	100	215	387 (2015)	12.0	12.4	13.8	18.3 (2015)
India	...	553,074	1,631,830	1,566,680	...	68.4	98.5	69.2
Maldives	...	...	...	...	...	...	...	...
Nepal	...	...	...	...	...	...	...	...
Sri Lanka	1,074	5,720	19,924	18,679	6.6	23.4	35.1	23.0
Southeast Asia								
Brunei Darussalam	...	...	...	...	...	...	...	...
Cambodia	...	...	...	...	...	...	...	...
Indonesia	26,813	81,428	360,388	425,768	16.2	28.5	47.7	45.7
Lao PDR	...	...	...	...	...	...	...	...
Malaysia	113,156	180,518	408,689	359,788	120.6	125.8	160.3	121.4
Myanmar	...	...	...	...	...	...	...	...
Philippines	25,981	39,799	157,321	239,738	32.1	38.6	78.8	78.6
Singapore	152,826	257,340	647,226	640,428	159.5	202.0	273.8	215.7
Thailand	29,217	123,885	277,732	432,956	23.1	65.4	81.4	106.4
Viet Nam	...	...	30,115	66,396	...	...	26.0	32.8
The Pacific								
Cook Islands	...	...	...	...	...	...	...	...
Fiji	244	587	419	...	14.5	19.5	13.3	...
Kiribati	...	...	...	...	...	...	...	...
Marshall Islands	...	...	...	...	...	...	...	...
Micronesia, Fed. States of	...	...	...	...	...	...	...	...
Nauru	...	...	...	...	...	...	...	...
Palau	...	...	...	...	...	...	...	...
Papua New Guinea	...	6,138	11,027	...	...	126.1	113.5	...
Samoa	...	...	...	...	...	...	...	...
Solomon Islands	...	...	...	...	...	...	...	...
Timor-Leste	...	...	...	...	...	...	...	...
Tonga	...	...	...	...	...	...	...	...
Tuvalu	...	...	...	...	...	...	...	...
Vanuatu	...	...	...	...	...	...	...	...
Developed Member Economies								
Australia	372,794	804,015	1,454,491	1,268,494	89.7	115.9	127.3	105.3
Japan	3,157,222	4,572,901	3,827,774	4,955,300	64.6	96.2	67.2	100.3
New Zealand	18,613	40,592	52,870 (2012)	80,048	35.4	35.4	30.0 (2012)	43.3

... = data not available at cutoff date, GDP = gross domestic product, Lao PDR = Lao People's Democratic Republic.

Sources: World Bank. World Development Indicators. http://databank.worldbank.org/data (accessed 26 July 2017); Asian Development Bank estimates using data from economy sources for Bhutan and Taipei,China.

Exchange Rates

Table 3.13: **Official Exchange Rate**
(local currency unit per $, period averages)

Regional Member	2000	2005	2010	2011	2012	2013	2014	2015	2016
Developing Member Economies									
Central and West Asia									
Afghanistan	47.36	49.49	46.45	46.75	50.92	55.38	57.25	61.14	67.87
Armenia	539.53	457.69	373.66	372.50	401.76	409.63	415.92	477.92	480.49
Azerbaijan	0.89	0.95	0.80	0.79	0.79	0.78	0.78	1.02	1.60
Georgia	1.98	1.81	1.78	1.69	1.65	1.66	1.77	2.27	2.37
Kazakhstan	142.13	132.88	147.36	146.62	149.11	152.13	179.19	221.73	342.16
Kyrgyz Republic	47.70	41.01	45.96	46.14	47.00	48.44	53.65	64.46	69.91
Pakistan	53.65	59.51	85.19	86.34	93.40	101.63	101.10	102.77	104.77
Tajikistan	2.08	3.12	4.38	4.61	4.74	4.76	4.94	6.16	7.84
Turkmenistan	1.04	1.26	2.85	2.85	2.85	2.85	2.85	3.50	3.50
Uzbekistan	236.61	1,106.10	1,578.42	1,706.61	1,897.56	2,097.20	2,319.55	2,583.54	2,984.70
East Asia									
China, People's Rep. of	8.28	8.19	6.77	6.46	6.31	6.20	6.14	6.23	6.64
Hong Kong, China	7.79	7.78	7.77	7.78	7.76	7.76	7.75	7.75	7.76
Korea, Rep. of	1,130.96	1,024.12	1,156.06	1,108.29	1,126.47	1,094.85	1,052.96	1,131.16	1,160.27
Mongolia	1,076.67	1,205.25	1,357.06	1,265.52	1,357.58	1,523.93	1,817.94	1,970.31	2,140.29
Taipei,China	31.23	32.17	31.64	29.46	29.61	29.77	30.37	31.90	32.32
South Asia									
Bangladesh	52.14	64.33	69.65	74.15	81.86	78.10	77.64	77.95	78.47
Bhutan	44.94	44.10	45.73	46.67	53.44	58.60	61.03	64.15	67.20
India	44.94	44.10	45.73	46.67	53.44	58.60	61.03	64.15	67.20
Maldives	11.77	12.80	12.80	14.60	15.36	15.37	15.38	15.37	15.37
Nepal	71.09	71.37	73.26	74.02	85.20	92.99	97.55	102.41	107.46
Sri Lanka	77.01	100.50	113.06	110.57	127.60	129.07	130.56	135.86	145.58
Southeast Asia									
Brunei Darussalam	1.72	1.66	1.36	1.26	1.25	1.25	1.27	1.37	1.38
Cambodia	3,840.75	4,092.50	4,184.92	4,058.50	4,033.00	4,027.25	4,037.50	4,067.75	4,058.69
Indonesia	8,421.78	9,704.74	9,090.43	8,770.43	9,386.63	10,461.24	11,865.21	13,389.41	13,308.33
Lao PDR	7,887.64	10,655.17	8,258.77	8,030.06	8,007.76	7,860.14	8,048.96	8,147.91	8,129.06
Malaysia	3.80	3.79	3.22	3.06	3.09	3.15	3.27	3.91	4.15
Myanmar[a]	6.52	5.82	5.63	5.44	640.65	933.57	984.35	1,162.62	1,234.87
Philippines	44.19	55.09	45.11	43.31	42.23	42.45	44.40	45.50	47.49
Singapore	1.72	1.66	1.36	1.26	1.25	1.25	1.27	1.37	1.38
Thailand	40.11	40.22	31.69	30.49	31.08	30.73	32.48	34.25	35.30
Viet Nam	14,167.75	15,858.92	18,612.92	20,509.75	20,828.00	20,933.42	21,148.00	21,697.57	21,935.00
The Pacific									
Cook Islands	2.20	1.42	1.39	1.27	1.23	1.22	1.21	1.43	1.44
Fiji	2.13	1.69	1.92	1.79	1.79	1.84	1.89	2.10	2.09
Kiribati	1.72	1.31	1.09	0.97	0.97	1.04	1.11	1.33	1.35
Marshall Islands[b]	1.00	1.00	1.00	1.00	1.00	1.00	1.00	1.00	1.00
Micronesia, Fed. States of[b]	1.00	1.00	1.00	1.00	1.00	1.00	1.00	1.00	1.00
Nauru	1.72	1.31	1.09	0.97	0.97	1.04	1.11	1.33	1.35
Palau[b]	1.00	1.00	1.00	1.00	1.00	1.00	1.00	1.00	1.00
Papua New Guinea	2.78	3.10	2.72	2.37	2.08	2.24	2.46	2.77	3.13
Samoa	3.29	2.71	2.48	2.32	2.29	2.31	2.33	2.56	2.56
Solomon Islands	5.09	7.53	8.06	7.64	7.36	7.30	7.38	7.91	7.95
Timor-Leste[b]	1.00	1.00	1.00	1.00	1.00	1.00	1.00	1.00	1.00
Tonga	1.76	1.94	1.93	1.83	1.70	1.73	1.82	1.94	2.22
Tuvalu	1.72	1.31	1.09	0.97	0.97	1.04	1.11	1.33	1.30
Vanuatu	137.64	109.25	96.91	89.47	92.64	94.54	97.07	108.99	108.48
Developed Member Economies									
Australia	1.72	1.31	1.09	0.97	0.97	1.04	1.11	1.33	1.35
Japan	107.77	110.22	87.78	79.81	79.79	97.60	105.94	121.04	108.79
New Zealand	2.20	1.42	1.39	1.27	1.23	1.22	1.21	1.43	1.44

Lao PDR = Lao People's Democratic Republic.

a Beginning 1 April 2012, the Central Bank of Myanmar adopted the managed float exchange rate regime for kyat vis-à-vis the US dollar.
b Unit of currency is the US dollar.

Sources: International Monetary Fund. International Financial Statistics. http://data.imf.org/ (accessed 2 June 2017); for Turkmenistan: United Nations National Accounts Main Aggregates Database and Interstate Statistical Committee of the Commonwealth of Independent States; for Uzbekistan: economy source, United Nations National Accounts Main Aggregates Database, and Interstate Statistical Committee of the Commonwealth of Independent States; for Taipei,China: economy source.

Table 3.14: **Purchasing Power Parity Conversion Factor**[a]
(local currency unit per $, period averages)

Regional Member	2000	2005	2010	2011	2012	2013	2014	2015	2016
Developing Member Economies									
Central and West Asia									
Afghanistan	9.89 (2002)	12.16	16.04	17.36	18.62	18.96	18.44	19.17	19.90
Armenia	144.93	157.74	183.12	187.10	193.53	196.87	197.87	198.07	196.50
Azerbaijan	0.17	0.21	0.30	0.36	0.36	0.36	0.35	0.32	0.36
Georgia	0.53	0.64	0.80	0.86	0.85	0.83	0.85	0.89	0.91
Kazakhstan	22.15	35.14	67.88	80.17	82.49	88.89	92.36	93.05	101.71
Kyrgyz Republic	8.11	9.26	14.80	17.76	18.94	19.24	20.49	20.96	21.20
Pakistan	11.12	12.92	20.77	24.35	25.33	26.67	28.14	28.98	28.76
Tajikistan	0.29	0.66	1.49	1.74	1.91	1.96	2.03	2.01	2.09
Turkmenistan	...	...	...	...	...	...	...	...	...
Uzbekistan	66.55	222.68	525.83	600.58	677.64	762.07	838.12	904.45	960.74
East Asia									
China, People's Rep. of	2.71	2.82	3.31	3.51	3.52	3.55	3.51	3.48	3.47
Hong Kong, China	7.44	5.69	5.37	5.46	5.55	5.56	5.62	5.76	5.79
Korea, Rep. of	747.23	788.92	840.57	854.59	854.89	869.08	870.74	890.72	893.75
Mongolia	138.38	223.58	476.22	537.13	594.84	602.41	635.89	639.72	645.65
Taipei,China	21.54	18.38	15.79	15.11	14.92	14.90	14.88	15.21	15.11
South Asia									
Bangladesh	15.68	17.33	21.90	23.15	24.58	25.93	26.92	28.19	29.70
Bhutan	12.27	13.66	15.84	16.86	18.07	18.83	19.84	20.36	21.55
India	10.14	11.06	14.21	15.11	16.01	16.73	16.94	17.06	17.45
Maldives	6.45 (2001)	6.30	7.87	8.53	8.84	9.22	9.47	10.10	10.56
Nepal	13.10	15.33	22.68	24.63	25.79	27.05	29.06	30.20	31.44
Sri Lanka	15.24	21.79	38.00	38.65	42.06	43.98	44.46	44.35	45.34
Southeast Asia									
Brunei Darussalam	0.48	0.59	0.61	0.72	0.71	0.68	0.66	0.54	0.48
Cambodia	1,062.54	1,106.83	1,330.18	1,347.11	1,340.27	1,349.27	1,347.84	1,350.34	1,379.79
Indonesia	1,427.63	2,013.80	3,425.30	3,606.57	3,674.27	3,795.44	3,931.64	4,046.50	4,091.83
Lao PDR	1,375.99	1,934.27	2,414.68	2,467.75	2,759.44	2,891.41	3,003.16	3,040.96	3,092.25
Malaysia	1.19	1.28	1.41	1.46	1.45	1.43	1.44	1.42	1.42
Myanmar	53.48	125.12	217.52	234.97	237.95	244.42	250.14	257.22	277.58
Philippines	13.71	15.47	17.52	17.85	17.88	17.95	18.19	17.89	17.95
Singapore	1.00	0.90	0.90	0.89	0.88	0.86	0.84	0.86	0.83
Thailand	11.06	11.34	12.17	12.37	12.38	12.40	12.33	12.28	12.33
Viet Nam	2,923.18	3,575.10	5,647.10	6,709.19	7,307.63	7,533.85	7,672.40	7,576.25	7,560.96
The Pacific									
Cook Islands	...	...	...	...	...	...	...	...	...
Fiji	0.89	0.94	1.02	1.04	1.06	1.06	1.08	1.11	1.13
Kiribati	0.86	0.90	0.96	0.96	0.95	0.94	0.96	0.95	0.95
Marshall Islands	...	...	...	...	...	...	...	...	...
Micronesia, Fed. States of	0.86	0.80	0.87	0.88	0.90	0.89	0.91	0.86	0.85
Nauru	...	...	0.86	1.00	1.22	0.94	0.81	0.74	0.77
Palau	0.72	0.74	0.74	0.75	0.76	0.82	0.85	0.88	0.89
Papua New Guinea	1.23	1.53	1.82	1.86	1.77	1.78	1.95	...	...
Samoa	1.43	1.48	1.66	1.66	1.70	1.70	1.67	1.70	1.66
Solomon Islands	3.91	4.66	5.87	6.37	6.66	6.53	6.96	6.96	7.18
Timor-Leste	0.38	0.40	0.47	0.52	0.54	0.52	0.52	0.51	...
Tonga	0.93	1.14	1.40	1.45	1.46	1.44	1.43	1.44	1.42
Tuvalu	1.04	1.11	1.12	1.11	1.10	1.10	1.10	1.12	1.14
Vanuatu	90.42	88.70	99.50	100.51	99.10	100.12	100.31	101.71	102.58
Developed Member Economies									
Australia	1.31	1.39	1.50	1.51	1.54	1.45	1.46	1.46	1.47
Japan	154.97	129.55	111.64	107.45	104.27	101.30	102.47	102.56	102.04
New Zealand	1.44	1.54	1.50	1.49	1.50	1.45	1.44	1.44	1.45

... = data not available at cutoff date, Lao PDR = Lao People's Democratic Republic.

a Purchasing power parity figures are extrapolated from the 2011 International Comparison Program benchmark estimates, or imputed using a statistical model based on these benchmark estimates.

Sources: World Bank. World Development Indicators. http://databank.worldbank.org/data/home.aspx (accessed 25 July 2016); Asian Development Bank estimates using data from economy sources and US Bureau of Economic Analysis for 2000–2016 in Afghanistan; Brunei Darussalam; Fiji; Pakistan; Taipei,China; Tajikistan; and 2016 in Maldives.

Table 3.15: **Price Level Indexes**
(PPPs to official exchange rates, period averages, United States = 100)

Regional Member	2000	2005	2010	2011	2012	2013	2014	2015	2016
Developing Member Economies									
Central and West Asia									
Afghanistan	20.93 (2002)	24.57	34.54	37.13	36.57	34.24	32.21	31.35	29.32
Armenia	26.86	34.46	49.01	50.23	48.17	48.06	47.57	41.44	40.90
Azerbaijan	18.54	22.02	37.39	45.64	46.33	45.86	44.81	30.94	22.47
Georgia	26.75	35.05	44.93	50.92	51.62	50.04	48.06	39.18	38.55
Kazakhstan	15.58	26.45	46.07	54.68	55.32	58.43	51.54	41.96	29.73
Kyrgyz Republic	17.01	22.58	32.19	38.48	40.30	39.71	38.18	32.52	30.33
Pakistan	20.73	21.71	24.38	28.20	27.12	26.24	27.83	28.20	27.45
Tajikistan	13.96	21.04	34.12	37.73	40.31	41.15	41.15	32.68	26.70
Turkmenistan	...	...	...	...	...	...	...	...	...
Uzbekistan	28.13	20.13	33.31	35.19	35.71	36.34	36.13	35.01	32.22
East Asia									
China, People's Rep. of	32.71	34.43	48.86	54.25	55.83	57.23	57.17	55.85	52.29
Hong Kong, China	95.53	73.14	69.06	70.16	71.59	71.73	72.50	74.36	74.60
Korea, Rep. of	66.07	77.03	72.71	77.11	75.89	79.38	82.69	78.74	77.03
Mongolia	12.85	18.55	35.09	42.44	43.82	39.53	34.98	32.47	30.17
Taipei,China	68.97	57.14	49.92	51.29	50.38	50.04	49.02	47.68	46.75
South Asia									
Bangladesh	30.07	26.94	31.45	31.21	30.03	33.20	34.67	36.17	37.85
Bhutan	27.30	30.97	34.64	36.12	33.82	32.13	32.51	31.73	32.07
India	22.56	25.08	31.07	32.37	29.97	28.56	27.76	26.59	25.96
Maldives	52.71 (2001)	49.21	61.45	58.39	57.51	60.00	61.56	65.74	68.72
Nepal	18.42	21.48	30.96	33.27	30.27	29.08	29.78	29.50	29.26
Sri Lanka	19.80	21.68	33.61	34.96	32.97	34.07	34.05	32.65	31.14
Southeast Asia									
Brunei Darussalam	27.69	35.33	44.69	57.03	57.07	54.50	51.89	38.99	34.79
Cambodia	27.66	27.05	31.79	33.19	33.23	33.50	33.38	33.20	34.00
Indonesia	16.95	20.75	37.68	41.12	39.14	36.28	33.14	30.22	30.75
Lao PDR	17.44	18.15	29.24	30.73	34.46	36.79	37.31	37.32	38.04
Malaysia	31.29	33.82	43.86	47.69	46.85	45.28	43.88	36.25	34.33
Myanmar[a]	7.70	20.17	36.20	40.48	37.14	26.18	25.41	22.12	22.48
Philippines	31.03	28.08	38.83	41.22	42.33	42.29	40.98	39.32	37.80
Singapore	58.06	54.14	65.92	70.88	70.30	68.93	66.60	62.27	60.28
Thailand	27.56	28.20	38.41	40.57	39.82	40.35	37.98	35.84	34.93
Viet Nam	20.63	22.54	30.34	32.71	35.09	35.99	36.28	34.92	34.47
The Pacific									
Cook Islands	...	...	...	...	...	...	...	...	...
Fiji	42.02	55.33	53.42	58.13	58.95	57.69	57.34	52.79	53.90
Kiribati	50.08	69.03	88.02	99.19	98.29	91.00	86.80	71.40	70.78
Marshall Islands	...	...	...	...	...	...	...	...	...
Micronesia, Fed. States of	86.48	80.03	86.81	87.93	90.16	89.15	91.34	86.23	85.40
Nauru	...	...	...	...	...	...	...	...	...
Palau	72.08	73.67	73.86	74.92	76.39	82.27	85.04	88.13	88.63
Papua New Guinea	44.23	49.20	66.85	78.41	85.16	79.52	79.06	...	...
Samoa	43.43	54.47	66.67	71.65	73.95	73.43	71.70	66.36	64.68
Solomon Islands	76.93	61.84	72.85	83.43	90.51	89.38	94.41	87.91	90.26
Timor-Leste	38.30	40.15	46.82	51.68	54.02	52.44	51.89	50.72	...
Tonga	52.72	58.77	72.53	79.20	86.03	83.24	78.89	74.08	63.94
Tuvalu	60.07	84.47	102.59	114.49	113.83	106.27	99.29	83.92	87.31
Vanuatu	65.69	81.19	102.68	112.34	106.98	105.90	103.33	93.32	94.57
Developed Member Economies									
Australia	75.83	106.02	137.84	155.87	159.47	139.68	131.53	109.87	108.97
Japan	143.80	117.54	127.18	134.64	130.68	103.80	96.72	84.73	93.79
New Zealand	65.61	108.08	107.77	117.39	121.17	118.58	119.69	100.67	100.94

... = data not available at cutoff date, Lao PDR = Lao People's Democratic Republic, PPP = purchasing power parity.

a The Central Bank of Myanmar devalued the local currency effective 1 April 2012. To achieve a consistent price series, the exchange rate used for estimating the price level index in prior years was extrapolated using the predevaluation exchange rate series.

Sources: Asian Development Bank estimates using economy sources, United States Bureau of Economic Analysis, and World Bank data.

IV. Globalization

Snapshot

- The People's Republic of China and Hong Kong, China were once again the recipients of the largest net foreign direct investment (FDI) inflows in nominal terms in 2016, while Hong Kong, China and Singapore were the largest recipients of FDI as a share of gross domestic product for economies with available data.
- While global trade growth remained sluggish in 2016, the total value of exports from Asia and the Pacific approached that of the world's export leader, Europe.
- Remittance flows to developing economies declined for the second straight year, dipping 2.4% in 2016 after declining 1.0% in 2015; nevertheless, remittances to economies in Asia and the Pacific have increased significantly since 2000 from about $36 billion to more than $253 billion in 2016.
- The People's Republic of China and Hong Kong, China together accounted for nearly 55% of developing member economies' total external debt in 2015.

Key Trends

The People's Republic of China and Hong Kong, China were once again the recipients of the largest net FDI inflows in nominal terms in 2016; Hong Kong, China and Singapore were the largest recipients of FDI as a share of gross domestic product for economies with available data. Based on data compiled by the United Nations Conference on Trade and Development (UNCTAD), global flows of FDI fell about 2% to $1.75 trillion between 2015 and 2016. Furthermore, investment in developing countries declined about 14% to $646 billion. While UNCTAD projects a modest recovery in 2017–2018, FDI flows are expected to remain well below their 2007 peak (UNCTAD 2017).

The impact of declining in FDI in developing economies of the world extends to Asia and the Pacific's developing economies which observed significant decline. In comparison to other developing regions, FDI flows to Latin America and the Caribbean (excluding Caribbean offshore financial centers) declined about 14% to $142 billion in 2016, while inflows to Africa declined about 3% to $59 billion.

By subregion, East Asia experienced declining FDI flows in 2016 following a corporate restructuring in Hong Kong, China in 2015 that resulted in a large, one-off surge in foreign investment. In Southeast Asia, several economies experienced declining inflows in 2016 due to global economic uncertainty. South Asia was the exception within the region because of stable FDI flows to India and increased flows to Pakistan arising from economic reform and improvements in security (ADB 2017).

The PRC ($170.6 billion); Hong Kong, China ($117.1 billion); Singapore ($61.6 billion); and India ($44.0 billion) ranked among the world's top 10 recipients of FDI in 2016 (Figure 4.1). Developed member economies Australia ($42.0 billion) and Japan ($34.9 billion) were the region's next largest recipients of FDI inflows in 2016 (Figure 4.2).

The two Asian economies with the highest levels of FDI as a proportion of gross domestic product (GDP) in 2016 were Hong Kong, China and Singapore, both of which also had high levels of FDI in nominal terms (Table 4.7).

Figure 4.1: Top 10 Economies in Terms of Net Inflows of Foreign Direct Investment, 2016
($ billion)

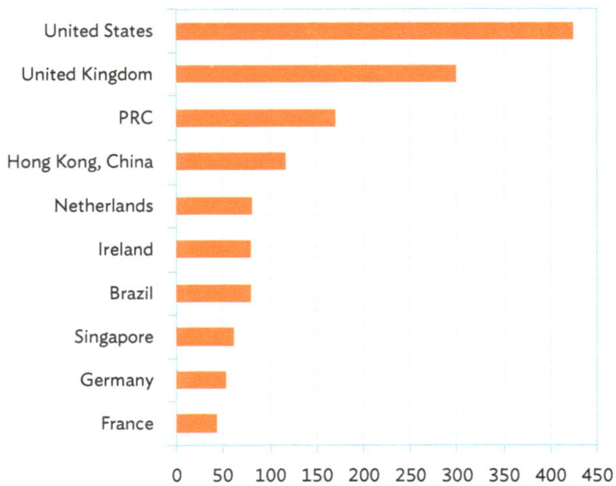

PRC = People's Republic of China.
Source: World Bank. World Development Indicators. 2017. http://data.worldbank.org/indicator/BX.KLT.DINV.CD.WD (accessed 25 July 2017).

Click here for figure data

Figure 4.2: Top 10 Economies in Asia and the Pacific in Terms of Net Inflows of Foreign Direct Investment, Latest Year
($ billion)

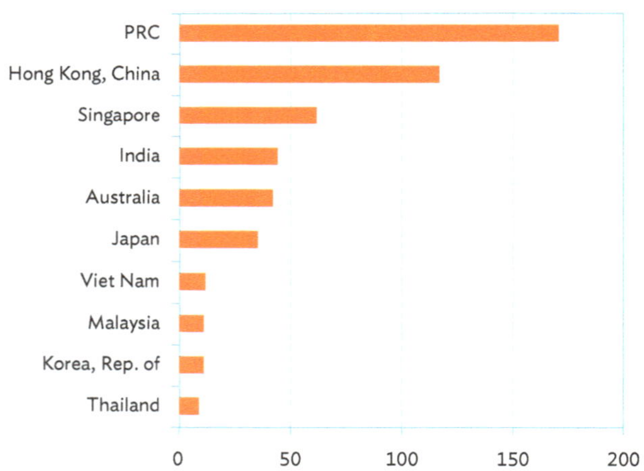

PRC = People's Republic of China
Source: Table 4.6.

Click here for figure data

While global trade growth remained sluggish in 2016, the total value of exports from Asia and the Pacific approached that of the world's export leader, Europe. Global trade growth in 2016 fell to its lowest level since the global financial crisis, with sluggishness in both developed and developing economies resulting from maturing global value chains, the slowing pace of trade liberalization, tepid global growth, depressed commodity prices, macroeconomic rebalancing in the PRC, and policy uncertainty in developed economies (Constantinescu, Mattoo, and Ruta 2017). Amid slowing growth in global trade, Asia and the Pacific (33.5%) was second only to Europe (37.1%) in terms of its share of global exports (Figure 4.3). The gap between the two regions has closed considerably since 2000 when the respective global export shares for Asia and the Pacific and Europe were 29.6% and 40.2%.

Within Asia and the Pacific, the PRC is the largest exporter, accounting for 36.8% of the region's total in 2016, followed by Japan (11.1%); the Republic of Korea (8.6%); Hong Kong, China (8.0%); and Singapore (5.7%) (Figure 4.3).

Of the economies of Asia and the Pacific for which data are available, Asia and the Pacific was the destination for at least 50% of their exports in 30 economies. On the other hand, Europe was the most frequent destination of exports of 10 economies of Asia and the Pacific while North America was the most frequent destination of exports from two regional economies.

The aggregate level of remittances in Asia and the Pacific increased significantly from about $36 billion in 2000 to $264 billion in 2015; but it dropped to nearly $254 billion in 2016. Globally, remittance flows to developing economies declined for the second straight year in 2016, dipping 2.4% after declining 1.0% in 2015. Amid this 2-year decline, remittance flows to developing economies

Figure 4.3: Shares in Total World Exports, Regions of the World; and Major Exporters in the Asia and Pacific Region, 2016
(%)

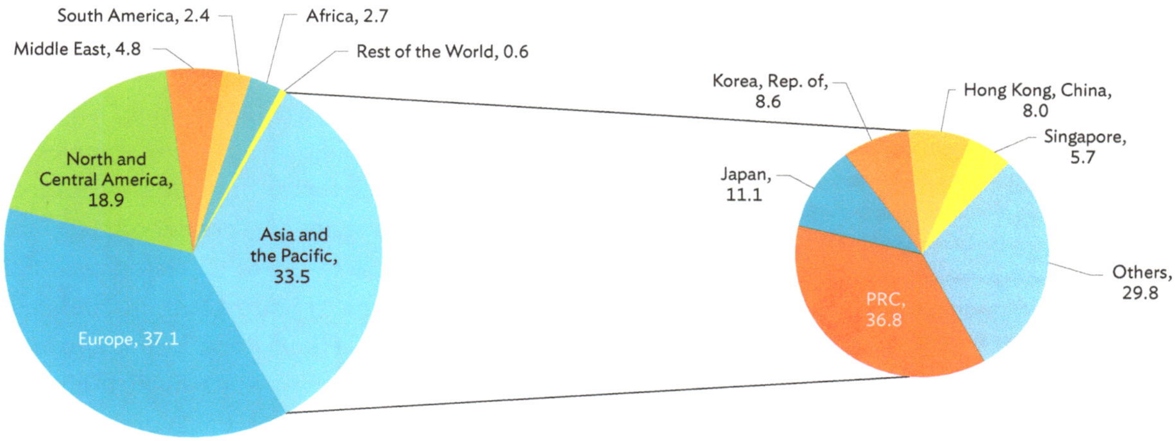

PRC = People's Republic of China.
Sources: International Monetary Fund. May 2017. *Direction of Trade Statistics* (CD-ROM). Washington DC; Table 4.13.

Click here for figure data

remained larger than official development assistance and more stable than private capital flows. Remittance growth to developing economies is expected to rebound to more than 3.0% in 2017 as oil prices stabilize (Global Knowledge Partnership on Migration and Development 2017).

In Asia and the Pacific, the aggregate level of remittances amount was estimated at $36 billion in 2000. This increased to $264 billion in 2015 but dropped to nearly $254 billion in 2016. Based on latest available data, India ($62.7 billion) and the PRC ($61.0 billion) received the most remittances in the region in nominal terms (Figure 4.4). Other regional economies receiving more than $10.0 billion in remittances in 2016 included the Philippines ($29.9 billion), Pakistan ($19.8 billion), Bangladesh ($13.7 billion), and Viet Nam ($13.4 billion).

India, the world's largest recipient of remittances, experienced an 8.9% decline in remittance inflows in 2016, resulting from low oil prices; weak economic growth in Gulf Cooperation Council countries and the Russian Federation; and depreciation of the euro, British pound, and ruble against the United States dollar. Dampened remittance flows were also observed in other developing economies. Despite this trend, remittances to the Philippines were resilient in 2016, with a recorded growth of 4.9% (ADB 2017).

Between 2000 (or the earliest year in which data are available) and 2016, the highest annual average rates of growth in remittances were observed in the Kyrgyz Republic, the Lao People's Democratic Republic, and the PRC (Table 4.4).[3] The only annual average declines during the review period were observed in Turkmenistan (–3.7%), Vanuatu (–1.9%), and Tuvalu (–1.7%).

As a share of GDP, the regional economies in which remittances accounted for more than one-quarter of GDP were the Kyrgyz Republic (30.5%), Nepal (30.0%), Tonga (29.8%), and Tajikistan (25.6%) (Table 4.5). The regional average in 2016 among developing members for which data are available was 1.3% of GDP.

3 Remittance growth in the Lao PDR came from a very low base of only $830,000 in 2005.

Figure 4.4: Worker's Remittances and Compensation of Employees Receipts
($ million)

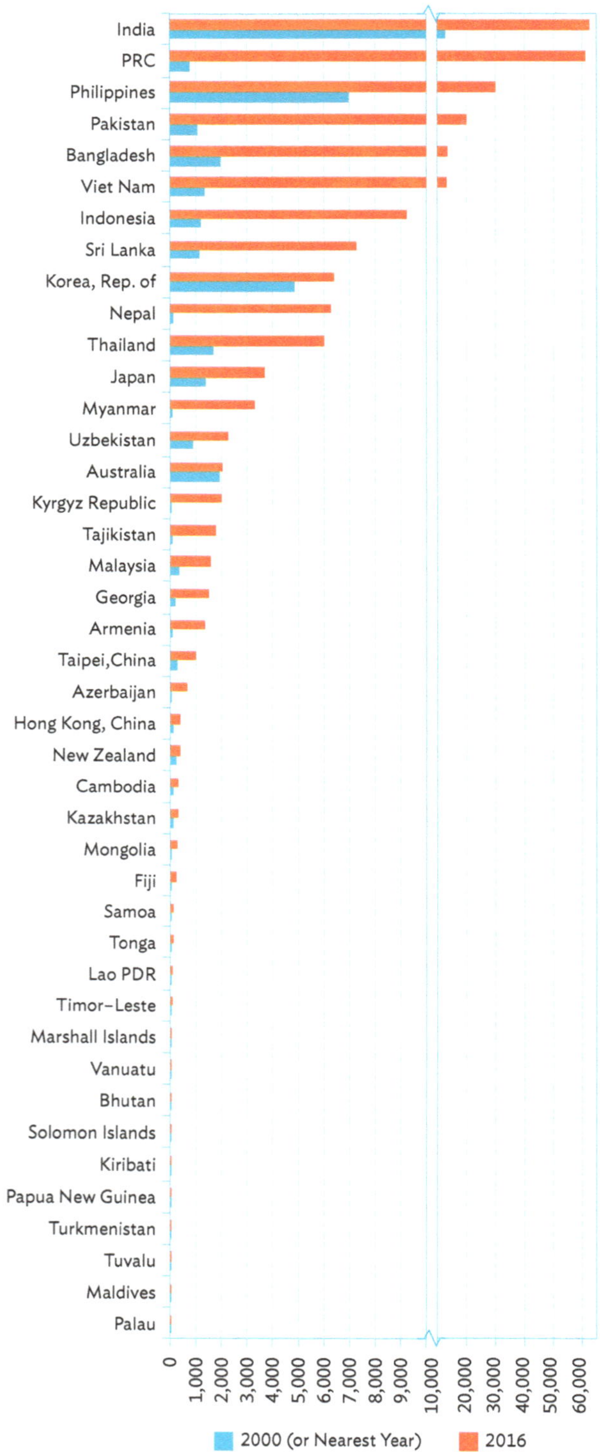

FSM = Federated States of Micronesia, Lao PDR = Lao People's Democratic Republic, PRC = People's Republic of China.
Note: Data for 2000 include economies with data from 2000 to 2006.
Source: Table 4.4.

Click here for figure data

The PRC and Hong Kong, China together accounted for nearly 55% of developing member economies' total external debt in 2015. The total external debt of the PRC and Hong Kong, China, respectively, comprised 28.3% and 26.5% of the total among developing member economies in 2015 (Table 4.19). External debt in Hong Kong, China, measured as a share of gross national income (GNI), reached 401.2% in 2016, the latest year for which data are available (Figure 4.5a). PRC-related lending drives much of Hong Kong, China's external debt, including lending to state-owned enterprises in the PRC (Development Bank of Singapore 2016). Mongolia had the region's second highest debt level in 2015 at 201.7% of GNI, followed by Papua New Guinea at 123.6%. The (arithmetic) average among developing member economies in 2015 (or the latest year for which data are available) was 58.1%.

The Lao People's Democratic Republic had the highest total external debt-to-GNI at 152.4% in 2000. The next highest ratios in 2000 were observed in the Kyrgyz Republic (150.5%) and Tajikistan (138.4%). The regional average among developing member economies was 57.1% in 2000. Among the region's top 10 economies with the highest external debt-to-GNI ratio in 2015, only the Lao People's Democratic Republic experienced a decline during the preceding decade.

Figure 4.5b shows the top 20 global rankings in terms of total external debt to GNI in 2000 and 2015. Hong Kong, China and Mongolia are in the top two spots in 2015, while Serbia and the Lao People's Democratic Republic were first and second, respectively, in 2000.

Figure 4.5a: Total External Debt of Developing Member Economies (% of GNI)

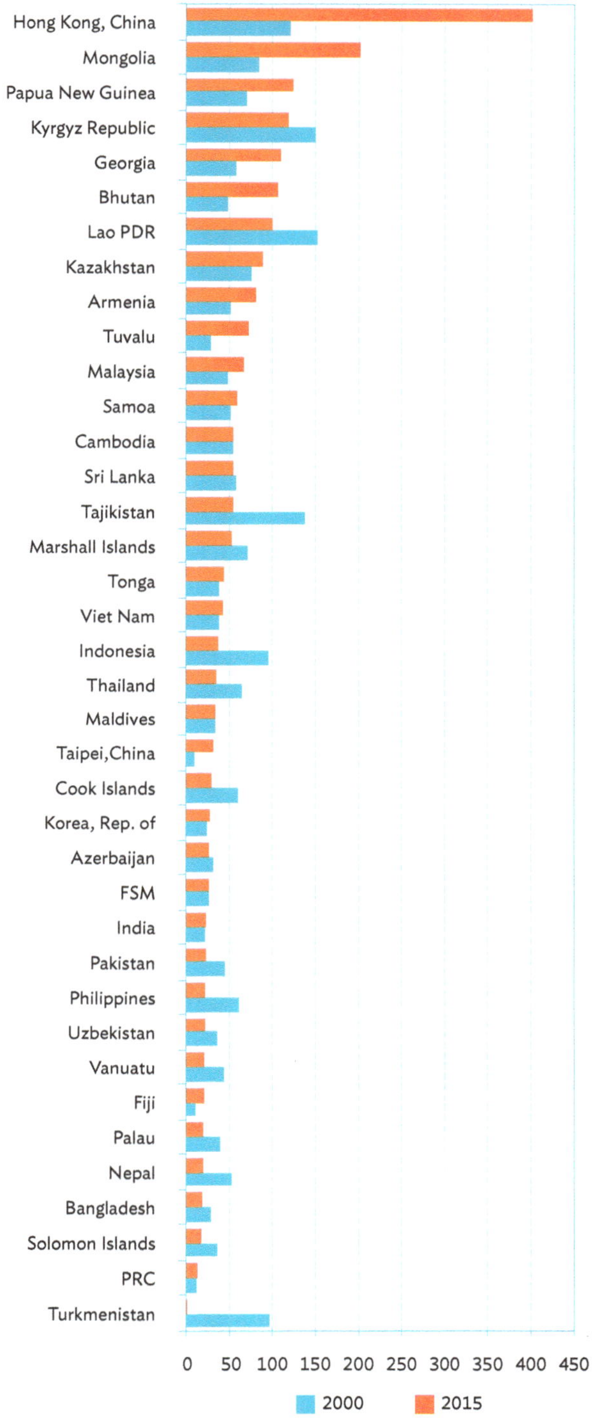

FSM = Federated States of Micronesia, Lao PDR = Lao People's Democratic Republic, PRC = People's Republic of China.
Notes: For Cook Islands; Hong Kong, China; Republic of Korea; Taipei,China; data refer to 2016. For Papua New Guinea, Tonga, and Vanuatu, data refer to 2014.
Source: Table 4.20.

Click here for figure data

Figure 4.5b: Total External Debt of Developing Economies—Top 20 Global Ranking (% of GNI)

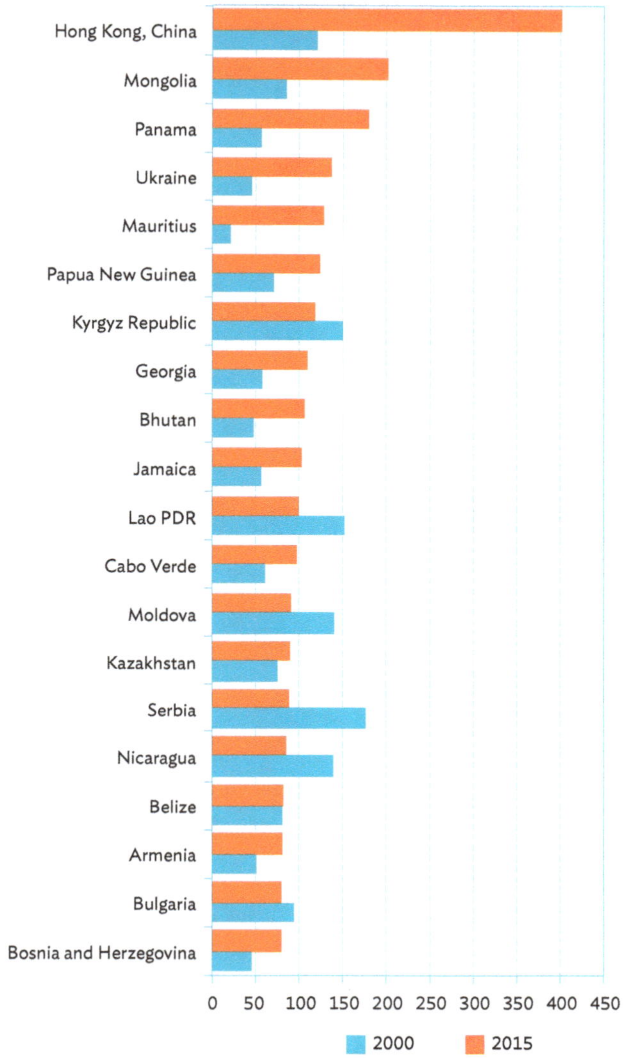

Lao PDR = Lao People's Democratic Republic.
Notes: For Hong Kong, China, data refer to 2016. For Papua New Guinea, data refer to 2014.
Sources: World Bank. World Development Indicators and International Debt Statistics. http://data.worldbank.org/data-catalog/world-development-indicators (accessed 7 July 2017); ADB estimates using economy sources.

Click here for figure data

Data Issues and Comparability

Most of the international transactions in this section are taken from balance of payments statistics. Economies follow IMF guidelines when compiling these statistics and meet regularly to discuss methodology, but many economies have difficulty accurately recording nonofficial transactions such as migrant workers' remittances and private capital flows, which is one of the reasons that the *Balance of Payments Manual* was updated to the 6th edition, the *Balance of Payments and International Investment Position Manual* (BPM6). Analysis for this section was based on balance of payments data as reported by the economies. A majority of countries use BPM5, some have shifted to BPM6, and a few continue to use BPM4. This affects the comparability of data across economies.

International trade statistics are closely monitored by the World Trade Organization and other international agencies. Common definitions are used by all countries, and the larger Asian economies use standard forms and procedures for data processing.

International tourist arrivals and receipts data come from the World Tourism Organization, which serves as a global forum for tourism policy issues and a practical source of information on this topic.

Table 4.1: **Trade in Goods Balance**
(% of GDP)

Regional Member	2000	2005	2010	2011	2012	2013	2014	2015	2016
Developing Member Economies									
Central and West Asia									
Afghanistan[a]	-28.4	-65.5	-26.7	-27.7	-25.9	-35.0	-27.4	-31.3	-27.4
Armenia	-24.4	-13.0	-22.3	-20.8	-19.9	-18.8	-17.7	-11.2	-8.9
Azerbaijan	6.1	24.9	37.3	36.9	31.8	28.8	25.2	11.0	11.1
Georgia	-17.5	-19.0	-22.6	-24.2	-26.7	-21.7	-26.0	-28.3	-26.6
Kazakhstan	12.2	18.1	19.3	23.3	18.3	14.7	16.4	6.9	7.0
Kyrgyz Republic	0.3	-17.0	-25.2	-26.2	-39.8	-38.6	-38.1	-34.3	-31.6
Pakistan	-2.0	-4.1	-6.6	-4.9	-7.3	-7.0	-6.7	-6.4	-6.7
Tajikistan	-9.5	-14.0	-36.0	-43.7	-45.3	-45.9	-32.5	-29.1	-27.5
Turkmenistan	...	14.1	10.1	21.5	18.6	10.3	9.5	-5.3	-15.6
Uzbekistan	3.6	10.0	7.6	7.3	3.0	4.1	4.4	...	...
East Asia									
China, People's Rep. of	2.5	5.4	3.9	3.0	3.6	3.7	4.2	5.2	4.4
Hong Kong, China	11.9	17.1	1.4	-3.0	-7.2	-10.1	-11.1	-7.4	-5.5
Korea, Rep. of	2.8	3.6	4.4	2.4	4.0	6.3	6.3	8.8	8.5
Mongolia	-6.4	-3.9	-2.4	-25.6	-24.6	-20.7	1.5	4.8	12.0
Taipei,China	5.8	6.5	8.3	8.2	10.0	10.7	11.5	13.9	13.1
South Asia									
Bangladesh	-4.0	-5.5	-4.5	-7.7	-7.0	-4.7	-3.9	-3.6	-2.8
Bhutan	-15.6	-30.7	-17.3	-24.5	-20.4	-19.7	-20.2	-20.2	-23.9
India	-2.7	-6.2	-7.4	-10.4	-10.7	-7.9	-7.1	-6.3	-5.0
Maldives	-37.4	-44.1	-45.6	-55.8	-50.3	-49.3	-53.8	-48.3	-48.8
Nepal	-14.4	-14.6	-25.5	-23.4	-24.4	-27.2	-30.4	-31.3	-30.2
Sri Lanka	-10.8	-10.3	-8.5	-14.9	-13.8	-10.2	-10.4	-10.4	-11.2
Southeast Asia									
Brunei Darussalam[b]	45.4	43.5	45.3	46.6	46.0	38.2	43.4	22.4	...
Cambodia	-14.7	-16.1	-16.5	-16.7	-17.9	-21.1	-19.1	-19.2	-17.1
Indonesia	15.2	6.0	4.1	3.8	0.9	0.6	0.8	1.6	1.7
Lao PDR	-12.5	-12.1	-4.7	-2.7	-7.7	-6.8	-12.1	-17.1	-8.7
Malaysia	22.2	23.9	15.1	15.4	11.6	9.5	10.2	9.4	8.2
Myanmar	-0.1	0.1	0.1	0.0	1.0	0.2	-2.8	-6.1	-5.3
Philippines	-7.4	-11.8	-8.4	-9.1	-7.6	-6.5	-6.1	-8.0	-11.2
Singapore	16.9	37.4	26.2	26.6	24.6	24.8	26.5	27.9	27.9
Thailand	4.3	1.8	7.8	3.3	0.0	0.0	4.2	6.7	8.8
Viet Nam	1.2	-4.2	-4.4	-0.3	5.6	5.1	6.5	3.8	6.8
The Pacific									
Cook Islands	-45.5	-41.6	-33.5	-37.2	-35.2	-35.0	-32.7	-33.5	-32.2
Fiji	-14.0	-26.0	-23.5	-22.6	-19.4	-27.8	-22.7	...	...
Kiribati	-52.2	-66.3	-41.7	-43.6	-50.4	-40.4	-50.5	-53.7	...
Marshall Islands	-54.7	-40.4	-55.5	-30.9	-26.9	-36.2	-37.5	-34.4	...
Micronesia, Fed. States of	-38.1	-42.7	-43.2	-43.1	-38.4	-40.7	-36.9	-40.6	...
Nauru	...	...	...	...	...	...	...	...	...
Palau	-79.5	-51.3	-50.3	-56.7	-58.3	-58.5	-64.9	-47.7	-45.6
Papua New Guinea	31.4	36.8	15.6	15.0	7.4	2.5	20.8	...	...
Samoa	-120.7	-31.5	-31.2	-29.3	-34.6	-37.5	-38.1	-34.1	-33.6
Solomon Islands	-8.1	-5.6	-23.4	-0.8	5.6	-2.5	...	...	...
Timor-Leste[c]	...	-3.7	-7.0	-6.6	-9.6	-11.0	-14.9	-20.5	...
Tonga	-27.4	-34.1	-27.6	-28.2	-29.9	-32.6	-31.1	-38.0	-34.5
Tuvalu[c]	-64.9	-40.5	-53.9	-19.7	-4.1	-34.7	-24.2	-29.2	...
Vanuatu	-18.2	-23.3	-27.1	-23.1	-25.4	-27.9	-24.2	...	...
Developed Member Economies									
Australia	-1.9	-2.6	-0.7	1.6	0.6	-0.2	0.6	-0.8	-1.6
Japan	2.4	2.2	1.9	-0.1	-0.9	-1.7	-2.0	-0.2	1.0
New Zealand	0.7	-2.1	1.1	0.7	0.2	0.9	-0.2	-0.7	...

... = data not available at cutoff date, 0.0 = magnitude is less than half of unit employed, GDP = gross domestic product, Lao PDR = Lao People's Democratic Republic.

a Data for 2000 refer to 2002.
b Data for 2000 refer to 2001.
c Data for 2005 refer to 2006.

Source: Economy sources.

Table 4.2: **Trade in Services Balance**
(% of GDP)

Regional Member	2000	2005	2010	2011	2012	2013	2014	2015	2016
Developing Member Economies									
Central and West Asia									
Afghanistan	...	-8.2|	4.4	3.9	-2.6	-6.0	-2.7	-3.6	-3.9
Armenia	-3.4	-3.0	-2.8	-0.6	-1.0	-1.1	-0.8	-0.9	-1.2
Azerbaijan	-4.3	-14.9	-3.3	-4.5	-4.2	-5.6	-8.1	-8.0	-8.3
Georgia	2.4	1.6	4.7	5.2	7.0	8.8	7.9	10.5	11.3
Kazakhstan	-5.3	-9.5	-4.9	-3.4	-3.8	-3.0	-2.8	-2.8	-3.5
Kyrgyz Republic	-12.2	-4.9	-4.2|	-1.7	-5.1	-0.7	-4.4	-2.8	-2.9
Pakistan	-3.5|	-2.8	-1.0	-1.0	-1.5	-0.7	-1.1	-1.1	-1.1
Tajikistan	-1.7	-4.5	-2.0	-3.0	-2.9	-3.3	-3.3	-3.1	-2.0
Turkmenistan	...	...	...	...	...	...	...	...	...
Uzbekistan[a,c]	-0.5	-1.1	-1.4	-1.6	-0.1	-0.4	-0.1	...	...
East Asia									
China, People's Rep. of	-0.1	0.0	-0.2	-0.6	-0.9	-1.3	-2.0	-2.0	-2.2
Hong Kong, China	-7.5	-4.9	4.4	6.9	8.3	10.7	11.3	9.8	7.5
Korea, Rep. of	-0.2	-1.0	-1.3	-1.0	-0.4	-0.5	-0.3	-1.1	-1.2
Mongolia	-7.5	0.5	-4.2|	-8.1	-11.6	-10.4	-10.5	-6.1	-12.0
Taipei,China	-3.8	-3.8	-2.5	-2.3	-3.5	-2.7	-1.9	-1.9	-2.1
South Asia									
Bangladesh	-1.4	-1.5	-1.1	-2.1	-2.3	-2.1	-2.4	-1.6	-1.3
Bhutan	-1.8	-4.8|	-4.5	-5.2	-4.7	-3.0	-3.3	-3.4	-2.3
India	0.3	2.8|	2.6	3.4	3.5	3.8	3.8	3.3	3.0
Maldives	33.4	7.0|	...	61.9	63.6	67.3	71.3	59.1	53.2
Nepal[b]	7.2	-0.4	-1.3	-0.6	1.0	0.5	1.1	1.3	0.4
Sri Lanka	0.2	1.4	1.2	1.7|	1.8	1.6	2.4	2.9	3.5
Southeast Asia									
Brunei Darussalam[d]	11.0	0.6|	-5.9	-7.1	-11.3	-13.1	-9.5	-7.8	...
Cambodia	-0.6	2.9|	9.3	10.9	11.8	11.3	11.5	11.3	10.4
Indonesia	-11.1|	-3.1	-1.3	-1.1	-1.2	-1.3	-1.1	-1.0	-0.7
Lao PDR	5.1	2.5	2.4	1.9	1.2	1.2	1.1	0.1	-0.3
Malaysia	-11.1|	-2.0	0.8	0.2	-0.9	-0.9	-1.0	-1.8	-1.6
Myanmar	0.0	-0.1	0.0	0.0	-0.4	0.4|	1.3	2.3	1.2
Philippines	-2.3	2.1|	2.9	2.9	2.5	2.6	1.6	1.9	2.3
Singapore	-4.6	-7.6	-0.2	0.4	-1.2	-2.4	-2.0	-2.0	-2.0
Thailand	3.7	-3.6	-2.1	-1.2	1.0	2.7	2.5	4.8	5.9
Viet Nam	-1.8	-0.5	-2.1	-2.3	-0.9	-1.8|	-1.9	-2.7	-2.6
The Pacific									
Cook Islands	...	...	...	...	...	...	...	...	...
Fiji	7.1	11.0|	17.1	16.7	16.3	15.0	14.9	...	...
Kiribati	-27.4	-30.3|	-25.3	-27.6	-28.1	-27.9	-41.6	-41.5	...
Marshall Islands[b]	-24.5	-24.1	-22.7	-23.3	-23.6	-26.2	-23.0	-21.6	...
Micronesia, Fed. States of	-15.3	-15.4	-14.0	-14.3	-13.2	-11.8	-10.1	-8.3	...
Nauru	...	...	...	...	-11.6	-7.4	-23.5	-13.4	-15.1
Palau	4.6	19.9	25.3	32.1	35.0	36.4	39.5	37.7	33.5
Papua New Guinea[b]	-21.2	-17.8	-17.2	-14.2	-15.3	-16.4	-9.0	...	...
Samoa	44.1	10.9	9.4	8.7	13.8	14.6	14.9	13.9	15.9
Solomon Islands	-8.2	1.5|	-13.8	-8.4	-9.2	-12.1	-10.7	-7.4	-8.6
Timor-Leste	...	...	-24.0	-24.9	-13.8	-7.6	-14.7	-18.7	...
Tonga	0.8	-6.1	-0.4	1.3	0.2|	0.8	-0.4	-0.9	1.9
Tuvalu[e]	-51.2	5.6	-3.8|	-80.5	-61.6	-63.1	-51.5	-60.1	...
Vanuatu	17.1	14.9	17.6|	16.4	19.9	24.8	19.3	...	...
Developed Member Economies									
Australia	-0.1	-0.1	-0.3	-0.5	-0.7	-1.0	-0.9	-0.6	-0.6
Japan	-1.0	-0.8	-0.5	-0.6	-0.8	-0.7	-0.6	-0.4	-0.2
New Zealand	1.4	1.5	0.9	0.6	0.5	0.4	0.9	1.7	...

... = data not available at cutoff date; | = marks break in series due to change in compilation methodology from *Balance of Payments Manual* (BPM), 5th edition to *Balance of Payments and International Investment Position Manual*, 6th edition; 0.0 = magnitude is less than half of unit employed; GDP = gross domestic product; Lao PDR = Lao People's Democratic Republic.

a For Uzbekistan, refers to BPM4 methodology.
b Refers to economies using BPM5 methodology.
c Includes other goods and income starting 2005.
d Data for 2000 refer to 2001.
e Data for 2005 refer to 2006.

Sources: Economy sources.

Table 4.3: **Current Account Balance**
(% of GDP)

Regional Member	2000	2005	2010	2011	2012	2013	2014	2015	2016
Developing Member Economies									
Central and West Asia									
Afghanistan	-3.5 (2002)	-2.7	-10.4	-14.5	-20.3	-26.1	-18.5	-22.9	-18.7
Armenia	-15.8	-2.5	-13.6	-10.4	-10.0	-7.6	-7.3	-2.6	-2.7
Azerbaijan	-3.2	1.3	28.4	26.0	21.4	17.6	13.9	-0.4	-3.6
Georgia	-5.8	-10.8	-10.3	-12.8	-11.7	-5.8	-10.7	-12.0	-13.3
Kazakhstan	2.0	-1.8	0.9	5.3	0.5	0.5	2.8	-2.8	-6.3
Kyrgyz Republic	-5.5	-1.4	-6.6	-8.1	-15.8	-14.1	-17.2	-16.2	-9.6
Pakistan	-0.3	-1.4	-2.3	0.1	-2.2	-1.1	-1.3	-1.0	-1.2
Tajikistan	-7.2	-0.8	-3.9	-7.1	-9.0	-7.7	-2.8	-6.4	-3.8
Turkmenistan	...	5.1	-10.6	2.0	0.0	-7.2	-6.7	-14.0	-21.0
Uzbekistan	1.6	13.5	6.1	5.7	2.7	3.4	4.1	...	...
East Asia									
China, People's Rep. of	1.7	5.8	3.9	1.8	2.5	1.5	2.3	2.7	1.8
Hong Kong, China	4.4	11.9	7.0	5.6	1.6	1.5	1.4	3.3	4.5
Korea, Rep. of	1.9	1.4	2.6	1.6	4.2	6.2	6.0	7.7	7.0
Mongolia	-6.1	3.5	-12.3	-43.3	-43.8	-37.6	-15.8	-8.1	-6.3
Taipei,China	2.5	4.0	8.3	7.8	8.9	10.1	11.8	14.3	13.4
South Asia									
Bangladesh	-0.9	-1.0	3.7	-1.3	-0.3	1.6	0.8	1.8	2.0
Bhutan	-9.4	-29.0	-20.5	-27.6	-20.0	-24.4	-24.8	-27.0	-27.7
India	-0.6	-1.2	-2.8	-4.2	-4.8	-1.7	-1.3	-1.1	-0.7
Maldives	-8.2	-24.4	-15.3	-15.6	-7.4	-4.6	-3.9	-8.8	-22.3
Nepal	-2.2	2.0	-2.3	-0.9	4.8	3.3	4.5	5.0	6.3
Sri Lanka	-6.4	-2.7	-1.9	-7.1	-5.8	-3.4	-2.5	-2.3	-2.4
Southeast Asia									
Brunei Darussalam	51.5 (2001)	47.3	36.5	34.8	29.8	20.9	30.6	15.9	...
Cambodia	-2.7	-3.6	-6.0	-6.0	-8.2	-13.0	-9.8	-9.3	-8.3
Indonesia	4.8	0.1	0.7	0.2	-2.7	-3.2	-3.1	-2.0	-1.8
Lao PDR	-0.3	-7.1	0.4	2.0	-4.0	-3.7	-8.9	-15.7	-7.8
Malaysia	9.0	14.4	10.1	10.9	5.2	3.5	4.4	3.0	2.4
Myanmar	-0.1	0.0	0.0	0.0	-1.5	-0.8	-2.8	-4.0	-2.8
Philippines	-2.7	1.9	3.6	2.5	2.8	4.2	3.8	2.5	0.2
Singapore	10.8	22.1	23.4	22.1	17.4	16.9	19.7	18.1	19.0
Thailand	7.4	-4.0	3.4	2.5	-0.4	-1.2	3.7	8.1	11.5
Viet Nam	4.2	-1.0	-3.7	0.2	5.9	4.5	4.9	-0.2	4.0
The Pacific									
Cook Islands	...	...	...	...	...	...	...	...	...
Fiji	-1.6	-11.3	-4.7	-5.1	-1.3	-9.8	-7.5	...	...
Kiribati	-3.2	-34.1	-2.2	-13.4	1.3	27.3	40.7	45.6	...
Marshall Islands	-15.1	5.8	-21.3	1.2	-3.2	-12.0	-3.4	14.8	...
Micronesia, Fed. States of	-13.4	-9.0	-15.4	-18.8	-13.4	-10.1	1.2	8.6	...
Nauru	...	...	...	...	38.1	18.8	-13.5	-9.5	1.7
Palau	-60.1	-21.2	-9.0	-11.8	-11.2	-11.6	-15.0	-7.7	-10.3
Papua New Guinea	10.1	13.3	-4.4	-1.0	-10.8	-16.3	10.5	...	...
Samoa	-3.3	-8.5	-5.4	-5.5	0.1	-5.6	-5.7	-3.7	-4.0
Solomon Islands	-12.9	-1.9	-20.8	-2.4	2.9	-3.8	-4.7	-3.4	-5.0
Timor-Leste[a]	...	19.3 (2006)	42.0	41.4	41.0	43.6	27.0	6.4	...
Tonga	-5.2	-9.4	-7.4	-9.3	-6.9	-8.7	-5.0	-9.0	-0.2
Tuvalu	54.5	-1.6 (2006)	-3.8	-37.0	18.1	1.3	19.3	7.0	...
Vanuatu	-5.0	-3.5	-5.8	-7.4	-8.8	-0.5	-0.3	...	...
Developed Member Economies									
Australia	-4.9	-6.5	-5.0	-3.1	-3.3	-3.7	-3.0	-3.6	-4.4
Japan	2.7	3.6	3.9	2.1	1.0	0.9	0.8	3.1	3.8
New Zealand	-1.0	-5.4	-2.0	-2.5	-3.0	-2.1	-2.8	-2.1	...

... = data not available at cutoff date, 0.0 = magnitude is less than half of unit employed, GDP = gross domestic product, Lao PDR = Lao People's Democratic Republic.

a GDP estimates refer to non-oil GDP. Before 2002, estimates include the value added of United Nations activities.

Source: Economy sources.

Table 4.4: **Workers' Remittances and Compensation of Employees, Receipts**
($ million)

Regional Member	2000	2005	2010	2011	2012	2013	2014	2015	2016
Developing Member Economies									
Central and West Asia									
Afghanistan	...	106 (2008)	342	185	252	314	268	301	312
Armenia	87	915	1,669	1,799	1,915	2,192	2,079	1,491	1,339
Azerbaijan	57	623	1,410	1,893	1,990	1,733	1,846	1,270	643
Georgia	210	446	1,184	1,547	1,770	1,945	1,986	1,459	1,491
Kazakhstan	122	62	226	180	178	207	229	194	308
Kyrgyz Republic	9	313	1,266	1,709	2,031	2,278	2,243	1,688	1,997
Pakistan	1,080	4,280	9,690	12,263	14,007	14,629	17,244	19,306	19,847
Tajikistan	79 (2002)	467	2,306	3,060	3,626	4,219	3,384	2,259	1,778
Turkmenistan	...	14 (2006)	35	35	37	40	30	16	9
Uzbekistan	...	898 (2006)	2,858	4,276	5,693	6,689	5,828	3,053	2,263
East Asia									
China, People's Rep. of	758	23,626	52,460	61,576	57,987	59,491	62,332	63,938	61,000
Hong Kong, China	136	297	340	352	367	360	372	387	401
Korea, Rep. of	4,862	5,178	5,836	6,582	6,571	6,455	6,551	6,454	6,395
Mongolia	12	180	266	279	320	256	255	261	263
Taipei,China	274	323	500	613	688	792	860	915	997
South Asia									
Bangladesh	1,969	4,642	10,850	12,071	14,120	13,867	14,988	15,388	13,680
Bhutan	...	2 (2006)	8	10	18	12	14	20	21
India	12,845	22,125	53,480	62,499	68,821	69,970	70,389	68,910	62,745
Maldives	2	2	3	3	3	3	3	4	4
Nepal	112	1,212	3,464	4,217	4,793	5,589	5,889	6,730	6,276
Sri Lanka	1,163	1,976	4,123	5,153	6,000	6,422	7,036	6,980	7,252
Southeast Asia									
Brunei Darussalam	...	...	...	...	...	...	...	...	...
Cambodia	121	164	153	160	172	176	377	395	323
Indonesia	1,190	5,420	6,916	6,924	7,212	7,614	8,551	9,659	9,234
Lao PDR	1	1	42	110	59	60	40	93	95
Malaysia	342	1,117	1,103	1,211	1,294	1,423	1,580	1,643	1,586
Myanmar	102	129	115	127	275	1,644	3,103	3,236	3,312
Philippines	6,957	13,733	20,563	21,922	23,352	25,369	27,273	28,483	29,878
Singapore	...	...	...	...	...	...	...	...	...
Thailand	1,700	1,187	3,580	4,554	4,713	5,690	5,655	5,895	6,025
Viet Nam	1,340	3,150	8,260	8,600	10,000	11,000	12,000	13,000	13,383
The Pacific									
Cook Islands	...	...	...	...	...	...	...	...	...
Fiji	44	204	174	160	191	204	206	251	255
Kiribati	...	12 (2006)	15	16	17	17	16	16	16
Marshall Islands	...	24	22	22	23	25	26	26	27
Micronesia, Fed. States of	...	...	18	19	21	22	23	23	24
Nauru	...	...	...	...	...	...	...	...	...
Palau	...	1	2	2	2	2	2	2	2
Papua New Guinea	7	7	3	17	14	14	10	10	11
Samoa	45 (1999)	82	139	160	178	165	141	131	132
Solomon Islands	4	7	14	17	21	21	16	19	20
Timor-Leste	...	4 (2006)	137	137	120	34	44	62	65
Tonga	53 (2001)	69	77	79	118	121	118	118	119
Tuvalu	...	5	4	5	4	4	4	4	4
Vanuatu	35	5	12	22	22	24	28	24	24
Developed Member Economies									
Australia	1,904	940	1,864	2,449	2,441	2,460	2,328	2,113	2,043
Japan	1,374	905	1,684	2,132	2,540	2,364	3,734	3,670	3,659
New Zealand	236	352	371	455	462	459	462	421	396
DEVELOPING MEMBER ECONOMIES[a]	**35,541**	**91,971**	**193,665**	**224,567**	**238,993**	**251,091**	**263,039**	**264,112**	**253,559**
REGIONAL MEMBERS[a]	**39,055**	**94,169**	**197,584**	**229,603**	**244,435**	**256,375**	**269,563**	**270,316**	**259,657**
WORLD	**126,750**	**282,536**	**462,146**	**524,414**	**544,903**	**574,016**	**596,588**	**582,449**	**575,191**

... = data not available at cutoff date, Lao PDR = Lao People's Democratic Republic.

a For reporting economies only.

Sources: World Bank. http://www.worldbank.org/en/topic/migrationremittancesdiasporaissues (accessed 14 June 2017); for Taipei,China: economy sources.

Table 4.5: **Workers' Remittances and Compensation of Employees, Receipts**
(% of GDP)

Regional Member	2000	2005	2010	2011	2012	2013	2014	2015	2016
Developing Member Economies									
Central and West Asia									
Afghanistan	...	1.0 (2008)	2.1	1.0	1.2	1.5	1.3	1.5	1.5
Armenia	4.6	18.7	18.0	17.7	18.0	19.7	17.9	14.1	12.7
Azerbaijan	1.1	4.7	2.7	2.9	2.9	2.3	2.5	2.4	1.7
Georgia	6.9	7.0	10.2	10.7	11.2	12.1	12.0	10.4	10.4
Kazakhstan	0.7	0.1	0.2	0.1	0.1	0.1	0.1	0.1	0.2
Kyrgyz Republic	0.6	12.7	26.4	27.6	30.8	31.1	30.0	25.3	30.5
Pakistan	1.4	3.6	5.6	5.8	6.5	6.6	6.9	7.2	7.1
Tajikistan	6.4 (2002)	20.2	40.9	46.9	47.5	49.6	36.6	28.8	25.6
Turkmenistan	...	0.1 (2006)	0.2	0.1	0.1	0.1	0.1	0.0	0.0
Uzbekistan	...	5.2 (2006)	7.2	9.3	11.0	11.6	9.3	4.6	3.4
East Asia									
China, People's Rep. of	0.1	1.0	0.9	0.8	0.7	0.6	0.6	0.6	0.5
Hong Kong, China	0.1	0.2	0.1	0.1	0.1	0.1	0.1	0.1	0.1
Korea, Rep. of	0.9	0.6	0.5	0.5	0.5	0.5	0.5	0.5	0.5
Mongolia	1.1	7.1	3.7	2.7	2.6	2.0	2.1	2.2	2.4
Taipei,China	0.1	0.1	0.1	0.1	0.1	0.2	0.2	0.2	0.2
South Asia									
Bangladesh	4.3	8.1	9.5	9.8	11.0	9.0	8.7	7.9	6.2
Bhutan	...	0.3 (2006)	0.5	0.6	1.0	0.7	0.7	1.0	0.9
India	2.7	2.6	3.1	3.3	3.7	3.6	3.5	3.2	2.8
Maldives	0.4	0.2	0.1	0.1	0.1	0.1	0.1	0.1	0.1
Nepal	2.1	14.7	21.3	22.8	26.7	30.7	29.2	32.4	30.0
Sri Lanka	7.0	8.1	7.3	7.9	8.8	8.6	8.9	8.7	8.9
Southeast Asia									
Brunei Darussalam	...	...	...	...	...	...	...	...	...
Cambodia	3.3	2.6	1.4	1.3	1.2	1.2	2.2	2.2	1.6
Indonesia	0.7	1.9	0.9	0.8	0.8	0.8	1.0	1.1	1.0
Lao PDR	0.0	0.0	0.6	1.4	0.6	0.5	0.3	0.6	0.6
Malaysia	0.4	0.8	0.4	0.4	0.4	0.4	0.5	0.6	0.5
Myanmar	0.0	0.0	0.0	0.0	0.3	2.6	4.7	5.2	5.1
Philippines	8.6	13.3	10.3	9.8	9.3	9.3	9.6	9.7	9.8
Singapore	...	...	...	...	...	...	...	...	...
Thailand	1.3	0.6	1.0	1.2	1.2	1.4	1.4	1.5	1.5
Viet Nam	4.3	5.5	7.1	6.3	6.4	6.4	6.4	6.7	6.5
The Pacific									
Cook Islands	...	...	...	...	...	...	...	...	...
Fiji	2.6	6.8	5.5	4.2	4.8	4.9	4.6	5.7	...
Kiribati	...	11.1 (2006)	9.7	9.2	9.1	9.4	9.0	9.6	...
Marshall Islands	...	17.2	13.5	12.8	12.6	12.9	14.2	14.5	...
Micronesia, Fed. States of	...	...	6.1	6.2	6.4	7.0	7.3	7.4	7.4
Nauru	...	...	...	...	...	...	...	...	...
Palau	...	0.8	0.9	1.0	1.1	1.0	0.9	0.8	0.7
Papua New Guinea	0.2	0.1	0.0	0.1	0.1	0.1	0.0	...	...
Samoa	19.5 (1999)	18.8	20.4	20.3	22.2	20.5	17.0	16.9	16.0
Solomon Islands	1.5	2.3	2.4	2.3	2.5	2.2	1.7	1.8	...
Timor-Leste	...	0.1 (2006)	3.4	2.4	1.8	0.6	1.1	2.0	...
Tonga	31.5 (2001)	26.0	21.0	18.6	25.0	26.9	26.6	27.0	29.8
Tuvalu	...	22.7	12.4	11.8	10.2	10.8	10.9	11.4	...
Vanuatu	12.7	1.3	1.7	2.7	2.8	3.0	3.5	...	...
Developed Member Economies									
Australia	0.5	0.1	0.2	0.2	0.2	0.2	0.2	0.2	0.2
Japan	0.0	0.0	0.0	0.0	0.0	0.0	0.1	0.1	0.1
New Zealand	0.4	0.3	0.3	0.3	0.3	0.2	0.2	0.2	...
DEVELOPING MEMBER ECONOMIES[a]	**0.9**	**1.2**	**1.0**	**1.0**	**1.5**	**1.5**	**1.4**	**1.4**	**1.3**
REGIONAL MEMBERS[a]	**0.4**	**0.7**	**0.8**	**0.7**	**1.0**	**1.1**	**1.1**	**1.1**	**1.0**

... = data not available at cutoff date, 0.0 = magnitude is less than half of unit employed, GDP = gross domestic product, Lao PDR = Lao People's Democratic Republic.

a For reporting economies only.

Sources: Economy sources; World Bank. http://www.worldbank.org/en/topic/migrationremittancesdiasporaissues (accessed 14 June 2017).

Table 4.6: **Foreign Direct Investment, Net Inflows**
($ million)

Regional Member	2000	2005	2010	2011	2012	2013	2014	2015	2016
Developing Member Economies									
Central and West Asia									
Afghanistan	50	271	54	58	47	38	44	163	...
Armenia	104	292	529	653	497	346	404	178	338
Azerbaijan	130	4,476	3,353	4,485	5,293	2,619	4,430	4,048	4,500
Georgia	131	453	869	1,084	831	956	1,750	1,571	...
Kazakhstan	1,371	2,546	7,456	13,760	13,648	10,011	7,091	6,585	...
Kyrgyz Republic	-2	43	402	701	324	640	353	1,139	...
Pakistan	308	2,201	2,022	1,326	859	1,333	1,867	979	...
Tajikistan	24	54	79	161	239	125	309	426	344
Turkmenistan	131	418	3,632	3,391	3,130	3,732	4,170	4,259	...
Uzbekistan	75	192	1,636	1,635	563	629	626	1,068	...
East Asia									
China, People's Rep. of	42,095	104,109	243,703	280,072	241,214	290,928	268,097	242,489	170,557
Hong Kong, China	70,496	40,963	82,709	96,135	74,887	76,857	129,847	181,047	117,110
Korea, Rep. of	11,509	13,643	9,497	9,773	9,496	12,767	9,274	4,104	10,827
Mongolia	54	188	1,691	4,571	4,272	2,060	338	94	...
Taipei,China	4,928	1,625	2,492	-1,957	3,207	3,598	2,839	2,413	8,334
South Asia									
Bangladesh	280	761	1,232	1,265	1,584	2,603	2,539	3,380	...
Bhutan	2 (2002)	6	75	31	24	20	29	11	8
India	3,584	7,269	27,397	36,499	23,996	28,153	34,577	44,009	...
Maldives	22	53	216	424	228	361	333	299	...
Nepal	-0	2	88	94	92	74	30	52	...
Sri Lanka	173	272	478	956	941	933	894	681	...
Southeast Asia									
Brunei Darussalam	61	175	481	691	865	776	568	173	...
Cambodia	118	377	735	795	1,441	1,345	1,730	1,701	...
Indonesia	-4,550	8,336	15,292	20,565	21,201	23,282	25,121	19,779	3,762
Lao PDR	34	28	279	301	294	427	913	1,079	...
Malaysia	3,788	3,925	10,886	15,119	8,896	11,296	10,619	10,963	...
Myanmar	255	235	901	2,520	1,334	2,255	2,175	4,084	...
Philippines	1,487	1,664	1,070	2,007	3,215	3,737	5,740	5,639	7,933
Singapore	15,515	18,090	55,076	49,156	56,237	64,685	73,987	70,580	61,597
Thailand	3,366	8,216	14,747	2,474	12,899	15,936	4,975	9,004	...
Viet Nam	1,298	1,954	8,000	7,430	8,368	8,900	9,200	11,800	...
The Pacific									
Cook Islands	...	...	...	...	...	...	...	...	...
Fiji	1	185	356	402	376	265	348	308	...
Kiribati	1	3	-7	1	-3	1	8	2	...
Marshall Islands	126	3	-9	-4	21	33	9	-54	...
Micronesia, Fed. States of	-0 (2001)	0	1	1	1	1	20	1	...
Nauru	1	1	1 (2009)	...	...	...	...	...	...
Palau	3	4	3	8	22	18	40	35	...
Papua New Guinea	96	32	29	-310	-64	18	-30	203	...
Samoa	-1	4	-1	9	14	14	23	41	...
Solomon Islands	2	1	166	120	24	53	21	32	...
Timor-Leste	1 (2002)	1	30	49	40	56	34	43	5
Tonga	9	7	9	4	2	7	56	13	...
Tuvalu	-0 (2001)	-0	0	-0	1	0	1	1	...
Vanuatu	20	13	63	61	60	59	13	31	...
Developed Member Economies									
Australia	14,893	-25,093	35,211	65,555	57,550	53,997	45,979	36,595	41,951
Japan	10,688	5,460	7,441	-851	547	10,648	19,752	5,585	34,905
New Zealand	-1,508	1,907	286	1,378	4,004	-70	3,296	-135	1,527
DEVELOPING MEMBER ECONOMIES[a]	**157,045**	**223,091**	**497,722**	**556,517**	**500,618**	**571,948**	**605,412**	**634,454**	**385,314**
REGIONAL MEMBERS[a]	**181,118**	**205,364**	**540,660**	**622,599**	**562,720**	**636,524**	**674,439**	**676,499**	**463,697**

... = data not available at cutoff date, 0 = magnitude is less than half of unit employed, Lao PDR = Lao People's Democratic Republic.

a For reporting economies only.

Sources: World Bank. World Development Indicators. http://data.worldbank.org/indicator/BX.KLT.DINV.CD.WD?locations=MH (accessed 25 July 2017); for Taipei,China: economy sources.

Table 4.7: **Foreign Direct Investment, Net Inflows**
(% of GDP)

Regional Member	2000	2005	2010	2011	2012	2013	2014	2015	2016
Developing Member Economies									
Central and West Asia									
Afghanistan	1.2 (2002)	4.1	0.3	0.3	0.2	0.2	0.2	0.8	...
Armenia	5.5	6.0	5.7	6.4	4.7	3.1	3.5	1.7	3.2
Azerbaijan	2.5	33.8	6.3	6.8	7.6	3.5	5.9	7.6	11.9
Georgia	4.3	7.1	7.5	7.5	5.2	5.9	10.6	11.2	...
Kazakhstan	7.5	4.5	5.0	7.1	6.6	4.2	3.2	3.6	...
Kyrgyz Republic	−0.2	1.7	8.4	11.3	4.9	8.7	4.7	17.1	...
Pakistan	0.0	0.0	0.0	0.1	0.1	0.1	0.1	0.2	0.1
Tajikistan	2.7	2.4	1.4	2.5	3.1	1.5	3.3	5.4	5.0
Turkmenistan	2.7	2.9	16.1	11.6	8.9	9.5	9.6	11.9	...
Uzbekistan	0.5	1.3	4.1	3.5	1.1	1.1	1.0	1.6	...
East Asia									
China, People's Rep. of	3.5	4.6	4.0	3.7	2.8	3.0	2.6	2.2	1.5
Hong Kong, China	41.1	22.6	36.2	38.7	28.5	27.9	44.6	58.5	36.5
Korea, Rep. of	2.0	1.5	0.9	0.8	0.8	1.0	0.7	0.3	0.8
Mongolia	4.7	7.4	23.5	43.9	34.8	16.4	2.8	0.8	...
Taipei,China	1.5	0.4	0.6	−0.4	0.6	0.7	0.5	0.5	1.6
South Asia									
Bangladesh	0.6	1.3	1.1	1.0	1.2	1.7	1.5	1.7	...
Bhutan	0.5 (2002)	0.8	4.7	1.7	1.3	1.1	1.5	0.5	0.4
India	0.7	0.9	1.6	1.9	1.3	1.5	1.7	2.1	...
Maldives	3.6	4.7	9.3	17.3	9.1	12.9	10.8	8.7	...
Nepal	0.0	0.0	0.5	0.5	0.5	0.4	0.2	0.2	...
Sri Lanka	1.0	1.1	0.8	1.5	1.4	1.3	1.1	0.8	...
Southeast Asia									
Brunei Darussalam	1.0	1.8	3.5	3.7	4.5	4.3	3.3	1.3	...
Cambodia	3.2	6.0	6.5	6.2	10.3	8.8	10.3	9.4	...
Indonesia	−2.8	2.9	2.0	2.3	2.3	2.6	2.8	2.3	0.4
Lao PDR	2.1	1.0	4.1	3.7	2.9	3.6	6.9	7.5	...
Malaysia	4.0	2.7	4.3	5.1	2.8	3.5	3.1	3.7	...
Myanmar	0.1	0.0	0.0	0.0	1.7	3.6	3.3	6.5	...
Philippines	1.8	1.6	0.5	0.9	1.3	1.4	2.0	1.9	2.6
Singapore	16.2	14.2	23.3	17.8	19.4	21.4	24.0	23.8	20.7
Thailand	2.7	4.3	4.3	0.7	3.2	3.8	1.2	2.3	...
Viet Nam	4.2	3.4	6.9	5.5	5.4	5.2	4.9	6.1	...
The Pacific									
Cook Islands	...	...	...	...	...	...	...	...	...
Fiji	0.0	6.2	11.3	10.7	9.5	6.3	7.8	7.0	...
Kiribati	1.1	2.3	−4.3	0.4	−1.8	0.6	4.6	1.0	...
Marshall Islands	113.3	2.4	−5.7	−2.5	11.5	17.0	4.9	−29.9	...
Micronesia, Fed. States of	−0.1 (2001)	0.0	0.3	0.3	0.3	0.3	6.4	0.3	...
Nauru	...	3.8	0.0 (2009)	...	...	...	...	...	...
Palau	2.1	2.1	1.5	4.2	10.1	7.9	16.2	11.6	...
Papua New Guinea	2.8	0.7	0.2	−1.7	−0.3	0.1	−0.1	...	...
Samoa	−0.5	0.9	−0.2	1.1	1.7	1.7	2.8	5.3	...
Solomon Islands	0.7	0.2	28.4	16.6	2.9	5.8	2.2	3.1	...
Timor-Leste	0.2 (2002)	0.0	0.8	0.9	0.6	1.0	0.8	1.4	...
Tonga	4.9	2.7	2.4	0.9	0.4	1.5	12.7	2.9	...
Tuvalu	−0.1 (2001)	−0.1	1.4	−0.3	3.5	0.9	1.7	1.7	...
Vanuatu	7.4	3.4	9.0	7.7	7.7	7.4	1.6	...	...
Developed Member Economies									
Australia	3.9	−3.6	3.0	4.5	3.7	3.7	3.2	3.0	3.4
Japan	0.2	0.1	0.1	0.0	0.0	0.2	0.4	0.1	0.7
New Zealand	−2.8	1.7	0.2	0.8	2.3	0.0	1.6	−0.1	...
DEVELOPING MEMBER ECONOMIES[a]	**4.0**	**2.8**	**2.6**	**2.4**	**3.2**	**3.3**	**3.3**	**3.4**	**2.0**
REGIONAL MEMBERS[a]	**2.0**	**1.5**	**2.1**	**2.0**	**2.4**	**2.7**	**2.7**	**2.7**	**1.8**

... = data not available at cutoff date, 0.0 = magnitude is less than half of unit employed, GDP = gross domestic product, Lao PDR = Lao People's Democratic Republic.

a For reporting economies only.

Sources: Economy sources; International Monetary Fund. International Financial Statistics. 2017. http://data.imf.org/ (accessed 25 July 2017); World Bank. World Development Indicators. 2017. http://data.worldbank.org/indicator/BX.KLT.DINV.CD.WD (accessed 25 July 2017).

Table 4.8: **Merchandise Exports**
($ million)

Regional Member	2000	2005	2010	2011	2012	2013	2014	2015	2016
Developing Member Economies									
Central and West Asia									
Afghanistan	137	384	388	376	415	515	571	571	596
Armenia	300	974	1,041	1,334	1,380	1,479	1,547	1,485	1,783
Azerbaijan	1,745	7,649	26,374	34,393	32,374	31,703	28,260	15,586	13,211
Georgia	324	865	1,677	2,186	2,377	2,911	2,861	2,205	2,113
Kazakhstan	8,812	27,849	60,271	84,336	86,449	84,700	79,460	45,956	36,776
Kyrgyz Republic	505	674	1,756	2,242	1,928	2,007	1,884	1,470	1,545
Pakistan	8,335	14,453	19,261	24,917	22,797	23,383	25,715	23,526	20,859
Tajikistan	784	909	1,195	1,257	1,358	1,162	977	891	899
Turkmenistan	2,508	4,944	9,679	16,751	19,987	18,854	19,782	12,164	7,520
Uzbekistan	3,265	5,409	13,023	15,021	13,600	14,323	13,546	12,508	12,179
East Asia									
China, People's Rep. of	249,203	761,953	1,577,754	1,898,381	2,048,714	2,209,004	2,342,293	2,273,468	2,098,154
Hong Kong, China	201,855	289,325	390,134	428,732	442,775	458,959	473,654	465,092	462,269
Korea, Rep. of	172,268	284,419	466,384	555,214	547,870	559,632	572,665	526,757	495,426
Mongolia	536	1,064	2,909	4,817	4,385	4,269	5,774	4,669	4,916
Taipei,China	151,458	199,807	277,413	312,051	306,269	310,237	318,871	283,467	279,521
South Asia									
Bangladesh	4,780	8,259	16,099	22,061	23,508	27,619	30,217	30,590	33,354
Bhutan	103	214	535	646	580	511	539	561	487
India	45,297	103,496	249,951	314,109	305,839	325,099	310,742	267,549	274,024
Maldives	109	162	62	115	162	166	145	144	...
Nepal	701	823	830	869	872	827	943	833	652
Sri Lanka	5,456	6,351	8,618	10,560	9,761	10,413	11,130	10,536	10,309
Southeast Asia									
Brunei Darussalam	3,906	6,247	8,887	12,464	12,980	11,436	10,601	6,338	4,876
Cambodia	1,397	2,908	3,906	5,035	5,633	6,530	7,407	8,453	9,233
Indonesia	62,124	85,660	157,779	203,497	190,032	182,552	175,981	150,366	144,490
Lao PDR	330	553	1,746	2,190	2,271	2,264	2,662	2,769	3,352
Malaysia	98,229	141,595	198,325	228,059	227,480	228,503	233,868	199,041	189,460
Myanmar	1,961	3,558	8,861	9,136	8,977	11,204	12,524	11,149	11,663
Philippines	38,078	41,255	51,498	48,305	52,100	56,698	62,102	58,648	56,313
Singapore	137,954	230,523	352,553	416,027	415,590	419,969	415,191	357,729	337,962
Thailand	69,152	110,360	192,937	219,994	227,721	227,524	226,662	214,120	214,054
Viet Nam	14,483	32,447	72,237	96,906	114,529	132,033	150,217	162,017	176,632
The Pacific									
Cook Islands	9	5	5	3	5	11	18	14	14
Fiji	543	705	837	1,073	1,224	1,137	1,220	896	...
Kiribati	4	4	4	9	7	7	10	9	...
Marshall Islands	25	34	34 (2009)	65	...	...	...	...	...
Micronesia, Fed. States of	17	13	30	43	52	35	32	40	...
Nauru	68	44	189	242	70	56	46	19	26
Palau	12	14	16	19	21	21	19	18	...
Papua New Guinea	2,089	3,311	5,737	6,907	6,323	5,942	8,786	8,417	7,919
Samoa	14	12	23	25	31	24	27	34	36
Solomon Islands	65	105	227	408	488	487	458	401	...
Timor-Leste	...	43	42	53	77	53	39	47	...
Tonga	9	10	8	15	16	18	19	...	...
Tuvalu	0	0	0	0	0	0	0	0	...
Vanuatu	26	46	48	67	55	39	63	39	50
Developed Member Economies									
Australia	63,980	106,211	212,027	269,941	256,522	252,894	239,708	187,525	191,218
Japan	479,320	595,696	767,825	821,312	798,937	714,931	689,916	624,681	643,753
New Zealand	13,292	21,698	31,365	37,685	37,321	39,434	41,541	34,152	33,750
DEVELOPING MEMBER ECONOMIES[a]	**1,288,974**	**2,379,437**	**4,181,284**	**4,980,911**	**5,139,079**	**5,374,315**	**5,549,527**	**5,160,592**	**4,912,670**
REGIONAL MEMBERS[a]	**1,845,566**	**3,103,042**	**5,192,501**	**6,109,849**	**6,231,859**	**6,381,574**	**6,520,692**	**6,006,950**	**5,781,391**

... = data not available at cutoff date, 0 = magnitude is less than half of unit employed, Lao PDR = Lao People's Democratic Republic.

a For reporting economies only.

Sources: Economy sources; International Monetary Fund. International Financial Statistics. http://data.imf.org/ (accessed 2 June 2017).

Table 4.9: **Growth Rates of Merchandise Exports**[a]
(%)

Regional Member	2000	2005	2010	2011	2012	2013	2014	2015	2016
Developing Member Economies									
Central and West Asia									
Afghanistan	-17.4	25.9	-3.7	-3.1	10.4	24.1	10.9	–	4.5
Armenia	29.7	34.7	46.6	28.2	3.4	7.1	4.6	-4.0	20.0
Azerbaijan	87.7	111.6	25.3	30.4	-5.9	-2.1	-10.9	-44.8	-15.2
Georgia	36.0	33.8	48.0	30.4	8.7	22.5	-1.7	-22.9	-4.2
Kazakhstan	50.1	38.6	39.5	39.9	2.5	-2.0	-6.2	-42.2	-20.0
Kyrgyz Republic	11.2	-6.5	5.0	27.7	-14.0	4.1	-6.1	-22.0	5.1
Pakistan	4.8	14.9	12.0	29.4	-8.5	2.6	10.0	-8.5	-11.3
Tajikistan	13.9	-0.7	18.3	5.2	8.0	-14.4	-15.9	-8.9	0.9
Turkmenistan	115.5	28.3	3.8	73.1	19.3	-5.7	4.9	-38.5	-38.2
Uzbekistan	0.9	11.5	10.6	15.3	-9.5	5.3	-5.4	-7.7	-2.6
East Asia									
China, People's Rep. of	27.8	28.4	31.3	20.3	7.9	7.8	6.0	-2.9	-7.7
Hong Kong, China	16.1	11.6	22.5	9.9	3.3	3.7	3.2	-1.8	-0.6
Korea, Rep. of	19.9	12.0	28.3	19.0	-1.3	2.1	2.3	-8.0	-5.9
Mongolia	18.0	22.4	54.3	65.6	-9.0	-2.6	35.3	-19.1	5.3
Taipei,China	22.6	8.6	35.1	12.5	-1.9	1.3	2.8	-11.1	-1.4
South Asia									
Bangladesh	12.5	11.3	3.7	37.0	6.6	17.5	9.4	1.2	9.0
Bhutan	-11.3	35.8	6.5	20.7	-10.2	-11.9	5.5	4.1	-13.2
India	22.2	25.0	43.1	25.7	-2.6	6.3	-4.4	-13.9	2.4
Maldives	18.8	-10.5	-63.6	86.5	40.6	2.8	-12.9	-0.6	...
Nepal	34.0	12.4	-4.9	4.7	0.3	-5.1	14.0	-11.6	-21.7
Sri Lanka	18.5	10.1	21.7	22.5	-7.6	6.7	6.9	-5.3	-2.2
Southeast Asia									
Brunei Darussalam	53.1	23.3	23.9	40.2	4.1	-11.9	-7.3	-40.2	-23.1
Cambodia	23.6	12.3	24.5	28.9	11.9	15.9	13.4	14.1	9.2
Indonesia	27.7	19.7	35.4	29.0	-6.6	-3.9	-3.6	-14.6	-3.9
Lao PDR	9.6	52.2	65.9	25.4	3.7	-0.3	17.6	4.0	21.1
Malaysia	16.1	11.8	26.5	15.0	-0.3	0.4	2.3	-14.9	-4.8
Myanmar	72.3	21.5	16.8	3.1	-1.7	24.8	11.8	-11.0	4.6
Philippines	8.7	4.0	34.0	-6.2	7.9	8.8	9.5	-5.6	-4.0
Singapore	20.3	15.7	30.5	18.0	-0.1	1.1	-1.1	-13.8	-5.5
Thailand	18.0	14.6	27.3	14.0	3.5	-0.1	-0.4	-5.5	0.0
Viet Nam	25.5	22.5	26.5	34.2	18.2	15.3	13.8	7.9	9.0
The Pacific									
Cook Islands	154.4	-26.9	88.0	-39.4	69.9	100.6	65.8	-20.3	-2.9
Fiji	-12.1	1.4	33.0	28.3	14.1	-7.1	7.3	-26.6	...
Kiribati	-59.1	58.2	-38.0	120.7	-18.3	-4.9	51.9	-11.0	...
Marshall Islands	48.7	14.0	5.6 (2009)	90.6	...	...	...	...	...
Micronesia, Fed. States of	...	-7.3	63.5	45.1	20.2	-33.3	-7.8	23.0	...
Nauru	-7.9	-15.3	58.0	27.8	-71.2	-19.5	-18.7	-58.9	36.2
Palau	65.9	116.9	15.9	16.4	12.2	-0.5	-8.7	-5.3	...
Papua New Guinea	7.3	26.8	30.9	20.4	-8.5	-6.0	47.9	-4.2	-5.9
Samoa	-24.9	0.6	114.4	6.3	26.8	-23.2	14.7	23.8	6.3
Solomon Islands	-48.1	22.3	37.4	80.0	19.7	-0.3	-5.9	-12.4	...
Timor-Leste	...	-58.9	20.7	27.8	44.4	-30.7	-26.7	19.8	...
Tonga	-27.1	-35.2	5.6	83.5	6.1	11.3	9.8	...	...
Tuvalu	-91.5	-54.0	55.5	-46.2	-83.7	4.4	464.8	-12.0	...
Vanuatu	2.8	-6.5	-14.8	38.7	-18.5	-29.4	62.6	-38.0	28.8
Developed Member Economies									
Australia	14.1	22.6	38.3	27.3	-5.0	-1.4	-5.2	-21.8	2.0
Japan	14.8	5.4	32.6	7.0	-2.7	-10.5	-3.5	-9.5	3.1
New Zealand	6.5	6.6	26.6	20.1	-1.0	5.7	5.3	-17.8	-1.2
DEVELOPING MEMBER ECONOMIES[b]	**21.0**	**18.3**	**30.2**	**19.1**	**3.2**	**4.6**	**3.3**	**-7.0**	**-4.8**
REGIONAL MEMBERS[b]	**19.0**	**15.6**	**30.8**	**17.7**	**2.0**	**2.4**	**2.2**	**-7.9**	**-3.8**

... = data not available at cutoff date, – = magnitude equals zero, Lao PDR = Lao People's Democratic Republic.

a Rates are based on US dollar values of exports.
b For reporting economies only.

Sources: Economy sources; International Monetary Fund. International Financial Statistics. http://data.imf.org/ (accessed 2 June 2017).

Table 4.10: **Merchandise Imports**
($ million)

Regional Member	2000	2005	2010	2011	2012	2013	2014	2015	2016
Developing Member Economies									
Central and West Asia									
Afghanistan	1,176	2,470	5,154	6,390	9,832	8,724	7,729	7,723	6,534
Armenia	885	1,802	3,749	4,145	4,261	4,386	4,424	3,239	3,292
Azerbaijan	1,172	4,350	6,662	10,056	10,192	10,321	9,332	9,774	9,004
Georgia	710	2,488	5,236	7,072	8,056	8,023	8,602	7,292	7,288
Kazakhstan	5,040	17,353	31,127	36,906	46,358	48,806	41,296	30,568	25,175
Kyrgyz Republic	554	1,189	3,223	4,261	5,576	5,987	5,735	4,070	3,919
Pakistan	9,967	20,630	34,169	40,042	42,960	42,802	45,820	45,394	44,665
Tajikistan	675	1,330	2,657	3,206	1,779	4,121	4,297	3,436	3,031
Turkmenistan	1,742	2,947	8,204	11,361	14,138	16,090	16,638	14,051	13,177
Uzbekistan	2,947	4,091	9,176	11,345	12,817	13,947	13,984	12,417	12,131
East Asia									
China, People's Rep. of	225,094	659,953	1,396,244	1,743,484	1,818,405	1,949,989	1,959,235	1,679,565	1,587,419
Hong Kong, China	212,800	299,520	433,102	483,633	504,377	523,558	544,107	522,001	516,395
Korea, Rep. of	160,481	261,238	425,212	524,413	519,584	515,586	525,515	436,499	406,193
Mongolia	615	1,177	3,200	6,598	6,738	6,358	5,237	3,798	3,358
Taipei,China	140,630	185,245	255,679	287,156	277,269	276,886	280,724	235,579	229,872
South Asia									
Bangladesh	8,080	12,575	23,581	34,715	35,219	38,738	41,031	40,562	42,810
Bhutan[a]	193	466	810	1,093	952	864	935	977	1,020
India	51,372	149,753	368,166	502,558	499,495	463,402	448,486	388,187	379,629
Maldives	389	683	909	1,329	1,554	1,728	1,990	1,893	...
Nepal	1,526	2,094	5,110	5,352	5,419	5,987	7,323	7,565	7,199
Sri Lanka	7,198	8,869	13,441	20,273	19,129	17,999	19,417	18,935	19,414
Southeast Asia									
Brunei Darussalam	1,107	1,448	2,535	3,600	3,565	3,613	3,596	3,235	2,671
Cambodia[a]	1,936	3,918	5,756	7,180	8,139	9,749	10,613	11,920	12,649
Indonesia	33,515	57,701	135,663	177,436	191,691	186,629	178,179	142,695	135,653
Lao PDR	535	882	2,060	2,404	3,055	3,081	4,271	5,233	4,739
Malaysia	81,963	114,302	164,177	187,460	196,412	205,875	208,667	175,593	168,422
Myanmar	2,319	1,984	6,413	9,035	9,069	13,760	16,633	16,578	17,180
Philippines[a]	34,491	47,418	54,933	60,496	62,129	62,411	65,398	71,067	80,834
Singapore	134,675	200,861	312,668	372,313	385,851	388,053	377,714	307,967	291,922
Thailand	62,180	118,200	184,834	229,004	227,564	227,071	209,392	187,079	178,307
Viet Nam	15,637	36,761	84,839	106,750	113,780	132,033	147,849	165,570	174,111
The Pacific									
Cook Islands	51	81	91	110	112	116	121	110	106
Fiji	856	1,610	1,806	2,182	2,254	2,823	2,656	2,080	...
Kiribati	39	76	73	92	109	107	107	...	...
Marshall Islands	116	132	...	176	...	...	...	...	...
Micronesia, Fed. States of	107	128	168	188	194	188	161	160	...
Nauru[a]	78	51	42	62	...	54	85	77	87
Palau	127	108	103	125	136	145	149	156	...
Papua New Guinea	999	1,519	3,522	4,232	4,757	5,410	4,000	2,551	1,823
Samoa	91	187	280	319	308	326	341	298	312
Solomon Islands	92	185	405	473	497	537	499	467	...
Timor-Leste	...	109	298	340	670	529	554	655	...
Tonga	70	121	156	181	202	203	222	...	...
Tuvalu	5	13	22	27	21	21	22	37	...
Vanuatu	84	165	284	305	296	314	314	367	416
Developed Member Economies									
Australia	67,806	118,924	193,081	234,046	250,419	232,685	227,859	200,643	189,042
Japan	379,884	516,697	692,242	853,449	885,928	832,440	810,886	647,744	607,043
New Zealand	13,963	26,248	30,523	37,048	38,256	39,646	42,523	36,618	35,935
DEVELOPING MEMBER ECONOMIES[b]	**1,204,318**	**2,228,185**	**3,995,937**	**4,909,876**	**5,054,921**	**5,207,345**	**5,223,397**	**4,567,417**	**4,390,756**
REGIONAL MEMBERS[b]	**1,665,972**	**2,890,053**	**4,911,783**	**6,034,418**	**6,229,525**	**6,312,116**	**6,304,665**	**5,452,423**	**5,222,776**

... = data not available at cutoff date, Lao PDR = Lao People's Democratic Republic.

a Compilation methodology shifted from cost, insurance and freight to free on board for Bhutan from 2003, Cambodia from 2005, and Nauru from 2012.
b For reporting economies only.

Sources: Economy sources; International Monetary Fund. International Financial Statistics. http://data.imf.org/ (accessed 2 June 2017).

Table 4.11: **Growth Rates of Merchandise Imports**[a]
(%)

Regional Member	2000	2005	2010	2011	2012	2013	2014	2015	2016
Developing Member Economies									
Central and West Asia									
Afghanistan	16.2	13.5	54.5	24.0	53.9	-11.3	-11.4	-0.1	-15.4
Armenia	9.1	33.4	12.9	10.6	2.8	2.9	0.9	-26.8	1.6
Azerbaijan	13.1	23.7	6.9	50.9	1.4	1.3	-9.6	4.7	-7.9
Georgia	2.9	34.9	17.0	35.1	13.9	-0.4	7.2	-15.2	-0.1
Kazakhstan	37.9	35.8	9.6	18.6	25.6	5.3	-15.4	-26.0	-17.6
Kyrgyz Republic	-7.6	25.5	6.0	32.2	30.9	7.4	-4.2	-29.0	-3.7
Pakistan	5.7	33.7	2.5	17.2	7.3	-0.4	7.1	-0.9	-1.6
Tajikistan	1.8	11.7	3.4	20.7	-44.5	131.6	4.3	-20.1	-11.8
Turkmenistan	26.8	-6.4	-8.8	38.5	24.4	13.8	3.4	-15.5	-6.2
Uzbekistan	-5.2	7.2	-2.8	23.6	13.0	8.8	0.3	-11.2	-2.3
East Asia									
China, People's Rep. of	35.8	17.6	38.8	24.9	4.3	7.2	0.5	-14.3	-5.5
Hong Kong, China	18.5	10.5	24.7	11.7	4.3	3.8	3.9	-4.1	-1.1
Korea, Rep. of	34.0	16.4	31.6	23.3	-0.9	-0.8	1.9	-16.9	-6.9
Mongolia	19.8	15.5	49.7	106.2	2.1	-5.6	-17.6	-27.5	-11.6
Taipei,China	26.3	7.8	44.3	12.3	-3.4	-0.1	1.4	-16.1	-2.4
South Asia									
Bangladesh	3.1	16.5	4.4	47.2	1.5	10.0	5.9	-1.1	5.5
Bhutan[b]	2.9	77.2	40.7	34.9	-12.9	-9.2	8.2	4.5	4.4
India	2.8	35.4	30.7	36.5	-0.6	-7.2	-3.2	-13.4	-2.2
Maldives	-3.4	21.3	-5.6	46.2	16.9	11.2	15.1	-4.9	...
Nepal	19.0	13.2	39.3	4.8	1.2	10.5	22.3	3.3	-4.8
Sri Lanka	20.5	10.7	31.8	50.8	-5.6	-5.9	7.9	-2.5	2.5
Southeast Asia									
Brunei Darussalam	-16.7	1.5	5.6	42.0	-1.0	1.4	-0.5	-10.0	-17.4
Cambodia[b]	21.6	...	18.0	24.7	13.4	19.8	8.9	12.3	6.1
Indonesia	39.6	24.0	40.1	30.8	8.0	-2.6	-4.5	-19.9	-4.9
Lao PDR	-3.4	23.8	41.0	16.7	27.1	0.8	38.6	22.5	-9.4
Malaysia	25.3	8.7	33.1	14.2	4.8	4.8	1.4	-15.9	-4.1
Myanmar	-11.0	0.6	53.4	40.9	0.4	51.7	20.9	-0.3	3.6
Philippines	5.9	2.9	19.7	10.1	2.7	0.5	4.8	8.7	13.7
Singapore	21.3	15.4	26.9	19.1	3.6	0.6	-2.7	-18.5	-5.2
Thailand	23.3	25.1	37.7	23.9	-0.6	-0.2	-7.8	-10.7	-4.7
Viet Nam	33.2	15.0	21.3	25.8	6.6	16.0	12.0	12.0	5.2
The Pacific									
Cook Islands	21.9	7.0	11.2	21.0	1.9	3.9	4.1	-9.3	-3.0
Fiji	-8.3	11.5	25.8	20.8	3.3	25.3	-5.9	-21.7	...
Kiribati	-4.2	28.7	5.4	25.5	18.4	-1.2	0.0	...	...
Marshall Islands	16.7	15.3	...	...	...	...	...	...	...
Micronesia, Fed. States of	...	-3.2	-1.8	12.0	3.0	-3.1	-14.3	-0.3	...
Nauru[b]	104.9	52.3	-79.4	48.8	-45.6	59.5	59.1	-10.3	14.1
Palau	-5.7	0.7	9.3	21.7	8.4	6.7	3.1	4.4	...
Papua New Guinea	-7.0	4.5	23.0	20.2	12.4	13.7	-26.1	-36.2	-28.5
Samoa	-21.7	20.7	36.6	14.1	-3.3	5.6	4.8	-12.7	4.8
Solomon Islands	-16.1	52.4	51.2	16.7	5.1	8.1	-7.0	-6.4	...
Timor-Leste	...	-25.3	1.0	13.9	97.3	-21.1	4.7	18.2	...
Tonga	-3.8	15.3	8.9	16.0	11.4	0.4	9.7	...	...
Tuvalu	-36.0	13.3	59.2	21.9	-22.9	-1.2	7.1	66.3	...
Vanuatu	-12.6	22.4	-2.5	7.3	-2.7	5.8	0.0	17.0	13.5
Developed Member Economies									
Australia	3.5	14.5	23.4	21.2	7.0	-7.1	-2.1	-11.9	-5.8
Japan	22.7	13.6	25.8	23.3	3.8	-6.0	-2.6	-20.1	-6.3
New Zealand	-2.7	13.4	21.5	21.4	3.3	3.6	7.3	-13.9	-1.9
DEVELOPING MEMBER ECONOMIES[c]	**24.3**	**16.2**	**32.6**	**22.9**	**3.0**	**3.0**	**0.3**	**-12.6**	**-3.9**
REGIONAL MEMBERS[c]	**22.6**	**15.6**	**31.1**	**22.9**	**3.2**	**1.3**	**-0.1**	**-13.5**	**-4.2**

... = data not available at cutoff date, Lao PDR = Lao People's Democratic Republic.

a Rates are based on US dollar values of exports.
b Compilation methodology shifted from cost, insurance, and freight to free on board for Bhutan from 2003, Cambodia from 2005, and Nauru from 2012.
c For reporting economies only.

Sources: Economy sources; International Monetary Fund. International Financial Statistics. http://data.imf.org/ (accessed 2 June 2017).

Table 4.12: **Trade in Goods**[a]
(% of GDP)

Regional Member	2000	2005	2010	2011	2012	2013	2014	2015	2016
Developing Member Economies									
Central and West Asia									
Afghanistan	...	43.1	34.5	35.3	48.0	42.8	38.9	40.2	35.2
Armenia	62.0	56.6	51.7	54.0	53.1	52.7	51.4	44.8	48.0
Azerbaijan	55.3	90.6	62.4	67.4	61.1	56.7	50.0	47.8	58.7
Georgia	33.8	52.3	59.4	64.1	65.8	67.7	69.4	67.9	65.6
Kazakhstan	75.7	79.1	61.7	62.9	63.9	56.4	54.5	41.5	45.9
Kyrgyz Republic	77.3	75.7	103.8	104.9	113.6	109.0	102.0	83.0	83.4
Pakistan	23.1	29.3	30.6	30.7	30.6	30.0	28.7	25.8	23.6
Tajikistan	169.6	96.8	68.3	68.4	41.1	62.1	57.1	55.1	56.5
Turkmenistan	86.2	55.6	79.2	96.2	97.0	89.1	83.8	73.1	...
Uzbekistan	45.1	66.0	56.2	57.1	51.2	49.1	43.8	37.5	...
East Asia									
China, People's Rep. of	39.2	62.2	48.7	48.1	45.2	43.3	41.0	35.7	32.9
Hong Kong, China	241.5	324.3	360.1	367.1	360.6	356.4	349.2	319.0	305.2
Korea, Rep. of	59.2	60.8	81.5	89.8	87.3	82.4	77.8	69.7	63.9
Mongolia	101.2	88.8	85.0	109.7	90.5	84.5	90.1	72.1	74.1
Taipei,China	88.1	102.4	119.5	123.4	117.7	114.8	113.0	98.8	96.2
South Asia									
Bangladesh	28.3	36.2	34.7	46.0	45.6	43.2	41.2	36.6	34.5
Bhutan	67.3	83.1	84.9	95.5	84.0	76.5	75.2	74.7	66.5
India	20.0	30.2	36.3	43.6	43.3	41.1	37.2	30.7	28.9
Maldives	79.7	75.4	41.8	59.0	68.1	67.8	69.0	59.3	...
Nepal	41.7	35.3	36.5	33.7	35.1	37.4	41.0	40.4	37.5
Sri Lanka	75.7	62.4	38.9	47.2	42.2	38.2	38.5	36.6	36.5
Southeast Asia									
Brunei Darussalam	83.5	80.7	83.3	86.7	86.9	83.2	83.0	74.0	66.2
Cambodia[b]	90.9	108.5	85.9	95.2	98.1	106.6	107.2	112.7	109.3
Indonesia	58.0	50.1	38.9	42.7	41.6	40.5	39.8	34.0	30.0
Lao PDR	52.9	52.8	56.5	57.0	52.3	44.8	52.3	55.6	50.9
Malaysia	192.1	178.3	142.1	139.5	134.8	134.4	130.9	126.4	120.8
Myanmar	1.1	0.3	0.2	0.2	22.6	40.2	44.0	44.3	44.7
Philippines	89.6	86.0	53.3	48.5	45.7	43.8	44.8	44.3	45.0
Singapore[c]	284.5	338.6	281.4	286.0	277.2	267.1	257.3	224.3	212.1
Thailand	103.9	120.7	110.7	121.1	114.5	108.1	107.3	100.5	96.4
Viet Nam	96.6	120.1	135.5	150.3	146.5	154.2	160.1	169.5	170.9
The Pacific									
Cook Islands	65.3	47.3	37.5	39.4	38.7	42.0	43.9	43.3	41.7
Fiji	83.3	77.7	84.2	86.3	87.6	94.5	86.7	67.8	...
Kiribati	63.6	72.0	50.2	56.9	62.1	62.3	66.0	...	...
Marshall Islands	127.0	120.1	...	139.6	...	...	...	...	...
Micronesia, Fed. States of	52.9	56.4	64.2	74.2	75.3	70.3	...	...	...
Nauru	...	360.0	366.6	351.1	85.1	107.4	114.0	105.6	108.3
Palau	94.1	63.8	64.8	71.8	72.8	72.6	68.3	58.4	...
Papua New Guinea	88.3	99.3	65.0	61.9	52.0	53.4	55.6	...	...
Samoa	45.1	45.9	44.5	43.6	42.4	43.5	44.7	42.9	42.4
Solomon Islands	55.1	68.3	91.1	106.9	108.0	101.4	92.2	84.6	...
Timor-Leste	...	8.2	8.5	6.9	11.2	10.3	14.7	22.6	...
Tonga	41.9	49.6	44.6	46.4	46.2	49.0	54.6	...	...
Tuvalu	37.3	59.8	71.9	70.9	55.7	55.3	60.0	104.4	...
Vanuatu	40.5	53.5	47.4	46.9	44.9	43.9	46.2	...	...
Developed Member Economies									
Australia	34.4	31.9	34.0	34.6	32.8	32.9	32.6	32.0	30.9
Japan	17.6	23.4	25.6	27.2	27.2	30.0	31.0	29.1	25.3
New Zealand	50.1	41.8	42.2	44.4	42.9	41.5	41.9	40.3	...
DEVELOPING MEMBER ECONOMIES[d]	**63.0**	**58.0**	**42.5**	**43.1**	**65.0**	**62.1**	**59.2**	**52.2**	**49.9**
REGIONAL MEMBERS[d]	**38.5**	**45.0**	**38.8**	**39.9**	**53.4**	**53.8**	**52.6**	**47.8**	**45.9**

... = data not available at cutoff date, Lao PDR = Lao People's Democratic Republic.

a The sum of merchandise exports and imports.
b Starting 2005, compilation methodology for imports shifted from cost, insurance and freight to free on board.
c Prior to 2003, data excluded Indonesia.
d For reporting economies only.

Sources: Economy sources; International Monetary Fund. International Financial Statistics. http://data.imf.org/ (accessed 2 June 2017).

Table 4.13: **Direction of Trade: Merchandise Exports**
(% of total merchandise exports)

To / From Regional Member	Asia		Europe		North and Central America		Middle East		South America		Africa		Oceania		Rest of the World	
	2000	2016	2000	2016	2000	2016	2000	2016	2000	2016	2000	2016	2000	2016	2000	2016
Developing Member Economies																
Central and West Asia																
Afghanistan	51.7	85.8	31.3	5.1	1.8	0.7	13.1	8.0	1.5	0.0	0.5	0.3	0.0	0.0	0.0	0.0
Armenia	8.5	18.0	56.1	52.9	12.9	10.1	12.5	18.2	0.0	0.0	0.0	0.0	0.0	0.0	9.9	0.8
Azerbaijan	13.4	19.6	76.4	66.5	0.5	5.5	8.6	5.7	0.4	0.0	0.6	2.6	0.0	0.0	0.1	0.0
Georgia	38.9	39.8	52.7	45.2	2.7	5.9	4.0	7.9	0.1	0.5	1.4	0.6	0.0	0.0	0.3	0.0
Kazakhstan	13.0	24.3	48.3	69.8	14.8	2.4	2.5	3.2	0.1	0.1	0.1	0.1	0.0	0.0	21.2	0.0
Kyrgyz Republic	39.4	34.1	58.3	60.8	0.6	0.1	1.7	3.4	0.0	0.0	0.0	1.5	0.0	0.0	0.0	0.0
Pakistan	24.3	33.0	28.6	29.8	28.1	17.8	12.4	9.8	1.2	1.2	3.6	6.5	1.6	1.1	0.1	0.9
Tajikistan	24.5	51.4	73.6	41.3	0.1	0.0	1.7	7.1	0.0	0.1	0.1	0.1	0.0	0.0	0.0	0.0
Turkmenistan	12.1	85.5	75.0	14.1	1.1	0.2	10.3	0.1	0.0	0.0	0.2	0.0	0.0	0.0	1.3	0.0
Uzbekistan	31.7	49.6	62.6	48.3	2.1	0.4	2.2	1.7	1.1	0.1	0.1	0.0	0.0	0.0	0.0	0.0
East Asia																
China, People's Rep. of	50.9	45.4	18.0	18.4	23.6	21.9	2.9	5.2	1.4	3.0	1.7	3.9	1.6	2.1	0.0	0.1
Hong Kong, China	52.7	73.3	16.5	10.4	26.1	10.9	1.4	2.5	1.1	0.9	0.7	0.9	1.5	1.2	0.0	0.0
Korea, Rep. of	48.0	59.9	15.6	11.2	26.4	17.5	4.3	5.0	2.2	2.0	1.5	2.2	1.8	2.1	0.2	0.0
Mongolia	55.5	86.9	17.5	12.4	24.6	0.4	0.1	0.3	0.0	0.0	0.0	0.0	2.3	0.1	0.0	0.0
Taipei,China	52.1	71.6	15.7	9.4	26.1	13.7	1.7	2.1	1.2	0.8	0.9	0.7	1.5	1.4	0.8	0.3
South Asia																
Bangladesh	7.1	12.5	41.0	45.0	33.8	15.7	2.4	2.4	0.2	0.6	0.6	0.3	0.4	1.9	14.5	21.6
Bhutan	99.3	99.0	0.2	0.6	0.1	0.3	0.0	0.0	0.0	0.0	0.3	0.1	0.0	0.0	0.0	0.0
India	26.0	30.6	27.9	19.4	23.7	18.6	12.2	19.3	1.3	2.1	4.5	7.8	1.2	1.3	3.3	0.9
Maldives	36.9	65.2	18.6	25.8	44.4	7.2	0.0	0.5	0.0	0.0	0.0	1.2	0.0	0.2	0.0	0.0
Nepal	46.0	69.1	23.9	13.5	28.1	12.6	0.1	0.4	0.0	0.3	0.0	0.1	0.3	1.0	1.6	3.0
Sri Lanka	14.3	21.2	31.6	34.0	42.2	30.6	7.5	9.7	0.6	1.4	0.7	1.4	1.1	1.9	2.0	0.0
Southeast Asia																
Brunei Darussalam	80.0	91.5	0.7	0.4	13.1	0.7	0.1	1.3	0.0	0.0	0.0	0.0	6.1	6.1	0.0	0.0
Cambodia	28.1	30.8	17.2	38.8	54.4	27.1	0.0	0.8	0.0	0.7	0.0	0.4	0.1	1.1	0.0	0.3
Indonesia	61.7	63.7	14.8	14.3	15.1	11.9	3.4	3.7	0.9	1.2	1.4	1.9	2.7	3.4	0.0	0.0
Lao PDR	58.3	90.6	38.0	7.4	3.2	1.6	0.1	0.0	0.0	0.0	0.2	0.0	0.2	0.3	0.0	0.0
Malaysia	57.3	67.2	14.3	10.9	22.3	11.8	2.0	3.2	0.6	0.7	0.6	2.1	2.9	4.1	0.0	0.0
Myanmar	74.0	87.3	8.4	7.5	16.6	2.2	0.0	1.7	0.2	0.1	0.6	1.0	0.1	0.1	0.0	0.0
Philippines	47.9	66.5	18.6	13.0	31.7	17.4	0.5	1.1	0.2	0.5	0.1	0.4	0.9	1.1	0.0	0.1
Singapore	59.9	72.8	14.5	10.7	19.2	9.2	1.7	2.1	0.4	0.4	1.1	1.0	3.0	3.8	0.1	0.0
Thailand	50.8	58.9	17.3	13.0	23.3	13.8	3.1	4.1	0.6	1.8	1.7	2.4	2.7	5.6	0.4	0.2
Viet Nam	57.1	48.3	22.9	19.4	6.3	22.9	2.9	4.4	0.3	1.7	0.8	1.5	8.9	1.9	0.6	0.0
The Pacific																
Cook Islands[a]	28.1	70.6	0.0	0.0	7.8	0.5	0.0	0.0	0.0	0.0	0.0	0.0	59.0	11.9	5.1	17.0
Fiji	10.2	16.1	20.7	8.5	24.3	21.6	0.0	0.2	0.1	0.0	0.0	0.2	44.7	53.4	0.0	0.0
Kiribati	37.5	22.7	0.0	0.0	0.1	7.4	0.0	0.0	12.1	0.0	0.0	15.4	50.2	54.5	0.0	0.0
Marshall Islands	0.0	16.3	43.4	78.0	56.6	1.6	0.0	2.6	0.0	0.0	0.0	0.3	0.0	1.3	0.0	0.0
Micronesia, Fed. States of	42.2	66.0	0.4	2.4	57.4	6.5	0.0	2.8	0.0	0.1	0.0	0.0	0.0	22.3	0.0	0.0
Nauru	38.7	25.7	1.3	0.3	7.5	3.6	0.0	0.2	0.1	0.8	7.0	46.9	45.4	22.4	0.0	0.0
Palau	64.6	2.7	7.0	57.7	12.3	20.8	0.0	0.0	1.4	0.0	14.7	0.0	0.0	18.9	0.0	0.0
Papua New Guinea	64.1	62.7	19.9	9.5	6.9	2.2	0.1	0.1	0.0	1.9	1.1	0.2	7.9	23.4	0.0	0.0
Samoa	1.1	15.7	1.6	1.0	24.4	6.0	0.1	0.2	0.0	3.0	0.1	0.1	72.7	73.9	0.0	0.0
Solomon Islands	87.1	83.0	0.6	13.4	0.0	0.2	0.0	0.1	0.0	0.0	0.9	0.1	11.4	3.2	0.0	0.0
Timor-Leste[b]	33.5	17.9	17.1	16.4	6.7	34.2	0.0	10.1	0.0	0.0	0.6	11.8	42.0	9.6	0.0	0.0
Tonga	40.1	54.6	1.2	1.5	21.5	13.6	0.1	0.0	0.0	0.0	15.6	0.2	21.6	30.1	0.0	0.0
Tuvalu	3.4	21.1	77.4	31.8	0.6	6.6	0.0	0.1	8.5	2.8	7.5	21.1	2.6	16.5	0.0	0.0
Vanuatu	24.6	15.1	60.9	7.4	1.1	48.6	0.0	0.0	0.1	6.8	0.0	0.4	13.3	21.6	0.0	0.0
Developed Member Economies																
Australia	58.7	69.6	12.2	11.2	11.6	7.6	5.1	2.9	0.8	0.8	1.9	0.9	8.0	4.5	1.7	2.6
Japan	41.6	53.8	17.7	12.9	34.3	24.5	2.3	3.9	1.2	1.1	0.9	1.0	2.1	2.6	0.0	0.0
New Zealand	36.5	45.7	16.5	10.7	18.0	13.7	2.8	4.5	1.5	0.9	0.9	3.0	22.6	19.8	1.1	1.6
DEVELOPING MEMBER ECONOMIES	**51.1**	**54.1**	**17.5**	**16.0**	**23.6**	**17.5**	**2.9**	**5.0**	**1.1**	**2.0**	**1.3**	**2.9**	**2.0**	**2.3**	**0.5**	**0.2**
REGIONAL MEMBERS	**48.8**	**54.5**	**17.3**	**15.5**	**26.0**	**17.9**	**2.8**	**4.8**	**1.1**	**1.9**	**1.2**	**2.6**	**2.4**	**2.5**	**0.4**	**0.3**
WORLD	**23.8**	**32.0**	**41.8**	**37.1**	**25.5**	**18.9**	**2.8**	**4.8**	**2.2**	**2.4**	**1.7**	**2.7**	**1.3**	**1.5**	**1.0**	**0.6**

0.0 = magnitude is less than half of unit employed, Lao PDR = Lao People's Democratic Republic.

a Data for 2016 refer to 2015.
b Data for 2000 refer to 2004.

Sources: International Monetary Fund. May 2017. *International Financial Statistics* (CD-ROM). Washington, DC; for the Cook Islands: economy source; and for Taipei,China: Ministry of Finance. http://www.mof.gov.tw/Eng/Pages/Detail.aspx?nodeid=259&pid=74391 (accessed 27 July 2017).

Table 4.14: **Direction of Trade: Merchandise Imports**
(% of total merchandise imports)

From / To Regional Member	Asia		Europe		North and Central America		Middle East		South America		Africa		Oceania		Rest of the World	
	2000	2016	2000	2016	2000	2016	2000	2016	2000	2016	2000	2016	2000	2016	2000	2016
Developing Member Economies																
Central and West Asia																
Afghanistan	96.1	59.9	3.6	3.5	0.1	5.5	0.2	29.2	0.0	0.2	0.0	1.2	0.0	0.5	0.0	0.0
Armenia	8.9	27.1	55.8	57.8	14.6	3.2	15.4	7.6	0.0	2.2	0.0	1.1	0.0	0.4	5.3	0.6
Azerbaijan	24.8	31.0	54.1	54.4	10.5	10.2	7.3	2.2	0.5	1.8	2.1	0.1	0.6	0.3	0.1	0.0
Georgia	33.1	33.2	51.2	41.9	10.2	20.8	4.2	2.6	0.9	1.2	0.1	0.2	0.2	0.0	0.1	0.0
Kazakhstan	14.4	29.0	75.7	62.7	7.0	5.9	1.1	0.8	1.0	0.9	0.5	0.6	0.1	0.1	0.2	0.0
Kyrgyz Republic	44.4	64.3	40.9	29.7	11.8	4.4	2.9	0.4	0.1	0.4	0.0	0.1	0.0	0.7	0.0	0.0
Pakistan	29.0	47.0	19.0	12.5	7.0	5.3	38.3	28.9	1.0	1.5	2.7	3.4	3.0	1.3	0.0	0.0
Tajikistan	57.7	36.8	40.5	52.1	0.1	1.8	1.6	7.9	0.0	1.5	0.1	0.0	0.0	0.0	0.0	0.0
Turkmenistan	31.8	54.4	44.8	43.1	3.5	2.4	13.5	0.1	0.1	0.0	0.0	0.0	0.0	0.0	6.2	0.0
Uzbekistan	38.5	53.5	49.8	42.4	11.0	3.3	0.7	0.1	0.1	0.6	0.0	0.0	0.0	0.0	0.0	0.0
East Asia																
China, People's Rep. of	55.6	43.7	17.6	18.1	11.9	10.4	4.5	5.4	2.1	5.6	2.4	3.5	2.6	5.0	3.2	8.2
Hong Kong, China	79.5	82.9	10.2	8.5	7.6	5.7	0.8	1.4	0.5	0.7	0.3	0.3	1.0	0.5	0.0	0.0
Korea, Rep. of	43.8	49.9	12.5	16.0	19.9	12.7	15.9	13.3	1.6	2.6	1.9	1.2	4.3	4.1	0.0	0.1
Mongolia	47.0	56.2	47.7	37.6	4.8	5.1	0.2	0.2	0.0	0.2	0.0	0.1	0.3	0.6	0.0	0.0
Taipei,China	56.1	59.9	13.6	12.5	19.4	13.6	4.8	7.7	1.0	1.6	2.3	1.3	2.8	3.3	0.0	0.0
South Asia																
Bangladesh	58.1	65.7	12.0	10.6	3.6	3.1	5.1	5.3	1.4	3.3	0.9	1.8	2.1	1.9	16.9	8.4
Bhutan	91.3	97.4	8.1	2.1	0.4	0.1	0.0	0.2	0.2	0.0	0.0	0.0	0.0	0.1	0.0	0.2
India	21.3	38.2	28.9	17.7	7.2	7.6	9.4	20.5	1.4	4.1	6.1	7.0	2.4	2.7	23.4	2.2
Maldives	73.3	63.4	10.5	12.6	3.7	2.3	8.7	18.3	0.1	0.8	0.4	0.7	2.9	1.8	0.4	0.0
Nepal	69.8	87.5	12.6	3.9	2.0	1.6	5.8	3.8	0.8	1.8	0.1	0.7	1.9	0.7	7.0	0.0
Sri Lanka	65.5	67.6	16.2	15.0	4.5	4.6	9.1	8.0	0.5	1.3	0.5	1.3	3.4	2.3	0.2	0.0
Southeast Asia																
Brunei Darussalam	74.4	58.8	11.1	6.8	9.9	28.4	0.2	0.3	0.1	0.3	0.0	0.3	4.0	4.4	0.3	0.8
Cambodia	88.3	90.9	8.2	5.2	2.8	2.3	0.1	0.2	0.1	0.1	0.0	0.1	0.5	0.7	0.0	0.4
Indonesia	54.7	72.0	13.9	9.3	12.3	6.3	8.4	4.0	1.5	2.9	2.4	1.1	5.8	4.3	0.9	0.1
Lao PDR	91.3	96.6	7.0	2.5	0.7	0.6	0.0	0.0	0.0	0.0	0.0	0.0	0.9	0.3	0.0	0.0
Malaysia	62.9	70.7	12.5	11.1	17.3	8.2	2.0	3.7	0.6	2.0	0.4	0.9	2.3	2.6	1.9	0.8
Myanmar	88.7	87.7	8.5	4.7	2.3	1.9	0.0	3.6	0.0	0.8	0.0	0.1	0.4	1.2	0.0	0.0
Philippines	55.4	76.2	10.7	8.4	19.4	9.0	10.5	3.4	0.7	1.1	0.2	0.1	3.0	1.8	0.0	0.1
Singapore	58.9	60.8	14.1	16.2	15.8	12.0	8.2	8.1	0.3	1.0	0.4	0.7	1.9	1.3	0.4	0.0
Thailand	58.0	66.2	12.6	12.6	12.6	7.1	10.2	7.6	1.1	1.7	1.3	1.0	2.3	2.2	2.0	1.5
Viet Nam	80.6	79.1	11.8	7.0	2.6	6.4	1.3	1.6	0.4	2.2	0.3	1.1	2.3	1.4	0.7	1.1
The Pacific																
Cook Islands[a]	1.9	2.8	0.2	0.1	8.6	6.1	0.0	0.0	0.0	0.0	0.0	0.0	85.0	69.1	4.3	21.9
Fiji	20.0	58.6	3.1	10.1	4.1	3.5	0.0	0.3	35.4	0.1	0.1	0.4	30.7	26.6	6.6	0.4
Kiribati	17.2	35.4	2.5	2.1	12.3	2.2	0.0	0.0	0.0	0.1	0.0	1.3	68.0	58.9	0.0	0.0
Marshall Islands	0.0	55.2	99.9	43.2	0.0	1.0	0.0	0.0	0.0	0.0	0.0	0.3	0.1	0.3	0.0	0.0
Micronesia, Fed. States of	0.0	25.8	2.0	0.6	0.0	23.7	0.0	0.2	0.0	0.3	0.0	0.5	98.0	35.9	0.0	13.0
Nauru	6.2	10.7	7.9	0.8	10.6	0.8	0.0	0.0	0.0	0.0	49.3	0.8	26.1	86.9	0.0	0.0
Palau	39.8	55.7	0.7	1.7	59.4	23.9	0.0	0.0	0.0	0.8	0.0	0.0	0.1	17.9	0.0	0.0
Papua New Guinea	39.3	51.6	3.2	6.0	2.3	3.1	0.0	0.0	0.2	0.1	0.1	0.3	54.8	38.9	0.0	0.0
Samoa	16.0	52.4	0.8	1.0	25.7	11.2	0.0	0.0	0.2	0.2	0.0	0.0	57.3	35.1	0.0	0.0
Solomon Islands	47.1	67.9	3.0	1.4	6.1	2.5	0.0	0.0	0.1	0.0	0.2	0.2	43.5	28.0	0.0	0.0
Timor-Leste[b]	76.3	90.5	5.3	4.6	0.6	0.3	0.0	0.1	0.1	1.4	0.1	0.3	17.7	2.8	0.0	0.0
Tonga	12.3	32.5	0.5	4.0	10.3	8.1	0.0	0.1	0.2	0.7	0.1	0.3	76.6	54.1	0.0	0.1
Tuvalu	15.9	62.2	32.6	1.1	0.2	6.5	0.0	0.3	1.0	0.0	0.0	6.7	50.2	23.2	0.0	0.0
Vanuatu	22.8	44.4	5.9	10.8	1.3	2.9	0.0	0.1	0.3	0.1	0.3	1.0	68.4	40.6	1.0	0.0
Developed Member Economies																
Australia	44.1	56.5	23.3	20.8	22.1	13.3	2.8	1.5	0.8	1.0	0.9	1.1	5.5	4.5	0.4	1.3
Japan	41.8	50.5	15.0	16.0	22.2	14.1	13.0	9.9	2.0	2.6	1.3	1.2	4.7	5.8	0.0	0.0
New Zealand	30.8	48.2	18.6	19.1	19.6	13.4	5.6	4.2	1.1	1.3	1.2	0.6	22.6	12.8	0.5	0.3
DEVELOPING MEMBER ECONOMIES	**57.9**	**56.3**	**14.6**	**15.1**	**13.6**	**9.3**	**6.7**	**7.2**	**1.1**	**3.3**	**1.5**	**2.3**	**2.6**	**3.3**	**2.0**	**3.4**
REGIONAL MEMBERS	**53.4**	**55.5**	**15.1**	**15.4**	**15.9**	**10.0**	**7.9**	**7.2**	**1.3**	**3.1**	**1.4**	**2.1**	**3.4**	**3.7**	**1.5**	**2.9**
WORLD	**28.3**	**35.4**	**40.2**	**37.4**	**20.0**	**13.9**	**4.1**	**4.4**	**2.6**	**2.9**	**2.2**	**2.2**	**1.3**	**1.5**	**1.3**	**2.1**

0.0 = magnitude is less than half of unit employed, Lao PDR = Lao People's Democratic Republic.

a Data for 2016 refer to 2015.
b Data for 2000 refer to 2004.

Sources: International Monetary Fund. May 2017. *International Financial Statistics* (CD-ROM). Washington, DC; for the Cook Islands: economy source; and for Taipei,China: Ministry of Finance. http://www.mof.gov.tw/Eng/Pages/Detail.aspx?nodeid=259&pid=74391 (accessed 27 July 2017).

Table 4.15: International Reserves and Ratio of International Reserves to Imports

Regional Member	International Reserves[a] (end of year; $ million)				Ratio of International Reserves to Imports[b] (months)			
	2000	2005	2010	2016	2000	2005	2010	2016
Developing Member Economies								
Central and West Asia								
Afghanistan	7(2002)	0	5,147	7,268	0.0(2002)	0.0	13.2	14.2
Armenia	314	669	1,866	2,200	4.8	4.8	6.9	9.3
Azerbaijan	680	1,178	6,409	7,142	5.3	3.2	11.5	9.5
Georgia	116	479	2,264	2,756	1.4	2.2	5.4	5.0
Kazakhstan	2,096	7,070	28,275	29,532	3.6	4.7	10.3	12.7
Kyrgyz Republic	262	612	1,720	1,970	6.2	6.6	6.9	6.4
Pakistan	2,056	10,948	17,210	22,050	2.6	6.9	6.6	6.5
Tajikistan	94	189	403	653	1.2	1.6	1.9	3.0
Turkmenistan	1,808	4,457	13,222(2007)	...	12.5	18.1	42.0(2007)	...
Uzbekistan	1,273	2,900	14,600	24,149(2014)	6.3	10.5	22.0	23.1(2014)
East Asia								
China, People's Rep. of	168,855	825,588	2,875,894	3,097,653	10.8	17.5	27.8	24.9
Hong Kong, China	107,560	124,278	268,743	386,241	7.9	6.1	8.4	8.9
Korea, Rep. of	96,198	210,391	291,571	371,103	7.5	10.0	8.4	11.4
Mongolia	202	333	2,288	1,304	4.0	3.4	8.9	4.5
Taipei,China	111,370	257,952	387,207	438,984	9.7	17.0	18.4	21.7
South Asia								
Bangladesh	1,516	2,825	11,178	32,279	2.4	2.9	6.3	9.8
Bhutan	318	467	1,002	1,103(2015)	20.6	12.2	15.1	13.1(2015)
India	40,155	136,026	297,746	359,729	8.3	10.4	9.3	11.0
Maldives	123	189	364	478	4.3	3.5	3.5	2.7
Nepal	952	1,504	2,939	7,945(2015)	7.3	8.9	7.2	12.5(2015)
Sri Lanka	1,147	2,735	7,196	6,019	1.9	3.7	6.4	3.7
Southeast Asia								
Brunei Darussalam	382(2001)	492	1,563	3,367(2015)	4.2(2001)	4.2	7.3	12.6(2015)
Cambodia	611	1,159	3,802	9,122	3.8	3.5	7.9	8.7
Indonesia	29,268	34,731	96,211	116,370	8.7	6.5	9.7	10.8
Lao PDR	140	239	713	69	3.1	3.3	4.2	0.2
Malaysia	28,624	70,152	106,525	94,501	4.4	7.8	8.6	8.0
Myanmar	234	782	5,729	3,817(2015)	1.3	5.3	16.0	3.2(2015)
Philippines	15,063	18,494	62,373	80,692	4.2	5.9	14.0	12.5
Singapore	80,170	116,172	225,715	246,576	6.9	7.2	8.8	10.6
Thailand	32,661	52,065	172,129	171,853	6.3	5.9	12.4	11.6
Viet Nam	3,510	9,216	12,926	28,616(2015)	3.0	3.2	2.0	2.2(2015)
The Pacific								
Cook Islands	...	...	...	...	...	...	...	...
Fiji	412	321	721	916(2014)	6.4	2.6	5.6	4.9(2014)
Kiribati	0	0	8(2012)	7(2015)	0.0	0.0	1.0(2012)	0.7(2015)
Marshall Islands	...	...	...	...	...	...	...	...
Micronesia, Fed. States of	113	50	56	135(2015)	12.4	4.8	4.2	9.7(2015)
Nauru	...	...	...	...	...	...	...	...
Palau	0	0	5	4	0.0	0.0	0.5	0.3
Papua New Guinea	296	749	3,092	1,656	3.5	5.9	10.5	10.9
Samoa	64	77	189	99	2.4	6.3	11.3	3.8
Solomon Islands	32	95	266	534(2015)	4.2	9.4	8.9	14.6(2015)
Timor-Leste	...	84(2006)	406	438(2015)	...	8.9(2006)	15.9	8.0(2015)
Tonga	25	47	105	176	4.7	5.0	11.5	14.6
Tuvalu	...	...	...	...	...	...	...	...
Vanuatu	39	67	161	302	6.1	6.2	8.1	11.7
Developed Member Economies								
Australia	18,817	43,257	42,268	55,069	3.5	4.5	2.6	3.3
Japan	361,639	846,896	1,096,185	1,216,843	12.9	21.9	21.0	25.0
New Zealand	3,952	8,893	16,723	14,700(2015)	3.7	4.2	6.5	5.1(2015)
DEVELOPING MEMBER ECONOMIES[c]	**728,742**	**1,895,784**	**4,929,939**	**5,559,810**	**7.7**	**11.1**	**15.9**	**15.8**
REGIONAL MEMBERS[c]	**1,113,150**	**2,794,830**	**6,085,114**	**6,846,422**	**8.6**	**12.7**	**16.0**	**16.3**

... = data not available at cutoff date, 0 or 0.0 = magnitude is less than half of unit employed, Lao PDR = Lao People's Democratic Republic.

a Data refer to international reserves with gold at national valuation unless otherwise specified. For Afghanistan (up to 2007), Kiribati, Palau, Samoa, Solomon Islands, Tonga, Turkmenistan, and Vanuatu, data refer to international reserves without gold.

b Merchandise imports from the balance of payments were used in the computation.

c For reporting economies only.

Sources: For international reserves: International Monetary Fund. May 2017. *International Financial Statistics* (CD-ROM). Washington, DC; for Taipei,China: economy source; for the reserves-to-imports ratio: Asian Development Bank estimates using data from International Monetary Fund. May 2017. *International Financial Statistics* (CD-ROM). Washington, DC; economy sources.

Table 4.16: **Official Flows[a] from All Sources to Developing Member Economies**
($ million)

Regional Member	2000	2005	2010	2011	2012	2013	2014	2015
Developing Member Economies								
Central and West Asia								
Afghanistan	136	2,838	6,470	6,866	6,667	5,153	4,945	4,239
Armenia	216	173	343	396	271	280	268	348
Azerbaijan	141	211	162	287	287	−71	217	70
Georgia	172	293	627	587	659	646	562	448
Kazakhstan	189	225	212	201	132	91	93	83
Kyrgyz Republic	215	267	384	523	470	539	627	770
Pakistan	707	1,617	3,021	3,498	2,017	2,194	3,615	3,790
Tajikistan	124	252	433	349	394	391	356	426
Turkmenistan	36	29	44	41	38	36	34	24
Uzbekistan	186	169	234	204	256	295	325	448
East Asia								
China, People's Rep. of	1,749	1,799	672	−603	−181	−657	−947	−332
Hong Kong, China	...	...	...	...	...	...	...	...
Korea, Rep. of	...	...	...	...	...	...	...	...
Mongolia	218	221	303	351	447	431	317	236
Taipei,China	...	...	...	...	...	...	...	...
South Asia								
Bangladesh	1,174	1,320	1,405	1,495	2,154	2,634	2,423	2,570
Bhutan	53	90	131	141	162	137	131	97
India	1,383	1,876	2,831	3,270	1,682	2,456	2,992	3,173
Maldives	19	77	112	54	57	22	23	27
Nepal	386	423	814	887	770	873	884	1,216
Sri Lanka	278	1,165	580	613	491	403	492	427
Southeast Asia								
Brunei Darussalam	...	...	...	...	...	...	...	...
Cambodia	396	539	734	792	808	808	803	677
Indonesia	1,663	2,537	1,390	402	69	69	−382	−33
Lao PDR	281	297	413	400	411	423	474	471
Malaysia	49	29	−6	41	18	−113	20	−1
Myanmar	106	145	355	380	505	3,936	1,385	1,169
Philippines	575	568	541	−184	−3	192	677	515
Singapore	...	...	...	...	...	...	...	...
Thailand	699	−167	−20	−134	−131	29	355	59
Viet Nam	1,683	1,911	2,948	3,619	4,113	4,086	4,216	3,157
The Pacific								
Cook Islands	4	8	14	27	21	16	27	24
Fiji	29	66	76	75	105	91	94	102
Kiribati	18	28	23	65	66	65	81	65
Marshall Islands	57	57	33	82	84	94	56	57
Micronesia, Fed. States of	102	106	63	133	143	143	117	81
Nauru	4	9	28	38	36	29	23	31
Palau	39	24	29	28	15	35	23	14
Papua New Guinea	275	267	512	613	670	657	580	590
Samoa	28	44	148	98	117	113	91	94
Solomon Islands	68	198	340	339	305	290	199	190
Timor-Leste	231	185	291	279	284	259	250	212
Tonga	19	32	70	93	78	81	80	68
Tuvalu[b]	4	9	14	39	25	28	34	50
Vanuatu	46	40	108	91	102	91	100	187
DEVELOPING MEMBER ECONOMIES[b]	**13,760**	**19,977**	**26,883**	**26,478**	**24,613**	**27,276**	**26,658**	**25,840**
DEVELOPING ECONOMIES[c]	**50,072**	**108,542**	**131,574**	**141,810**	**133,752**	**151,138**	**161,703**	**152,603**

... = data not available at cutoff date, Lao PDR = Lao People's Democratic Republic.

a Refers to net official development assistance only, i.e., concessional flows to developing economies and multilateral institutions provided by official agencies, including state and local governments, or by their executing agencies, administered with the objective of promoting the economic development and welfare of developing economies, and containing a grant element of at least 25%.
b For reporting economies only.
c Includes data for all developing economies as reported in Organisation for Economic Co-operation and Development. *Geographical Distribution of Financial Flows to Aid Recipients*. Paris.

Source: Organisation for Economic Co-operation and Development. OECD.Stat Online. http://stats.oecd.org (accessed 27 June 2017).

Table 4.17: **Net Private Flows[a] from All Sources to Developing Member Economies**
($ million)

Regional Member	2000	2005	2010	2011	2012	2013	2014	2015
Developing Member Economies								
Central and West Asia								
Afghanistan	21	-12	-22	7	-11	26	32	-5
Armenia	-21	54	40	19	-90	207	-1	65
Azerbaijan	467	1,193	724	885	136	927	-143	635
Georgia	24	-33	27	146	190	48	-75	1,241
Kazakhstan	473	2,341	-1,349	1,786	223	3,629	1,951	2,870
Kyrgyz Republic	11	2	23	15	15	19	18	-0
Pakistan	-596	883	134	472	533	-550	83	46
Tajikistan	-8	-1	14	5	14	60	-9	-10
Turkmenistan	93	-69	680	3	-458	156	1,162	2,231
Uzbekistan	123	-151	29	-58	119	264	-391	110
East Asia								
China, People's Rep. of	-308	21,264	46,798	48,961	18,773	53,944	60,986	17,443
Hong Kong, China	...	...	...	...	...	...	...	...
Korea, Rep. of	...	...	...	...	...	...	...	...
Mongolia	-6	-17	20	65	425	582	480	249
Taipei,China	...	...	...	...	...	...	...	...
South Asia								
Bangladesh	63	232	-82	373	805	-17	446	60
Bhutan	-9	1	26	-5	107	-165	6	16
India	1,122	5,815	20,931	14,685	15,721	7,659	12,232	7,096
Maldives	-5	8	29	-80	-32	25	90	103
Nepal	-4	-2	-11	-7	78	123	5	-8
Sri Lanka	99	19	213	179	421	654	507	484
Southeast Asia								
Brunei Darussalam	...	...	...	...	...	...	...	...
Cambodia	9	2	253	124	271	312	401	396
Indonesia	43	7,115	3,509	10,242	7,123	6,995	11,827	9,674
Lao PDR	6	–	78	26	345	58	45	-22
Malaysia	-189	1,263	6,569	7,001	10,582	10,085	7,935	3,503
Myanmar	-70	14	293	499	323	597	-148	853
Philippines	1,048	3,299	2,296	2,368	4,889	2,067	4,959	1,860
Singapore	...	...	...	...	...	...	...	...
Thailand	-137	11,062	6,109	10,550	5,888	7,074	9,620	-2,002
Viet Nam	-182	349	3,209	3,751	4,604	8,846	3,678	3,901
The Pacific								
Cook Islands	-31	-29	-0	8	-1	3	-2	-2
Fiji	1	42	-3	51	163	65	115	48
Kiribati	0	1	-0	3	0	0	3	3
Marshall Islands	108	2,737	973	2,968	2,122	-1,069	-256	2,250
Micronesia, Fed. States of	...	0	3	599	5	92	320	798
Nauru	-2	2	...	-0	...	...	...	...
Palau	18	1	3	6	22	2	-5	7
Papua New Guinea	-24	232	4,108	-172	3,062	1,016	-3,311	-2,931
Samoa	1	29	22	7	7	-32	35	1
Solomon Islands	-15	-17	3	8	-463	4	23	11
Timor-Leste	...	0	-4	-1	3	25	2	17
Tonga	-7	2	-10	-3	0	1	1	-1
Tuvalu	-4	-1	...	1	-0	-2	-1	0
Vanuatu	25	11	31	-23	86	43	15	-5
DEVELOPING MEMBER ECONOMIES[b]	**2,136**	**57,640**	**95,668**	**105,466**	**76,001**	**103,774**	**112,635**	**50,985**
DEVELOPING ECONOMIES[c]	**81,273**	**178,572**	**351,214**	**337,663**	**309,244**	**267,476**	**414,153**	**133,010**

... = data not available at cutoff date, – = magnitude equals zero, 0 = magnitude is less than half of unit employed, Lao PDR = Lao People's Democratic Republic.

a Refers to the sum of direct investment, portfolio investment, and private net export credits of Development Assistance Committee economies only. The list of Development Assistance Committee economies is available at http://www.oecd.org/dac/dacmembers.htm

b For reporting economies only.

c Includes data for all developing economies as reported in Organisation for Economic Co-operation and Development. *Geographical Distribution of Financial Flows to Aid Recipients*. Paris.

Source: Organisation for Economic Co-operation and Development. OECD.Stat Online. http://stats.oecd.org (accessed 27 June 2017).

Table 4.18: **Aggregate Net Resource Flows[a] from All Sources to Developing Member Economies**
($ million)

Regional Member	2000	2005	2010	2011	2012	2013	2014	2015
Developing Member Economies								
Central and West Asia								
Afghanistan	157	2,826	6,448	6,873	6,655	5,178	4,977	4,234
Armenia	194	226	382	415	180	488	266	413
Azerbaijan	608	1,404	886	1,172	422	856	74	705
Georgia	196	261	654	733	849	694	487	1,689
Kazakhstan	662	2,566	–1,137	1,987	355	3,720	2,044	2,952
Kyrgyz Republic	226	270	407	539	485	558	644	770
Pakistan	110	2,500	3,155	3,970	2,550	1,645	3,698	3,836
Tajikistan	116	251	448	354	409	451	348	417
Turkmenistan	129	–40	723	44	–420	192	1,197	2,255
Uzbekistan	310	18	264	146	375	559	–66	558
East Asia								
China, People's Rep. of	1,441	23,063	47,470	48,358	18,593	53,287	60,039	17,111
Hong Kong, China	...	...	...	...	...	...	...	...
Korea, Rep. of	...	...	...	...	...	...	...	...
Mongolia	213	204	323	417	871	1,013	797	485
Taipei,China	...	...	...	...	...	...	...	...
South Asia								
Bangladesh	1,237	1,553	1,323	1,868	2,959	2,617	2,869	2,631
Bhutan	44	91	157	137	268	–28	136	113
India	2,505	7,691	23,762	17,955	17,403	10,116	15,224	10,269
Maldives	14	85	140	–26	25	46	113	130
Nepal	383	421	803	879	848	996	889	1,208
Sri Lanka	377	1,184	793	792	912	1,057	999	911
Southeast Asia								
Brunei Darussalam	...	...	...	...	...	...	...	...
Cambodia	405	540	987	917	1,078	1,121	1,204	1,073
Indonesia	1,706	9,651	4,899	10,644	7,192	7,065	11,445	9,641
Lao PDR	287	297	492	425	755	481	519	450
Malaysia	–141	1,292	6,563	7,042	10,600	9,971	7,955	3,502
Myanmar	35	158	648	879	828	4,533	1,236	2,021
Philippines	1,623	3,867	2,837	2,184	4,886	2,259	5,636	2,375
Singapore	...	...	...	...	...	...	...	...
Thailand	562	10,895	6,088	10,416	5,757	7,102	9,975	–1,943
Viet Nam	1,501	2,260	6,157	7,370	8,717	12,931	7,895	7,059
The Pacific								
Cook Islands	–27	–21	13	36	20	18	25	22
Fiji	30	108	73	127	268	157	209	151
Kiribati	18	29	23	68	66	65	84	68
Marshall Islands	165	2,794	1,006	3,050	2,206	–975	–200	2,307
Micronesia, Fed. States of	...	106	67	733	149	235	437	879
Nauru	2	12	...	37	...	...	...	...
Palau	57	25	32	34	37	38	18	21
Papua New Guinea	251	499	4,621	441	3,732	1,674	–2,731	–2,341
Samoa	28	73	170	105	125	81	126	95
Solomon Islands	54	182	344	348	–158	293	222	201
Timor-Leste	...	185	287	278	286	284	252	229
Tonga	12	34	61	91	78	82	82	68
Tuvalu	–0	8	...	40	25	26	34	50
Vanuatu	71	51	139	68	188	134	116	181
DEVELOPING MEMBER ECONOMIES[b]	**15,896**	**77,617**	**122,550**	**131,944**	**100,614**	**131,049**	**139,293**	**76,824**
DEVELOPING ECONOMIES[c]	**131,345**	**287,114**	**482,788**	**479,472**	**442,996**	**418,614**	**575,855**	**285,613**

... = data not available at cutoff date, 0 = magnitude is less than half of unit employed, Lao PDR = Lao People's Democratic Republic.

a Refers to the sum of official and net private flows.
b For reporting economies only.
c Includes data for all developing economies as reported in Organisation for Economic Co-operation and Development. *Geographical Distribution of Financial Flows to Aid Recipients*. Paris.

Source: Organisation for Economic Co-operation and Development. OECD.Stat Online. http://stats.oecd.org (accessed 27 June 2017).

Table 4.19: **Total External Debt of Developing Member Economies**[a]
($ million)

Regional Member	Total External Debt				External Debt, Public and Publicly Guaranteed			
	2000	2005	2010	2015	2000	2005	2010	2015
Developing Member Economies								
Central and West Asia								
Afghanistan	...	969 (2006)	2,425	2,489	...	911 (2006)	1,966	1,959
Armenia	1,010	1,968	6,304	8,925	675	923	2,557	3,992
Azerbaijan	1,585	2,247	7,159	13,215	794	1,491	3,720	8,505
Georgia	1,826	2,151	9,656	14,854	1,274	1,531	4,141	5,664
Kazakhstan	12,890	43,857	119,145	154,288	3,623	2,177	3,845	20,070
Kyrgyz Republic	1,938	2,257	4,114	7,504	1,220	1,665	2,442	3,393
Pakistan	33,022	34,018	64,003	65,482	27,192	30,089	43,403	48,212
Tajikistan	1,141	1,121	3,562	5,100	755	826	1,806	1,954
Turkmenistan	2,627	1,153	529	403	2,271	878	359	234
Uzbekistan	4,948	4,632	7,802	14,838	3,766	3,626	3,423	6,498
East Asia								
China, People's Rep. of	145,666	283,310	734,465	1,418,291	94,489	84,212	94,003	158,402
Hong Kong, China[b]	208,260	470,288	879,034	1,330,055 (2016)	...	...	...	...
Korea, Rep. of	135,208	161,956	355,911	380,949 (2016)	52,128	39,665	120,636	158,701
Mongolia	960	1,396	5,928	21,542	833	1,267	1,782	3,596
Taipei,China	34,757	86,732	101,581	172,238 (2016)	23	222	8,035	1,109 (2016)
South Asia								
Bangladesh	15,603	18,506	26,881	38,640	14,992	17,441	21,453	27,101
Bhutan	212	657	935	1,956	202	636	919	1,945
India	101,131	121,195	290,428	479,559	81,196	54,726	100,563	175,718
Maldives	203	362	917	943	185	300	628	633
Nepal	2,878	3,191	3,789	4,155	2,826	3,112	3,509	3,612
Sri Lanka	9,250	11,300	21,684	43,920	7,945	9,658	16,430	27,448
Southeast Asia								
Brunei Darussalam	...	...	...	...	...	...	...	...
Cambodia	1,946	2,769	3,685	9,319	1,853	2,666	2,874	5,420
Indonesia	144,032	142,120	198,268	308,540	70,025	77,705	103,387	160,038
Lao PDR	2,531	3,279	6,525	11,645	2,474	2,354	3,771	6,657
Malaysia	41,946	64,911	133,800	190,951	19,125	34,387	61,858	66,385
Myanmar	5,875	6,674	8,217	6,401	5,328	5,815	6,646	5,240
Philippines	58,456	58,693	65,303	77,725	33,744	35,364	45,039	36,145
Singapore	...	...	...	...	...	...	...	...
Thailand	79,830	58,467	106,358	129,654	29,462	12,602	15,929	22,420
Viet Nam	12,785	18,530	44,902	77,798	11,584	16,219	32,764	46,335
The Pacific								
Cook Islands	55	71	76	85 (2016)	...	...	...	...
Fiji	195	303	570	871	174	185	388	697
Kiribati	8	11	14	36	...	...	...	...
Marshall Islands	105	92	105	95	...	...	...	...
Micronesia, Fed. States of	63	62	86	81	...	...	...	...
Nauru	...	...	...	...	...	...	...	...
Palau	58	60	67	60	...	...	...	...
Papua New Guinea	2,325	1,871	5,987	20,031	1,454	1,264	1,042	1,501
Samoa	139	169	325	437	138	167	299	408
Solomon Islands	156	167	231	207	121	144	125	81
Timor-Leste	...	...	...	...	...	...	...	...
Tonga	74	89	154	173	65	80	144	164
Tuvalu	4	10 (2006)	16	14 (2013)	...	...	...	...
Vanuatu	112	100	174	170	73	72	99	74
DEVELOPING MEMBER ECONOMIES[c]	**1,065,811**	**1,611,715**	**3,221,113**	**5,013,640**	**472,010**	**444,378**	**709,986**	**1,010,310**
DEVELOPING ECONOMIES[d]	**2,469,681**	**3,245,953**	**5,872,519**	**8,552,978**	**1,323,338**	**1,325,514**	**1,796,923**	**2,571,498**

... = data not available at cutoff date, Lao PDR = Lao People's Democratic Republic.

a Refers to the sum of public and publicly guaranteed long-term debt, private nonguaranteed long-term debt, use of International Monetary Fund credit, and estimated short-term debt.

b Data in 2000, 2005, and onward are not comparable due to a change in coverage or compilation methodology.

c For reporting economies only.

d Includes data for all developing economies as reported in World Bank. International Debt Statistics. For developing member economies not covered by the World Bank, data are from economy sources.

Sources: World Bank. International Debt Statistics. http://data.worldbank.org/data-catalog/international-debt-statistics (accessed 7 July 2017); Asian Development Bank estimates; economy sources.

External Indebtedness

Table 4.20: **Total External Debt of Developing Member Economies**
(% of GNI)

Regional Member	Total External Debt				External Debt, Public and Publicly Guaranteed			
	2000	2005	2010	2015	2000	2005	2010	2015
Developing Member Economies								
Central and West Asia								
Afghanistan	...	13.6 (2006)	15.2	12.6	...	12.8 (2006)	12.3	10.0
Armenia	51.4	38.5	64.9	81.3	34.4	18.1	26.3	36.4
Azerbaijan	31.8	19.4	14.5	25.8	15.9	12.9	7.5	16.6
Georgia	57.5	33.2	85.6	109.4	40.1	23.7	36.7	41.7
Kazakhstan	75.7	84.7	92.6	89.3	21.3	4.2	3.0	11.6
Kyrgyz Republic	150.5	95.1	91.7	118.6	94.8	70.2	54.4	53.6
Pakistan	45.2	30.4	34.8	22.9	37.2	26.9	23.6	16.8
Tajikistan	138.4	50.2	64.0	54.4	91.6	37.0	25.9	20.4
Turkmenistan	96.3	15.3	2.6	1.1	83.3	11.6	1.7	0.7
Uzbekistan	36.5	32.4	19.3	21.8	27.8	25.4	8.5	9.6
East Asia								
China, People's Rep. of	12.2	12.6	12.2	13.1	7.9	3.7	1.5	1.4
Hong Kong, China[a]	120.3	257.7	376.5	401.2 (2016)	...	...	...	...
Korea, Rep. of	24.2	18.2	32.5	27.0 (2016)	9.3	4.5	11.0	11.4
Mongolia	84.8	56.5	89.9	201.7	73.6	51.2	27.0	33.4
Taipei,China	10.3	22.5	22.1	31.5 (2016)	0.0	0.1	1.7	0.2
South Asia								
Bangladesh	28.3	25.5	21.6	18.6	27.2	24.1	17.2	13.0
Bhutan	48.2	81.3	62.4	105.8	46.1	78.7	61.4	103.7
India	21.4	14.6	17.2	23.4	17.2	6.6	6.1	8.5
Maldives	34.2	33.3	45.6	33.5	31.1	27.5	31.2	20.5
Nepal	52.2	39.1	23.5	19.6	51.2	38.2	21.8	16.8
Sri Lanka	57.8	46.9	38.6	54.6	49.6	40.1	29.3	34.1
Southeast Asia								
Brunei Darussalam	...	...	...	...	...	...	...	...
Cambodia	55.1	46.1	34.3	54.6	52.4	44.4	26.8	31.8
Indonesia	95.8	52.3	27.0	37.0	45.4	28.6	14.1	19.2
Lao PDR	152.4	122.8	97.2	99.6	149.0	88.2	56.5	56.7
Malaysia	48.7	47.3	54.2	66.3	22.2	25.1	25.1	23.1
Myanmar	...	...	...	...	59.9	48.5	13.4	8.9
Philippines	61.6	45.2	24.6	22.0	35.5	27.2	16.9	10.2
Singapore	...	...	...	...	...	...	...	...
Thailand	64.4	32.3	32.6	35.2	23.8	7.0	4.9	6.0
Viet Nam	38.5	32.8	40.3	42.5	34.9	28.7	29.4	25.2
The Pacific								
Cook Islands[b]	60.1	38.7	29.7	29.5 (2016)	...	...	...	...
Fiji	11.3	9.9	18.7	20.9	10.1	6.1	12.8	16.6
Kiribati	...	7.1	6.3	10.7	...	...	...	...
Marshall Islands	71.2	51.5	53.0	52.7	...	...	...	...
Micronesia, Fed. States of	26.4	23.9	27.8	25.8	...	...	...	...
Nauru	...	...	...	...	...	...	...	...
Palau[b]	39.6	31.1	36.3	20.1	...	...	...	...
Papua New Guinea	70.4	41.3	65.6	123.6 (2014)	44.0	27.9	11.4	8.3 (2014)
Samoa	51.7	38.3	50.9	59.5	51.2	37.9	46.9	55.4
Solomon Islands	35.9	40.3	46.5	18.0	27.7	34.7	25.2	7.2
Timor-Leste	...	...	...	...	...	...	...	...
Tonga	38.7	34.4	40.3	44.1 (2014)	32.2	30.1	37.6	37.4
Tuvalu[b]	28.9	45.7 (2006)	49.4	72.5	...	...	...	...
Vanuatu	43.3	27.2	25.8	21.1 (2014)	28.2	19.5	14.7	9.4 (2014)

... = data not available at cutoff date, 0.0 = magnitude is less than half of unit employed, GNI = gross national income, Lao PDR = Lao People's Democratic Republic.

a Data in 2000 and 2005 onward are not comparable due to a change in coverage or compilation methodology.
b For total external debt as a percentage of GNI, gross domestic product is used in lieu of GNI.

Sources: World Bank. World Development Indicators and International Debt Statistics. http://data.worldbank.org/data-catalog/world-development-indicators (accessed 7 July 2017); Asian Development Bank estimates using economy sources.

Table 4.21: **Total External Debt of Developing Member Economies**
(% of exports of goods, services, and primary income)

Regional Member	2000	2005	2010	2011	2012	2013	2014	2015
Developing Member Economies								
Central and West Asia								
Afghanistan	...	...	91.6	78.3	126.7	147.1	123.2	164.9
Armenia	181.0	101.3	193.4	194.5	189.4	196.5	188.7	221.9
Azerbaijan	72.9	26.9	24.8	19.2	27.3	27.2	34.4	62.1
Georgia	183.7	89.1	210.3	189.3	174.7	166.3	174.0	211.6
Kazakhstan	123.0	139.8	174.7	135.5	144.4	160.5	177.2	281.0
Kyrgyz Republic	328.5	234.4	181.0	169.6	170.6	176.5	218.9	285.9
Pakistan	326.5	172.1	222.7	203.0	194.4	196.6	200.2	224.5
Tajikistan	...	88.7	158.3	132.8	130.9	130.4	162.5	198.9
Turkmenistan	...	...	...	...	...	...	...	...
Uzbekistan	...	...	...	...	...	...	...	...
East Asia								
China, People's Rep. of	71.9	34.9	42.1	48.5	48.6	57.9	64.1	53.4
Hong Kong, China[a, b]	76.8	121.2	149.2	148.1	145.6	152.0	166.2	174.1 (2016)
Korea, Rep. of[a]	64.6	46.5	62.5	56.7	55.5	56.3	56.4	60.7 (2016)
Mongolia	153.2	93.6	173.3	208.3	340.8	416.9	339.4	414.6
Taipei,China[a]	19.3	35.9	29.9	32.1	29.2	38.4	39.6	44.9 (2016)
South Asia								
Bangladesh	214.0	163.4	123.5	100.5	102.8	107.0	107.6	110.6
Bhutan	...	...	154.0	140.6	194.2	233.9	270.6	269.1
India	161.9	75.6	81.1	73.2	86.5	89.1	91.8	108.2
Maldives	43.4	73.1	45.6	35.9	35.6	30.8	31.7	29.9
Nepal	212.5	224.2	212.7	178.0	178.6	162.5	143.1	155.0
Sri Lanka	141.7	141.9	189.8	182.8	260.2	257.8	250.2	257.9
Southeast Asia								
Brunei Darussalam	...	...	...	...	...	...	...	...
Cambodia	102.8	67.6	61.2	54.0	70.7	70.7	69.5	74.5
Indonesia	197.1	146.5	117.6	101.9	118.2	127.8	145.8	177.9
Lao PDR	493.1	430.1	282.7	307.6	280.4	302.3	293.3	317.3
Malaysia	36.7	38.9	57.2	53.4	73.7	72.8	74.0	85.6
Myanmar	273.9	173.9	104.7	94.6	80.5	58.5	46.6	45.2
Philippines	189.8	152.4	106.6	102.0	92.4	86.9	91.7	94.8
Singapore	...	...	...	...	...	...	...	...
Thailand	92.8	44.4	45.7	40.8	47.0	46.9	46.7	46.2
Viet Nam	73.1	50.1	56.0	50.7	49.4	45.8	44.8	44.8
The Pacific								
Cook Islands	...	...	...	...	...	...	...	...
Fiji	19.0	17.9	30.2	36.2	29.7	32.2	34.0	39.5
Kiribati[a]	16.3	17.6	...	...	11.2	9.5	7.4	17.0
Marshall Islands[a]	141.1	98.0	97.7	75.6	67.7	62.3	65.6	60.4
Micronesia, Fed. States of[a]	100.3	98.2	91.9	88.9	69.3	65.6	65.8	52.7
Nauru	...	...	...	...	...	...	...	...
Palau[a]	119.0	69.2	65.4	51.4	48.6	43.9	37.5	31.2
Papua New Guinea	98.2	51.3	98.2	170.5	217.7	337.3	227.4	205.6
Samoa	...	114.8	161.1	173.9	177.7	179.4	185.3	195.5
Solomon Islands	121.3	108.1	68.9	45.5	35.0	33.7	30.5	35.9
Timor-Leste	...	...	...	...	...	...	...	...
Tonga	...	151.0	224.7	191.6	174.8	177.4	265.3	227.9
Tuvalu[a]	85.9	54.9	65.0	67.6	48.1	47.3	...	...
Vanuatu	63.9	49.0	48.0	43.5	88.5	41.8	39.7	47.5

... = data not available at cutoff date, Lao PDR = Lao People's Democratic Republic.

a External debt as percent of exports of goods, services, and primary income was derived using balance of payments data. The 2005 data for Tuvalu refer to 2006.
b Data prior to 2005 are not comparable with the rest of the series due to a change in coverage or compilation methodology.

Sources: World Bank. World Development Indicators and International Debt Statistics. http://data.worldbank.org/data-catalog/world-development-indicators (accessed 7 July 2017); Asian Development Bank estimates; economy sources.

Table 4.22: **Total Debt Service Paid**

Regional Member	Debt Service Payment ($ million)				Debt Service Payment (% of exports of goods, services, and primary income)			
	2000	2005	2010	2015	2000	2005	2010	2015
Developing Member Economies								
Central and West Asia								
Afghanistan	...	11 (2006)	10	44	...	...	0.4	2.9
Armenia	51	142	969	1,556	9.1	7.3	29.7	38.7
Azerbaijan	138	242	432	1,106	6.4	2.9	1.5	5.2
Georgia	126	195	803	2,082	12.7	8.1	17.5	29.7
Kazakhstan	3,392	13,158	39,474	34,951	32.4	41.9	57.9	63.6
Kyrgyz Republic	178	143	557	412	30.2	14.8	24.5	15.7
Pakistan	2,871	2,466	4,273	3,751	28.4	12.5	14.9	12.9
Tajikistan	68	73	695	430	...	5.8	30.9	16.8
Turkmenistan	472	310	155	54	...	...	...	...
Uzbekistan	908	795	618	1,269	...	...	...	...
East Asia								
China, People's Rep. of	26,610	27,469	51,992	123,858	13.1	3.4	3.0	4.7
Hong Kong, China	...	...	...	...	...	...	...	...
Korea, Rep. of[a, b]	22,905	7,224	2,843	...	10.9	2.1	0.5	...
Mongolia	41	45	239	1,754	6.6	3.0	7.0	33.8
Taipei,China[a, b]	45	11,006	3,630	6,150	0.0	4.6	1.1	1.5
South Asia								
Bangladesh	773	812	1,106	1,438	10.6	7.2	5.1	4.1
Bhutan	7	7	87	129	...	...	14.4	17.8
India	10,668	23,922	24,413	48,379	17.1	14.9	6.8	10.9
Maldives	20	31	81	110	4.2	6.3	4.0	3.5
Nepal	103	120	188	222	7.6	8.5	10.6	8.3
Sri Lanka	791	441	1,408	3,182	12.1	5.5	12.3	18.7
Southeast Asia								
Brunei Darussalam	...	...	...	...	...	...	...	...
Cambodia	13	30	65	774	0.7	0.7	1.1	6.2
Indonesia	16,696	20,281	29,343	55,719	22.8	20.9	17.4	32.1
Lao PDR	41	136	302	398	8.0	17.8	13.1	10.9
Malaysia	6,441	9,381	5,575	13,503	5.6	5.6	2.4	6.1
Myanmar	9	5	4	76	0.4	0.1	0.0	0.5
Philippines	7,066	9,528	11,461	8,104	22.9	24.7	18.7	9.9
Singapore	...	...	...	...	...	...	...	...
Thailand	14,013	18,044	10,965	19,281	16.3	13.7	4.7	6.9
Viet Nam	1,306	946	1,873	6,624	7.5	2.6	2.3	3.8
The Pacific								
Cook Islands[a]	1	3	2	5	...	...	...	...
Fiji	26	15	24	48	2.6	0.9	1.2	2.2
Kiribati[b]	1	1	1	1	1.7	1.9	...	0.2
Marshall Islands[b]	22	4	9	7	29.8	4.8	8.0	4.5
Micronesia, Fed. States of[b]	23	2	5	8	36.1	3.9	5.3	5.4
Nauru	...	...	...	...	...	...	...	...
Palau	...	...	...	...	...	...	...	...
Papua New Guinea	305	308	812	1,102	12.9	8.4	13.3	11.3
Samoa	6	6	11	21	...	3.9	5.3	9.4
Solomon Islands	9	14	21	14	7.1	9.1	6.2	2.4
Timor-Leste	...	...	...	...	...	...	...	...
Tonga	5	5	5	15	...	8.8	7.4	20.2
Tuvalu	...	...	...	...	...	...	...	...
Vanuatu	3	3	6	5	1.6	1.6	1.6	1.4

... = data not available at cutoff date, 0.0 = magnitude is less than half of unit employed, Lao PDR = Lao People's Democratic Republic.

a Refers to principal repayments on long-term debts plus interests on short-term and long-term debts.
b Debt service payment as percent of exports of goods, services, and primary income was derived from the balance of payments data.

Sources: World Bank. World Development Indicators and International Debt Statistics. http://data.worldbank.org/data-catalog/world-development-indicators (accessed 7 July 2017); Asian Development Bank estimates; economy sources.

Table 4.23: **International Tourist Arrivals**[a]
(thousand)

Regional Member	2000	2005	2010	2015	2016
Developing Member Economies					
Central and West Asia[b]	**3,404**	**6,086**	**8,922**	**14,386**	**6,020**
Afghanistan	...	...	...	...	...
Armenia	45	319	687	1,192	1,260
Azerbaijan	576 (2002)	693	1,280	1,922	2,045
Georgia	387	560	1,067	2,282	2,715
Kazakhstan	1,471	3,143	2,991	4,560 (2014)	...
Kyrgyz Republic	59	319 |	855	3,051	...
Pakistan	557	798	907	965 (2014)	...
Tajikistan	4	...	160	414	...
Turkmenistan	3	12	...	...	...
Uzbekistan	302	242	975	...	...
East Asia	**48,126**	**71,322**	**90,571**	**107,630**	**114,159**
China, People's Rep. of	31,229	46,809	55,665	56,886	59,270
Hong Kong, China	8,814	14,773	20,085	26,686	26,553
Korea, Rep. of	5,322	6,023	8,798	13,232	17,242
Mongolia	137	339	456	386	404
Taipei,China	2,624	3,378	5,567	10,440	10,690
South Asia[b]	**4,187**	**5,460**	**8,169**	**17,135**	**18,869**
Bangladesh	199	208	303	125 (2014)	...
Bhutan	8	14	41	155	210
India	2,649	3,919	5,776 |	13,284	14,569
Maldives	467	395	792	1,234	1,286
Nepal	464	375	603	539	753
Sri Lanka	400	549	654	1,798	2,051
Southeast Asia[b]	**35,458**	**43,540**	**63,428**	**104,181**	**96,784**
Brunei Darussalam	...	126	214	218	219
Cambodia	...	1,333	2,508	4,775	5,012
Indonesia	5,064	...	...	9,963	...
Lao PDR	191	672	1,670	3,543	3,315
Malaysia	10,222	16,431	24,577	25,721	26,757
Myanmar	208	232	792	4,681	...
Philippines	1,992	2,623	3,520	5,361	5,967
Singapore	6,062	7,079	9,161	12,052	12,913
Thailand	9,579	11,567	15,936	29,923	32,588
Viet Nam	2,140	3,477	5,050	7,944	10,013
The Pacific[b]	**701**	**1,046**	**1,345**	**1,629**	**1,367**
Cook Islands	73	88	104	125	146
Fiji	294	545	632	755	792
Kiribati	5	5	5	4	5
Marshall Islands	5	9	5	6	10
Micronesia, Fed. States of	21	19	45	30	24
Nauru	...	...	...	...	...
Palau	58	81	85	162	138
Papua New Guinea	58	69	140	184	...
Samoa	88	102	122	134	...
Solomon Islands	5	9	21	22	22
Timor-Leste	...	14 (2006)	40	61	72
Tonga	35	42	47	54	61
Tuvalu	1	1	2	2	2
Vanuatu	58	62	97	90	95
Developed Member Economies[b]	**11,475**	**14,544**	**16,836**	**30,220**	**32,302**
Australia	4,931	5,463	5,790	7,444	8,263
Japan	4,757	6,728	8,611	19,737	24,039
New Zealand	1,787	2,353	2,435	3,039	...
DEVELOPING MEMBER ECONOMIES[b]	**91,876**	**127,454**	**172,435**	**244,961**	**237,199**
REGIONAL MEMBERS[b]	**103,351**	**141,998**	**189,271**	**275,181**	**269,501**

... = data not available at cutoff date, | = marks break in series, Lao PDR = Lao People's Democratic Republic.

a For Australia; Japan; the Republic of Korea; the Kyrgyz Republic; Taipei,China; Tajikistan; and Viet Nam, data refer to international visitor arrivals at frontiers (including tourists and same-day visitors). For the rest of the economies, data refer to international tourist arrivals at frontiers (overnight visitors, i.e., excluding same-day visitors).
b For reporting economies only. Regional aggregates include data for nearest years as reported in the table.

Source: World Tourism Organization. June 2017. *UNWTO World Tourism Barometer and Statistical Annex.* Volume 15.

Table 4.24: **International Tourism Receipts**
($ million)

Regional Member	2000	2005	2010	2015	2016
Developing Member Economies					
Central and West Asia[a]	**679**	**1,526**	**3,639**	**7,540**	**8,201**
Afghanistan	...	...	86	82	49
Armenia	38	223	646	936	968
Azerbaijan	63	78	657	2,309	2,714
Georgia	97	241	659	1,936	2,166
Kazakhstan	356	701	1,005	1,534	1,549
Kyrgyz Republic	15	73	160	426	432
Pakistan	81	182	305	317	323
Tajikistan	2 (2002)	...	...	...	...
Turkmenistan	...	...	...	...	...
Uzbekistan	27	28	121	...	...
East Asia	**32,707**	**50,550**	**87,307**	**110,966**	**108,201**
China, People's Rep. of	16,231	29,296	45,814 |	44,969	44,432
Hong Kong, China	5,868	10,294	22,200	36,150	32,860
Korea, Rep. of	6,834	5,806	10,328	15,214	17,210
Mongolia	36	177	244	246	316
Taipei,China	3,738	4,977	8,721	14,387	13,383
South Asia	**4,247**	**8,974**	**17,249**	**27,288**	**29,386**
Bangladesh	50	75	87	150	175
Bhutan	10	19	40	94	90
India	3,460	7,493	14,490	21,013	22,427
Maldives	321	826	1,713	2,569	2,730
Nepal	158	132	343	481	446
Sri Lanka	248	429	576	2,981	3,518
Southeast Asia[a]	**25,502**	**34,986**	**68,423**	**108,502**	**116,453**
Brunei Darussalam	155 (2001)	191	...	140	...
Cambodia	304	840	1,519	3,130	3,207
Indonesia	4,975	4,522	6,958	10,761	11,349
Lao PDR	114	147	382	679	...
Malaysia	5,011	8,847	18,115	17,584	18,074
Myanmar	162	67	72	2,101	2,177
Philippines	2,156	2,287	2,645	5,272	5,139
Singapore	5,142	6,209	14,178	16,563	18,386
Thailand	7,483	9,576	20,104	44,922	49,871
Viet Nam	...	2,300	4,450	7,350	8,250
The Pacific[a]	**416**	**859**	**1,296**	**1,574**	**1,028**
Cook Islands	36	91	111	175 (2014)	...
Fiji	189	485	634	744	765
Kiribati	3	4	4	3 (2014)	...
Marshall Islands	3	3	4	5 (2014)	...
Micronesia, Fed. States of	17	16	24	25 (2014)	...
Nauru	...	...	...	...	...
Palau	53	60	73	149	...
Papua New Guinea	7	4	2	2	1
Samoa	41	73	123	141	151
Solomon Islands	4	2	44	51	53
Timor-Leste	...	20 (2006)	31	51	58
Tonga	7	15	27	...	...
Tuvalu	...	1	2	...	...
Vanuatu	56	85	217	228	...
Developed Member Economies	**14,934**	**29,851**	**48,319**	**62,905**	**72,739**
Australia	9,289	16,748	28,598	28,872	32,423
Japan	3,373	6,630	13,199	24,983	30,678
New Zealand	2,272	6,473	6,522	9,050	9,638
DEVELOPING MEMBER ECONOMIES[a]	**63,550**	**96,895**	**177,914**	**255,870**	**263,269**
REGIONAL MEMBERS[a]	**78,484**	**126,746**	**226,233**	**318,775**	**336,008**

... = data not available at cutoff date, | = marks break in series, Lao PDR = Lao People's Democratic Republic.

a For reporting economies only. Regional aggregates include data for nearest years as reported in the table.

Source: World Tourism Organization. June 2017. *UNWTO World Tourism Barometer and Statistical Annex*. Volume 15.

V. Transport and Communications

Snapshot

- In 2013, occupants of four-wheeled vehicles comprised a plurality of traffic-related deaths in 15 of 35 regional economies for which data are available.
- Air carrier departures increased between 2000 and 2016 in 31 out of 39 economies in Asia and the Pacific for which data are available.
- The People's Republic of China and India together accounted for nearly one-third of the world's mobile phone subscriptions in 2015.
- While the People's Republic of China led the region in fixed broadband subscriptions in 2015 by a wide margin, the Republic of Korea; Hong Kong, China; and New Zealand had the highest subscription rates per 100 inhabitants.

Key Trends

In 2013, occupants of four-wheeled vehicles comprised a plurality of traffic-related deaths in 15 of 35 regional economies for which data are available. The highest percentages of occupants of four-wheeled vehicles as a share of total road-user deaths in 2013 were in Bhutan (94.9%), Turkmenistan (74.7%), and the Kyrgyz Republic (67.3%).

Occupants of two- and three-wheeled vehicles comprised a plurality of road deaths in 11 regional economies, with Thailand (72.8%), Cambodia (70.4%), and the Lao People's Democratic Republic (66.9%) reporting the highest percentages of such road deaths. Pedestrians comprised the highest share of total of road-user deaths in nine regional economies, led by Palau (100.0%), Samoa (76.5%), and Kiribati (66.7%).

By subregion, occupants of four-wheeled vehicles accounted for 62.0% of road-user deaths in Central and West Asia, 19.6% in East Asia, 19.3% in South Asia, 13.8% in Southeast Asia, 46.8% in the Pacific, and 38.9% in developed member economies. Occupants of two- and three-wheeled vehicles comprised 1.2% of road-user deaths in Central and West Asia, 26.6% in East Asia, 31.9% in South Asia, 49.0% in Southeast Asia, 0.4% in the Pacific, and 17.4% in developed member economies. Pedestrians accounted for 27.1% of road-user deaths in Central and West Asia, 26.4% in East Asia, 11.6% in South Asia, 16.6% in Southeast Asia, 32.0% in the Pacific, and 31.5% in developed member economies.

Air carrier departures increased between 2000 and 2016 in 29 out of 39 Asia and the Pacific economies for which data are available. With the exception of a 2-year dip in 2002–2003, global air carrier departures grew steadily between 2000 and 2016, rising an average of 5.5% per year to reach more than 34 million annually (WB 2017). In Asia and the Pacific, air carrier departures increased in 29 out of 39 economies between 2000 and 2016, or the most recent year for which data are available (Table 5.6). The largest average annual increases (Figure 5.2) during the review period were seen in Bangladesh (15.1%), Kazakhstan (14.8%), and Viet Nam (14.5%). The largest average annual declines during the review period were observed in Armenia (–11.9%), Fiji (–6.2%), and Turkmenistan (–3.2%).

Figure 5.1: Distribution of Road Deaths by Type of Vehicle, 2013

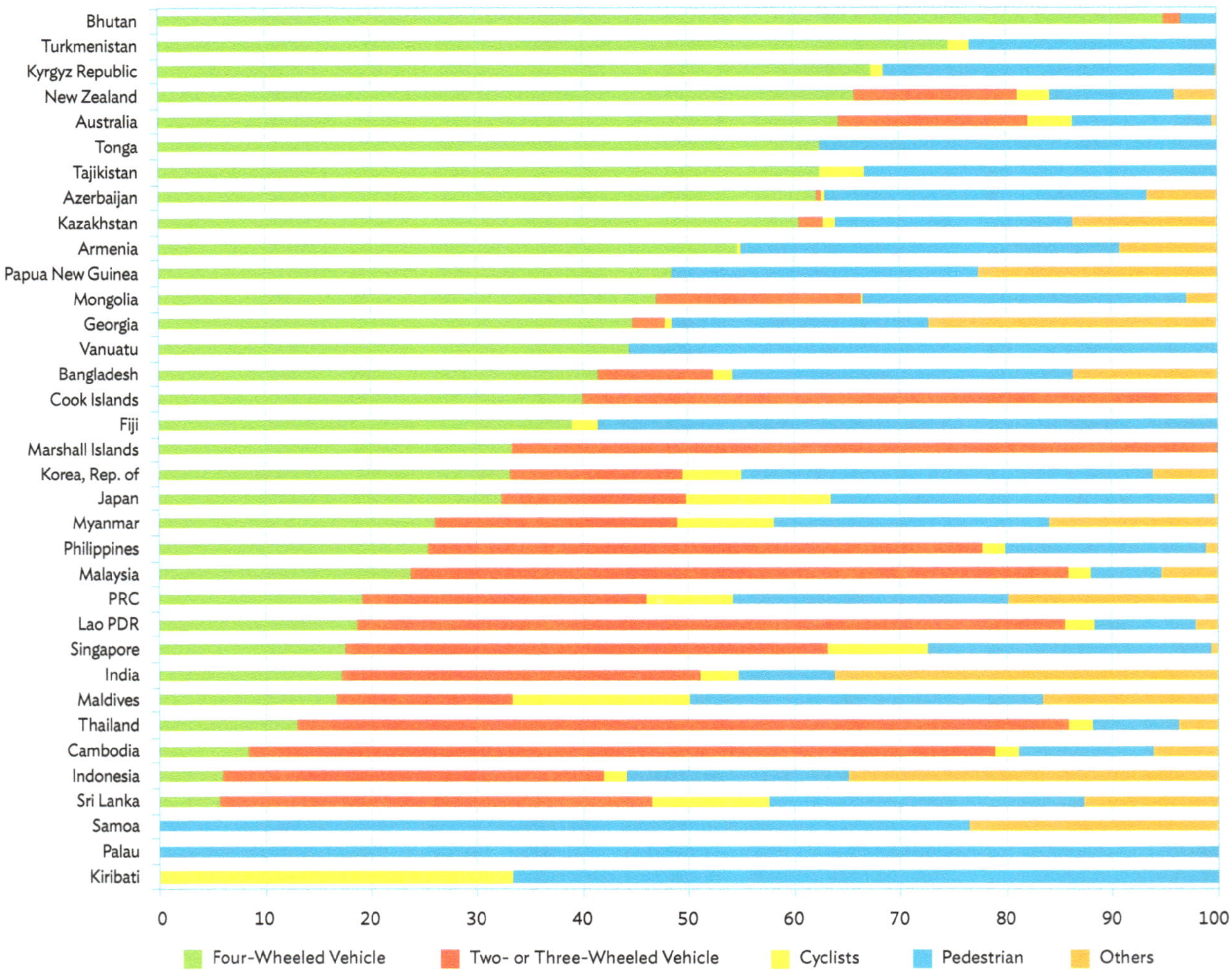

Lao PDR = Lao People's Democratic Republic, PRC = People's Republic of China.
Source: Table 5.3.

Figure 5.2: Annual Percentage Change in Air Carrier Departures
(%)

PRC = People's Republic of China.
Note: This chart includes economies with available data between 2000 and 2016.
Source: Table 5.6.

The PRC and India together account for nearly one-third of the world's mobile phone subscriptions. In 2016, the PRC (1.36 billion) and India (1.13 billion) led the world in terms of mobile cellular subscriptions (Table 5.8), together accounting for 33.2% of the global total (ITU 2017). However, the highest rates of subscription per 100 people were observed in Hong Kong, China (234); Maldives (223); and Thailand (173). The lowest rates (Figure 5.3) were found in Kiribati (51), Papua New Guinea (49), and the Federated States of Micronesia (22).

Asia and the Pacific led all regions of the globe with 4.106 billion mobile cellular subscriptions in 2016 (Table 5.8). Within the region, East Asia has the most mobile cellular subscriptions (1.48 billion), followed by South Asia (1.31 billion), Southeast Asia (861 billion), Central and West Asia (252 million), developed member economies (197 million), and the Pacific (7.15 million). However, East Asia's average of 98.9 mobile cellular subscriptions per 100 inhabitants exceeded only that of Central and West Asia (81.7), South Asia (86.9), and the Pacific (63.1), while it trailed the averages of the Southeast Asia (136) and the developed member economies.[4]

[4] The numbers are based on the weighted average using the figures provided in Tables 5.8 and 5.9.

Figure 5.3: Mobile Telephone Subscriptions per 100 Inhabitants, 2016

FSM = Federated States of Micronesia, Lao PDR = Lao People's Democratic Republic, PRC = People's Republic of China.
Source: Table 5.9.

While the PRC led the region in fixed broadband subscriptions in 2016 by a wide margin, the Republic of Korea; Hong Kong, China; and New Zealand had the highest subscription rates per 100 inhabitants. The number of fixed broadband subscriptions in the PRC in 2016 exceeded 323 million, more than twice as many as total fixed broadband subscriptions in the rest of Asia and the Pacific combined (Table 5.8). The list of other economies with high fixed broadband subscriptions also includes Japan (39.8 million), the Republic of Korea (20.6 million), and India (18.7 million). On the basis of fixed broadband subscriptions per 100 inhabitants (Figure 5.4), the highest rates in 2016 were observed in the Republic of Korea (41.1); Hong Kong, China (35.5); and New Zealand (32.4). The fewest number of subscriptions per 100 inhabitants were seen in Tajikistan (0.07), Myanmar (0.06), and Afghanistan (0.03).

Figure 5.4: Fixed Broadband Subscriptions per 100 Inhabitants, 2016

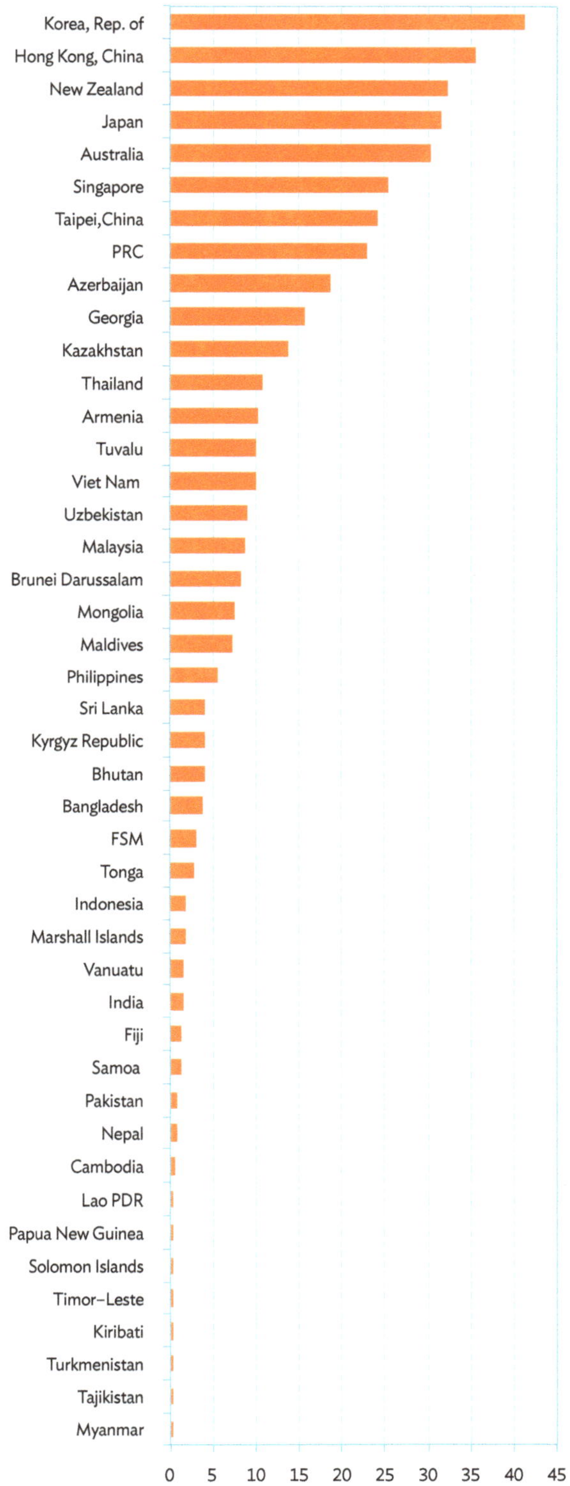

FSM = Federated States of Micronesia, Lao PDR = Lao People's Democratic Republic, PRC = People's Republic of China.
Source: Table 5.9.

Data Issues and Comparability

Recent and complete data for all types of road indicators are scarce. Some subregions, especially the Pacific, have incomplete or no data. In addition, the definition of road traffic fatalities varies across economies. Some economies report deaths caused by road accidents if the person died within 24 hours; some are within 30 days; some are within a year or more. Data are usually reported by the police authorities and hospitals and later compiled by the relevant government agencies. The issues with data organization, collection, compilation, and dissemination pose a continuing challenge and affect the availability, quality, and timeliness of statistics.

Most data on telephone and internet subscriptions come from questionnaires the International Telecommunication Union sends to participating economies. ADB other information and reports are sourced from the ministries in charge of telecommunications, and staff estimates.

Table 5.1: Road Indicators—Network[a]
(kilometers)

Regional Member	Primary		Class I		Class II		Class III		Below III		Other		Total[b]	
	2004	2015	2004	2015	2004	2015	2004	2015	2004	2015	2004	2015	2004	2015
Developing Member Economies														
Central and West Asia														
Afghanistan	...	...	...	10	621	2,549	77	...	3,549	1,461	...	...	4,247	4,020
Armenia	...	...	142	147	377	721	479	58	...	40	...	...	998	966
Azerbaijan	...	...	82	291	1,012	1,174	348	...	...	...	228	...	1,670	1,465
Georgia	...	...	8	64	788	877	358	160	...	...	...	...	1,154	1,101
Kazakhstan	...	...	72	557	767	5,407	10,004	6,389	2,346	475	...	...	13,189	12,828
Kyrgyz Republic	...	...	...	...	464	303	511	1,324	720	136	...	...	1,695	1,763
Pakistan	358	357	1,116	1,116	160	275	2,569	2,442	1,174	1,138	...	...	5,377	5,328
Tajikistan	...	...	...	20	289	978	603	...	1,033	914	...	...	1,925	1,912
Turkmenistan	...	...	...	60	...	...	2,180	2,120	24	24	...	...	2,204	2,204
Uzbekistan	...	...	255	1,195	765	1,101	1,618	670	328	...	...	...	2,966	2,966
East Asia														
China, People's Rep. of[c]	4,140	8,437	189	230	2,749	1,855	2,008	321	1,443	5	15,400	...	25,929	10,847
Hong Kong, China	...	...	...	...	...	...	...	...	...	...	...	...	...	...
Korea, Rep. of	466	457	197	423	244	40	...	...	...	...	...	...	907	920
Mongolia	...	...	...	8	440	1,702	345	158	3,501	2,450	...	...	4,286	4,318
Taipei,China	...	...	...	...	...	...	...	...	...	...	...	...	...	...
South Asia														
Bangladesh	...	...	20	311	441	1,400	476	44	868	5	...	...	1,805	1,760
Bhutan	...	...	...	7	6	116	...	...	161	47	...	...	167	170
India	...	90	484	7,067	...	1,071	10,869	3,556	105	117	...	160	11,458	11,901
Maldives	...	...	...	...	...	...	...	...	...	...	...	...	...	...
Nepal	...	...	...	...	311	218	1,003	1,082	12	13	...	...	1,326	1,313
Sri Lanka	...	...	...	60	269	519	190	71	191	...	...	...	650	650
Southeast Asia														
Brunei Darussalam	...	...	...	...	...	...	...	...	...	...	...	...	...	...
Cambodia	...	...	...	...	398	610	743	1,346	199	...	...	...	1,340	1,956
Indonesia	335	409	18	603	1,600	3,045	1,965	...	...	...	34	34	3,952	4,091
Lao PDR	...	...	...	...	...	244	2,375	2,307	...	306	3	...	2,378	2,857
Malaysia	795	795	67	61	733	817	...	...	...	...	...	...	1,595	1,673
Myanmar	...	...	147	320	144	575	983	1,702	1,729	1,928	...	...	3,003	4,525
Philippines	...	...	17	380	27	2,310	2,872	691	451	451	150	...	3,517	3,381
Singapore	11	13	8	6	...	...	...	...	...	...	...	...	19	19
Thailand	182	617	2,572	4,123	1,226	598	1,128	202	...	2	4	...	5,112	5,540
Viet Nam	...	...	408	968	1,915	1,872	104	282	251	76	...	...	2,678	3,121
The Pacific														
Cook Islands	...	...	...	...	...	...	...	...	...	...	...	...	...	...
Fiji	...	...	...	...	...	...	...	...	...	...	...	...	...	...
Kiribati	...	...	...	...	...	...	...	...	...	...	...	...	...	...
Marshall Islands	...	...	...	...	...	...	...	...	...	...	...	...	...	...
Micronesia, Fed. States of	...	...	...	...	...	...	...	...	...	...	...	...	...	...
Nauru	...	...	...	...	...	...	...	...	...	...	...	...	...	...
Palau	...	...	...	...	...	...	...	...	...	...	...	...	...	...
Papua New Guinea	...	...	...	...	...	...	...	...	...	...	...	...	...	...
Samoa	...	...	...	...	...	...	...	...	...	...	...	...	...	...
Solomon Islands	...	...	...	...	...	...	...	...	...	...	...	...	...	...
Timor-Leste	...	...	...	...	...	...	...	...	...	...	...	...	...	...
Tonga	...	...	...	...	...	...	...	...	...	...	...	...	...	...
Tuvalu	...	...	...	...	...	...	...	...	...	...	...	...	...	...
Vanuatu	...	...	...	...	...	...	...	...	...	...	...	...	...	...
Developed Member Economies														
Australia	...	...	...	...	...	...	...	...	...	...	...	...	...	...
Japan	1,111	1,138	...	...	...	...	...	...	...	...	...	...	1,111	1,138
New Zealand	...	...	...	...	...	...	...	...	...	...	...	...	...	...

... = data not available at cutoff date, Lao PDR = Lao People's Democratic Republic.

a The road network refers to the Asian Highway that consists of highway routes of international importance within Asia, including highway routes substantially crossing more than one subregion; highway routes within subregions that connected neighboring subregions; and highway routes located within member states that provide access to (i) capital cities; (ii) main industrial and agricultural centers; (iii) major air, sea, and river ports; (iv) major container terminals and depots; and (v) major tourist attractions. "Primary" class in the classification is access-controlled motorways. Access-controlled motorways are used exclusively by automobiles. Motorcycles, bicycles, and pedestrians will not be allowed to enter the motorway to ensure traffic safety and the high running speed of automobiles.
Class I refers to asphalt, cement, or concrete roads with four or more lanes.
Class II refers to double bituminous treated roads with two lanes.
Class III is regarded as the minimum desirable standard usually described as a two-lane (narrow) road.
Roads classified below class III are road sections below the minimum desirable standard.

b Sum of reported available data.

c Initial and latest year estimates may not be comparable. Estimates for 2015 do not include approximately 15,400 kilometers of potential Asian Highway routes based on the electronic files provided by the United Nations Economic and Social Commission for Asia and the Pacific Statistics Division on 30 June 2017.

Source: United Nations Economic and Social Commission for Asia and the Pacific. ESCAP Online Statistical Database. http://data.unescap.org/escap_stat/ (accessed 26 June 2017).

Table 5.2: **Road Indicators—Vehicles**

Regional Member	Number of Registered Vehicles in 2013						
	Total		By Type[a]				
	(thousand)	(per 1,000 people)[b]	Cars and Four-Wheeled	Two- or Three-Wheeled	Heavy Trucks	Buses	Others
Developing Member Economies							
Central and West Asia							
Afghanistan	655,357	23.8	407,608	68,090	81,416	20,589	77,654
Armenia	300,091 (2010)	92.3	247,723	28	40,924	11,396	20
Azerbaijan	1,135,936 (2012)	122.3	958,594	2,067	130,019	29,647	15,609
Georgia	951,649	212.2	774,453	4,830	151,057	21,309	–
Kazakhstan	3,926,487	230.5	3,190,057	74,762	398,753	94,417	168,498
Kyrgyz Republic	958,187	169.2	777,847	21,696	114,853	34,561	9,230
Pakistan	9,080,437 (2011)	51.3	3,095,900	5,560,218	223,152	201,167	–
Tajikistan	411,548	50.4	353,919	4,925	36,942	15,762	–
Turkmenistan	847,874 (2014)	159.7	676,622	37,275	114,004	19,973	–
Uzbekistan	...	...	...	...	...	...	...
East Asia							
China, People's Rep. of[c]	250,138,212	183.8	137,406,846	95,326,138	5,069,292	...	12,335,936
Hong Kong, China	...	...	...	...	...	...	...
Korea, Rep. of	23,150,619	461.0	15,078,354	2,117,035	970,805	4,984,425	–
Mongolia	675,064	232.9	491,771	25,771	151,530	5,992	–
Taipei,China[d]	21,400,863 (2015)	911.0	6,573,746	13,661,719	1,069,434	33,890	62,074
South Asia		...					
Bangladesh	2,088,566 (2014)	13.4	547,423	1,336,339	141,850	59,500	3,454
Bhutan	68,173 (2014)	91.5	46,575	9,758	9,397	475	1,968
India	159,490,578 (2012)	129.1	38,338,015	115,419,175	4,056,885	1,676,503	–
Maldives	61,412	141.3	10,256	50,775	145	140	96
Nepal	1,178,911 (2011)	44.3	133,992	891,018	47,930	35,100	70,871
Sri Lanka	5,203,678	252.9	832,840	3,566,184	329,648	93,428	381,578
Southeast Asia							
Brunei Darussalam	349,279 (2010)	903.0	...	...	...	...	...
Cambodia	2,457,569	164.9	67,645	2,068,937	45,625	4,473	270,889
Indonesia	104,211,132	418.8	10,838,592	86,253,257	5,156,362	1,962,921	–
Lao PDR	1,439,481	215.5	276,493	1,120,673	38,454	3,861	–
Malaysia	23,819,256	796.1	10,689,450	11,087,878	1,116,167	62,784	862,977
Myanmar	4,310,112 (2014)	83.7	386,049	3,712,220	127,947	22,253	61,643
Philippines	7,690,038	79.0	3,009,116	4,250,667	358,445	31,665	40,145
Singapore	974,170	180.4	763,008	144,934	48,719	17,065	444
Thailand	32,476,977 (2012)	488.4	11,829,221	19,169,418	901,014	137,609	439,715
Viet Nam	40,790,841	454.7	798,592	38,643,091	696,316	111,030	541,812
The Pacific							
Cook Islands	12,453	669.5	5,085	6,846	491	31	–
Fiji	86,535	100.4	...	...	...	...	...
Kiribati	3,452	31.4	1,926	701	536	289	–
Marshall Islands	2,116	39.5	1,917	52	26	63	58
Micronesia, Fed. States of	8,337 (2010)	81.1	7,356	96	747	138	–
Nauru	...	...	...	...	...	...	...
Palau	7,102	405.1	...	...	...	...	...
Papua New Guinea	94,297 (2014)	12.4	61,255	1,155	21,075	10,812	–
Samoa	17,449	91.5	16,243	97	873	236	–
Solomon Islands	45,000	79.5	...	...	...	...	...
Timor-Leste[e]	63,553	53.9	14,621	48,143	651	138	–
Tonga	8,154	78.8	6,039	184	1,882	49	–
Tuvalu	...	...	...	...	...	...	...
Vanuatu	14,000	52.9	...	...	...	...	...
Developed Member Economies							
Australia	17,180,596	742.9	15,871,827	744,732	416,902	93,034	54,101
Japan	91,377,312	717.6	76,137,715	11,948,432	...	...	3,291,072
New Zealand	3,250,066 (2012)	737.3	2,643,624	114,930	112,856	8,286	370,370

... = data not available at cutoff date, – = magnitude equals zero, Lao PDR = Lao People's Democratic Republic.

a Figures refer to the same year indicated in the column for "Total" unless otherwise specified.
b Computed by dividing the total number of registered vehicles by the midyear population in thousands.
c Computation per 1,000 people used end-year population data instead of midyear data.
d Combination of trucks and wagons in the category "Heavy Trucks."
e There is no renewal process for vehicles in Timor-Leste; hence, 2013 data refer to the total number of vehicles from 2006 to 2013.

Sources: All economies use World Health Organization. 2015. *Global Status Report on Road Safety 2015*. Geneva, except for Armenia and Brunei Darussalam, which use the *Global Status Report on Road Safety 2013*; Asian Development Bank estimates; for Taipei,China: Directorate-General of Budget, Accounting and Statistics. 2016. *Statistical Yearbook 2015*. Nantou City.

Table 5.3: **Road Indicators—Safety**

Regional Member	Estimated Road Traffic Deaths in 2013		Road Users Deaths in 2013 (%)				
	Total	Death Rate (per 100,000 population)	Four-Wheeled Vehicle	Two- or Three-Wheeled Vehicle	Cyclists	Pedestrian	Others
Developing Member Economies							
Central and West Asia							
Afghanistan	4,734	16	...	...	...	...	...
Armenia	546	18	54.7	–	0.3	35.8	9.2
Azerbaijan	943	10	62.1	0.5	0.3	30.5	6.7
Georgia	514	12	44.7	3.1	0.6	24.3	27.2
Kazakhstan	3,983	24	60.5	2.3	1.1	22.5	13.5
Kyrgyz Republic	1,220	22	67.3	–	1.1	31.6	0.1
Pakistan	25,781	14	...	...	...	...	...
Tajikistan	1,543	19	62.5	–	4.2	33.3	–
Turkmenistan	914	17	74.7	–	1.9	23.4	–
Uzbekistan	3,240	11	...	...	...	...	...
East Asia							
China, People's Rep. of	261,367	19	19.2	26.8	8.1	26.1	19.8
Hong Kong, China	...	...	...	...	...	...	...
Korea, Rep. of	5,931	12	33.2	16.3	5.5	38.9	6.1
Mongolia	597	21	47.0	19.3	0.2	30.6	2.9
Taipei,China	...	...	...	...	...	...	...
South Asia							
Bangladesh	21,316	14	41.5	10.8	1.8	32.2	13.7
Bhutan	114	15	94.9	1.7	–	3.4	–
India	207,551	17	17.2	33.9	3.5	9.1	36.2
Maldives	12	4	16.7	16.7	16.7	33.3	16.7
Nepal	4,713	17	...	...	...	...	...
Sri Lanka	3,691	17	5.7	40.8	11.0	29.8	12.7
Southeast Asia							
Brunei Darussalam	...	...	...	...	...	...	...
Cambodia	2,635	17	8.5	70.4	2.3	12.7	6.1
Indonesia	38,279	15	6.0	36.0	2.0	21.0	35.0
Lao PDR	971	14	18.7	66.9	2.7	9.6	2.1
Malaysia	7,129	24	23.7	62.1	2.2	6.6	5.5
Myanmar	10,809	20	26.0	23.0	9.0	26.0	16.0
Philippines	10,379	11	25.3	52.5	2.0	19.0	1.1
Singapore	197	4	17.5	45.6	9.4	26.9	0.6
Thailand	24,237	36	13.0	72.8	2.3	8.1	3.8
Viet Nam	22,419	25	...	...	...	...	...
The Pacific							
Cook Islands	5	24	40.0	60.0	–	–	–
Fiji	51	6	39.0	–	2.4	58.5	–
Kiribati	3	3	–	–	33.3	66.7	–
Marshall Islands	3	6	33.3	66.7	–	–	–
Micronesia, Fed. States of	2	2	...	...	...	...	...
Nauru	...	...	...	...	...	...	...
Palau	1	5	–	–	–	100.0	–
Papua New Guinea	1,232	17	48.4	–	–	29.0	22.6
Samoa	30	16	–	–	–	76.5	23.5
Solomon Islands	108	19	...	...	...	...	...
Timor-Leste	188	17	...	...	...	...	...
Tonga	8	8	62.5	–	–	37.5	–
Tuvalu	...	...	...	...	...	...	...
Vanuatu	42	17	44.4	–	–	55.6	–
Developed Member Economies							
Australia	1,252	5	64.2	17.9	4.2	13.2	0.6
Japan	5,971	5	32.4	17.4	13.7	36.2	0.3
New Zealand	272	6	65.7	15.4	3.1	11.8	3.9

... = data not available at cutoff date, – = magnitude equals zero, Lao PDR = Lao People's Democratic Republic.

Source: World Health Organization. 2015. *Global Status Report on Road Safety 2015*. Geneva.

Table 5.4: **Rail Indicators**

Regional Member	Rail Lines (total route, kilometers)				Rail Network, Length per Land Area (kilometers per thousand square kilometers)			
	2000	2005	2010	2015	2000	2005	2010	2015
Developing Member Economies								
Central and West Asia								
Afghanistan	...	...	...	...	...	...	...	...
Armenia	842.0	732.0	826.0	703.2	29.6	25.7	29.0	24.7
Azerbaijan	2,116.0	2,122.0	2,079.0	2,067.8	25.6	25.7	25.2	25.0
Georgia	1,562.0	1,513.0 (2007)	1,566.0	1,491.0	22.5	21.8 (2007)	22.5	21.5
Kazakhstan	13,545.0	14,204.0	14,202.0	14,767.1	5.0	5.3	5.3	5.5
Kyrgyz Republic	...	417.0 (2007)	417.0	417.0 (2014)	...	2.2 (2007)	2.2	2.2 (2014)
Pakistan	7,791.0	7,791.0	7,791.0	9,255.0	10.1	10.1	10.1	12.0
Tajikistan	...	616.0	621.0	621.0 (2014)	...	4.4	4.4	4.5 (2014)
Turkmenistan	...	2,529.0	3,115.0	3,115.0 (2014)	...	5.4	6.6	6.6 (2014)
Uzbekistan	3,645.0	4,014.0	4,227.0	4,192.0 (2014)	8.6	9.4	9.9	9.9 (2014)
East Asia								
China, People's Rep. of	58,656.0	62,200.0	66,239.0	67,212.0	6.2	6.6	7.1	7.2
Hong Kong, China	...	...	...	...	...	...	...	...
Korea, Rep. of	3,123.0	3,392.0	3,379.0	3,909.2	32.4	35.0	34.8	40.1
Mongolia	1,810.0	1,810.0	1,814.0	1,810.0	1.2	1.2	1.2	1.2
Taipei,China	1,190.0	1,336.0	1,743.0	1,771.0	80.0	87.0	109.0	111.0 (2014)
South Asia								
Bangladesh	2,768.0	2,855.0	2,835.0	2,835.0 (2014)	21.3	21.9	21.8	21.8 (2014)
Bhutan	...	...	...	...	...	...	...	...
India	62,759.0	63,465.0	63,974.0	66,030.0	21.1	21.3	21.5	22.2
Maldives	...	...	...	...	...	...	...	...
Nepal	...	...	...	...	...	...	...	...
Sri Lanka	...	1,449.0 (2004)	1,463.0 (2008)	...	...	23.1 (2004)	23.3 (2008)	...
Southeast Asia								
Brunei Darussalam	...	...	...	...	...	...	...	...
Cambodia	601.0	650.0	...	...	3.4	3.7	...	...
Indonesia	...	...	4,684.0 (2012)	4,684.0 (2014)	...	...	2.6 (2012)	2.6 (2014)
Lao PDR	...	...	...	...	...	...	...	...
Malaysia	1,622.0	1,657.0	1,665.0	2,250.0 (2014)	4.9	5.0	5.1	6.8 (2014)
Myanmar	...	...	...	...	...	...	...	...
Philippines	491.0	491.0 (2004)	479.0 (2008)	...	1.6	1.6 (2004)	1.6 (2008)	...
Singapore	...	...	...	...	...	...	...	...
Thailand	4,103.0	4,044.0 (2004)	4,429.0	5,327.0 (2014)	8.0	7.9 (2004)	8.7	10.4 (2014)
Viet Nam	2,545.0 (2002)	2,671.0	2,347.0	3,186.0	8.2 (2002)	8.6	7.6	10.3
The Pacific								
Cook Islands	...	...	...	...	...	...	...	...
Fiji	...	...	...	...	...	...	...	...
Kiribati	...	...	...	...	...	...	...	...
Marshall Islands	...	...	...	...	...	...	...	...
Micronesia, Fed. States of	...	...	...	...	...	...	...	...
Nauru	...	...	...	...	...	...	...	...
Palau	...	...	...	...	...	...	...	...
Papua New Guinea	...	...	...	...	...	...	...	...
Samoa	...	...	...	...	...	...	...	...
Solomon Islands	...	...	...	...	...	...	...	...
Timor-Leste	...	...	...	...	...	...	...	...
Tonga	...	...	...	...	...	...	...	...
Tuvalu	...	...	...	...	...	...	...	...
Vanuatu	...	...	...	...	...	...	...	...
Developed Member Economies								
Australia	9,499.0	9,528.0	9,674.0 (2009)	...	1.2	1.2	1.3 (2009)	...
Japan	20,165.0	20,096.0	20,035.0	16,704.4	55.3	55.1	55.0	45.8
New Zealand	...	...	...	...	...	...	...	...

... = data not available at cutoff date, Lao PDR = Lao People's Democratic Republic.

Sources: World Bank. World Development Indicators. http://data.worldbank.org/indicator (accessed 12 July 2017); Asian Development Bank estimates; for Taipei,China: National Development Council. 2016. *Statistical Data Book*. Taipei City.

Table 5.5: **Railways, Passengers Carried, and Goods Transported**

Regional Member	Passenger Carried (million passenger-kilometers)				Goods Transported (million ton-kilometers)			
	2000	2005	2010	2015	2000	2005	2010	2015
Developing Member Economies								
Central and West Asia								
Afghanistan	...	...	...	...	...	...	...	...
Armenia	47	30	50	44	354	654	346	640
Azerbaijan	493	789	917	495	5,770	10,374 (2007)	8,250	6,211
Georgia	453	720	655	465	3,912	6,127	6,228	4,261
Kazakhstan	10,215	12,129	15,448	17,085	124,983	171,855	213,174	189,759
Kyrgyz Republic	...	60 (2007)	99	75 (2014)	...	752 (2007)	738	922 (2014)
Pakistan	18,495	23,045	24,731	20,288	3,754	4,796	6,187	3,301
Tajikistan	...	50	33	24 (2014)	1,326	1,274 (2007)	808	554 (2014)
Turkmenistan	...	1,286	1,811	1,811 (2014)	...	8,670	11,992	11,992 (2014)
Uzbekistan	2,163	2,012	2,905	3,437 (2014)	15,441	18,007	22,282	22,686 (2014)
East Asia								
China, People's Rep. of	441,468	583,320	791,158	723,006	1,333,606	1,934,612	2,451,185	1,980,061
Hong Kong, China	...	...	...	...	...	...	...	...
Korea, Rep. of	28,097	31,004	33,027	23,450	10,803	10,108	9,452	9,479
Mongolia	1,070	1,228	1,220	997	4,293	8,361 (2007)	10,287	11,463
Taipei,China	12,624	12,255	20,931	27,111	1,179	982	873	636
South Asia								
Bangladesh	3,941	4,340	7,305	7,305 (2014)	777	896	710	710 (2014)
Bhutan	...	...	...	...	...	...	...	...
India	430,666	575,702	903,465	1,147,190	305,201	407,398	600,548	681,696
Maldives	...	...	...	...	...	...	...	...
Nepal	...	...	...	...	...	...	...	...
Sri Lanka	...	4,682	4,767 (2008)	...	88	138	135 (2008)	...
Southeast Asia								
Brunei Darussalam	...	...	...	...	...	...	...	...
Cambodia	45	45	...	...	92	92	...	...
Indonesia	...	25,535	20,283 (2012)	20,283 (2014)	...	4,698	7,166 (2012)	7,166 (2014)
Lao PDR	...	...	...	...	...	...	...	...
Malaysia	1,312	1,181	1,527	3,293 (2014)	907	1,178	1,384	3,071 (2014)
Myanmar	...	4,163 (2006)	...	...	...	885 (2006)	...	...
Philippines	171	83 (2006)	...	...	...	1 (2004)	...	...
Singapore	...	...	...	...	...	...	...	...
Thailand	9,935	9,195	8,037	7,504 (2014)	3,384	4,037	3,161	2,455 (2014)
Viet Nam	3,200	4,558	4,378	4,234	1,902	2,928	3,901	4,125
The Pacific								
Cook Islands	...	...	...	...	...	...	...	...
Fiji	...	...	...	...	...	...	...	...
Kiribati	...	...	...	...	...	...	...	...
Marshall Islands	...	...	...	...	...	...	...	...
Micronesia, Fed. States of	...	...	...	...	...	...	...	...
Nauru	...	...	...	...	...	...	...	...
Palau	...	...	...	...	...	...	...	...
Papua New Guinea	...	...	...	...	...	...	...	...
Samoa	...	...	...	...	...	...	...	...
Solomon Islands	...	...	...	...	...	...	...	...
Timor-Leste	...	...	...	...	...	...	...	...
Tonga	...	...	...	...	...	...	...	...
Tuvalu	...	...	...	...	...	...	...	...
Vanuatu	...	...	...	...	...	...	...	...
Developed Member Economies								
Australia	1,265	1,290	1,500	...	34,050	46,164	64,172	59,649 (2014)
Japan	240,793	239,246	244,235	206,722	22,313	21,900	20,432	20,255 (2014)
New Zealand	...	...	...	...	4,078	...	...	...

... = data not available at cutoff date, Lao PDR = Lao People's Democratic Republic.

Sources: World Bank. World Development Indicators. http://data.worldbank.org/indicator (accessed 14 July 2017); for Taipei,China: Directorate-General of Budget, Accounting and Statistics. 2016. *Statistical Yearbook 2015*. Nantou City.

Table 5.6: Air Transport

Regional Member	Carrier Departure Worldwide (number of takeoffs)				Freight (million ton-kilometers)				Passenger Carried (thousand)			
	2000	2005	2010	2016	2000	2005	2010	2016	2000	2005	2010	2016
Developing Member Economies												
Central and West Asia												
Afghanistan	3,409	...	21,677	22,771	7.8	...	108.0	29.0	150	...	1,999	1,918
Armenia	4,406	5,939	8,761	852 (2013)	8.8	7.0	6.0	1.0 (2013)	298	556	705	45 (2013)
Azerbaijan	8,012	12,470	9,885	24,009	47.2	11.9	7.8	732.8	546	1,134	797	1,962
Georgia	1,906	4,673	2,803	3,200	2.0	2.8	0.9	0.2	118	249	164	220
Kazakhstan	8,041	17,302	33,483	73,188	11.8	15.8	42.4	38.9	461	1,160	3,098	5,008
Kyrgyz Republic	6,051	5,228	7,371	17,904	3.7	2.0	1.3	0.1	241	226	376	584
Pakistan	63,956	48,905	64,932	70,005	340.3	407.9	333.0	175.5	5,294	5,364	6,588	9,628
Tajikistan	3,953	6,987	5,710	6,472	2.0	3.7	1.0	1.5	168	479	617	1,038
Turkmenistan	21,858	14,094	3,221	12,890	11.9	10.1	6.2	6.0	1,284	1,654	301	1,318
Uzbekistan	30,075	22,183	22,924	21,486	79.6	71.6	153.7	112.3	1,745	1,639	2,114	2,384
East Asia												
China, People's Rep. of	572,921	1,349,269	2,377,789	3,952,098	3,900.1	7,579.4	17,193.9	21,304.6	61,892	136,722	266,293	487,960
Hong Kong, China	79,182	122,705	158,255	235,385	5,111.5	7,763.9	10,373.4	11,409.1	14,378	20,230	28,348	43,454
Korea, Rep. of	226,910	221,424	280,427	433,525	7,651.3	7,432.6	12,942.7	11,484.9	34,331	33,888	36,988	77,134
Mongolia	6,200	5,332	6,528	6,009	8.4	6.1	3.9	8.1	254	295	391	538
Taipei,China[a]	586,560	479,499	360,409	481,028 (2015)	1.3	1.8	2.3	2.2 (2015)	48,407	44,268	41,091	58,156 (2015)
South Asia												
Bangladesh	6,313	7,399	19,300	59,728	193.9	183.5	164.4	54.0	1,331	1,634	1,819	3,816
Bhutan	1,138	2,467	3,053	6,065	–	0.3	0.4	0.7	34	49	182	224
India	198,426	330,484	623,197	917,625	547.7	774.0	1,631.0	1,893.9	17,299	27,879	64,374	119,578
Maldives	5,970	4,520	26,849	33,006	13.2	0.0	...	6.9	315	82	1,025	1,410
Nepal	12,130	6,255	45,990	24,063	17.0	6.9	6.5	4.9	643	480	918	634
Sri Lanka	5,206	19,712	20,921	40,711	255.7	310.4	339.0	403.1	1,756	2,818	3,008	5,285
Southeast Asia												
Brunei Darussalam	12,739	11,808	12,333	11,058	140.2	134.1	148.5	124.3	864	978	1,263	1,169
Cambodia	4,648	3,207	5,105	11,933	4.1	1.2	0.0	1.4	125	169	278	1,047
Indonesia	159,027	320,724	520,932	762,715	408.5	439.8	665.7	931.3	9,916	26,836	59,384	96,529
Lao PDR	6,411	9,002	11,374	9,985	1.7	2.5	0.1	1.5	211	293	444	1,220
Malaysia	169,263	176,152	302,185	447,000	1,863.8	2,577.6	2,564.7	1,149.9	16,561	20,369	34,239	53,817
Myanmar	10,329	26,460	20,485	60,627	0.8	2.7	2.1	5.1	438	1,504	924	2,598
Philippines	44,547	58,944	205,318	345,773	289.9	322.7	460.2	646.0	5,756	8,057	22,575	40,051
Singapore	71,042	77,119	131,722	188,576	6,004.9	7,571.3	7,121.4	6,423.2	16,704	17,744	24,860	34,969
Thailand	101,591	124,347	201,306	405,393	1,712.9	2,002.4	2,938.7	2,160.1	17,392	18,903	28,781	60,455
Viet Nam	28,999	54,415	109,176	252,441	117.3	230.2	426.9	459.0	2,878	5,454	14,378	37,937
The Pacific												
Cook Islands	...	...	...	...	...	...	...	...	...	...	...	...
Fiji	57,776	41,886	26,127	20,906	90.8	92.1	77.1	87.0	586	871	1,259	1,403
Kiribati	...	...	...	...	...	...	...	...	...	...	...	...
Marshall Islands	2,324	3,083	...	...	0.2	0.3	...	...	16	26	...	...
Micronesia, Fed. States of	...	...	...	...	...	...	...	...	...	...	...	...
Nauru	...	...	...	...	...	...	...	...	...	...	...	...
Palau	...	...	...	...	...	...	...	...	...	...	...	...
Papua New Guinea	27,512	19,606	32,741	31,745	22.3	21.1	28.5	34.5	1,100	819	1,405	2,061
Samoa	10,877	11,439	9,144	13,805	2.2	1.8	0.0	0.0	164	267	77	116
Solomon Islands	11,481	12,318	7,388	13,711	1.0	0.8	2.5	3.6	75	91	143	373
Timor-Leste	...	...	...	...	...	...	...	...	...	...	...	...
Tonga	3,814	...	...	...	0.0	...	...	...	52	...	...	...
Tuvalu	...	...	...	...	...	...	...	...	...	...	...	...
Vanuatu	1,402	1,580	17,212	9,037	1.8	1.8	0.2	1.2	102	112	248	299
Developed Member Economies												
Australia	382,514	342,509	572,906	676,526	1,730.7	2,444.6	2,938.3	1,902.1	32,578	44,657	60,641	72,598
Japan	645,087	651,858	934,487	984,303	8,672.0	8,549.2	7,698.8	9,360.9	109,123	102,279	109,617	117,706
New Zealand	240,046	209,469	207,872	178,594	817.1	781.5	468.6	1,232.7	10,781	11,952	13,295	15,243

... = data not available at cutoff date, – = magnitude equals zero, 0.0 = magnitude is less than half of unit employed, Lao PDR = Lao People's Democratic Republic.

a Carried departure worldwide is based on the number of aircraft movements both domestic and international; freight is based on million ton.

Sources: World Bank. World Development Indicators. http://databank.worldbank.org/data/reports.aspx?source=world-development-indicators (accessed 17 July 2017); for Taipei,China: Directorate-General of Budget, Accounting and Statistics. 2016. *Statistical Yearbook 2015*. Nantou City.

Table 5.7: **Container Port Traffic**
(thousand teu)

Regional Member	2000	2005	2006	2007	2008	2009	2010	2011	2012	2013	2014
Developing Member Economies											
Central and West Asia											
Afghanistan	...	...	...	...	...	...	...	...	...	...	...
Armenia	...	...	...	...	...	...	...	...	...	...	...
Azerbaijan	...	...	...	...	...	...	...	...	...	...	...
Georgia	...	...	...	185	254	182	226	239	257	277	291
Kazakhstan	...	...	...	...	...	...	...	...	...	...	...
Kyrgyz Republic	...	...	...	...	...	...	...	...	...	...	...
Pakistan	...	1,686	1,777	1,936	1,938	2,058	2,149	2,193	2,375	2,485	2,597
Tajikistan	...	...	...	...	...	...	...	...	...	...	...
Turkmenistan	...	...	...	...	...	...	...	...	...	...	...
Uzbekistan	...	...	...	...	...	...	...	...	...	...	...
East Asia											
China, People's Rep. of	41,000	67,245	84,811	103,823	115,942	108,800	130,290	144,642	161,319	170,859	181,635
Hong Kong, China	...	22,602	23,539	23,998	24,494	21,040	23,699	24,384	23,117	22,352	22,300
Korea, Rep. of	9,030	15,113	15,514	17,086	17,418	15,700	18,543	20,834	21,610	22,588	23,797
Mongolia	...	...	...	...	...	...	...	...	...	...	...
Taipei,China	...	12,791	13,102	13,720	12,971	11,352	12,737	14,076	14,976	15,353	16,431
South Asia											
Bangladesh	456	809	902	978	1,091	1,182	1,356	1,432	1,436	1,500	1,655
Bhutan	...	...	...	...	...	...	...	...	...	...	...
India	2,451	4,982	6,141	7,398	7,672	8,014	9,753	10,285	10,279	10,883	11,656
Maldives	...	...	...	48	54	56	65	69	74	80	84
Nepal	...	...	...	...	...	...	...	...	...	...	...
Sri Lanka	1,733	2,455	3,079	3,687	3,687	3,464	4,000	4,263	4,321	4,306	4,908
Southeast Asia											
Brunei Darussalam	...	...	...	...	90	86	99	105	113	122	128
Cambodia	...	...	...	253	259	208	224	237	255	275	289
Indonesia	3,798	5,503	4,316	6,583	7,405	7,255	8,483	8,966	9,639	11,273	11,901
Lao PDR	...	...	...	...	...	...	...	...	...	...	...
Malaysia	4,642	12,198	13,419	14,829	16,094	15,923	18,267	20,139	20,873	21,169	22,719
Myanmar	...	...	...	170	180	164	190	201	216	233	245
Philippines	3,032	3,634	3,676	4,351	4,471	4,307	4,947	5,289	5,686	5,860	5,869
Singapore	17,100	23,192	24,792	28,768	30,891	26,593	29,179	30,728	32,499	33,516	34,832
Thailand	3,179	5,115	5,574	6,339	6,726	5,898	6,649	7,171	7,469	7,702	8,284
Viet Nam	1,190	2,537	3,000	4,009	4,394	4,937	5,984	6,930	7,548	9,137	9,531
The Pacific											
Cook Islands	...	...	...	...	...	...	...	...	...	...	...
Fiji	...	...	...	...	...	...	...	...	...	...	...
Kiribati	...	...	...	...	...	...	...	...	...	...	...
Marshall Islands	...	...	...	...	...	...	...	...	...	...	...
Micronesia, Fed. States of	...	...	...	...	...	...	...	...	...	...	...
Nauru	...	...	...	...	...	...	...	...	...	...	...
Palau	...	...	...	...	...	...	...	...	...	...	...
Papua New Guinea	...	...	...	282	255	262	295	314	337	364	382
Samoa	...	...	...	...	...	...	...	...	...	...	...
Solomon Islands	...	...	...	...	...	...	...	...	...	...	...
Timor-Leste	...	...	...	...	...	...	...	...	...	...	...
Tonga	...	...	...	...	...	...	...	...	...	...	...
Tuvalu	...	...	...	...	...	...	...	...	...	...	...
Vanuatu	...	...	...	...	...	...	...	...	...	...	...
Developed Member Economies											
Australia	3,543	5,191	5,742	6,290	6,102	6,200	6,668	7,012	7,155	7,313	7,524
Japan	13,100	17,055	18,470	19,165	18,944	16,286	18,098	19,422	20,115	20,486	20,744
New Zealand	1,067	1,603	1,807	2,312	2,318	2,325	2,463	2,517	2,867	3,093	3,251

... = data not available at cutoff date, teu = twenty-foot equivalent unit, Lao PDR = Lao People's Democratic Republic.

Sources: World Bank. World Development Indicators. http://data.worldbank.org/indicator (accessed 18 July 2017); for Taipei,China in 2005–2007: United Nations Conference on Trade and Development. 2008 and 2010. *Review of Maritime Transport*. New York; for 2008–2014: UNCTADstat. http://unctadstat.unctad.org/EN/Index.html (accessed 18 July 2017).

Table 5.8: **Access to Fixed Telephone, Mobile Phones, and Internet**
(thousand)

Regional Member	Fixed Telephone		Mobile Cellular		Fixed Broadband	
	2000	2016	2000	2016	2000	2016
Developing Member Economies						
Central and West Asia						
Afghanistan	29.0	114.2	25.0 (2002)	21,603.0	0.2 (2004)	8.8
Armenia	533.4	531.6	17.5	3,434.6	0.0 (2001)	303.0
Azerbaijan	801.2	1,700.2	420.4	10,316.0	1.0 (2002)	1,803.7
Georgia	508.8	831.3	194.7	5,532.7	0.4 (2001)	677.6
Kazakhstan	1,834.2	3,931.1	197.3	25,395.0	1.0 (2003)	2,316.3
Kyrgyz Republic	376.1	382.1	9.0	7,613.5	0.0 (2002)	236.2
Pakistan	3,053.5	3,067.9	306.5	136,489.0	14.6 (2005)	1,642.8
Tajikistan	218.5	468.0	1.2	9,400.0	0.0 (2003)	6.0
Turkmenistan	364.4	665.0	7.5	8,575.0	...	4.0
Uzbekistan	1,655.0	3,412.9	53.1	23,265.4	2.8 (2003)	2,746.4
East Asia						
China, People's Rep. of	144,829.0	206,624.0	85,260.0	1,364,934.0	22.7	322,597.0
Hong Kong, China	3,925.8	4,323.3	5,447.3	17,233.3	444.5	2,611.7
Korea, Rep. of	25,863.0	28,035.6	26,816.4	61,295.5	3,870.0	20,555.7
Mongolia	117.5	225.3	154.6	3,367.6	0.0 (2001)	226.1
Taipei,China	12,642.2	13,771.0	17,873.8	29,244.3	229.0	5,686.0
South Asia						
Bangladesh	491.3	772.4	279.0	126,391.3	43.7 (2007)	6,112.7
Bhutan	14.1	21.1	–	698.4	...	31.0
India	32,436.1	24,404.0	3,577.1	1,127,809.0	50.0 (2001)	18,733.5
Maldives	24.4	21.1	7.6	812.1	0.2 (2002)	26.3
Nepal	266.9	858.2	10.2	32,120.3	1.0 (2006)	224.2
Sri Lanka	767.4	2,479.8	430.2	25,797.2	0.3 (2001)	892.2
Southeast Asia						
Brunei Darussalam	80.5	74.2	95.0	523.5	1.9 (2001)	36.1
Cambodia	30.9	227.3	130.5	19,915.5	0.1 (2002)	96.7
Indonesia	6,662.6	10,372.9	3,669.3	385,573.4	4.0	4,897.9
Lao PDR	40.9	1,266.6	12.7	3,958.5	0.0 (2003)	24.4
Malaysia	4,628.0	4,510.2	5,121.7	43,912.6	4.0 (2001)	2,718.8
Myanmar	271.4	514.4	13.4	48,728.4	0.2 (2005)	30.2
Philippines	3,061.4	3,835.9	6,454.4	113,000.0	10.0 (2001)	5,649.4
Singapore	1,946.0	2,003.2	2,747.4	8,399.7	69.0	1,454.8
Thailand	5,591.1	4,706.0	3,056.0	116,606.0	1.6 (2001)	7,219.0
Viet Nam	2,542.7	5,598.0	788.6	120,600.2	1.1 (2002)	9,335.2
The Pacific						
Cook Islands	5.7	7.8	0.6	11.5	0.0	2.7
Fiji	86.4	74.2	55.1	927.8	7.0 (2005)	12.3
Kiribati	3.4	1.0	0.3	55.0	0.3 (2005)	0.1
Marshall Islands	4.0	2.4 (2014)	0.4	15.5 (2015)	...	1.0
Micronesia, Fed. States of	9.6	6.9	–	23.4	0.0 (2003)	3.2
Nauru	1.8	1.9 (2009)	1.2	9.9	...	1.0 (2010)
Palau	...	...	...	...	...	...
Papua New Guinea	64.8	154.0	8.6	3,782.0	...	17.0
Samoa	8.5	7.2	2.5	134.6	0.0 (2004)	2.4
Solomon Islands	7.7	7.4	1.2	416.6	0.2 (2004)	1.3
Timor-Leste	2.0 (2003)	2.7	20.1 (2003)	1,492.1	0.0 (2003)	1.0
Tonga	9.7	11.0	0.2	80.0	0.0 (2002)	3.0
Tuvalu	0.7	2.0	0.5 (2004)	7.6	0.1 (2004)	1.0
Vanuatu	6.6	4.3	0.4	192.2	0.0 (2003)	4.4
Developed Member Economies						
Australia	10,050.0	8,180.0	8,562.0	26,550.0	122.8 (2001)	7,374.0
Japan	61,957.1	64,024.9	66,784.4	164,265.1	854.7	39,842.1
New Zealand	1,831.0	1,820.0	1,542.0	5,800.0	4.7	1,503.6

... = data not available at cutoff date, 0.0 = magnitude is less than half of unit employed, – = magnitude equals zero, Lao PDR = Lao People's Democratic Republic.

Source: International Telecommunication Union. World Telecommunication/ICT Indicators Database. http://www.itu.int/en/ITU-D/Statistics/Pages/stat/default.aspx (accessed 17 July 2017).

Table 5.9: **Access to Fixed Telephone, Mobile Phones, and Internet**
(per 100 people)

Regional Member	Fixed Telephone				Mobile Cellular				Fixed Broadband				Internet Users[a]			
	2000	2005	2010	2016	2000	2005	2010	2016	2000	2005	2010	2016	2000	2005	2010	2016
Developing Member Economies																
Central and West Asia																
Afghanistan	0.1	...	0.1	0.3	–	4.8	36.0	66.0	...	0.0	0.0	0.0	...	1.2	4.0	10.6
Armenia	17.3	19.7	20.0	17.8	0.6	10.5	130.4	114.8	...	0.1	3.2	10.1	1.3	5.3	25.0	62.0
Azerbaijan	9.9	12.8	16.6	17.5	5.2	26.2	100.1	106.3	...	0.0	5.2	18.6	0.1	8.0	46.0	78.2
Georgia	10.7	12.7	25.3	19.4	4.1	26.2	90.6	129.1	...	0.1	4.2	15.8	0.5	6.1	26.9	50.0
Kazakhstan	12.6	18.0	25.5	23.2	1.4	35.8	121.9	150.0	...	0.0	5.5	13.7	0.7	3.0	31.6	76.8
Kyrgyz Republic	7.6	8.7	9.2	6.6	0.2	10.7	98.9	131.4	...	0.0	0.4	4.1	1.0	10.5	16.3	34.5
Pakistan	2.1	3.3	3.5	1.6	0.2	8.1	57.3	71.4	...	0.0	0.5	0.9	...	6.3	8.0	15.5
Tajikistan	3.5	4.1	4.8	5.3	0.0	3.9	77.9	106.7	...	...	0.1	0.1	0.0	0.3	11.6	20.5
Turkmenistan	8.1	8.4	10.3	12.2	0.2	2.2	63.4	157.7	...	...	0.0	0.1	0.1	1.0	3.0	18.0
Uzbekistan	6.7	6.9	6.8	11.3	0.2	2.8	75.5	77.3	...	0.0	0.4	9.1	0.5	3.3	15.9	46.8
East Asia																
China, People's Rep. of	11.3	26.6	21.6	14.7	6.7	29.8	63.2	96.9	0.0	2.8	9.3	22.9	1.8	8.5	34.3	53.2
Hong Kong, China	57.4	55.0	61.9	58.7	79.7	123.9	195.7	234.0	6.5	24.1	30.7	35.5	27.8	56.9	72.0	87.3
Korea, Rep. of	56.3	50.8	58.9	56.1	58.3	81.5	104.8	122.7	8.4	25.9	35.5	41.1	44.7	73.5	83.7	92.7
Mongolia	4.9	6.2	7.1	7.6	6.4	22.1	92.5	113.6	...	0.1	2.8	7.6	1.3	...	10.2	22.3
Taipei,China	57.6	63.7	70.8	58.7	81.5	97.5	119.9	124.6	1.0	19.1	22.9	24.2	28.1	58.0	71.5	79.7
South Asia																
Bangladesh	0.4	0.7	0.8	0.5	0.2	6.3	44.9	77.9	...	...	0.3	3.8	0.1	0.2	3.7	18.2
Bhutan	2.5	5.1	3.7	2.7	–	5.5	55.0	88.8	...	...	1.2	3.9	0.4	3.8	13.6	41.8
India	3.1	4.5	2.9	1.9	0.3	8.0	62.4	87.0	...	0.1	0.9	1.4	0.5	2.4	7.5	29.5
Maldives	9.0	10.9	8.7	5.8	2.8	68.4	151.8	223.0	...	1.1	4.8	7.2	2.2	6.9	26.5	59.1
Nepal	1.2	1.9	3.1	3.0	0.0	0.9	34.3	111.7	...	...	0.2	0.8	0.2	0.8	7.9	19.7
Sri Lanka	4.1	6.2	17.2	11.4	2.3	16.8	83.6	118.5	...	0.1	1.1	4.1	0.6	1.8	12.0	32.1
Southeast Asia																
Brunei Darussalam	24.3	22.8	19.9	17.1	28.6	63.3	108.6	120.7	...	2.2	5.4	8.3	9.0	36.5	53.0	75.0
Cambodia	0.3	0.2	2.5	1.4	1.1	8.0	56.7	124.9	...	0.0	0.2	0.6	0.0	0.3	1.3	25.6
Indonesia	3.2	6.0	17.0	4.0	1.8	20.9	87.8	149.1	0.0	0.0	0.9	1.9	0.9	3.6	10.9	25.4
Lao PDR	0.8	1.6	1.6	17.7	0.2	11.4	62.6	55.4	...	0.0	0.1	0.3	0.1	0.9	7.0	21.9
Malaysia	19.8	16.9	16.3	14.5	21.9	75.6	119.7	141.2	...	1.9	7.4	8.7	21.4	48.6	56.3	78.8
Myanmar	0.6	1.0	0.9	0.9	0.0	0.3	1.1	89.3	...	0.0	0.0	0.1	...	0.1	0.3	25.1
Philippines	3.9	3.9	3.6	3.7	8.3	40.5	89.0	109.2	...	0.1	...	5.5	2.0	5.4	25.0	55.5
Singapore	49.7	41.0	39.3	35.0	70.1	97.5	145.4	146.9	1.8	14.6	26.4	25.4	36.0	61.0	71.0	81.0
Thailand	9.0	10.7	10.3	7.0	4.9	46.5	108.0	172.6	...	0.8	4.9	10.7	3.7	15.0	22.4	47.5
Viet Nam	3.1	...	16.1	5.9	1.0	...	...	...	...	0.2	4.1	9.9	0.3	12.7	30.7	46.5
The Pacific																
Cook Islands	31.9	34.2	35.6	...	3.1	20.6	38.5	...	...	0.3	8.3	...	15.7	26.2	35.7	54.0
Fiji	10.6	13.7	15.1	8.3	6.8	24.9	81.1	103.3	...	0.9	2.7	1.4	1.5	8.5	20.0	46.5
Kiribati	4.1	4.6	8.6	0.9	0.4	0.7	10.8	51.3	...	0.4	0.9	0.1	1.8	4.0	9.1	13.7
Marshall Islands	7.7	...	...	...	0.9	1.3	...	...	...	...	...	1.9	1.5	3.9	7.0	29.8
Micronesia, Fed. States of	9.0	11.7	8.2	6.5	–	13.3	26.6	22.2	...	0.0	1.0	3.0	3.7	11.9	20.0	33.4
Nauru	17.9	17.8	–	...	11.9	...	61.8	97.3	...	...	9.5	...	...	...	...	...
Palau	...	...	...	...	...	...	...	...	...	...	...	...	...	...	...	...
Papua New Guinea	1.2	1.0	1.8	2.0	0.2	1.2	27.8	48.6	...	...	0.1	0.2	0.8	1.7	1.3	9.6
Samoa	4.9	10.8	4.3	3.7	1.4	13.3	48.4	69.2	...	0.0	0.1	1.2	0.6	3.4	7.0	29.4
Solomon Islands	1.9	1.6	1.6	1.2	0.3	1.3	21.9	69.9	...	0.1	0.5	0.2	0.5	0.8	5.0	11.0
Timor-Leste	...	0.2	0.3	0.2	...	3.3	43.8	125.0	...	0.0	0.0	0.1	...	0.1	3.0	25.2
Tonga	9.9	13.6	29.8	10.3	0.2	29.6	52.2	74.7	...	0.6	1.1	2.8	2.4	4.9	16.0	40.0
Tuvalu	7.0	9.2	12.2	20.1	–	13.4	16.3	76.4	...	1.5	2.4	10.1	5.2	...	25.0	46.0
Vanuatu	3.6	3.3	3.0	1.6	0.2	6.1	71.9	71.3	...	0.0	0.2	1.6	2.1	5.1	8.0	24.0
Developed Member Economies																
Australia	52.2	49.3	47.4	33.8	44.5	89.8	100.4	109.6	...	9.8	24.6	30.4	46.8	63.0	76.0	88.2
Japan	49.3	45.7	51.5	50.6	53.1	76.0	96.8	129.8	0.7	18.4	26.8	31.5	30.0	66.9	78.2	92.0
New Zealand	47.5	41.8	43.0	39.2	40.0	85.4	107.8	125.0	0.1	7.8	25.0	32.4	47.4	62.7	80.5	88.5

... = data not available at cutoff date, 0.0 = magnitude is less than half of unit employed, – = magnitude equals zero, Lao PDR = Lao People's Democratic Republic.

a The reference population differs across economies. For example, some economies refer to population of people aged 6 years and above, others use 7 years and above, or between 16 to 74 years. The details are provided in the documentation of the International Telecommunication Union.

Source: International Telecommunication Union. World Telecommunication/ICT Indicators Database. http://www.itu.int/en/ITU-D/Statistics/Pages/stat/default.aspx (accessed 17 July 2017).

VI. Energy and Electricity

Snapshot

- Asia and the Pacific accounted for nearly 44% of global energy use in 2014, more than twice as much as any other region.
- The region led the world by a wide margin in energy production in 2014, comprising 35.6% of the global total.
- Since 2000, per capita electricity consumption rose in 38 out of the 41 developing member economies for which data are available, and declined in all three developed members.
- Asia and the Pacific improved its energy efficiency more rapidly than the global average between 2000 and 2014.
- Coal remained the dominant source of electricity among six of the region's top 10 electricity producers in 2014.

Key Trends

Asia and the Pacific accounted for nearly 44% of global energy use in 2014, more than twice as much as any other region. The economies of Asia and the Pacific collectively accounted for 43.8% of total global energy use in 2014, surpassing all other regions by a wide margin (Figure 6.1). The region consuming the next largest amount of energy was Europe and Central Asia (19.7%), followed by North America (18.7%), West Asia and Africa (11.4%), and Latin America and the Caribbean (6.5%).

The region's global share of energy consumption is expected to increase in the decades ahead due to continued rapid gains in gross domestic product (GDP) per capita and increased use of energy-consuming goods (ADB 2013).

Figure 6.1: Energy Use by Global Region and by Economy in Asia and the Pacific, 2014
(kilotons of oil equivalent, %)

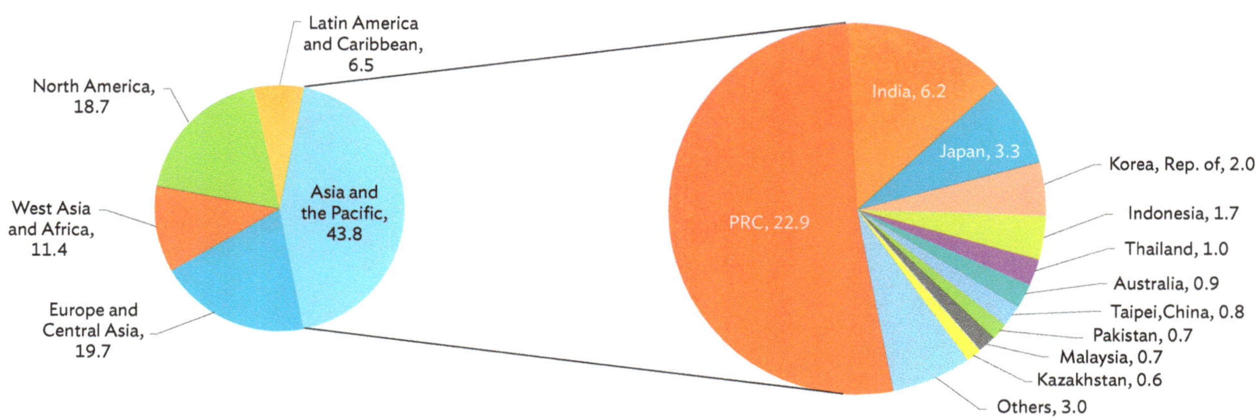

PRC = People's Republic of China.
Sources: Table 6.3 and International Energy Agency.

The People's Republic of China (PRC) accounted for most of the energy demand in Asia and the Pacific, comprising 52.3% of the regional total and 22.9% of the world total in 2014, up from 36.2% and 11.6%, respectively, in 2000. While energy consumption continues to rise in the PRC, energy intensity, which refers to the physical energy required to generate each unit of GDP, has fallen in the PRC by more than 37% since peaking in 2005 (ADB 2017).

The next largest regional consumers of energy in 2014 were India with a global share of 6.2%, up from 4.6% in 2000; and Japan with a global share of 3.3%, down from 5.3% in 2000.

The region led the world by a wide margin in energy production in 2014, comprising 35.6% of the global total. Relative to other regions, Asia and the Pacific's 35.6% share of global energy production in 2014 (Figure 6.2) was followed by West Asia and Africa (21.3%), North America (18.0%), Europe and Central Asia (17.6%), and Latin America and the Caribbean (7.5%). The PRC led all regional economies in production in 2014, accounting for more than half of the regional total and 18.8% of the global total. The next largest energy producers and their respective global shares in 2014 were India (3.9%), Indonesia (3.3%), and Australia (2.6%).

In 2000, Asia and the Pacific accounted for a 26.2% share of global energy production. The increase of more than 9 percentage points between 2000 and 2014 was led by the PRC, whose share of global energy production increased more than 7 percentage points from 11.2% in 2000. India (from 3.5% to 3.9%), Indonesia (from 2.4% to 3.3%), and Australia (from 2.3% to 2.6%) also experienced gains in their respective global energy production shares during the review period.

Since 2000, per capita electricity consumption rose in 38 out of the 42 developing member economies for which data are available, and declined in all three developed members. Figure 6.3 shows that between 2000 and 2014 (or between the earliest and latest years for which data are available), per capita electricity consumption increased on an average annual basis in all developing member economies except Uzbekistan (–0.5%), Solomon Islands (–0.8%), and Tajikistan (–2.6%). In addition, all three developed member economies

Figure 6.2: Energy Production by Global Region and by Economy in Asia and the Pacific, 2014
(kilotons of oil equivalent, %)

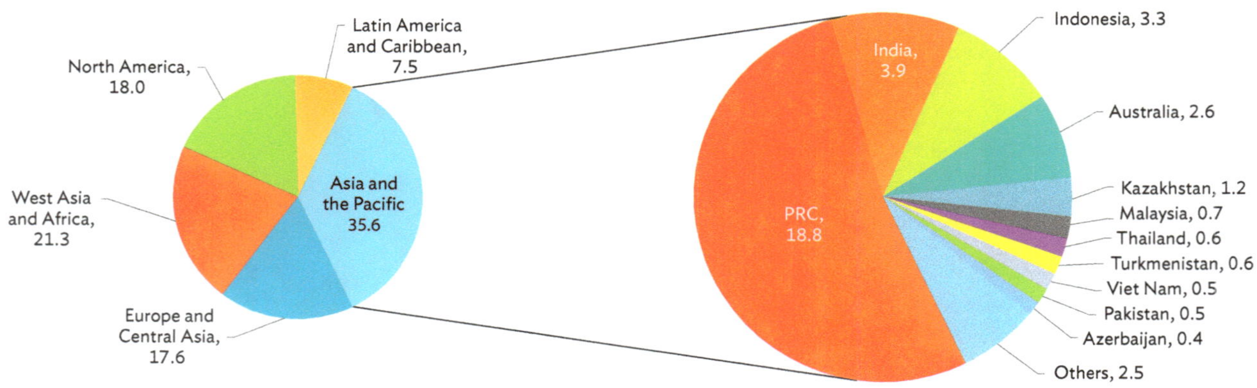

PRC = People's Republic of China.
Sources: Table 6.4 and International Energy Agency.

Figure 6.3: Per Capita Electric Power Consumption
(kWh)

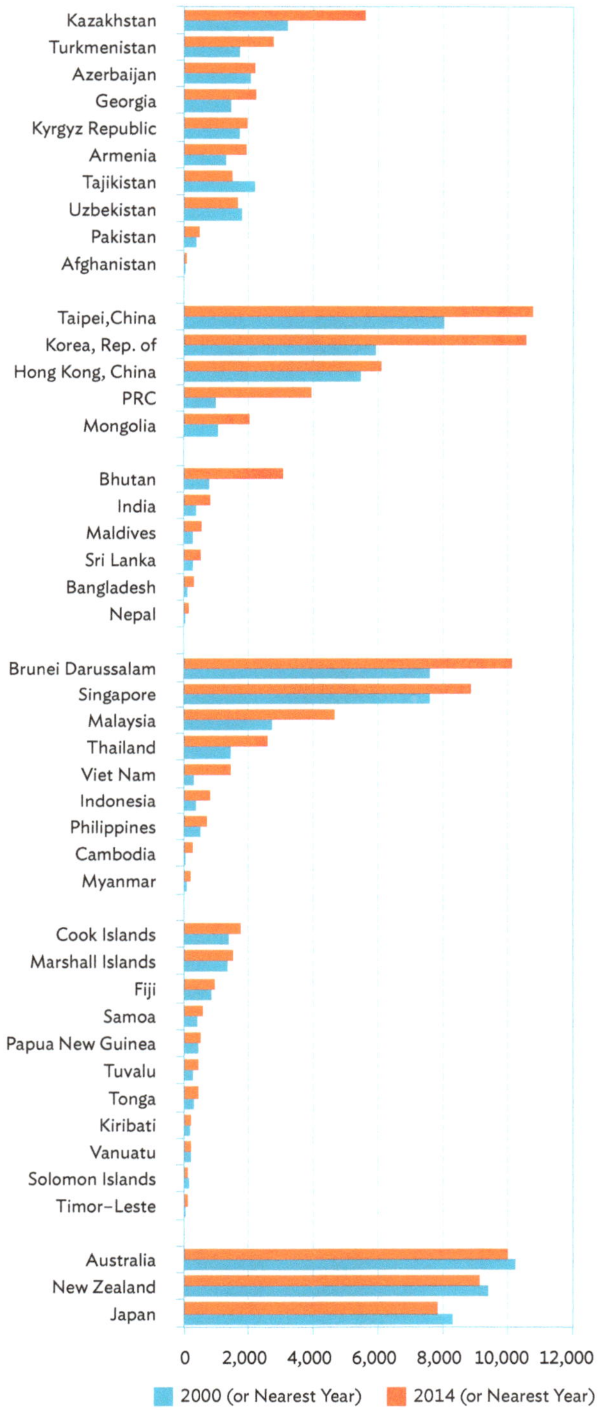

kWh = kilowatt-hour, PRC = People's Republic of China.
Notes: Earliest year: 2000 except for Afghanistan (2001) and Timor-Leste (2006). Latest year: 2016 for Afghanistan, the Cook Islands, Solomon Islands, and Vanuatu; 2015 for Bhutan, Fiji, Maldives, Samoa, and Timor-Leste; 2006 for the Marshall Islands; and 2014 for the rest of the economies.
Source: Table 6.2.

experienced average annual declines in per capita electricity consumption during the review period: Australia (–0.1%), New Zealand (–0.2%), and Japan (–0.4%). The largest average annual gains in per capita electricity consumption occurred in Cambodia (17.0%), Timor-Leste (18.9%), and Viet Nam (11.9%), although Cambodia's and Timor-Leste's per capita consumption continue to be low.

Table 6.2 shows that in 2014, the Asia and Pacific region's economies with the highest levels of per capita electricity consumption, measured in terms of kilowatts per hour (kWh), were Taipei,China (10,740 kWh); the Republic of Korea (10,560 kWh); and Brunei Darussalam (10,110 kWh). The region's economies with the lowest levels of per capita electricity consumption in 2014 were Afghanistan (98 kWh), Solomon Islands (118 kWh), and Timor-Leste (129 kWh).

Asia and the Pacific improved its energy efficiency more rapidly than the global average between 2000 and 2014. The level of energy efficiency—measured as the amount of GDP per unit of energy use—in Asia and the Pacific was \$7.2 in 2014, which trailed the global average of \$7.7 (Figure 6.4, Table 6.3).[5] By comparison, the most energy-efficient region in 2014 was Latin America and the Caribbean (\$9.9), followed by Europe and Central Asia (\$9.4), North America (\$7.2), and West Asia and Africa (\$7.1). Asia and the Pacific increased energy efficiency relatively well between 2000 and 2014 with annual average gains of 1.5%. The rest of the regions registered the following average annual gains: Europe and Central Asia (2.0%), North America (1.9%), West Asia and Africa (1.5%), and Latin America and the Carribean (0.6%).

5 Energy efficiency measured in constant 2011 prices (at purchasing power parity) per kilogram of oil equivalent.

Figure 6.4: Gross Domestic Product per Unit of Energy Use
(constant 2011 PPP $ per kilogram of oil equivalent)

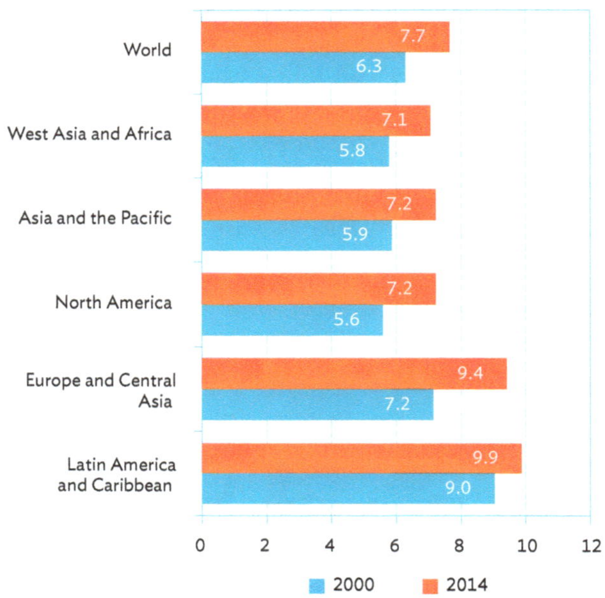

PPP = purchasing power parity.
Sources: Table 6.3 and International Energy Agency.

Of the 40 economies in Asia and the Pacific for which data are available, 32 increased their level of energy efficiency between 2000 and 2014 (Table 6.3). High-income Hong Kong, China led all economies in the region ($26.8). This was followed by lower-middle-income Sri Lanka ($20.7) and the Lao People's Democratic Republic ($18.1).

Coal remained the dominant source of electricity among 6 of the region's top 10 electricity producers in 2014. In Asia and the Pacific's three largest electricity producers—the PRC, India, and Australia—coal accounted for 72.5%, 75.1%, and 33.5% of electricity production in 2014, respectively, compared with shares of 78.2%, 68.5%, and 21.3% in 2000 (Figure 6.5, Table 6.1).

Among the region's top 10 electricity producers, Viet Nam depends most on renewable source of energy as its primary source of electricity generation, with hydropower accounting for 41.6% of

Figure 6.5: Sources of Electricity (Top Producers), 2014
(%)

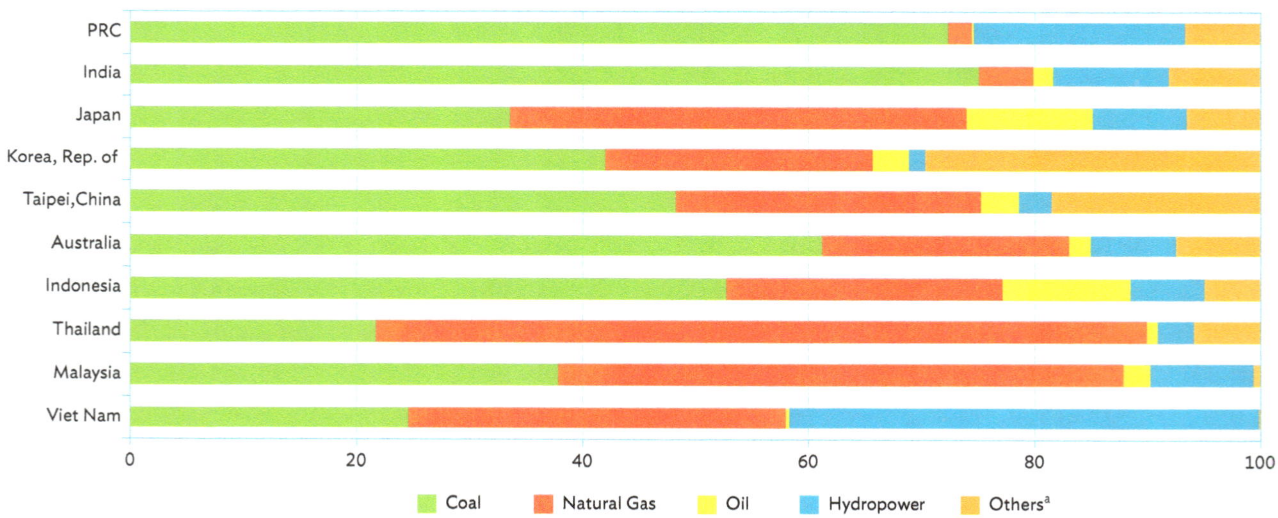

PRC = People's Republic of China.
[a] Computed as a residual that includes combustible renewables and waste; and generation by nuclear power, geothermal, solar, wind, and tide and wave energy.
Source: Table 6.1.

the total electricity produced in the country in 2014. However, this figure was down from 54.8% in 2000, while the share of natural gas in domestic electricity production more than doubled from 16.4% to 33.5% during the same period.

Among the remainder of the region's top 10 electricity producers, natural gas was the biggest contributor to electricity production in 2014 in Japan (40.4%), Malaysia (50.1%), and Thailand (68.3%).

Data Issues and Comparability

Most of the energy data are compiled by the International Energy Agency (IEA) using standard procedures and conversion factors. However, breaks in the series cannot be avoided as IEA revises its time series occasionally to improve the coverage and methodology with the availability of more detailed energy accounts (WB 2017b). For economies without IEA data, these are obtained either from the Energy Balances or the Energy Statistics Yearbook of the United Nations Statistics Division (UNSD). Where data are obtained from the Energy Statistics Yearbook (for earlier years), some degree of precision may be lost with the conversion from petajoules (reported in whole numbers) to kilotons of oil equivalent. The use of mixed data sources (IEA and UNSD) has minimal implications on comparability as the energy balances of IEA and UNSD are found to correspond fairly closely with each other (Treanton 2011, Quadrelli 2015). Users are advised to visit the IEA and UNSD websites for the detailed differences in energy balances and estimates between these two organizations.

Data for the indicator household electrification rate are lacking. Rather than having data for one starting and one ending year across all economies, data for each economy are posted over different ranges of years depending on data availability; thus, the data may not be comparable. This could indicate infrequent or irregular timing in the generation of data, making data inconsistent and limiting possibilities for analysis.

Similarly, data on the sources of electricity are incomplete. For the Pacific island economies, which have limited resources for power generation, no data on the source of electricity generated is available.

Table 6.1: **Electricity Production and Sources**

Regional Member	Total Electricity Production (billion kWh)		Sources of Electricity (% of total) Coal		Natural Gas		Oil		Hydropower		Others[a]	
	2000	2014	2000	2014	2000	2014	2000	2014	2000	2014	2000	2014
Developing Member Economies												
Central and West Asia												
Afghanistan	0.7	1.1 (2016)	...	...	...	...	...	...	...	...	...	...
Armenia	6.0	7.8	–	–	45.2	42.4	–	–	21.2	25.7	33.7	31.9
Azerbaijan	18.7	24.7	–	–	19.8	93.9	72.0	0.2	8.2	5.3	–	0.7
Georgia	7.4	10.4	–	–	17.4	19.6	3.7	–	78.9	80.4	–	–
Kazakhstan	51.3	105.1	69.5	71.9	10.7	19.2	5.2	1.0	14.7	7.9	–	–
Kyrgyz Republic	14.9	14.6	4.3	7.4	9.8	0.8	–	0.6	85.9	91.3	–	–
Pakistan	68.1	105.3	0.4	0.2	32.0	25.1	39.5	39.7	25.2	29.8	2.9	5.2
Tajikistan	14.2	16.5	–	–	1.6	2.9	–	–	98.4	97.1	–	–
Turkmenistan	9.8	20.4	–	–	100.0	100.0	–	–	–	–	–	–
Uzbekistan	46.9	55.4	4.1	4.1	73.3	74.2	10.1	0.4	12.5	21.4	–	–
East Asia												
China, People's Rep. of	1,355.7	5,678.9	78.2	72.5	0.4	2.0	3.5	0.2	16.4	18.7	1.5	6.6
Hong Kong, China	31.3	39.9	98.2	76.2	–	23.0	1.8	0.6	–	–	–	0.2
Korea, Rep. of	290.1	550.9	38.4	42.0	10.2	23.7	11.9	3.2	1.9	1.4	37.6	29.7
Mongolia	2.9	5.4	97.0	92.3	–	–	3.0	4.5	–	–	–	3.2
Taipei,China	184.9	260.0	47.8	48.2	9.5	27.1	16.2	3.3	4.8	2.9	21.7	18.5
South Asia												
Bangladesh	15.8	55.8	–	2.0	88.8	82.0	6.5	14.7	4.7	1.1	–	0.3
Bhutan	1.9	7.4 (2015)	...	...	...	...	...	...	...	...	...	...
India	569.7	1,287.4	68.5	75.1	9.8	4.9	5.1	1.8	13.1	10.2	3.5	8.0
Maldives	0.1	0.4 (2015)	...	...	...	...	...	...	...	...	...	...
Nepal	1.7	3.8	–	–	–	–	1.6	0.0	98.4	99.8	–	0.2
Sri Lanka	7.0	12.5	–	25.7	–	–	54.2	35.1	45.6	36.5	0.2	2.7
Southeast Asia												
Brunei Darussalam	2.5	4.5	–	–	99.1	99.0	0.9	1.0	–	–	–	0.0
Cambodia	0.2	3.1	–	28.2	–	–	100.0	10.7	–	60.5	–	0.6
Indonesia	93.3	228.6	36.4	52.6	28.0	24.6	19.7	11.3	10.7	6.6	5.2	4.8
Lao PDR	3.7	14.9	...	...	...	...	...	...	...	...	...	...
Malaysia	69.3	147.5	11.1	37.9	73.6	50.1	5.2	2.4	10.1	9.1	–	0.6
Myanmar	5.1	14.2	–	2.0	49.5	35.2	13.5	0.5	37.0	62.4	–	–
Philippines	45.3	77.3	36.8	42.8	0.0	24.2	20.3	7.4	17.2	11.8	25.7	13.8
Singapore	31.7	49.4	–	1.1	18.5	95.3	80.0	0.7	–	–	1.5	2.9
Thailand	96.0	173.6	18.5	21.6	64.2	68.3	10.4	1.0	6.3	3.2	0.5	5.9
Viet Nam	26.6	140.9	11.8	24.5	16.4	33.5	17.0	0.3	54.8	41.5	–	0.1
The Pacific												
Cook Islands	0.0	0.0 (2016)	...	...	...	...	...	...	...	...	...	...
Fiji	0.7	0.9 (2015)	...	...	...	...	...	...	...	...	...	...
Kiribati	0.0	0.0	...	...	...	...	...	...	...	...	...	...
Marshall Islands	0.1	...	...	...	...	...	...	...	...	...	...	...
Micronesia, Fed. States of	0.1	0.1 (2011)	...	...	...	...	...	...	...	...	...	...
Nauru	0.0	...	...	...	...	...	...	...	...	...	...	...
Palau	0.1	0.1 (2011)	...	...	...	...	...	...	...	...	...	...
Papua New Guinea	2.4	4.2	...	...	...	...	...	...	...	...	...	...
Samoa	0.1	0.1 (2015)	...	...	...	...	...	...	...	...	...	...
Solomon Islands	0.1	0.1 (2016)	...	...	...	...	...	...	...	...	...	...
Timor-Leste	0.1(2006)	0.4 (2015)	...	...	...	...	...	...	...	...	...	...
Tonga	0.0	0.1	...	...	...	...	...	...	...	...	...	...
Tuvalu	...	...	...	...	...	...	...	...	...	...	...	...
Vanuatu	0.0	0.1 (2016)	...	...	...	...	...	...	...	...	...	...
Developed Member Economies												
Australia	210.2	248.3	82.9	61.2	7.7	21.9	0.8	2.0	8.0	7.4	0.6	7.5
Japan	1,099.7	1,040.7	21.3	33.5	23.1	40.4	16.3	11.2	8.8	8.4	30.6	6.5
New Zealand	39.2	43.6	3.9	4.5	24.4	16.3	–	0.0	62.3	55.9	9.4	23.3

... = data not available at cutoff date, – = magnitude equals zero, 0.0 = magnitude is less than half of unit employed, kWh = kilowatt-hour, Lao PDR = Lao People's Democratic Republic.

a Computed as residual that includes combustible renewables and waste; and generation by nuclear power, geothermal, solar, wind, and tide and wave energy.

Sources: International Energy Agency. http://www.iea.org/statistics/statisticssearch/ (accessed 16 June 2017); economy sources for Afghanistan, Bhutan, the Lao PDR, Maldives, and the Pacific economies.

Table 6.2: **Electric Power Consumption and Electrification**

Regional Member	Electric Power Consumption (per capita kWh)		Household Electrification Rate (% of households)	
	2000	2014	Earliest Year	Latest Year
Developing Member Economies				
Central and West Asia				
Afghanistan	21 (2001)	98 (2016)	...	71.5 (2015)
Armenia	1,290	1,900	98.9 (2000)	99.8 (2010)
Azerbaijan	2,040	2,200	99.5 (2006)	...
Georgia	1,450	2,220	...	...
Kazakhstan	3,170	5,600	...	...
Kyrgyz Republic	1,700	1,940	...	99.8 (2012)
Pakistan	370	470	89.2 (2006)	93.6 (2012)
Tajikistan	2,170	1,490	...	99.1 (2012)
Turkmenistan	1,700	2,760	99.6 (2000)	...
Uzbekistan	1,780	1,650	99.7 (2002)	...
East Asia				
China, People's Rep. of	990	3,930	...	...
Hong Kong, China	5,450	6,070	...	...
Korea, Rep. of	5,910	10,560	...	...
Mongolia	1,050	2,030	67.3 (2000)	...
Taipei,China	8,030	10,740	...	...
South Asia				
Bangladesh	100	310	32.0 (2000)	62.4 (2014)
Bhutan	773	3,039 (2015)	41.1 (2003)	...
India	390	800	67.9 (2006)	...
Maldives	273	558 (2015)	83.8 (2000)	99.8 (2009)
Nepal	60	140	24.6 (2001)	76.3 (2011)
Sri Lanka	290	530	80.7 (2002)	...
Southeast Asia				
Brunei Darussalam	7,600	10,110	...	...
Cambodia	30	270	16.6 (2000)	56.1 (2014)
Indonesia	390	810	90.7 (2003)	96.0 (2012)
Lao PDR	...	...	46.3 (2002)	...
Malaysia	2,720	4,650	...	...
Myanmar	70	210	47.0 (2002)	55.6 (2016)
Philippines	500	710	76.6 (2003)	87.5 (2013)
Singapore	7,580	8,840	...	...
Thailand	1,450	2,570	...	...
Viet Nam	300	1,440	89.1 (2002)	...
The Pacific				
Cook Islands	1,372	1,750 (2016)	97.0 (2006)	99.0 (2010)
Fiji	858	950 (2015)	...	84.0 (2008)
Kiribati	169	211	...	62.0 (2010)
Marshall Islands	1,352	1,516 (2006)	72.0 (2007)	90.0 (2011)
Micronesia, Fed. States of	...	...	46.0 (2000)	65.0 (2010)
Nauru	...	...	100.0 (2002)	100.0 (2011)
Palau	...	...	99.0 (2005)	98.0 (2012)
Papua New Guinea	457	523	12.0 (2006)	19.5 (2010)
Samoa	400	594 (2015)	98.0 (2006)	96.4 (2011)
Solomon Islands	134	118 (2016)	...	21.0 (2009)
Timor-Leste	27 (2006)	129 (2015)	27.0 (2002)	38.0 (2009)
Tonga	324	461	89.0 (2006)	97.0 (2011)
Tuvalu	289	453	94.0 (2005)	98.0 (2012)
Vanuatu	214	232 (2016)	...	33.0 (2009)
Developed Member Economies				
Australia	10,210	10,000	...	...
Japan	8,300	7,830	...	...
New Zealand	9,370	9,130	...	...

... = data not available at cutoff date, kWh = kilowatt-hour, Lao PDR = Lao People's Democratic Republic.

Sources: For electric power consumption: International Energy Agency. http://www.iea.org/statistics/statisticssearch/ (accessed 16 June 2017); economy sources for Afghanistan, Bhutan, the Lao PDR, Maldives, and the Pacific economies. For household electrification rate: International Development Association. Results Measurement System Online. http://data.worldbank.org/data-catalog/IDA-results-measurement (accessed 16 June 2017); United States Agency for International Development, Demographic and Health Surveys Program. The DHS Program STAT compiler. http://www.statcompiler.com/ (accessed 16 June 2017); Secretariat of the Pacific Community, Pacific Regional Information System. National Minimum Development Indicators. http://www.spc.int/nmdi/MdiHome.aspx (accessed 16 June 2017).

Table 6.3: **Use of Energy**

Regional Member	Energy Use (kilotons of oil equivalent)				GDP per Unit of Energy Use (constant 2011 PPP $ per kilogram of oil equivalent)			
	2000	2005	2010	2014	2000	2005	2010	2014
Developing Member Economies								
Central and West Asia								
Afghanistan	597	860	3,339	3,674	...	33.1	13.9	15.9
Armenia	2,015	2,512	2,483	2,959	4.5	6.4	7.8	7.8
Azerbaijan	11,296	13,427	11,585	14,322	3.2	5.0	12.5	11.1
Georgia	2,869	2,841	3,122	4,390	5.0	7.2	8.5	7.4
Kazakhstan	35,679	50,878	69,121	76,667	4.2	4.8	4.7	5.3
Kyrgyz Republic	2,319	2,574	2,753	3,795	4.4	4.8	5.5	4.9
Pakistan	64,063	76,512	85,020	89,887	7.6	8.1	8.6	9.4
Tajikistan	2,149	2,340	2,176	2,805	3.4	5.0	7.4	7.6
Turkmenistan	14,880	19,175	22,685	26,749	1.6	1.6	2.2	2.9
Uzbekistan	50,868	47,085	43,210	43,677	1.2	1.7	2.8	3.8
East Asia								
China, People's Rep. of	1,135,102	1,816,983	2,614,842	3,051,504	4.1	4.1	4.9	5.7
Hong Kong, China	13,590	12,567	13,674	14,246	16.7	22.2	24.7	26.8
Korea, Rep. of	188,158	210,288	250,025	268,413	5.2	5.8	6.0	6.3
Mongolia	2,397	2,996	3,942	5,375	4.7	5.1	5.3	6.2
Taipei,China	84,840	102,370	111,445	110,232	...	...	...	...
South Asia								
Bangladesh	18,262	22,794	30,513	35,423	11.8	12.1	12.2	13.4
Bhutan	1,051	1,146	1,403	1,507	1.9	2.6	3.3	3.8
India	448,096	516,156	693,238	824,743	5.9	7.0	7.8	8.5
Maldives	143	215	366	457	...	11.9	10.5	10.4
Nepal	8,108	9,132	10,211	11,690	4.5	4.7	5.3	5.5
Sri Lanka	8,326	9,001	9,741	10,711	12.5	14.0	17.7	20.7
Southeast Asia								
Brunei Darussalam	2,385	2,218	3,240	3,554	11.5	13.7	9.7	8.8
Cambodia	3,412	3,436	5,299	6,367	4.9	7.6	6.8	7.5
Indonesia	155,656	179,767	212,107	225,513	7.9	8.6	9.6	11.3
Lao PDR	1,624	1,767	1,810	1,867	7.7	9.6	13.7	18.1
Malaysia	48,889	65,729	73,382	89,703	7.7	7.3	8.1	8.2
Myanmar	12,842	14,896	14,021	19,309	4.7	7.4	13.3	12.8
Philippines	39,990	38,854	40,397	47,673	8.2	10.6	13.0	13.8
Singapore	18,668	21,568	25,417	28,015	11.2	12.3	14.4	15.7
Thailand	72,285	99,005	117,840	134,756	8.0	7.6	7.7	7.5
Viet Nam	28,736	41,252	58,912	66,620	7.2	7.0	6.6	7.3
The Pacific								
Cook Islands	9	20	...	24	...	...	...	...
Fiji	534	776	669	553	10.1	7.9	9.5	13.4
Kiribati	11	8	...	22	15.4	22.8	...	9.3
Marshall Islands	...	...	24	24	...	...	7.6	8.1
Micronesia, Fed. States of	45	38	...	54	7.6	9.2	...	6.1
Nauru	44	46	...	54	...	...	...	2.8
Palau	67	66	74	87	3.9	4.5	3.4	3.2
Papua New Guinea	1,123	1,797	1,249	2,479	8.9	6.2	11.9	8.2
Samoa	67	74	...	108	11.3	13.0	...	9.8
Solomon Islands	134	138	...	148	5.3	5.4	...	7.9
Timor-Leste	...	...	96	182	...	...	21.5	14.1
Tonga	41	58	...	39	11.0	8.6	...	13.8
Tuvalu	...	...	...	...	...	...	...	...
Vanuatu	48	39	...	77	10.9	14.0	...	9.7
Developed Member Economies	**643,196**	**649,546**	**644,625**	**587,544**	**7.9**	**8.4**	**8.7**	**10.1**
Australia	108,101	113,478	127,632	125,235	6.3	7.0	7.1	8.1
Japan	518,005	519,139	498,611	441,745	8.3	8.8	9.2	10.8
New Zealand	17,090	16,929	18,382	20,564	6.4	7.8	7.6	7.6
DEVELOPING MEMBER ECONOMIES[a]	**2,481,418**	**3,393,405**	**4,539,430**	**5,230,454**	**5.3**	**5.5**	**6.2**	**6.9**
REGIONAL MEMBER ECONOMIES[a]	**3,124,614**	**4,042,951**	**5,184,055**	**5,817,998**	**5.9**	**6.0**	**6.5**	**7.2**
WORLD	**10,036,889**	**11,532,975**	**12,951,898**	**13,699,127**	**6.3**	**6.6**	**7.0**	**7.7**

... = data not available at cutoff date, GDP = gross domestic product, Lao PDR = Lao People's Democratic Republic, PPP = purchasing power parity.

a For reporting economies only.

Sources: For GDP per unit use of energy: Asian Development Bank estimates; for energy use: International Energy Agency. Statistics. http://www.iea.org/statistics/statisticssearch/ (accessed 16 June 2017); for Papua New Guinea: Asia-Pacific Economic Cooperation. Expert Group on Energy Data Analysis Database. http://www.egeda.ewg.apec.org/ (accessed 20 June 2017); for Afghanistan, Bhutan, the Lao PDR, Maldives, and the Pacific economies except Papua New Guinea: ADB. *Energy Statistics in Asia and the Pacific 1990–2009*. Manila; United Nations Statistics Division. 2014. *Energy Balances*. New York; United Nations Statistics Division. 2011, 2013, and 2014. *Energy Statistics Yearbook*. New York.

Table 6.4: **Energy Production and Imports**

Regional Member	Energy Production (kiloton of oil equivalent)				Energy Imports, Net (% of energy use)			
	2000	2005	2010	2014	2000	2005	2010	2014
Developing Member Economies								
Central and West Asia								
Afghanistan	...	...	1,064	1,515	...	...	68.1	58.8
Armenia	643	869	878	848	68.0	65.4	64.7	71.3
Azerbaijan	18,808	27,253	65,514	58,777	-66.5	-103.0	-465.5	-310.4
Georgia	1,324	980	1,312	1,372	53.9	65.5	58.0	68.7
Kazakhstan	78,575	118,644	156,875	166,284	-120.2	-133.2	-127.0	-116.9
Kyrgyz Republic	1,369	1,324	1,270	1,915	40.9	48.6	53.9	49.6
Pakistan	46,890	60,991	64,989	68,203	26.8	20.3	23.6	24.1
Tajikistan	1,264	1,546	1,542	1,788	41.1	34.0	29.1	36.2
Turkmenistan	45,968	61,602	47,247	77,976	-208.9	-221.3	-108.3	-191.5
Uzbekistan	55,085	56,535	55,133	55,845	-8.3	-20.1	-27.6	-27.9
East Asia								
China, People's Rep. of	1,128,877	1,706,943	2,315,537	2,593,113	0.5	6.1	11.4	15.0
Hong Kong, China	50	51	96	188	99.6	99.6	99.3	98.7
Korea, Rep. of	34,445	42,982	44,955	49,108	81.7	79.6	82.0	81.7
Mongolia	1,949	3,848	15,674	14,410	18.7	-28.4	-297.6	-168.1
Taipei,China	11,793	12,485	12,957	13,636	86.1	87.8	88.4	87.6
South Asia								
Bangladesh	15,156	19,364	26,080	29,457	17.0	15.0	14.5	16.8
Bhutan	1,115	1,284	1,749	1,781	-4.6	-4.1	-24.7	-18.2
India	350,752	402,330	496,722	541,811	20.1	22.1	28.3	34.3
Maldives	–	–	...	4	100.0	100.0	...	99.2
Nepal	7,138	8,152	8,876	9,740	12.0	10.7	13.1	16.7
Sri Lanka	4,748	4,920	5,544	5,327	43.0	45.3	43.1	50.3
Southeast Asia								
Brunei Darussalam	19,684	21,060	18,573	16,256	-725.4	-849.5	-473.2	-357.4
Cambodia	2,718	2,496	3,621	4,258	20.3	27.4	31.7	33.1
Indonesia	237,479	280,282	379,769	457,998	-52.6	-55.9	-79.0	-103.1
Lao PDR	...	...	1,878	1,712	...	...	-3.8	8.3
Malaysia	77,545	95,568	89,308	94,641	-58.6	-45.4	-21.7	-5.5
Myanmar	15,419	22,277	22,559	25,675	-20.1	-49.6	-60.9	-33.0
Philippines	19,549	21,396	23,548	25,854	51.1	44.9	41.7	45.8
Singapore	202	394	588	649	98.9	98.2	97.7	97.7
Thailand	43,948	55,188	70,578	78,740	39.2	44.3	40.1	41.6
Viet Nam	39,919	60,759	66,388	71,198	-38.9	-47.3	-12.7	-6.9
The Pacific								
Cook Islands	–	–	–	–	100.0	100.0	100.0	100.0
Fiji	269	250	143	186	49.6	67.8	78.6	66.3
Kiribati	–	–	...	1	100.0	100.0	...	96.9
Marshall Islands	...	–	–	–	...	100.0	100.0	100.0
Micronesia, Fed. States of	–	–	...	1	100.0	100.0	...	98.6
Nauru	–	–	–	–	100.0	100.0	100.0	100.0
Palau	2	2	–	–	97.0	97.0	100.0	100.0
Papua New Guinea	3,866	2,775	1,458	2,772	-244.3	-54.4	-16.7	-11.8
Samoa	21	21	...	39	68.7	71.6	...	63.9
Solomon Islands	79	79	...	77	41.0	42.8	...	47.8
Timor-Leste	...	...	4,443	3,405	...	...	-4,550.0	-1,771.7
Tonga	–	1	...	1	100.0	98.3	...	98.3
Tuvalu	...	...	...	...	...	...	...	...
Vanuatu	20	20	...	23	58.3	48.7	...	70.5
Developed Member Economies	**352,439**	**377,053**	**439,572**	**409,345**				
Australia	233,552	265,161	323,683	365,707	-116.1	-133.7	-153.6	-192.0
Japan	104,596	99,030	99,004	26,587	79.8	80.9	80.3	94.0
New Zealand	14,291	12,862	16,885	17,051	16.4	24.0	8.1	17.1
DEVELOPING MEMBER ECONOMIES[a]	**2,266,669**	**3,094,671**	**4,006,868**	**4,476,583**				
REGIONAL MEMBER ECONOMIES[a]	**2,619,108**	**3,471,724**	**4,446,440**	**4,885,928**				
WORLD	**10,031,786**	**11,588,027**	**12,868,539**	**13,805,443**				

... = data not available at cutoff date, – = magnitude equals zero, Lao PDR = Lao People's Democratic Republic.

a For reporting economies only.

Sources: For production: International Energy Agency. Statistics. http://www.iea.org/statistics/statisticssearch/ (accessed 16 June 2017); for Papua New Guinea: Asia-Pacific Economic Cooperation. Expert Group on Energy Data Analysis Database. http://www.egeda.ewg.apec.org/ (accessed 20 June 2017); for Afghanistan, Bhutan, the Lao PDR, Maldives, and the Pacific economies except Papua New Guinea: Asian Development Bank. *Energy Statistics in Asia and the Pacific 1990–2009*. Manila; United Nations Statistics Division. 2014. *Energy Balances*. New York; United Nations Statistics Division. 2013 and 2014. *Energy Statistics Yearbook*. New York; for net energy imports as % of energy use: Asian Development Bank estimates.

Table 6.5: **Retail Prices of Fuel Energy**
($ per liter)

Regional Member	Gasoline (Premium)				Diesel			
	2000	2005	2010	2016	2000	2005	2010	2016
Developing Member Economies								
Central and West Asia								
Afghanistan	...	...	...	...	...	...	...	...
Armenia	0.51	0.73	1.01	0.78	0.34	0.60	0.92	0.72
Azerbaijan	...	...	...	...	...	...	...	...
Georgia	...	...	...	...	...	...	...	...
Kazakhstan	0.35	0.47	0.58	0.39	0.30	0.39	0.53	0.38
Kyrgyz Republic	...	...	...	...	...	...	...	...
Pakistan	0.48	0.82	0.80	0.73	0.22	0.54	0.83	0.77
Tajikistan	...	...	...	...	...	...	...	...
Turkmenistan	...	...	...	...	...	...	...	...
Uzbekistan	0.44	0.33 (2004)	...	...	...	...	...	...
East Asia								
China, People's Rep. of	...	...	...	...	...	...	...	...
Hong Kong, China	1.32	1.60	1.75	1.70	0.80	1.00	1.25	1.38
Korea, Rep. of	1.10	1.40	1.48	1.21	0.54	1.05	1.30	1.02
Mongolia	0.33	0.56	1.01	0.68	0.38	0.81 (2006)	0.96	0.98
Taipei,China	0.57	0.73	0.94	0.69	0.44	0.60	0.82	0.61
South Asia								
Bangladesh	...	...	...	...	...	...	...	...
Bhutan	...	...	...	...	...	...	...	...
India	0.58	0.86	1.05	1.18 (2014)	0.32	0.64	0.83	0.91 (2014)
Maldives	...	...	...	...	...	...	...	...
Nepal	0.58	0.87	1.22	1.30 (2014)	0.33	0.58	0.95	1.08 (2014)
Sri Lanka	0.65	0.80	1.02	0.86 (2015)	0.32	0.50	0.65	0.70 (2015)
Southeast Asia								
Brunei Darussalam	...	...	...	...	...	...	...	...
Cambodia	...	...	...	...	...	...	...	...
Indonesia	0.14	0.30	0.50	0.58 (2014)	0.07	0.27	0.50	0.48 (2014)
Lao PDR	...	...	...	...	...	...	...	...
Malaysia	0.29	0.40	0.67	0.51	0.18	0.29	0.57	0.39
Myanmar	...	1.84 (2007)	1.41	0.76 (2015)	...	1.62 (2007)	1.37	0.80 (2015)
Philippines	0.37	0.57	0.96	0.84	0.28	0.51	0.76	0.54
Singapore	0.81	0.83 (2004)	...	...	0.33	0.56	0.89	0.75
Thailand	0.39	0.59	1.12 (2009)	...	0.32	0.50	0.90	0.73 (2015)
Viet Nam	...	...	0.99 (2011)	0.85 (2015)	...	...	0.93 (2011)	0.68 (2015)
The Pacific								
Cook Islands	...	...	...	...	...	...	...	...
Fiji	...	...	...	...	...	...	...	...
Kiribati	...	...	...	...	...	...	...	...
Marshall Islands	...	...	...	...	...	...	...	...
Micronesia, Fed. States of	...	...	...	...	...	...	...	...
Nauru	...	...	...	...	...	...	...	...
Palau	...	...	...	...	...	...	...	...
Papua New Guinea	...	...	...	...	...	...	...	...
Samoa	...	...	...	...	...	...	...	...
Solomon Islands	...	...	...	...	...	...	...	...
Timor-Leste	...	...	...	...	...	...	...	...
Tonga	...	...	...	...	...	...	...	...
Tuvalu	...	...	...	...	...	...	...	...
Vanuatu	0.78	1.23	1.50	...	...	...	...	...
Developed Member Economies								
Australia	0.49	0.82	1.09	0.79	...	0.87	1.09	0.76
Japan	1.05	1.23	1.64	1.21	0.76	0.91	1.28	0.94
New Zealand	0.51	0.97	1.34	1.33	0.33	0.64	0.85	0.70

... = data not available at cutoff date, Lao PDR = Lao People's Democratic Republic.

Source: Economy sources.

VII. Environment

Snapshot

- Economic progress in Asia and the Pacific has been accompanied by rising carbon dioxide emissions. Based on latest data, the region was responsible for 47.4% of total global carbon dioxide emissions.
- Deforestation was reported in almost one-third of the Asia and Pacific region's economies but large economies like India and the People's Republic of China experienced an increase in total forested land in 2014.
- Between 2000 and 2014, almost the same number of economies from the region experienced an increase in the share of land devoted to agriculture as those that experienced a decrease (21 and 24 economies, respectively), while in three economies there was no change during the review period.
- Between 2002 and 2014, the internal renewable freshwater resources of the Asia and Pacific region's economies declined on a per capita basis in all but two (Armenia and Georgia) of the 37 economies for which data are available.

Key Trends

Economic progress in Asia and the Pacific has been accompanied by rising carbon dioxide emissions. Based on latest data, the region was responsible for 47.4% of total global carbon dioxide emissions. Climate change threatens access to water, food production, health, use of land, and physical and natural capital (OECD 2012). In 2011–2015, 45% of the world's nearly 700 climate-related disasters occurred in Asia and the Pacific (UN ESCAP 2017). The region accounted for 47.4% of total global carbon dioxide emissions in 2013, with its top five emitters—the People's Republic of China, India, Japan, the Republic of Korea, and Indonesia—responsible for more than two-thirds of the regional total (Figure 7.1). Since 2000, Asia and the Pacific's share to total global carbon dioxide emissions has increased by roughly 15 percentage points.

Figure 7.1: Emissions of Carbon Dioxide Accounted for by Asia and the Pacific, 2013
(% of global carbon dioxide emissions)

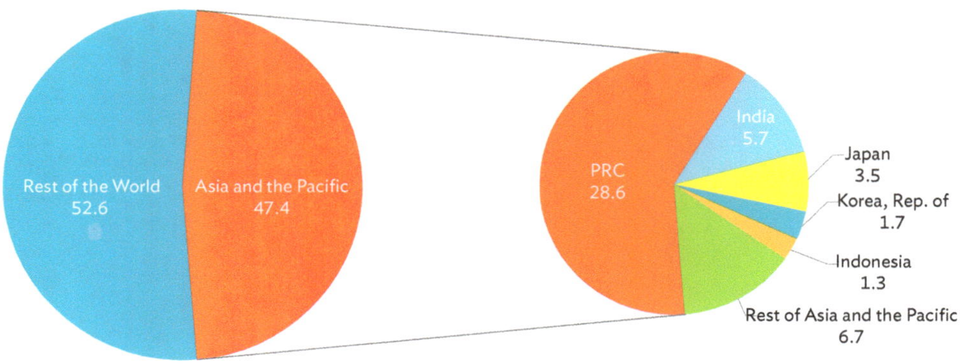

PRC = People's Republic of China.
Sources: Table 7.2; World Bank. World Development Indicators. http://data.worldbank.org/indicator (accessed 9 August 2017).

Deforestation was reported in almost one-third of the Asia and Pacific region's economies but large economies like India and the People's Republic of China experienced an increase in total forested land in 2014. In 2014, 16 out of 46 regional economies for which data are available expanded their forested area (Figure 7.2), up slightly from 18 in 2000. Asia's total forest area has expanded since 1990 on an aggregate basis, albeit with subregional variations (UNEP 2016). The largest annual increases in forested area in 2014 occurred in Taipei,China (4.5%); the Philippines (3.2%); and Azerbaijan (2.4%). In the same year, the highest annual deforestation rates were observed in Pakistan (2.8%), Myanmar (1.8%), and Timor-Leste (1.6%). In addition, large economies like the PRC and India also experienced an increase in their respective total forested land in 2014.

Between 2000 and 2014, almost the same number of economies from the region experienced an increase in the share of land devoted to agriculture as those that experienced a decrease (21 and 24 economies, respectively), while in three economies there was no change during the review period. Two factors that contribute to the expansion of agricultural land as a percentage of total land area are an expanding population and increased meat consumption. At the same time, urbanization and the development of rural areas reduce the area for agriculture (Chakravorty, Moreaux, and Nostbakken 2010).

Figure 7.2: Deforestation Rates, Latest Year
(%)

FSM = Federated States of Micronesia, Lao PDR = Lao People's Democratic Republic, PRC = People's Republic of China.
Note: This chart includes economies with available data between 2014–2015. Deforestation rates for Afghanistan, Brunei Darussalam, the Cook Islands, Georgia, Kazakhstan, Kiribati, Maldives, the Marshall Islands, Nepal, Palau, Samoa, Singapore, Tonga, Turkmenistan, Tuvalu, and Vanuatu are zero.
Source: Table 7.2.

Out of all 48 regional economies, 21 saw an increase in the percentage of land devoted to agriculture between 2000 and 2014, 24 experienced a decline, and 3 had no change (Figure 7.3). The largest percentage point gains occurred in Armenia, where the size of agricultural land as a share of total land rose 2.6 percentage points during the review period (Table 7.3). This was followed by gains in Viet Nam (6.8 percentage points), and Sri Lanka (6.2 percentage points). The most significant declines were observed in New Zealand (–16.3 percentage points); the Cook Islands (–13.8 percentage points), and Mongolia (–11.3 percentage points).

Between 2002 and 2014, the internal renewable freshwater resources of the Asia and Pacific region's economies declined on a per capita basis in all but two (Armenia and Georgia) of the 37 economies for which data are available. In Armenia, per capita freshwater resources increased 1.0% during the review period but population growth was negative; in Georgia, there was very little population growth as freshwater resources expanded 15.7% on a per capita basis (Figure 7.4, Table 1.1). Among the region's economies experiencing a decrease in per capita internal renewable freshwater resources in 2014 as a percentage of the values in 2002, Afghanistan's was the most significant (–33.9%), followed by Vanuatu (–26.7%), and Singapore (–26.2%). In terms of levels of internal renewable freshwater resources per capita, the decline was most pronounced in Bhutan, Papua New Guinea, and Solomon Islands.

Figure 7.3: Agricultural Land
(% of land area)

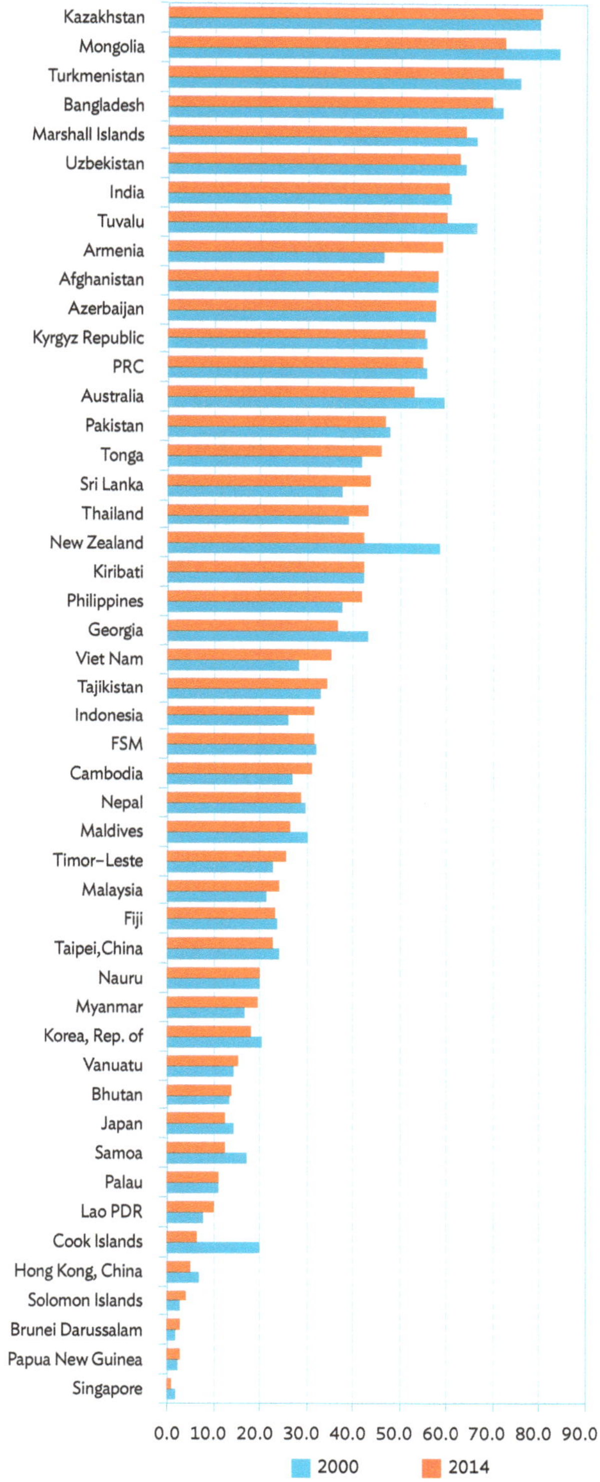

FSM = Federated States of Micronesia, Lao PDR = Lao People's Democratic Republic, PRC = People's Republic of China.
Source: Table 7.1.

Asia and the Pacific is home to 55% of the world's population but less than one-third of the globe's internal renewable freshwater resources (Chakravorty, Moreaux, and Nostbakken 2010). There is extreme variation within Asia and the Pacific in terms of per capita freshwater resources. The region's (arithmetic) average freshwater resources per capita in 2014 was 17,151 cubic meters (m^3), with values greater than 75,000 m^3 in Papua New Guinea, Bhutan, and Solomon Islands. The bottom three countries for this indicator include Maldives, Singapore, and Turkmenistan. (Table 7.3).

Data Issues and Comparability

In previous issues of Key Indicators for Asia and the Pacific, data from the World Development Indicators for GHG emissions were compiled from the International Energy Agency. Starting in 2016, World Development Indicators data were compiled from the European Commission Joint Research Centre's Emissions Database for Global Atmospheric Research, which consistently applies a technology-based emissions factor approach for all economies when calculating emissions.

The Food and Agriculture Organization of the United Nations monitors land use and forestry data using country reports and satellite imagery.

Figure 7.4: Internal Renewable Freshwater Resources Per Capita
(cubic meters/year per inhabitant)

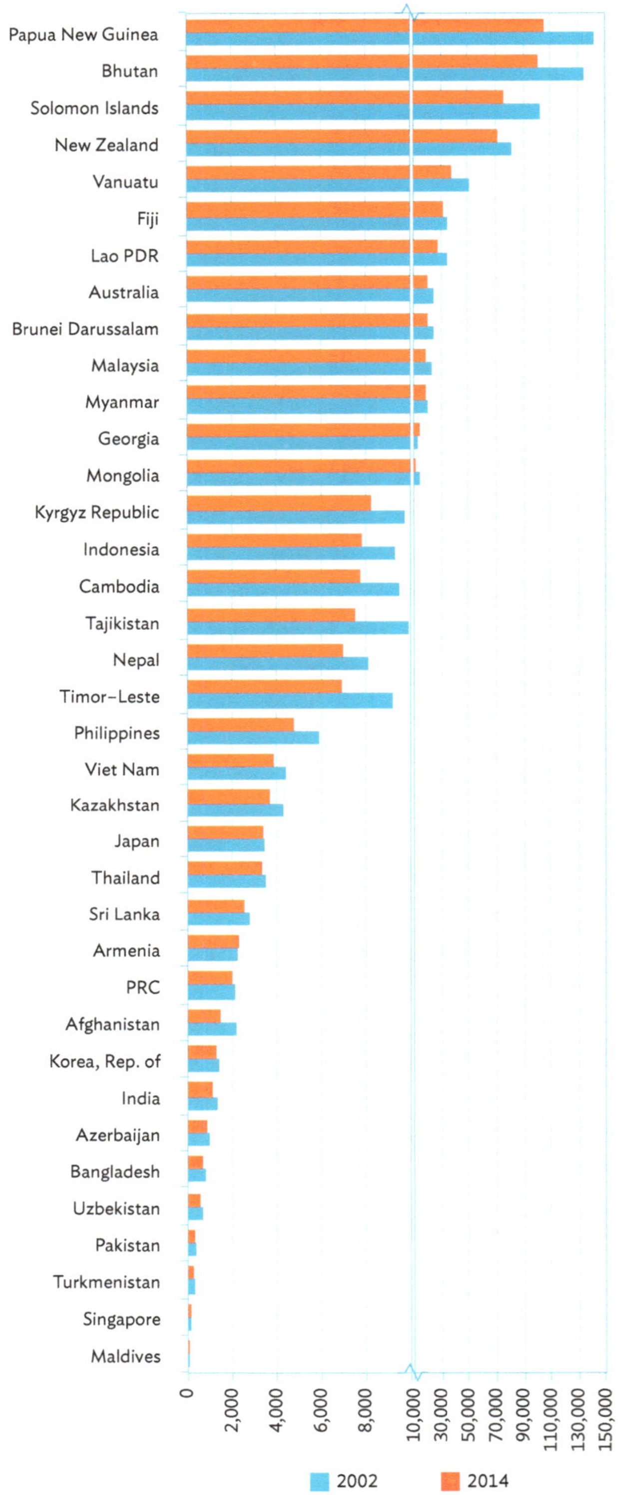

Lao PDR = Lao People's Democratic Republic, PRC = People's Republic of China.
Source: Table 7.3.

Table 7.1: **Agriculture Land Use**
(% of land area)

Regional Member	Agricultural Land				Arable Land				Permanent Cropland			
	2000	2005	2010	2014	2000	2005	2010	2014	2000	2005	2010	2014
Developing Member Economies												
Central and West Asia												
Afghanistan	57.8	58.1	58.1	58.1	11.8	12.0	11.9	11.9	0.1	0.2	0.2	0.2
Armenia	46.5	56.4	60.9	59.0	15.8	16.0	15.8	15.7	1.3	1.8	1.9	2.0
Azerbaijan	57.4	57.6	57.7	57.7	22.1	22.3	22.8	23.3	2.9	2.7	2.8	2.8
Georgia	43.2	36.3	35.7	36.8	11.4	6.8	6.0	6.6	3.9	1.6	1.8	2.3
Kazakhstan	79.8	78.6	80.4	80.4	11.2	10.6	10.6	10.9	0.1	0.0	0.0	0.0
Kyrgyz Republic	55.9	56.0	55.3	55.0	7.1	6.7	6.7	6.7	0.3	0.4	0.4	0.4
Pakistan	47.6	46.7	45.7	47.0	40.3	39.1	38.1	39.5	0.9	1.0	1.1	1.1
Tajikistan	32.7	33.4	34.0	34.2	5.6	5.4	5.4	5.3	0.7	0.8	0.9	1.0
Turkmenistan	75.5	74.2	72.4	72.0	4.1	4.3	4.1	4.1	0.1	0.1	0.1	0.1
Uzbekistan	64.2	62.9	62.7	62.9	10.5	10.3	10.2	10.3	0.8	0.8	0.8	0.9
East Asia												
China, People's Rep. of	55.6	55.1	54.8	54.8	12.6	12.0	11.4	11.3	1.2	1.3	1.5	1.7
Hong Kong, China	6.7	6.7	5.2	4.9	4.8	4.8	3.3	3.0	1.0	1.0	1.0	1.0
Korea, Rep. of	20.5	19.4	18.2	17.9	17.8	17.0	15.5	15.1	2.1	1.9	2.1	2.2
Mongolia	84.0	73.0	73.1	72.7	0.8	0.4	0.4	0.4	0.0	0.0	0.0	0.0
Taipei,China	24.0	23.5	23.0	22.6	17.5	17.0	16.9	16.8	6.5	6.5	6.1	5.8
South Asia												
Bangladesh	72.2	71.5	71.0	69.9	64.1	60.8	59.9	58.9	3.5	6.1	6.5	6.4
Bhutan	13.3	15.6	13.6	13.8	2.7	4.4	2.6	2.6	0.5	0.5	0.3	0.3
India	60.9	60.6	60.4	60.4	54.1	53.6	52.8	52.6	3.1	3.4	4.1	4.4
Maldives	30.0	30.0	26.3	26.3	10.0	10.0	13.0	13.0	16.7	16.7	10.0	10.0
Nepal	29.6	29.3	28.8	28.7	16.4	15.9	15.2	14.7	0.8	0.9	1.1	1.5
Sri Lanka	37.5	40.0	41.8	43.7	14.6	17.5	19.1	20.7	15.9	15.5	15.6	15.9
Southeast Asia												
Brunei Darussalam	1.9	2.1	2.5	2.7	0.4	0.4	0.8	0.9	0.8	0.9	1.1	1.1
Cambodia	27.0	30.3	30.9	30.9	21.0	21.0	21.5	21.5	0.8	0.9	0.9	0.9
Indonesia	26.0	28.6	30.7	31.5	11.3	12.7	13.0	13.0	8.6	9.9	11.6	12.4
Lao PDR	7.8	8.6	9.6	10.3	4.0	5.0	6.1	6.6	0.4	0.4	0.6	0.7
Malaysia	21.4	21.7	22.7	23.9	2.9	2.9	2.8	2.9	17.6	18.0	19.0	20.1
Myanmar	16.5	17.2	19.2	19.4	15.2	15.4	16.5	16.5	0.9	1.4	2.2	2.4
Philippines	37.7	38.1	40.6	41.7	16.9	16.8	17.8	18.7	15.8	16.3	17.8	17.9
Singapore	1.8	1.1	1.1	0.9	1.5	1.0	0.9	0.8	0.3	0.1	0.1	0.1
Thailand	38.8	38.4	41.2	43.3	30.6	29.8	30.8	32.9	6.6	7.1	8.8	8.8
Viet Nam	28.2	32.4	34.7	35.1	19.9	20.5	20.8	20.7	6.2	9.8	11.9	12.3
The Pacific												
Cook Islands	20.0	11.4	5.6	6.3	7.5	5.2	2.9	4.2	12.5	6.2	2.7	2.1
Fiji	23.4	23.4	23.3	23.3	9.3	9.3	9.0	9.0	4.5	4.5	4.7	4.7
Kiribati	42.0	42.0	42.0	42.0	2.5	2.5	2.5	2.5	39.5	39.5	39.5	39.5
Marshall Islands	66.7	72.2	72.2	63.9	5.6	11.1	11.1	11.1	44.4	44.4	44.4	36.1
Micronesia, Fed. States of	32.1	32.1	31.4	31.4	3.6	3.6	2.9	2.9	24.3	24.3	24.3	24.3
Nauru	20.0	20.0	20.0	20.0	–	–	–	–	20.0	20.0	20.0	20.0
Palau	10.9	10.9	10.9	10.9	2.2	2.2	2.2	2.2	4.3	4.3	4.3	4.3
Papua New Guinea	2.2	2.3	2.6	2.6	0.5	0.5	0.7	0.7	1.4	1.3	1.5	1.5
Samoa	17.0	14.8	12.4	12.4	4.9	3.9	2.8	2.8	11.0	9.5	7.8	7.8
Solomon Islands	2.7	3.2	3.8	3.9	0.5	0.6	0.7	0.7	2.0	2.3	2.9	2.9
Timor-Leste	22.7	25.9	25.0	25.6	8.1	11.4	10.1	10.4	4.5	4.4	4.8	5.0
Tonga	41.7	41.7	44.4	45.8	20.8	20.8	23.6	25.0	15.3	15.3	15.3	15.3
Tuvalu	66.7	56.7	60.0	60.0	–	–	–	–	66.7	56.7	60.0	60.0
Vanuatu	14.4	15.0	15.3	15.3	1.6	1.6	1.6	1.6	9.3	9.9	10.3	10.3
Developed Member Economies												
Australia	59.3	57.9	51.9	52.9	6.2	6.4	5.5	6.1	0.0	0.0	0.1	0.0
Japan	14.4	12.9	12.6	12.4	12.3	12.0	11.7	11.6	1.0	0.9	0.9	0.8
New Zealand	58.5	44.5	43.3	42.2	5.7	1.6	1.9	2.2	0.2	0.2	0.3	0.3

– = magnitude equals zero, 0.0 = magnitude is less than half of unit employed, Lao PDR = Lao People's Democratic Republic.

Source: Food and Agriculture Organization of the United Nations. FAOSTAT Database. http://www.faostat.fao.org (accessed 4 July 2017).

Table 7.2: **Deforestation and Pollution**

Regional Member	Deforestation Rate[a] (average % change)		Carbon Dioxide Emissions[b] (thousand metric tons)		Nitrous Oxide Emissions (thousand metric tons CO_2 equivalent)	
	2000	2014	2000	2013	2000	2012
Developing Member Economies						
Central and West Asia						
Afghanistan	–	–	774	21,269	3,317	3,424
Armenia	0.06	-0.06	3,465	5,497	462	1,023
Azerbaijan	-0.23	-2.41	29,508	35,643	2,030	2,673
Georgia	-0.03	–	4,536	7,510	2,437	2,352
Kazakhstan	0.17	–	118,099	262,902	14,865	17,822
Kyrgyz Republic	-0.26	1.23	4,635	9,842	1,452	1,567
Pakistan	1.91	2.76	106,449	153,369	26,350	30,651
Tajikistan	-0.05	-0.10	2,237	3,586	1,110	1,848
Turkmenistan	–	–	37,539	66,893	3,046	4,924
Uzbekistan	-0.52	0.34	121,059	103,226	9,610	13,192
East Asia						
China, People's Rep. of	-1.13	-0.75	3,405,180	10,249,463	414,138	587,166
Hong Kong, China	...	...	40,440	44,994	513	476
Korea, Rep. of	0.13	0.12	447,561	592,499	18,576	14,979
Mongolia	0.69	0.76	7,506	41,591	5,058	3,548
Taipei,China	–	-4.54 (2015)	227,109	269,627	3,816	4,594 (2013)
South Asia						
Bangladesh	0.18	0.18	27,869	68,951	20,770	26,683
Bhutan	-0.38	-0.36	396	884	281	555
India	-0.22	-0.25	1,031,853	2,034,752	207,700	239,755
Maldives	–	–	451	1,049	12	27
Nepal	2.30	–	3,069	6,502	4,232	4,598
Sri Lanka	0.42	0.32	10,238	16,025	2,044	2,174
Southeast Asia						
Brunei Darussalam	0.40	–	4,712	7,785	395	342
Cambodia	1.20	1.31	1,977	5,574	3,295	16,685
Indonesia	1.89	0.74	263,419	479,365	94,933	93,139
Lao PDR	0.67	-1.03	939	2,175	3,265	8,987
Malaysia	0.36	-0.06	125,734	236,510	13,822	15,310
Myanmar	1.23	1.81	10,088	12,603	31,300	26,783
Philippines	-0.68	-3.17	73,307	98,239	12,365	12,762
Singapore	–	–	49,006	50,557	6,635	1,909
Thailand	-1.80	-0.18	181,271	303,118	18,677	30,833
Viet Nam	-2.06	-0.89	53,645	152,624	19,746	34,494
The Pacific						
Cook Islands	-0.47	–	...	...	...	...
Fiji	-0.28	-0.48	865	1,709	343	344
Kiribati	–	–	33	62	3	4
Marshall Islands	–	–	77	103	0	0
Micronesia, Fed. States of	-0.05	-0.05	136	147	11	11
Nauru	...	...	84	44	0	0
Palau	-0.38	–	114	224	0	0
Papua New Guinea	0.01	0.01	2,666	6,073	1,613	1,234
Samoa	-2.46	–	139	238	37	40
Solomon Islands	0.25	0.25	147	198	2,425	2,656
Timor-Leste	1.29	1.58	...	440	164	226
Tonga	–	–	95	209	22	22
Tuvalu	–	–	...	...	1	1
Vanuatu	–	–	84	106	118	109
Developed Member Economies						
Australia	-0.02	-0.25	329,443	377,906	75,581	54,247
Japan	0.03	0.01	1,220,528	1,243,384	30,411	24,911
New Zealand	-0.48	-0.00	32,981	33,960	11,549	11,880

continued

Table 7.2: **Deforestation and Pollution** *(continued)*

Regional Member	Methane Emissions (thousand metric tons CO_2 equivalent)		Other Greenhouse Gases[c] (thousand metric tons CO_2 equivalent)	
	2000	2012	2000	2012
Developing Member Economies				
Central and West Asia				
Afghanistan	9,384	13,763	126	349
Armenia	2,565	3,426	112	710
Azerbaijan	9,955	19,955	464	1,142
Georgia	4,137	5,019	3	227
Kazakhstan	38,779	71,350	14,065	30,363
Kyrgyz Republic	3,486	4,291	93	68
Pakistan	117,125	158,337	757	1,159
Tajikistan	3,304	5,408	798	367
Turkmenistan	21,241	22,009	124	595
Uzbekistan	37,233	47,333	298	989
East Asia				
China, People's Rep. of	1,043,400	1,752,290	104,677	251,254
Hong Kong, China	2,695	3,147	155	150
Korea, Rep. of	30,916	32,625	14,934	8,968
Mongolia	9,218	6,257	26,233	2,216
Taipei,China	13,490	5,927(2013)	2,452	3,632(2013)
South Asia				
Bangladesh	89,247	105,142	686	1,329
Bhutan	1,032	1,770	644	488
India	561,733	636,396	56,626	153,658
Maldives	34	52	0	-0
Nepal	21,206	23,982	2,443	7,995
Sri Lanka	9,606	11,864	441	91
Southeast Asia				
Brunei Darussalam	3,882	4,539	101	427
Cambodia	14,985	35,915	23,021	73,300
Indonesia	170,032	223,316	63,048	2,556
Lao PDR	7,219	15,011	13,588	136,841
Malaysia	29,309	34,271	5,144	3,866
Myanmar	66,942	80,637	78,176	406,274
Philippines	49,911	57,170	12,487	3,891
Singapore	1,684	2,386	1,410	3,299
Thailand	83,564	106,499	8,756	45,556
Viet Nam	75,430	113,564	5,782	25,707
The Pacific				
Cook Islands	...	...	...	...
Fiji	705	715	9	52
Kiribati	13	16	–	-0
Marshall Islands	6	8	...	...
Micronesia, Fed. States of	28	30	...	...
Nauru	3	3	-0	-0
Palau	1	1	...	...
Papua New Guinea	2,001	2,143	1,949	2,188
Samoa	116	133	-0	0
Solomon Islands	1,394	1,449	0	0
Timor-Leste	450	732	–	-0
Tonga	58	61	-0	0
Tuvalu	3	3	-0	0
Vanuatu	267	254	0	-0
Developed Member Economies				
Australia	128,133	125,588	520,911	174,653
Japan	47,496	38,957	51,527	71,746
New Zealand	26,584	28,658	1,506	1,764

... = data not available at cutoff date, – = magnitude equals zero, CO_2 = carbon dioxide, Lao PDR = Lao People's Democratic Republic.

a Rate refers to percentage change over previous year. A negative value indicates that the deforestation rate is decreasing (i.e., reforestation).
b Data from the World Bank are expressed in kiloton (kt), while data provided in the table are expressed in thousand metric tons using 1 kt = 1000 metric tons conversion factor.
c Other greenhouse gas emissions refer to hydrofluorocarbons, perfluorocarbons, and sulfur hexafluoride.

Sources: Food and Agriculture Organization of the United Nations. FAOSTAT Database. http://www.fao.org/faostat/en/#data/RL (accessed 9 August 2017); World Bank. World Development Indicators. http://data.worldbank.org/indicator (accessed 9 August 2017); for Taipei,China: Directorate General of Budget, Accounting and Statistics. *Statistical Yearbook 2015*. http://ebook.dgbas.gov.tw/public/Data/610281138403HCL2D3O.pdf.

Table 7.3: **Freshwater Resources**

Regional Member	Internal Renewable Freshwater Resources (billion cubic meters per year) 2002	2014	Internal Renewable Freshwater Resources (cubic meters per inhabitant per year) 2002	2014	Annual Freshwater Withdrawals (billion cubic meters)	Water Productivity[a] 2002	2014
Developing Member Economies	**11,043**	**11,040**	**3,228**	**2,808**			
Central and West Asia	**370**	**370**	**1,554**	**1,210**			
Afghanistan	47	47	2,194	1,450	20 (2000)	0	1
Armenia	7	7	2,251	2,273	3 (2012)	3	4
Azerbaijan	8	8	980	832	12 (2012)	2	5
Georgia	58	58	12,555	14,532	2 (2008)	...	8
Kazakhstan	64	64	4,287	3,651	20 (2010)	4	9
Kyrgyz Republic	49	49	9,732	8,237	8 (2006)	0	1
Pakistan	55	55	381	291	184 (2008)	1	1
Tajikistan	63	63	9,905	7,482	11 (2006)	0	1
Turkmenistan	1	1	305	261	28 (2004)	0	1
Uzbekistan	16	16	651	547	49 (2005)	0	1
East Asia	**2,913**	**2,913**	**2,137**	**1,994**			
China, People's Rep. of	2,813	2,813	2,141	1,999	604 (2013)	...	14
Hong Kong, China	...	...	...	...	...	...	...
Korea, Rep. of	65	65	1,387	1,289	29 (2005)	27	42
Mongolia	35	35	14,239	11,761	1 (2009)	...	21
Taipei,China	...	...	...	...	...	...	...
South Asia	**1,883**	**1,880**	**1,482**	**1,235**			
Bangladesh	105	105	771	652	36 (2008)	...	4
Bhutan	81	78	135,361	100,671	0 (2008)	...	6
India	1,446	1,446	1,326	1,103	648 (2010)	1	3
Maldives	0	0	103	82	0 (2008)	...	487
Nepal	198	198	8,084	6,951	9 (2006)	1	2
Sri Lanka	53	53	2,770	2,549	13 (2005)	3	6
Southeast Asia	**4,985**	**4,985**	**9,223**	**7,884**			
Brunei Darussalam	9	9	24,752	20,085	0 (1994)	...	149
Cambodia	121	121	9,510	7,742	2 (2006)	...	7
Indonesia	2,019	2,019	9,288	7,839	113 (2000)	4	8
Lao PDR	190	190	34,606	27,992	3 (2005)	...	3
Malaysia	580	580	23,769	19,122	11 (2005)	19	28
Myanmar	1,003	1,003	20,600	18,610	33 (2000)	1	2
Philippines	479	479	5,892	4,757	82 (2009)	...	3
Singapore	1	1	145	107	...	...	1,493
Thailand	225	225	3,500	3,303	57 (2007)	...	7
Viet Nam	359	359	4,387	3,846	82 (2005)	...	2
The Pacific	**892**	**892**	**104,114**	**79,857**			
Cook Islands	...	...	...	...	...	...	...
Fiji	29	29	35,001	32,003	0 (2005)	35	43
Kiribati	...	...	...	...	...	...	...
Marshall Islands	...	...	...	...	...	...	...
Micronesia, Fed. States of	...	...	...	...	...	...	...
Nauru	...	...	...	...	...	...	...
Palau	...	...	...	...	...	...	...
Papua New Guinea	801	801	141,695	105,132	0 (2005)	24	34
Samoa	...	...	...	...	...	...	...
Solomon Islands	45	45	102,782	76,594	...	...	...
Timor-Leste	8	8	9,181	6,932	1 (2004)	...	1
Tonga	...	...	...	...	...	...	...
Tuvalu	...	...	...	...	...	...	...
Vanuatu	10	10	51,546	37,793	...	...	...
Developed Member Economies	**1,249**	**1,249**	**8,342**	**8,054**			
Australia	492	492	25,213	20,527	19 (2013)	41	65
Japan	430	430	3,406	3,397	81 (2009)	64	73
New Zealand	327	327	82,534	72,201	5 (2010)	39	31

... = data not available at cutoff date, 0 = magnitude is less than half of unit employed, Lao PDR = Lao People's Democratic Republic.

a Gross domestic product in constant 2010 US dollars per cubic meter of total freshwater withdrawal.

Sources: Food and Agriculture Organization of the United Nations. AQUASTAT Database. http://www.fao.org/nr/water/aquastat/data/query/index.html (accessed 20 July 2017); World Bank. World Development Indicators. http://data.worldbank.org/indicator (accessed 20 July 2017).

VIII. Government and Governance

Snapshot

- Based on latest data, three-quarters of the economies in Asia and the Pacific incurred fiscal deficits. Fiscal deficits also exceeded 2% of gross domestic product (GDP) in half of the region's economies.
- Tax revenue as a share of GDP rose between 2015 and 2016 in 19 of 34 economies for which data are available.
- Government expenditure as a share of GDP rose between 2015 and 2016 in more than half of the economies in the region.
- The (arithmetic) average number of days required to start a business in developing member economies for which data are available declined from 50 days in 2005 to 19 days in 2016, compared with a decline in the global average from 51 days to 21 days during the same period.
- On a scale from 0 (highly corrupt) to 100 (very clean), the average score for 37 economies in Asia and the Pacific with available data in Transparency International's Corruption Perceptions Index was 42 in 2016, up from 40 in 2015.

Key Trends

Based on latest data, three-quarters of the economies in Asia and the Pacific incurred fiscal deficits. Fiscal deficits also exceeded 2% of gross domestic product (GDP) in half of the region's economies. Figure 8.1 shows that three-quarters of the Asia and Pacific region's economies for which data are available had a fiscal deficit in 2016. In half of the economies, fiscal deficit exceeded 2% of GDP. As a percentage of GDP, the largest deficits were in Mongolia (15.4%), Tajikistan (10.4%), and Myanmar (6.0%). The largest surpluses as a percentage of GDP were in the Federated States of Micronesia (11.0%); Palau (4.3%); and Hong Kong, China (3.7%).

Afghanistan, Bhutan, and Solomon Islands all posted fiscal deficits in 2016 after running surpluses in 2015 (Table 8.1). The largest shift from surplus to deficit, measured as a percentage of GDP, occurred in Solomon Islands (5.7 percentage points). Brunei Darussalam, the Republic of Korea, Tonga, and Turkmenistan each ran fiscal surpluses in 2016 after posting deficits in 2015. The largest fiscal shift in this direction occurred in Brunei Darussalam (16.9 percentage points).

Figure 8.1: Fiscal Balance as a Percentage of GDP, 2016
(%)

FSM = Federated States of Micronesia, GDP = gross domestic product, PRC = People's Republic of China.
Source: Table 8.1.

Tax revenue as a share of GDP rose between 2015 and 2016 in 19 of 34 economies for which data are available. Figure 8.2 shows government tax revenue—including value-added tax, sales tax, import duties, income tax, profit tax, property tax, capital gains tax, and compulsory social security charges, among others—as a percentage of GDP in both 2015 and 2016.[6] The largest increase in tax revenue during the review period, measured as a percentage of GDP, occurred in Nauru (3.7 percentage points), followed by Tonga (1.8 percentage points) and Nepal and Pakistan (1.6 percentage points each). The largest declines occurred in Solomon Islands (3.3 percentage points), Afghanistan (2.1 percentage points), and Tajikistan (1.3 percentage points).

Government expenditure as a share of GDP rose between 2015 and 2016 in more than half of the economies in the region. Table 8.4 shows that the largest gains in government expenditure between 2015 and 2016, measured as a share of GDP, were in Nauru (19.3 percentage points), Mongolia (7.0 percentage points), and Nepal (6.3 percentage points). The largest declines during the review period were in Azerbaijan (4.8 percentage points), Solomon Islands (3.7 percentage points), and Turkmenistan (3.2 percentage points).

Developed economies and societies with relatively older populations tend to spend more on health and social security and welfare (ADB 2016). Latest available data show that in Asia and the Pacific, Japan (7.6%) and New Zealand (7.0%) were among the regional leaders in public spending on health when measured as a share of GDP (Table 8.5).

6 Caution should be exercised when making intercountry comparisons of tax revenue-to-GDP ratios due to differences in the definition of tax revenue employed in each economy. For instance, some economies consider revenues from mandatory social contribution as part of tax revenue while others do not. The country tables accompanying this publication provide details on the composition of tax revenue in each member economy of ADB.

Figure 8.2: Tax Revenue as a Percentage of GDP
(%)

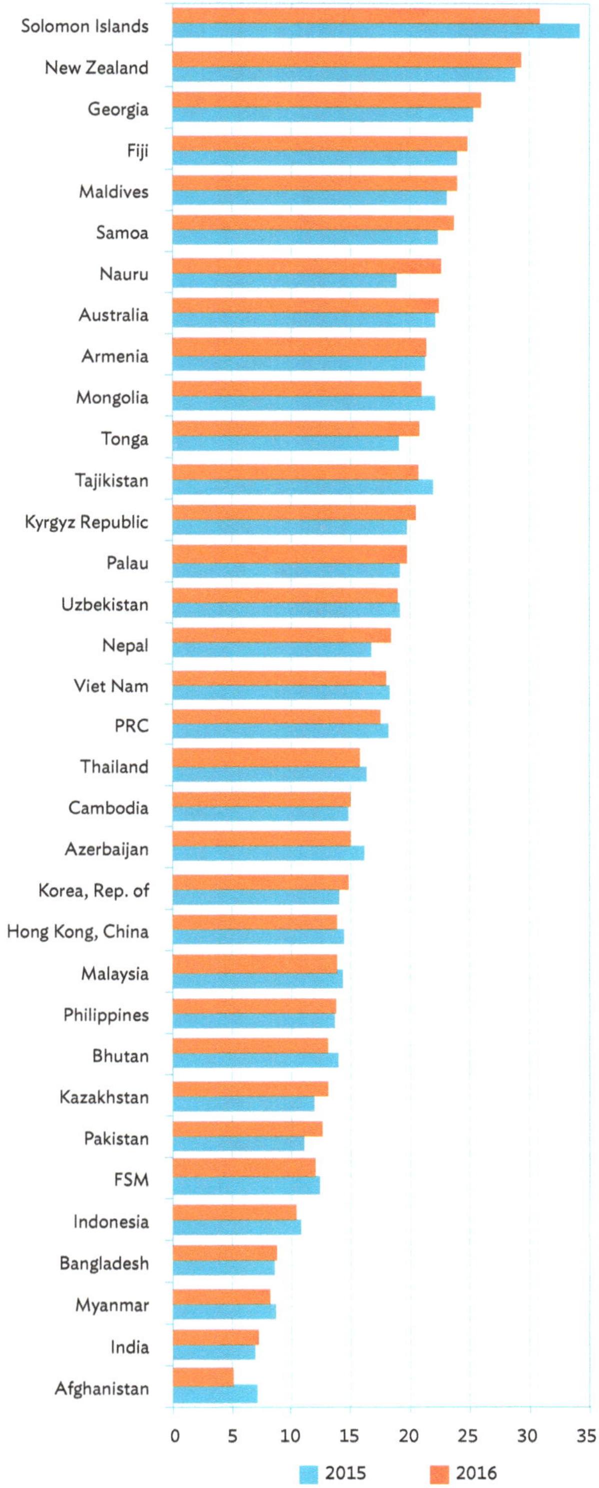

FSM = Federated States of Micronesia, GDP = gross domestic product, PRC = People's Republic of China.
Note: This chart includes economies with available data for both 2015 and 2016.
Source: Table 8.2.

At the same time, Kiribati led all regional economies with an 8.0% share of GDP allocated to spending on health, resulting from large inflows of international aid. Japan (16.0%) and New Zealand (11.4%) led the region in terms of social security and welfare spending as a percentage of GDP based on latest data. The only other two economies in the region to exceed 10% of GDP on social security and welfare spending were Timor-Leste (10.9%) and Mongolia (10.3%).

The (arithmetic) average number of days required to start a business in developing member economies for which data are available declined from 50 days in 2005 to 19 days in 2016, compared with a decline in the global average from 51 days to 21 days during the same period. Between 2005 and 2016, the time required to start a business in the region's developing member economies for which data are available fell in 34 instances, rose in 3, and remained unchanged in 3 (Figure 8.3). The largest declines between 2005 and 2016 in the number of days required occurred in Timor-Leste (158 days), Indonesia (139 days), and Azerbaijan (110 days). Increases in the number of days required to start a business were observed in Cambodia (12 days), Palau (4 days), and Maldives (3 days); no change was observed in Kiribati, the Marshall Islands, and the Federated States of Micronesia. Reforms that facilitate the start-up process include online business registration, a single office for business start-up permits, and reduced minimum capital requirements (WB 2016).

By subregion, the (arithmetic) average number of days required to start a business in 2016 was 32 in Southeast Asia, 21 in the Pacific, 16 in South Asia, 10 in East Asia, and 9 in Central and West Asia (Table 8.6).

Figure 8.3: Number of Days Required to Start a Business

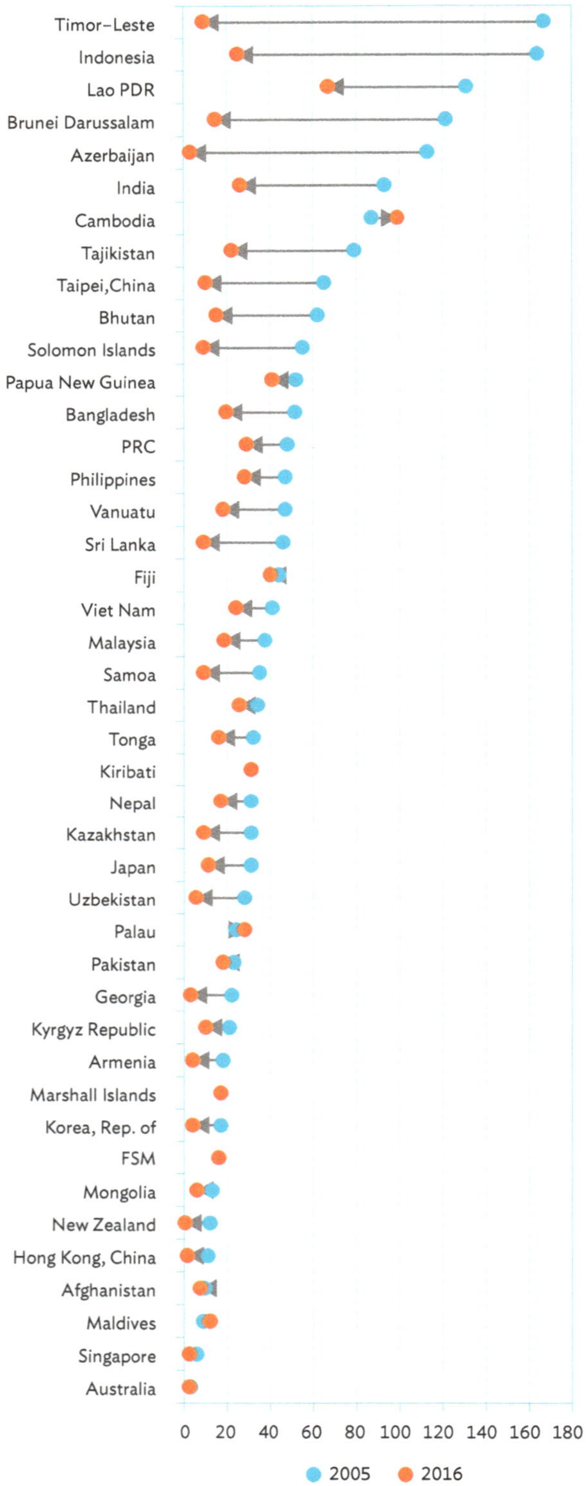

FSM = Federated States of Micronesia, Lao PDR = Lao People's Democratic Republic, PRC = People's Republic of China.
Note: This chart includes economies with available data between 2005 and 2016.
Source: Table 8.6.

On a scale from 0 (highly corrupt) to 100 (very clean), the (arithmetic) average score for 34 economies in Asia and the Pacific with available data in Transparency International's Corruption Perceptions Index was 42 in 2016, up from 40 in 2015. Transparency International's 2016 Corruption Perceptions Index assessed 176 economies for levels of corruption. Although the average score out of 100 for Asia and the Pacific economies was 42, about two-thirds of the region's economies had scores below the regional average in 2016 (Table 8.7). New Zealand moved up three spots to attain the number one global ranking in 2016. The region's developing member economies with the highest global rankings were Singapore (7th); Hong Kong, China (15th); and Bhutan (27th). The region's lowest rankings belonged to Afghanistan (169th) and Cambodia and Uzbekistan (tied for 156th).

A correlation between GDP per capita and perceived corruption persisted in Asia and the Pacific economies in 2016. Figure 8.4 shows a correlation between higher levels of GDP per capita (in constant 2011 dollars at purchasing power parity) and lower levels of perceived corruption. This correlation is partially explained by the tendency of corruption to reduce the effectiveness of governance and impede the efficient allocation of resources within an economy (IMF 2016b). The region's two developing member economies with the highest scores in the 2016 Corruption Perceptions Index—Singapore and Hong Kong, China—were first and third, respectively, among developing members in terms of GDP per capita (in constant 2011 dollars at purchasing power parity).

Figure 8.4: Corruption Perceptions Index (score) **and GDP per Capita at PPP** (constant 2011 PPP$), **2016**

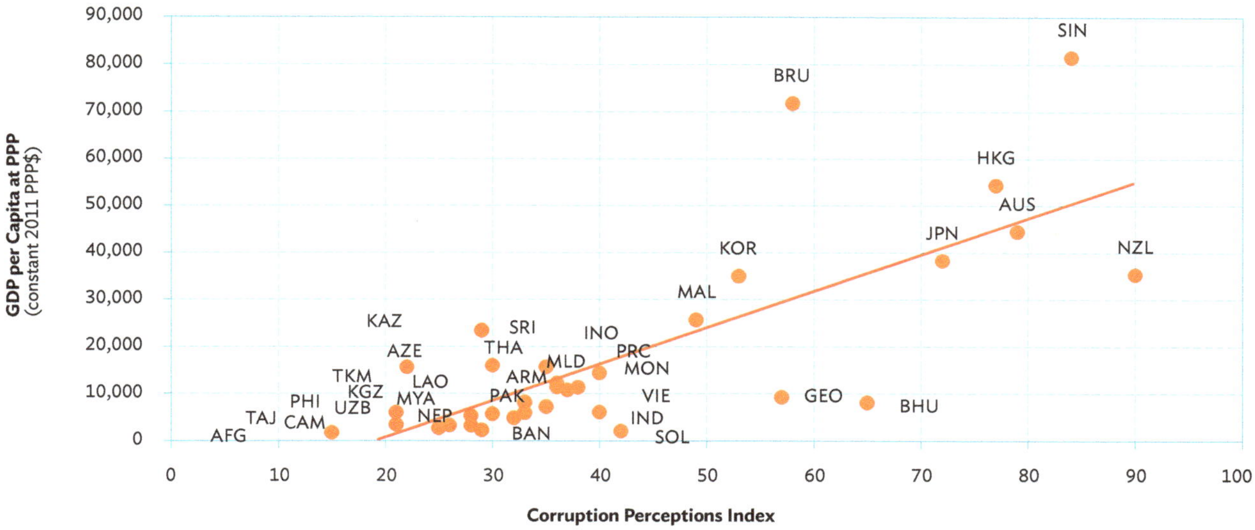

AFG = Afghanistan, ARM = Armenia, AUS = Australia, AZE = Azerbaijan, BAN = Bangladesh, BHU = Bhutan, BRU = Brunei Darussalam, CAM = Cambodia, GDP = Gross Domestic Product, GEO = Georgia, IND = India, INO = Indonesia, JPN = Japan, KAZ = Kazakhstan, KGZ = Kyrgyz Republic, HKG = Hong Kong, China, KOR = Republic of Korea, LAO = Lao People's Democratic Republic, MAL = Malaysia, MLD = Maldives, MON = Mongolia, MYA = Myanmar, NEP = Nepal, NZL = New Zealand, PAK = Pakistan, PHI = Philippines, PRC = People's Republic of China, PPP= Purchasing Power Parity, SIN = Singapore, SOL = Solomon Islands, SRI = Sri Lanka, TAJ = Tajikistan, THA = Thailand, TKM = Turkmenistan, UZB = Uzbekistan, VIE = Viet Nam.

Sources: Table 8.7; World Bank. World Development Indicators. http://databank.worldbank.org/data/reports.aspx?source=world-development-indicators (accessed 5 July 2017).

Data Issues and Comparability

Data on government expenditure and revenue are from economy sources. The coverage of the budget data is not standard throughout the region. Data from different economies refer only to the central government, except for Bangladesh, Georgia, Kiribati, the Kyrgyz Republic, Mongolia, Pakistan, and Tajikistan, where data refer to consolidated government or general government. For Australia, data refer to the Commonwealth government. Most economies try to follow the International Monetary Fund's Government Finance Statistics guidelines, while some economies are still using the 1986 version and others have switched to the 2001 guidelines. Most economies record their transactions on a cash basis, and a few on accrual. Few economies include revenues from social contributions as part of tax revenue, others lump it under nontax revenue; and some countries do not include social contributions as part of revenue.

Statistics on the time and cost for registering new businesses and on perceived corruption are taken from nonofficial sources. Common procedures are used in all economies and the researchers producing these data have refined their procedures over several surveys. However, because of the subjective nature of much of the data, they can only be used to give a broad idea of trends, levels, and rankings; small changes from one year to the next should be interpreted with care. For more details on the methodology, refer to the methodological notes of the World Bank's Doing Business database and Transparency International.

Table 8.1: **Fiscal Balance**[a]
(% of GDP)

Regional Member	2000	2005	2010	2011	2012	2013	2014	2015	2016
Developing Member Economies									
Central and West Asia									
Afghanistan[b]	-1.2 (2002)	-4.5	2.5	-0.2	-0.5	2.3	-1.7	1.6	-0.1
Armenia	-4.9	-1.9	-5.0	-2.8	-1.4	-1.6	-1.9	-4.8	-3.4
Azerbaijan	-1.0	-0.7	-0.9	0.6	-0.2	0.6	-0.5	-0.5	-0.4
Georgia	-1.3	1.2	-5.6	-2.1	-1.7	-2.1	-2.8	-2.6	-2.9
Kazakhstan	-0.1	0.6	-2.4	-2.0	-2.9	-1.9	-2.7	-2.2	-1.6
Kyrgyz Republic	-2.0	0.2	-4.9	-4.8	-6.5	-0.7	-0.5	-1.4	-4.6
Pakistan[c]	-5.4	-3.0	-5.9	-6.3	-8.6	-8.1	-4.7	-5.2	-4.5
Tajikistan	-0.6	0.2	-7.1	-5.8	-3.4	-5.4	-3.8	-7.8	-10.4
Turkmenistan	-0.3	0.8	2.0	3.5	6.4	1.5	0.9	-0.7	0.6
Uzbekistan	-1.0	0.1	0.3	0.4	0.4	0.3	1.3	0.1	0.1
East Asia									
China, People's Rep. of	-2.8	-1.2	-1.6	-1.1	-1.6	-1.8	-1.8	-3.4	-3.8
Hong Kong, China[d]	-0.6	1.0	4.2	3.8	3.2	1.0	3.6	0.6	3.7
Korea, Rep. of	1.0	0.4	1.3	1.4	1.3	1.0	0.6	-0.0	1.0
Mongolia	-5.7	2.4	0.4	-6.4	-6.8	-1.2	-3.9	-5.0	-15.4
Taipei,China	-4.5	-0.3	-2.6	-1.5	-2.8	-1.0	-0.8	0.2	...
South Asia									
Bangladesh[c]	-4.5	-3.7	-2.8	-3.6	-3.2	-3.3	-3.1	-3.9	-3.7
Bhutan[c]	-3.9	-6.6	1.5	-2.0	-1.1	-4.0	3.6	1.4	-1.0
India[d]	-5.5	-4.0	-4.8	-5.9	-4.9	-4.5	-4.1	-3.9	-3.5
Maldives	-4.4	-7.3	-14.4	-6.6	-7.7	-4.1	-2.9	-6.8	-5.8
Nepal[e]	-4.7	-2.4	-1.9	-2.4	-2.0	0.6	0.9	-0.7	-4.5
Sri Lanka	-9.3	-7.0	-7.0	-6.2	-5.6	-5.4	-5.7	-7.4	...
Southeast Asia									
Brunei Darussalam[f]	10.9	21.1	15.6	25.6	15.7	10.1	-0.7	-14.0	2.9
Cambodia	-2.1	-0.7	-8.8	-7.6	-6.8	-6.9	-3.8	-2.6	-1.5
Indonesia	-1.1	-0.5	-0.7	-1.1	-1.8	-2.2	-2.1	-2.6	-2.5
Lao PDR[g]	-4.6	-4.5	-2.2	-1.6	-1.0	-5.2	-3.2	-3.4	...
Malaysia	-5.5	-3.4	-5.3	-4.7	-4.3	-3.8	-3.4	-3.2	-3.1
Myanmar[d]	0.7	-4.3 (2006)	-4.6	-3.8	-4.7	-5.4	-1.1	-4.3	-6.0
Philippines	-3.7	-2.6	-3.5	-2.0	-2.3	-1.4	-0.6	-0.9	-2.4
Singapore[d]	9.7	6.4	7.6	9.2	8.6	8.2	7.3	4.4	...
Thailand[g]	-2.8	0.1	-2.9	-1.6	-2.2	-0.7	-2.0	-1.3	-0.7
Viet Nam[h]	-4.3	-1.0	-2.1	-0.5	-3.4	-5.0	-4.4	-4.6	-4.2
The Pacific									
Cook Islands[c]	-1.5	2.1	6.4	3.7	4.1	2.6	...	...	...
Fiji[i]	-3.1	-3.4	-2.2	-1.4	-1.1	-0.5	-4.0	-3.2	-1.6
Kiribati	42.3	7.0	16.9 (2008)	...	...	...	...	...	...
Marshall Islands[g]	8.1	-22.3	3.4	2.1	-0.7	-0.2	3.2	2.8	...
Micronesia, Fed. States of[g]	-3.5	-5.6	0.5	-0.6	0.9	2.9	11.2	10.5	11.0
Nauru[c]	...	4.3	0.1	...	...	...	0.1	...	-0.1
Palau[g]	-12.9	1.6	-1.0	1.3	1.0	0.7	3.6	4.8	4.3
Papua New Guinea	-2.0	0.1	0.5	-0.2	-3.1	-5.6	-5.3	...	...
Samoa[c]	-0.7	2.0	-5.6	-5.1	-7.2	-3.7	-5.1	-3.8	-0.4
Solomon Islands	-0.6	-0.9	8.3	6.4	6.6	5.0	2.9	1.1	-4.6
Timor-Leste	...	3.9	3.7	-11.7	-31.6	-29.5	-54.9	-76.1	...
Tonga[c]	-0.3	3.0	-2.7	-7.6	-7.1	-0.8	1.9	-0.1	2.6
Tuvalu	-2.0	-7.8	-0.1	-8.9	9.3	26.3	36.4	7.2	...
Vanuatu	-6.2	2.9	4.9	1.8	1.6	0.9	0.7	...	...
Developed Member Economies									
Australia[c]	1.8	1.5	-3.5	-3.3	-2.7	-1.4	-2.0	-2.3	-2.1
Japan[d]	-6.1	-3.9	-7.5	-8.3	-7.4	-6.8	-5.2	-4.5	...
New Zealand[j]	2.0	6.1	0.9	0.4	0.5	0.6	0.8	0.9	1.1

... = data not available at cutoff date, -0.0 = magnitude is less than half of unit employed, GDP = gross domestic product, Lao PDR = Lao People's Democratic Republic.

a Data refer to central government, except for Bangladesh, Georgia, the Federated States of Micronesia, Kiribati, the Kyrgyz Republic, Mongolia, Pakistan, and Tajikistan, where data refer to consolidated government or general government. For the People's Republic of China, data refer to consolidated central and local governments. For Australia, data refer to the Commonwealth government.

b For 2012, government finance covers 9 months only (21 March to 20 December) due to the change of Afghanistan's fiscal year effective FY1391 (2012). From 2013 onward, the fiscal year begins on 21 December and ends on 20 December.

c Data are based on fiscal year ending 30 June.

d Data are based on fiscal year beginning 1 April.

e Data are based on fiscal year ending 15 July.

f Data for 2005 onward are based on fiscal year beginning 1 April.

g Data are based on fiscal year ending 30 September.

h Tax revenue includes local government taxes.

i Data for 2015 onward are based on fiscal year ending 31 July.

j Data for 2000–2008 refer to fiscal year ending 31 March, and for 2009–2016 to fiscal year ending 30 June.

Source: Economy sources.

Table 8.2: **Tax Revenue**[a]
(% of GDP)

Regional Member	2000	2005	2010	2011	2012	2013	2014	2015	2016
Developing Member Economies									
Central and West Asia									
Afghanistan[b]	...	3.8	8.9	8.4	5.5	6.7	6.4	7.1	5.0
Armenia	14.8	14.3	20.2	20.6	20.6	22.0	22.0	21.2	21.3
Azerbaijan	12.2	14.0	12.4	12.3	12.7	13.2	14.2	16.2	15.0
Georgia	14.6	20.8	23.5	25.2	25.5	24.8	24.8	25.2	25.9
Kazakhstan	20.2	26.3	13.4	14.1	13.2	13.3	12.9	11.9	13.0
Kyrgyz Republic	11.7	16.2	17.9	18.5	20.6	20.5	20.6	19.7	20.5
Pakistan[c]	10.6	10.1	9.9	9.3	10.2	9.8	10.2	11.0	12.6
Tajikistan	13.1	16.5	18.0	19.5	19.6	20.8	22.7	21.9	20.6
Turkmenistan	23.0	20.9 (2004)	...	17.5	20.2	17.7	17.0	15.6	...
Uzbekistan	23.4 (2001)	20.6	20.0	19.5	19.6	19.6	19.6	19.1	18.9
East Asia									
China, People's Rep. of	12.5	15.4	17.7	18.3	18.6	18.6	18.5	18.1	17.5
Hong Kong, China[d]	9.7	12.3	13.6	14.2	13.7	13.5	15.7	14.4	13.9
Korea, Rep. of	17.0	13.9	14.0	14.4	14.7	14.1	13.8	14.0	14.8
Mongolia	22.4	22.8	27.6	27.8	25.2	26.5	23.2	22.1	20.9
Taipei,China	13.1	8.8	7.6	8.4	8.4	8.0	8.4	8.7	...
South Asia									
Bangladesh[c]	6.8	8.6	7.8	8.7	9.0	9.0	8.6	8.5	8.8
Bhutan[c]	10.0	9.4	13.3	13.6	15.1	14.6	13.5	13.9	13.1
India[d]	6.3	7.3	7.3	7.2	7.5	7.3	7.3	6.9	7.2
Maldives	13.8	12.0	9.9	13.7	17.8	20.7	22.8	23.0	23.9
Nepal[e]	8.7	9.2	13.4	13.0	13.9	15.3	15.9	16.7	18.3
Sri Lanka	14.2	13.7	11.3	11.7	10.4	10.5	10.1	12.1	...
Southeast Asia									
Brunei Darussalam[f]	23.4	33.1	24.0 (2009)	...	...	...	...	...	...
Cambodia	7.3	7.7	10.1	10.2	11.4	11.9	13.8	14.7	15.0
Indonesia	8.3	12.5	10.5	11.2	11.4	11.3	10.9	10.8	10.4
Lao PDR[g]	10.6	9.7	13.5	14.1	13.4	13.5	13.6	13.4	...
Malaysia	13.2	14.8	13.3	14.8	15.6	15.3	14.8	14.3	13.8
Myanmar[d]	2.0	4.3 (2006)	3.2	3.7	3.8	6.3	10.0	8.7	8.2
Philippines	12.8	12.4	12.1	12.4	12.9	13.3	13.6	13.6	13.7
Singapore[d]	14.9	11.6	13.0	13.3	13.9	13.5	13.9	13.6	...
Thailand[g]	12.8	15.2	14.6	15.9	15.1	16.9	15.6	16.3	15.7
Viet Nam[h]	18.0	21.0	22.4	22.3	19.0	19.1	18.2	18.2	17.9
The Pacific									
Cook Islands[c]	22.3	25.3	25.5	25.1	23.6	25.5	...	...	...
Fiji[i]	20.0	21.1	21.6	23.5	24.2	24.3	24.8	23.9	24.8
Kiribati	21.5	20.8	17.1	18.1	17.7	17.7	16.1	17.5	...
Marshall Islands[g]	15.4	18.3	17.1	16.8	15.8	15.9	15.9	17.2	...
Micronesia, Fed. States of[g]	11.9	11.7	12.0	12.0	11.6	12.1	19.0	12.4	12.0
Nauru[c]	...	...	...	...	8.0	15.3	14.9	18.8	22.5
Palau[g]	16.1	16.7	17.0	17.3	18.1	18.2	19.2	19.1	19.7
Papua New Guinea	23.8	24.8	16.6	18.5	18.4	18.0	16.9	...	...
Samoa[c]	20.6	20.6	20.9	18.8	19.7	21.8	22.4	22.3	23.6
Solomon Islands	19.1	24.3	34.0	36.9	37.3	37.2	35.0	34.2	30.8
Timor-Leste	...	1.5	1.2	2.1	3.5	4.7	7.5	8.0	...
Tonga[c]	15.8	19.2	16.1	17.0	15.9	17.0	17.0	19.0	20.8
Tuvalu	21.5	21.5	16.3	16.9	15.0	19.0	18.0	19.4	...
Vanuatu	15.7	16.4	16.3	16.4	16.5	17.2	17.2	...	...
Developed Member Economies									
Australia[c]	23.2	24.8	20.7	20.6	21.4	22.2	22.2	22.1	22.4
Japan[d]	10.0	9.8	8.6	9.1	9.4	10.0	11.1	11.1	...
New Zealand[j]	32.7	35.9	27.0	26.5	27.1	28.3	27.8	28.8	29.3

... = data not available at cutoff date, GDP = gross domestic product, Lao PDR = Lao People's Democratic Republic.

a Data refer to central government, except for Bangladesh, Georgia, the Federated States of Micronesia, Kiribati, the Kyrgyz Republic, Mongolia, Pakistan, and Tajikistan, where data refer to consolidated government or general government. For the People's Republic of China, data refer to consolidated central and local governments. For Australia, data refer to the Commonwealth government.

b For 2012, government finance covers 9 months only (21 March to 20 December) due to the change of Afghanistan's fiscal year effective FY1391 (2012). From 2013 onward, the fiscal year begins on 21 December and ends on 20 December.

c Data are based on fiscal year ending 30 June.

d Data are based on fiscal year beginning 1 April.

e Data are based on fiscal year ending 15 July.

f Data for 2005 onward are based on fiscal year beginning 1 April.

g Data are based on fiscal year ending 30 September.

h Tax revenue includes local government taxes.

i Data for 2015 onward are based on fiscal year ending 31 July.

j Data for 2000–2008 refer to fiscal year ending 31 March, and for 2009–2016 to fiscal year ending 30 June.

Source: Economy sources.

Table 8.3: **Total Government Revenue**[a]
(% of GDP)

Regional Member	2000	2005	2010	2011	2012	2013	2014	2015	2016
Developing Member Economies									
Central and West Asia									
Afghanistan[b]	2.9 (2002)	6.9	10.8	11.1	7.5	9.2	8.2	9.7	10.3
Armenia	15.9	16.2	21.7	21.8	21.8	23.3	23.4	22.7	22.6
Azerbaijan	14.7	16.3	26.8	30.1	31.6	33.5	31.2	32.2	29.0
Georgia	15.5	27.1	27.1	28.9	28.9	27.3	27.3	28.3	28.7
Kazakhstan	22.9	27.6	14.2	14.8	14.3	13.8	13.5	12.7	14.0
Kyrgyz Republic	14.2	19.8	23.1	24.2	26.2	26.1	27.3	27.7	26.4
Pakistan[c]	13.4	13.8	14.0	12.3	12.8	13.3	14.5	14.3	15.3
Tajikistan	14.1	19.2	19.3	21.1	21.5	22.7	25.1	25.0	23.4
Turkmenistan	23.5	20.5	16.1	18.1	21.0	18.4	17.9	16.6	14.7
Uzbekistan	28.0	21.6	21.8	21.7	21.7	21.7	21.8	21.2	20.6
East Asia									
China, People's Rep. of	13.4	16.9	20.1	21.2	21.7	21.7	21.8	22.1	21.4
Hong Kong, China[d]	16.8	17.5	21.2	22.6	21.7	21.3	21.2	18.8	22.5
Korea, Rep. of	21.4	20.8	21.4	21.9	22.6	22.0	21.6	21.8	22.7
Mongolia	27.8	27.4	31.6	32.2	29.1	31.0	28.2	25.6	24.2
Taipei,China	17.7	14.3	10.7	11.8	11.0	11.5	10.9	11.6	...
South Asia									
Bangladesh[c]	8.5	10.6	9.5	10.2	10.9	10.8	10.5	9.7	10.0
Bhutan[c]	23.2	17.0	27.4	20.8	20.7	20.0	19.7	19.9	17.8
India[d]	9.5	9.7	10.6	9.0	9.3	9.4	9.3	9.2	9.8
Maldives	30.0	26.4	21.5	25.6	25.3	27.4	31.5	31.5	37.1
Nepal[e]	11.3	11.9	14.9	14.5	16.0	17.6	18.8	19.3	20.5
Sri Lanka	16.4	15.5	12.7	13.4	12.0	11.9	11.4	13.0	...
Southeast Asia									
Brunei Darussalam[f]	49.1	53.2	49.0	55.3	46.8	37.9	31.1	20.3	13.8
Cambodia	10.0	10.6	12.6	12.4	14.4	14.3	17.1	16.8	17.6
Indonesia	14.7	17.8	14.5	15.4	15.5	15.0	14.6	13.0	12.5
Lao PDR[g]	13.1	11.7	15.3	15.7	15.2	15.6	16.1	15.5	...
Malaysia	17.4	19.6	19.4	20.3	21.4	20.9	19.9	18.9	17.3
Myanmar[d]	4.2	17.6 (2006)	14.2	14.7	23.0	24.4	25.1	21.7	19.8
Philippines	14.3	14.4	13.4	14.0	14.5	14.9	15.1	15.8	15.2
Singapore[d]	29.3	20.9	22.1	23.8	22.9	22.2	22.2	22.5	...
Thailand[g]	14.7	17.3	16.8	17.8	17.1	19.4	18.2	19.2	18.8
Viet Nam[h]	20.1	25.7	26.7	25.5	22.3	22.8	22.0	23.5	24.3
The Pacific									
Cook Islands[c]	27.0	29.3	34.1	35.1	33.4	35.3	...	...	...
Fiji[i]	25.5	24.2	25.4	26.6	27.0	27.0	27.6	26.5	29.1
Kiribati	94.4	65.2	52.4 (2009)	...	88.8	86.6	114.3	126.2	...
Marshall Islands[g]	22.0	22.0	19.9	20.0	19.2	21.4	23.8	27.1	...
Micronesia, Fed. States of[g]	22.5	19.7	21.4	20.6	22.8	26.7	36.9	37.1	35.1
Nauru[c]	...	33.1	39.2	...	31.9	39.1	60.0	64.7	94.1
Palau[g]	22.4	19.1	19.7	20.6	21.8	22.0	24.1	23.9	25.1
Papua New Guinea	25.7	26.8	17.8	19.4	19.5	18.8	18.8	...	...
Samoa[c]	25.6	24.1	23.6	21.9	22.7	23.8	24.6	24.9	26.1
Solomon Islands	21.6	26.7	37.0	40.4	43.0	51.4	47.2	46.6	40.3
Timor-Leste	...	9.5	22.7	17.0	5.4	6.5	10.2	12.0	...
Tonga[c]	21.1	22.8	20.1	19.6	18.1	19.7	20.1	22.3	24.7
Tuvalu	215.6	55.7	52.2	47.8	56.5	82.9	74.2	105.5	...
Vanuatu	18.7	18.5	18.1	18.1	18.8	19.2	19.1	...	...
Developed Member Economies									
Australia[c]	25.3	26.2	22.6	22.0	22.7	23.7	23.6	23.6	23.9
Japan[d]	11.7	11.5	9.9	10.4	10.8	11.6	12.5	12.7	...
New Zealand[j]	37.6	41.9	33.5	35.1	33.5	34.5	33.9	34.5	35.5

... = data not available at cutoff date, GDP = gross domestic product, Lao PDR = Lao People's Democratic Republic.

a Data refer to central government, except for Bangladesh, Georgia, the Federated States of Micronesia, Kiribati, the Kyrgyz Republic, Mongolia, Pakistan, and Tajikistan, where data refer to consolidated government or general government. For the People's Republic of China, data refer to consolidated central and local governments. For Australia, data refer to the Commonwealth government.

b For 2012, government finance covers 9 months only (21 March to 20 December) due to the change of Afghanistan's fiscal year effective FY1391 (2012). From 2013 onward, the fiscal year begins on 21 December and ends on 20 December.

c Data are based on fiscal year ending 30 June.

d Data are based on fiscal year beginning 1 April.

e Data are based on fiscal year ending 15 July.

f Data for 2005 onward are based on fiscal year beginning 1 April.

g Data are based on fiscal year ending 30 September.

h Tax revenue includes local government taxes.

i Data for 2015 onward are based on fiscal year ending 31 July.

j Data for 2000–2008 refers to fiscal year ending 31 March, and for 2009–2016 refers to fiscal year ending 30 June.

Source: Economy sources.

Table 8.4: **Total Government Expenditure**[a]
(% of GDP)

Regional Member	2000	2005	2010	2011	2012	2013	2014	2015	2016
Developing Member Economies									
Central and West Asia									
Afghanistan[b]	7.7 (2002)	16.5	20.6	22.0	17.4	23.2	24.6	25.5	25.7
Armenia	20.1	18.0	27.6	26.2	23.6	25.1	25.6	28.0	26.3
Azerbaijan	16.2	16.8	27.6	29.2	31.6	31.4	31.1	31.7	26.9
Georgia	16.3	26.6	34.0	30.7	30.6	29.4	30.3	30.5	31.1
Kazakhstan	22.2	25.6	22.0	20.8	21.5	19.6	21.1	20.7	21.2
Kyrgyz Republic	18.0	20.4	31.2	32.0	34.5	29.3	30.3	31.3	33.1
Pakistan[c]	18.9	18.0	20.2	18.6	21.2	19.8	20.4	20.2	20.6
Tajikistan	14.7	19.4	25.1	27.4	25.1	28.5	28.8	33.6	33.8
Turkmenistan	23.9	19.7	14.1	14.6	14.7	16.9	17.0	17.3	14.1
Uzbekistan	28.9	21.5	21.5	21.2	21.3	21.4	20.4	21.1	20.5
East Asia									
China, People's Rep. of	16.1	18.1	21.8	22.3	23.3	23.6	23.6	25.5	25.2
Hong Kong, China[d]	17.4	16.5	17.0	18.8	18.5	20.3	17.5	18.2	18.7
Korea, Rep. of	17.2	20.1	19.8	20.2	20.8	21.1	21.0	21.2	20.9
Mongolia	28.6	22.7	29.2	34.3	35.5	31.5	31.8	30.7	37.8
Taipei,China	22.2	14.6	13.3	13.3	13.7	12.5	11.7	11.4	...
South Asia									
Bangladesh[c]	14.5	15.0	12.7	13.0	13.0	13.3	13.5	13.0	13.7
Bhutan[c]	42.2	35.4	35.6	34.8	35.8	34.7	29.0	27.6	29.4
India[d]	15.0	13.7	15.4	14.9	14.2	13.9	13.4	13.1	13.4
Maldives	37.3	40.3	37.0	35.4	34.1	31.8	34.8	40.3	45.0
Nepal[e]	17.5	15.3	19.0	18.8	19.3	17.8	18.8	20.1	26.4
Sri Lanka	25.0	23.8	19.3	19.4	17.5	17.3	17.1	20.5	...
Southeast Asia									
Brunei Darussalam[f]	40.6	32.1	33.3	29.7	31.0	27.8	31.8	34.3	38.2
Cambodia	14.8	13.2	21.4	20.0	21.2	21.1	20.9	19.4	19.1
Indonesia	15.8	18.4	15.2	16.5	17.3	17.3	16.8	15.7	15.0
Lao PDR[g]	20.8	18.4	24.2	23.3	22.1	26.3	24.8	23.5	...
Malaysia	22.9	23.0	24.7	25.0	25.7	24.7	23.3	22.1	20.4
Myanmar[d]	3.5	19.2	18.9	18.5	27.6	29.8	26.2	26.0	25.8
Philippines	18.1	16.9	16.8	15.9	16.6	16.1	15.6	16.7	17.5
Singapore[d]	18.2	14.5	14.5	14.6	14.3	14.0	15.0	18.1	...
Thailand[g]	16.8	17.2	19.7	19.4	19.4	20.0	20.3	20.5	19.5
Viet Nam[h]	22.6	25.1	27.2	25.4	28.2	28.8	26.4	28.5	28.7
The Pacific									
Cook Islands[c]	31.0	33.3	33.0	39.7	36.5	41.2	...	...	...
Fiji[i]	28.6	27.6	27.7	28.0	28.3	27.6	31.3	29.9	30.8
Kiribati	87.4	100.2	86.9	92.3	104.5	97.4	105.4	86.3	...
Marshall Islands[g]	58.6	85.3	57.9	55.8	52.0	53.7	50.0	55.8	...
Micronesia, Fed. States of[g]	67.2	59.1	67.0	65.2	65.0	59.1	53.6	55.5	53.4
Nauru[c]	...	28.5	83.6	...	44.7	57.4	51.8	72.4	91.7
Palau[g]	56.5	38.9	47.7	42.3	43.2	39.6	39.7	33.7	36.7
Papua New Guinea	32.9	35.2	20.9	22.0	24.7	26.2	25.6	...	...
Samoa[c]	31.2	32.7	30.0	33.0	32.6	30.1	34.0	30.8	28.6
Solomon Islands	31.6	34.6	39.7	41.2	41.9	58.4	54.5	55.0	51.3
Timor-Leste	...	5.6	19.0	28.7	37.0	35.9	65.0	88.1	...
Tonga[c]	22.2	21.2	28.0	32.4	29.5	25.5	26.7	35.8	39.4
Tuvalu	186.3	78.6	104.7	77.9	75.0	81.2	86.8	116.3	...
Vanuatu	26.0	18.4	22.2	21.8	21.8	20.6	21.4	...	...
Developed Member Economies									
Australia[c]	23.5	24.8	26.1	25.3	25.4	25.1	25.5	25.9	26.0
Japan[d]	17.8	15.4	17.3	18.8	18.3	18.4	17.8	17.2	...
New Zealand[j]	35.7	35.8	35.9	42.0	35.7	35.4	33.9	33.7	33.3

... = data not available at cutoff date, GDP = gross domestic product, Lao PDR = Lao People's Democratic Republic.

a Data refer to central government, except for Bangladesh, Georgia, the Federated States of Micronesia, Kiribati, the Kyrgyz Republic, Mongolia, Pakistan, and Tajikistan, where data refer to consolidated government or general government. For the People's Republic of China, data refer to consolidated central and local governments. For Australia, data refer to the Commonwealth government.
b For 2012, government finance covers 9 months only (21 March to 20 December) due to the change of Afghanistan's fiscal year effective FY1391 (2012). From 2013 onward, the fiscal year begins on 21 December and ends on 20 December.
c Data are based on fiscal year ending 30 June.
d Data are based on fiscal year beginning 1 April.
e Data are based on fiscal year ending 15 July.
f Data for 2005 onward are based on fiscal year beginning 1 April.
g Data are based on fiscal year ending 30 September.
h Total expenditure includes local government expenditure.
i Data for 2015 onward are based on fiscal year ending 31 July.
j Data for 2000–2008 refer to fiscal year ending 31 March, and for 2009–2016 to fiscal year ending 30 June.

Source: Economy sources.

Table 8.5: **Government Expenditure by Economic Activity**[a]
(% of GDP)

Regional Member	Health			Education			Social Security and Welfare		
	2000	2010	2016	2000	2010	2016	2000	2010	2016
Developing Member Economies									
Central and West Asia									
Afghanistan	...	...	...	...	...	...	...	...	...
Armenia	1.0	1.6	1.6	2.8	2.8	2.4	2.1	7.1	7.8
Azerbaijan	0.9	1.0	1.2	3.9	2.8	2.9	3.0	2.6	4.4
Georgia	0.6	2.2	3.1	2.2	2.9	3.8	4.3	6.9	7.8
Kazakhstan	...	...	...	...	...	...	...	...	...
Kyrgyz Republic	2.0	2.9	2.9	3.5	5.4	6.6	1.7	5.0	5.5
Pakistan[b]	...	...	...	...	...	...	...	...	...
Tajikistan[c]	0.9	1.4	2.1	2.3	4.0	5.8	1.8	3.5	5.0
Turkmenistan	...	...	...	...	...	...	...	...	...
Uzbekistan	...	2.8	3.0 (2015)	...	7.2	7.1 (2015)	...	2.2	1.3 (2015)
East Asia									
China, People's Rep. of	...	1.2	1.8	3.3 (2002)	3.0	3.8	0.7	2.2	2.9
Hong Kong, China[d]	2.4	2.2	2.7	3.9	3.4	3.3	2.1	2.3	2.7
Korea, Rep. of	0.1	0.2	0.3 (2015)	3.1	3.0	3.2 (2015)	3.0	4.5	5.6 (2015)
Mongolia	3.8	2.5	2.9 (2014)	6.7	5.1	8.8 (2014)	6.2	11.1	10.3 (2014)
Taipei,China	0.2	0.2	0.1 (2015)	2.3	1.7	1.5 (2015)	5.6	3.1	3.5 (2015)
South Asia									
Bangladesh[b]	1.0	0.8	0.7	2.0	2.0	2.3	0.1	0.9	0.9
Bhutan[b]	...	3.0	2.7	...	6.7	5.9	...	3.1	3.0
India[d,e]	0.7	0.7	1.2 (2014)	3.2	1.9	4.6 (2014)	0.8	0.4	1.9 (2014)
Maldives	4.1	3.3	4.2 (2015)	7.4	5.5	5.6 (2015)	1.0	1.9	6.3 (2015)
Nepal[f]	0.9	1.5	1.5	2.4	3.9	4.0	0.9	0.8	0.9
Sri Lanka	1.6	1.2	1.6 (2015)	2.4	1.6	2.0 (2015)	2.8	1.7	2.1 (2015)
Southeast Asia									
Brunei Darussalam[g]	2.1	1.8	...	4.2	3.6	...	1.2	0.8	...
Cambodia	0.9	1.3	1.3	1.3	1.6	2.3	0.2	0.5	0.8
Indonesia	...	...	...	...	...	...	...	...	...
Lao PDR[h]	1.0	...	...	1.0	...	...	...	...	...
Malaysia	1.5	2.0	1.9	5.6	6.1	4.5	0.9	1.2	0.9
Myanmar[d]	...	...	...	...	...	...	...	...	...
Philippines	0.4	0.3	0.9	3.3	2.5	3.5	0.7	0.5	0.8
Singapore[d]	0.9	1.2	2.2 (2015)	3.9	3.0	3.0 (2015)	0.6	1.1	1.9 (2015)
Thailand[h]	1.3	1.9	1.2	3.9	4.1	3.7	0.9	1.7	2.4
Viet Nam[i]	...	...	...	...	...	...	...	...	...
The Pacific									
Cook Islands[b]	3.1	3.3	...	3.2	4.9	...	...	...	...
Fiji[j]	2.3	2.1	2.1 (2015)	4.3	3.5	3.2 (2015)	0.1	0.1	0.1 (2015)
Kiribati	7.6	8.6	8.0 (2015)	11.0	10.1	8.9 (2015)	0.9	1.6	1.3 (2015)
Marshall Islands[h]	...	...	...	...	...	...	...	...	...
Micronesia, Fed. States of[h]	...	...	...	...	...	...	...	...	...
Nauru[b]	...	...	...	...	...	...	...	...	...
Palau[h]	...	...	...	...	...	...	...	...	...
Papua New Guinea	1.6	...	...	5.1	...	...	...	...	...
Samoa[b]	4.0	3.7	4.1	4.9	4.3	4.1	1.1	1.2	1.5
Solomon Islands	...	...	...	...	...	...	...	...	...
Timor-Leste	...	0.9	3.8 (2015)	...	1.7	7.6 (2015)	...	3.5	10.9 (2015)
Tonga[b]	4.8	...	...	4.4	...	...	...	...	...
Tuvalu	...	...	...	...	...	...	...	...	...
Vanuatu	2.4	...	...	4.9	...	...	0.0	...	...
Developed Member Economies									
Australia[b]	3.9	4.0	4.2	1.6	2.8	2.0	8.6	8.4	9.2
Japan[d]	6.1	7.1	7.6 (2015)	3.7	2.9	2.8 (2015)	10.2	15.8	16.0 (2015)
New Zealand[k]	5.3	7.1	7.0	4.9	6.8	6.2	11.7	12.6	11.4

... = data not available at cutoff date, 0.0 = magnitude is less than half of unit employed, GDP = gross domestic product, Lao PDR = Lao People's Democratic Republic.

a Data refer to central government, except for Bangladesh, Georgia, the Federated States of Micronesia, Kiribati, the Kyrgyz Republic, Mongolia, Pakistan, and Tajikistan, where data refer to consolidated government or general government. For the People's Republic of China, data refer to consolidated central and local governments. For Australia, data refer to the Commonwealth government.
b Data are based on fiscal year ending 30 June.
c Data for social security and welfare include defense.
d Data are based on fiscal year beginning 1 April.
e For 2012 to 2016, data for general government relate to administrative departments (current and capital expenditure) excluding the local bodies.
f Data are based on fiscal year ending 15 July.
g Data for 2005 onward are based on fiscal year beginning 1 April.
h Data are based on fiscal year ending 30 September.
i Total expenditure includes local government expenditure.
j Data for 2015 onward are based on fiscal year ending 31 July.
k Data for 2000–2008 refer to fiscal year ending 31 March, and for 2009–2016 to fiscal year ending 30 June.

Source: Economy sources.

Table 8.6: **Doing Business Start-Up Indicators**

Regional Member	Cost of Business Start-Up Procedure (% of GNI per capita)			Time Required to Start a Business (days)		
	2005	2010	2016	2005	2010	2016
Developing Member Economies						
Central and West Asia[a]	**27.8**	**12.0**	**6.6**	**38**	**14**	**9**
Afghanistan	75.2	26.7	19.9	10	8	8
Armenia	6.1	3.1	0.9	18	14	4
Azerbaijan	12.3	3.1	1.3	113	8	3
Georgia	13.7	5.0	2.4	22	4	3
Kazakhstan	9.9	1.0	0.3	31	25	9
Kyrgyz Republic	10.4	3.7	2.0	21	14	10
Pakistan	25.6	17.8	12.4	23	20	18
Tajikistan	85.1	36.9	16.8	79	16	22
Turkmenistan	...	...	...	...	...	...
Uzbekistan	11.5	10.8	3.2	28	14	6
East Asia[a]	**9.3**	**5.7**	**3.9**	**31**	**17**	**10**
China, People's Rep. of	13.6	4.5	0.7	48	38	29
Hong Kong, China	3.4	2.0	0.6	11	6	2
Korea, Rep. of	15.7	14.7	14.6	17	14	4
Mongolia	9.6	3.2	1.5	13	13	6
Taipei,China	4.4	4.0	2.1	65	15	10
South Asia[a]	**44.8**	**28.0**	**12.5**	**49**	**31**	**16**
Bangladesh	56.1	21.2	13.8	52	27	20
Bhutan	16.9	6.1	3.8	62	46	15
India	62.0	50.5	13.8	93	30	26
Maldives	14.0	9.4	5.2	9	12	12
Nepal	69.9	46.6	26.1	31	31	17
Sri Lanka	50.0	33.9	12.2	46	38	9
Southeast Asia[a]	**55.6**	**39.4**	**15.7**	**74**	**55**	**32**
Brunei Darussalam	8.9 (2006)	13.7	1.6	122 (2006)	109	15
Cambodia	276.1	127.5	57.2	87	102	99
Indonesia	101.7	25.8	19.4	164	49	25
Lao PDR	17.4	8.9	4.6	131	85	67
Malaysia	26.6	17.5	6.2	38	18	19
Myanmar	...	157.7 (2012)	40.4	...	76 (2012)	13
Philippines	23.9	22.1	15.8	47	37	28
Singapore	0.9	0.7	0.6	6	3	3
Thailand	17.3	7.7	6.6	34	33	26
Viet Nam	27.6	12.1	4.6	41	36	24
The Pacific[a]	**59.4**	**37.1**	**28.5**	**47**	**39**	**21**
Cook Islands	...	...	...	...	...	...
Fiji	28.4	23.8	17.9	44	44	40
Kiribati	40.3	47.1	36.3	31	31	31
Marshall Islands	22.4	17.6	12.5	17	17	17
Micronesia, Fed. States of	127.6	137.8	140.4	16	16	16
Nauru	...	...	...	...	...	...
Palau	4.7	5.7	2.9	24	28	28
Papua New Guinea	27.7	27.0	15.6	52	52	41
Samoa	46.4	9.8	7.7	35	9	9
Solomon Islands	135.5	78.5	28.5	55	55	9
Timor-Leste	125.4	5.7	0.5	167	110	9
Tonga	11.7	7.0	6.8	32	25	16
Tuvalu	...	...	...	...	...	...
Vanuatu	83.5	48.2	44.3	47	47	18
Developed Member Economies[a]	**4.3**	**2.9**	**2.8**	**15**	**9**	**5**
Australia	1.9	0.7	0.7	3	3	3
Japan	10.7	7.5	7.5	31	23	11
New Zealand	0.2	0.4	0.3	12	1	1
DEVELOPING MEMBER ECONOMIES[a]	**43.0**	**27.0**	**15.2**	**50**	**33**	**19**
REGIONAL MEMBERS[a]	**40.3**	**25.3**	**14.4**	**47**	**32**	**18**
WORLD	**80.1**	**42.9**	**25.9**	**51**	**35**	**21**

... = data not available at cutoff date, GNI = gross national income, Lao PDR = Lao People's Democratic Republic.

a Arithmetic average of reporting economies only.

Source: World Bank. Doing Business Online. http://data.worldbank.org/indicator (accessed 4 July 2017).

Table 8.7: Corruption Perceptions Index[a]

Regional Member	2000	2005	2010	2011	2012	2013	2014	2015	2016	Rank in 2015[b]	Rank in 2016[b]
Developing Member Economies											
Central and West Asia											
Afghanistan	...	2.5	1.4	1.5	8	8	12	11	15	166	169
Armenia	2.5	2.9	2.6	2.6	34	36	37	35	33	95	113
Azerbaijan	1.5	2.2	2.4	2.4	27	28	29	29	30	119	123
Georgia	2.4 (2002)	2.3	3.8	4.1	52	49	52	52	57	48	44
Kazakhstan	3.0	2.6	2.9	2.7	28	26	29	28	29	123	131
Kyrgyz Republic	...	2.3	2.0	2.1	24	24	27	28	28	123	136
Pakistan	2.3 (2001)	2.1	2.3	2.5	27	28	29	30	32	117	116
Tajikistan	...	2.1	2.1	2.3	22	22	23	26	25	136	151
Turkmenistan	...	1.8	1.6	1.6	17	17	17	18	22	154	154
Uzbekistan	2.4	2.2	1.6	1.6	17	17	18	19	21	153	156
East Asia											
China, People's Rep. of	3.1	3.2	3.5	3.6	39	40	36	37	40	83	79
Hong Kong, China	7.7	8.3	8.4	8.4	77	75	74	75	77	18	15
Korea, Rep. of	4.0	5.0	5.4	5.4	56	55	55	56	53	37	52
Mongolia	...	3.0	2.7	2.7	36	38	39	39	38	72	87
Taipei,China	5.5	5.9	5.8	6.1	61	61	61	62	61	30	31
South Asia											
Bangladesh	0.4 (2001)	1.7	2.4	2.7	26	27	25	25	26	139	145
Bhutan	...	6.0 (2006)	5.7	5.7	63	63	65	65	65	27	27
India	2.8	2.9	3.3	3.1	36	36	38	38	40	76	79
Maldives	...	3.3 (2007)	2.3	2.5	...	...	...	...	36	...	95
Nepal	...	2.5	2.2	2.2	27	31	29	27	29	130	131
Sri Lanka	3.7 (2002)	3.2	3.2	3.3	40	37	38	37	36	83	95
Southeast Asia											
Brunei Darussalam	...	...	5.5	5.2	55	60	...	...	58	...	41
Cambodia	...	2.3	2.1	2.1	22	20	21	21	21	150	156
Indonesia	1.7	2.2	2.8	3.0	32	32	34	36	37	88	90
Lao PDR	...	3.3	2.1	2.2	21	26	25	25	30	139	123
Malaysia	4.8	5.1	4.4	4.3	49	50	52	50	49	54	55
Myanmar	...	1.8	1.4	1.5	15	21	21	22	28	147	136
Philippines	2.8	2.5	2.4	2.6	34	36	38	35	35	95	101
Singapore	9.1	9.4	9.3	9.2	87	86	84	85	84	8	7
Thailand	3.2	3.8	3.5	3.4	37	35	38	38	35	76	101
Viet Nam	2.5	2.6	2.7	2.9	31	31	31	31	33	112	113
The Pacific											
Cook Islands	...	...	...	...	...	...	...	...	...	...	...
Fiji	...	4.0	...	...	...	...	...	...	...	...	...
Kiribati	...	3.3 (2007)	3.2	3.1	...	...	...	...	...	...	...
Marshall Islands	...	...	...	...	...	...	...	...	...	...	...
Micronesia, Fed. States of	...	...	...	...	...	...	...	...	...	...	...
Nauru	...	...	...	...	...	...	...	...	...	...	...
Palau	...	...	...	...	...	...	...	...	...	...	...
Papua New Guinea	...	2.3	2.1	2.2	25	25	25	25	28	139	136
Samoa	...	4.5 (2007)	4.1	3.9	...	...	52	...	...	...	...
Solomon Islands	...	2.8 (2007)	2.8	2.7	...	...	...	...	42	...	72
Timor-Leste	...	2.6 (2006)	2.5	2.4	33	30	28	28	35	123	101
Tonga	...	1.7 (2007)	3.0	3.1	...	...	...	...	...	...	...
Tuvalu	...	...	...	...	...	...	...	...	...	...	...
Vanuatu	...	3.1 (2007)	3.6	3.5	...	...	...	...	...	...	...
Developed Member Economies											
Australia	8.3	8.8	8.7	8.8	85	81	80	79	79	13	13
Japan	6.4	7.3	7.8	8.0	74	74	76	75	72	18	20
New Zealand	9.4	9.6	9.3	9.5	90	91	91	88	90	4	1

... = data not available at cutoff date, Lao PDR = Lao People's Democratic Republic.

a For 2000–2011, score relates to perception of the degree of corruption as seen by businesspeople and country analysts and are not comparable over time; score ranges from 10 (highly clean) to 0 (highly corrupt). Starting 2012, computation of the score used an updated methodology and is now presented on a 100 (very clean) to 0 (highly corrupt) scale. Scores from 2011 and previous years should not be compared with scores from 2012 onward due to differences in methodology.

b Based on Transparency International, an economy's rank indicates its position relative to the other countries in the index; 2016 rankings are based on 176 economies while 2015 rankings are based on 168 economies of the world.

Source: Transparency International. http://files.transparency.org/content/download/2060/13252/file/CPI2016_FullDataSetWithRegionalTables.xlsx (accessed 5 July 2017).

References

Asian Development Bank. 2013. *Asian Development Outlook 2013*. Manila.

Asian Development Bank. 2016. *Asian Development Outlook 2016*. Manila.

Asian Development Bank. 2017. *Asian Development Outlook 2017*. Manila.

U. Chakravorty, M. Moreaux, and L. Nostbakken. 2010. Will Biofuel Mandates Raise Food Prices. *TSE Working Papers*. No. 10-212. Toulouse: Toulouse School of Economics.

C. Constantinescu, A. Mattoo, and M. Ruta. 2017. *Global Trade Watch: Trade Developments in 2016*. Washington, DC: World Bank.

Development Bank of Singapore. 2016. *Hong Kong: Cautious Outlook*. Singapore.

Global Knowledge Partnership on Migration and Development. 2017. Migration and Remittances: Recent Developments and Outlook. *Migration and Development Brief*. No. 27. Washington, DC: World Bank.

T. Hesketh and Z. Xing. 2006. Abnormal Sex Ratios in Human Populations: Causes and Consequences. *Proceedings of the National Academy of Sciences of the United States of America*. 103 (36). pp. 13271–75.

International Monetary Fund. 2016a. *Monetary and Financial Statistics Manual and Compilation Guide*. Washington, DC.

International Monetary Fund. 2016b. Corruption: Costs and Mitigating Strategies. *IMF Staff Discussion Note*. Washington, DC.

International Telecommunication Union. 2017. ICT Statistics Database. http://www.itu.int/en/ITUD/Statistics/Pages/default.aspx (accessed 11 July 2017).

I. Loudiyi. 2010. World Bank Blog on Growth and Crisis: *The Past and Future of Export-Led Growth*. http://blogs.worldbank.org/growth/past-and-futureexport-led-growth

W. McMahon. 1998. Education and Growth in East Asia. *Economics of Education Review*. 17 (2). pp. 159–172.

Organisation for Economic Co-operation and Development. 2012. *Environmental Outlook to 2050*. Paris.

R. Quadrelli. 2015. Energy Balances across Organizations. Presentation at the 2015 Interenerstat Meeting. September 2015. IEA, Paris. https://www.iea.org/media/workshops/2015/edc/Session_6_IEA_balances.pdf

J. Smith and M. Majmundar, eds. 2012. *Aging in Asia: Findings from New and Emerging Data Initiatives*. Washington, DC: National Academies Press.

Standard Chartered Bank. 2016. Asia Leverage—After the Boom. https://www. sc.com/BeyondBorders/wp-content/uploads/2016/04/2016-04-01-BeyondBorders-Report-Asialeverage.pdf

K. Treanton. 2011. Comparing the UNSD, IEA and Eurostat Balances. Presentation at the 6th Meeting of the Oslo City Group. 2–5 May 2011. Canberra, Australia. https://unstats.un.org/oslogroup/meetings/og-06/

United Nations Conference on Trade and Development. 2017. *World Investment Report 2017*. http://unctad.org/en/PublicationChapters/wir2017ch2_en.pdf

United Nations, Department of Economic and Social Affairs, Population Division. 2014. *World Urbanization Prospects, 2014 Revision*. https://esa.un.org/unpd/wup/

United Nations, Department of Economic and Social Affairs, Population Division. *World Population Prospects, 2017 Revision*. https://esa.un.org/unpd/wpp/

United Nations Economic and Social Commission for Asia and the Pacific. 2017. *Statistical Yearbook for Asia and the Pacific 2016*. Bangkok.

United Nations Environment Programme. 2016. *Global Environment Outlook: GEO-6 Regional Assessment for Asia and the Pacific*. Nairobi.

World Bank. 2016. *Doing Business 2016: Measuring Regulatory Quality and Efficiency*. http://www.doingbusiness.org/~/media/GIAWB/Doing%20Business/Documents/AnnualReports/English/DB16-Full-Report.pdf

World Bank. 2017a. *World Bank Open Data*. http://data.worldbank.org/

World Bank. 2017b. *World Development Indicators: Metadata on Energy Use Indicator*. http://data.worldbank.org/indicator/EG.USE.PCAP.KG.OE

PART III
Global Value Chains

Asia's Emerging Role in International Production Sharing Agreements: From Factories in Asia to Markets in Asia

Snapshot

- Statistics on global value chain participation show that an increase in the domestic content of exports helped mitigate the impact of the global trade slowdown on incomes in the economies of the Asia and the Pacific region.
- Strong economic growth, despite lower values of trade in final and intermediate products, contributed to increasing localization of value chain processes in many economies in the region.

Introduction

The Asian Development Bank produces multiregional input-output tables (MRIOT) and trade in value-added statistics to illuminate the complex production sharing arrangements among economies.[1] The analysis of these for 2000 to 2015 as published in *Key Indicators for Asia and the Pacific 2016* (KI 2016) depicted a region-wide tendency toward localization of production for domestic consumption, with economies experiencing healthy growth. This occurred even as the pace of expansion in cross-border trade has decelerated markedly since 2011. Other studies, such as ADB (2016b and 2016c) have also discerned similar trends.

This Part summarizes the analysis based on MRIOTs and trade in value-added statistics, focusing on the period 2014–2016, to examine movements in global value chain participation (i.e., the sum of the share of foreign value-added, returned domestic value-added, and double counted value-added) by select economies in the Asia and Pacific region in recent years.[2] It should be noted that since the release of the KI 2016, the ADB's MRIOT database has been expanded with the addition of detailed product supply and use data of ten more Asian economies for the years 2014-2016 enabling a geographically wider analysis. The economies covered in this study are: Bangladesh; Bhutan; Brunei Darussalam; the People's Republic of China (PRC); Cambodia; Fiji; India; Indonesia; Japan; Kazakhstan; the Republic of Korea; the Kyrgyz Republic; the Lao People's Democratic Republic (Lao PDR); Malaysia; Maldives; Mongolia; Nepal; Pakistan; the Philippines; Sri Lanka; Taipei,China; Thailand; and Viet Nam.[3]

Trends in Value-Added Exports: Larger Economies Adjusting to Global and Local Conditions

From 2014 to 2016, value-added exports declined markedly across the region consequent to the global trade slowdown (Tables 3.1a–3.1f). Notable exceptions, such as Japan and Thailand, bucked the trend largely by augmenting the proportion of domestic content in their exports, for example, by undertaking greater value-adding activities in the production and supply chains that they are part of, and by localizing additional components of

1 The data can be downloaded from https://www.adb.org/data/icp/input-output-tables.

2 The definition of the GVC related terms and indicators are provided in Box Table 3.1.

3 The data presented in this Part III are not official statistics. Production and trade data from various sources were integrated into the input–output economic framework and adjusted as required to conform with specific macroeconomic concepts. As such, data and statistics presented here could differ from relevant official statistics.

Box Table 3.1: Definitions of Global Value Chains Terms and Indicators

Indicator	Definition
Domestic Value Added (DVA)	Domestic inputs of goods and services in the overall exports of an economy.
Domestic Value Added Absorbed Abroad (VAX_G)	All domestic value added embodied in the gross exports and ultimately absorbed abroad.
Domestic Value Added First Exported then Returned Home (RDV_B)	Domestic value added that are exported first, but then return to the home economy for domestic consumption. This would happen, for example, when the Philippines export electronic parts to the PRC for final assembly of laptops, which then return to the Philippines for final consumption.
Foreign Value Added (FVA)	Imported inputs of goods and services in the overall exports of an economy.
Global Value Chains (GVCs)	A network of interlinked stages of production for goods and services that straddles international borders. Typically, a GVC involves combining imported and domestically produced goods and services into products that are then exported for use as intermediates in the subsequent stage of production or as final consumption products.
GVC participation	There are various ways to measure economies' participation in GVCs. A simple metric is the share of foreign value added in total exports. It reflects the extent to which an economy uses foreign inputs in producing for exports. A more rigorous measure is Vertical Specialization (VS), which is the share of foreign value added and pure double counted terms in total exports.
Pure Double-Counted Terms (PDC)	In a GVC, some goods or services may cross the same national border for three or more times.
Revealed Comparative Advantage (RCA)	It is an index, introduced by Bela Balassa, to calculate the relative advantage an economy has in the export of any given good or service. An economy is said to have an RCA in a product if it exports more than its "fair share", or a share that is equal to or greater than the share of total world trade that the product represents.
Value Added Exports by Forward Industrial Linkages (VAX_F)	Domestic value added that is originated from a particular sector and ultimately absorbed abroad via the exports of all sectors in the source economy. For example, besides direct export, the value added of German business services sector may be exported as an input to German automobiles. This indicator is useful in understanding the contribution of a given sector to the economy's aggregate exports.
Value Added Exports by Backward Industrial Linkages (VAX_B)	Value added that is originated from all domestic sectors and ultimately absorbed abroad via the export of a particular sector in the source economy. For example, the domestic value added of German automobile exports includes that of all German sectors (e.g., business service, computers) used as inputs.

Source: Asian Development Bank. 2015. *Key Indicators for Asia and the Pacific 2015*. https://www.adb.org/publications/key-indicators-asia-and-pacific-2015

such chains. On the other hand, the uptick seen in India's value-added exports in 2016 occurred even as the share of local content in (goods and services) exports noticeably decreased. This was due possibly to India's greater participation in global value chains (GVCs) and expanded supply to foreign markets.

Although manufacturing continued to dominate the PRC exports and GVC participation, services were gaining strength, with their share in value-added exports increasing from 17% in 2014 to 23% in 2016. In both gross and value terms, the PRC's services exports continued to grow during the period while primary and manufacturing exports declined overall, indicating a definite movement toward greater participation in the services components of GVCs. The expansion was driven particularly by transportation, finance, and business support service industries. However, the contribution of the complex technology-based telecommunication industry to the PRC's exports continues to be relatively minor.

The key trend discernible from the MRIOT data is that while domestic expenditure on goods and services in the PRC grew at a healthy rate from 2014 to 2016, imports and exports declined, implying that bourgeoning domestic demand for final and intermediate products were increasingly being supplied by value chains, of which the final portions (such as assembly and packaging processes) are

Box Table 3.2: Sector Aggregation	
Aggregate Economic Sectors	**Industry Sectors used by the World Input-Output Database**
Primary Sector	Consists of the sectors Agriculture, Hunting, Forestry, and Fishing; Mining and Quarrying.
Low Technology Sector	Consists of the sectors Food, Beverages, and Tobacco; Textiles and Textile Products; Leather, Leather Products, and Footwear; Wood and Products of Wood and Cork; Pulp, Paper, Paper Products, Printing, and Publishing; Rubber and Plastics; Manufacturing, NEC; Recycling; Electricity, Gas, and Water Supply; Construction.
High and Medium Technology Sector	Consists of the sectors Coke, Refined Petroleum, and Nuclear Fuel; Chemicals and Chemical Products; Other Non-Metallic Mineral; Basic Metals and Fabricated Metals; Machinery, NEC; Electrical and Optical Equipment; Transport Equipment.
Business Services Sector	Consists of the sectors Sale, Maintenance, and Repair of Motor Vehicles and Motorcycles; Retail Trade, Except of Motor Vehicles and Motorcycles; Repair of Household Goods; Hotels and Restaurants; Inland Transport; Water Transport; Air Transport; Other Supporting and Auxiliary Transport Activities; Activities of Travel Agencies; Post and Telecommunications; Financial Intermediation; Real Estate Activities; Renting of Machinery and Equipment; Other Business Activities.
Personal Services Sector	Consists of the sectors Public Administration and Defense; Compulsory Social Security; Education; Health and Social Work; Other Community, Social, and Personal Services; Private Households with Employed persons.

Source: Asian Development Bank. 2015. *Key Indicators for Asia and the Pacific 2015.* https://www.adb.org/publications/key-indicators-asia-and-pacific-2015

located within the country. The domestically created value returning to the PRC embedded in imports to be ultimately consumed in the country, and the value added, domestic as well as foreign, which crosses the borders multiple times due to geographically dispersed multistage production processes continued to be low (the sum of the two indicators was less than 10% of gross exports in any given sector[4]) and invariant. This is a further indication of sluggish growth in GVC participation by the PRC's sectors.

Trends in Value-Added Exports: Asia's Advanced Economies Looking More Locally

Of the advanced economies in the region, the Republic of Korea and Taipei,China saw their value-added exports declining in proportion to the drop in their gross exports from 2014 to 2016, yet the relative shares of the various value-added segments in gross exports remained more or less stable during the period. Even though these two economies' participation in GVCs was quite high and robust in every sector compared to the other Asian economies, virtually no change was seen in their participation indices during this period. As was the case in the PRC, their gross domestic product (GDP) grew, while gross exports and imports as well as their corresponding value-added shrank considerably. This shows that even in these economies that are highly integrated into the global production networks, the domestic demand was being increasingly met by local suppliers.

Interestingly, in Japan, another advanced economy of the region that is well integrated into the global supply chains (indicated by its lower share of domestic valued-added in gross exports ultimately consumed abroad), the orientation toward localization of the markets was also quite evident from the data. The portion of domestic valued-added in a unit value of exports has been rising sharply in Japan, especially in the crucial medium- and high-technology manufacturing sector (from 74% in 2014 to 79% in 2016). Thailand treaded pretty much the same path as Japan, with the local content in exports expanding in virtually every sector.

4 The industry composition of aggregate economic sector categories is given in Box Table 3.2.

Trends in Value-Added Exports: Local Components of Global Value Chains Lengthening in Southeast Asia

For Indonesia, Malaysia, and the Philippines, GVC participation indicators remained stable from 2014 to 2016, but the data show signs of a domestic demand-driven expansion in the economy increasingly supported by local supply, consistent with the fact that these economies posted healthy GDP growth while their imports were relatively stagnant. However, the decline in trade (imports as well as exports) in most of the sectors in the largest economies of the Association of Southeast Asian Nations could adversely affect predominantly export-dependent economies, particularly those with direct trade linkages to countries like Indonesia. This requires further examination of the economic interlinkages and dependencies of potentially vulnerable countries (along the lines ADB [2016d], which analyzed inter-economy and inter-sectoral input-output linkages to look at the implications for developing Asia of moderating growth in the PRC).

It is noteworthy that, from 2014 to 2016, the business services sector exports of the Philippines grew by over 10%, both in gross and value-added terms, while the exports of all the other broad sector categories declined, underlining the importance of business processing services to the country's economy. Likewise, in Malaysia, this sector experienced a sharp increase in exports in 2016 after declining significantly in 2015. Although the domestic content in the exports of the sector was quite high (over 80% in Malaysia and 90% in the Philippines) much of the value-added exports were embedded in intermediates such as business support operations, which points to the extent of the business services sector's contribution to the relevant GVCs.

Unlike many of the region's economies, Viet Nam saw its exports grow sharply in 2015 across the board, and the local contribution to the production process also expanded notably. In 2016, Viet Nam's exports declined markedly from the previous year's levels but the share of domestic content was relatively stable. Once again, the strong economic growth exhibited by the country during this period when its trade in final and intermediate products was contracting overall provides a definite indication of the development and maturation of local value chains.

Trends in Value-Added Exports: Smaller Economies Looking for their Global Value Chain Niche

Among the smaller[5] economies, namely, Bhutan, Brunei Darussalam, Fiji, the Kyrgyz Republic, the Lao PDR, Maldives, Mongolia, and Nepal, only Brunei Darussalam, the Lao PDR, and Mongolia participated in GVCs in any meaningful way, due to their export of primary resources that enter various production processes located abroad as intermediates. Yet, their participation in the GVCs is quite likely to be at the extreme upstream, perhaps in the relatively lower value-adding segments.

In almost all other economies, tourism was the single largest exporting sector due to its supply of services to nonresidents. The Kyrgyz Republic's exports of agricultural products and minerals enable it to participate in a limited scale in a few regional value chains at the upstream end. Moreover, the relatively significant share of import content in the exports of these countries resulted more likely from their need to import the intermediates required to produce the final goods and services largely meant for domestic consumption, due to the non-availability of these locally, rather than from any conscious decision to enter GVCs. However, these economies could potentially leverage their pivotal locations and proximity to much larger and fast-developing countries, and develop specific advantages to attract at least certain segments of the value chains.

5 The relative sizes of the economies are determined in terms of the magnitude of their respective gross domestic products.

Cambodia's value-added exports increased primarily due to its expanding contribution to the textiles GVCs and its bourgeoning tourism sector. Bangladesh continued to be a major participant in the textiles GVCs from 2014 to 2016, although the local content in textiles exports increased notably, implying localization of additional components of the supply chain. However, as can be seen from the MRIOTs, total exports of Bangladesh declined significantly, while the local content of its products and its GDP rose, pointing to the increasing diversion of local resources to ultimately meet growing domestic demand for final goods and services. As was the case with Bangladesh, Sri Lanka's participation in GVCs in a meaningful way was only in the textiles sector. Besides textiles, only the tourism industry posted a notable increase in exports from 2014 to 2016. Local content in exports remained high and invariant during the period across all sectors in Sri Lanka, except for those involving complex technology inputs—which have relatively low output and exports anyway.

Trends in Valued-Added Exports: Limited Global Value Chain Participation by Central and West Asia

Kazakhstan's enduring dependence on primary resources is quite evident from the data. The overall level of gross and value-added exports of the country was intrinsically linked to the global demand for fuel and minerals. Even the exports of the country's business services sector were closely connected to the activities in the resource sector. Thus, the economy participated in GVCs by incorporating its resources as intermediates and contributed support services such as transportation, distribution, business processing, and finance. Kazakhstan became more integrated into global production and supply networks in 2014–2016. Its GVC participation indicators increased from 9% to 14%. However, much of the increase came through the growth in the foreign content (including double counted value produced abroad) in exports, illustrating the growing importance of the country to the chains supplying primary-resource-based products to the regional and global markets.

Pakistan's exports from almost every sector declined from 2014 to 2016. Even in the primary sector, which posted a significant increase in gross and value-added exports in 2015, there was a considerable decline in 2016. The domestic content in the output of most of the sectors remained quite high (above 90%). Even in the high-technology industries, such as electrical and optical equipment manufacturing where the domestic content of the products tends to be comparatively lower, the share was well above 80%, indicating the relative upstream position of Pakistan's sectors in the GVCs they participate in. As in many other economies, Pakistan also experienced economic growth from 2014 to 2016 even as trade contracted, pointing to the movement toward the localization of supply to serve domestic demand.

Changes in Indirect Exports: Stagnating Global Value Chain Participation

The sector-specific value-added exports measured by both forward and backward linkage methods, while at times varying significantly in value, also point to the generally declining trend in exports (Tables 3.2a–3.2f). It certainly is possible for both measures to show different trends for any given sector of an economy. This was seen in Bangladesh during 2000–2015,[6] where gross exports (measured through backward linkage methods) of many sectors declined, while indirect value-added exports (measured by forward linkage methods) increased markedly due to their contribution to the country's fast expanding, export-oriented textiles sector. However, in 2014–2016, both measures exhibited the same globally declining trend in value-added exports. The healthy

6 Data and analysis for the 2000–2015 period were provided in ADB (2016).

economic growth that many economies, including the major ones like the PRC and India, posted even as gross imports and exports, as well as value-added trade, stagnated or even declined, proves that the value created domestically was increasingly being used to serve local demand.

The value created by other sectors of an economy that is embedded in the exports of any given sector of that economy is known as the backward-linked indirect export. Conversely, the value created by any given sector that is incorporated into the exported products of other sectors is known as forward-linked indirect export. An increasing share of indirect value-added in a sector's backward-linked exports generally implies that imported intermediates are being replaced by local goods and services in the production processes of that sector. A growing proportion of indirect valued-added in the forward-linked exports suggests that a sector's output is being used increasingly in the local production processes as intermediates, rather than being exported directly to be used in production abroad. Thus, the magnitude and share of indirect value-added in exports provide a reasonably reliable indicator of localization.

The direct and indirect value-added export estimates are provided in Tables 3.3a–3.3f by aggregate economic sectors for each of the Asian economies studied. No region-wide tendency was discernible from the data; the direct–indirect value-added export ratios varied little in certain economies but changed drastically in others. The changes also seem sector-specific, even measure-specific (whether forward or backward) in many economies. For example, the estimates related to the medium- and high-technology manufacturing sector in the Republic of Korea; Taipei,China; and Thailand show a clear tendency toward further localization, while the relevant statistics in Viet Nam indicate increasing integration of the country's medium- and high-technology manufacturing sector into the global supply chains.

Evolution in Revealed Comparative Advantages: Increasing Localization of Global Value Chain Processes

The revealed comparative advantages (RCA) of each of the economies are given in Table 3.4 by broad economic sector categories. Estimates both by the traditional gross exports-based method and the new forward-linked value-added exports-based method proposed by Wang, Wei, and Zhu (2014) are provided. Clearly, a larger number of sectors increased their RCA as per the latter method from 2014 to 2016. Even where the RCA declined under both the approaches, the loss in comparative advantage under the value-added method was generally smaller. This trend suggests that additional components of global or regional value chains were being localized, and the internally produced intermediates were being used to meet the demands of the newly localized processes of the chains.

It is worth noting that the changes in the RCA using both methods move in the same direction for several sectors, possibly due to the large direct value-added component—the common element in both measures—in the sectors' exports. The bigger the direct component in the gross exports, the less sophisticated the product is likely to be, and the more upstream the sector tends to be in the value chains. Further, the larger the direct component, the lower the probability that the other processes in the economy are using the product. Thus, when the estimates from both methods move in unison, the relevant sector's output tends to be basic; and, the economy is not likely to have the production processes to absorb it as intermediate. It is also likely, as was the case with the low-technology manufacturing sector in the Philippines, that the gross export based RCA decreases when the value-added based indicator increases. This implies that while gross exports of the sector might have gone down comparatively, the products of the sector were increasingly being used in export-oriented local processes, suggesting that such processes were now being localized, and that products were being used locally as intermediates, rather than exported to be processed abroad.

However, in certain sectors such as low-technology manufacturing in Japan and Thailand, and primary resources processing in the PRC and Japan, the reverse was apparent. This indicates that the economy was scaling back on the value chain segments involved in the processing of those intermediates and were exporting them directly abroad to be treated there. This trend usually sets in when an economy moves up the value chains and orients its resources toward higher value-adding activities. Consequently, the relatively lower value-adding processes tend to be moved down to low-income economies. Further, from 2014 to 2016, the changes in RCA by the value-added approach was numerically larger (higher positive or lower negative) than those tracked through the gross exports method in most of the sectors analyzed, suggesting increasing indirect value-added exports and greater localization of value chain components.

Trends in Vertical Specialization: Markets Turning Inward

The vertical specialization (VS) indicators, calculated as the total share of foreign content in exports (FVA) and double counted domestic (DDC) and foreign value-added (FDC) for 2014, 2015, and 2016 are shown in Tables 3.5a–3.5c for the 35 aggregate industries of each of the economies studied. Additional details are provided in Tables 3.6a–3.6w for select industries in the economies. The changes in the VS indicators between the years are provided in Tables 3.7a–3.7b. It is evident from the tables that, while there were industry-specific exceptions in economies such as the PRC, India, and Indonesia, there was a general stagnation, even decrease, in the VS measures in 2014–2016. Among the larger economies, the biggest increase in the index was posted by the fuel production sector in Kazakhstan, which was noted earlier as increasingly getting involved in specific cross-country production processes. The relatively large year-to-year variations seen in small economies like Maldives are generally due to the low base values of exports and the value-added components therein, which are prone to wide fluctuations in terms of proportions. Given that VS is generally regarded as a representative measure of GVC participation, the data clearly point to a stagnation, at best sluggish growth, in some economies, in a plethora of international production sharing arrangements. Thus, the trends seen in VS indicators across sectors and economies over the 2014–2016 period, coupled with the movements related to other economic indicators discussed earlier such as GDP and trade growth, point to a strong emergence of local value chains.

Summary

The phenomenon of globalization, evidenced by bourgeoning trade in intermediates and globally provisioned final products, has fueled economic growth in many economies in the Asia and Pacific region. However, as reported by many institutions, including the Asian Development Bank, growth in trade has decelerated considerably since 2011, fueling concerns of a global economic slowdown. Since trade in intermediates is intrinsically related to value chains, the observed deceleration in the growth in GVC participation rate has also raised concern, especially among economies that have benefited considerably from value chain participation at various levels. However, data also show that since 2011, many Asian economies have been growing at a healthy rate, despite the decline in trade. Increasingly, domestic demand is driving economic activity in many countries, and the resources used to supply foreign demand are now being diverted to meet local demand. These emerging trends need to be studied closely to inform the design and implementation of policies that enable developing countries to maximize the gains from trade.

References

ADB. 2016a. Part III—Asia's Evolving Role in International Production-Sharing Arrangements: Reemergence of the Local Market. In *Key Indicators for Asia and the Pacific 2016*. Manila.

ADB. 2016b. Part 2 – Trade and Global Value Chain. In *Asian Economic Integration Report 2016*. Manila

ADB. 2016c. *Changing Patterns of Trade and Global Value Chains in Post crisis Asia*. ADB Briefs No 53. Manila

ADB. 2016d. *Structural Change and Moderating Growth in the People's Republic of China: Implications for Developing Asia and Beyond*. Manila

Z. Wang, S. Wei, and K. Zhu. 2014. Quantifying International Production Sharing at the Bilateral and Sector Levels. *NBER Working Paper*. No. 19677. Cambridge, MA: National Bureau of Economic Research.

Table 3.1a: Value Added Decomposition of Exports—Primary Sector

	Exports	VAX_G	RDV_B	FVA	PDC	VAX_G	RDV_B	FVA	PDC
	($ million)					(% share in exports)			
Bangladesh									
2014	1,164	1,109	2	40	12	95.30	0.19	3.47	1.04
2015	1,070	1,033	1	31	6	96.48	0.06	2.92	0.54
2016	1,081	1,049	1	29	3	97.00	0.05	2.67	0.29
Bhutan									
2014	66	61	0	4	1	92.50	0.02	6.71	0.78
2015	72	68	0	4	1	93.46	0.02	5.51	1.02
2016	71	66	0	5	1	92.59	0.02	6.40	0.99
Brunei Darussalam									
2014	5,491	5,083	0	273	135	92.56	0.01	4.97	2.46
2015	3,675	3,339	0	221	115	90.85	0.01	6.02	3.12
2016	3,547	3,144	0	270	133	88.63	0.01	7.62	3.75
Cambodia									
2014	1,316	1,203	1	84	29	91.38	0.05	6.39	2.19
2015	1,241	1,087	1	115	38	87.56	0.08	9.29	3.07
2016	1,056	966	1	71	19	91.45	0.05	6.70	1.79
China, People's Rep. of									
2014	34,516	30,764	1,023	1,858	871	89.13	2.96	5.38	2.52
2015	31,816	28,309	963	1,704	840	88.98	3.03	5.36	2.64
2016	33,059	29,096	941	2,117	905	88.01	2.84	6.40	2.74
Fiji									
2014	116	84	0	27	5	72.30	0.01	23.68	4.02
2015	125	91	0	28	5	73.03	0.01	22.75	4.21
2016	118	87	0	27	4	73.87	0.01	22.44	3.69
India									
2014	22,655	21,493	177	702	283	94.87	0.78	3.10	1.25
2015	18,087	17,232	111	545	200	95.27	0.61	3.01	1.11
2016	29,525	27,776	286	1,023	440	94.08	0.97	3.46	1.49
Indonesia									
2014	50,483	46,302	618	1,977	1,586	91.72	1.22	3.92	3.14
2015	39,770	36,253	426	1,675	1,415	91.16	1.07	4.21	3.56
2016	39,555	36,395	409	1,538	1,213	92.01	1.04	3.89	3.07
Japan									
2014	5,425	2,878	87	1,655	804	53.05	1.61	30.52	14.83
2015	5,414	2,834	77	1,694	808	52.34	1.43	31.29	14.93
2016	5,892	3,495	84	1,587	727	59.31	1.42	26.93	12.34
Kazakhstan									
2014	42,859	39,003	57	2,259	1,539	91.00	0.13	5.27	3.59
2015	25,237	22,299	36	1,701	1,202	88.36	0.14	6.74	4.76
2016	24,558	20,827	25	2,176	1,530	84.81	0.10	8.86	6.23
Korea, Rep. of									
2014	1,067	886	7	140	34	83.04	0.68	13.10	3.18
2015	1,014	830	7	140	38	81.85	0.67	13.77	3.71
2016	1,049	850	7	153	39	80.97	0.66	14.62	3.75
Kyrgyz Republic									
2014	331	259	0	54	18	78.30	0.07	16.27	5.36
2015	297	233	0	41	23	78.49	0.04	13.69	7.78
2016	352	264	0	59	29	75.01	0.02	16.69	8.28

continued on next page

Table 3.1a: continued

Table 3.1a: Value Added Decomposition of Exports—Primary Sector									
	Exports	VAX_G	RDV_B	FVA	PDC	VAX_G	RDV_B	FVA	PDC
	($ million)					(% share in exports)			
Lao PDR									
2014	3,320	2,905	1	308	106	87.51	0.03	9.28	3.19
2015	3,478	3,092	1	282	102	88.93	0.03	8.10	2.94
2016	3,567	3,212	1	265	89	90.06	0.02	7.44	2.49
Malaysia									
2014	13,096	12,000	61	678	356	91.63	0.47	5.18	2.72
2015	10,665	9,367	37	818	442	87.83	0.35	7.67	4.15
2016	10,311	9,043	35	834	398	87.70	0.34	8.09	3.86
Maldives									
2014	28	18	0	9	2	63.54	0.01	31.06	5.39
2015	26	13	0	11	2	52.00	0.00	40.92	7.08
2016	36	19	0	14	3	53.85	0.00	38.97	7.17
Mongolia									
2014	4,227	3,015	1	881	331	71.33	0.02	20.83	7.82
2015	4,186	3,225	0	709	251	77.05	0.01	16.94	6.00
2016	4,255	3,227	0	771	256	75.85	0.01	18.12	6.02
Nepal									
2014	84	78	0	5	0	93.06	0.07	6.50	0.38
2015	92	86	0	6	0	93.43	0.05	6.18	0.33
2016	110	103	0	7	0	93.13	0.06	6.47	0.34
Pakistan									
2014	1,800	1,750	2	38	10	97.24	0.09	2.10	0.57
2015	6,215	6,051	4	122	37	97.37	0.06	1.97	0.60
2016	5,717	5,504	3	163	46	96.27	0.06	2.86	0.81
Philippines									
2014	1,586	1,476	3	79	28	93.06	0.20	4.96	1.78
2015	1,445	1,329	3	84	28	92.01	0.19	5.84	1.96
2016	1,397	1,266	3	98	30	90.64	0.20	7.01	2.16
Sri Lanka									
2014	723	647	0	66	9	89.46	0.04	9.19	1.31
2015	652	584	0	56	11	89.59	0.03	8.66	1.73
2016	632	561	0	59	12	88.81	0.04	9.27	1.88
Taipei,China									
2014	2,084	1,586	4	394	100	76.10	0.20	18.91	4.79
2015	2,007	1,450	4	430	123	72.25	0.18	21.45	6.13
2016	2,212	1,637	3	457	115	74.02	0.14	20.64	5.20
Thailand									
2014	7,165	6,163	27	737	238	86.01	0.38	10.28	3.33
2015	3,003	2,589	13	294	107	86.21	0.43	9.78	3.57
2016	3,410	2,969	11	345	85	87.06	0.33	10.11	2.50
Viet Nam									
2014	39,641	31,407	94	6,330	1,809	79.23	0.24	15.97	4.56
2015	40,998	33,245	93	5,838	1,823	81.09	0.23	14.24	4.45
2016	39,185	31,405	128	5,902	1,750	80.15	0.33	15.06	4.47

0 = magnitude is less than half of unit employed, FVA = foreign value added, Lao PDR = Lao People's Democratic Republic, PDC = pure double counted terms, RDV_B = domestic value added first exported then returned home, VAX_G = domestic value added absorbed abroad.

Source: ADB Multi Region Input-Output Tables Database.

Table 3.1b: Value Added Decomposition of Exports—Low-Technology Manufacturing Sector

	Exports	VAX_G	RDV_B	FVA	PDC	VAX_G	RDV_B	FVA	PDC
	($ million)					(% share in exports)			
Bangladesh									
2014	35,153	31,186	23	3,416	527	88.72	0.07	9.72	1.50
2015	28,305	25,893	12	2,116	284	91.48	0.04	7.48	1.00
2016	27,763	26,553	8	1,067	135	95.64	0.03	3.84	0.49
Bhutan									
2014	228	198	0	26	4	86.64	0.00	11.43	1.93
2015	248	221	0	22	5	89.08	0.00	8.73	2.19
2016	226	191	0	31	4	84.44	0.00	13.60	1.96
Brunei Darussalam									
2014	79	54	0	23	3	68.00	0.00	28.76	3.23
2015	112	71	0	38	4	63.07	0.00	33.48	3.44
2016	109	71	0	34	5	64.57	0.02	31.23	4.18
Cambodia									
2014	3,682	2,363	0	1,247	72	64.17	0.00	33.87	1.95
2015	4,097	2,683	0	1,319	95	65.49	0.01	32.19	2.32
2016	4,505	2,950	0	1,435	120	65.48	0.01	31.85	2.66
China, People's Rep. of									
2014	561,310	494,411	6,235	51,469	9,196	88.08	1.11	9.17	1.64
2015	547,199	479,098	6,860	51,437	9,804	87.55	1.25	9.40	1.79
2016	520,542	452,497	5,919	52,641	9,486	86.93	1.14	10.11	1.82
Fiji									
2014	355	259	0	83	12	73.05	0.00	23.50	3.45
2015	327	241	0	74	12	73.63	0.00	22.63	3.73
2016	358	267	0	79	12	74.57	0.00	21.98	3.45
India									
2014	79,263	67,566	210	9,559	1,928	85.24	0.27	12.06	2.43
2015	73,260	63,478	162	8,048	1,572	86.65	0.22	10.99	2.15
2016	92,677	78,561	255	11,569	2,293	84.77	0.27	12.48	2.47
Indonesia									
2014	84,176	68,203	207	12,760	3,006	81.02	0.25	15.16	3.57
2015	82,203	66,077	212	12,729	3,185	80.38	0.26	15.49	3.87
2016	80,551	65,605	209	11,873	2,865	81.44	0.26	14.74	3.56
Japan									
2014	51,849	41,308	736	6,739	3,065	79.67	1.42	13.00	5.91
2015	53,705	41,360	628	8,197	3,519	77.01	1.17	15.26	6.55
2016	49,244	41,327	636	5,061	2,221	83.92	1.29	10.28	4.51
Kazakhstan									
2014	1,882	1,587	10	235	50	84.34	0.52	12.49	2.65
2015	1,679	1,367	8	237	66	81.41	0.50	14.14	3.95
2016	1,601	1,304	5	230	62	81.43	0.33	14.38	3.86
Korea, Rep. of									
2014	51,041	36,488	279	10,156	4,118	71.49	0.55	19.90	8.07
2015	46,172	32,442	241	9,408	4,080	70.26	0.52	20.38	8.84
2016	44,884	32,005	221	8,972	3,686	71.31	0.49	19.99	8.21
Kyrgyz Republic									
2014	153	97	0	30	26	63.29	0.18	19.74	16.79
2015	221	132	0	58	31	59.82	0.07	26.10	14.01
2016	74	43	0	10	21	57.53	0.16	13.72	28.59

continued on next page

Table 3.1b: continued

Table 3.1b: Value Added Decomposition of Exports—Low-Technology Manufacturing Sector									
	Exports	VAX_G	RDV_B	FVA	PDC	VAX_G	RDV_B	FVA	PDC
	($ million)					(% share in exports)			
Lao PDR									
2014	1,149	898	0	201	50	78.15	0.02	17.47	4.36
2015	1,166	886	0	218	62	75.96	0.03	18.73	5.29
2016	970	794	0	137	39	81.84	0.02	14.14	4.00
Malaysia									
2014	45,697	32,880	67	9,972	2,777	71.95	0.15	21.82	6.08
2015	45,229	31,929	65	10,019	3,217	70.59	0.14	22.15	7.11
2016	39,702	28,209	63	8,348	3,082	71.05	0.16	21.03	7.76
Maldives									
2014	99	54	0	42	3	54.36	0.00	42.18	3.45
2015	342	246	0	89	7	71.97	0.00	26.02	2.01
2016	281	206	0	71	4	73.31	0.00	25.13	1.56
Mongolia									
2014	388	284	0	80	25	73.17	0.02	20.49	6.32
2015	374	292	0	63	19	78.25	0.01	16.75	4.99
2016	392	303	0	67	21	77.34	0.01	17.19	5.45
Nepal									
2014	250	188	0	57	5	75.31	0.02	22.81	1.86
2015	249	187	0	57	5	75.16	0.02	22.83	1.98
2016	261	195	0	61	5	74.73	0.02	23.38	1.86
Pakistan									
2014	14,534	13,098	6	1,072	357	90.12	0.04	7.38	2.46
2015	10,001	9,038	4	720	238	90.38	0.04	7.20	2.38
2016	9,825	8,881	3	722	219	90.39	0.03	7.35	2.23
Philippines									
2014	12,700	11,172	9	1,334	185	87.97	0.07	10.51	1.46
2015	12,599	10,807	9	1,530	253	85.78	0.07	12.14	2.01
2016	11,438	9,571	6	1,606	255	83.67	0.05	14.04	2.23
Sri Lanka									
2014	6,185	5,184	1	896	104	83.81	0.02	14.49	1.69
2015	6,274	5,215	1	927	130	83.13	0.02	14.78	2.08
2016	6,756	5,562	1	1,053	140	82.33	0.02	15.58	2.08
Taipei,China									
2014	25,320	14,825	35	7,624	2,836	58.55	0.14	30.11	11.20
2015	25,622	14,515	33	8,005	3,069	56.65	0.13	31.24	11.98
2016	35,176	20,299	27	12,004	2,845	57.71	0.08	34.13	8.09
Thailand									
2014	71,072	53,076	136	14,049	3,811	74.68	0.19	19.77	5.36
2015	69,510	52,661	120	13,052	3,678	75.76	0.17	18.78	5.29
2016	67,722	52,990	105	11,229	3,398	78.25	0.16	16.58	5.02
Viet Nam									
2014	34,509	19,383	18	13,450	1,658	56.17	0.05	38.97	4.80
2015	40,453	23,764	34	13,767	2,887	58.75	0.08	34.03	7.14
2016	37,829	22,526	44	12,866	2,392	59.55	0.12	34.01	6.32

0 = magnitude is less than half of unit employed, FVA = foreign value added, Lao PDR = Lao People's Democratic Republic, PDC = pure double counted terms, RDV_B = domestic value added first exported then returned home, VAX_G = domestic value added absorbed abroad.

Source: ADB Multi Region Input-Output Tables Database.

Table 3.1c: Value Added Decomposition of Exports—Medium- and High-Technology Manufacturing Sector

	Exports	VAX_G	RDV_B	FVA	PDC	VAX_G	RDV_B	FVA	PDC
	($ million)					(% share in exports)			
Bangladesh									
2014	2,273	1,794	3	406	69	78.94	0.13	17.88	3.05
2015	1,916	1,568	2	299	47	81.84	0.11	15.60	2.46
2016	1,432	1,259	1	151	21	87.92	0.08	10.55	1.45
Bhutan									
2014	73	57	0	15	1	77.26	0.02	20.80	1.92
2015	73	58	0	14	2	78.49	0.02	19.38	2.11
2016	93	69	0	21	2	74.52	0.01	22.96	2.51
Brunei Darussalam									
2014	4,771	4,209	1	362	200	88.21	0.01	7.58	4.19
2015	3,161	2,740	0	274	147	86.70	0.01	8.65	4.64
2016	3,271	2,810	0	295	165	85.92	0.01	9.02	5.06
Cambodia									
2014	75	45	0	23	6	60.64	0.06	31.36	7.94
2015	68	43	0	20	5	63.30	0.07	29.38	7.24
2016	88	52	0	29	7	58.69	0.06	33.30	7.96
China, People's Rep. of									
2014	1,451,565	1,111,360	41,606	221,197	77,402	76.56	2.87	15.24	5.33
2015	1,409,298	1,056,457	43,692	226,705	82,444	74.96	3.10	16.09	5.85
2016	1,342,004	993,965	38,911	229,067	80,062	74.07	2.90	17.07	5.97
Fiji									
2014	36	21	0	13	2	58.65	0.00	37.09	4.26
2015	32	18	0	12	2	57.68	0.00	37.27	5.04
2016	31	18	0	12	1	58.37	0.00	37.07	4.56
India									
2014	154,828	97,011	668	41,761	15,387	62.66	0.43	26.97	9.94
2015	142,369	94,358	588	33,738	13,684	66.28	0.41	23.70	9.61
2016	175,920	108,067	834	48,441	18,578	61.43	0.47	27.54	10.56
Indonesia									
2014	65,689	49,502	266	11,679	4,242	75.36	0.40	17.78	6.46
2015	59,630	44,479	216	10,755	4,180	74.59	0.36	18.04	7.01
2016	56,317	42,782	199	9,781	3,555	75.97	0.35	17.37	6.31
Japan									
2014	618,131	454,234	6,143	114,480	43,273	73.49	0.99	18.52	7.00
2015	577,217	410,810	5,072	116,486	44,850	71.17	0.88	20.18	7.77
2016	561,728	441,444	4,873	83,840	31,572	78.59	0.87	14.93	5.62
Kazakhstan									
2014	11,599	10,569	37	633	360	91.12	0.32	5.46	3.10
2015	9,708	8,356	32	755	565	86.07	0.33	7.78	5.82
2016	9,670	8,314	21	739	596	85.98	0.21	7.64	6.17
Korea, Rep. of									
2014	550,894	337,366	1,879	157,600	54,048	61.24	0.34	28.61	9.81
2015	515,126	305,948	1,690	153,402	54,085	59.39	0.33	29.78	10.50
2016	488,149	299,017	1,500	139,913	47,719	61.26	0.31	28.66	9.78
Kyrgyz Republic									
2014	669	498	1	107	63	74.47	0.08	15.99	9.45
2015	544	398	0	73	73	73.20	0.04	13.34	13.42
2016	553	391	0	87	74	70.75	0.03	15.76	13.47

continued on next page

Table 3.1c: continued

Table 3.1c: Value Added Decomposition of Exports—Medium- and High-Technology Manufacturing Sector									
	Exports	VAX_G	RDV_B	FVA	PDC	VAX_G	RDV_B	FVA	PDC
	($ million)					(% share in exports)			
Lao PDR									
2014	32	20	0	7	4	63.05	0.08	23.14	13.74
2015	35	24	0	7	4	69.05	0.09	19.39	11.48
2016	60	40	0	13	7	67.13	0.09	21.74	11.05
Malaysia									
2014	80,584	49,302	186	22,275	8,821	61.18	0.23	27.64	10.95
2015	71,709	42,341	140	20,798	8,430	59.05	0.19	29.00	11.76
2016	69,022	41,665	138	19,653	7,566	60.36	0.20	28.47	10.96
Maldives									
2014	3	2	0	1	0	60.98	0.00	37.29	1.73
2015	1	1	0	0	0	73.47	0.00	25.54	0.99
2016	6	4	0	2	0	69.29	0.00	30.41	0.30
Mongolia									
2014	165	121	0	37	8	72.85	0.00	22.10	5.04
2015	133	103	0	23	6	77.83	0.00	17.47	4.70
2016	100	77	0	16	7	76.92	0.00	15.70	7.38
Nepal									
2014	99	59	0	35	5	59.70	0.09	35.60	4.61
2015	98	60	0	35	4	60.77	0.09	35.24	3.90
2016	122	73	0	43	6	59.46	0.08	35.54	4.93
Pakistan									
2014	1,063	903	1	133	27	84.90	0.06	12.53	2.51
2015	977	824	1	128	25	84.30	0.05	13.11	2.54
2016	877	721	0	133	22	82.22	0.04	15.20	2.54
Philippines									
2014	22,899	13,321	31	6,275	3,272	58.17	0.14	27.40	14.29
2015	21,536	12,494	27	5,975	3,040	58.01	0.13	27.74	14.12
2016	20,480	11,371	33	6,152	2,925	55.52	0.16	30.04	14.28
Sri Lanka									
2014	473	290	0	154	29	61.37	0.03	32.55	6.05
2015	308	190	0	96	23	61.53	0.03	31.07	7.37
2016	325	210	0	92	24	64.46	0.03	28.23	7.27
Taipei,China									
2014	273,496	144,231	627	85,671	42,967	52.74	0.23	31.32	15.71
2015	267,580	137,028	557	86,995	43,000	51.21	0.21	32.51	16.07
2016	257,196	132,915	551	83,858	39,873	51.68	0.21	32.60	15.50
Thailand									
2014	75,679	39,223	154	26,964	9,337	51.83	0.20	35.63	12.34
2015	67,368	36,755	120	22,669	7,825	54.56	0.18	33.65	11.61
2016	68,869	39,170	114	22,450	7,135	56.88	0.17	32.60	10.36
Viet Nam									
2014	11,999	6,016	13	4,737	1,232	50.14	0.11	39.48	10.27
2015	17,628	9,580	21	5,936	2,092	54.34	0.12	33.67	11.87
2016	15,921	8,894	35	5,272	1,721	55.86	0.22	33.11	10.81

0 = magnitude is less than half of unit employed, FVA = foreign value added, Lao PDR = Lao People's Democratic Republic, PDC = pure double counted terms, RDV_B = domestic value added first exported then returned home, VAX_G = domestic value added absorbed abroad.

Source: ADB Multi Region Input-Output Tables Database.

Table 3.1d: Value Added Decomposition of Exports—Business Services Sector

	Exports	VAX_G	RDV_B	FVA	PDC	VAX_G	RDV_B	FVA	PDC
	($ million)					(% share in exports)			
Bangladesh									
2014	1,160	1,072	1	69	18	92.46	0.08	5.93	1.53
2015	1,256	1,168	1	69	18	93.00	0.06	5.52	1.43
2016	962	918	1	33	10	95.47	0.06	3.43	1.03
Bhutan									
2014	154	125	0	24	5	81.15	0.00	15.35	3.50
2015	158	126	0	27	5	80.06	0.00	16.86	3.08
2016	132	104	0	24	5	78.54	0.00	17.77	3.68
Brunei Darussalam									
2014	336	263	0	57	16	78.20	0.00	16.98	4.81
2015	308	240	0	52	16	77.92	0.01	16.94	5.13
2016	312	238	0	59	15	76.28	0.00	18.82	4.90
Cambodia									
2014	2,604	1,882	0	550	172	72.29	0.01	21.10	6.60
2015	2,591	1,926	0	486	179	74.32	0.01	18.75	6.93
2016	3,203	2,339	0	642	222	73.03	0.01	20.04	6.93
China, People's Rep. of									
2014	372,768	330,815	12,329	20,589	9,035	88.75	3.31	5.52	2.42
2015	387,574	342,112	13,708	21,606	10,149	88.27	3.54	5.57	2.62
2016	474,586	417,417	16,237	27,947	12,985	87.95	3.42	5.89	2.74
Fiji									
2014	1,159	799	0	304	56	68.95	0.01	26.22	4.82
2015	1,086	746	0	285	55	68.75	0.01	26.21	5.04
2016	1,075	758	0	265	52	70.53	0.01	24.64	4.83
India									
2014	104,232	97,508	538	5,029	1,158	93.55	0.52	4.82	1.11
2015	86,337	81,342	441	3,609	945	94.21	0.51	4.18	1.09
2016	77,457	71,346	437	4,486	1,187	92.11	0.56	5.79	1.53
Indonesia									
2014	11,002	9,746	31	982	242	88.59	0.28	8.93	2.20
2015	12,668	10,911	52	1,256	449	86.13	0.41	9.91	3.54
2016	12,169	10,520	50	1,187	412	86.45	0.41	9.75	3.39
Japan									
2014	147,043	131,619	1,597	10,701	3,126	89.51	1.09	7.28	2.13
2015	160,942	145,339	1,899	10,142	3,562	90.31	1.18	6.30	2.21
2016	170,290	156,629	2,289	8,400	2,972	91.98	1.34	4.93	1.75
Kazakhstan									
2014	20,735	18,633	183	1,411	508	89.86	0.88	6.81	2.45
2015	19,031	17,280	169	1,109	472	90.80	0.89	5.83	2.48
2016	14,998	13,258	99	1,195	446	88.40	0.66	7.96	2.97
Korea, Rep. of									
2014	91,692	75,425	436	12,137	3,695	82.26	0.48	13.24	4.03
2015	87,186	70,472	431	12,135	4,147	80.83	0.49	13.92	4.76
2016	84,800	68,082	413	12,241	4,064	80.29	0.49	14.44	4.79
Kyrgyz Republic									
2014	408	282	0	89	36	69.26	0.05	21.88	8.81
2015	448	311	0	104	34	69.34	0.02	23.10	7.53
2016	505	356	0	114	35	70.52	0.03	22.55	6.90

continued on next page

Table 3.1d: continued

Table 3.1d: Value Added Decomposition of Exports—Business Services Sector

	Exports	VAX_G	RDV_B	FVA	PDC	VAX_G	RDV_B	FVA	PDC
	($ million)					(% share in exports)			
Lao PDR									
2014	472	389	0	62	20	82.47	0.03	13.23	4.27
2015	496	418	0	59	19	84.28	0.02	11.83	3.87
2016	407	347	0	45	15	85.18	0.02	11.09	3.71
Malaysia									
2014	47,659	39,854	77	6,048	1,681	83.62	0.16	12.69	3.53
2015	37,490	30,710	56	5,061	1,663	81.92	0.15	13.50	4.44
2016	42,837	35,984	63	5,129	1,659	84.00	0.15	11.97	3.87
Maldives									
2014	2,611	1,645	0	772	194	63.01	0.00	29.57	7.42
2015	2,471	1,673	0	621	177	67.71	0.00	25.12	7.18
2016	2,543	1,712	0	652	178	67.33	0.00	25.65	7.01
Mongolia									
2014	771	604	0	133	34	78.41	0.03	17.19	4.37
2015	689	580	0	85	23	84.22	0.02	12.35	3.41
2016	713	599	0	90	24	83.94	0.02	12.66	3.38
Nepal									
2014	479	396	0	69	13	82.76	0.04	14.49	2.71
2015	450	374	0	63	13	83.10	0.04	14.04	2.82
2016	490	403	0	73	14	82.15	0.04	14.97	2.85
Pakistan									
2014	9,195	8,851	6	282	56	96.26	0.07	3.06	0.61
2015	8,235	7,900	5	272	58	95.93	0.07	3.30	0.70
2016	6,878	6,581	4	239	53	95.69	0.06	3.47	0.78
Philippines									
2014	23,843	22,044	23	1,394	382	92.45	0.10	5.85	1.60
2015	26,083	24,041	30	1,509	502	92.17	0.12	5.79	1.92
2016	26,539	24,470	29	1,551	489	92.20	0.11	5.84	1.84
Sri Lanka									
2014	5,348	4,716	1	519	112	88.17	0.03	9.70	2.10
2015	5,246	4,654	1	479	112	88.71	0.02	9.14	2.13
2016	6,028	5,390	2	509	127	89.42	0.03	8.45	2.10
Taipei,China									
2014	69,755	54,238	185	11,744	3,588	77.75	0.27	16.84	5.14
2015	65,863	51,043	190	10,874	3,755	77.50	0.29	16.51	5.70
2016	63,063	48,846	211	10,481	3,525	77.46	0.33	16.62	5.59
Thailand									
2014	53,272	45,595	95	5,979	1,602	85.59	0.18	11.22	3.01
2015	58,598	51,072	114	5,700	1,712	87.16	0.20	9.73	2.92
2016	61,253	54,390	90	5,244	1,529	88.80	0.15	8.56	2.50
Viet Nam									
2014	21,827	17,425	14	3,955	433	79.83	0.06	18.12	1.99
2015	24,578	20,778	23	3,279	497	84.54	0.09	13.34	2.02
2016	25,101	20,790	35	3,752	524	82.82	0.14	14.95	2.09

0 = magnitude is less than half of unit employed, FVA = foreign value added, Lao PDR = Lao People's Democratic Republic, PDC = pure double counted terms, RDV_B = domestic value added first exported then returned home, VAX_G = domestic value added absorbed abroad.

Source: ADB Multi Region Input-Output Tables Database.

Table 3.1e: Value Added Decomposition of Exports—Personal Services Sector

	Exports	VAX_G	RDV_B	FVA	PDC	VAX_G	RDV_B	FVA	PDC
	($ million)					(% share in exports)			
Bangladesh									
2014	712	683	0	25	4	95.85	0.06	3.54	0.55
2015	1,242	1,168	5	42	28	93.99	0.37	3.36	2.28
2016	1,104	1,072	2	21	10	97.12	0.14	1.88	0.87
Bhutan									
2014	49	43	0	6	1	86.23	0.00	12.48	1.29
2015	13	11	0	2	0	82.59	0.00	15.32	2.09
2016	70	59	0	10	1	83.79	0.00	14.40	1.80
Brunei Darussalam									
2014	24	21	0	3	0	87.03	0.00	11.14	1.83
2015	70	58	0	12	1	82.61	0.00	16.57	0.81
2016	94	76	0	17	1	81.19	0.01	17.78	1.02
Cambodia									
2014	128	109	0	16	4	84.75	0.02	12.30	2.93
2015	126	108	0	14	4	85.70	0.02	11.46	2.82
2016	158	134	0	19	5	85.06	0.01	12.07	2.86
China, People's Rep. of									
2014	13,886	12,590	129	1,014	154	90.66	0.93	7.30	1.11
2015	26,229	23,493	509	1,782	446	89.57	1.94	6.79	1.70
2016	29,503	26,440	560	2,017	486	89.62	1.90	6.84	1.65
Fiji									
2014	55	45	0	8	1	82.57	0.00	15.11	2.32
2015	26	22	0	4	0	85.06	0.00	14.29	0.65
2016	61	51	0	9	1	82.61	0.00	15.11	2.27
India									
2014	9,976	9,612	0	363	0	96.35	0.00	3.64	0.00
2015	13,884	13,471	0	413	0	97.02	0.00	2.97	0.00
2016	13,851	13,314	0	536	0	96.12	0.00	3.87	0.00
Indonesia									
2014	1,614	1,459	3	134	19	90.40	0.16	8.28	1.16
2015	1,662	1,509	2	132	19	90.79	0.15	7.92	1.15
2016	1,622	1,475	2	125	19	90.96	0.15	7.72	1.16
Japan									
2014	2,972	2,738	17	187	30	92.14	0.57	6.28	1.01
2015	19,160	17,942	146	857	215	93.65	0.76	4.47	1.12
2016	14,315	13,401	128	621	166	93.61	0.89	4.34	1.16
Kazakhstan									
2014	540	493	0	43	3	91.36	0.07	8.01	0.56
2015	485	442	0	40	3	91.11	0.07	8.18	0.64
2016	434	390	0	41	3	89.85	0.06	9.38	0.71
Korea, Rep. of									
2014	4,563	3,862	17	572	113	84.63	0.36	12.53	2.47
2015	4,189	3,486	17	555	131	83.22	0.40	13.24	3.13
2016	3,829	3,207	15	504	104	83.74	0.39	13.15	2.73
Kyrgyz Republic									
2014	220	186	0	28	7	84.38	0.01	12.56	3.05
2015	229	193	0	30	6	84.23	0.00	13.01	2.75
2016	234	196	0	32	6	83.71	0.00	13.54	2.74

continued on next page

Table 3.1e: continued

Table 3.1e: Value Added Decomposition of Exports—Personal Services Sector									
	Exports	VAX_G	RDV_B	FVA	PDC	VAX_G	RDV_B	FVA	PDC
	($ million)					(% share in exports)			
Lao PDR									
2014	117	104	0	12	1	88.97	0.01	9.88	1.14
2015	117	104	0	12	1	88.67	0.01	10.37	0.96
2016	124	113	0	10	1	91.07	0.01	8.24	0.68
Malaysia									
2014	2,924	2,445	2	436	41	83.61	0.07	14.92	1.40
2015	4,902	3,991	6	791	114	81.42	0.12	16.14	2.33
2016	5,038	4,183	5	738	112	83.03	0.10	14.64	2.23
Maldives									
2014	126	97	0	22	6	77.21	0.00	17.73	5.05
2015	61	44	0	12	4	73.03	0.00	19.90	7.07
2016	80	61	0	15	4	76.29	0.00	18.24	5.47
Mongolia									
2014	103	87	0	14	1	84.75	0.00	14.07	1.17
2015	87	75	0	11	1	86.40	0.00	13.00	0.59
2016	118	103	0	13	1	87.65	0.00	11.35	1.00
Nepal									
2014	404	375	0	24	5	92.68	0.05	5.98	1.29
2015	397	370	0	22	5	93.21	0.04	5.45	1.29
2016	429	396	0	27	6	92.33	0.05	6.20	1.42
Pakistan									
2014	2,255	2,196	1	53	5	97.38	0.03	2.37	0.22
2015	2,174	2,121	1	48	5	97.54	0.03	2.22	0.22
2016	2,126	2,065	1	55	6	97.10	0.03	2.60	0.27
Philippines									
2014	1,080	988	1	69	23	91.44	0.07	6.37	2.12
2015	807	741	1	48	18	91.73	0.08	5.97	2.23
2016	810	744	1	48	18	91.75	0.08	5.97	2.19
Sri Lanka									
2014	1,072	957	0	100	15	89.28	0.02	9.33	1.38
2015	1,051	942	0	92	16	89.65	0.02	8.79	1.54
2016	602	541	0	50	11	89.85	0.02	8.30	1.82
Taipei,China									
2014	1,764	1,472	1	271	20	83.43	0.08	15.34	1.15
2015	1,526	1,243	1	262	19	81.50	0.07	17.20	1.23
2016	1,550	1,288	1	246	15	83.11	0.07	15.86	0.97
Thailand									
2014	4,457	3,506	4	854	93	78.65	0.09	19.16	2.10
2015	5,250	4,271	9	855	114	81.37	0.16	16.29	2.18
2016	4,971	4,092	3	778	98	82.32	0.07	15.65	1.96
Viet Nam									
2014	4,021	3,368	3	560	90	83.75	0.08	13.93	2.24
2015	4,399	3,806	4	492	97	86.52	0.09	11.18	2.21
2016	5,081	4,305	6	647	124	84.72	0.12	12.73	2.43

0 = magnitude is less than half of unit employed, FVA = foreign value added, Lao PDR = Lao People's Democratic Republic, PDC = pure double counted terms, RDV_B = domestic value added first exported then returned home, VAX_G = domestic value added absorbed abroad.

Source: ADB Multi Region Input-Output Tables Database.

Table 3.1f: Value Added Decomposition of Exports—Total Economy

	Exports	VAX_G	RDV_B	FVA	PDC	VAX_G	RDV_B	FVA	PDC
	($ million)					(% share in exports)			
Bangladesh									
2014	40,461	35,844	30	3,957	630	88.59	0.07	9.78	1.56
2015	33,789	30,829	20	2,558	383	91.24	0.06	7.57	1.13
2016	32,342	30,851	12	1,300	178	95.39	0.04	4.02	0.55
Bhutan									
2014	571	483	0	76	12	84.60	0.01	13.23	2.16
2015	565	483	0	68	13	85.59	0.01	12.13	2.28
2016	593	489	0	90	14	82.47	0.01	15.22	2.30
Brunei Darussalam									
2014	10,701	9,628	1	717	354	89.98	0.01	6.70	3.31
2015	7,326	6,448	1	596	282	88.01	0.01	8.14	3.84
2016	7,333	6,338	0	675	319	86.44	0.01	9.20	4.35
Cambodia									
2014	7,805	5,602	1	1,920	282	71.77	0.01	24.60	3.61
2015	8,124	5,847	2	1,954	321	71.97	0.02	24.06	3.95
2016	9,010	6,441	1	2,196	372	71.49	0.01	24.37	4.13
China, People's Rep. of									
2014	2,434,045	1,979,939	61,321	296,127	96,658	81.34	2.52	12.17	3.97
2015	2,402,115	1,929,468	65,732	303,233	103,682	80.32	2.74	12.62	4.32
2016	2,399,694	1,919,415	62,567	313,788	103,924	79.99	2.61	13.08	4.33
Fiji									
2014	1,720	1,208	0	436	76	70.24	0.01	25.36	4.39
2015	1,595	1,119	0	402	74	70.13	0.01	25.23	4.64
2016	1,644	1,181	0	391	71	71.87	0.01	23.78	4.35
India									
2014	370,954	293,190	1,594	57,414	18,757	79.04	0.43	15.48	5.06
2015	333,937	269,881	1,303	46,352	16,401	80.82	0.39	13.88	4.91
2016	389,429	299,063	1,811	66,056	22,499	76.80	0.47	16.96	5.78
Indonesia									
2014	212,964	175,212	1,124	27,533	9,095	82.27	0.53	12.93	4.27
2015	195,933	159,229	909	26,547	9,248	81.27	0.46	13.55	4.72
2016	190,214	156,777	870	24,504	8,064	82.42	0.46	12.88	4.24
Japan									
2014	825,419	632,778	8,580	133,763	50,298	76.66	1.04	16.21	6.09
2015	816,438	618,285	7,822	137,377	52,954	75.73	0.96	16.83	6.49
2016	801,470	656,295	8,009	99,509	37,657	81.89	1.00	12.42	4.70
Kazakhstan									
2014	77,614	70,286	287	4,582	2,460	90.56	0.37	5.90	3.17
2015	56,141	49,744	246	3,842	2,309	88.61	0.44	6.84	4.11
2016	51,261	44,093	150	4,381	2,637	86.02	0.29	8.55	5.14
Korea, Rep. of									
2014	699,257	454,027	2,618	180,605	62,008	64.93	0.37	25.83	8.87
2015	653,686	413,179	2,387	175,640	62,481	63.21	0.37	26.87	9.56
2016	622,712	403,160	2,157	161,783	55,613	64.74	0.35	25.98	8.93
Kyrgyz Republic									
2014	1,780	1,322	1	308	149	74.26	0.07	17.29	8.38
2015	1,740	1,268	1	304	167	72.87	0.03	17.49	9.61
2016	1,719	1,251	1	302	166	72.75	0.03	17.56	9.66

continued on next page

Table 3.1f: continued

Table 3.1f: Value Added Decomposition of Exports—Total Economy									
	Exports	VAX_G	RDV_B	FVA	PDC	VAX_G	RDV_B	FVA	PDC
	($ million)					(% share in exports)			
Lao PDR									
2014	5,089	4,316	1	590	182	84.81	0.03	11.60	3.57
2015	5,292	4,524	1	578	188	85.50	0.03	10.92	3.56
2016	5,127	4,506	1	471	150	87.87	0.02	9.18	2.93
Malaysia									
2014	189,960	136,481	393	39,410	13,676	71.85	0.21	20.75	7.20
2015	169,996	118,339	303	37,487	13,867	69.61	0.18	22.05	8.16
2016	166,910	119,085	305	34,703	12,818	71.35	0.18	20.79	7.68
Maldives									
2014	2,867	1,816	0	846	205	63.34	0.00	29.51	7.15
2015	2,900	1,977	0	732	190	68.18	0.00	25.25	6.56
2016	2,946	2,003	0	753	190	67.99	0.00	25.57	6.44
Mongolia									
2014	5,654	4,111	1	1,144	398	72.71	0.02	20.23	7.05
2015	5,469	4,277	1	891	300	78.20	0.01	16.30	5.49
2016	5,577	4,309	1	958	310	77.26	0.01	17.17	5.56
Nepal									
2014	1,315	1,096	1	191	28	83.32	0.04	14.53	2.10
2015	1,287	1,077	1	182	27	83.72	0.04	14.15	2.09
2016	1,413	1,169	1	212	31	82.76	0.04	14.98	2.22
Pakistan									
2014	28,847	26,798	15	1,578	456	92.90	0.05	5.47	1.58
2015	27,602	25,934	14	1,291	363	93.96	0.05	4.68	1.31
2016	25,423	23,752	12	1,313	346	93.43	0.05	5.17	1.36
Philippines									
2014	62,108	49,000	67	9,151	3,890	78.89	0.11	14.73	6.26
2015	62,470	49,412	70	9,147	3,841	79.10	0.11	14.64	6.15
2016	60,665	47,422	71	9,455	3,717	78.17	0.12	15.59	6.13
Sri Lanka									
2014	13,802	11,794	3	1,735	269	85.45	0.02	12.57	1.95
2015	13,530	11,584	3	1,651	292	85.62	0.02	12.20	2.16
2016	14,343	12,263	3	1,763	313	85.50	0.02	12.29	2.19
Taipei,China									
2014	372,420	216,352	853	105,703	49,511	58.09	0.23	28.38	13.29
2015	362,597	205,278	785	106,567	49,966	56.61	0.22	29.39	13.78
2016	359,196	204,985	793	107,045	46,373	57.07	0.22	29.80	12.91
Thailand									
2014	211,646	147,563	417	48,583	15,083	69.72	0.20	22.95	7.13
2015	203,729	147,348	375	42,570	13,436	72.33	0.18	20.90	6.59
2016	206,224	153,610	323	40,045	12,245	74.49	0.16	19.42	5.94
Viet Nam									
2014	111,998	77,600	143	29,032	5,223	69.29	0.13	25.92	4.66
2015	128,055	91,173	174	29,311	7,397	71.20	0.14	22.89	5.78
2016	123,118	87,920	248	28,439	6,510	71.41	0.20	23.10	5.29

0 = magnitude is less than half of unit employed, FVA = foreign value added, Lao PDR = Lao People's Democratic Republic, PDC = pure double counted terms, RDV_B = domestic value added first exported then returned home, VAX_G = domestic value added absorbed abroad.

Source: ADB Multi Region Input-Output Tables Database.

Table 3.2a: Value-Added Exports by Various Measures—Primary Sector											
	Exports	VAX_G	DVA_B	DVA_F	VAX_B	VAX_F	VAX_G	DVA_B	DVA_F	VAX_B	VAX_F
	($ million)						Value-Added Export Measure to Gross Exports Ratio (%)				
Bangladesh											
2014	1,164	1,109	1,112	2,750	1,109	2,746	95.30	95.50	236.27	95.30	235.91
2015	1,070	1,033	1,033	2,344	1,033	2,343	96.48	96.54	218.99	96.48	218.92
2016	1,081	1,049	1,049	2,292	1,049	2,291	97.00	97.05	212.05	97.00	211.97
Bhutan											
2014	66	61	61	73	61	73	92.50	92.51	110.53	92.50	110.51
2015	72	68	68	75	68	75	93.46	93.47	104.00	93.46	103.99
2016	71	66	66	75	66	75	92.59	92.61	105.04	92.59	105.02
Brunei Darussalam											
2014	5,491	5,083	5,083	6,689	5,083	6,688	92.56	92.57	121.81	92.56	121.80
2015	3,675	3,339	3,339	4,391	3,339	4,391	90.85	90.86	119.48	90.85	119.47
2016	3,547	3,144	3,144	4,266	3,144	4,266	88.63	88.63	120.27	88.63	120.26
Cambodia											
2014	1,316	1,203	1,203	1,252	1,203	1,252	91.38	91.43	95.17	91.38	95.12
2015	1,241	1,087	1,088	1,157	1,087	1,156	87.56	87.65	93.19	87.56	93.12
2016	1,056	966	966	1,065	966	1,065	91.45	91.51	100.91	91.45	100.86
China, People's Rep. of											
2014	34,516	30,764	31,882	290,287	30,764	282,077	89.13	92.37	841.02	89.13	817.24
2015	31,816	28,309	29,349	238,028	28,309	230,943	88.98	92.25	748.15	88.98	725.88
2016	33,059	29,096	30,107	226,214	29,096	219,840	88.01	91.07	684.28	88.01	665.00
Fiji											
2014	116	84	84	131	84	131	72.30	72.30	113.55	72.30	113.54
2015	125	91	91	137	91	137	73.03	73.04	109.19	73.03	109.18
2016	118	87	87	136	87	136	73.87	73.87	115.05	73.87	115.04
India											
2014	22,655	21,493	21,683	41,638	21,493	41,368	94.87	95.71	183.79	94.87	182.60
2015	18,087	17,232	17,350	36,352	17,232	36,151	95.27	95.92	200.98	95.27	199.87
2016	29,525	27,776	28,087	50,903	27,776	50,506	94.08	95.13	172.41	94.08	171.06
Indonesia											
2014	50,483	46,302	46,952	69,633	46,302	68,960	91.72	93.01	137.93	91.72	136.60
2015	39,770	36,253	36,704	56,657	36,253	56,179	91.16	92.29	142.46	91.16	141.26
2016	39,555	36,395	36,827	56,210	36,395	55,752	92.01	93.10	142.10	92.01	140.95
Japan											
2014	5,425	2,878	2,969	7,245	2,878	7,104	53.05	54.74	133.56	53.05	130.95
2015	5,414	2,834	2,915	6,057	2,834	5,952	52.34	53.85	111.88	52.34	109.93
2016	5,892	3,495	3,582	6,138	3,495	6,039	59.31	60.80	104.18	59.31	102.49
Kazakhstan											
2014	42,859	39,003	39,059	34,340	39,003	34,283	91.00	91.13	80.12	91.00	79.99
2015	25,237	22,299	22,334	18,909	22,299	18,873	88.36	88.49	74.92	88.36	74.78
2016	24,558	20,827	20,851	17,100	20,827	17,077	84.81	84.91	69.63	84.81	69.54
Korea, Rep. of											
2014	1,067	886	894	6,702	886	6,663	83.04	83.80	627.99	83.04	624.37
2015	1,014	830	837	6,412	830	6,374	81.85	82.59	632.53	81.85	628.85
2016	1,049	850	857	6,283	850	6,248	80.97	81.70	598.74	80.97	595.39
Kyrgyz Republic											
2014	331	259	259	206	259	206	78.30	78.37	62.24	78.30	62.18
2015	297	233	234	188	233	188	78.49	78.53	63.20	78.49	63.16
2016	352	264	264	205	264	205	75.01	75.04	58.23	75.01	58.21

continued on next page

Table 3.2a: continued

Table 3.2a: Value-Added Exports by Various Measures—Primary Sector											
	Exports	VAX_G	DVA_B	DVA_F	VAX_B	VAX_F	VAX_G	DVA_B	DVA_F	VAX_B	VAX_F
	($ million)						Value-Added Export Measure to Gross Exports Ratio (%)				
Lao PDR											
2014	3,320	2,905	2,906	2,679	2,905	2,679	87.51	87.53	80.70	87.51	80.67
2015	3,478	3,092	3,093	2,830	3,092	2,829	88.93	88.96	81.37	88.93	81.34
2016	3,567	3,212	3,213	2,848	3,212	2,847	90.06	90.08	79.85	90.06	79.83
Malaysia											
2014	13,096	12,000	12,072	35,385	12,000	35,268	91.63	92.18	270.20	91.63	269.31
2015	10,665	9,367	9,412	29,578	9,367	29,496	87.83	88.25	277.33	87.83	276.56
2016	10,311	9,043	9,084	28,350	9,043	28,271	87.70	88.11	274.96	87.70	274.19
Maldives											
2014	28	18	18	140	18	140	63.54	63.55	500.38	63.54	500.35
2015	26	13	13	82	13	82	52.00	52.01	316.22	52.00	316.21
2016	36	19	19	88	19	88	53.85	53.86	244.75	53.85	244.74
Mongolia											
2014	4,227	3,015	3,016	2,091	3,015	2,091	71.33	71.35	49.48	71.33	49.47
2015	4,186	3,225	3,226	2,058	3,225	2,058	77.05	77.06	49.17	77.05	49.16
2016	4,255	3,227	3,228	2,058	3,227	2,058	75.85	75.86	48.37	75.85	48.36
Nepal											
2014	84	78	78	127	78	127	93.06	93.13	151.40	93.06	151.30
2015	92	86	86	132	86	132	93.43	93.49	144.00	93.43	143.93
2016	110	103	103	152	103	152	93.13	93.19	137.90	93.13	137.82
Pakistan											
2014	1,800	1,750	1,752	7,982	1,750	7,978	97.24	97.33	443.43	97.24	443.18
2015	6,215	6,051	6,055	9,994	6,051	9,989	97.37	97.43	160.81	97.37	160.72
2016	5,717	5,504	5,507	9,267	5,504	9,262	96.27	96.33	162.09	96.27	162.01
Philippines											
2014	1,586	1,476	1,479	5,900	1,476	5,893	93.06	93.27	372.00	93.06	371.58
2015	1,445	1,329	1,332	5,341	1,329	5,335	92.01	92.21	369.70	92.01	369.29
2016	1,397	1,266	1,269	4,772	1,266	4,766	90.64	90.84	341.48	90.64	341.10
Sri Lanka											
2014	723	647	647	1,126	647	1,125	89.46	89.50	155.69	89.46	155.63
2015	652	584	584	1,180	584	1,180	89.59	89.62	181.06	89.59	181.01
2016	632	561	561	1,119	561	1,118	88.81	88.85	177.12	88.81	177.06
Taipei,China											
2014	2,084	1,586	1,590	2,645	1,586	2,639	76.10	76.30	126.92	76.10	126.60
2015	2,007	1,450	1,453	2,528	1,450	2,522	72.25	72.42	125.99	72.25	125.68
2016	2,212	1,637	1,640	2,643	1,637	2,637	74.02	74.17	119.51	74.02	119.25
Thailand											
2014	7,165	6,163	6,194	25,130	6,163	25,053	86.01	86.45	350.72	86.01	349.64
2015	3,003	2,589	2,604	22,070	2,589	22,011	86.21	86.72	734.86	86.21	732.89
2016	3,410	2,969	2,982	22,670	2,969	22,619	87.06	87.44	664.83	87.06	663.32
Viet Nam											
2014	39,641	31,407	31,526	32,394	31,407	32,306	79.23	79.53	81.72	79.23	81.50
2015	40,998	33,245	33,358	34,873	33,245	34,783	81.09	81.36	85.06	81.09	84.84
2016	39,185	31,405	31,551	32,656	31,405	32,534	80.15	80.52	83.34	80.15	83.03

DVA_B = domestic value added exports by backward industrial linkages, DVA_F = domestic value added exports by forward industrial linkages, Lao PDR = Lao People's Democratic Republic, VAX_B = value added exports by backward industrial linkages, VAX_F = value added exports by forward industrial linkages, VAX_G = domestic value added absorbed abroad.

Source: ADB Multi Region Input-Output Tables Database.

Table 3.2b: Value-Added Exports by Various Measures—Low-Technology Manufacturing Sector

	Exports	VAX_G	DVA_B	DVA_F	VAX_B	VAX_F	VAX_G	DVA_B	DVA_F	VAX_B	VAX_F
	($ million)						Value-Added Export Measure to Gross Exports Ratio (%)				
Bangladesh											
2014	35,153	31,186	31,209	15,699	31,186	15,688	88.72	88.78	44.66	88.72	44.63
2015	28,305	25,893	25,904	13,124	25,893	13,118	91.48	91.52	46.37	91.48	46.34
2016	27,763	26,553	26,561	12,896	26,553	12,892	95.64	95.67	46.45	95.64	46.44
Bhutan											
2014	228	198	198	200	198	200	86.64	86.64	87.81	86.64	87.81
2015	248	221	221	228	221	228	89.08	89.08	91.97	89.08	91.97
2016	226	191	191	202	191	202	84.44	84.44	89.33	84.44	89.33
Brunei Darussalam											
2014	79	54	54	72	54	72	68.00	68.00	91.15	68.00	91.15
2015	112	71	71	61	71	61	63.07	63.07	54.01	63.07	54.00
2016	109	71	71	65	71	65	64.57	64.59	59.41	64.57	59.40
Cambodia											
2014	3,682	2,363	2,363	1,990	2,363	1,990	64.17	64.17	54.04	64.17	54.04
2015	4,097	2,683	2,683	2,240	2,683	2,239	65.49	65.49	54.67	65.49	54.66
2016	4,505	2,950	2,950	2,441	2,950	2,441	65.48	65.49	54.20	65.48	54.19
China, People's Rep. of											
2014	561,310	494,411	500,230	362,655	494,411	355,317	88.08	89.12	64.61	88.08	63.30
2015	547,199	479,098	485,566	353,276	479,098	345,257	87.55	88.74	64.56	87.55	63.10
2016	520,542	452,497	457,971	339,886	452,497	332,598	86.93	87.98	65.29	86.93	63.89
Fiji											
2014	355	259	259	194	259	194	73.05	73.05	54.74	73.05	54.74
2015	327	241	241	182	241	182	73.63	73.64	55.86	73.63	55.85
2016	358	267	267	200	267	200	74.57	74.57	55.76	74.57	55.76
India											
2014	79,263	67,566	67,755	35,252	67,566	35,106	85.24	85.48	44.47	85.24	44.29
2015	73,260	63,478	63,623	33,211	63,478	33,093	86.65	86.85	45.33	86.65	45.17
2016	92,677	78,561	78,790	44,816	78,561	44,617	84.77	85.02	48.36	84.77	48.14
Indonesia											
2014	84,176	68,203	68,388	38,408	68,203	38,288	81.02	81.24	45.63	81.02	45.49
2015	82,203	66,077	66,270	37,319	66,077	37,200	80.38	80.62	45.40	80.38	45.25
2016	80,551	65,605	65,797	36,944	65,605	36,827	81.44	81.68	45.86	81.44	45.72
Japan											
2014	51,849	41,308	42,090	62,098	41,308	61,159	79.67	81.18	119.77	79.67	117.96
2015	53,705	41,360	42,020	59,751	41,360	58,933	77.01	78.24	111.26	77.01	109.74
2016	49,244	41,327	41,994	62,659	41,327	61,843	83.92	85.28	127.24	83.92	125.58
Kazakhstan											
2014	1,882	1,587	1,596	2,320	1,587	2,308	84.34	84.81	123.27	84.34	122.65
2015	1,679	1,367	1,375	1,666	1,367	1,657	81.41	81.87	99.25	81.41	98.70
2016	1,601	1,304	1,309	1,489	1,304	1,483	81.43	81.73	92.97	81.43	92.62
Korea, Rep. of											
2014	51,041	36,488	36,787	44,299	36,488	44,005	71.49	72.07	86.79	71.49	86.21
2015	46,172	32,442	32,701	41,312	32,442	41,041	70.26	70.82	89.47	70.26	88.89
2016	44,884	32,005	32,243	41,533	32,005	41,282	71.31	71.84	92.53	71.31	91.97
Kyrgyz Republic											
2014	153	97	97	81	97	81	63.29	63.48	53.04	63.29	52.89
2015	221	132	132	105	132	105	59.82	59.90	47.39	59.82	47.33
2016	74	43	43	46	43	46	57.53	57.70	62.11	57.53	61.98

continued on next page

Table 3.2b: continued

Table 3.2b: Value-Added Exports by Various Measures—Low-Technology Manufacturing Sector											
	Exports	VAX_G	DVA_B	DVA_F	VAX_B	VAX_F	VAX_G	DVA_B	DVA_F	VAX_B	VAX_F
	($ million)						Value-Added Export Measure to Gross Exports Ratio (%)				
Lao PDR											
2014	1,149	898	898	866	898	866	78.15	78.17	75.38	78.15	75.36
2015	1,166	886	886	887	886	887	75.96	75.98	76.07	75.96	76.05
2016	970	794	794	863	794	863	81.84	81.86	88.98	81.84	88.97
Malaysia											
2014	45,697	32,880	32,944	14,858	32,880	14,824	71.95	72.09	32.51	71.95	32.44
2015	45,229	31,929	31,993	14,872	31,929	14,838	70.59	70.74	32.88	70.59	32.81
2016	39,702	28,209	28,273	13,254	28,209	13,221	71.05	71.21	33.38	71.05	33.30
Maldives											
2014	99	54	54	97	54	97	54.36	54.36	97.56	54.36	97.56
2015	342	246	246	395	246	395	71.97	71.97	115.66	71.97	115.66
2016	281	206	206	382	206	382	73.31	73.31	135.72	73.31	135.71
Mongolia											
2014	388	284	284	313	284	313	73.17	73.19	80.72	73.17	80.71
2015	374	292	292	339	292	339	78.25	78.26	90.65	78.25	90.63
2016	392	303	303	352	303	351	77.34	77.35	89.70	77.34	89.69
Nepal											
2014	250	188	188	139	188	138	75.31	75.34	55.51	75.31	55.49
2015	249	187	187	136	187	136	75.16	75.18	54.76	75.16	54.74
2016	261	195	195	143	195	143	74.73	74.75	54.96	74.73	54.94
Pakistan											
2014	14,534	13,098	13,105	5,053	13,098	5,051	90.12	90.16	34.77	90.12	34.75
2015	10,001	9,038	9,042	3,722	9,038	3,720	90.38	90.42	37.22	90.38	37.20
2016	9,825	8,881	8,884	3,667	8,881	3,666	90.39	90.42	37.32	90.39	37.31
Philippines											
2014	12,700	11,172	11,180	8,750	11,172	8,742	87.97	88.03	68.90	87.97	68.84
2015	12,599	10,807	10,816	8,721	10,807	8,712	85.78	85.85	69.22	85.78	69.15
2016	11,438	9,571	9,576	8,464	9,571	8,456	83.67	83.72	73.99	83.67	73.93
Sri Lanka											
2014	6,185	5,184	5,185	4,277	5,184	4,276	83.81	83.83	69.15	83.81	69.13
2015	6,274	5,215	5,216	4,276	5,215	4,275	83.13	83.14	68.16	83.13	68.14
2016	6,756	5,562	5,563	4,422	5,562	4,421	82.33	82.34	65.45	82.33	65.44
Taipei,China											
2014	25,320	14,825	14,858	16,453	14,825	16,404	58.55	58.68	64.98	58.55	64.79
2015	25,622	14,515	14,545	16,903	14,515	16,854	56.65	56.77	65.97	56.65	65.78
2016	35,176	20,299	20,308	19,535	20,299	19,490	57.71	57.73	55.54	57.71	55.41
Thailand											
2014	71,072	53,076	53,218	31,957	53,076	31,879	74.68	74.88	44.96	74.68	44.85
2015	69,510	52,661	52,783	31,662	52,661	31,594	75.76	75.94	45.55	75.76	45.45
2016	67,722	52,990	53,101	32,033	52,990	31,972	78.25	78.41	47.30	78.25	47.21
Viet Nam											
2014	34,509	19,383	19,382	13,883	19,383	13,868	56.17	56.16	40.23	56.17	40.19
2015	40,453	23,764	23,781	18,072	23,764	18,046	58.75	58.79	44.67	58.75	44.61
2016	37,829	22,526	22,555	16,917	22,526	16,880	59.55	59.62	44.72	59.55	44.62

DVA_B = domestic value added exports by backward industrial linkages, DVA_F = domestic value added exports by forward industrial linkages, Lao PDR = Lao People's Democratic Republic, VAX_B = value added exports by backward industrial linkages, VAX_F = value added exports by forward industrial linkages, VAX_G = domestic value added absorbed abroad.

Source: ADB Multi Region Input-Output Tables Database.

Table 3.2c: Value-Added Exports by Various Measures—Medium- and High-Technology Manufacturing Sector											
	Exports	VAX_G	DVA_B	DVA_F	VAX_B	VAX_F	VAX_G	DVA_B	DVA_F	VAX_B	VAX_F
	($ million)						Value-Added Export Measure to Gross Exports Ratio (%)				
Bangladesh											
2014	2,273	1,794	1,797	874	1,794	873	78.94	79.07	38.45	78.94	38.39
2015	1,916	1,568	1,570	1,215	1,568	1,214	81.84	81.95	63.42	81.84	63.36
2016	1,432	1,259	1,261	1,199	1,259	1,198	87.92	88.00	83.69	87.92	83.64
Bhutan											
2014	73	57	57	34	57	34	77.26	77.28	45.61	77.26	45.61
2015	73	58	58	33	58	33	78.49	78.51	45.64	78.49	45.63
2016	93	69	69	41	69	41	74.52	74.53	44.15	74.52	44.15
Brunei Darussalam											
2014	4,771	4,209	4,209	2,243	4,209	2,242	88.21	88.22	47.00	88.21	47.00
2015	3,161	2,740	2,741	1,472	2,740	1,472	86.70	86.70	46.56	86.70	46.55
2016	3,271	2,810	2,810	1,461	2,810	1,461	85.92	85.92	44.67	85.92	44.66
Cambodia											
2014	75	45	45	65	45	65	60.64	60.71	87.56	60.64	87.50
2015	68	43	43	65	43	65	63.30	63.38	95.23	63.30	95.16
2016	88	52	52	76	52	76	58.69	58.75	85.96	58.69	85.90
China, People's Rep. of											
2014	1,451,565	1,111,360	1,151,727	646,998	1,111,360	625,040	76.56	79.34	44.57	76.56	43.06
2015	1,409,298	1,056,457	1,098,796	607,550	1,056,457	584,858	74.96	77.97	43.11	74.96	41.50
2016	1,342,004	993,965	1,030,958	581,530	993,965	560,822	74.07	76.82	43.33	74.07	41.79
Fiji											
2014	36	21	21	30	21	30	58.65	58.66	83.22	58.65	83.21
2015	32	18	18	25	18	25	57.68	57.68	77.86	57.68	77.85
2016	31	18	18	27	18	27	58.37	58.37	85.33	58.37	85.32
India											
2014	154,828	97,011	97,655	59,936	97,011	59,541	62.66	63.07	38.71	62.66	38.46
2015	142,369	94,358	94,933	54,381	94,358	54,065	66.28	66.68	38.20	66.28	37.98
2016	175,920	108,067	108,870	69,045	108,067	68,543	61.43	61.89	39.25	61.43	38.96
Indonesia											
2014	65,689	49,502	49,758	33,089	49,502	32,917	75.36	75.75	50.37	75.36	50.11
2015	59,630	44,479	44,688	30,581	44,479	30,432	74.59	74.94	51.29	74.59	51.03
2016	56,317	42,782	42,974	29,622	42,782	29,482	75.97	76.31	52.60	75.97	52.35
Japan											
2014	618,131	454,234	460,221	307,966	454,234	303,914	73.49	74.45	49.82	73.49	49.17
2015	577,217	410,810	415,640	270,368	410,810	267,129	71.17	72.01	46.84	71.17	46.28
2016	561,728	441,444	446,135	297,311	441,444	294,017	78.59	79.42	52.93	78.59	52.34
Kazakhstan											
2014	11,599	10,569	10,606	8,329	10,569	8,300	91.12	91.43	71.80	91.12	71.56
2015	9,708	8,356	8,388	6,122	8,356	6,099	86.07	86.40	63.06	86.07	62.82
2016	9,670	8,314	8,335	5,701	8,314	5,687	85.98	86.19	58.95	85.98	58.80
Korea, Rep. of											
2014	550,894	337,366	339,126	248,001	337,366	246,615	61.24	61.56	45.02	61.24	44.77
2015	515,126	305,948	307,523	216,394	305,948	215,204	59.39	59.70	42.01	59.39	41.78
2016	488,149	299,017	300,412	210,374	299,017	209,320	61.26	61.54	43.10	61.26	42.88
Kyrgyz Republic											
2014	669	498	498	494	498	494	74.47	74.56	73.88	74.47	73.82
2015	544	398	399	406	398	405	73.20	73.24	74.54	73.20	74.51
2016	553	391	391	392	391	392	70.75	70.78	70.96	70.75	70.94

continued on next page

Table 3.2c: continued

Table 3.2c: Value-Added Exports by Various Measures—Medium- and High-Technology Manufacturing Sector											
	Exports	VAX_G	DVA_B	DVA_F	VAX_B	VAX_F	VAX_G	DVA_B	DVA_F	VAX_B	VAX_F
	($ million)						Value-Added Export Measure to Gross Exports Ratio (%)				
Lao PDR											
2014	32	20	20	65	20	65	63.05	63.13	207.11	63.05	207.00
2015	35	24	24	66	24	66	69.05	69.14	189.14	69.05	189.04
2016	60	40	40	80	40	80	67.13	67.22	134.52	67.13	134.43
Malaysia											
2014	80,584	49,302	49,477	32,300	49,302	32,183	61.18	61.40	40.08	61.18	39.94
2015	71,709	42,341	42,471	28,664	42,341	28,574	59.05	59.23	39.97	59.05	39.85
2016	69,022	41,665	41,792	28,025	41,665	27,936	60.36	60.55	40.60	60.36	40.47
Maldives											
2014	3	2	2	4	2	4	60.98	60.98	115.26	60.98	115.26
2015	1	1	1	9	1	9	73.47	73.47	1,027.35	73.47	1,027.32
2016	6	4	4	11	4	11	69.29	69.29	176.97	69.29	176.97
Mongolia											
2014	165	121	121	180	121	180	72.85	72.85	108.67	72.85	108.66
2015	133	103	103	164	103	164	77.83	77.83	123.59	77.83	123.57
2016	100	77	77	156	77	156	76.92	76.92	156.41	76.92	156.39
Nepal											
2014	99	59	59	55	59	55	59.70	59.79	55.50	59.70	55.43
2015	98	60	60	55	60	55	60.77	60.85	56.09	60.77	56.03
2016	122	73	73	65	73	65	59.46	59.54	53.12	59.46	53.06
Pakistan											
2014	1,063	903	903	809	903	808	84.90	84.96	76.07	84.90	76.02
2015	977	824	824	739	824	738	84.30	84.35	75.61	84.30	75.57
2016	877	721	722	682	721	682	82.22	82.26	77.75	82.22	77.71
Philippines											
2014	22,899	13,321	13,351	8,815	13,321	8,796	58.17	58.30	38.50	58.17	38.41
2015	21,536	12,494	12,519	8,467	12,494	8,450	58.01	58.13	39.32	58.01	39.23
2016	20,480	11,371	11,402	7,704	11,371	7,684	55.52	55.67	37.62	55.52	37.52
Sri Lanka											
2014	473	290	291	396	290	396	61.37	61.40	83.78	61.37	83.75
2015	308	190	190	264	190	264	61.53	61.55	85.58	61.53	85.56
2016	325	210	210	312	210	312	64.46	64.49	96.03	64.46	96.00
Taipei,China											
2014	273,496	144,231	144,835	124,137	144,231	123,592	52.74	52.96	45.39	52.74	45.19
2015	267,580	137,028	137,556	112,800	137,028	112,335	51.21	51.41	42.16	51.21	41.98
2016	257,196	132,915	133,445	109,905	132,915	109,443	51.68	51.88	42.73	51.68	42.55
Thailand											
2014	75,679	39,223	39,356	31,038	39,223	30,924	51.83	52.00	41.01	51.83	40.86
2015	67,368	36,755	36,849	29,479	36,755	29,390	54.56	54.70	43.76	54.56	43.63
2016	68,869	39,170	39,260	31,206	39,170	31,123	56.88	57.01	45.31	56.88	45.19
Viet Nam											
2014	11,999	6,016	6,027	5,176	6,016	5,166	50.14	50.23	43.14	50.14	43.06
2015	17,628	9,580	9,598	7,971	9,580	7,955	54.34	54.45	45.22	54.34	45.13
2016	15,921	8,894	8,927	7,606	8,894	7,581	55.86	56.07	47.77	55.86	47.62

DVA_B = domestic value added exports by backward industrial linkages, DVA_F = domestic value added exports by forward industrial linkages, Lao PDR = Lao People's Democratic Republic, VAX_B = value added exports by backward industrial linkages, VAX_F = value added exports by forward industrial linkages, VAX_G = domestic value added absorbed abroad.

Source: ADB Multi Region Input-Output Tables Database.

Table 3.2d: Value-Added Exports by Various Measures—Business Services Sector

	Exports	VAX_G	DVA_B	DVA_F	VAX_B	VAX_F	VAX_G	DVA_B	DVA_F	VAX_B	VAX_F
	($ million)						Value-Added Export Measure to Gross Exports Ratio (%)				
Bangladesh											
2014	1,160	1,072	1,073	13,384	1,072	13,373	92.46	92.54	1,154.01	92.46	1,153.08
2015	1,256	1,168	1,168	12,235	1,168	12,229	93.00	93.05	974.41	93.00	973.88
2016	962	918	919	11,206	918	11,202	95.47	95.53	1,165.28	95.47	1,164.86
Bhutan											
2014	154	125	125	142	125	142	81.15	81.15	92.18	81.15	92.17
2015	158	126	126	137	126	137	80.06	80.06	87.11	80.06	87.10
2016	132	104	104	126	104	126	78.54	78.55	95.19	78.54	95.19
Brunei Darussalam											
2014	336	263	263	562	263	562	78.20	78.21	167.12	78.20	167.11
2015	308	240	240	446	240	446	77.92	77.93	144.84	77.92	144.83
2016	312	238	238	454	238	454	76.28	76.28	145.54	76.28	145.53
Cambodia											
2014	2,604	1,882	1,883	2,180	1,882	2,179	72.29	72.30	83.70	72.29	83.69
2015	2,591	1,926	1,926	2,263	1,926	2,262	74.32	74.32	87.31	74.32	87.30
2016	3,203	2,339	2,339	2,720	2,339	2,719	73.03	73.04	84.91	73.03	84.90
China, People's Rep. of											
2014	372,768	330,815	344,717	699,641	330,815	676,999	88.75	92.48	187.69	88.75	181.61
2015	387,574	342,112	357,444	744,130	342,112	717,849	88.27	92.23	192.00	88.27	185.22
2016	474,586	417,417	435,892	779,232	417,417	752,699	87.95	91.85	164.19	87.95	158.60
Fiji											
2014	1,159	799	799	807	799	807	68.95	68.96	69.64	68.95	69.64
2015	1,086	746	746	748	746	748	68.75	68.75	68.91	68.75	68.90
2016	1,075	758	758	767	758	767	70.53	70.53	71.35	70.53	71.34
India											
2014	104,232	97,508	98,081	145,228	97,508	144,466	93.55	94.10	139.33	93.55	138.60
2015	86,337	81,342	81,809	131,068	81,342	130,418	94.21	94.76	151.81	94.21	151.06
2016	77,457	71,346	71,817	119,691	71,346	119,001	92.11	92.72	154.53	92.11	153.64
Indonesia											
2014	11,002	9,746	9,777	32,621	9,746	32,472	88.59	88.86	296.51	88.59	295.16
2015	12,668	10,911	10,964	32,996	10,911	32,842	86.13	86.55	260.46	86.13	259.25
2016	12,169	10,520	10,570	32,335	10,520	32,188	86.45	86.87	265.72	86.45	264.52
Japan											
2014	147,043	131,619	133,322	249,448	131,619	246,193	89.51	90.67	169.64	89.51	167.43
2015	160,942	145,339	147,428	261,880	145,339	258,514	90.31	91.60	162.72	90.31	160.63
2016	170,290	156,629	159,056	273,809	156,629	270,278	91.98	93.40	160.79	91.98	158.72
Kazakhstan											
2014	20,735	18,633	18,819	25,164	18,633	24,975	89.86	90.76	121.36	89.86	120.45
2015	19,031	17,280	17,451	22,951	17,280	22,773	90.80	91.70	120.60	90.80	119.66
2016	14,998	13,258	13,359	19,638	13,258	19,531	88.40	89.07	130.94	88.40	130.23
Korea, Rep. of											
2014	91,692	75,425	75,957	142,438	75,425	141,623	82.26	82.84	155.34	82.26	154.45
2015	87,186	70,472	70,999	136,994	70,472	136,188	80.83	81.43	157.13	80.83	156.20
2016	84,800	68,082	68,581	132,890	68,082	132,150	80.29	80.87	156.71	80.29	155.84
Kyrgyz Republic											
2014	408	282	283	385	282	385	69.26	69.31	94.52	69.26	94.42
2015	448	311	311	408	311	408	69.34	69.36	91.04	69.34	91.01
2016	505	356	357	442	356	442	70.52	70.55	87.46	70.52	87.42

continued on next page

Table 3.2d: continued

Table 3.2d: Value-Added Exports by Various Measures—Business Services Sector

	Exports	VAX_G	DVA_B	DVA_F	VAX_B	VAX_F	VAX_G	DVA_B	DVA_F	VAX_B	VAX_F
	($ million)						Value-Added Export Measure to Gross Exports Ratio (%)				
Lao PDR											
2014	472	389	389	622	389	622	82.47	82.50	131.87	82.47	131.82
2015	496	418	418	659	418	659	84.28	84.30	132.77	84.28	132.74
2016	407	347	347	625	347	624	85.18	85.20	153.29	85.18	153.27
Malaysia											
2014	47,659	39,854	39,935	50,963	39,854	50,844	83.62	83.79	106.93	83.62	106.68
2015	37,490	30,710	30,770	41,402	30,710	41,312	81.92	82.07	110.44	81.92	110.20
2016	42,837	35,984	36,052	45,439	35,984	45,343	84.00	84.16	106.07	84.00	105.85
Maldives											
2014	2,611	1,645	1,645	1,477	1,645	1,477	63.01	63.01	56.58	63.01	56.58
2015	2,471	1,673	1,673	1,359	1,673	1,359	67.71	67.71	54.98	67.71	54.98
2016	2,543	1,712	1,712	1,376	1,712	1,376	67.33	67.34	54.12	67.33	54.11
Mongolia											
2014	771	604	605	1,419	604	1,419	78.41	78.44	184.16	78.41	184.11
2015	689	580	580	1,592	580	1,591	84.22	84.24	230.97	84.22	230.93
2016	713	599	599	1,600	599	1,600	83.94	83.95	224.26	83.94	224.23
Nepal											
2014	479	396	396	467	396	466	82.76	82.80	97.50	82.76	97.45
2015	450	374	374	448	374	448	83.10	83.14	99.50	83.10	99.46
2016	490	403	403	486	403	486	82.15	82.19	99.20	82.15	99.15
Pakistan											
2014	9,195	8,851	8,857	10,959	8,851	10,952	96.26	96.33	119.19	96.26	119.11
2015	8,235	7,900	7,905	9,552	7,900	9,546	95.93	96.00	116.00	95.93	115.92
2016	6,878	6,581	6,586	8,263	6,581	8,258	95.69	95.75	120.14	95.69	120.07
Philippines											
2014	23,843	22,044	22,068	24,401	22,044	24,369	92.45	92.56	102.34	92.45	102.21
2015	26,083	24,041	24,074	25,919	24,041	25,883	92.17	92.30	99.37	92.17	99.23
2016	26,539	24,470	24,501	25,464	24,470	25,427	92.20	92.32	95.95	92.20	95.81
Sri Lanka											
2014	5,348	4,716	4,717	5,116	4,716	5,114	88.17	88.20	95.65	88.17	95.62
2015	5,246	4,654	4,655	5,000	4,654	4,998	88.71	88.74	95.31	88.71	95.29
2016	6,028	5,390	5,392	5,806	5,390	5,804	89.42	89.45	96.32	89.42	96.30
Taipei,China											
2014	69,755	54,238	54,451	69,625	54,238	69,384	77.75	78.06	99.81	77.75	99.47
2015	65,863	51,043	51,266	69,376	51,043	69,125	77.50	77.84	105.33	77.50	104.95
2016	63,063	48,846	49,096	68,868	48,846	68,600	77.46	77.85	109.20	77.46	108.78
Thailand											
2014	53,272	45,595	45,703	55,828	45,595	55,688	85.59	85.79	104.80	85.59	104.53
2015	58,598	51,072	51,205	59,935	51,072	59,787	87.16	87.38	102.28	87.16	102.03
2016	61,253	54,390	54,496	63,657	54,390	63,534	88.80	88.97	103.92	88.80	103.72
Viet Nam											
2014	21,827	17,425	17,436	23,201	17,425	23,174	79.83	79.88	106.29	79.83	106.17
2015	24,578	20,778	20,800	27,022	20,778	26,983	84.54	84.63	109.94	84.54	109.79
2016	25,101	20,790	20,823	27,198	20,790	27,140	82.82	82.96	108.35	82.82	108.12

DVA_B = domestic value added exports by backward industrial linkages, DVA_F = domestic value added exports by forward industrial linkages, Lao PDR = Lao People's Democratic Republic, VAX_B = value added exports by backward industrial linkages, VAX_F = value added exports by forward industrial linkages, VAX_G = domestic value added absorbed abroad.

Source: ADB Multi Region Input-Output Tables Database.

Table 3.2e: Value-Added Exports by Various Measures—Personal Services Sector

	Exports	VAX_G	DVA_B	DVA_F	VAX_B	VAX_F	VAX_G	DVA_B	DVA_F	VAX_B	VAX_F
	($ million)						Value-Added Export Measure to Gross Exports Ratio (%)				
Bangladesh											
2014	712	683	683	3,168	683	3,165	95.85	95.91	444.81	95.85	444.47
2015	1,242	1,168	1,173	3,345	1,168	3,341	93.99	94.38	269.28	93.99	268.88
2016	1,104	1,072	1,074	3,270	1,072	3,268	97.12	97.26	296.23	97.12	296.04
Bhutan											
2014	49	43	43	34	43	34	86.23	86.23	69.35	86.23	69.35
2015	13	11	11	9	11	9	82.59	82.59	68.96	82.59	68.96
2016	70	59	59	45	59	45	83.79	83.79	64.15	83.79	64.15
Brunei Darussalam											
2014	24	21	21	64	21	64	87.03	87.03	268.03	87.03	268.01
2015	70	58	58	79	58	79	82.61	82.62	112.42	82.61	112.41
2016	94	76	76	93	76	93	81.19	81.19	99.08	81.19	99.06
Cambodia											
2014	128	109	109	116	109	116	84.75	84.77	90.32	84.75	90.30
2015	126	108	108	125	108	125	85.70	85.72	98.74	85.70	98.71
2016	158	134	134	139	134	139	85.06	85.07	88.31	85.06	88.29
China, People's Rep. of											
2014	13,886	12,590	12,704	41,681	12,590	40,507	90.66	91.49	300.16	90.66	291.71
2015	26,229	23,493	24,044	52,215	23,493	50,562	89.57	91.67	199.07	89.57	192.77
2016	29,503	26,440	27,054	55,119	26,440	53,456	89.62	91.70	186.83	89.62	181.19
Fiji											
2014	55	45	45	46	45	46	82.57	82.57	83.49	82.57	83.48
2015	26	22	22	27	22	27	85.06	85.06	103.27	85.06	103.27
2016	61	51	51	52	51	52	82.61	82.61	85.11	82.61	85.11
India											
2014	9,976	9,612	9,610	12,730	9,612	12,709	96.35	96.33	127.61	96.35	127.40
2015	13,884	13,471	13,469	16,172	13,471	16,153	97.02	97.01	116.48	97.02	116.34
2016	13,851	13,314	13,311	16,420	13,314	16,395	96.12	96.10	118.55	96.12	118.37
Indonesia											
2014	1,614	1,459	1,462	2,585	1,459	2,575	90.40	90.55	160.13	90.40	159.53
2015	1,662	1,509	1,512	2,585	1,509	2,576	90.79	90.93	155.50	90.79	154.98
2016	1,622	1,475	1,478	2,536	1,475	2,528	90.96	91.11	156.39	90.96	155.87
Japan											
2014	2,972	2,738	2,755	14,600	2,738	14,409	92.14	92.72	491.34	92.14	484.90
2015	19,160	17,942	18,103	28,050	17,942	27,757	93.65	94.49	146.40	93.65	144.87
2016	14,315	13,401	13,536	24,387	13,401	24,119	93.61	94.56	170.35	93.61	168.48
Kazakhstan											
2014	540	493	493	420	493	419	91.36	91.39	77.81	91.36	77.72
2015	485	442	442	342	442	342	91.11	91.16	70.55	91.11	70.47
2016	434	390	390	315	390	315	89.85	89.88	72.76	89.85	72.69
Korea, Rep. of											
2014	4,563	3,862	3,881	15,205	3,862	15,121	84.63	85.04	333.21	84.63	331.36
2015	4,189	3,486	3,506	14,454	3,486	14,371	83.22	83.69	345.05	83.22	343.07
2016	3,829	3,207	3,223	14,237	3,207	14,161	83.74	84.17	371.76	83.74	369.78
Kyrgyz Republic											
2014	220	186	186	157	186	157	84.38	84.39	71.19	84.38	71.18
2015	229	193	193	162	193	162	84.23	84.24	70.74	84.23	70.73
2016	234	196	196	166	196	166	83.71	83.71	70.67	83.71	70.67

continued on next page

Table 3.2e: continued

Table 3.2e: Value-Added Exports by Various Measures—Personal Services Sector											
	Exports	VAX_G	DVA_B	DVA_F	VAX_B	VAX_F	VAX_G	DVA_B	DVA_F	VAX_B	VAX_F
	($ million)						Value-Added Export Measure to Gross Exports Ratio (%)				
Lao PDR											
2014	117	104	104	85	104	85	88.97	88.98	72.34	88.97	72.34
2015	117	104	104	84	104	84	88.67	88.68	72.03	88.67	72.03
2016	124	113	113	91	113	91	91.07	91.08	73.31	91.07	73.30
Malaysia											
2014	2,924	2,445	2,446	3,368	2,445	3,362	83.61	83.65	115.17	83.61	114.96
2015	4,902	3,991	3,996	4,125	3,991	4,118	81.42	81.53	84.15	81.42	84.00
2016	5,038	4,183	4,188	4,321	4,183	4,314	83.03	83.12	85.76	83.03	85.62
Maldives											
2014	126	97	97	98	97	98	77.21	77.21	78.09	77.21	78.08
2015	61	44	44	133	44	133	73.03	73.04	219.15	73.03	219.14
2016	80	61	61	146	61	146	76.29	76.30	183.60	76.29	183.59
Mongolia											
2014	103	87	87	108	87	108	84.75	84.75	105.29	84.75	105.28
2015	87	75	75	125	75	125	86.40	86.40	143.26	86.40	143.25
2016	118	103	103	144	103	144	87.65	87.65	122.70	87.65	122.69
Nepal											
2014	404	375	375	310	375	309	92.68	92.73	76.53	92.68	76.49
2015	397	370	371	306	370	306	93.21	93.26	77.00	93.21	76.97
2016	429	396	396	323	396	323	92.33	92.38	75.29	92.33	75.25
Pakistan											
2014	2,255	2,196	2,197	2,010	2,196	2,010	97.38	97.41	89.14	97.38	89.12
2015	2,174	2,121	2,122	1,942	2,121	1,941	97.54	97.57	89.29	97.54	89.26
2016	2,126	2,065	2,065	1,885	2,065	1,884	97.10	97.13	88.66	97.10	88.63
Philippines											
2014	1,080	988	989	1,200	988	1,199	91.44	91.51	111.12	91.44	111.02
2015	807	741	741	1,034	741	1,033	91.73	91.81	128.09	91.73	127.95
2016	810	744	744	1,090	744	1,088	91.75	91.83	134.46	91.75	134.31
Sri Lanka											
2014	1,072	957	957	883	957	882	89.28	89.30	82.31	89.28	82.29
2015	1,051	942	942	867	942	867	89.65	89.67	82.51	89.65	82.49
2016	602	541	541	608	541	608	89.85	89.87	100.92	89.85	100.89
Taipei,China											
2014	1,764	1,472	1,472	4,346	1,472	4,334	83.43	83.46	246.31	83.43	245.63
2015	1,526	1,243	1,244	4,456	1,243	4,443	81.50	81.51	292.07	81.50	291.24
2016	1,550	1,288	1,288	4,827	1,288	4,814	83.11	83.13	311.48	83.11	310.64
Thailand											
2014	4,457	3,506	3,509	4,027	3,506	4,019	78.65	78.73	90.34	78.65	90.17
2015	5,250	4,271	4,281	4,577	4,271	4,565	81.37	81.55	87.19	81.37	86.97
2016	4,971	4,092	4,095	4,368	4,092	4,362	82.32	82.38	87.89	82.32	87.76
Viet Nam											
2014	4,021	3,368	3,371	3,088	3,368	3,085	83.75	83.84	76.80	83.75	76.72
2015	4,399	3,806	3,810	3,410	3,806	3,406	86.52	86.62	77.51	86.52	77.42
2016	5,081	4,305	4,311	3,791	4,305	3,785	84.72	84.84	74.61	84.72	74.49

DVA_B = domestic value added exports by backward industrial linkages, DVA_F = domestic value added exports by forward industrial linkages, Lao PDR = Lao People's Democratic Republic, VAX_B = value added exports by backward industrial linkages, VAX_F = value added exports by forward industrial linkages, VAX_G = domestic value added absorbed abroad.

Source: ADB Multi Region Input-Output Tables Database.

Table 3.2f: Value-Added Exports by Various Measures—All Sectors

	Exports	VAX_G	DVA_B	DVA_F	VAX_B	VAX_F	VAX_G	DVA_B	DVA_F	VAX_B	VAX_F
	($ million)						Value-Added Export Measure to Gross Exports Ratio (%)				
Bangladesh											
2014	40,461	35,844	35,874	35,874	35,844	35,844	88.59	88.66	88.66	88.59	88.59
2015	33,789	30,829	30,848	30,848	30,829	30,829	91.24	91.30	91.30	91.24	91.24
2016	32,342	30,851	30,863	30,863	30,851	30,851	95.39	95.43	95.43	95.39	95.39
Bhutan											
2014	571	483	483	483	483	483	84.60	84.60	84.60	84.60	84.60
2015	565	483	483	483	483	483	85.59	85.60	85.60	85.59	85.59
2016	593	489	489	489	489	489	82.47	82.48	82.48	82.47	82.47
Brunei Darussalam											
2014	10,701	9,628	9,629	9,629	9,628	9,628	89.98	89.99	89.99	89.98	89.98
2015	7,326	6,448	6,448	6,448	6,448	6,448	88.01	88.02	88.02	88.01	88.01
2016	7,333	6,338	6,339	6,339	6,338	6,338	86.44	86.44	86.44	86.44	86.44
Cambodia											
2014	7,805	5,602	5,603	5,603	5,602	5,602	71.77	71.79	71.79	71.77	71.77
2015	8,124	5,847	5,848	5,848	5,847	5,847	71.97	71.99	71.99	71.97	71.97
2016	9,010	6,441	6,442	6,442	6,441	6,441	71.49	71.50	71.50	71.49	71.49
China, People's Rep. of											
2014	2,434,045	1,979,939	2,041,261	2,041,261	1,979,939	1,979,939	81.34	83.86	83.86	81.34	81.34
2015	2,402,115	1,929,468	1,995,200	1,995,200	1,929,468	1,929,468	80.32	83.06	83.06	80.32	80.32
2016	2,399,694	1,919,415	1,981,982	1,981,982	1,919,415	1,919,415	79.99	82.59	82.59	79.99	79.99
Fiji											
2014	1,720	1,208	1,208	1,208	1,208	1,208	70.24	70.25	70.25	70.24	70.24
2015	1,595	1,119	1,119	1,119	1,119	1,119	70.13	70.13	70.13	70.13	70.13
2016	1,644	1,181	1,182	1,182	1,181	1,181	71.87	71.87	71.87	71.87	71.87
India											
2014	370,954	293,190	294,784	294,784	293,190	293,190	79.04	79.47	79.47	79.04	79.04
2015	333,937	269,881	271,184	271,184	269,881	269,881	80.82	81.21	81.21	80.82	80.82
2016	389,429	299,063	300,874	300,874	299,063	299,063	76.80	77.26	77.26	76.80	76.80
Indonesia											
2014	212,964	175,212	176,336	176,336	175,212	175,212	82.27	82.80	82.80	82.27	82.27
2015	195,933	159,229	160,138	160,138	159,229	159,229	81.27	81.73	81.73	81.27	81.27
2016	190,214	156,777	157,647	157,647	156,777	156,777	82.42	82.88	82.88	82.42	82.42
Japan											
2014	825,419	632,778	641,358	641,358	632,778	632,778	76.66	77.70	77.70	76.66	76.66
2015	816,438	618,285	626,107	626,107	618,285	618,285	75.73	76.69	76.69	75.73	75.73
2016	801,470	656,295	664,304	664,304	656,295	656,295	81.89	82.89	82.89	81.89	81.89
Kazakhstan											
2014	77,614	70,286	70,573	70,573	70,286	70,286	90.56	90.93	90.93	90.56	90.56
2015	56,141	49,744	49,990	49,990	49,744	49,744	88.61	89.04	89.04	88.61	88.61
2016	51,261	44,093	44,243	44,243	44,093	44,093	86.02	86.31	86.31	86.02	86.02
Korea, Rep. of											
2014	699,257	454,027	456,645	456,645	454,027	454,027	64.93	65.30	65.30	64.93	64.93
2015	653,686	413,179	415,566	415,566	413,179	413,179	63.21	63.57	63.57	63.21	63.21
2016	622,712	403,160	405,316	405,316	403,160	403,160	64.74	65.09	65.09	64.74	64.74
Kyrgyz Republic											
2014	1,780	1,322	1,323	1,323	1,322	1,322	74.26	74.33	74.33	74.26	74.26
2015	1,740	1,268	1,269	1,269	1,268	1,268	72.87	72.90	72.90	72.87	72.87
2016	1,719	1,251	1,251	1,251	1,251	1,251	72.75	72.78	72.78	72.75	72.75

continued on next page

Table 3.2f: continued

Table 3.2f: Value-Added Exports by Various Measures—All Sectors

	Exports	VAX_G	DVA_B	DVA_F	VAX_B	VAX_F	VAX_G	DVA_B	DVA_F	VAX_B	VAX_F
	($ million)						Value-Added Export Measure to Gross Exports Ratio (%)				
Lao PDR											
2014	5,089	4,316	4,318	4,318	4,316	4,316	84.81	84.84	84.84	84.81	84.81
2015	5,292	4,524	4,526	4,526	4,524	4,524	85.50	85.52	85.52	85.50	85.50
2016	5,127	4,506	4,507	4,507	4,506	4,506	87.87	87.89	87.89	87.87	87.87
Malaysia											
2014	189,960	136,481	136,874	136,874	136,481	136,481	71.85	72.05	72.05	71.85	71.85
2015	169,996	118,339	118,642	118,642	118,339	118,339	69.61	69.79	69.79	69.61	69.61
2016	166,910	119,085	119,389	119,389	119,085	119,085	71.35	71.53	71.53	71.35	71.35
Maldives											
2014	2,867	1,816	1,816	1,816	1,816	1,816	63.34	63.34	63.34	63.34	63.34
2015	2,900	1,977	1,977	1,977	1,977	1,977	68.18	68.18	68.18	68.18	68.18
2016	2,946	2,003	2,003	2,003	2,003	2,003	67.99	67.99	67.99	67.99	67.99
Mongolia											
2014	5,654	4,111	4,112	4,112	4,111	4,111	72.71	72.73	72.73	72.71	72.71
2015	5,469	4,277	4,277	4,277	4,277	4,277	78.20	78.21	78.21	78.20	78.20
2016	5,577	4,309	4,310	4,310	4,309	4,309	77.26	77.27	77.27	77.26	77.26
Nepal											
2014	1,315	1,096	1,097	1,097	1,096	1,096	83.32	83.37	83.37	83.32	83.32
2015	1,287	1,077	1,078	1,078	1,077	1,077	83.72	83.76	83.76	83.72	83.72
2016	1,413	1,169	1,170	1,170	1,169	1,169	82.76	82.81	82.81	82.76	82.76
Pakistan											
2014	28,847	26,798	26,814	26,814	26,798	26,798	92.90	92.95	92.95	92.90	92.90
2015	27,602	25,934	25,949	25,949	25,934	25,934	93.96	94.01	94.01	93.96	93.96
2016	25,423	23,752	23,764	23,764	23,752	23,752	93.43	93.47	93.47	93.43	93.43
Philippines											
2014	62,108	49,000	49,067	49,067	49,000	49,000	78.89	79.00	79.00	78.89	78.89
2015	62,470	49,412	49,482	49,482	49,412	49,412	79.10	79.21	79.21	79.10	79.10
2016	60,665	47,422	47,493	47,493	47,422	47,422	78.17	78.29	78.29	78.17	78.17
Sri Lanka											
2014	13,802	11,794	11,797	11,797	11,794	11,794	85.45	85.47	85.47	85.45	85.45
2015	13,530	11,584	11,587	11,587	11,584	11,584	85.62	85.64	85.64	85.62	85.62
2016	14,343	12,263	12,267	12,267	12,263	12,263	85.50	85.53	85.53	85.50	85.50
Taipei,China											
2014	372,420	216,352	217,206	217,206	216,352	216,352	58.09	58.32	58.32	58.09	58.09
2015	362,597	205,278	206,063	206,063	205,278	205,278	56.61	56.83	56.83	56.61	56.61
2016	359,196	204,985	205,778	205,778	204,985	204,985	57.07	57.29	57.29	57.07	57.07
Thailand											
2014	211,646	147,563	147,980	147,980	147,563	147,563	69.72	69.92	69.92	69.72	69.72
2015	203,729	147,348	147,723	147,723	147,348	147,348	72.33	72.51	72.51	72.33	72.33
2016	206,224	153,610	153,934	153,934	153,610	153,610	74.49	74.64	74.64	74.49	74.49
Viet Nam											
2014	111,998	77,600	77,742	77,742	77,600	77,600	69.29	69.41	69.41	69.29	69.29
2015	128,055	91,173	91,348	91,348	91,173	91,173	71.20	71.33	71.33	71.20	71.20
2016	123,118	87,920	88,168	88,168	87,920	87,920	71.41	71.61	71.61	71.41	71.41

DVA_B = domestic value added exports by backward industrial linkages, DVA_F = domestic value added exports by forward industrial linkages, Lao PDR = Lao People's Democratic Republic, VAX_B = value added exports by backward industrial linkages, VAX_F = value added exports by forward industrial linkages, VAX_G = domestic value added absorbed abroad.

Source: ADB Multi Region Input-Output Tables Database.

Table 3.3a: Direct and Indirect Value-Added Exports—Primary Sector

	Gross Exports	VAX_F	VAX_B	Direct Exports	Indirect Exports (Forward Linkage)	Indirect Exports (Backward Linkage)	Share of Direct Exports in VAX_F	Share of Indirect Exports in VAX_F	Share of Direct Exports in VAX_B	Share of Indirect Exports in VAX_B
	($ million)						(%)			
Bangladesh										
2014	1,164	2,746	1,109	699	2,046	410	25.47	74.53	63.05	36.95
2015	1,070	2,343	1,033	659	1,684	374	28.11	71.89	63.78	36.22
2016	1,081	2,291	1,049	652	1,640	397	28.44	71.56	62.14	37.86
Bhutan										
2014	66	73	61	54	20	8	73.09	26.91	87.33	12.67
2015	72	75	68	60	15	7	79.92	20.08	88.92	11.08
2016	71	75	66	58	17	8	77.43	22.57	87.83	12.17
Brunei Darussalam										
2014	5,491	6,688	5,083	4,752	1,936	330	71.05	28.95	93.50	6.50
2015	3,675	4,391	3,339	3,120	1,270	218	71.07	28.93	93.46	6.54
2016	3,547	4,266	3,144	2,939	1,327	205	68.90	31.10	93.49	6.51
Cambodia										
2014	1,316	1,252	1,203	1,112	140	90	88.85	11.15	92.49	7.51
2015	1,241	1,156	1,087	1,002	154	85	86.68	13.32	92.19	7.81
2016	1,056	1,065	966	889	176	77	83.48	16.52	92.07	7.93
China, People's Rep. of										
2014	34,516	282,077	30,764	22,047	260,029	8,717	7.82	92.18	71.67	28.33
2015	31,816	230,943	28,309	20,572	210,370	7,736	8.91	91.09	72.67	27.33
2016	33,059	219,840	29,096	20,976	198,864	8,120	9.54	90.46	72.09	27.91
Fiji										
2014	116	131	84	62	69	22	47.08	52.92	73.93	26.07
2015	125	137	91	70	67	21	51.24	48.76	76.60	23.40
2016	118	136	87	67	70	21	48.92	51.08	76.18	23.82
India										
2014	22,655	41,368	21,493	18,588	22,781	2,905	44.93	55.07	86.48	13.52
2015	18,087	36,151	17,232	14,607	21,544	2,625	40.41	59.59	84.77	15.23
2016	29,525	50,506	27,776	23,834	26,673	3,942	47.19	52.81	85.81	14.19
Indonesia										
2014	50,483	68,960	46,302	41,064	27,896	5,237	59.55	40.45	88.69	11.31
2015	39,770	56,179	36,253	32,054	24,125	4,200	57.06	42.94	88.42	11.58
2016	39,555	55,752	36,395	32,180	23,572	4,215	57.72	42.28	88.42	11.58
Japan										
2014	5,425	7,104	2,878	1,860	5,243	1,017	26.19	73.81	64.65	35.35
2015	5,414	5,952	2,834	1,555	4,396	1,279	26.13	73.87	54.88	45.12
2016	5,892	6,039	3,495	1,769	4,270	1,726	29.29	70.71	50.61	49.39
Kazakhstan										
2014	42,859	34,283	39,003	31,481	2,802	7,522	91.83	8.17	80.71	19.29
2015	25,237	18,873	22,299	16,890	1,983	5,408	89.49	10.51	75.75	24.25
2016	24,558	17,077	20,827	15,447	1,630	5,380	90.46	9.54	74.17	25.83
Korea, Rep. of										
2014	1,067	6,663	886	647	6,016	239	9.71	90.29	73.04	26.96
2015	1,014	6,374	830	605	5,769	225	9.49	90.51	72.93	27.07
2016	1,049	6,248	850	611	5,637	239	9.77	90.23	71.87	28.13
Kyrgyz Republic										
2014	331	206	259	190	16	70	92.13	7.87	73.15	26.85
2015	297	188	233	170	18	64	90.32	9.68	72.68	27.32
2016	352	205	264	193	13	72	93.88	6.12	72.85	27.15

continued on next page

Table 3.3a: continued

Table 3.3a: Direct and Indirect Value-Added Exports—Primary Sector

	Gross Exports	VAX_F	VAX_B	Direct Exports	Indirect Exports (Forward Linkage)	Indirect Exports (Backward Linkage)	Share of Direct Exports in VAX_F	Share of Indirect Exports in VAX_F	Share of Direct Exports in VAX_B	Share of Indirect Exports in VAX_B
	($ million)						(%)			
Lao PDR										
2014	3,320	2,679	2,905	2,542	137	364	94.89	5.11	87.48	12.52
2015	3,478	2,829	3,092	2,707	122	385	95.70	4.30	87.54	12.46
2016	3,567	2,847	3,212	2,725	123	487	95.69	4.31	84.83	15.17
Malaysia										
2014	13,096	35,268	12,000	10,744	24,524	1,256	30.46	69.54	89.53	10.47
2015	10,665	29,496	9,367	8,308	21,189	1,060	28.16	71.84	88.69	11.31
2016	10,311	28,271	9,043	8,000	20,271	1,042	28.30	71.70	88.47	11.53
Maldives										
2014	28	140	18	14	126	3	10.34	89.66	81.39	18.61
2015	26	82	13	11	71	2	13.49	86.51	82.01	17.99
2016	36	88	19	16	72	3	18.04	81.96	81.99	18.01
Mongolia										
2014	4,227	2,091	3,015	1,996	95	1,020	95.44	4.56	66.18	33.82
2015	4,186	2,058	3,225	1,954	104	1,271	94.95	5.05	60.58	39.42
2016	4,255	2,058	3,227	1,958	100	1,270	95.15	4.85	60.66	39.34
Nepal										
2014	84	127	78	70	57	8	54.94	45.06	89.33	10.67
2015	92	132	86	77	56	9	57.99	42.01	89.34	10.66
2016	110	152	103	92	60	11	60.40	39.60	89.39	10.61
Pakistan										
2014	1,800	7,978	1,750	1,613	6,365	138	20.21	79.79	92.12	7.88
2015	6,215	9,989	6,051	5,618	4,371	434	56.24	43.76	92.83	7.17
2016	5,717	9,262	5,504	5,110	4,152	394	55.17	44.83	92.84	7.16
Philippines										
2014	1,586	5,893	1,476	1,206	4,687	270	20.46	79.54	81.69	18.31
2015	1,445	5,335	1,329	1,087	4,248	242	20.38	79.62	81.80	18.20
2016	1,397	4,766	1,266	1,023	3,743	244	21.46	78.54	80.75	19.25
Sri Lanka										
2014	723	1,125	647	559	567	88	49.66	50.34	86.39	13.61
2015	652	1,180	584	505	675	79	42.79	57.21	86.46	13.54
2016	632	1,118	561	489	630	72	43.69	56.31	87.10	12.90
Taipei,China										
2014	2,084	2,639	1,586	1,192	1,447	394	45.17	54.83	75.14	24.86
2015	2,007	2,522	1,450	1,082	1,440	368	42.91	57.09	74.65	25.35
2016	2,212	2,637	1,637	1,216	1,421	421	46.10	53.90	74.27	25.73
Thailand										
2014	7,165	25,053	6,163	4,876	20,176	1,287	19.46	80.54	79.12	20.88
2015	3,003	22,011	2,589	2,042	19,970	548	9.27	90.73	78.85	21.15
2016	3,410	22,619	2,969	2,325	20,294	644	10.28	89.72	78.31	21.69
Viet Nam										
2014	39,641	32,306	31,407	26,983	5,323	4,424	83.52	16.48	85.91	14.09
2015	40,998	34,783	33,245	28,533	6,250	4,712	82.03	17.97	85.83	14.17
2016	39,185	32,534	31,405	26,874	5,660	4,531	82.60	17.40	85.57	14.43

Lao PDR = Lao People's Democratic Republic, VAX_B = value added exports by backward industrial linkages, VAX_F = value added exports by forward industrial linkages.

Source: ADB Multi Region Input-Output Tables Database.

Table 3.3b: Direct and Indirect Value-Added Exports—Low-Technology Manufacturing Sector

	Gross Exports	VAX_F	VAX_B	Direct Exports	Indirect Exports (Forward Linkage)	Indirect Exports (Backward Linkage)	Share of Direct Exports in VAX_F	Share of Indirect Exports in VAX_F	Share of Direct Exports in VAX_B	Share of Indirect Exports in VAX_B
	($ million)						(%)			
Bangladesh										
2014	35,153	15,688	31,186	13,590	2,098	17,596	86.63	13.37	43.58	56.42
2015	28,305	11,703	25,893	10,893	809	15,000	93.08	6.92	42.07	57.93
2016	27,763	12,892	26,553	12,014	877	14,539	93.19	6.81	45.25	54.75
Bhutan										
2014	228	200	198	167	33	30	83.56	16.44	84.69	15.31
2015	248	228	221	199	28	21	87.52	12.48	90.37	9.63
2016	226	202	191	165	37	26	81.50	18.50	86.22	13.78
Brunei Darussalam										
2014	79	72	54	25	47	28	34.98	65.02	46.89	53.11
2015	112	61	71	28	32	42	46.91	53.09	40.16	59.84
2016	109	65	71	31	34	39	48.42	51.58	44.54	55.46
Cambodia										
2014	3,682	1,990	2,363	1,868	122	495	93.88	6.12	79.05	20.95
2015	4,097	2,239	2,683	2,102	137	581	93.88	6.12	78.36	21.64
2016	4,505	2,441	2,950	2,283	159	667	93.51	6.49	77.38	22.62
China, People's Rep. of										
2014	561,310	355,317	494,411	189,270	166,046	305,140	53.27	46.73	38.28	61.72
2015	547,199	345,257	479,098	182,065	163,192	297,034	52.73	47.27	38.00	62.00
2016	520,542	332,598	452,497	173,073	159,525	279,424	52.04	47.96	38.25	61.75
Fiji										
2014	355	194	259	139	55	120	71.85	28.15	53.84	46.16
2015	327	182	241	135	47	105	74.11	25.89	56.22	43.78
2016	358	200	267	150	50	118	74.93	25.07	56.03	43.97
India										
2014	79,263	35,106	67,566	22,262	12,844	45,304	63.41	36.59	32.95	67.05
2015	73,260	33,093	63,478	20,587	12,506	42,891	62.21	37.79	32.43	67.57
2016	92,677	44,617	78,561	27,212	17,405	51,349	60.99	39.01	34.64	65.36
Indonesia										
2014	84,176	38,288	68,203	33,424	4,864	34,779	87.30	12.70	49.01	50.99
2015	82,203	37,200	66,077	32,437	4,763	33,640	87.20	12.80	49.09	50.91
2016	80,551	36,827	65,605	32,121	4,706	33,483	87.22	12.78	48.96	51.04
Japan										
2014	51,849	61,159	41,308	20,896	40,263	20,412	34.17	65.83	50.59	49.41
2015	53,705	58,933	41,360	20,884	38,050	20,476	35.44	64.56	50.49	49.51
2016	49,244	61,843	41,327	22,282	39,561	19,045	36.03	63.97	53.92	46.08
Kazakhstan										
2014	1,882	2,308	1,587	976	1,332	611	42.28	57.72	61.49	38.51
2015	1,679	1,657	1,367	862	795	505	52.04	47.96	63.09	36.91
2016	1,601	1,483	1,304	798	685	506	53.83	46.17	61.22	38.78
Korea, Rep. of										
2014	51,041	44,005	36,488	17,529	26,476	18,959	39.83	60.17	48.04	51.96
2015	46,172	41,041	32,442	15,327	25,714	17,115	37.35	62.65	47.24	52.76
2016	44,884	41,282	32,005	14,877	26,405	17,128	36.04	63.96	46.48	53.52
Kyrgyz Republic										
2014	153	81	97	59	22	38	72.99	27.01	61.01	38.99
2015	221	105	132	80	25	52	76.37	23.63	60.43	39.57
2016	74	46	43	20	25	22	44.56	55.44	48.00	52.00

continued on next page

Table 3.3b: continued

Table 3.3b: Direct and Indirect Value-Added Exports—Low-Technology Manufacturing Sector

	Gross Exports	VAX_F	VAX_B	Direct Exports	Indirect Exports (Forward Linkage)	Indirect Exports (Backward Linkage)	Share of Direct Exports in VAX_F	Share of Indirect Exports in VAX_F	Share of Direct Exports in VAX_B	Share of Indirect Exports in VAX_B
	($ million)						(%)			
Lao PDR										
2014	1,149	866	898	653	213	245	75.43	24.57	72.74	27.26
2015	1,166	887	886	639	248	247	72.03	27.97	72.12	27.88
2016	970	863	794	572	291	222	66.26	33.74	72.03	27.97
Malaysia										
2014	45,697	14,824	32,880	9,118	5,706	23,762	61.51	38.49	27.73	72.27
2015	45,229	14,838	31,929	9,712	5,126	22,217	65.45	34.55	30.42	69.58
2016	39,702	13,221	28,209	8,047	5,173	20,162	60.87	39.13	28.53	71.47
Maldives										
2014	99	97	54	27	70	27	27.94	72.06	50.13	49.87
2015	342	395	246	174	221	72	44.00	56.00	70.71	29.29
2016	281	382	206	145	237	61	38.01	61.99	70.37	29.63
Mongolia										
2014	388	313	284	152	162	132	48.38	51.62	53.36	46.64
2015	374	339	292	144	195	148	42.51	57.49	49.23	50.77
2016	392	351	303	155	196	148	44.10	55.90	51.14	48.86
Nepal										
2014	250	138	188	102	36	86	73.68	26.32	54.28	45.72
2015	249	136	187	101	35	86	74.10	25.90	53.97	46.03
2016	261	143	195	104	39	91	72.46	27.54	53.28	46.72
Pakistan										
2014	14,534	5,051	13,098	4,485	566	8,613	88.80	11.20	34.24	65.76
2015	10,001	3,720	9,038	3,236	484	5,802	86.99	13.01	35.81	64.19
2016	9,825	3,666	8,881	3,197	469	5,684	87.22	12.78	36.00	64.00
Philippines										
2014	12,700	8,742	11,172	5,188	3,554	5,984	59.34	40.66	46.44	53.56
2015	12,599	8,712	10,807	5,110	3,602	5,697	58.66	41.34	47.29	52.71
2016	11,438	8,456	9,571	4,747	3,709	4,823	56.14	43.86	49.60	50.40
Sri Lanka										
2014	6,185	4,276	5,184	3,695	581	1,489	86.40	13.60	71.27	28.73
2015	6,274	4,275	5,215	3,586	689	1,629	83.88	16.12	68.76	31.24
2016	6,756	4,421	5,562	3,850	571	1,712	87.08	12.92	69.21	30.79
Taipei,China										
2014	25,320	16,404	14,825	8,511	7,894	6,315	51.88	48.12	57.41	42.59
2015	25,622	16,854	14,515	8,127	8,727	6,388	48.22	51.78	55.99	44.01
2016	35,176	19,490	20,299	10,305	9,185	9,994	52.87	47.13	50.77	49.23
Thailand										
2014	71,072	31,879	53,076	23,233	8,646	29,843	72.88	27.12	43.77	56.23
2015	69,510	31,594	52,661	22,534	9,059	30,126	71.33	28.67	42.79	57.21
2016	67,722	31,972	52,990	22,351	9,621	30,639	69.91	30.09	42.18	57.82
Viet Nam										
2014	34,509	13,868	19,383	9,509	4,359	9,874	68.57	31.43	49.06	50.94
2015	40,453	18,046	23,764	12,201	5,844	11,563	67.61	32.39	51.34	48.66
2016	37,829	16,880	22,526	11,592	5,288	10,934	68.67	31.33	51.46	48.54

Lao PDR = Lao People's Democratic Republic, VAX_B = value added exports by backward industrial linkages, VAX_F = value added exports by forward industrial linkages.

Source: ADB Multi Region Input-Output Tables Database.

Table 3.3c: Direct and Indirect Value-Added Exports—Medium- and High-Technology Manufacturing Sector										
	Gross Exports	VAX_F	VAX_B	Direct Exports	Indirect Exports (Forward Linkage)	Indirect Exports (Backward Linkage)	Share of Direct Exports in VAX_F	Share of Indirect Exports in VAX_F	Share of Direct Exports in VAX_B	Share of Indirect Exports in VAX_B
	($ million)						(%)			
Bangladesh										
2014	2,273	873	1,794	410	463	1,384	46.99	53.01	22.85	77.15
2015	1,916	1,214	1,568	467	748	1,102	38.43	61.57	29.75	70.25
2016	1,432	1,198	1,259	414	784	845	34.56	65.44	32.87	67.13
Bhutan										
2014	73	34	57	27	7	30	79.91	20.09	47.17	52.83
2015	73	33	58	29	4	29	86.73	13.27	50.42	49.58
2016	93	41	69	35	6	34	85.38	14.62	50.58	49.42
Brunei Darussalam										
2014	4,771	2,242	4,209	2,103	140	2,106	93.77	6.23	49.96	50.04
2015	3,161	1,472	2,740	1,374	97	1,366	93.38	6.62	50.14	49.86
2016	3,271	1,461	2,810	1,374	87	1,437	94.03	5.97	48.88	51.12
Cambodia										
2014	75	65	45	39	26	6	60.40	39.60	87.15	12.85
2015	68	65	43	37	28	6	57.01	42.99	85.70	14.30
2016	88	76	52	44	32	8	58.32	41.68	85.36	14.64
China, People's Rep. of										
2014	1,451,565	625,040	1,111,360	381,255	243,785	730,105	61.00	39.00	34.31	65.69
2015	1,409,298	584,858	1,056,457	354,749	230,109	701,708	60.66	39.34	33.58	66.42
2016	1,342,004	560,822	993,965	336,583	224,239	657,382	60.02	39.98	33.86	66.14
Fiji										
2014	36	30	21	15	15	6	49.29	50.71	69.93	30.07
2015	32	25	18	13	11	5	53.56	46.44	72.29	27.71
2016	31	27	18	13	13	5	49.73	50.27	72.70	27.30
India										
2014	154,828	59,541	97,011	45,465	14,075	51,546	76.36	23.64	46.87	53.13
2015	142,369	54,065	94,358	40,429	13,636	53,929	74.78	25.22	42.85	57.15
2016	175,920	68,543	108,067	50,575	17,968	57,491	73.79	26.21	46.80	53.20
Indonesia										
2014	65,689	32,917	49,502	27,330	5,587	22,172	83.03	16.97	55.21	44.79
2015	59,630	30,432	44,479	24,552	5,880	19,927	80.68	19.32	55.20	44.80
2016	56,317	29,482	42,782	23,557	5,925	19,225	79.90	20.10	55.06	44.94
Japan										
2014	618,131	303,914	454,234	250,157	53,757	204,078	82.31	17.69	55.07	44.93
2015	577,217	267,129	410,810	221,261	45,868	189,549	82.83	17.17	53.86	46.14
2016	561,728	294,017	441,444	244,591	49,426	196,853	83.19	16.81	55.41	44.59
Kazakhstan										
2014	11,599	8,300	10,569	6,044	2,256	4,525	72.82	27.18	57.19	42.81
2015	9,708	6,099	8,356	4,549	1,550	3,807	74.59	25.41	54.44	45.56
2016	9,670	5,687	8,314	4,315	1,371	3,999	75.89	24.11	51.90	48.10
Korea, Rep. of										
2014	550,894	246,615	337,366	187,837	58,779	149,529	76.17	23.83	55.68	44.32
2015	515,126	215,204	305,948	164,605	50,599	141,343	76.49	23.51	53.80	46.20
2016	488,149	209,320	299,017	158,790	50,530	140,227	75.86	24.14	53.10	46.90
Kyrgyz Republic										
2014	669	494	498	472	22	26	95.56	4.44	94.73	5.27
2015	544	405	398	377	28	21	93.02	6.98	94.68	5.32
2016	553	392	391	370	22	21	94.31	5.69	94.57	5.43

continued on next page

Table 3.3c: continued

Table 3.3c: Direct and Indirect Value-Added Exports—Medium- and High-Technology Manufacturing Sector

	Gross Exports	VAX_F	VAX_B	Direct Exports	Indirect Exports (Forward Linkage)	Indirect Exports (Backward Linkage)	Share of Direct Exports in VAX_F	Share of Indirect Exports in VAX_F	Share of Direct Exports in VAX_B	Share of Indirect Exports in VAX_B
	($ million)						(%)			
Lao PDR										
2014	32	65	20	18	48	2	27.00	73.00	88.65	11.35
2015	35	66	24	19	46	5	29.45	70.55	80.63	19.37
2016	60	80	40	31	49	9	39.09	60.91	78.28	21.72
Malaysia										
2014	80,584	32,183	49,302	22,847	9,336	26,455	70.99	29.01	46.34	53.66
2015	71,709	28,574	42,341	20,053	8,521	22,288	70.18	29.82	47.36	52.64
2016	69,022	27,936	41,665	19,506	8,430	22,159	69.82	30.18	46.82	53.18
Maldives										
2014	3	4	2	2	2	1	37.96	62.04	71.76	28.24
2015	1	9	1	0	8	0	5.41	94.59	75.63	24.37
2016	6	11	4	3	7	1	30.46	69.54	77.79	22.21
Mongolia										
2014	165	180	121	79	101	42	43.80	56.20	65.32	34.68
2015	133	164	103	63	101	41	38.16	61.84	60.59	39.41
2016	100	156	77	48	108	29	30.68	69.32	62.38	37.62
Nepal										
2014	99	55	59	42	13	17	76.55	23.45	71.07	28.93
2015	98	55	60	43	12	17	77.87	22.13	71.79	28.21
2016	122	65	73	52	13	21	80.18	19.82	71.55	28.45
Pakistan										
2014	1,063	808	903	356	452	547	44.04	55.96	39.43	60.57
2015	977	738	824	335	403	489	45.35	54.65	40.65	59.35
2016	877	682	721	298	384	423	43.70	56.30	41.31	58.69
Philippines										
2014	22,899	8,796	13,321	7,003	1,793	6,318	79.62	20.38	52.57	47.43
2015	21,536	8,450	12,494	6,896	1,553	5,598	81.62	18.38	55.20	44.80
2016	20,480	7,684	11,371	6,280	1,404	5,091	81.73	18.27	55.23	44.77
Sri Lanka										
2014	473	396	290	199	197	91	50.20	49.80	68.50	31.50
2015	308	264	190	124	140	65	47.11	52.89	65.51	34.49
2016	325	312	210	174	138	36	55.77	44.23	83.06	16.94
Taipei,China										
2014	273,496	123,592	144,231	110,130	13,462	34,101	89.11	10.89	76.36	23.64
2015	267,580	112,335	137,028	100,029	12,306	36,999	89.05	10.95	73.00	27.00
2016	257,196	109,443	132,915	96,316	13,127	36,599	88.01	11.99	72.46	27.54
Thailand										
2014	75,679	30,924	39,223	21,650	9,274	17,573	70.01	29.99	55.20	44.80
2015	67,368	29,390	36,755	19,680	9,710	17,075	66.96	33.04	53.54	46.46
2016	68,869	31,123	39,170	20,569	10,554	18,600	66.09	33.91	52.51	47.49
Viet Nam										
2014	11,999	5,166	6,016	2,199	2,967	3,816	42.57	57.43	36.56	63.44
2015	17,628	7,955	9,580	4,216	3,739	5,364	52.99	47.01	44.01	55.99
2016	15,921	7,581	8,894	3,682	3,899	5,212	48.56	51.44	41.40	58.60

0 = magnitude is less than half of unit employed, Lao PDR = Lao People's Democratic Republic, VAX_B = value added exports by backward industrial linkages, VAX_F = value added exports by forward industrial linkages.

Source: ADB Multi Region Input-Output Tables Database.

Table 3.3d: Direct and Indirect Value-Added Exports—Business Services Sector

	Gross Exports	VAX_F	VAX_B	Direct Exports	Indirect Exports (Forward Linkage)	Indirect Exports (Backward Linkage)	Share of Direct Exports in VAX_F	Share of Indirect Exports in VAX_F	Share of Direct Exports in VAX_B	Share of Indirect Exports in VAX_B
	($ million)						(%)			
Bangladesh										
2014	1,160	13,373	1,072	765	12,608	307	5.72	94.28	71.35	28.65
2015	1,256	12,229	1,168	810	11,418	357	6.63	93.37	69.39	30.61
2016	962	11,202	918	619	10,583	299	5.53	94.47	67.46	32.54
Bhutan										
2014	154	142	125	93	49	32	65.48	34.52	74.38	25.62
2015	158	137	126	99	39	27	71.91	28.09	78.23	21.77
2016	132	126	104	83	44	21	65.49	34.51	79.36	20.64
Brunei Darussalam										
2014	336	562	263	143	419	120	25.42	74.58	54.31	45.69
2015	308	446	240	137	309	103	30.74	69.26	57.14	42.86
2016	312	454	238	141	313	97	31.08	68.92	59.30	40.70
Cambodia										
2014	2,604	2,179	1,882	1,440	739	443	66.07	33.93	76.49	23.51
2015	2,591	2,262	1,926	1,459	803	467	64.51	35.49	75.77	24.23
2016	3,203	2,719	2,339	1,778	941	561	65.38	34.62	76.01	23.99
China, People's Rep. of										
2014	372,768	676,999	330,815	195,205	481,794	135,611	28.83	71.17	59.01	40.99
2015	387,574	717,849	342,112	202,029	515,820	140,082	28.14	71.86	59.05	40.95
2016	474,586	752,699	417,417	240,873	511,827	176,544	32.00	68.00	57.71	42.29
Fiji										
2014	1,159	807	799	573	234	226	71.04	28.96	71.75	28.25
2015	1,086	748	746	577	172	170	77.07	22.93	77.24	22.76
2016	1,075	767	758	585	182	173	76.24	23.76	77.13	22.87
India										
2014	104,232	144,466	97,508	82,079	62,387	15,428	56.82	43.18	84.18	15.82
2015	86,337	130,418	81,342	68,232	62,186	13,110	52.32	47.68	83.88	16.12
2016	77,457	119,001	71,346	59,546	59,455	11,800	50.04	49.96	83.46	16.54
Indonesia										
2014	11,002	32,472	9,746	6,006	26,466	3,741	18.50	81.50	61.62	38.38
2015	12,668	32,842	10,911	6,563	26,278	4,348	19.99	80.01	60.15	39.85
2016	12,169	32,188	10,520	6,348	25,840	4,172	19.72	80.28	60.34	39.66
Japan										
2014	147,043	246,193	131,619	93,618	152,575	38,002	38.03	61.97	71.13	28.87
2015	160,942	258,514	145,339	102,574	155,939	42,765	39.68	60.32	70.58	29.42
2016	170,290	270,278	156,629	111,612	158,666	45,017	41.30	58.70	71.26	28.74
Kazakhstan										
2014	20,735	24,975	18,633	14,392	10,583	4,241	57.62	42.38	77.24	22.76
2015	19,031	22,773	17,280	13,646	9,127	3,634	59.92	40.08	78.97	21.03
2016	14,998	19,531	13,258	10,317	9,214	2,941	52.82	47.18	77.81	22.19
Korea, Rep. of										
2014	91,692	141,623	75,425	50,320	91,303	25,104	35.53	64.47	66.72	33.28
2015	87,186	136,188	70,472	46,759	89,429	23,713	34.33	65.67	66.35	33.65
2016	84,800	132,150	68,082	44,688	87,462	23,394	33.82	66.18	65.64	34.36
Kyrgyz Republic										
2014	408	385	282	241	144	41	62.65	37.35	85.41	14.59
2015	448	408	311	261	147	50	63.89	36.11	83.85	16.15
2016	505	442	356	296	145	60	67.08	32.92	83.17	16.83

continued on next page

Table 3.3d: continued

Table 3.3d: Direct and Indirect Value-Added Exports—Business Services Sector

	Gross Exports	VAX_F	VAX_B	Direct Exports	Indirect Exports (Forward Linkage)	Indirect Exports (Backward Linkage)	Share of Direct Exports in VAX_F	Share of Indirect Exports in VAX_F	Share of Direct Exports in VAX_B	Share of Indirect Exports in VAX_B
	($ million)						(%)			
Lao PDR										
2014	472	622	389	314	308	75	50.54	49.46	80.79	19.21
2015	496	659	418	331	328	87	50.27	49.73	79.18	20.82
2016	407	624	347	272	353	75	43.50	56.50	78.27	21.73
Malaysia										
2014	47,659	50,844	39,854	28,112	22,732	11,741	55.29	44.71	70.54	29.46
2015	37,490	41,312	30,710	21,355	19,957	9,355	51.69	48.31	69.54	30.46
2016	42,837	45,343	35,984	25,074	20,269	10,910	55.30	44.70	69.68	30.32
Maldives										
2014	2,611	1,477	1,645	998	479	647	67.54	32.46	60.64	39.36
2015	2,471	1,359	1,673	1,012	346	661	74.51	25.49	60.51	39.49
2016	2,543	1,376	1,712	1,031	345	681	74.93	25.07	60.22	39.78
Mongolia										
2014	771	1,419	604	455	965	150	32.03	67.97	75.22	24.78
2015	689	1,591	580	405	1,186	175	25.47	74.53	69.83	30.17
2016	713	1,600	599	424	1,176	175	26.51	73.49	70.81	29.19
Nepal										
2014	479	466	396	313	154	83	67.02	32.98	78.92	21.08
2015	450	448	374	294	154	80	65.59	34.41	78.50	21.50
2016	490	486	403	319	167	84	65.55	34.45	79.12	20.88
Pakistan										
2014	9,195	10,952	8,851	6,738	4,214	2,113	61.52	38.48	76.12	23.88
2015	8,235	9,546	7,900	5,952	3,594	1,948	62.35	37.65	75.34	24.66
2016	6,878	8,258	6,581	4,916	3,342	1,665	59.54	40.46	74.70	25.30
Philippines										
2014	23,843	24,369	22,044	15,107	9,262	6,936	61.99	38.01	68.53	31.47
2015	26,083	25,883	24,041	17,035	8,848	7,007	65.82	34.18	70.86	29.14
2016	26,539	25,427	24,470	17,224	8,202	7,245	67.74	32.26	70.39	29.61
Sri Lanka										
2014	5,348	5,114	4,716	3,535	1,579	1,181	69.13	30.87	74.97	25.03
2015	5,246	4,998	4,654	3,462	1,537	1,192	69.26	30.74	74.39	25.61
2016	6,028	5,804	5,390	4,175	1,630	1,215	71.93	28.07	77.46	22.54
Taipei,China										
2014	69,755	69,384	54,238	40,816	28,568	13,422	58.83	41.17	75.25	24.75
2015	65,863	69,125	51,043	37,439	31,686	13,604	54.16	45.84	73.35	26.65
2016	63,063	68,600	48,846	35,612	32,988	13,234	51.91	48.09	72.91	27.09
Thailand										
2014	53,272	55,688	45,595	28,791	26,896	16,804	51.70	48.30	63.15	36.85
2015	58,598	59,787	51,072	31,876	27,911	19,196	53.32	46.68	62.41	37.59
2016	61,253	63,534	54,390	34,010	29,524	20,380	53.53	46.47	62.53	37.47
Viet Nam										
2014	21,827	23,174	17,425	13,025	10,149	4,400	56.21	43.79	74.75	25.25
2015	24,578	26,983	20,778	16,336	10,648	4,443	60.54	39.46	78.62	21.38
2016	25,101	27,140	20,790	16,040	11,099	4,750	59.10	40.90	77.15	22.85

Lao PDR = Lao People's Democratic Republic, VAX_B = value added exports by backward industrial linkages, VAX_F = value added exports by forward industrial linkages.

Source: ADB Multi Region Input-Output Tables Database.

Table 3.3e: Direct and Indirect Value-Added Exports—Personal Services Sector										
	Gross Exports	VAX_F	VAX_B	Direct Exports	Indirect Exports (Forward Linkage)	Indirect Exports (Backward Linkage)	Share of Direct Exports in VAX_F	Share of Indirect Exports in VAX_F	Share of Direct Exports in VAX_B	Share of Indirect Exports in VAX_B
	($ million)						(%)			
Bangladesh										
2014	712	3,165	683	513	2,652	169	16.22	83.78	75.21	24.79
2015	1,242	3,341	1,168	865	2,475	302	25.90	74.10	74.10	25.90
2016	1,104	3,268	1,072	804	2,464	268	24.59	75.41	74.96	25.04
Bhutan										
2014	49	34	43	31	4	12	89.57	10.43	72.04	27.96
2015	13	9	11	8	1	3	89.62	10.38	74.83	25.17
2016	70	45	59	44	1	15	97.34	2.66	74.52	25.48
Brunei Darussalam										
2014	24	64	21	17	47	4	26.94	73.06	82.95	17.05
2015	70	79	58	44	35	14	56.14	43.86	76.38	23.62
2016	94	93	76	60	33	16	64.49	35.51	78.69	21.31
Cambodia										
2014	128	116	109	91	25	18	78.59	21.41	83.73	16.27
2015	126	125	108	99	25	9	79.69	20.31	91.79	8.21
2016	158	139	134	113	27	21	80.94	19.06	84.02	15.98
China, People's Rep. of										
2014	13,886	40,507	12,590	6,667	33,840	5,923	16.46	83.54	52.95	47.05
2015	26,229	50,562	23,493	11,789	38,773	11,703	23.32	76.68	50.18	49.82
2016	29,503	53,456	26,440	13,752	39,704	12,688	25.73	74.27	52.01	47.99
Fiji										
2014	55	46	45	38	8	7	82.68	17.32	83.60	16.40
2015	26	27	22	18	9	4	67.76	32.24	82.27	17.73
2016	61	52	51	43	9	7	82.98	17.02	85.49	14.51
India										
2014	9,976	12,709	9,612	8,508	4,201	1,104	66.95	33.05	88.52	11.48
2015	13,884	16,153	13,471	11,931	4,222	1,540	73.86	26.14	88.57	11.43
2016	13,851	16,395	13,314	11,904	4,491	1,410	72.61	27.39	89.41	10.59
Indonesia										
2014	1,614	2,575	1,459	1,085	1,491	375	42.12	57.88	74.33	25.67
2015	1,662	2,576	1,509	1,135	1,441	374	44.07	55.93	75.23	24.77
2016	1,622	2,528	1,475	1,111	1,416	364	43.97	56.03	75.34	24.66
Japan										
2014	2,972	14,409	2,738	1,687	12,722	1,051	11.71	88.29	61.63	38.37
2015	19,160	27,757	17,942	13,676	14,081	4,266	49.27	50.73	76.22	23.78
2016	14,315	24,119	13,401	10,071	14,047	3,329	41.76	58.24	75.15	24.85
Kazakhstan										
2014	540	419	493	344	75	149	82.09	17.91	69.84	30.16
2015	485	342	442	305	37	137	89.14	10.86	68.95	31.05
2016	434	315	390	252	64	138	79.84	20.16	64.59	35.41
Korea, Rep. of										
2014	4,563	15,121	3,862	2,664	12,457	1,198	17.62	82.38	68.97	31.03
2015	4,189	14,371	3,486	2,417	11,954	1,069	16.82	83.18	69.34	30.66
2016	3,829	14,161	3,207	2,189	11,971	1,017	15.46	84.54	68.27	31.73
Kyrgyz Republic										
2014	220	157	186	153	3	32	97.85	2.15	82.54	17.46
2015	229	162	193	158	4	35	97.57	2.43	81.93	18.07
2016	234	166	196	161	5	36	96.95	3.05	81.84	18.16

continued on next page

Table 3.3e: continued

Table 3.3e: Direct and Indirect Value-Added Exports—Personal Services Sector

	Gross Exports	VAX_F	VAX_B	Direct Exports	Indirect Exports (Forward Linkage)	Indirect Exports (Backward Linkage)	Share of Direct Exports in VAX_F	Share of Indirect Exports in VAX_F	Share of Direct Exports in VAX_B	Share of Indirect Exports in VAX_B
	($ million)						(%)			
Lao PDR										
2014	117	85	104	84	1	21	98.75	1.25	80.29	19.71
2015	117	84	104	83	1	21	98.65	1.35	80.13	19.87
2016	124	91	113	90	1	23	98.58	1.42	79.34	20.66
Malaysia										
2014	2,924	3,362	2,445	1,651	1,710	794	49.12	50.88	67.54	32.46
2015	4,902	4,118	3,991	2,661	1,457	1,330	64.62	35.38	66.67	33.33
2016	5,038	4,314	4,183	2,776	1,537	1,407	64.36	35.64	66.37	33.63
Maldives										
2014	126	98	97	76	22	21	77.23	22.77	78.10	21.90
2015	61	133	44	36	97	8	26.98	73.02	80.97	19.03
2016	80	146	61	49	97	12	33.53	66.47	80.69	19.31
Mongolia										
2014	103	108	87	68	40	19	63.30	36.70	78.64	21.36
2015	87	125	75	54	71	21	43.22	56.78	71.66	28.34
2016	118	144	103	74	70	29	51.40	48.60	71.94	28.06
Nepal										
2014	404	309	375	300	9	75	96.96	3.04	80.03	19.97
2015	397	306	370	297	9	74	96.96	3.04	80.06	19.94
2016	429	323	396	313	10	83	96.89	3.11	78.96	21.04
Pakistan										
2014	2,255	2,010	2,196	1,841	169	355	91.61	8.39	83.83	16.17
2015	2,174	1,941	2,121	1,798	143	323	92.65	7.35	84.79	15.21
2016	2,126	1,884	2,065	1,756	129	309	93.17	6.83	85.05	14.95
Philippines										
2014	1,080	1,199	988	706	493	281	58.91	41.09	71.52	28.48
2015	807	1,033	741	536	497	205	51.85	48.15	72.33	27.67
2016	810	1,088	744	542	547	202	49.79	50.21	72.88	27.12
Sri Lanka										
2014	1,072	882	957	645	237	312	73.11	26.89	67.38	32.62
2015	1,051	867	942	636	231	306	73.36	26.64	67.51	32.49
2016	602	608	541	374	233	167	61.60	38.40	69.18	30.82
Taipei,China										
2014	1,764	4,334	1,472	1,145	3,189	327	26.42	73.58	77.79	22.21
2015	1,526	4,443	1,243	963	3,480	280	21.68	78.32	77.49	22.51
2016	1,550	4,814	1,288	1,000	3,815	288	20.76	79.24	77.60	22.40
Thailand										
2014	4,457	4,019	3,506	2,070	1,950	1,436	51.49	48.51	59.03	40.97
2015	5,250	4,565	4,271	2,558	2,008	1,714	56.02	43.98	59.88	40.12
2016	4,971	4,362	4,092	2,279	2,084	1,813	52.23	47.77	55.68	44.32
Viet Nam										
2014	4,021	3,085	3,368	2,694	392	674	87.31	12.69	79.98	20.02
2015	4,399	3,406	3,806	2,988	417	818	87.74	12.26	78.51	21.49
2016	5,081	3,785	4,305	3,385	400	919	89.44	10.56	78.64	21.36

Lao PDR = Lao People's Democratic Republic, VAX_B = value added exports by backward industrial linkages, VAX_F = value added exports by forward industrial linkages.

Source: ADB Multi Region Input–Output Tables Database.

Table 3.3f: Direct and Indirect Value-Added Exports—Total Economy

	Gross Exports	VAX_F	VAX_B	Direct Exports	Indirect Exports (Forward Linkage)	Indirect Exports (Backward Linkage)	Share of Direct Exports in VAX_F	Share of Indirect Exports in VAX_F	Share of Direct Exports in VAX_B	Share of Indirect Exports in VAX_B
	($ million)						(%)			
Bangladesh										
2014	40,461	35,844	35,844	15,978	19,866	19,866	44.58	55.42	44.58	55.42
2015	33,789	30,829	30,829	13,694	17,135	17,135	44.42	55.58	44.42	55.58
2016	32,342	30,851	30,851	14,503	16,348	16,348	47.01	52.99	47.01	52.99
Bhutan										
2014	571	483	483	371	112	112	76.84	23.16	76.84	23.16
2015	565	483	483	396	88	88	81.88	18.12	81.88	18.12
2016	593	489	489	384	105	105	78.54	21.46	78.54	21.46
Brunei Darussalam										
2014	10,701	9,628	9,628	7,040	2,589	2,589	73.12	26.88	73.12	26.88
2015	7,326	6,448	6,448	4,704	1,744	1,744	72.96	27.04	72.96	27.04
2016	7,333	6,338	6,338	4,545	1,793	1,793	71.71	28.29	71.71	28.29
Cambodia										
2014	7,805	5,602	5,602	4,551	1,052	1,052	81.23	18.77	81.23	18.77
2015	8,124	5,847	5,847	4,700	1,147	1,147	80.38	19.62	80.38	19.62
2016	9,010	6,441	6,441	5,107	1,334	1,334	79.29	20.71	79.29	20.71
China, People's Rep. of										
2014	2,434,045	1,979,939	1,979,939	794,444	1,185,496	1,185,496	40.12	59.88	40.12	59.88
2015	2,402,115	1,929,468	1,929,468	771,204	1,158,264	1,158,264	39.97	60.03	39.97	60.03
2016	2,399,694	1,919,415	1,919,415	785,257	1,134,158	1,134,158	40.91	59.09	40.91	59.09
Fiji										
2014	1,720	1,208	1,208	827	381	381	68.47	31.53	68.47	31.53
2015	1,595	1,119	1,119	813	306	306	72.69	27.31	72.69	27.31
2016	1,644	1,181	1,181	857	324	324	72.57	27.43	72.57	27.43
India										
2014	370,954	293,190	293,190	176,902	116,287	116,287	60.34	39.66	60.34	39.66
2015	333,937	269,881	269,881	155,786	114,095	114,095	57.72	42.28	57.72	42.28
2016	389,429	299,063	299,063	173,071	125,992	125,992	57.87	42.13	57.87	42.13
Indonesia										
2014	212,964	175,212	175,212	108,908	66,304	66,304	62.16	37.84	62.16	37.84
2015	195,933	159,229	159,229	96,742	62,487	62,487	60.76	39.24	60.76	39.24
2016	190,214	156,777	156,777	95,318	61,459	61,459	60.80	39.20	60.80	39.20
Japan										
2014	825,419	632,778	632,778	368,218	264,560	264,560	58.19	41.81	58.19	41.81
2015	816,438	618,285	618,285	359,951	258,334	258,334	58.22	41.78	58.22	41.78
2016	801,470	656,295	656,295	390,325	265,970	265,970	59.47	40.53	59.47	40.53
Kazakhstan										
2014	77,614	70,286	70,286	53,237	17,048	17,048	75.74	24.26	75.74	24.26
2015	56,141	49,744	49,744	36,253	13,491	13,491	72.88	27.12	72.88	27.12
2016	51,261	44,093	44,093	31,129	12,963	12,963	70.60	29.40	70.60	29.40
Korea, Rep. of										
2014	699,257	454,027	454,027	258,997	195,029	195,029	57.04	42.96	57.04	42.96
2015	653,686	413,179	413,179	229,714	183,465	183,465	55.60	44.40	55.60	44.40
2016	622,712	403,160	403,160	221,154	182,005	182,005	54.86	45.14	54.86	45.14
Kyrgyz Republic										
2014	1,780	1,322	1,322	1,115	207	207	84.33	15.67	84.33	15.67
2015	1,740	1,268	1,268	1,046	222	222	82.46	17.54	82.46	17.54
2016	1,719	1,251	1,251	1,040	211	211	83.15	16.85	83.15	16.85

continued on next page

Table 3.3f: continued

Table 3.3f: Direct and Indirect Value-Added Exports—Total Economy										
	Gross Exports	VAX_F	VAX_B	Direct Exports	Indirect Exports (Forward Linkage)	Indirect Exports (Backward Linkage)	Share of Direct Exports in VAX_F	Share of Indirect Exports in VAX_F	Share of Direct Exports in VAX_B	Share of Indirect Exports in VAX_B
	($ million)						(%)			
Lao PDR										
2014	5,089	4,316	4,316	3,610	706	706	83.65	16.35	83.65	16.35
2015	5,292	4,524	4,524	3,780	745	745	83.54	16.46	83.54	16.46
2016	5,127	4,506	4,506	3,689	817	817	81.87	18.13	81.87	18.13
Malaysia										
2014	189,960	136,481	136,481	72,472	64,009	64,009	53.10	46.90	53.10	46.90
2015	169,996	118,339	118,339	62,088	56,250	56,250	52.47	47.53	52.47	47.53
2016	166,910	119,085	119,085	63,404	55,681	55,681	53.24	46.76	53.24	46.76
Maldives										
2014	2,867	1,816	1,816	1,116	699	699	61.48	38.52	61.48	38.52
2015	2,900	1,977	1,977	1,234	744	744	62.38	37.62	62.38	37.62
2016	2,946	2,003	2,003	1,244	758	758	62.14	37.86	62.14	37.86
Mongolia										
2014	5,654	4,111	4,111	2,749	1,362	1,362	66.86	33.14	66.86	33.14
2015	5,469	4,277	4,277	2,620	1,657	1,657	61.26	38.74	61.26	38.74
2016	5,577	4,309	4,309	2,659	1,650	1,650	61.70	38.30	61.70	38.30
Nepal										
2014	1,315	1,096	1,096	826	270	270	75.39	24.61	75.39	24.61
2015	1,287	1,077	1,077	811	266	266	75.27	24.73	75.27	24.73
2016	1,413	1,169	1,169	879	290	290	75.19	24.81	75.19	24.81
Pakistan										
2014	28,847	26,798	26,798	15,033	11,766	11,766	56.09	43.91	56.09	43.91
2015	27,602	25,934	25,934	16,939	8,996	8,996	65.31	34.69	65.31	34.69
2016	25,423	23,752	23,752	15,277	8,475	8,475	64.32	35.68	64.32	35.68
Philippines										
2014	62,108	49,000	49,000	29,210	19,789	19,789	59.61	40.39	59.61	40.39
2015	62,470	49,412	49,412	30,664	18,748	18,748	62.06	37.94	62.06	37.94
2016	60,665	47,422	47,422	29,817	17,605	17,605	62.88	37.12	62.88	37.12
Sri Lanka										
2014	13,802	11,794	11,794	8,633	3,162	3,162	73.19	26.81	73.19	26.81
2015	13,530	11,584	11,584	8,313	3,271	3,271	71.76	28.24	71.76	28.24
2016	14,343	12,263	12,263	9,061	3,202	3,202	73.89	26.11	73.89	26.11
Taipei,China										
2014	372,420	216,352	216,352	161,794	54,558	54,558	74.78	25.22	74.78	25.22
2015	362,597	205,278	205,278	147,641	57,638	57,638	71.92	28.08	71.92	28.08
2016	359,196	204,985	204,985	144,449	60,536	60,536	70.47	29.53	70.47	29.53
Thailand										
2014	211,646	147,563	147,563	80,620	66,943	66,943	54.63	45.37	54.63	45.37
2015	203,729	147,348	147,348	78,689	68,659	68,659	53.40	46.60	53.40	46.60
2016	206,224	153,610	153,610	81,534	72,077	72,077	53.08	46.92	53.08	46.92
Viet Nam										
2014	111,998	77,600	77,600	54,411	23,189	23,189	70.12	29.88	70.12	29.88
2015	128,055	91,173	91,173	64,274	26,899	26,899	70.50	29.50	70.50	29.50
2016	123,118	87,920	87,920	61,573	26,347	26,347	70.03	29.97	70.03	29.97

Lao PDR = Lao People's Democratic Republic, VAX_B = value added exports by backward industrial linkages, VAX_F = value added exports by forward industrial linkages.

Source: ADB Multi Region Input-Output Tables Database.

Table 3.4: Revealed Comparative Advantage by Aggregate Sector

	RCA Calculated through Traditional Method			RCA Calculated through Value-Added Export Method		
	2014	2015	2016	2014	2015	2016
	(ratio)			(ratio)		
Bangladesh						
Business Services Sector	0.12	0.15	0.11	0.93	0.94	0.86
Low-Technology Manufacturing Sector	4.09	4.94	5.36	2.63	2.78	3.13
Medium- and High-Technology Manufacturing Sector	0.11	0.13	0.10	0.13	0.16	0.16
Personal Services Sector	0.88	1.19	1.14	2.36	2.26	2.26
Primary Sector	0.26	0.31	0.32	0.48	0.49	0.51
Bhutan						
Business Services Sector	1.12	1.10	0.86	0.73	0.68	0.61
Low-Technology Manufacturing Sector	2.43	2.67	2.39	3.10	3.50	3.10
Medium- and High-Technology Manufacturing Sector	0.28	0.29	0.35	0.26	0.28	0.34
Personal Services Sector	4.30	0.77	3.98	1.89	0.40	1.97
Primary Sector	1.05	1.23	1.15	0.94	1.03	1.04
Brunei Darussalam						
Business Services Sector	0.13	0.17	0.16	0.14	0.16	0.17
Low-Technology Manufacturing Sector	0.04	0.09	0.09	0.06	0.07	0.08
Medium- and High-Technology Manufacturing Sector	0.96	0.96	1.00	0.88	0.93	0.93
Personal Services Sector	0.11	0.31	0.43	0.18	0.25	0.31
Primary Sector	4.64	4.82	4.64	4.33	4.51	4.60
Cambodia						
Business Services Sector	1.38	1.26	1.36	0.97	0.92	1.00
Low-Technology Manufacturing Sector	2.87	3.07	3.12	2.65	2.85	2.84
Medium- and High-Technology Manufacturing Sector	0.02	0.02	0.02	0.04	0.05	0.05
Personal Services Sector	0.82	0.50	0.59	0.55	0.44	0.46
Primary Sector	1.52	1.47	1.12	1.39	1.31	1.13
China, People's Rep. of						
Business Services Sector	0.63	0.64	0.76	0.85	0.89	0.93
Low-Technology Manufacturing Sector	1.40	1.39	1.35	1.33	1.32	1.29
Medium- and High-Technology Manufacturing Sector	1.29	1.31	1.26	1.19	1.24	1.18
Personal Services Sector	0.28	0.35	0.41	0.55	0.55	0.59
Primary Sector	0.13	0.13	0.13	0.89	0.79	0.78
Fiji						
Business Services Sector	2.79	2.68	2.50	1.66	1.59	1.53
Low-Technology Manufacturing Sector	1.26	1.25	1.36	1.20	1.21	1.27
Medium- and High-Technology Manufacturing Sector	0.04	0.04	0.04	0.09	0.09	0.09
Personal Services Sector	1.58	0.53	1.25	1.01	0.50	0.94
Primary Sector	0.61	0.75	0.69	0.68	0.81	0.79
India						
Business Services Sector	1.16	1.02	0.76	1.22	1.15	0.94
Low-Technology Manufacturing Sector	1.30	1.34	1.49	0.89	0.91	1.12
Medium- and High-Technology Manufacturing Sector	0.90	0.95	1.02	0.77	0.81	0.92
Personal Services Sector	1.34	1.35	1.19	1.15	1.24	1.16
Primary Sector	0.55	0.52	0.73	0.88	0.89	1.16
Indonesia						
Business Services Sector	0.21	0.25	0.24	0.46	0.49	0.48
Low-Technology Manufacturing Sector	2.41	2.55	2.65	1.63	1.73	1.76
Medium- and High-Technology Manufacturing Sector	0.67	0.68	0.67	0.71	0.78	0.75
Personal Services Sector	0.38	0.27	0.29	0.39	0.34	0.34
Primary Sector	2.14	1.95	1.99	2.46	2.35	2.44
Japan						
Business Services Sector	0.74	0.78	0.81	0.97	1.00	0.97
Low-Technology Manufacturing Sector	0.38	0.40	0.38	0.72	0.71	0.71
Medium- and High-Technology Manufacturing Sector	1.62	1.58	1.58	1.81	1.75	1.80
Personal Services Sector	0.18	0.76	0.60	0.61	0.93	0.78
Primary Sector	0.06	0.06	0.07	0.07	0.06	0.06

continued on next page

Table 3.4: continued

Table 3.4: Revealed Comparative Advantage by Aggregate Sector

	RCA Calculated through Traditional Method			RCA Calculated through Value-Added Export Method		
	2014	2015	2016	2014	2015	2016
	(ratio)			(ratio)		
Kazakhstan						
Business Services Sector	1.11	1.34	1.12	0.89	1.09	1.05
Low-Technology Manufacturing Sector	0.15	0.18	0.20	0.25	0.25	0.25
Medium- and High-Technology Manufacturing Sector	0.32	0.39	0.42	0.44	0.50	0.52
Personal Services Sector	0.35	0.28	0.28	0.16	0.14	0.15
Primary Sector	4.99	4.32	4.59	3.03	2.51	2.64
Korea, Rep. of						
Business Services Sector	0.54	0.53	0.52	0.77	0.78	0.77
Low-Technology Manufacturing Sector	0.44	0.43	0.45	0.73	0.74	0.77
Medium- and High-Technology Manufacturing Sector	1.70	1.76	1.76	2.05	2.12	2.08
Personal Services Sector	0.33	0.21	0.21	0.89	0.72	0.75
Primary Sector	0.01	0.01	0.02	0.09	0.10	0.11
Kyrgyz Republic						
Business Services Sector	0.95	1.02	1.13	0.72	0.77	0.83
Low-Technology Manufacturing Sector	0.52	0.77	0.27	0.46	0.61	0.28
Medium- and High-Technology Manufacturing Sector	0.81	0.70	0.72	1.41	1.30	1.26
Personal Services Sector	6.15	4.27	4.57	3.16	2.67	2.82
Primary Sector	1.68	1.64	1.97	0.97	0.98	1.12
Lao People's Democratic Republic						
Business Services Sector	0.38	0.37	0.30	0.36	0.35	0.33
Low-Technology Manufacturing Sector	1.38	1.34	1.18	1.50	1.46	1.44
Medium- and High-Technology Manufacturing Sector	0.01	0.01	0.03	0.06	0.06	0.07
Personal Services Sector	1.14	0.72	0.81	0.52	0.39	0.43
Primary Sector	5.90	6.32	6.67	3.87	4.14	4.32
Malaysia						
Business Services Sector	1.04	0.87	0.98	0.92	0.83	0.90
Low-Technology Manufacturing Sector	1.47	1.62	1.49	0.81	0.93	0.83
Medium- and High-Technology Manufacturing Sector	0.92	0.94	0.93	0.89	0.98	0.94
Personal Services Sector	0.77	0.93	1.01	0.66	0.72	0.77
Primary Sector	0.62	0.60	0.59	1.61	1.65	1.62
Maldives						
Business Services Sector	3.77	3.36	3.30	2.02	1.63	1.62
Low-Technology Manufacturing Sector	0.21	0.72	0.60	0.40	1.48	1.43
Medium- and High-Technology Manufacturing Sector	0.00	0.00	0.00	0.01	0.02	0.02
Personal Services Sector	2.18	0.68	0.91	1.44	1.40	1.55
Primary Sector	0.09	0.09	0.12	0.48	0.27	0.30
Mongolia						
Business Services Sector	0.56	0.50	0.49	0.86	0.89	0.88
Low-Technology Manufacturing Sector	0.42	0.42	0.44	0.57	0.59	0.61
Medium- and High-Technology Manufacturing Sector	0.06	0.05	0.04	0.16	0.16	0.15
Personal Services Sector	0.91	0.52	0.71	0.70	0.61	0.71
Primary Sector	6.76	7.36	7.31	3.17	3.19	3.26
Nepal						
Business Services Sector	1.51	1.38	1.33	1.06	0.99	0.98
Low-Technology Manufacturing Sector	1.16	1.18	1.15	0.94	0.94	0.92
Medium- and High-Technology Manufacturing Sector	0.16	0.17	0.19	0.19	0.21	0.22
Personal Services Sector	15.32	10.00	10.18	7.54	5.91	5.88
Primary Sector	0.58	0.69	0.75	0.72	0.81	0.89
Pakistan						
Business Services Sector	1.32	1.18	1.04	1.01	0.88	0.82
Low-Technology Manufacturing Sector	3.07	2.21	2.41	1.41	1.07	1.16
Medium- and High-Technology Manufacturing Sector	0.08	0.08	0.08	0.11	0.12	0.12
Personal Services Sector	3.89	2.55	2.80	2.00	1.56	1.69
Primary Sector	0.56	2.16	2.16	1.85	2.55	2.66

continued on next page

Table 3.4: continued

Table 3.4: Revealed Comparative Advantage by Aggregate Sector

	RCA Calculated through Traditional Method			RCA Calculated through Value-Added Export Method		
	2014	2015	2016	2014	2015	2016
	(ratio)			(ratio)		
Philippines						
Business Services Sector	1.59	1.65	1.67	1.23	1.25	1.26
Low-Technology Manufacturing Sector	1.25	1.23	1.18	1.33	1.31	1.34
Medium- and High-Technology Manufacturing Sector	0.80	0.77	0.76	0.68	0.70	0.65
Personal Services Sector	0.87	0.42	0.45	0.65	0.44	0.49
Primary Sector	0.23	0.22	0.22	0.75	0.72	0.69
Sri Lanka						
Business Services Sector	1.60	1.53	1.61	1.08	1.03	1.12
Low-Technology Manufacturing Sector	2.73	2.82	2.94	2.71	2.74	2.70
Medium- and High-Technology Manufacturing Sector	0.07	0.05	0.05	0.13	0.09	0.10
Personal Services Sector	3.87	2.51	1.41	2.00	1.56	1.06
Primary Sector	0.47	0.46	0.42	0.59	0.68	0.62
Taipei,China						
Business Services Sector	0.78	0.72	0.67	0.80	0.80	0.79
Low-Technology Manufacturing Sector	0.41	0.43	0.61	0.57	0.61	0.71
Medium- and High-Technology Manufacturing Sector	1.58	1.65	1.61	2.15	2.22	2.14
Personal Services Sector	0.24	0.14	0.14	0.53	0.45	0.50
Primary Sector	0.05	0.05	0.06	0.08	0.08	0.09
Thailand						
Business Services Sector	1.04	1.13	1.14	0.94	0.97	0.97
Low-Technology Manufacturing Sector	2.05	2.08	2.05	1.61	1.59	1.56
Medium- and High-Technology Manufacturing Sector	0.77	0.74	0.75	0.79	0.81	0.81
Personal Services Sector	1.05	0.83	0.81	0.73	0.65	0.60
Primary Sector	0.31	0.14	0.16	1.06	0.99	1.01
Viet Nam						
Business Services Sector	0.81	0.76	0.78	0.74	0.70	0.73
Low-Technology Manufacturing Sector	1.88	1.92	1.92	1.34	1.47	1.44
Medium- and High-Technology Manufacturing Sector	0.23	0.31	0.29	0.25	0.35	0.35
Personal Services Sector	1.79	1.11	1.38	1.06	0.78	0.92
Primary Sector	3.20	3.08	3.05	2.60	2.53	2.53

RCA = revealed comparative advantage.

Source: ADB Multi Region Input–Output Tables Database.

Table 3.5a: Vertical Specialization by Sector, 2014

	Bangladesh	Bhutan	Brunei Darussalam	Cambodia	China, People's Rep. of	Fiji	India	Indonesia	Japan	Kazakhstan	Korea, Rep. of	Kyrgyz Republic
	(% of gross exports)											
Agriculture, Hunting, Forestry, and Fishing	4.47	3.29	25.61	8.57	5.64	18.62	3.06	4.00	12.83	10.41	16.43	21.45
Air Transport	25.48	50.17	25.03	14.41	16.77	57.58	9.25	21.53	15.43	13.21	33.05	39.76
Basic Metals and Fabricated Metal	11.52	30.54	26.66	36.41	19.98	47.30	33.60	22.62	34.73	7.68	38.38	24.80
Chemicals and Chemical Products	8.07	23.24	11.54	32.67	16.98	33.86	26.69	23.28	29.16	11.74	40.48	37.69
Coke, Refined Petroleum, and Nuclear Fuel	36.58	–	11.54	58.16	24.15	89.20	57.73	11.84	56.31	4.93	72.73	37.55
Construction	9.21	30.59	39.78	21.83	13.97	30.22	15.81	21.03	17.09	15.26	27.23	39.13
Education	3.02	7.20	16.95	5.70	6.43	12.27	1.55	10.18	3.96	9.77	9.05	10.55
Electrical and Optical Equipment	14.50	30.54	26.65	47.32	23.23	68.52	24.30	37.34	22.53	12.71	34.51	34.13
Electricity, Gas, and Water Supply	5.36	5.57	17.50	56.90	16.68	48.81	20.12	17.29	39.01	13.16	43.24	39.34
Financial Intermediation	3.32	4.47	9.01	3.16	4.03	15.57	2.51	4.49	4.18	6.78	10.78	11.69
Food, Beverages, and Tobacco	6.35	22.33	40.73	32.51	7.65	27.80	8.83	10.89	12.97	14.00	24.69	28.28
Health and Social Work	2.57	14.55	21.40	5.11	9.84	13.51	10.64	13.49	10.98	20.29	17.76	12.67
Hotels and Restaurants	4.88	10.04	30.18	23.06	6.09	23.21	8.27	9.67	9.75	12.43	14.90	28.45
Inland Transport	3.38	27.14	13.75	14.41	7.86	35.18	16.06	17.77	9.44	14.05	26.24	40.28
Leather, Leather Products, and Footwear	6.46	18.91	13.15	36.63	11.00	31.08	14.02	27.50	20.69	27.34	31.58	34.02
Machinery, nec	16.23	30.54	26.65	65.53	16.53	31.54	24.89	47.44	19.09	18.66	30.16	34.13
Manufacturing, nec; Recycling	23.29	23.24	26.66	41.13	10.58	20.55	20.91	19.81	17.53	27.09	28.78	44.43
Mining and Quarrying	6.53	12.27	7.37	9.06	11.74	42.70	6.62	7.38	53.12	8.82	15.83	26.79
Other Community, Social, and Personal Services	2.93	14.60	7.07	12.84	8.60	38.17	3.64	8.29	6.29	7.23	16.04	25.44
Other Nonmetallic Mineral	8.64	12.40	29.76	31.44	14.75	33.50	23.08	18.16	24.90	14.93	33.57	33.51
Other Supporting and Auxiliary Transport Activities; Activities of Travel Agencies	5.29	5.07	24.72	14.41	10.17	24.29	7.31	8.45	8.26	8.79	19.87	39.73
Post and Telecommunications	1.67	15.39	24.98	17.77	6.39	16.12	5.49	5.97	5.02	9.64	16.53	32.34
Private Households with Employed Persons	–	–	–	–	–	–	–	–	–	–	–	–
Public Administration and Defense; Compulsory Social Security	6.52	13.99	17.01	15.05	6.77	13.79	0.00	9.30	6.82	13.45	8.24	15.63
Pulp, Paper, Paper Products, Printing, and Publishing	10.01	30.85	30.02	32.99	14.28	33.31	20.16	19.20	12.17	23.99	20.49	42.13
Real Estate Activities	1.61	2.31	3.39	17.53	2.04	10.69	1.13	3.76	1.83	4.94	4.34	0.54
Renting of Machinery and Equipment and Other Business Activities	5.14	15.28	22.92	13.53	11.55	18.88	5.18	10.72	4.84	13.58	12.91	38.96
Retail Trade, except of Motor Vehicles and Motorcycles; Repair of Household Goods	2.54	10.06	17.50	36.43	5.18	17.11	2.59	8.02	5.20	8.18	12.07	23.28
Rubber and Plastics	10.14	37.95	29.76	32.98	16.25	55.38	23.88	25.61	20.94	23.15	32.55	33.27
Sale, Maintenance, and Repair of Motor Vehicles and Motorcycles; Retail Sale of Fuel	7.52	10.06	29.18	40.46	–	17.11	2.57	9.58	17.29	13.43	11.81	16.62
Textiles and Textile Products	8.46	18.92	13.15	36.63	9.56	15.86	12.39	28.57	16.09	16.65	27.19	33.28
Transport Equipment	19.72	30.54	26.66	40.18	15.22	30.54	26.78	17.59	21.24	22.58	31.01	34.13
Water Transport	13.99	27.14	16.81	14.41	9.69	46.42	12.98	19.22	28.24	14.60	31.05	39.76
Wholesale Trade and Commission Trade, except of Motor Vehicles and Motorcycles	1.67	10.06	17.51	40.46	5.28	20.85	2.59	8.01	5.03	8.09	11.21	18.86
Wood and Products of Wood and Cork	6.37	16.22	30.02	20.26	12.62	22.84	9.09	11.30	17.85	19.09	28.56	63.93

continued on next page

Table 3.5a: continued

Table 3.5a: Vertical Specialization by Sector, 2014											
	Lao PDR	Malaysia	Maldives	Mongolia	Nepal	Pakistan	Philippines	Sri Lanka	Taipei,China	Thailand	Viet Nam
	(% of gross exports)										
Agriculture, Hunting, Forestry, and Fishing	5.60	13.20	36.45	9.78	6.79	2.86	5.67	11.60	23.52	14.03	29.10
Air Transport	88.13	30.54	40.65	32.94	18.58	9.60	30.56	32.88	52.65	19.04	40.77
Basic Metals and Fabricated Metal	52.25	44.84	46.43	33.05	44.88	14.87	42.67	50.84	49.06	53.86	56.22
Chemicals and Chemical Products	26.38	32.40	–	23.77	31.44	8.15	20.15	31.10	63.43	30.84	42.02
Coke, Refined Petroleum, and Nuclear Fuel	35.26	20.34	96.88	22.77	30.92	18.25	49.06	46.75	76.58	29.60	44.82
Construction	39.14	30.66	46.91	40.71	25.44	11.60	20.09	18.14	40.20	36.87	38.78
Education	5.60	8.02	10.19	9.38	5.65	1.46	4.55	–	7.65	6.40	12.15
Electrical and Optical Equipment	32.93	43.61	67.58	33.19	46.49	17.84	45.20	33.09	40.37	53.62	55.30
Electricity, Gas, and Water Supply	11.72	19.72	60.22	22.72	20.87	28.91	9.34	18.78	53.68	15.92	19.19
Financial Intermediation	8.91	9.47	11.02	8.59	9.42	0.98	4.03	4.56	7.05	6.12	7.12
Food, Beverages, and Tobacco	19.56	25.69	43.46	11.48	13.91	8.38	9.47	11.40	31.03	19.74	46.50
Health and Social Work	17.54	25.12	19.46	22.18	14.19	5.34	8.40	4.99	16.68	19.65	27.53
Hotels and Restaurants	16.56	18.11	38.04	21.10	14.52	11.33	9.90	10.32	18.78	14.05	29.74
Inland Transport	25.63	22.29	35.79	33.54	34.61	6.67	22.85	13.84	29.75	26.53	22.10
Leather, Leather Products, and Footwear	20.46	26.29	73.86	19.47	23.61	6.73	23.99	15.42	36.61	25.48	50.61
Machinery, nec	34.22	45.06	–	33.51	21.57	13.44	34.50	16.12	42.11	48.48	56.19
Manufacturing, nec; Recycling	22.72	26.11	21.58	35.37	34.03	9.82	19.61	27.21	44.74	37.11	41.93
Mining and Quarrying	15.26	6.63	–	29.68	9.55	1.35	11.83	6.42	28.37	11.16	13.36
Other Community, Social, and Personal Services	12.24	17.89	25.40	15.66	7.47	1.48	10.91	10.70	17.64	19.70	17.27
Other Nonmetallic Mineral	27.58	30.55	41.96	30.01	29.12	10.91	28.93	26.79	44.15	24.52	42.01
Other Supporting and Auxiliary Transport Activities; Activities of Travel Agencies	75.48	21.88	27.47	35.73	17.53	3.72	11.92	–	17.09	10.87	20.61
Post and Telecommunications	11.70	16.74	23.87	26.42	12.87	3.07	10.56	25.65	16.92	9.31	18.80
Private Households with Employed Persons	–	–	–	–	–	–	–	–	–	–	–
Public Administration and Defense; Compulsory Social Security	11.69	16.66	17.30	18.05	6.72	7.17	3.82	–	9.73	0.01	14.56
Pulp, Paper, Paper Products, Printing, and Publishing	17.25	31.17	34.93	36.10	32.18	7.28	15.96	23.15	31.32	24.17	44.86
Real Estate Activities	3.44	7.39	12.82	7.46	6.42	0.05	3.08	4.64	5.16	2.81	9.24
Renting of Machinery and Equipment and Other Business Activities	9.20	14.21	11.00	24.36	15.61	0.97	5.72	12.12	17.49	18.25	20.01
Retail Trade, except of Motor Vehicles and Motorcycles; Repair of Household Goods	13.46	13.12	22.03	14.90	5.59	2.64	4.74	5.82	10.42	5.15	12.66
Rubber and Plastics	44.76	33.45	–	20.09	33.71	9.54	25.04	18.78	47.84	29.37	47.95
Sale, Maintenance, and Repair of Motor Vehicles and Motorcycles; Retail Sale of Fuel	17.60	17.55	38.87	14.93	4.03	4.45	9.96	5.44	27.60	17.31	25.43
Textiles and Textile Products	20.70	31.76	27.13	30.55	27.53	10.21	20.51	17.64	39.94	23.01	50.60
Transport Equipment	57.48	52.67	37.17	34.63	39.19	22.60	25.63	32.60	41.23	42.86	50.77
Water Transport	86.58	21.18	50.41	33.07	–	8.60	23.99	11.30	55.08	18.58	30.51
Wholesale Trade and Commission Trade, except of Motor Vehicles and Motorcycles	10.57	12.30	15.31	14.99	4.30	1.13	5.49	5.01	12.50	5.14	25.43
Wood and Products of Wood and Cork	17.76	26.23	31.70	34.67	21.76	8.69	12.61	15.60	44.61	16.74	44.17

– = magnitude equals zero, Lao PDR = Lao People's Democratic Republic.

Source: ADB Multi Region Input–Output Tables Database.

Table 3.5b: Vertical Specialization by Sector, 2015

	Bangladesh	Bhutan	Brunei Darussalam	Cambodia	China, People's Rep. of	Fiji	India	Indonesia	Japan	Kazakhstan	Korea, Rep. of	Kyrgyz Republic
	(% of gross exports)											
Agriculture, Hunting, Forestry, and Fishing	3.47	3.37	26.49	12.38	5.64	18.60	3.15	4.13	14.11	14.23	17.88	21.09
Air Transport	26.04	52.98	28.40	13.34	17.82	61.76	7.83	16.92	13.27	10.85	33.88	41.77
Basic Metals and Fabricated Metal	13.39	30.18	27.92	36.18	21.47	48.37	30.59	24.88	35.84	12.07	41.53	26.41
Chemicals and Chemical Products	11.38	18.60	12.39	34.03	18.06	34.37	24.17	24.55	32.76	19.53	40.78	34.86
Coke, Refined Petroleum, and Nuclear Fuel	33.13	–	13.08	40.06	27.07	86.65	52.10	14.18	58.01	16.02	74.63	34.74
Construction	8.24	34.84	41.78	19.21	14.64	29.51	15.36	19.50	18.17	16.53	27.97	42.61
Education	2.97	–	16.92	–	5.99	13.99	1.37	9.89	3.75	10.63	9.56	10.34
Electrical and Optical Equipment	18.12	–	26.91	47.59	24.56	–	21.31	35.35	25.04	14.84	36.19	34.37
Electricity, Gas and Water Supply	4.87	5.17	20.52	54.76	18.38	51.36	20.17	24.06	35.59	16.72	41.98	36.19
Financial Intermediation	4.89	8.00	9.20	2.82	3.50	16.08	4.01	5.88	4.01	2.64	12.57	19.38
Food, Beverages, and Tobacco	10.68	25.18	40.94	34.92	7.47	28.26	8.24	10.32	13.94	17.21	25.43	28.14
Health and Social Work	2.13	–	22.63	9.85	10.13	13.93	8.87	13.02	10.84	22.98	18.34	–
Hotels and Restaurants	6.85	11.32	30.62	20.86	6.24	23.06	7.62	12.62	10.34	14.31	15.30	28.36
Inland Transport	2.55	28.59	14.22	13.24	7.97	33.57	13.86	14.92	8.73	13.62	26.57	40.89
Leather, Leather Products, and Footwear	4.31	19.52	16.91	34.26	11.37	31.52	12.70	29.34	16.75	26.36	35.04	33.68
Machinery, nec	18.44	30.24	27.10	64.02	17.48	32.15	21.64	45.01	21.18	18.54	31.62	33.23
Manufacturing, nec; Recycling	27.19	20.15	27.09	39.98	11.12	20.07	18.78	19.62	20.61	23.67	29.80	43.85
Mining and Quarrying	7.19	8.74	9.07	8.10	14.81	41.39	5.97	8.28	53.80	11.37	16.20	26.01
Other Community, Social, and Personal Services	5.54	20.69	9.14	14.74	8.35	39.21	3.07	7.87	6.05	6.97	17.56	26.06
Other Nonmetallic Mineral	5.73	9.02	34.77	30.22	15.91	33.41	21.10	19.52	25.15	22.72	34.57	33.83
Other Supporting and Auxiliary Transport Activities; Activities of Travel Agencies	4.48	9.36	25.03	13.26	10.65	23.23	5.93	7.92	7.47	10.22	21.76	40.30
Post and Telecommunications	4.01	18.99	26.87	16.91	6.00	16.00	4.62	5.82	4.55	11.03	18.06	33.33
Private Households with Employed Persons	–	–	–	–	–	–	–	–	–	–	–	–
Public Administration and Defense; Compulsory Social Security	6.31	17.23	18.22	–	6.70	–	0.00	9.07	6.70	15.58	9.14	15.94
Pulp, Paper, Paper Products, Printing, and Publishing	13.54	32.72	31.55	33.31	14.96	35.31	17.31	22.00	15.59	25.35	20.33	41.10
Real Estate Activities	1.17	2.18	6.24	–	2.04	10.49	3.39	3.35	1.91	5.18	5.11	–
Renting of Machinery and Equipment and Other Business Activities	3.23	18.49	22.97	12.59	12.02	18.68	4.44	14.34	4.75	14.43	14.01	–
Retail Trade, except of Motor Vehicles and Motorcycles; Repair of Household Goods	2.25	7.13	20.85	35.43	5.33	15.28	2.74	12.13	4.92	8.18	13.33	24.31
Rubber and Plastics	10.93	37.10	33.73	30.61	16.65	57.19	21.21	25.00	25.61	34.89	33.63	33.64
Sale, Maintenance, and Repair of Motor Vehicles and Motorcycles; Retail Sale of Fuel	6.95	11.56	30.56	38.45	–	15.30	3.97	10.43	16.92	10.28	12.97	14.99
Textiles and Textile Products	7.89	20.24	14.82	35.38	9.93	15.79	11.22	28.81	17.65	13.92	29.04	32.94
Transport Equipment	19.91	–	25.85	38.98	16.06	31.48	23.39	17.37	24.23	14.27	33.20	33.23
Water Transport	11.45	31.99	17.32	13.29	10.08	47.28	10.41	18.85	26.51	14.97	30.95	41.79
Wholesale Trade and Commission Trade, except of Motor Vehicles and Motorcycles	1.35	6.98	18.64	39.15	5.35	18.94	2.72	12.22	4.46	6.94	12.08	18.30
Wood and Products of Wood and Cork	10.04	17.71	31.69	18.40	13.19	23.05	8.53	14.67	18.93	19.85	30.03	44.41

continued on next page

Table 3.5b: continued

Table 3.5b: Vertical Specialization by Sector, 2015											
	Lao PDR	Malaysia	Maldives	Mongolia	Nepal	Pakistan	Philippines	Sri Lanka	Taipei,China	Thailand	Viet Nam
	(% of gross exports)										
Agriculture, Hunting, Forestry, and Fishing	6.61	13.44	48.00	8.56	6.44	2.59	7.05	11.77	27.55	13.64	26.06
Air Transport	84.62	31.04	36.74	23.62	18.39	10.24	33.64	32.12	51.30	17.22	33.66
Basic Metals and Fabricated Metal	43.08	48.71	31.03	27.30	43.25	14.57	42.74	50.88	50.63	51.71	51.96
Chemicals and Chemical Products	23.15	33.86	–	21.66	31.13	7.87	27.83	37.09	66.94	29.72	39.83
Coke, Refined Petroleum, and Nuclear Fuel	30.94	23.55	–	18.09	30.74	19.21	50.82	48.11	79.01	28.06	40.06
Construction	33.12	31.13	25.80	31.94	25.17	11.57	19.58	17.36	40.90	33.13	33.24
Education	5.39	12.50	12.17	7.43	5.65	1.29	4.33	–	8.20	5.89	9.83
Electrical and Optical Equipment	27.17	45.34	–	25.38	46.34	20.47	44.73	20.59	41.33	50.67	51.96
Electricity, Gas and Water Supply	9.86	20.09	71.43	16.88	21.65	28.44	9.31	15.11	53.97	14.97	16.31
Financial Intermediation	8.69	9.93	13.12	5.65	9.24	0.84	4.06	4.99	9.36	5.55	4.90
Food, Beverages, and Tobacco	30.18	26.87	37.65	9.28	13.40	7.76	11.66	14.82	34.68	18.48	42.86
Health and Social Work	15.51	29.11	20.39	15.41	14.39	5.23	9.59	4.92	17.31	18.05	20.19
Hotels and Restaurants	23.40	19.24	32.91	15.30	14.50	11.00	9.57	10.06	19.27	12.58	24.80
Inland Transport	23.66	21.94	32.74	24.68	33.94	7.14	26.04	13.49	29.76	24.31	17.76
Leather, Leather Products, and Footwear	21.74	30.12	91.57	17.35	23.66	5.85	23.77	14.96	39.52	23.86	46.79
Machinery, nec	30.21	48.31	–	26.46	24.88	14.37	34.70	13.47	43.88	45.48	51.58
Manufacturing, nec; Recycling	26.74	30.17	13.22	29.20	32.70	10.42	21.88	22.63	44.27	35.68	39.83
Mining and Quarrying	12.82	11.26	–	23.77	9.48	1.13	10.76	5.67	28.18	11.61	10.91
Other Community, Social, and Personal Services	15.01	19.00	41.42	11.57	7.02	1.34	10.38	10.41	19.47	18.27	13.89
Other Nonmetallic Mineral	21.38	34.26	27.85	24.43	28.11	10.64	33.06	29.48	44.30	25.80	39.66
Other Supporting and Auxiliary Transport Activities; Activities of Travel Agencies	69.23	22.13	24.59	26.21	17.28	3.30	11.68	–	16.98	9.83	17.26
Post and Telecommunications	12.11	18.70	17.28	19.68	12.75	2.93	10.78	25.06	18.75	8.37	17.07
Private Households with Employed Persons	–	–	–	–	–	–	–	–	–	–	–
Public Administration and Defense; Compulsory Social Security	12.34	18.43	13.42	15.21	6.10	6.78	4.74	–	11.02	0.53	10.53
Pulp, Paper, Paper Products, Printing, and Publishing	27.21	33.47	25.85	28.40	31.56	8.17	14.42	13.72	30.55	23.94	42.30
Real Estate Activities	3.89	8.14	–	7.17	–	0.06	3.38	4.45	6.57	2.57	8.10
Renting of Machinery and Equipment and Other Business Activities	9.09	18.43	32.32	17.34	15.33	0.74	5.82	10.79	18.61	16.86	16.58
Retail Trade, except of Motor Vehicles and Motorcycles; Repair of Household Goods	11.56	14.44	28.99	10.15	5.51	2.43	4.66	5.41	13.02	4.66	11.32
Rubber and Plastics	39.28	34.27	–	15.20	33.38	9.55	29.83	17.93	48.53	27.52	45.52
Sale, Maintenance, and Repair of Motor Vehicles and Motorcycles; Retail Sale of Fuel	15.12	17.93	50.47	10.70	3.77	4.15	–	5.09	30.86	15.55	23.59
Textiles and Textile Products	21.95	30.59	17.72	23.84	26.72	9.65	20.54	17.40	43.48	21.73	46.81
Transport Equipment	47.47	53.56	24.65	26.87	38.38	25.72	27.02	20.48	43.53	40.28	47.24
Water Transport	82.52	21.20	47.35	22.90	–	9.15	28.22	9.01	49.43	16.91	23.67
Wholesale Trade and Commission Trade, except of Motor Vehicles and Motorcycles	9.09	14.91	18.51	10.40	4.10	0.96	5.55	4.91	12.49	4.63	23.84
Wood and Products of Wood and Cork	28.07	28.35	22.72	26.94	20.76	9.68	14.43	20.34	42.84	16.16	42.23

– = magnitude equals zero, Lao PDR = Lao People's Democratic Republic.

Source: ADB Multi Region Input–Output Tables Database.

Table 3.5c: Vertical Specialization by Sector, 2016

	Bangladesh	Bhutan	Brunei Darussalam	Cambodia	China, People's Rep. of	Fiji	India	Indonesia	Japan	Kazakhstan	Korea, Rep. of	Kyrgyz Republic
	(% of gross exports)											
Agriculture, Hunting, Forestry, and Fishing	2.92	4.81	27.75	8.50	6.38	17.44	3.66	4.44	11.17	16.12	19.21	24.77
Air Transport	18.90	53.59	28.59	13.56	18.04	58.75	10.62	16.73	10.61	14.42	31.60	41.98
Basic Metals and Fabricated Metal	8.63	35.48	27.49	35.17	22.56	47.27	34.06	22.50	29.67	13.58	40.93	28.88
Chemicals and Chemical Products	6.73	24.55	10.53	32.00	20.26	33.49	26.27	22.79	23.61	15.75	37.63	34.96
Coke, Refined Petroleum, and Nuclear Fuel	24.08	–	13.70	40.44	29.42	79.45	59.84	12.46	53.80	13.47	72.48	35.39
Construction	5.38	35.02	42.59	19.98	15.29	29.09	15.84	19.12	15.21	18.04	25.87	40.62
Education	1.65	8.02	19.71	5.47	5.78	13.42	1.61	9.52	3.53	13.67	11.09	10.55
Electrical and Optical Equipment	11.86	30.81	25.99	46.32	25.29	0.00	24.80	34.43	18.18	13.96	34.19	35.94
Electricity, Gas, and Water Supply	2.49	5.42	16.97	55.46	19.13	51.29	16.33	23.68	30.57	18.95	39.08	35.94
Financial Intermediation	1.63	6.84	12.89	2.57	3.81	15.24	2.21	5.82	3.12	3.55	14.08	10.61
Food, Beverages and Tobacco	5.81	25.14	39.67	30.13	8.28	26.45	9.24	10.17	11.01	17.37	24.92	29.10
Health and Social Work	0.99	15.25	24.58	5.40	11.07	13.51	12.29	12.77	8.68	20.35	16.64	14.06
Hotels and Restaurants	3.03	9.59	32.40	22.14	6.60	21.79	11.31	11.82	8.92	15.05	14.80	28.99
Inland Transport	1.58	29.07	12.92	13.57	8.33	38.67	17.34	14.44	6.78	16.41	27.68	42.02
Leather, Leather Products, and Footwear	2.58	19.67	–	35.40	11.94	30.28	14.11	26.86	15.33	19.34	33.91	34.81
Machinery, nec	11.47	30.52	27.93	64.52	18.13	32.79	25.03	44.47	14.88	16.91	32.57	34.03
Manufacturing, nec; Recycling	18.42	20.97	30.13	40.70	11.67	19.36	19.60	18.34	13.61	19.01	30.92	44.86
Mining and Quarrying	3.31	9.14	11.21	7.34	16.56	40.05	6.67	7.35	46.24	15.05	15.64	27.49
Other Community, Social, and Personal Services	2.56	17.85	11.32	14.18	8.52	39.76	4.05	7.87	5.51	7.63	16.81	28.92
Other Nonmetallic Mineral	3.45	12.30	37.28	30.39	16.87	32.64	23.41	18.95	20.49	18.57	32.83	34.20
Other Supporting and Auxiliary Transport Activities; Activities of Travel Agencies	1.90	4.67	26.64	13.57	10.87	21.87	8.30	7.79	5.61	12.82	21.72	41.89
Post and Telecommunications	0.93	17.69	23.07	17.23	6.51	15.89	7.27	5.74	3.76	17.11	19.74	33.42
Private Households with Employed Persons	–	–	–	–	–	–	–	–	–	–	–	–
Public Administration and Defense; Compulsory Social Security	3.39	16.20	20.75	14.83	6.40	13.04	0.00	8.83	6.88	19.12	9.82	16.12
Pulp, Paper, Paper Products, Printing, and Publishing	8.47	34.66	33.86	32.28	18.29	33.91	21.36	19.90	8.73	22.94	19.93	43.82
Real Estate Activities	0.51	4.28	7.31	14.99	2.03	10.29	1.02	3.26	1.83	9.61	4.50	21.39
Renting of Machinery and Equipment and Other Business Activities	1.61	15.60	26.21	11.95	11.82	18.60	6.53	14.09	3.30	15.57	15.36	21.60
Retail Trade, except of Motor Vehicles and Motorcycles; Repair of Household Goods	1.44	9.11	17.40	38.07	5.40	14.58	2.99	11.97	4.50	12.04	15.21	24.40
Rubber and Plastics	5.82	41.81	35.59	32.05	17.91	56.86	24.42	23.39	16.18	27.32	31.07	33.97
Sale, Maintenance, and Repair of Motor Vehicles and Motorcycles; Retail Sale of Fuel	4.78	6.83	32.90	40.46	–	16.06	2.96	10.30	13.11	12.78	14.86	16.81
Textiles and Textile Products	4.00	20.05	14.36	35.40	10.50	14.95	13.06	27.99	13.28	12.80	27.87	36.81
Transport Equipment	13.76	30.68	25.99	39.45	17.50	34.68	27.02	16.45	16.61	12.30	32.13	33.83
Water Transport	7.63	28.62	19.68	13.56	10.53	46.15	17.17	18.33	21.30	16.54	29.32	43.31
Wholesale Trade and Commission Trade, except of Motor Vehicles and Motorcycles	0.70	7.22	20.36	41.48	5.35	17.89	2.99	7.69	3.57	9.70	13.70	19.48
Wood and Products of Wood and Cork	5.58	19.86	35.03	18.34	13.83	21.36	9.65	11.52	14.98	20.78	32.39	51.58

continued on next page

Table 3.5c: continued

Table 3.5c: Vertical Specialization by Sector, 2016

	Lao PDR	Malaysia	Maldives	Mongolia	Nepal	Pakistan	Philippines	Sri Lanka	Taipei,China	Thailand	Viet Nam
	(% of gross exports)										
Agriculture, Hunting, Forestry, and Fishing	5.09	14.88	46.14	8.85	6.76	3.75	8.61	12.44	25.74	12.82	26.81
Air Transport	84.37	29.39	37.27	24.24	18.79	10.24	32.73	31.48	51.55	15.52	37.82
Basic Metals and Fabricated Metal	41.24	47.90	32.44	31.72	45.00	15.82	48.31	51.22	49.51	47.69	49.79
Chemicals and Chemical Products	20.29	32.98	–	20.66	32.66	7.68	29.01	54.75	65.74	26.76	37.73
Coke, Refined Petroleum, and Nuclear Fuel	27.86	23.03	99.85	18.84	31.09	25.43	50.20	29.11	78.54	27.15	40.00
Construction	30.18	31.13	24.51	36.58	25.54	10.87	19.86	17.25	43.50	29.52	34.22
Education	4.45	7.87	10.00	7.90	5.74	1.25	4.32	0.67	9.21	5.22	10.53
Electrical and Optical Equipment	26.78	43.42	0.00	25.72	46.83	20.34	47.66	21.96	41.25	48.07	48.91
Electricity, Gas, and Water Supply	8.07	19.58	71.10	17.16	20.97	28.25	9.34	14.41	52.92	13.36	17.27
Financial Intermediation	7.24	9.68	9.61	5.94	9.30	0.79	4.31	4.87	8.23	4.84	6.25
Food, Beverages and Tobacco	25.85	25.96	37.18	10.38	14.18	8.20	14.46	16.12	32.13	16.80	42.66
Health and Social Work	13.94	25.03	18.95	19.21	14.54	6.27	10.33	5.64	17.95	16.11	24.73
Hotels and Restaurants	16.40	18.35	33.37	15.77	14.85	10.55	10.64	10.80	18.53	11.00	26.92
Inland Transport	19.96	21.26	35.84	24.24	34.87	7.26	27.12	12.76	29.58	22.42	19.31
Leather, Leather Products, and Footwear	17.00	25.47	90.67	18.46	24.06	6.28	24.44	15.49	39.71	21.48	46.53
Machinery, nec	29.83	47.21	–	32.03	21.42	13.71	38.72	54.36	43.63	42.91	49.77
Manufacturing, nec; Recycling	20.34	24.70	14.80	32.26	33.81	11.15	22.19	17.03	40.47	31.40	40.25
Mining and Quarrying	10.94	10.87	–	25.03	9.50	1.17	11.49	5.62	28.80	10.69	12.39
Other Community, Social, and Personal Services	9.71	20.79	40.52	11.89	7.99	1.66	10.51	10.66	17.44	16.26	14.74
Other Nonmetallic Mineral	20.42	34.11	29.13	27.68	29.03	11.58	35.88	31.99	45.71	20.91	38.50
Other Supporting and Auxiliary Transport Activities; Activities of Travel Agencies	68.79	20.58	25.07	26.73	17.47	3.10	11.23	8.85	16.21	8.59	18.07
Post and Telecommunications	9.13	14.02	18.36	20.28	13.05	3.09	11.30	22.76	17.85	7.19	16.50
Private Households with Employed Persons	–	–	–	–	–	–	–	–	–	–	–
Public Administration and Defense; Compulsory Social Security	9.98	17.04	13.24	12.71	6.75	6.54	4.47	1.87	11.48	0.00	12.68
Pulp, Paper, Paper Products, Printing, and Publishing	13.07	31.74	27.07	31.97	31.97	7.55	15.61	14.76	31.29	20.82	39.72
Real Estate Activities	2.62	9.52	10.41	8.97	6.39	0.09	3.40	4.40	7.31	2.28	8.83
Renting of Machinery and Equipment and Other Business Activities	7.37	16.81	32.71	17.99	15.58	0.59	5.85	12.35	18.98	14.89	18.60
Retail Trade, except of Motor Vehicles and Motorcycles; Repair of Household Goods	10.18	13.09	28.98	11.26	5.58	2.26	5.22	5.65	12.09	3.98	11.74
Rubber and Plastics	33.75	34.13	–	17.78	34.18	9.24	30.55	20.65	48.36	25.55	43.09
Sale, Maintenance, and Repair of Motor Vehicles and Motorcycles; Retail Sale of Fuel	13.37	17.03	52.31	11.39	3.99	3.95	9.81	5.26	29.14	13.41	23.61
Textiles and Textile Products	17.80	29.19	18.75	27.21	27.46	9.56	21.07	18.40	43.41	19.32	45.23
Transport Equipment	47.45	52.56	27.10	27.07	41.49	24.77	30.06	20.99	43.26	37.83	45.43
Water Transport	82.31	20.52	47.39	30.25	–	9.14	28.01	8.37	49.09	15.48	27.23
Wholesale Trade and Commission Trade, except of Motor Vehicles and Motorcycles	7.86	12.26	17.55	11.51	4.26	1.17	6.22	4.77	12.27	3.97	25.11
Wood and Products of Wood and Cork	19.11	26.29	23.57	31.07	21.68	9.05	15.65	21.36	43.74	14.01	38.99

– = magnitude equals zero, Lao PDR = Lao People's Democratic Republic.

Source: ADB Multi Region Input–Output Tables Database.

Table 3.6a: Vertical Specialization, Disaggregated (People's Republic of China)

	Gross Export	VS	FVA_FIN	FVA_INT	DDC	FDC	VS	FVA_FIN	FVA_INT	DDC	FDC
	($ million)						(% of gross export)	(% of VS)			
Chemicals and Chemical Products											
2014	117,913	20,019	2,845	9,440	1,399	6,334	16.98	14.21	47.16	6.99	31.64
2015	109,934	19,850	2,820	9,040	1,344	6,646	18.06	14.21	45.54	6.77	33.48
2016	97,660	19,790	2,864	9,324	1,191	6,412	20.26	14.47	47.12	6.02	32.40
Electrical and Optical Equipment											
2014	781,726	181,585	98,291	38,251	10,092	34,952	23.23	54.13	21.07	5.56	19.25
2015	776,278	190,634	104,745	38,002	9,679	38,208	24.56	54.95	19.93	5.08	20.04
2016	777,183	196,559	109,528	38,854	9,728	38,449	25.29	55.72	19.77	4.95	19.56
Post and Telecommunications											
2014	2,205	141	43	67	11	20	6.39	30.64	47.19	8.06	14.11
2015	6,539	393	57	227	43	67	6.00	14.42	57.74	10.88	16.96
2016	6,227	406	65	231	42	67	6.51	16.12	56.97	10.44	16.47
Renting of Machinery and Equipment and Other Business Activities											
2014	81,077	9,366	1,781	4,391	682	2,511	11.55	19.01	46.89	7.28	26.81
2015	85,874	10,322	1,986	4,517	755	3,064	12.02	19.24	43.76	7.31	29.69
2016	138,998	16,427	3,818	6,895	1,285	4,430	11.82	23.24	41.97	7.82	26.97
Textiles and Textile Products											
2014	242,244	23,163	17,353	3,033	448	2,330	9.56	74.92	13.09	1.93	10.06
2015	223,008	22,145	16,251	2,875	472	2,548	9.93	73.38	12.98	2.13	11.51
2016	219,384	23,033	16,979	3,176	474	2,404	10.50	73.71	13.79	2.06	10.44

DDC = domestic value added double counted in exports, FDC = foreign value added double counted in exports, FVA_FIN = foreign value added in exports for final consumption, FVA_INT = foreign value added in intermediate exports, VS = vertical specialization.

Source: ADB Multi Region Input-Output Tables Database.

Table 3.6b: Vertical Specialization, Disaggregated (Indonesia)

	Gross Export	VS	FVA_FIN	FVA_INT	DDC	FDC	VS	FVA_FIN	FVA_INT	DDC	FDC
	($ million)						(% of gross export)	(% of VS)			
Coke, Refined Petroleum, and Nuclear Fuel											
2014	14,210	1,682	382	824	12	463	11.84	22.74	49.01	0.73	27.52
2015	12,094	1,714	384	822	11	497	14.18	22.40	47.97	0.62	29.01
2016	11,320	1,411	321	687	9	394	12.46	22.72	48.71	0.63	27.94
Electrical and Optical Equipment											
2014	15,982	5,967	3,609	1,287	15	1,056	37.34	60.48	21.56	0.25	17.70
2015	14,947	5,283	3,215	1,103	12	953	35.35	60.85	20.88	0.23	18.04
2016	14,609	5,030	3,105	1,032	11	883	34.43	61.72	20.52	0.21	17.55
Food, Beverages, and Tobacco											
2014	32,955	3,589	957	1,948	20	664	10.89	26.66	54.28	0.56	18.50
2015	29,113	3,005	858	1,551	16	580	10.32	28.55	51.61	0.53	19.31
2016	28,748	2,924	798	1,564	15	547	10.17	27.30	53.49	0.50	18.72
Hotels and Restaurants											
2014	3,506	339	114	170	2	53	9.67	33.57	50.28	0.55	15.61
2015	2,692	340	129	153	2	56	12.62	38.05	45.09	0.45	16.42
2016	2,181	258	105	112	1	39	11.82	40.79	43.56	0.42	15.23
Mining and Quarrying											
2014	45,665	3,370	4	1,826	50	1,490	7.38	0.13	54.17	1.49	44.21
2015	34,887	2,889	4	1,517	37	1,330	8.28	0.15	52.50	1.30	46.05
2016	34,113	2,509	5	1,341	33	1,129	7.35	0.21	53.46	1.32	45.01

DDC = domestic value added double counted in exports, FDC = foreign value added double counted in exports, FVA_FIN = foreign value added in exports for final consumption, FVA_INT = foreign value added in intermediate exports, VS = vertical specialization.

Source: ADB Multi Region Input-Output Tables Database.

Table 3.6c: Vertical Specialization, Disaggregated (India)

	Gross Export	VS	FVA_FIN	FVA_INT	DDC	FDC	VS	FVA_FIN	FVA_INT	DDC	FDC
	($ million)						(% of gross export)	(% of VS)			
Electrical and Optical Equipment											
2014	9,331	2,268	945	783	9	530	24.30	41.69	34.55	0.39	23.37
2015	8,987	1,915	817	629	7	462	21.31	42.66	32.86	0.35	24.13
2016	13,239	3,284	1,488	1,003	14	779	24.80	45.31	30.55	0.42	23.72
Manufacturing, nec; Recycling											
2014	16,194	3,386	2,092	879	12	403	20.91	61.77	25.96	0.37	11.90
2015	14,903	2,799	1,796	692	8	303	18.78	64.18	24.72	0.28	10.82
2016	20,908	4,099	2,889	825	12	372	19.60	70.48	20.13	0.30	9.09
Renting of Machinery and Equipment and Other Business Activities											
2014	68,124	3,529	1,815	1,167	33	515	5.18	51.41	33.07	0.93	14.59
2015	62,436	2,775	1,390	888	26	471	4.44	50.09	32.00	0.93	16.98
2016	60,529	3,952	1,847	1,353	40	713	6.53	46.73	34.23	1.01	18.03
Textiles and Textile Products											
2014	30,540	3,784	2,384	751	12	637	12.39	63.00	19.85	0.32	16.83
2015	29,286	3,286	2,162	586	9	529	11.22	65.78	17.85	0.27	16.10
2016	35,692	4,660	2,972	943	16	728	13.06	63.78	20.23	0.35	15.63
Transport Equipment											
2014	28,871	7,731	5,409	1,411	16	894	26.78	69.97	18.25	0.21	11.57
2015	27,119	6,343	4,413	1,121	12	797	23.39	69.57	17.68	0.19	12.56
2016	36,383	9,830	7,094	1,601	21	1,114	27.02	72.16	16.28	0.21	11.34

DDC = domestic value added double counted in exports, FDC = foreign value added double counted in exports, FVA_FIN = foreign value added in exports for final consumption, FVA_INT = foreign value added in intermediate exports, VS = vertical specialization.

Source: ADB Multi Region Input–Output Tables Database.

Table 3.6d: Vertical Specialization, Disaggregated (Japan)

	Gross Export	VS	FVA_FIN	FVA_INT	DDC	FDC	VS	FVA_FIN	FVA_INT	DDC	FDC
	($ million)						(% of gross export)	(% of VS)			
Basic Metals and Fabricated Metal											
2014	105,020	36,469	3,082	20,240	546	12,601	34.73	8.45	55.50	1.50	34.55
2015	94,107	33,732	2,707	18,454	481	12,090	35.84	8.03	54.71	1.43	35.84
2016	84,826	25,164	1,930	14,003	370	8,861	29.67	7.67	55.65	1.47	35.21
Electrical and Optical Equipment											
2014	171,789	38,697	13,518	12,742	867	11,570	22.53	34.93	32.93	2.24	29.90
2015	160,266	40,137	13,994	13,256	808	12,079	25.04	34.87	33.03	2.01	30.09
2016	145,719	26,487	8,966	8,913	590	8,018	18.18	33.85	33.65	2.23	30.27
Machinery, nec											
2014	66,837	12,760	7,178	3,286	142	2,154	19.09	56.26	25.75	1.11	16.88
2015	64,168	13,593	7,590	3,517	135	2,350	21.18	55.84	25.88	0.99	17.29
2016	57,045	8,488	4,627	2,283	95	1,483	14.88	54.51	26.90	1.12	17.47
Transport Equipment											
2014	182,407	38,745	27,167	7,529	267	3,782	21.24	70.12	19.43	0.69	9.76
2015	167,878	40,684	27,872	8,217	270	4,325	24.23	68.51	20.20	0.66	10.63
2016	192,382	31,955	21,851	6,365	231	3,508	16.61	68.38	19.92	0.72	10.98
Wholesale Trade and Commission Trade, except of Motor Vehicles and Motorcycles											
2014	78,774	3,966	2,122	1,149	90	605	5.03	53.50	28.98	2.27	15.25
2015	78,042	3,483	1,825	931	122	605	4.46	52.40	26.74	3.50	17.37
2016	87,018	3,104	1,599	855	98	553	3.57	51.50	27.53	3.14	17.82

DDC = domestic value added double counted in exports, FDC = foreign value added double counted in exports, FVA_FIN = foreign value added in exports for final consumption, FVA_INT = foreign value added in intermediate exports, VS = vertical specialization.

Source: ADB Multi Region Input–Output Tables Database.

Table 3.6e: Vertical Specialization, Disaggregated (Republic of Korea)

	Gross Export	VS	FVA_FIN	FVA_INT	DDC	FDC	VS	FVA_FIN	FVA_INT	DDC	FDC
	($ million)						(% of gross export)	(% of VS)			
Basic Metals and Fabricated Metal											
2014	51,297	19,690	2,191	10,979	219	6,301	38.38	11.13	55.76	1.11	32.00
2015	47,229	19,615	2,026	10,843	192	6,554	41.53	10.33	55.28	0.98	33.41
2016	45,921	18,795	1,898	10,597	163	6,137	40.93	10.10	56.38	0.87	32.65
Chemicals and Chemical Products											
2014	68,996	27,931	1,405	16,433	280	9,814	40.48	5.03	58.83	1.00	35.14
2015	69,430	28,315	1,328	16,795	259	9,932	40.78	4.69	59.32	0.91	35.08
2016	65,621	24,693	1,116	15,140	208	8,228	37.63	4.52	61.32	0.84	33.32
Electrical and Optical Equipment											
2014	203,505	70,224	25,490	23,271	990	20,472	34.51	36.30	33.14	1.41	29.15
2015	189,086	68,432	25,260	22,626	838	19,707	36.19	36.91	33.06	1.23	28.80
2016	184,964	63,237	23,745	20,906	731	17,854	34.19	37.55	33.06	1.16	28.23
Transport Equipment											
2014	128,425	39,825	30,304	6,287	114	3,121	31.01	76.09	15.79	0.29	7.84
2015	115,253	38,266	28,409	6,333	109	3,416	33.20	74.24	16.55	0.28	8.93
2016	104,382	33,537	24,340	5,910	95	3,193	32.13	72.57	17.62	0.28	9.52
Water Transport											
2014	12,933	4,016	1,405	1,582	36	992	31.05	34.99	39.40	0.89	24.71
2015	13,751	4,256	1,539	1,508	38	1,171	30.95	36.17	35.43	0.89	27.51
2016	13,787	4,042	1,463	1,441	38	1,100	29.32	36.20	35.64	0.93	27.22

DDC = domestic value added double counted in exports, FDC = foreign value added double counted in exports, FVA_FIN = foreign value added in exports for final consumption, FVA_INT = foreign value added in intermediate exports, VS = vertical specialization.

Source: ADB Multi Region Input-Output Tables Database.

Table 3.6f: Vertical Specialization, Disaggregated (Taipei,China)

	Gross Export	VS	FVA_FIN	FVA_INT	DDC	FDC	VS	FVA_FIN	FVA_INT	DDC	FDC
	($ million)						(% of gross export)	(% of VS)			
Air Transport											
2014	6,290	3,312	909	1,863	10	530	52.65	27.46	56.25	0.29	16.01
2015	6,512	3,341	905	1,848	9	579	51.30	27.08	55.32	0.27	17.34
2016	6,436	3,318	927	1,823	8	559	51.55	27.94	54.94	0.26	16.86
Basic Metals and Fabricated Metal											
2014	28,525	13,994	1,256	8,079	63	4,596	49.06	8.97	57.73	0.45	32.84
2015	28,975	14,670	1,334	8,374	61	4,901	50.63	9.09	57.08	0.42	33.41
2016	28,256	13,991	1,261	8,080	56	4,593	49.51	9.02	57.75	0.40	32.83
Chemicals and Chemical Products											
2014	37,441	23,750	850	15,068	95	7,738	63.43	3.58	63.44	0.40	32.58
2015	37,207	24,905	841	16,089	92	7,883	66.94	3.38	64.60	0.37	31.65
2016	35,909	23,608	772	15,609	82	7,144	65.74	3.27	66.12	0.35	30.26
Electrical and Optical Equipment											
2014	150,906	60,927	11,669	25,396	845	23,016	40.37	19.15	41.68	1.39	37.78
2015	146,890	60,715	12,182	25,389	724	22,420	41.33	20.06	41.82	1.19	36.93
2016	140,881	58,108	11,882	24,577	639	21,011	41.25	20.45	42.29	1.10	36.16
Renting of Machinery and Equipment and Other Business Activities											
2014	5,888	1,030	221	593	10	206	17.49	21.45	57.56	0.95	20.05
2015	5,259	979	201	554	8	216	18.61	20.56	56.58	0.84	22.02
2016	5,017	952	193	545	7	207	18.98	20.29	57.23	0.78	21.70

DDC = domestic value added double counted in exports, FDC = foreign value added double counted in exports, FVA_FIN = foreign value added in exports for final consumption, FVA_INT = foreign value added in intermediate exports, VS = vertical specialization.

Source: ADB Multi Region Input-Output Tables Database.

Table 3.6g: Vertical Specialization, Disaggregated (Bangladesh)

	Gross Export	VS	FVA_FIN	FVA_INT	DDC	FDC	VS	FVA_FIN	FVA_INT	DDC	FDC
	($ million)						(% of gross export)	(% of VS)			
Leather, Leather Products, and Footwear											
2014	820	53	48	2	0	3	6.46	90.80	3.57	0.03	5.61
2015	860	37	33	1	0	3	4.31	87.95	3.85	0.03	8.17
2016	975	25	21	1	0	3	2.58	84.25	4.82	0.04	10.89
Manufacturing, nec; Recycling											
2014	1,571	366	287	48	0	30	23.29	78.40	13.24	0.04	8.31
2015	502	136	82	31	0	23	27.19	59.85	22.99	0.05	17.11
2016	483	89	53	21	0	14	18.42	60.07	23.66	0.03	16.24
Post and Telecommunications											
2014	653	11	2	7	0	2	1.67	15.48	63.61	0.27	20.63
2015	678	27	6	15	0	6	4.01	23.24	56.02	0.08	20.65
2016	397	4	1	2	0	1	0.93	15.47	60.32	0.13	24.08
Textiles and Textile Products											
2014	22,602	1,913	1,419	256	3	235	8.46	74.17	13.39	0.15	12.28
2015	22,411	1,767	1,341	216	2	208	7.89	75.89	12.24	0.10	11.77
2016	24,431	978	758	118	1	102	4.00	77.45	12.02	0.07	10.45
Water Transport											
2014	298	42	7	25	0	9	13.99	16.59	60.74	0.09	22.58
2015	321	37	5	23	0	9	11.45	14.39	61.38	0.05	24.18
2016	368	28	5	16	0	7	7.63	16.38	58.83	0.04	24.75

0 = magnitude is less than half of unit employed, DDC = domestic value added double counted in exports, FDC = foreign value added double counted in exports, FVA_FIN = foreign value added in exports for final consumption, FVA_INT = foreign value added in intermediate exports, VS = vertical specialization.

Source: ADB Multi Region Input–Output Tables Database.

Table 3.6h: Vertical Specialization, Disaggregated (Malaysia)

	Gross Export	VS	FVA_FIN	FVA_INT	DDC	FDC	VS	FVA_FIN	FVA_INT	DDC	FDC
	($ million)						(% of gross export)	(% of VS)			
Agriculture, Hunting, Forestry, and Fishing											
2014	2,528	334	49	211	2	72	13.20	14.80	63.15	0.59	21.46
2015	2,767	372	55	233	2	83	13.44	14.71	62.60	0.50	22.20
2016	2,791	415	77	251	2	86	14.88	18.55	60.37	0.41	20.67
Coke, Refined Petroleum, and Nuclear Fuel											
2014	16,357	3,326	659	1,707	16	944	20.34	19.83	51.33	0.48	28.37
2015	14,251	3,355	699	1,706	14	937	23.55	20.82	50.85	0.40	27.92
2016	14,202	3,270	628	1,721	12	909	23.03	19.22	52.61	0.38	27.79
Electrical and Optical Equipment											
2014	31,036	13,536	5,416	3,589	52	4,478	43.61	40.01	26.52	0.39	33.08
2015	28,123	12,750	5,206	3,365	40	4,139	45.34	40.83	26.39	0.32	32.46
2016	25,309	10,989	4,689	2,905	35	3,359	43.42	42.67	26.43	0.32	30.57
Financial Intermediation											
2014	3,029	287	51	157	2	77	9.47	17.76	54.81	0.68	26.75
2015	2,768	275	52	146	2	75	9.93	18.88	53.12	0.55	27.45
2016	2,737	265	49	142	1	72	9.68	18.49	53.61	0.52	27.38
Post and Telecommunications											
2014	10,888	1,822	145	1,362	10	306	16.74	7.94	74.75	0.54	16.78
2015	5,535	1,035	95	731	5	204	18.70	9.22	70.62	0.47	19.69
2016	8,253	1,157	101	834	5	217	14.02	8.72	72.09	0.45	18.74

DDC = domestic value added double counted in exports, FDC = foreign value added double counted in exports, FVA_FIN = foreign value added in exports for final consumption, FVA_INT = foreign value added in intermediate exports, VS = vertical specialization.

Source: ADB Multi Region Input–Output Tables Database.

Table 3.6i: Vertical Specialization, Disaggregated (Philippines)

	Gross Export	VS	FVA_FIN	FVA_INT	DDC	FDC	VS	FVA_FIN	FVA_INT	DDC	FDC
	($ million)						(% of gross export)	(% of VS)			
Basic Metals and Fabricated Metal											
2014	1,959	836	206	392	1	237	42.67	24.62	46.92	0.07	28.39
2015	1,938	828	202	385	1	241	42.74	24.39	46.47	0.08	29.06
2016	1,657	800	147	407	1	246	48.31	18.35	50.82	0.08	30.75
Electrical and Optical Equipment											
2014	15,791	7,137	2,561	1,867	17	2,692	45.20	35.89	26.17	0.24	37.71
2015	15,050	6,732	2,516	1,686	16	2,514	44.73	37.37	25.04	0.24	37.35
2016	13,752	6,554	2,557	1,658	14	2,326	47.66	39.01	25.29	0.21	35.49
Food, Beverages, and Tobacco											
2014	9,707	920	454	350	1	115	9.47	49.33	38.05	0.07	12.55
2015	9,304	1,085	535	397	1	152	11.66	49.35	36.61	0.06	13.98
2016	8,554	1,237	609	450	1	178	14.46	49.18	36.36	0.05	14.41
Renting of Machinery and Equipment and Other Business Activities											
2014	13,846	792	82	487	2	222	5.72	10.33	61.41	0.28	27.97
2015	11,477	668	67	396	2	203	5.82	10.01	59.36	0.27	30.36
2016	12,320	721	70	427	2	222	5.85	9.76	59.23	0.28	30.73
Textiles and Textile Products											
2014	1,238	254	229	13	0	11	20.51	90.21	5.30	0.01	4.48
2015	1,227	252	229	12	0	11	20.54	90.80	4.64	0.01	4.55
2016	1,209	255	231	12	0	11	21.07	90.76	4.77	0.01	4.46

DDC = domestic value added double counted in exports, FDC = foreign value added double counted in exports, FVA_FIN = foreign value added in exports for final consumption, FVA_INT = foreign value added in intermediate exports, VS = vertical specialization.

Source: ADB Multi Region Input–Output Tables Database.

Table 3.6j: Vertical Specialization, Disaggregated (Thailand)

	Gross Export	VS	FVA_FIN	FVA_INT	DDC	FDC	VS	FVA_FIN	FVA_INT	DDC	FDC
	($ million)						(% of gross export)	(% of VS)			
Electrical and Optical Equipment											
2014	42,918	23,014	9,622	6,611	89	6,692	53.62	41.81	28.73	0.39	29.08
2015	38,739	19,630	8,390	5,406	74	5,760	50.67	42.74	27.54	0.38	29.34
2016	40,020	19,239	8,777	5,147	72	5,243	48.07	45.62	26.75	0.38	27.25
Food, Beverages, and Tobacco											
2014	28,137	5,555	3,244	1,717	15	580	19.74	58.40	30.90	0.26	10.44
2015	26,329	4,865	2,894	1,424	13	534	18.48	59.50	29.27	0.26	10.97
2016	26,794	4,502	2,604	1,361	12	526	16.80	57.83	30.23	0.26	11.68
Post and Telecommunications											
2014	1,272	118	19	76	1	23	9.31	15.66	64.16	0.77	19.41
2015	1,303	109	20	65	1	24	8.37	17.90	59.60	0.79	21.70
2016	1,304	94	17	56	1	21	7.19	17.89	59.33	0.80	21.99
Renting of Machinery and Equipment and Other Business Activities											
2014	6,358	1,160	202	651	6	301	18.25	17.43	56.09	0.54	25.93
2015	6,124	1,033	155	575	6	297	16.86	15.02	55.68	0.55	28.75
2016	5,897	878	135	491	5	247	14.89	15.42	55.93	0.56	28.08
Textiles and Textile Products											
2014	9,651	2,220	1,513	371	4	332	23.01	68.14	16.69	0.19	14.97
2015	9,261	2,012	1,364	332	4	312	21.73	67.81	16.50	0.19	15.49
2016	9,402	1,817	1,247	300	3	267	19.32	68.64	16.49	0.19	14.68

DDC = domestic value added double counted in exports, FDC = foreign value added double counted in exports, FVA_FIN = foreign value added in exports for final consumption, FVA_INT = foreign value added in intermediate exports, VS = vertical specialization.

Source: ADB Multi Region Input–Output Tables Database.

Table 3.6k: Vertical Specialization, Disaggregated (Viet Nam)											
	Gross Export	VS	FVA_FIN	FVA_INT	DDC	FDC	VS	FVA_FIN	FVA_INT	DDC	FDC
	($ million)						(% of gross export)	(% of VS)			
Agriculture, Hunting, Forestry, and Fishing											
2014	18,056	5,255	1,872	2,455	16	912	29.10	35.63	46.72	0.30	17.35
2015	21,044	5,483	1,715	2,626	17	1,126	26.06	31.28	47.88	0.30	20.54
2016	19,401	5,201	1,739	2,464	15	983	26.81	33.44	47.37	0.29	18.91
Financial Intermediation											
2014	4,250	302	140	112	1	49	7.12	46.35	36.91	0.38	16.35
2015	5,201	255	81	112	2	60	4.90	31.73	44.15	0.61	23.51
2016	5,579	349	109	155	2	83	6.25	31.26	44.33	0.52	23.88
Hotels and Restaurants											
2014	8,244	2,451	1,988	321	1	141	29.74	81.11	13.09	0.06	5.75
2015	8,039	1,994	1,628	244	1	121	24.80	81.65	12.24	0.06	6.05
2016	8,713	2,346	1,964	251	1	130	26.92	83.72	10.68	0.05	5.55
Leather, Leather Products, and Footwear											
2014	700	354	286	33	0	35	50.61	80.77	9.18	0.12	9.93
2015	718	336	252	40	1	44	46.79	74.85	11.97	0.16	13.02
2016	687	320	253	33	0	34	46.53	79.00	10.35	0.14	10.52
Textiles and Textile Products											
2014	8,716	4,411	3,626	359	5	421	50.60	82.21	8.13	0.11	9.55
2015	11,468	5,368	3,612	952	9	796	46.81	67.27	17.73	0.18	14.82
2016	10,357	4,684	3,397	730	7	550	45.23	72.52	15.59	0.15	11.74

0 = magnitude is less than half of unit employed, DDC = domestic value added double counted in exports, FDC = foreign value added double counted in exports, FVA_FIN = foreign value added in exports for final consumption, FVA_INT = foreign value added in intermediate exports, VS = vertical specialization.

Source: ADB Multi Region Input–Output Tables Database.

Table 3.6l: Vertical Specialization, Disaggregated (Mongolia)											
	Gross Export	VS	FVA_FIN	FVA_INT	DDC	FDC	VS	FVA_FIN	FVA_INT	DDC	FDC
	($ million)						(% of gross export)	(% of VS)			
Agriculture, Hunting, Forestry, and Fishing											
2014	218	21	9	9	0	3	9.78	40.71	43.78	0.01	15.49
2015	227	19	8	9	0	3	8.56	39.15	44.05	0.01	16.79
2016	235	21	8	9	0	4	8.85	37.41	45.68	0.01	16.90
Electricity, Gas, and Water Supply											
2014	209	48	5	28	0	14	22.72	9.77	59.88	0.02	30.33
2015	179	30	3	17	0	10	16.88	9.98	56.09	0.02	33.91
2016	210	36	4	20	0	12	17.16	10.83	56.50	0.02	32.64
Leather, Leather Products, and Footwear											
2014	64	12	2	4	0	6	19.47	17.26	33.19	0.02	49.52
2015	62	11	2	4	0	5	17.35	16.71	33.99	0.02	49.29
2016	63	12	2	3	0	6	18.46	17.24	27.88	0.02	54.86
Mining and Quarrying											
2014	4,009	1,190	67	796	0	327	29.68	5.62	66.87	0.03	27.48
2015	3,959	941	48	645	0	248	23.77	5.11	68.55	0.03	26.31
2016	4,020	1,006	47	706	0	252	25.03	4.72	70.17	0.02	25.09
Wholesale Trade and Commission Trade, except of Motor Vehicles and Motorcycles											
2014	199	30	3	18	0	9	14.99	10.19	59.83	0.03	29.95
2015	168	17	2	10	0	6	10.40	10.81	54.40	0.03	34.76
2016	185	21	4	11	0	7	11.51	17.65	51.40	0.02	30.93

0 = magnitude is less than half of unit employed, DDC = domestic value added double counted in exports, FDC = foreign value added double counted in exports, FVA_FIN = foreign value added in exports for final consumption, FVA_INT = foreign value added in intermediate exports, VS = vertical specialization.

Source: ADB Multi Region Input–Output Tables Database.

Table 3.6m: Vertical Specialization, Disaggregated (Sri Lanka)

	Gross Export	VS	FVA_FIN	FVA_INT	DDC	FDC	VS	FVA_FIN	FVA_INT	DDC	FDC
	($ million)						(% of gross export)	(% of VS)			
Agriculture, Hunting, Forestry, and Fishing											
2014	569	66	41	16	0	8	11.60	62.49	24.81	0.01	12.69
2015	504	59	35	14	0	10	11.77	59.18	24.17	0.02	16.63
2016	512	64	37	16	0	11	12.44	58.19	24.90	0.02	16.89
Food, Beverages, and Tobacco											
2014	2,085	238	156	56	0	26	11.40	65.52	23.71	0.01	10.76
2015	2,247	333	216	74	0	43	14.82	64.96	22.22	0.01	12.81
2016	2,164	349	229	76	0	44	16.12	65.48	21.80	0.01	12.71
Hotels and Restaurants											
2014	983	101	67	22	0	12	10.32	66.54	21.55	0.01	11.89
2015	951	96	56	26	0	14	10.06	58.14	26.69	0.01	15.16
2016	614	66	37	18	0	11	10.80	55.90	27.50	0.02	16.59
Rubber and Plastics											
2014	227	43	20	13	0	10	18.78	46.95	29.58	0.01	23.46
2015	226	41	22	10	0	9	17.93	54.54	24.16	0.01	21.29
2016	422	87	59	14	0	14	20.65	67.47	16.59	0.01	15.93
Textiles and Textile Products											
2014	3,314	585	440	88	0	56	17.64	75.36	15.12	0.02	9.50
2015	3,037	528	398	79	0	51	17.40	75.37	15.03	0.02	9.59
2016	3,514	647	492	94	0	60	18.40	76.15	14.58	0.02	9.25

0 = magnitude is less than half of unit employed, DDC = domestic value added double counted in exports, FDC = foreign value added double counted in exports, FVA_FIN = foreign value added in exports for final consumption, FVA_INT = foreign value added in intermediate exports, VS = vertical specialization.

Source: ADB Multi Region Input–Output Tables Database.

Table 3.6n: Vertical Specialization, Disaggregated (Bhutan)

	Gross Export	VS	FVA_FIN	FVA_INT	DDC	FDC	VS	FVA_FIN	FVA_INT	DDC	FDC
	($ million)						(% of gross export)	(% of VS)			
Agriculture, Hunting, Forestry, and Fishing											
2014	35	1	0	1	0	0	3.29	37.79	48.40	0.02	13.79
2015	30	1	0	1	0	0	3.37	34.57	51.44	0.02	13.97
2016	29	1	0	1	0	0	4.81	19.25	65.00	0.02	15.73
Basic Metals and Fabricated Metal											
2014	37	11	5	5	0	1	30.54	42.03	47.79	0.01	10.17
2015	40	12	5	6	0	1	30.18	41.94	46.83	0.00	11.23
2016	47	17	7	8	0	2	35.48	41.04	47.43	0.00	11.52
Electricity, Gas, and Water Supply											
2014	154	9	1	5	0	3	5.57	13.70	55.07	0.01	31.23
2015	195	10	3	4	0	3	5.17	29.17	42.62	0.00	28.21
2016	144	8	1	4	0	3	5.42	11.77	54.07	0.01	34.15
Mining and Quarrying											
2014	31	4	0	3	0	0	12.27	2.52	88.10	0.01	9.36
2015	43	4	0	3	0	1	8.74	7.78	76.18	0.01	16.03
2016	42	4	0	3	0	0	9.14	7.08	80.38	0.02	12.53
Other Nonmetallic Mineral											
2014	28	4	3	0	0	0	12.40	97.42	2.12	0.00	0.45
2015	26	2	2	0	0	0	9.02	95.87	3.16	0.00	0.97
2016	35	4	4	0	0	0	12.30	96.93	2.38	0.00	0.69

0 = magnitude is less than half of unit employed, DDC = domestic value added double counted in exports, FDC = foreign value added double counted in exports, FVA_FIN = foreign value added in exports for final consumption, FVA_INT = foreign value added in intermediate exports, VS = vertical specialization.

Source: ADB Multi Region Input–Output Tables Database.

Table 3.6o: Vertical Specialization, Disaggregated (Brunei Darussalam)											
	Gross Export	VS	FVA_FIN	FVA_INT	DDC	FDC	VS	FVA_FIN	FVA_INT	DDC	FDC
	($ million)						(% of gross export)	(% of VS)			
Chemicals and Chemical Products											
2014	88	10	1	6	0	4	11.54	5.28	59.82	0.03	34.87
2015	58	7	0	4	0	3	12.39	5.36	57.85	0.02	36.77
2016	61	6	0	4	0	2	10.53	4.84	57.17	0.02	37.97
Coke, Refined Petroleum, and Nuclear Fuel											
2014	4,609	532	(0)	336	0	196	11.54	(0.02)	63.21	0.03	36.78
2015	3,053	399	9	247	0	143	13.08	2.23	61.90	0.01	35.86
2016	3,101	425	10	260	0	155	13.70	2.35	61.21	0.01	36.43
Mining and Quarrying											
2014	5,472	403	4	265	0	135	7.37	1.01	65.61	0.03	33.35
2015	3,660	332	3	215	0	114	9.07	0.78	64.90	0.02	34.30
2016	3,513	394	2	261	0	130	11.21	0.62	66.38	0.01	32.99
Other Supporting and Auxiliary Transport Activities; Activities of Travel Agencies											
2014	99	25	7	12	0	6	24.72	27.48	47.35	0.02	25.14
2015	81	20	6	9	0	5	25.03	28.32	45.23	0.01	26.43
2016	70	19	6	8	0	5	26.64	31.28	44.24	0.01	24.46
Water Transport											
2014	47	8	3	3	0	3	16.81	31.91	32.28	0.02	35.79
2015	39	7	2	2	0	2	17.32	32.47	30.69	0.01	36.83
2016	36	7	2	2	0	3	19.68	33.71	29.58	0.01	36.70

0 = magnitude is less than half of unit employed, DDC = domestic value added double counted in exports, FDC = foreign value added double counted in exports, FVA_FIN = foreign value added in exports for final consumption, FVA_INT = foreign value added in intermediate exports, VS = vertical specialization.

Source: ADB Multi Region Input–Output Tables Database.

Table 3.6p: Vertical Specialization, Disaggregated (Cambodia)											
	Gross Export	VS	FVA_FIN	FVA_INT	DDC	FDC	VS	FVA_FIN	FVA_INT	DDC	FDC
	($ million)						(% of gross export)	(% of VS)			
Agriculture, Hunting, Forestry, and Fishing											
2014	1,309	112	43	41	0	29	8.57	37.99	36.52	0.08	25.41
2015	1,237	153	63	52	0	38	12.38	41.19	34.01	0.10	24.70
2016	1,052	89	43	28	0	19	8.50	48.05	30.84	0.10	21.01
Hotels and Restaurants											
2014	1,191	275	162	71	0	41	23.06	59.15	25.76	0.01	15.08
2015	1,221	255	145	66	0	44	20.86	56.78	25.87	0.02	17.34
2016	1,455	322	186	82	0	53	22.14	57.83	25.59	0.01	16.57
Leather, Leather Products, and Footwear											
2014	136	50	45	3	0	2	36.63	90.24	5.61	0.01	4.15
2015	146	50	44	3	0	3	34.26	87.35	6.92	0.01	5.73
2016	168	59	48	7	0	5	35.40	80.83	11.03	0.01	8.12
Post and Telecommunications											
2014	98	17	2	11	0	4	17.77	13.98	64.19	0.02	21.81
2015	101	17	3	11	0	4	16.91	14.84	61.48	0.03	23.65
2016	129	22	3	14	0	5	17.23	14.50	62.40	0.03	23.07
Textiles and Textile Products											
2014	3,168	1,160	1,046	66	0	49	36.63	90.11	5.67	0.01	4.22
2015	3,502	1,239	1,077	90	0	71	35.38	86.97	7.26	0.01	5.76
2016	3,916	1,386	1,161	137	0	88	35.40	83.74	9.90	0.01	6.35

0 = magnitude is less than half of unit employed, DDC = domestic value added double counted in exports, FDC = foreign value added double counted in exports, FVA_FIN = foreign value added in exports for final consumption, FVA_INT = foreign value added in intermediate exports, VS = vertical specialization.

Source: ADB Multi Region Input–Output Tables Database.

Table 3.6q: Vertical Specialization, Disaggregated (Fiji)

	Gross Export	VS	FVA_FIN	FVA_INT	DDC	FDC	VS	FVA_FIN	FVA_INT	DDC	FDC
	($ million)						(% of gross export)	(% of VS)			
Agriculture, Hunting, Forestry, and Fishing											
2014	72	13	5	6	0	2	18.62	40.02	44.81	0.01	15.16
2015	79	15	7	6	0	2	18.60	44.89	40.08	0.01	15.02
2016	73	13	6	5	0	2	17.44	49.35	37.30	0.01	13.34
Air Transport											
2014	276	159	34	101	0	24	57.58	21.47	63.52	0.00	15.01
2015	241	149	31	96	0	23	61.76	20.47	64.07	0.00	15.46
2016	232	136	34	79	0	24	58.75	25.02	57.63	0.00	17.34
Food, Beverages, and Tobacco											
2014	235	65	32	25	0	9	27.80	48.52	37.86	0.00	13.61
2015	243	69	31	27	0	10	28.26	45.92	40.02	0.01	14.05
2016	237	63	29	25	0	9	26.45	45.96	39.11	0.00	14.93
Hotels and Restaurants											
2014	458	106	62	31	0	13	23.21	58.74	29.15	0.01	12.10
2015	462	107	63	30	0	14	23.06	58.98	27.95	0.01	13.07
2016	468	102	63	27	0	13	21.79	61.43	26.28	0.01	12.29
Other Supporting and Auxiliary Transport Activities; Activities of Travel Agencies											
2014	135	33	10	15	0	8	24.29	30.55	45.85	0.01	23.59
2015	130	30	10	13	0	7	23.23	32.37	43.35	0.01	24.26
2016	130	28	11	11	0	6	21.87	38.80	38.38	0.01	22.81

0 = magnitude is less than half of unit employed, DDC = domestic value added double counted in exports, FDC = foreign value added double counted in exports, FVA_FIN = foreign value added in exports for final consumption, FVA_INT = foreign value added in intermediate exports, VS = vertical specialization.

Source: ADB Multi Region Input-Output Tables Database.

Table 3.6r: Vertical Specialization, Disaggregated (Kazakhstan)

	Gross Export	VS	FVA_FIN	FVA_INT	DDC	FDC	VS	FVA_FIN	FVA_INT	DDC	FDC
	($ million)						(% of gross export)	(% of VS)			
Agriculture, Hunting, Forestry, and Fishing											
2014	1,238	129	85	30	0	13	10.41	66.12	23.52	0.33	10.02
2015	1,194	170	120	33	0	17	14.23	70.52	19.26	0.16	10.05
2016	1,004	162	106	37	0	18	16.12	65.56	22.96	0.15	11.33
Basic Metals and Fabricated Metal											
2014	7,574	582	16	253	4	308	7.68	2.72	43.53	0.77	52.99
2015	6,814	822	22	321	4	475	12.07	2.71	39.08	0.43	57.78
2016	6,709	911	33	350	2	525	13.58	3.60	38.47	0.25	57.68
Coke, Refined Petroleum, and Nuclear Fuel											
2014	2,106	104	33	49	1	21	4.93	31.64	47.26	0.76	20.35
2015	1,456	233	74	106	1	52	16.02	31.74	45.61	0.27	22.38
2016	1,603	216	78	95	0	43	13.47	36.04	44.00	0.22	19.73
Mining and Quarrying											
2014	41,620	3,670	229	1,915	30	1,496	8.82	6.25	52.17	0.82	40.76
2015	24,043	2,733	171	1,377	17	1,168	11.37	6.25	50.40	0.63	42.72
2016	23,553	3,544	222	1,811	12	1,500	15.05	6.26	51.10	0.34	42.31
Wholesale Trade and Commission Trade, except of Motor Vehicles and Motorcycles											
2014	15,935	1,289	39	881	10	360	8.09	3.01	68.33	0.76	27.90
2015	14,196	986	35	615	7	329	6.94	3.56	62.34	0.71	33.39
2016	11,617	1,127	47	751	5	324	9.70	4.16	66.69	0.41	28.74

0 = magnitude is less than half of unit employed, DDC = domestic value added double counted in exports, FDC = foreign value added double counted in exports, FVA_FIN = foreign value added in exports for final consumption, FVA_INT = foreign value added in intermediate exports, VS = vertical specialization.

Source: ADB Multi Region Input-Output Tables Database.

Table 3.6s: Vertical Specialization, Disaggregated (Kyrgyz Republic)

	Gross Export	VS	FVA_FIN	FVA_INT	DDC	FDC	VS	FVA_FIN	FVA_INT	DDC	FDC
	($ million)						(% of gross export)	(% of VS)			
Agriculture, Hunting, Forestry, and Fishing											
2014	320	69	27	25	0	16	21.45	39.13	36.87	0.02	23.97
2015	274	58	14	23	0	22	21.09	23.36	39.42	0.02	37.21
2016	327	81	27	26	0	27	24.77	33.84	32.36	0.01	33.79
Basic Metals and Fabricated Metal											
2014	624	155	51	57	0	48	24.80	32.66	36.65	0.01	30.68
2015	519	137	14	59	0	64	26.41	10.17	43.00	0.01	46.82
2016	519	150	30	54	0	67	28.88	19.75	35.74	0.01	44.50
Construction											
2014	89	35	14	14	0	6	39.13	41.22	40.70	0.02	18.05
2015	165	70	45	18	0	8	42.61	64.15	25.09	0.01	10.75
2016	94	38	20	12	0	5	40.62	53.15	32.78	0.01	14.07
Inland Transport											
2014	104	42	11	22	0	10	40.28	25.32	51.59	0.02	23.07
2015	109	45	11	22	0	12	40.89	25.53	48.41	0.01	26.05
2016	109	46	13	22	0	11	42.02	27.62	48.18	0.01	24.18
Post and Telecommunications											
2014	86	28	6	15	0	7	32.34	22.99	53.31	0.01	23.69
2015	62	21	5	10	0	5	33.33	23.49	50.15	0.01	26.35
2016	60	20	5	10	0	5	33.42	23.82	50.89	0.01	25.28

0 = magnitude is less than half of unit employed, DDC = domestic value added double counted in exports, FDC = foreign value added double counted in exports, FVA_FIN = foreign value added in exports for final consumption, FVA_INT = foreign value added in intermediate exports, VS = vertical specialization.

Source: ADB Multi Region Input–Output Tables Database.

Table 3.6t: Vertical Specialization, Disaggregated (Lao People's Democratic Republic)

	Gross Export	VS	FVA_FIN	FVA_INT	DDC	FDC	VS	FVA_FIN	FVA_INT	DDC	FDC
	($ million)						(% of gross export)	(% of VS)			
Agriculture, Hunting, Forestry, and Fishing											
2014	961	54	5	29	0	21	5.60	8.65	53.19	0.05	38.11
2015	993	66	6	33	0	27	6.61	9.48	50.01	0.06	40.45
2016	622	32	5	15	0	12	5.09	15.63	47.95	0.04	36.37
Electricity, Gas, and Water Supply											
2014	374	44	8	24	0	12	11.72	17.74	54.18	0.02	28.06
2015	314	31	6	16	0	10	9.86	18.16	50.54	0.03	31.27
2016	350	28	5	14	0	9	8.07	18.89	50.89	0.02	30.19
Mining and Quarrying											
2014	2,359	360	101	173	0	85	15.26	28.16	48.18	0.01	23.65
2015	2,484	318	90	153	0	76	12.82	28.15	48.09	0.02	23.74
2016	2,945	322	85	160	0	77	10.94	26.36	49.68	0.02	23.95
Textiles and Textile Products											
2014	120	25	21	2	0	2	20.70	83.69	8.85	0.00	7.45
2015	131	29	24	2	0	2	21.95	83.70	8.32	0.00	7.97
2016	108	19	16	2	0	2	17.80	80.74	10.16	0.00	9.10
Wood and Products of Wood and Cork											
2014	173	31	3	22	0	6	17.76	8.85	71.52	0.04	19.58
2015	188	53	5	36	0	12	28.07	8.86	68.18	0.04	22.92
2016	118	23	2	15	0	6	19.11	6.86	68.14	0.04	24.96

0 = magnitude is less than half of unit employed, DDC = domestic value added double counted in exports, FDC = foreign value added double counted in exports, FVA_FIN = foreign value added in exports for final consumption, FVA_INT = foreign value added in intermediate exports, VS = vertical specialization.

Source: ADB Multi Region Input–Output Tables Database.

Table 3.6u: Vertical Specialization, Disaggregated (Maldives)

	Gross Export	VS	FVA_FIN	FVA_INT	DDC	FDC	VS	FVA_FIN	FVA_INT	DDC	FDC
	($ million)						(% of gross export)	(% of VS)			
Agriculture, Hunting, Forestry, and Fishing											
2014	28	10	4	4	0	2	36.45	42.58	42.63	0.01	14.78
2015	26	12	5	6	0	2	48.00	38.65	46.61	0.01	14.74
2016	36	17	7	7	0	3	46.14	39.65	44.80	0.01	15.54
Air Transport											
2014	93	38	14	21	0	3	40.65	36.96	56.22	0.01	6.81
2015	33	12	4	7	0	1	36.74	35.27	57.59	0.01	7.13
2016	35	13	6	6	0	1	37.27	44.15	46.60	0.01	9.24
Food, Beverages, and Tobacco											
2014	37	16	12	4	0	1	43.46	72.42	21.64	0.00	5.95
2015	29	11	10	1	0	0	37.65	90.16	7.89	0.00	1.95
2016	31	12	10	1	0	0	37.18	86.44	10.58	0.00	2.99
Hotels and Restaurants											
2014	2,265	861	389	298	0	174	38.04	45.11	34.64	0.01	20.25
2015	2,255	742	325	253	0	164	32.91	43.81	34.12	0.00	22.06
2016	2,301	768	347	258	0	163	33.37	45.23	33.55	0.01	21.22
Post and Telecommunications											
2014	40	10	2	5	0	3	23.87	22.27	51.20	0.01	26.52
2015	57	10	2	5	0	3	17.28	19.71	49.74	0.01	30.54
2016	62	11	2	6	0	4	18.36	19.76	49.28	0.01	30.96

0 = magnitude is less than half of unit employed, DDC = domestic value added double counted in exports, FDC = foreign value added double counted in exports, FVA_FIN = foreign value added in exports for final consumption, FVA_INT = foreign value added in intermediate exports, VS = vertical specialization.
Source: ADB Multi Region Input-Output Tables Database.

Table 3.6v: Vertical Specialization, Disaggregated (Nepal)

	Gross Export	VS	FVA_FIN	FVA_INT	DDC	FDC	VS	FVA_FIN	FVA_INT	DDC	FDC
	($ million)						(% of gross export)	(% of VS)			
Agriculture, Hunting, Forestry, and Fishing											
2014	81	6	3	2	0	0	6.79	61.34	33.22	0.01	5.42
2015	90	6	4	2	0	0	6.44	66.63	28.37	0.01	4.98
2016	108	7	5	2	0	0	6.76	65.49	29.48	0.01	5.02
Basic Metals and Fabricated Metal											
2014	67	30	12	14	0	4	44.88	40.49	46.70	0.01	12.81
2015	68	30	14	12	0	3	43.25	47.20	41.82	0.01	10.97
2016	83	37	15	17	0	5	45.00	39.82	46.31	0.01	13.87
Food, Beverages, and Tobacco											
2014	62	9	7	2	0	0	13.91	78.61	18.39	0.00	3.00
2015	56	7	6	1	0	0	13.40	78.27	18.80	0.00	2.93
2016	66	9	7	2	0	0	14.18	76.45	20.42	0.01	3.12
Inland Transport											
2014	128	44	21	18	0	5	34.61	47.62	41.42	0.00	10.95
2015	116	39	18	17	0	4	33.94	46.17	42.55	0.00	11.27
2016	141	49	25	19	0	5	34.87	51.07	37.83	0.00	11.10
Textiles and Textile Products											
2014	73	20	16	2	0	1	27.53	81.03	11.77	0.00	7.20
2015	73	19	16	2	0	1	26.72	82.61	10.75	0.00	6.64
2016	74	20	17	2	0	1	27.46	81.12	12.05	0.00	6.83

0 = magnitude is less than half of unit employed, DDC = domestic value added double counted in exports, FDC = foreign value added double counted in exports, FVA_FIN = foreign value added in exports for final consumption, FVA_INT = foreign value added in intermediate exports, VS = vertical specialization.

Source: ADB Multi Region Input-Output Tables Database.

Table 3.6w: Vertical Specialization, Disaggregated (Pakistan)											
	Gross Export	VS	FVA_FIN	FVA_INT	DDC	FDC	VS	FVA_FIN	FVA_INT	DDC	FDC
	($ million)						(% of gross export)	(% of VS)			
Agriculture, Hunting, Forestry, and Fishing											
2014	1,574	45	13	22	0	10	2.86	28.55	49.44	0.09	21.93
2015	6,139	159	64	57	0	37	2.59	40.39	36.21	0.06	23.34
2016	5,528	208	87	74	0	46	3.75	42.15	35.67	0.04	22.14
Food, Beverages, and Tobacco											
2014	2,293	192	93	68	0	31	8.38	48.49	35.27	0.02	16.21
2015	310	24	17	4	0	2	7.76	72.59	18.04	0.01	9.36
2016	336	28	18	6	0	3	8.20	66.97	22.67	0.01	10.35
Inland Transport											
2014	2,698	180	74	81	0	25	6.67	41.15	44.86	0.03	13.95
2015	2,897	207	85	91	0	31	7.14	40.87	44.09	0.03	15.01
2016	2,582	188	83	75	0	30	7.26	44.20	39.99	0.02	15.78
Textiles and Textile Products											
2014	10,882	1,111	515	296	0	300	10.21	46.38	26.62	0.02	26.98
2015	8,480	818	394	211	0	213	9.65	48.16	25.75	0.02	26.07
2016	8,316	795	388	213	0	194	9.56	48.84	26.74	0.02	24.40
Wholesale Trade and Commission Trade, except of Motor Vehicles and Motorcycles											
2014	2,032	23	3	12	0	8	1.13	11.44	53.42	0.18	34.96
2015	1,948	19	2	9	0	7	0.96	12.12	48.92	0.19	38.77
2016	1,685	20	2	9	0	8	1.17	10.17	47.72	0.16	41.95

0 = magnitude is less than half of unit employed, DDC = domestic value added double counted in exports, FDC = foreign value added double counted in exports, FVA_FIN = foreign value added in exports for final consumption, FVA_INT = foreign value added in intermediate exports, VS = vertical specialization.

Source: ADB Multi Region Input–Output Tables Database.

Table 3.7a: Vertical Specialization Index: Difference between 2014 and 2015 (percentage points)

Industries	PRC	INO	IND	JPN	KOR	TAP	BAN	MAL	PHI	THA	VIE	MON	SRI	BHU	BRU	CAM	FIJ	KAZ	KGZ	LAO	MLD	NEP	PAK
Agriculture, Hunting, Forestry, and Fishing	0	1	0	1	1	4	(1)	0	1	(0)	(3)	(1)	0	0	1	4	(0)	4	(0)	1	12	(0)	(0)
Air Transport	1	1	(1)	(2)	1	(1)	1	0	3	(2)	(7)	(9)	(1)	3	3	(1)	4	(2)	2	(4)	(4)	(0)	1
Basic Metals and Fabricated Metal	1	1	(3)	1	3	2	2	4	0	(2)	(4)	(6)	0	(0)	1	(0)	1	4	2	(9)	(15)	(2)	(0)
Chemicals and Chemical Products	1	1	(3)	4	0	4	3	1	8	(1)	(2)	(2)	6	(5)	1	1	1	8	(3)	(3)	–	(0)	(0)
Coke, Refined Petroleum, and Nuclear Fuel	3	1	(6)	2	2	2	(3)	3	2	(2)	(5)	(5)	1	–	2	(18)	(3)	11	(3)	(4)	(97)	(0)	1
Construction	1	1	(0)	1	1	1	(1)	0	(1)	(4)	(6)	(9)	(1)	4	2	(3)	(1)	1	3	(6)	(21)	(0)	(0)
Education	(0)	1	(0)	(0)	1	1	(0)	4	(0)	(1)	(2)	(2)	–	(7)	(0)	(6)	2	1	(0)	(0)	2	0	(0)
Electrical and Optical Equipment	1	1	(3)	3	2	1	4	2	(0)	(3)	(3)	(8)	(13)	(31)	0	0	(69)	2	0	(6)	(68)	(0)	3
Electricity, Gas, and Water Supply	2	1	0	(3)	(1)	0	(0)	0	(0)	(1)	(3)	(6)	(4)	(0)	3	(2)	3	4	(3)	(2)	11	1	(0)
Financial Intermediation	(1)	1	2	(0)	2	2	2	0	0	(1)	(2)	(3)	0	4	0	(0)	1	(4)	8	(0)	2	(0)	(0)
Food, Beverages, and Tobacco	(0)	1	(1)	1	1	4	4	1	2	(1)	(4)	(2)	3	3	0	2	0	3	(0)	11	(6)	(1)	(1)
Health and Social Work	0	1	(2)	(0)	1	1	(0)	4	1	(2)	(7)	(7)	(0)	(15)	1	5	0	3	(13)	(2)	1	0	(0)
Hotels and Restaurants	0	1	(1)	1	0	0	2	1	(0)	(1)	(5)	(6)	(0)	1	0	(2)	(0)	2	(0)	7	(5)	(0)	(0)
Inland Transport	0	1	(2)	(1)	0	0	(1)	(0)	3	(2)	(4)	(9)	(0)	1	0	(1)	(2)	(0)	1	(2)	(3)	(1)	0
Leather, Leather Products, and Footwear	0	1	(1)	(4)	3	3	(2)	4	(0)	(2)	(4)	(2)	(0)	1	4	(2)	0	(1)	(0)	1	18	0	(1)
Machinery, nec	1	1	(3)	2	1	2	2	3	0	(3)	(5)	(7)	(3)	(0)	0	(2)	1	(0)	(1)	(4)	–	3	1
Manufacturing, nec; Recycling	1	1	(2)	3	1	(0)	4	4	2	(1)	(2)	(6)	(5)	(3)	0	(1)	(0)	(3)	(1)	4	(8)	(1)	1
Mining and Quarrying	3	1	(1)	1	0	(0)	1	5	(1)	0	(2)	(6)	(1)	(4)	2	(1)	(1)	3	(1)	(2)	–	(0)	(0)
Other Community, Social, and Personal Services	(0)	1	(1)	(0)	2	2	3	1	(1)	(1)	(3)	(4)	(0)	6	2	2	1	(0)	1	3	16	(0)	(0)
Other Nonmetallic Mineral	1	1	(2)	0	1	0	(3)	4	4	1	(2)	(6)	3	(3)	5	(1)	(0)	8	0	(6)	(14)	(1)	(0)
Other Supporting and Auxiliary Transport Activities; Activities of Travel Agencies	0	1	(1)	(1)	2	(0)	(1)	0	(0)	(1)	(3)	(10)	–	4	0	(1)	(1)	1	1	(6)	(3)	(0)	(0)
Post and Telecommunications	(0)	1	(1)	(0)	2	2	2	2	0	(1)	(2)	(7)	(1)	4	2	(1)	(0)	1	1	0	(7)	(0)	(0)
Private Households with Employed Persons	–	1	–	–	–	–	–	–	–	–	–	–	–	–	–	–	–	–	–	–	–	–	–
Public Administration and Defense; Compulsory Social Security	(0)	1	(0)	(0)	1	1	(0)	2	1	1	(4)	(3)	–	3	1	(15)	(14)	2	0	1	(4)	(1)	(0)
Pulp, Paper, Paper Products, Printing, and Publishing	1	1	(3)	3	(0)	(1)	4	2	(2)	(0)	(3)	(8)	(9)	2	2	0	2	1	(1)	10	(9)	(1)	1
Real Estate Activities	0	1	2	0	1	1	(0)	1	0	(0)	(1)	(0)	(0)	(0)	3	(18)	(0)	0	(1)	0	(13)	(6)	0
Renting of M&Eq and Other Business Activities	0	1	(1)	(0)	1	1	(2)	4	0	(1)	(3)	(7)	(1)	3	0	(1)	(0)	1	(39)	(0)	21	(0)	(0)
Retail Trade, except of Motor Vehicles and Motorcycles; Repair of Household Goods	0	1	0	(0)	1	3	(0)	1	(0)	(0)	(1)	(5)	(0)	(3)	3	(1)	(2)	(0)	1	(2)	7	(0)	(0)
Rubber and Plastics	0	1	(3)	5	1	1	1	1	5	(2)	(2)	(5)	(1)	(1)	4	(2)	2	12	0	(5)	–	(0)	0
Sale, Maintenance, and Repair of Motor Vehicles and Motorcycles; Retail Sale of Fuel	–	1	1	(0)	1	3	(1)	0	(10)	(2)	(2)	(4)	(0)	1	1	(2)	(2)	(3)	(2)	(2)	12	(0)	(0)
Textiles and Textile Products	0	1	(1)	2	2	4	(1)	(1)	0	(1)	(4)	(7)	(0)	1	2	(1)	(0)	(3)	(0)	1	(9)	(1)	(1)
Transport Equipment	1	1	(3)	3	2	2	0	1	1	(3)	(4)	(8)	(12)	(31)	(1)	(1)	1	(8)	(1)	(10)	(13)	(1)	3
Water Transport	0	1	(3)	(2)	(0)	(6)	(3)	0	4	(2)	(7)	(10)	(2)	5	1	(1)	1	0	2	(4)	(3)	–	1
Wholesale Trade and Commission Trade, except of Motor Vehicles and Motorcycles	0	1	0	(1)	1	(0)	(0)	3	0	(1)	(2)	(5)	(0)	(3)	1	(1)	(2)	(1)	(1)	(1)	3	(0)	(0)
Wood and Products of Wood and Cork	1	1	(1)	1	1	(2)	4	2	2	(1)	(2)	(8)	5	1	2	(2)	0	1	(20)	10	(9)	(1)	1

– = magnitude equals zero, 0 = magnitude is less than half of unit employed, ( ) = indicates less than zero or negative; BAN = Bangladesh; BHU = Bhutan; BRU = Brunei Darussalam; CAM = Cambodia; FIJ = Fiji; IND = India; INO = Indonesia; JPN = Japan; KAZ = Kazakhstan; KGZ = Kyrgyz Republic; KOR = Republic of Korea; LAO = Lao People's Democratic Republic; MAL = Malaysia; MLD = Maldives; MON = Mongolia; NEP = Nepal; PAK = Pakistan; PHI = Philippines; PRC = People's Republic of China; SRI = Sri Lanka; TAP = Taipei,China; THA = Thailand; VIE = Viet Nam.

Source: ADB Multi Region Input–Output Tables Database.

Table 3.7b: Vertical Specialization Index: Difference between 2015 and 2016 (percentage points)

Industries	PRC	INO	IND	JPN	KOR	TAP	BAN	MAL	PHI	THA	VIE	MON	SRI	BHU	BRU	CAM	FIJ	KAZ	KGZ	LAO	MLD	NEP	PAK
Agriculture, Hunting, Forestry, and Fishing	1	0	1	(3)	1	(2)	(1)	1	2	(1)	1	0	1	1	1	(4)	(1)	2	4	(2)	(2)	0	1
Air Transport	0	(0)	3	(3)	(2)	0	(7)	(2)	(1)	(2)	4	1	(1)	1	0	0	(3)	4	0	(0)	1	0	(0)
Basic Metals and Fabricated Metal	1	(2)	3	(6)	(1)	(1)	(5)	(1)	6	(4)	(2)	4	0	5	(0)	(1)	(1)	2	2	(2)	1	2	1
Chemicals and Chemical Products	2	(2)	2	(9)	(3)	(1)	(5)	(1)	1	(3)	(2)	(1)	18	6	(2)	(2)	(1)	(4)	0	(3)	–	2	(0)
Coke, Refined Petroleum, and Nuclear Fuel	2	(2)	8	(4)	(2)	(0)	(9)	(1)	(1)	(1)	(0)	1	(19)	–	1	0	(7)	(3)	1	(3)	100	0	6
Construction	1	(0)	0	(3)	(2)	3	(3)	0	0	(4)	1	5	(0)	0	1	1	(0)	2	(2)	(3)	(1)	0	(1)
Education	(0)	(0)	0	(0)	2	1	(1)	(5)	(0)	(1)	1	0	1	8	3	5	(1)	3	0	(1)	(2)	0	(0)
Electrical and Optical Equipment	1	(1)	3	(7)	(2)	(0)	(6)	(2)	3	(3)	(3)	0	1	31	(1)	(1)	0	(1)	2	(0)	0	0	(0)
Electricity, Gas, and Water Supply	1	(0)	(4)	(5)	(3)	(1)	(2)	(1)	0	(2)	1	0	(1)	0	(4)	1	(0)	2	(0)	(2)	(0)	(1)	(0)
Financial Intermediation	0	(0)	(2)	(1)	2	(1)	(3)	(0)	0	(1)	1	0	(0)	(1)	4	(0)	(1)	1	(9)	(1)	(4)	0	(0)
Food, Beverages, and Tobacco	1	(0)	1	(3)	(1)	(3)	(5)	(1)	3	(2)	(0)	1	1	(0)	(1)	(5)	(2)	0	1	(4)	(0)	1	0
Health and Social Work	1	(0)	3	(2)	(2)	1	(1)	(4)	1	(2)	5	4	1	15	2	(4)	(0)	(3)	14	(2)	(1)	0	1
Hotels and Restaurants	0	(1)	4	(1)	(0)	(1)	(4)	(1)	1	(2)	2	0	1	(2)	2	1	(1)	1	1	(7)	0	0	(0)
Inland Transport	0	(0)	3	(2)	1	(0)	(1)	(1)	1	(2)	2	(0)	(1)	0	(1)	0	5	3	1	(4)	3	1	0
Leather, Leather Products, and Footwear	1	(2)	1	(1)	(1)	0	(2)	(5)	1	(2)	(0)	1	1	0	(17)	1	(1)	(7)	1	(5)	(1)	0	0
Machinery, nec	1	(1)	3	(6)	1	(0)	(7)	(1)	4	(3)	(2)	6	41	0	1	0	1	(2)	1	(0)	–	(3)	(1)
Manufacturing, nec; Recycling	1	(1)	1	(7)	1	(4)	(9)	(5)	0	(4)	0	3	(6)	1	3	1	(1)	(5)	1	(6)	2	1	1
Mining and Quarrying	2	(1)	1	(8)	(1)	1	(4)	(0)	1	(1)	1	1	(0)	0	2	(1)	(1)	4	1	(2)	–	0	0
Other Community, Social, and Personal Services	0	(0)	1	(1)	(1)	(2)	(3)	2	0	(2)	1	0	0	(3)	2	(1)	1	1	3	(5)	(1)	1	0
Other Nonmetallic Mineral	1	(1)	2	(5)	(2)	1	(2)	(0)	3	(5)	(1)	3	3	3	3	0	(1)	(4)	0	(1)	1	1	1
Other Supporting and Auxiliary Transport Activities; Activities of Travel Agencies	0	(0)	2	(2)	(0)	(1)	(3)	(2)	(0)	(1)	1	1	9	(5)	2	0	(1)	3	2	(0)	0	0	(0)
Post and Telecommunications	1	(0)	3	(1)	2	(1)	(3)	(5)	1	(1)	(1)	1	(2)	(1)	(4)	0	(0)	6	0	(3)	1	0	0
Private Households with Employed Persons	–	–	–	–	–	–	–	–	–	–	–	–	–	–	–	–	–	–	–	–	–	–	–
Public Administration and Defense; Compulsory Social Security	(0)	(0)	0	0	1	0	(3)	(1)	(0)	(1)	2	(3)	2	(1)	3	15	13	4	0	(2)	(0)	1	(0)
Pulp, Paper, Paper Products, Printing, and Publishing	3	(2)	4	(7)	(0)	1	(5)	(2)	1	(3)	(3)	4	1	2	2	(1)	(1)	(2)	3	(14)	1	0	(1)
Real Estate Activities	(0)	(0)	(2)	(0)	(1)	1	(1)	1	0	(0)	1	2	(0)	2	1	15	(0)	4	21	(1)	10	6	0
Renting of M&Eq and Other Business Activities	(0)	(0)	2	(1)	1	0	(2)	(2)	0	(2)	2	1	2	(3)	3	(1)	(0)	1	22	(2)	0	0	(0)
Retail Trade, except of Motor Vehicles and Motorcycles; Repair of Household Goods	0	(0)	0	(0)	2	(1)	(1)	(1)	1	(1)	0	1	0	2	(3)	3	(1)	4	0	(1)	(0)	0	(0)
Rubber and Plastics	1	(2)	3	(9)	(3)	(0)	(5)	(0)	1	(2)	(2)	3	3	5	2	1	(0)	(8)	0	(6)	–	1	(0)
Sale, Maintenance, and Repair of Motor Vehicles and Motorcycles; Retail Sale of Fuel	–	(0)	(1)	(4)	2	(2)	(2)	(1)	10	(2)	0	1	0	(5)	2	2	1	2	2	(2)	2	0	(0)
Textiles and Textile Products	1	(1)	2	(4)	(1)	(0)	(4)	(1)	1	(2)	(2)	3	1	(0)	(0)	0	(1)	(1)	4	(4)	1	1	(0)
Transport Equipment	1	(1)	4	(8)	(1)	(0)	(6)	(1)	3	(2)	(2)	0	1	31	0	0	3	(2)	1	(0)	2	3	(1)
Water Transport	0	(1)	7	(5)	(2)	(0)	(4)	(1)	(0)	(1)	4	7	(1)	(3)	2	0	(1)	2	2	(0)	0	–	(0)
Wholesale Trade and Commission Trade, except of Motor Vehicles and Motorcycles	0	(5)	0	(1)	2	(0)	(1)	(3)	1	(1)	1	1	(0)	0	2	2	(1)	3	1	(1)	(1)	0	0
Wood and Products of Wood and Cork	1	(3)	1	(4)	2	1	(4)	(2)	1	(2)	(3)	4	1	2	3	(0)	(2)	1	7	(9)	1	1	(1)

– = magnitude equals zero, 0 = magnitude is less than half of unit employed, ( ) = indicates less than zero or negative; BAN = Bangladesh; BHU = Bhutan; BRU = Brunei Darussalam; CAM = Cambodia; FIJ = Fiji; IND = India; INO = Indonesia; JPN = Japan; KAZ = Kazakhstan; KGZ = Kyrgyz Republic; KOR = Republic of Korea; LAO = Lao People's Democratic Republic; MAL = Malaysia; MLD = Maldives; MON = Mongolia; NEP = Nepal; PAK = Pakistan; PHI = Philippines; PRC = People's Republic of China; SRI = Sri Lanka; TAP = Taipei,China; THA = Thailand; VIE = Viet Nam.

Source: ADB Multi Region Input–Output Tables Database.

Definitions

This section contains the definitions of statistical indicators that are covered in Part I - Sustainable Development Goals (SDGs) and Part II - Regional Trends and Tables. The definitions are taken mostly from the Asian Development Bank's Development Indicators Reference Manual, including websites and publications of international and private organizations such as the Food and Agriculture Organization of the United Nations (FAO); International Labour Organization (ILO); International Monetary Fund (IMF); International Telecommunication Union (ITU); Organisation for Economic Co-operation and Development (OECD); Transparency International; United Nations Children's Fund (UNICEF); United Nations Educational, Scientific and Cultural Organization (UNESCO); United Nations Population Division (UNPD); United Nations Statistics Division (UNSD); World Bank; World Health Organization (WHO); and United Nations World Tourism Organization (UNWTO). The SDG indicators are arranged according to their respective goals and targets before they are defined, while the indicators for the Regional Trends and Tables are grouped according to their themes and subtopics before they are defined. In many instances, the indicators themselves, rather than their growth rates or ratios to another indicator, are defined.

Sustainable Development Goals

Goals and Targets	Statistical Indicators	Definition
Goal 1: End poverty in all its forms everywhere		
Target 1.1: By 2030, eradicate extreme poverty for all people everywhere, currently measured as people living on less than $1.90 a day.	1.1.1a Proportion of population below the international poverty line, by sex, age, employment status and geographical location (urban/rural)	Proportion of the population living on less than $1.90 a day, measured at 2011 international prices. Note: The $1.90-a-day poverty line is expressed in 2011 purchasing power parity terms. The PPP conversion factor for private consumption is the number of units of a country's currency required to buy the same amount of goods and services in the domestic market as a United States (US) dollar would buy in the US.
	1.1.1b Proportion of employed population below the international poverty line, by sex	Proportion of the employed population living in households with per capita consumption or income that is below the international poverty line at $1.90 a day. Note: The proportion of working poor in total employment (also known as the working poverty rate) combines data on household income or consumption with labor force framework variables measured at the individual level, and sheds light on the relationship between household poverty and employment. The numbers are modeled estimates by the International Labour Organization.
Target 1.2: By 2030, reduce at least by half the proportion of men, women and children of all ages living in poverty in all its dimensions according to national definitions.	1.2.1 Proportion of population living below the national poverty line, by sex, age, and geographical location (urban/rural)	Percentage of the total population living below the national poverty line. Note: National poverty rate is defined at country-specific poverty lines in local currencies, which are different in real terms across countries and different from the $1.90-a-day international poverty line. Thus, national poverty rates cannot be compared across countries or with the $1.90-a-day poverty rate.
Goal 2: End hunger, achieve food security and improved nutrition and promote sustainable agriculture		
Target 2.1: By 2030, end hunger and ensure access by all people, in particular the poor and people in vulnerable situations, including infants, to safe, nutritious and sufficient food all year round.	2.1.1 Prevalence of undernourishment	Proportion of the population whose habitual food consumption is insufficient to provide the dietary energy levels that are required to maintain a normal active and healthy life. Note: Undernourishment is defined as the condition by which a person has access, on a regular basis, to amounts of food that are insufficient to provide the energy required for conducting a normal, healthy and active life, given his or her own dietary energy requirements.

(continued on next page)

Goals and Targets	Statistical Indicators	Definition
Target 2.2: By 2030, end all forms of malnutrition, including achieving, by 2025, the internationally agreed targets on stunting and wasting in children under 5 years of age, and address the nutritional needs of adolescent girls, pregnant and lactating women and older persons.	2.2.1 Prevalence of stunting (height for age <–2 standard deviation from the median of the World Health Organization (WHO) Child Growth Standards) among children under 5 years of age	Prevalence of stunting (height-for-age <–2 standard deviation from the median of the WHO Child Growth Standards) among children under 5 years of age. Note: Stunting refers to the impaired growth and development that children experience from poor nutrition, repeated infection, and inadequate psychosocial stimulation.
	2.2.2.a Prevalence of malnutrition (weight for height <–2 standard deviation from the median of the WHO Child Growth Standards) among children under 5 years of age (wasting)	Prevalence of wasting (weight for height <–2 standard deviation from the median of the WHO Child Growth Standards) among children under 5 years of age.
	2.2.2.b Prevalence of malnutrition (weight for height >+2 standard deviation from the median of the WHO Child Growth Standards) among children under 5 years of age (overweight)	Prevalence of overweight (weight for height >+2 standard deviation from the median of the WHO Child Growth Standards) among children under 5 years of age.
Target 2.a: Increase investment, including through enhanced international cooperation, in rural infrastructure, agricultural research and extension services, technology development and plant and livestock gene banks in order to enhance agricultural productive capacity in developing countries, in particular least developed countries.	2.a.1 The agriculture orientation index for government expenditures	Agriculture share of government expenditures, divided by the agriculture share of gross domestic product, where agriculture refers to the agriculture, forestry, fishing, and hunting sector. The measure is a currency-free index, calculated as the ratio of these two shares.
	2.a.2 Total official flows (official development assistance plus other official flows) to the agriculture sector	Gross disbursements of total official development assistance (ODA) and other official flows (OOF) from all donors to the agriculture sector. Note: Total ODA and OOF to developing countries quantify the public effort (excluding export credits) that donors provide to developing countries for agriculture.
Goal 3: Ensure healthy lives and promote well-being for all at all ages		
Target 3.1: By 2030, reduce the global maternal mortality ratio to less than 70 per 100,000 live births.	3.1.1 Maternal mortality ratio	Number of maternal deaths during a given time period per 100,000 live births during the same time period. Note: Maternal deaths refer to the annual number of female deaths from any cause related to or aggravated by pregnancy or its management (excluding accidental or incidental causes) during pregnancy and childbirth, or within 42 days of termination of pregnancy, irrespective of the duration and site of the pregnancy, expressed per 100,000 live births, for a specified time period.
	3.1.2 Proportion of births attended by skilled health personnel	Percentage of deliveries attended by health personnel trained in providing life-saving obstetric care, including giving the necessary supervision, care, and advice to women during pregnancy, labor, and the postpartum period, conducting deliveries on their own, and caring for newborns. Traditional birth attendants, even if they receive a short training course, are not included. Note: Having a skilled attendant at the time of delivery is an important life-saving intervention for both mothers and babies. Not having access to this key assistance is detrimental to women's health and gender empowerment because it could cause the death of the mother or long- lasting disability, especially in marginalized settings.

(continued on next page)

Goals and Targets	Statistical Indicators	Definition
Target 3.2: By 2030, end preventable deaths of newborns and children under 5 years of age, with all countries aiming to reduce neonatal mortality to at least as low as 12 per 1,000 live births and under-5 mortality to at least as low as 25 per 1,000 live births.	3.2.1 Under-five mortality rate	Probability of a child born in a specific year or period dying before reaching the age of 5 years, if subject to age specific mortality rates of that period, expressed per 1,000 live births. Note: The under-five mortality rate as defined here is, strictly speaking, not a rate (i.e., the number of deaths divided by the number of population at risk during a certain period of time) but a probability of death derived from a life table and expressed as a rate per 1,000 live births.
	3.2.2 Neonatal mortality rate	The probability that a child born in a specific year or period will die during the first 28 completed days of life if subject to age-specific mortality rates of that period, expressed per 1,000 live births. Note: Neonatal deaths (deaths among live births during the first 28 completed days of life) may be subdivided into early neonatal deaths, occurring during the first 7 days of life, and late neonatal deaths, occurring after the 7th day but before the 28th completed day of life.
Target 3.3: By 2030, end the epidemics of AIDS, tuberculosis, malaria and neglected tropical diseases and combat hepatitis, water-borne diseases, and other communicable diseases.	3.3.1 Number of new HIV infections per 1,000 uninfected population, by sex, age and key populations	Number of new HIV infections per 1,000 person-years among the uninfected population.
	3.3.2 Tuberculosis incidence per 100,000 population	Estimated number of new and relapse tuberculosis cases (all forms of tuberculosis, including cases in people living with HIV) arising in a given year, expressed as a rate per 100,000 population.
	3.3.3 Malaria incidence per 1,000 population	Number of reported new cases of malaria per 1,000 people each year.
Target 3.4: By 2030, reduce by one third premature mortality from noncommunicable diseases through prevention and treatment and promote mental health and well-being.	3.4.1 Mortality rate attributed to cardiovascular disease, cancer, diabetes or chronic respiratory disease	Probability of dying between the ages of 30 and 70 years from cardiovascular diseases, cancer, diabetes, or chronic respiratory diseases, defined as the percentage of 30-year-old-people who would die before their 70th birthday from cardiovascular disease, cancer, diabetes, or chronic respiratory disease, assuming that he or she would experience current mortality rates at every age and would not die from any other cause of death (e.g., injuries or HIV/AIDS).
Target 3.6: By 2020, halve the number of global deaths and injuries from road traffic accidents.	3.6.1 Death rate due to road traffic injuries	Number of road traffic fatal injury deaths per 100,000 population.
Target 3.7: By 2030, ensure universal access to sexual and reproductive health-care services, including for family planning, information and education, and the integration of reproductive health into national strategies and programmes.	3.7.2 Adolescent birth rate (aged 15–19 years) per 1,000 women in that age group	Annual number of births to females aged 15–19 years per 1,000 females in the respective age group. Note: The adolescent birth rate among women aged 15–19 years is also referred to as the age-specific fertility rate for women aged 15–19.

(continued on next page)

Goals and Targets	Statistical Indicators	Definition
Target 3.9: By 2030, substantially reduce the number of deaths and illnesses from hazardous chemicals and air, water and soil pollution and contamination.	3.9.1 Mortality rate attributed to household and ambient air pollution	Expressed as number of deaths and death rate. Death rates are calculated by dividing the number of deaths by the total population (or indicated if a different population group is used, e.g., children under 5 years). Note: Evidence from epidemiological studies have shown that exposure to air pollution is linked, among others, to the important diseases taken into account in this estimate: - acute respiratory infections in young children (estimated under 5 years of age); - cerebrovascular diseases (stroke) in adults (estimated above 25 years); - ischaemic heart diseases in adults (estimated above 25 years); - chronic obstructive pulmonary disease (COPD) in adults (estimated above 25 years); and - lung cancer in adults (estimated above 25 years).
	3.9.2 Mortality rate attributed to unsafe water, unsafe sanitation and lack of hygiene (exposure to unsafe Water, Sanitation and Hygiene for All (WASH) services)	Number of deaths from unsafe water, unsafe sanitation, and lack of hygiene (exposure to unsafe WASH services) in a year, divided by the population, and multiplied by 100,000.
Goal 4: Ensure inclusive and equitable quality education and promote lifelong learning opportunities for all		
Target 4.1: By 2030, ensure that all girls and boys complete free, equitable and quality primary and secondary education leading to relevant and effective learning outcomes.	4.1.1 Proportion of children and young people: (a) at the end of primary; and (b) at the end of lower secondary achieving at least a minimum proficiency level in (i) reading and (ii) mathematics, by sex	Percentage of children and young people at the end of primary education and the end of lower secondary education achieving at least a minimum proficiency level in reading and mathematics. Note: The minimum proficiency level is measured relative to new common reading and mathematics scales currently in development. The actual SDG indicator is the proportion of children and young people (i) in grades 2 or 3; (ii) at the end or primary; and (iii) at the end of lower secondary school achieving at least a minimum proficiency level in reading and mathematics. This indicator is calculated as the percentage of children and/or young people at the relevant stage of education achieving or exceeding a predefined proficiency level in a given subject.
Target 4.2: By 2030, ensure that all girls and boys have access to quality early childhood development, care and pre-primary education so that they are ready for primary education.	4.2.2 Participation rate in organized learning (one year before the official primary entry age), by sex	Percentage of children in the given age range who participate in one or more organized learning programs, including programs that offer a combination of education and care. Note: An organized learning program is one that consists of a coherent set or sequence of educational activities designed with the intention of achieving predetermined learning outcomes or the accomplishment of a specific set of educational tasks. Early childhood and primary education programs are examples of organized learning programs. The official primary entry age is the age at which children are obliged to start primary education according to national legislation or policies.
Target 4.c: By 2030, substantially increase the supply of qualified teachers, including through international cooperation for teacher training in developing countries, especially least developed countries and small island developing States.	4.c.1.a Proportion of teachers in preprimary education who have received at least the minimum organized teacher training 4.c.1.b Proportion of teachers in primary education who have received at least the minimum organized teacher training 4.c.1.c Proportion of teachers in lower secondary education who have received at least the minimum organized teacher training 4.c.1.d Proportion of teachers in upper secondary education who have received at least the minimum organized teacher training	Percentage of teachers by level of education taught (preprimary, primary, lower secondary, and upper secondary education) who have received at least the minimum organized pedagogical teacher preservice and in-service training required for teaching at the relevant level in a given country. Number of teachers in a given level of education who are trained is expressed as a percentage of all teachers in that level of education. The percentage of trained teachers should not exceed 100%. When feasible, the number of part-time teachers should be converted to "full-time equivalent" numbers of teachers; a double-shift teacher should be counted twice, etc. Ideally, all staff involved in direct classroom-teaching roles should be included in the calculations.

(continued on next page)

Goals and Targets	Statistical Indicators	Definition
Goal 5: Achieve gender equality and empower all women and girls		
Target 5.3: Eliminate all harmful practices, such as child, early and forced marriage and female genital mutilation.	5.3.1 Proportion of women aged 20–24 years who were married or in a union before age 15 and before age 18	Proportion of women aged 20–24 years who were married or in a union by age 15 and by age 18. Note: Both formal (i.e., marriages) and informal unions are covered under this indicator. Informal unions are generally defined as those in which a couple lives together for some time, intends to have a lasting relationship, but for which there has been no formal civil or religious ceremony (i.e., cohabitation).
Target 5.5: Ensure women's full and effective participation and equal opportunities for leadership at all levels of decision-making in political, economic and public life.	5.5.1 Proportion of seats held by women in (a) national parliaments and (b) local governments	Number of seats held by women members in single or lower chambers of national parliaments, expressed as a percentage of all occupied seats. Note: National parliaments can be bicameral or unicameral. This indicator covers the single chamber in unicameral parliaments and the lower chamber in bicameral parliaments. It does not cover the upper chamber of bicameral parliaments. Seats are usually won by members in general parliamentary elections. Seats may also be filled by nomination, appointment, indirect election, rotation of members, and by election. Seats refer to the number of parliamentary mandates, or the number of members of parliament.
	5.5.2 Proportion of women in managerial positions	Proportion of females in the total number of persons employed in senior and middle management. Senior and middle management correspond to major group 1 in both ISCO-08 and ISCO-88, minus category 14 in ISCO-08 (hospitality, retail and other services managers) and minus category 13 in ISCO-88 (general managers), since these comprise mainly managers of small enterprises. Note: The indicator provides information on the proportion of women who are employed in decision making and management roles in government, large enterprises, and institutions, thus providing some insight into women's power in decision making and in the economy (especially compared to men's power in those areas).
Goal 6: Ensure availability and sustainable management of water and sanitation for all		
Target 6.1: By 2030, achieve universal and equitable access to safe and affordable drinking water for all.	6.1.1 Proportion of population using safely managed drinking water services	Proportion of population using an improved basic drinking water source that is located on premises, available when needed, and free of fecal (and priority chemical) contamination. Note: Improved drinking water sources include the following: piped water into dwelling, yard, or plot; public taps or standpipes; boreholes or tubewells; protected dug wells; protected springs; and rainwater. Packaged drinking water is considered improved if households use an improved water source for other domestic purposes. The WHO/UNICEF Joint Monitoring Programme for Water Supply and Sanitation (JMP) estimates access to basic services for each country, separately in urban and rural areas, by fitting a regression line to a series of data points from household surveys and censuses. This approach was used to report on use of "improved water" sources for Millennium Development Goal (MDG) monitoring. The JMP is evaluating the use of alternative statistical estimation methods as more data become available.
Target 6.2: By 2030, achieve access to adequate and equitable sanitation and hygiene for all and end open defecation, paying special attention to the needs of women and girls and those in vulnerable situations.	6.2.1 Proportion of population using safely managed sanitation services, including a hand-washing facility with soap and water	Proportion of the population using an improved basic sanitation facility at the household level, which is not shared with other households and where excreta is safely disposed in situ or treated off-site. Note: "Improved" source is as defined for MDG monitoring, i.e., flush or pour flush toilets to sewer systems, septic tanks, or pit latrines; ventilated improved pit latrines; pit latrines with a slab; and composting toilets. A handwashing facility is a device to contain, transport, or regulate the flow of water to facilitate handwashing.

(continued on next page)

Goals and Targets	Statistical Indicators	Definition
Target 6.4: By 2030, substantially increase water-use efficiency across all sectors and ensure sustainable withdrawals and supply of freshwater to address water scarcity and substantially reduce the number of people suffering from water scarcity.	6.4.2 Level of water stress: freshwater withdrawal as a proportion of available freshwater resources	Ratio between total freshwater withdrawn by all major sectors and total renewable freshwater resources, after taking into account environmental water requirements. Note: Total freshwater withdrawal is the volume of freshwater extracted from its source (rivers, lakes, aquifers) for agriculture, industries, and municipalities. Freshwater withdrawal includes primary freshwater (not withdrawn before); secondary freshwater (previously withdrawn and returned to rivers and groundwater, such as discharged wastewater and agricultural drainage water); and fossil groundwater. Main sectors, as defined by ISIC standards, include agriculture, forestry, and fishing; manufacturing; electricity industry; and services. Environmental water requirements are the quantities of water required to sustain freshwater and estuarine ecosystems. This indicator is also known as water withdrawal intensity.
Target 6.a: By 2030, expand international cooperation and capacity-building support to developing countries in water- and sanitation-related activities and programmes, including water harvesting, desalination, water efficiency, wastewater treatment, recycling and reuse technologies.	6.a.1 Amount of water- and sanitation-related official development assistance that is part of a government-coordinated spending plan	Proportion of total water and sanitation-related official development assistance (ODA) disbursements that are included in the government budget. Note: The amount of water and sanitation-related ODA is a quantifiable measurement as a proxy for "international cooperation and capacity development support" in financial terms. A low value of this indicator (near 0%) would suggest that international donors are investing in water- and sanitation-related activities and programs in the country outside the purview of the national government. A high value (near 100%) would indicate that donors are aligned with national government policies and plans for water and sanitation.
Goal 7: Ensure access to affordable, reliable, sustainable and modern energy for all		
Target 7.1: By 2030, ensure universal access to affordable, reliable and modern energy services.	7.1.1 Proportion of population with access to electricity	Percentage of the population with access to electricity. Access to electricity addresses major critical issues in all the dimensions of sustainable development. The target has a wide range of social and economic impacts, including facilitating development of household-based income generating activities and lightening the burden of household tasks.
	7.1.2 Proportion of population with primary reliance on clean fuels and technology	Number of people using clean fuels and technologies for cooking, heating, and lighting divided by total population reporting any cooking, heating, or lighting, expressed in percentage. "Clean" is defined by the emission rate targets and specific fuel recommendations (i.e., against unprocessed coal and kerosene) included in the normative guidance WHO guidelines for indoor air quality: household fuel combustion.
Target 7.2: By 2030, increase substantially the share of renewable energy in the global energy mix.	7.2.1 Renewable energy share in the total final energy consumption	Percentage of final consumption of energy that is derived from renewable resources. Note: Renewable energy consumption includes consumption of energy derived from: hydro, solid biofuels, wind, solar, liquid biofuels, biogas, geothermal, marine, and waste. Total final energy consumption is calculated from national balances and statistics as total final consumption minus non-energy use.
Target 7.3: By 2030, double the global rate of improvement in energy efficiency.	7.3.1 Energy intensity measured in terms of primary energy and GDP	The energy supplied to the economy per unit value of economic output. Energy supplied to the economy per unit value of economic output. Note: Total energy supply, as defined by the International Recommendations for Energy Statistics, is made up of production plus net imports minus international marine and aviation bunkers plus stock changes. Gross domestic product (GDP) is the measure of economic output. For international comparison purposes, GDP is measured in constant terms at purchasing power parity.
Goal 8: Promote sustained, inclusive and sustainable economic growth, full and productive employment and decent work for all		
Target 8.1: Sustain per capita economic growth in accordance with national circumstances and, in particular, at least 7 per cent gross domestic product growth per annum in the least developed countries.	8.1.1 Annual growth rate of real GDP per capita	Percentage change in the real GDP per capita between two consecutive years. Note: Real GDP per capita is calculated by dividing GDP at constant prices by the population of a country or area. The data for real GDP are measured in constant US dollars to facilitate the calculation of country growth rates and aggregation of the country data.

(continued on next page)

Goals and Targets	Statistical Indicators	Definition
Target 8.2: Achieve higher levels of economic productivity through diversification, technological upgrading and innovation, including through a focus on high-value added and labour-intensive sectors.	8.2.1 Annual growth rate of real GDP per employed person	Annual percentage change in real GDP per employed person.
Target 8.5: By 2030, achieve full and productive employment and decent work for all women and men, including for young people and persons with disabilities, and equal pay for work of equal value.	8.5.2 Unemployment rate, by sex and age	Percentage of persons in the labor force who are unemployed.
Target 8.6: By 2020, substantially reduce the proportion of youth not in employment, education or training.	8.6.1 Proportion of youth (aged 15–24 years) not in education, employment or training	Also known as "the NEET rate", expressed as a percentage of the total youth population.
Target 8.7: Take immediate and effective measures to eradicate forced labour, end modern slavery and human trafficking and secure the prohibition and elimination of the worst forms of child labour, including recruitment and use of child soldiers, and by 2025 end child labour in all its forms.	8.7.1 Proportion of children aged 5–17 years engaged in child labor	Number of children aged 5–17 years who are reported to have been engaged in child labor in the past week divided by the total number of children aged 5–17 in the population.
Target 8.10: Strengthen the capacity of domestic financial institutions to encourage and expand access to banking, insurance and financial services for all.	8.10.1 Number of commercial bank branches and automated teller machines (ATMs) per 100,000 adults	The number of commercial bank branches per 100,000 adults refers to the number of commercial banks branches per year reported by the Central Bank or the main financial regulator of the country. To make it comparable, this number is presented as a reference per 100,000 adults in the respective country. The number of ATMs per 100,000 adults, refers to the number of ATMs in the country for all types of institutions such as commercial banks, nondeposit-taking microfinance institutions, deposit-taking microfinance institutions, credit unions and financial cooperatives, etc. This information is reported every year by the central bank or the main financial regulator of the country. To make it comparable, this number is presented as a reference per 100,000 adults in the respective country.
	8.10.2 Proportion of adults (15 years and older) with an account at a bank or other financial institution or with a mobile-money-service provider	Percentage of adults (ages 15+) who report having an account (by themselves or together with someone else) at a bank or other type of financial institution or personally using a mobile money service in the past 12 months.
Goal 9: Build resilient infrastructure, promote inclusive and sustainable industrialization and foster innovation		
Target 9.1: Develop quality, reliable, sustainable and resilient infrastructure, including regional and trans-border infrastructure, to support economic development and human well-being, with a focus on affordable and equitable access for all.	9.1.2 Passenger volume, by road transport (thousand passenger kilometers) 9.1.2 Freight volume, by road transport (thousand ton kilometers) 9.1.2 Passenger volume, by air transport (thousand passenger kilometers) 9.1.2 Freight volume, by air transport (metric tons)	Passenger and freight volumes is the sum of the passenger and freight volumes reported for the air carriers in terms of number of people and metric tons of cargo, respectively. The International Transport Forum collects data on transport (rail and road) statistics on an annual basis from all its member countries. Data are collected from transport ministries, statistical offices, and other institutions designated as official data source. Although there are clear definitions for all the terms used in this survey, countries might have different methodologies to calculate ton-kilometers and passenger-kilometres. Methods could be based on traffic or mobility surveys, and may use very different sampling methods and estimating techniques that could affect the comparability of their statistics.

(continued on next page)

Goals and Targets	Statistical Indicators	Definition
Target 9.2: Promote inclusive and sustainable industrialization and, by 2030, significantly raise industry's share of employment and gross domestic product, in line with national circumstances, and double its share in least developed countries.	9.2.1 Manufacturing value added as a proportion of GDP and per capita	Manufacturing value added (MVA) as a proportion of gross domestic product (GDP) is a ratio between MVA and GDP, both reported in constant 2010 US dollars. MVA per capita is calculated by dividing MVA in constant 2010 US dollars by the population of a country or area.
	9.2.2 Manufacturing employment as a proportion of total employment	Share of manufacturing employment in total employment.
Target 9.3: By 2030, upgrade infrastructure and retrofit industries to make them sustainable, with increased resource-use efficiency and greater adoption of clean and environmentally sound technologies and industrial processes, with all countries taking action in accordance with their respective capabilities.	9.4.1 CO_2 emission per unit of value added	Carbon dioxide (CO_2) emissions per unit value added is an indicator computed as a ratio between CO_2 emissions from fuel combustion and the value added of associated economic activities. The indicator can be computed for the whole economy (total CO_2 emissions/GDP) or for specific sectors, notably the manufacturing sector (CO_2 emissions from manufacturing industries per MVA). CO_2 emissions per unit of GDP are expressed in kilograms of CO_2 per US dollar at constant 2010 purchasing power parity GDP. CO_2 emissions from manufacturing industries per unit of MVA are measured in kilograms of CO_2 equivalent per unit of MVA in constant 2010 US dollars.
Target 9.5: Enhance scientific research, upgrade the technological capabilities of industrial sectors in all countries, in particular developing countries, including, by 2030, encouraging innovation and substantially increasing the number of research and development workers per 1 million people and public and private research and development spending.	9.5.1 Research and development expenditure as a proportion of GDP	Amount of research and development (R&D) expenditure divided by the total output of the economy.
	9.5.2 Researchers (in full-time equivalent) per million inhabitants	Number of R&D workers per 1 million people.
Target 9.a: Facilitate sustainable and resilient infrastructure development in developing countries through enhanced financial, technological and technical support to African countries, least developed countries, landlocked developing countries and small island developing States.	9.a.1 Total official international support (official development assistance plus other official flows) to infrastructure	Gross disbursements of total official development assistance and other official flows from all donors in support of infrastructure.
Target 9.b: Support domestic technology development, research and innovation in developing countries, including by ensuring a conducive policy environment for, inter alia, industrial diversification and value addition to commodities.	9.b.1 Proportion of medium and high-tech industry value added in total value added	Proportion of medium- and high-technology industry (MHT) value added in total MVA. Note: Industrial development generally entails a structural transition from resource-based and low technology activities to MHT activities. A modern, highly complex production structure offers better opportunities for skills development and technological innovation. MHT activities are also the high value addition industries of manufacturing with higher technological intensity and labor productivity. Increasing the share of MHT sectors also reflects the impact of innovation.

(continued on next page)

Goals and Targets	Statistical Indicators	Definition
Target 9.c: Significantly increase access to information and communications technology and strive to provide universal and affordable access to the Internet in least developed countries by 2020.	9.c.1 Proportion of population covered by a mobile network, by technology	Percentage of inhabitants living within range of a mobile cellular signal, irrespective whether they are mobile phone subscribers or users. This is calculated by dividing the number of inhabitants within range of a mobile cellular signal by the total population and multiplying by 100. Note: Coverage refer to (i) LTE, (ii) broadband (3G), and (iii) narrowband (2G) mobile-cellular technologies. (i) 2G mobile population coverage refers to the percentage of inhabitants within range of a mobile network with access to data communications (e.g., internet) at downstream speeds below 256 Kbit/s. This includes mobile cellular technologies such as GPRS, CDMA2000 1x and most EDGE implementations. (ii) 3G population coverage refers to the percentage of inhabitants that are within range of at least a 3G mobile-cellular signal, irrespective whether or not they are subscribers. (iii) LTE population coverage refers to the percentage of inhabitants that live within range of LTE/LTE-Advanced, mobile WiMAX/WirelessMAN, or other more advanced mobile cellular networks, irrespective whether or not they are subscribers.
Goal 10: Reduce inequality within and among countries		
Target 10.1: By 2030, progressively achieve and sustain income growth of the bottom 40 per cent of the population at a rate higher than the national average.	10.1.1.a Growth rates of household expenditure or income per capita among the bottom 40% of the population	The growth rate in the welfare aggregate of the bottom 40% is computed as the annualized average growth rate in per capita real consumption or income of the bottom 40% of the income distribution in a country using household surveys over a roughly 5-year period.
	10.1.1.b Growth rates of household expenditure or income per capita	The national average growth rate in the welfare aggregate is computed as the annualized average growth rate in per capita real consumption or income of the total population in a country using household surveys over roughly a 5-year period.
Goal 11: Make cities and human settlements inclusive, safe, resilient and sustainable		
Target 11.1: By 2030, ensure access for all to adequate, safe and affordable housing and basic services and upgrade slums.	11.1.1: Proportion of urban population living in slums, informal settlements or inadequate housing	Proportion of urban population living in slums, informal settlements, or inadequate housing is currently being measured by the proportion of urban population living in slums. This indicator integrates the component of the slums and informal settlements that has been monitored for the last 15 years by UN-Habitat in mostly developing countries with a new component—inadequate housing—that applies largely to the developed countries. By integrating these two components, the indicator is now universal and can be monitored in both developing and developed regions. The inadequate housing component allows capturing housing informality in more developed countries and wealthier urban contexts.
Target 11.6: By 2030, reduce the adverse per capita environmental impact of cities, including by paying special attention to air quality and municipal and other waste management.	11.6.2 Annual mean levels of fine particulate matter (e.g., PM2.5 and PM10) in cities (population weighted)	The mean annual concentration of fine suspended particles of less than 2.5 microns in diameter (PM2.5) is a common measure of air pollution. Note: The mean is a population-weighted average for urban population in a country, and is expressed in micrograms per cubic meter (µg/m^3).
Goal 12: Ensure sustainable consumption and production patterns		
Target 12.2: By 2030, achieve the sustainable management and efficient use of natural resources.	12.2.1 Material footprint, material footprint per capita, and material footprint per GDP	Material footprint is the attribution of global material extraction to domestic final demand of a country. The total material footprint is the sum of the material footprint for biomass, fossil fuels, metal ores, and nonmetal ores.
	12.2.2 Domestic material consumption, domestic material consumption per capita, and domestic material consumption per GDP	Domestic material consumption (DMC) is a standard material flow accounting (MFA) indicator and reports the apparent consumption of materials in a national economy.

(continued on next page)

Goals and Targets	Statistical Indicators	Definition
Goal 13: Take urgent action to combat climate change and its impacts		
Target 13.1: Strengthen resilience and adaptive capacity to climate-related hazards and natural disasters in all countries.	13.1.2 Number of countries that adopt and implement national disaster risk reduction strategies in line with the Sendai Framework for Disaster Risk Reduction 2015–2030	Note: An open-ended intergovernmental expert working group on indicators and terminology relating to disaster risk reduction established by the General Assembly (resolution 69/284) is developing a set of indicators to measure global progress in the implementation of the Sendai Framework. These indicators will eventually reflect the agreements on the Sendai Framework indicators.
Goal 14: Conserve and sustainably use the oceans, seas and marine resources for sustainable development		
Target 14.5: By 2020, conserve at least 10 per cent of coastal and marine areas, consistent with national and international law and based on the best available scientific information.	14.5.1 Coverage of protected areas in relation to marine areas	The indicator coverage of protected areas in relation to marine areas shows temporal trends in the mean percentage of important sites for marine biodiversity (i.e., those that contribute significantly to the global persistence of biodiversity) that are wholly covered by designated protected areas.
Goal 15: Protect, restore and promote sustainable use of terrestrial ecosystems, sustainably manage forests, combat desertification, and halt and reverse land degradation and halt biodiversity loss		
Target 15.1: By 2020, ensure the conservation, restoration and sustainable use of terrestrial and inland freshwater ecosystems and their services, in particular forests, wetlands, mountains and drylands, in line with obligations under international agreements.	15.1.1 Forest area as a proportion of total land area	Size of forest cover in relation to total land area.
Target 15.5: Take urgent and significant action to reduce the degradation of natural habitats, halt the loss of biodiversity and, by 2020, protect and prevent the extinction of threatened species.	15.5.1 Red List Index	The Red List Index measures change in aggregate extinction risk across groups of species. It is based on genuine changes in the number of species in each category of extinction risk on the IUCN Red List of Threatened Species (IUCN 2015), which is expressed as changes in an index ranging from 0 to 1. Note: The Red List Index value ranges from 1 (all species are categorized as "Least Concern") to 0 (all species are categorized as "Extinct"), and thus indicates how far the set of species has moved overall toward extinction.
Goal 16: Promote peaceful and inclusive societies for sustainable development, provide access to justice for all and build effective, accountable and inclusive institutions at all levels		
Targets 16.1: Significantly reduce all forms of violence and related death rates everywhere.	16.1.1 Number of victims of intentional homicide (per 100,000 population)	Total count of victims of intentional homicide divided by the total population, expressed per 100,000 population. Intentional homicide is defined as the unlawful death inflicted upon a person with the intent to cause death or serious injury (International Classification of Crime for Statistical Purposes 2015); population refers to total resident population in a given country in a given year. Note: This indicator is widely used at national and international levels to measure the most extreme form of violent crime, and also provides a direct indication of lack of security.
Target 16.3: Promote the rule of law at the national and international levels and ensure equal access to justice for all.	16.3.2 Unsentenced detainees as a proportion of overall prison population	Total number of persons held in detention who have not yet been sentenced, as a percentage of the total number of persons held in detention, on a specified date.

(continued on next page)

Goals and Targets	Statistical Indicators	Definition
Target 16.5: Substantially reduce corruption and bribery in all their forms.	16.5.2 Proportion of businesses that had at least one contact with a public official and that paid a bribe to a public official, or were asked for a bribe by those public officials during the previous 12 months	Proportion of firms that asked for a gift or informal payment when meeting with tax officials. Note: This indicator aims to ascertain whether firms were solicited for gifts or informal payments (i.e., bribes) when meeting with tax officials. Paying taxes are required in most countries and hence the rational for this indicator is to measure the incidence of corruption during this routine interaction.
Target 16.9: By 2030, provide legal identity for all, including birth registration.	16.9.1 Proportion of children under 5 years of age whose births have been registered with a civil authority, by age	Proportion of children under 5 years of age whose births have been registered with a civil authority.
Goal 17: Strengthen the means of implementation and revitalize the Global Partnership for Sustainable Development		
Target 17.9: Enhance international support for implementing effective and targeted capacity-building in developing countries to support national plans to implement all the Sustainable Development Goals, including through North–South, South–South and triangular cooperation.	17.9.1 Dollar value of financial and technical assistance (including through North–South, South–South and triangular cooperation) committed to developing countries	Gross disbursements of total official development assistance (ODA) and other official flows from all donors for capacity building and national planning. Note: ODA refers to those flows to countries and territories on the DAC List of ODA Recipients and to multilateral institutions, which are (i) provided by official agencies, including state and local governments, or by their executive agencies; (ii) where each transaction is administered with the promotion of the economic development and welfare of developing countries as its main objective; and (iii) is concessional in character and conveys a grant element of at least 25% (calculated at a rate of discount of 10%). Other official flows (excluding officially supported export credits) are defined as transactions by the official sector that do not meet the conditions for eligibility as ODA, either because they are not primarily aimed at development, or because they are not sufficiently concessional.
Target 17.18: By 2020, enhance capacity-building support to developing countries, including for least developed countries and small island developing States, to increase significantly the availability of high-quality, timely and reliable data disaggregated by income, gender, age, race, ethnicity, migratory status, disability, geographic location and other characteristics relevant in national contexts.	17.18.3 Number of countries with a national statistical plan that is fully funded and under implementation, by source of funding	Count of countries that are either (i) implementing a strategy, (ii) designing one, or (iii) awaiting adoption of the strategy in the current year. Note: The indicator is based on the annual Status Report on National Strategies for the Development of Statistics. In collaboration with its partners, PARIS21 reports on country progress in designing and implementing national statistical plans. This indicator can be disaggregated by geographical area. Regional-level aggregates are based on the total count of national strategies.
Target 17.19: By 2030, build on existing initiatives to develop measurements of progress on sustainable development that complement gross domestic product, and support statistical capacity-building in developing countries.	17.19.1 Dollar value of all resources made available to strengthen statistical capacity in developing countries	Ongoing statistical support in developing countries, expressed in US dollars. Note: The indictor is based on the Partner Report on Support to Statistics designed and administered by PARIS21 to provide a snapshot of the US dollar value of ongoing statistical support in developing countries.
	17.19.2 Number of countries that have conducted at least one population and housing census in the last 10 years	This includes countries that compile their detailed population and housing statistics from population registers, administrative records, sample surveys, other sources, or a combination of those sources.

Regional Trends and Tables

Indicator	Definition
PEOPLE	
Population	
Midyear Population	Estimates of the midyear defacto population. Defacto population includes all persons physically present in the country during the census day, including foreign, military, and diplomatic personnel and their accompanying household members; and transient foreign visitors in the country or in harbors.
Growth Rates in Population	Number of people added to (or subtracted from) a population over a given period of time because of natural increase and net migration expressed as a percentage of the population at the given period of time.
Net International Migration Rate	Number of immigrants minus the specified number of emigrants over a period, divided by the person-years lived by the population of the receiving country over that period. It is expressed as net number of migrants per 1,000 population.
Urban Population	Population living in urban areas, defined in accordance with the national definition or as used in the most recent population census. Because of national differences in the characteristics that distinguish urban from rural areas, the distinction between urban and rural populations is not amenable to a single definition that would be applicable to all countries. National definitions are most commonly based on size of locality. Population that is not urban is considered rural.
Urban Population (as % of total population)	The estimated population living in urban areas at midyear as a percentage of the total midyear population in a country.
Age Dependency Ratio	Ratio of the nonworking-age population to the working-age population. Since countries define working age differently, a straightforward application of the definition will lead to noncomparable data. ADB therefore uses the following UN definition that can be computed directly from an age distribution: $\frac{\text{Population aged (0–14) + (65 and over) years x 100}}{\text{Population aged (15–64) years}}$
Labor Force and Employment	
Labor Force Participation Rate	Percentage of the labor force to the working-age population. The labor force is the sum of those employed and unemployed seeking work. The labor force participation rate measures the extent of economically active working-age population in an economy. It provides an indication of the relative size of the supply of labor available for the production of goods and services in the economy. It must be noted that the definition of working-age population varies across countries.
Employment in Agriculture, Forestry, and Fishing	Employment in agriculture, forestry, and fishing that corresponds to division 1 (International Standard of Industrial Classification [ISIC] revision 2), tabulation categories A and B (ISIC revision 3), and category A of ISIC revision 4.
Employment in Mining and Quarrying	Employment in mining and quarrying that corresponds to division 2 (ISIC revision 2), tabulation category C (ISIC revision 3), and category B of ISIC revision 4.
Employment in Manufacturing	Employment in manufacturing that corresponds to division 3 (ISIC revision 2), tabulation category D (ISIC revision 3), and category C of ISIC revision 4.
Employment in Electricity, Gas, Steam, and Air-Conditioning Supply; Water Supply; Sewerage, Waste Management and Remediation Activities	Employment in electricity, gas, steam and air conditioning supply; water supply, sewerage, waste management and remediation activities that corresponds to division 4 (ISIC revision 2), tabulation category E (ISIC revision 3), and categories D and E of ISIC revision 4.
Employment in Construction	Employment in construction that corresponds to division 5 (ISIC revision 2), tabulation category F (ISIC revisions 3), and category F of ISIC revision 4.
Employment in Wholesale and Retail Trade; Repair of Motor Vehicles and Motorcycles	Employment in wholesale and retail trade; repair of motor vehicles and motorcycles that corresponds to division 6 (subdivisions 61 and 62, ISIC revision 2); tabulation category G (ISIC revision 3); and category G of ISIC revision 4.
Employment in Accommodation and Food Service Activities	Employment in accommodation and food service activities that corresponds to division 6 (subdivision 63, ISIC revision 2); tabulation category H (ISIC revision 3); and category I of ISIC revision 4.

(continued on next page)

Indicator	Definition
Employment in Transportation and Storage	Employment in transport and storage that corresponds to division 7 (subdivision 71, ISIC revision 2); tabulation category I (subcategories 60–63, ISIC revision 3); and category H of ISIC revision 4.
Employment in Information and Communication	Employment in information and communication that corresponds to division 7 (subdivision 72, ISIC revision 2); tabulation category I (subcategory 64, ISIC revision 3); and category J of ISIC revision 4.
Employment in Financial and Insurance Activities	Employment in financial and insurance activities that corresponds to division 8 (subdivisions 81–82, ISIC revision 2), tabulation category J (ISIC revision 3), and category K of ISIC revision 4.
Employment in Real Estate Activities	Employment in real estate activities that corresponds to division 8 (subdivision 83, ISIC revision 2); tabulation category K (subcategory 70, ISIC revision 3); and category L of ISIC revision 4.
Employment in Other Services	Employment in other services that corresponds to divisions 9 and 0 (ISIC revision 2), tabulation categories L to Q (ISIC revision 3), and categories M to U of ISIC revision 4.
Poverty Indicators	
Proportion of Population Living below $3.10 a day (2011 PPP)	Percentage of the population living on less than $3.10 a day at 2011 purchasing power parity (PPP).
Income Ratio of Highest 20% to Lowest 20%	Income or consumption share that accrues to the richest 20% of the population divided by the income share of the lowest 20% of the population.
Gini Coefficient or Index	Measure of the degree to which an economy's income distribution diverges from perfect equal distribution. A value of zero (0) implies perfect equality while a value of one (1) implies perfect inequality.
Human Development Index	Composite index of long and healthy life (measured by life expectancy at birth), knowledge (measured by expected years of schooling and mean years of schooling), and decent standard of living (measured by gross national income per capita in PPP US dollars).
Social Indicators	
Life Expectancy at Birth	Number of years that a newborn is expected to live if prevailing patterns of mortality at the time of his or her birth are to stay the same throughout his or her life.
Crude Birth Rate	Ratio of the total number of live births in a given period to the midyear total population of the same period, expressed per 1,000 people.
Crude Death Rate	Ratio of the number of deaths occurring within a given period to the midyear total population of the same period, expressed per 1,000 people.
Total Fertility Rate	Number of children that would be born to a woman if she were to live to the end of her childbearing years and bear children in accordance with current age-specific fertility rates.
Primary Education Completion Rate	Total number of new entrants in the last grade of primary education, regardless of age, expressed as percentage of the total population of the theoretical entrance age to the last grade of primary. This indicator is also known as "gross intake rate to the last grade of primary." The ratio can exceed 100% due to overaged and underaged children who enter primary school late, early, and/or repeat grades.
Adult Literacy Rate	The percentage of population aged 15 years and over who can both read and write with understanding a short simple statement on his or her everyday life. Generally, literacy also encompasses numeracy, the ability to make simple arithmetic calculations.
Primary Pupil–Teacher Ratio	Average number of pupils (students) per teacher at the primary level of education in a given school year. This indicator is used to measure the level of human resources input in terms of number of teachers in relation to the size of the primary pupil population.
Secondary Pupil–Teacher Ratio	Average number of pupils (students) per teacher at the secondary level of education in a given school year. This indicator is used to measure the level of human resources input in terms of number of teachers in relation to the size of the secondary pupil population.
Physicians	Physicians, including generalist and specialist medical practitioners, expressed in terms of 1,000 people.
Hospital Beds	In-patient beds for both acute and chronic care available in public, private, general, and specialized hospitals and rehabilitation centers expressed in terms of 1,000 people.
Number of Adults Living with HIV	All adults, defined as men and women aged 15 and over years old, with HIV infection, whether or not they have developed symptoms of AIDS.

(continued on next page)

Indicator	Definition
ECONOMY AND OUTPUT	
National Accounts	
Gross Domestic Product	Unduplicated market value of the total production activity of all resident producer units within the economic territory of a country during a given period. It is calculated without making deductions for depreciation of fabricated assets or for depletion and degradation of natural resources. Transfer payments are excluded from the calculation of gross domestic product (GDP). GDP can be computed using the production, expenditure, and income approaches. Production-based GDP is the sum of the gross value added by all resident producers in the economy plus any taxes and minus any subsidies not included in the value of the products. Gross value added is the net output of an industry after adding up all outputs and subtracting intermediate inputs. Income-based GDP is the sum of the compensation of employees, mixed income, operating surplus, consumption of fixed capital, and taxes less subsidies on production and imports. Expenditure-based GDP is the sum of final consumption expenditure of households, nonprofit institutions serving households, and the government; gross capital formation; and exports minus imports of goods and services. GDP can be measured at current prices (the prices of the current reporting period), and constant prices (obtained by expressing values in terms of a base period and chain volume measure).
GDP at PPP	Measures obtained by using PPP to convert the GDP into a common currency, and by valuing them at a uniform price level. They are the spatial equivalent of a time series of GDP for a single country expressed at constant prices. At the level of GDP, they are used to compare the economic size of countries.
GDP per Capita at PPP	GDP at PPP divided by the midyear population.
GNI per Capita, Atlas Method	The gross national income (GNI) converted to US dollars using the World Bank Atlas method, divided by the midyear population. GNI is the sum of value added by all resident producers plus any product taxes (less subsidies) not included in the valuation of output plus net receipts of primary income (compensation of employees and property income) from abroad. GNI, calculated in national currency, is usually converted to US dollars at official exchange rates for comparisons across economies, although an alternative rate is used when the official exchange rate is judged to diverge by an exceptionally large margin from the rate actually applied in international transactions. To smooth fluctuations in prices and exchange rates, a special Atlas method of conversion is used by the World Bank. This applies a conversion factor that averages the exchange rate for a given year and the two preceding years, adjusted for differences in rates of inflation between the country, and the G-5 countries (France, Germany, Japan, the United Kingdom, and the United States).
Agriculture Value Added	The gross output of agriculture less the corresponding value of intermediate consumption. The industrial origin of value added is determined by ISIC revision 4 where agriculture corresponds to ISIC Section A and includes agriculture, forestry, and fishing.
Industry Value Added	The gross output of industry sectors less the corresponding value of intermediate consumption. The industrial origin of value added is determined by ISIC revision 4 where industry corresponds to ISIC Sections B-F and includes mining and quarrying (B); manufacturing (C); electricity, gas steam and air conditioning supply (D); water supply, sewage waste management, and remediation activities (E); and construction (F).
Services Value Added	The gross output of services sectors less the corresponding value of intermediate consumption. The industrial origin of value added is determined by ISIC revision 4. Services corresponds to ISIC Sections G-U and includes wholesale and retail trade, repair of motor vehicles and motorcycles (G); transport and storage (H); accommodation and food service activities (I); information and communication (J); financial and insurance activities (K); real estate activities (L); professional, scientific, and technical activities (M); administrative and support service activities (N); public administration and defense, compulsory social security (O); education (P); human health and social work activities (Q); arts, entertainment, and recreation (R); other service activities (S); activities of households as employers, undifferentiated goods, and services-producing activities of households for own use (T); and activities of extraterritorial organizations and bodies (U).

(continued on next page)

Indicator	Definition
Household Consumption Expenditure	Market value of all goods and services, including durable products (such as cars, washing machines, and home computers), purchased or received as income in kind by households. It excludes purchases of dwellings but includes imputed rent for owner-occupied dwellings. It also includes payments and fees to governments to obtain permits and licenses. The expenditure of nonprofit institutions serving households is generally recorded as the consumption of households for most economies.
Government Consumption Expenditure	Includes all current outlays on purchases of goods and services (including wages and salaries). It also includes most expenditure on national defense and security, but excludes government military expenditures that are part of public investment.
Gross Capital Formation	Total value of gross fixed capital formation, changes in inventories, and acquisitions less disposals of valuables. Gross fixed capital formation is the value of acquisitions less disposals of tangible goods such as buildings and intangible goods such as computer software that are intended for use in production during several accounting periods. Changes in inventories are changes in stocks of produced goods and goods for intermediate consumption, and the net increase in the value of work in progress. Valuables are goods such as precious metals and works of art that are acquired in the expectation that they will retain or increase their value over time.
Exports of Goods and Services	Consist of sales, barter, or gifts or grants, of goods and services from residents to nonresidents. The treatment of exports in the System of National Accounts is generally identical with that in the balance of payments accounts as described in the *Balance of Payments Manual*.
Imports of Goods and Services	Consist of purchases, barter, or receipts of gifts or grants, of goods and services by residents from nonresidents. The treatment of imports in the System of National Accounts is generally identical with that in the balance of payments accounts as described in the *Balance of Payments Manual*.
Gross Domestic Saving	Difference between GDP and final consumption expenditure, where final consumption expenditure is the sum of the final consumption of household, nonprofit institutions serving households, and the government.
Production	
Agriculture Production Index	Relative level of the aggregate volume of agricultural production for each year in comparison with the base period. It is based on the sum of price-weighted quantities of different agricultural commodities produced after deductions of quantities used as seed and feed weighted in a similar manner. The resulting aggregate represents, therefore, disposable production for any use except as seed and feed.
Manufacturing Production Index	An index covering production in manufacturing. The exact coverage, the weighting system, and the methods of calculation vary from country to country but the divergences are less important than, for example, in the case of price and wage indexes.
MONEY, FINANCE, AND PRICES	
Prices	
Consumer Price Index	An index that measures changes in prices against a reference period of a basket of goods and services purchased by households. Based on the purpose of the consumer price index, a different basket of goods and services can be selected. For macroeconomic purposes, a broad-based basket is used to represent the relative price movement of household final consumption expenditure.
Food Consumer Price Index	An index that measures the change over time in the general level of prices of food and nonalcoholic beverage items that households acquire, use, or pay for consumption. This is done by measuring the cost of purchasing a fixed basket of consumer food and beverage of constant quality and similar characteristics, with the products in the basket being selected to be representative of households' expenditure during a specified period.
Nonfood Consumer Price Index	An index that measures the change over time, in general level, the prices of nonfood items that households acquire, use, or pay for consumption. Nonfood index includes items such as clothing, housing and repairs, water, electricity, fuel, services and miscellaneous goods or all items in the basket of goods and services other than food and nonalcoholic beverages.
Wholesale Price Index	A measure that reflects changes in the prices paid for goods at various stages of distribution up to the point of retail. It can include prices of raw materials for intermediate and final consumption, prices of intermediate or unfinished goods, and prices of finished goods. The goods are usually valued at purchasers' prices.

(continued on next page)

Indicator	Definition
Producer Price Index	A measure of the change in the prices of goods and services either as they leave their place of production or as they enter the production process. A measure of the change in the prices received by domestic producers for their outputs or of the change in the prices paid by domestic producers for their intermediate inputs.
GDP Deflator	A measure of the annual rate of price change in the economy as a whole for the period shown obtained by dividing GDP at current prices by GDP at constant prices.
Money and Finance	
Money Supply	Refers to total amount of money in circulation in a specific country. Money supply can be measured in different ways: M1 (Narrow Money) is a measure of money supply that includes all coins and notes (M0) as well as personal money in current accounts. M2 (Intermediate Money) is the sum of M1 and personal money in deposit accounts. M3 (Broad Money) is the sum of M2 and government and other deposits. According to the Organization for Economic Co-operation and Development, M3 includes currency, deposits with an agreed maturity of up to 2 years, deposits redeemable at notice of up to 3 months and repurchase agreements, money market fund shares or units, and debt securities up to 2 years. Not all countries publish the same types of aggregates, and even when aggregates have the same name (e.g., M1, M2, M3, etc.) their asset composition often differs significantly. Cross-country differences in national definitions of lowered-ordered aggregates also arise from differences in the maturity categories of nontransferable deposits included in a particular money aggregate. For example, the definition of M2 in one country may include time deposits with maturities of 1 year or less, whereas another country's M2 definition may include time deposits with maturities of 2 years or less. When the monetary policy strategy consists of monetary aggregate targeting, the choice of the definition of the targeted aggregate is guided mainly by two considerations. The aggregate should be sufficiently sensitive to interest rate changes for the central bank to be able to control it and display a stable relationship over time to the movement of the overall price level.
Interest Rate on Savings Deposits	Rate paid by commercial and similar banks for savings deposits.
Interest Rate on Time Deposits	Rate paid by commercial and similar banks for time deposits.
Lending Interest Rate	Bank rate that usually meets the short- and medium-term financing needs of the private sector. This rate is normally differentiated according to creditworthiness of borrowers and objectives of financing.
Yield on Short-Term Treasury Bills	Rate at which short-term securities are issued or traded in the market.
Domestic Credit Provided by Banking Sector	Includes all credits to various sectors on a gross basis, except credit to the central government, which is net. The banking sector includes monetary authorities, deposit money banks, and other banking institutions for which data are available (including institutions that do not accept transferable deposits but do incur such liabilities as time and savings deposits). Examples of other banking institutions are savings and mortgage loan institutions and building and loan associations.
Ratio of Bank Nonperforming Loans to Total Gross Loans	Value of nonperforming loans divided by the total value of the loan portfolio (including nonperforming loans before the deduction of loan loss provisions). The amount recorded as nonperforming should be the gross value of the loan as recorded in the balance sheet, not just the amount that is overdue.
Stock Market Price Index	Index that measures changes in the prices of stocks traded in the stock exchange. The price changes of the stocks are usually weighted by their market capitalization.
Stock Market Capitalization	The share price times the number of shares outstanding (also known as market value).
Exchange Rates	
Official Exchange Rate	The exchange rate determined by national authorities or the rate determined in the legally sanctioned exchange market. It is calculated as an annual average based on the monthly averages (local currency units relative to the US dollar).
Purchasing Power Parity Conversion Factor	Number of units of country B's currency that are needed in country B to purchase the same quantity of an individual good or service, which one unit of country A's currency can purchase in country A.

(continued on next page)

Indicator	Definition
Price Level Index	Ratio of the relevant PPP to the exchange rate. It is expressed as an index on a base of 100. A price level index (PLI) greater than 100 is an indication that when the national average prices are converted at exchange rates, the resulting prices tend to be higher on average than prices in the base country (or countries) of the region (and vice versa). At the level of GDP, PLIs provide a measure of the differences in the general price levels of countries. PLIs are also referred to as comparative price levels.
GLOBALIZATION	
Balance of Payments	
Trade in Goods Balance	Difference between exports and imports of goods.
Trade in Services Balance	Difference between exports and imports of services.
Current Account Balance	Sum of net exports of goods, services, net income, and net current transfers.
Workers' Remittances and Compensation of Employees, Receipts	Consist of (i) Current transfers from migrant workers who are residents of the host country to recipients in their country of origin. To count as resident, the workers must have been living in the host country for more than a year. (ii) Compensation of employees of migrants who have lived in the host country for less than a year. (iii) Migrants' transfers defined as the net worth of migrants who are expected to remain in the host country for more than 1 year and which is transferred from one country to another at the time of migration.
Foreign Direct Investment	Refers to net inflows of investment to acquire a lasting management interest (10% or more of voting stock) in an enterprise operating in an economy other than that of the investor. It is the sum of equity capital, reinvestment of earnings, other long-term capital, and short-term capital as shown in the balance of payments.
External Trade	
Merchandise Exports or Imports	Covers all movable goods, with a few specified exceptions, the ownership of which changes between a resident and a foreigner. For merchandise exports, it represents the value of the goods and related distributive services at the customs frontier of the exporting economy, i.e., the free-on-board value. Merchandise imports, on the other hand, are reported in cost, insurance, and freight values.
Trade in Goods	Sum of merchandise exports and merchandise imports.
International Reserves	
International Reserves	External assets that are readily available to and controlled by monetary authorities for meeting balance of payments financing needs, for intervention in exchange markets to affect the currency exchange rate, and for other related purposes (such as maintaining confidence in the currency and the economy, and serving as a basis for foreign borrowing). Consist of monetary gold, special drawing rights (SDR) holdings, reserve position in the International Monetary Fund (IMF), currency and deposits, securities (including debt and equity securities), financial derivatives, and other claims (loans and other financial instruments).
Ratio of International Reserves to Imports	International reserves outstanding at the end of the year as a ratio to imports of goods from the balance of payments during the year, where imports of goods are expressed in terms of monthly average. It is a useful measure for reserve needs of countries with limited access to capital markets.
Capital Flows	
Official Flows	Flows of official financing administered with the promotion of the economic development and welfare of developing countries as the main objective, and which are concessional in character with a grant element of at least 25% (using a fixed 10% rate of discount). By convention, ODA flows comprise contributions of donor government agencies, at all levels, to developing countries ("bilateral ODA") and to multilateral institutions. ODA receipts comprise disbursements by bilateral donors and multilateral institutions. Lending by export credit agencies—with the pure purpose of export promotion—is excluded.

(continued on next page)

Indicator	Definition
Net Private Flows	Sum of direct investment, portfolio investment, and private net export credits of Development Assistance Committee economies only. Direct investment is a category of international investment made by a resident entity in one economy (direct investor) with the objective of establishing a lasting interest in an enterprise resident in an economy other than that of the investor (direct investment enterprise). "Lasting interest" implies the existence of a long-term relationship between the direct investor and the enterprise and a significant degree of influence by the direct investor on the management of the direct investment enterprise. Direct investment involves both the initial transaction between the two entities and all subsequent capital transactions between them and among affiliated enterprises, both incorporated and unincorporated. Portfolio investment is the category of international investment that covers investment in equity and debt securities, excluding any such instruments that are classified as direct investment or reserve assets.
Aggregate Net Resource Flows	Sum of net official and private capital flows. Net flow is disbursements less principal repayments.
External Indebtedness	
Total External Debt	Debt owed to nonresidents repayable in currency, goods, or services. It is the sum of public, publicly guaranteed, and private nonguaranteed long-term debt, use of IMF credit, and short-term debt. Short-term debt includes all debt having an original maturity of 1 year or less and interest in arrears on long-term debt.
Public and Publicly Guaranteed Debt	Public and publicly guaranteed debt comprises long-term external obligations of public debtors, including the national government, political subdivisions (or an agency of either), and autonomous public bodies, and external obligations of private debtors that are guaranteed for repayment by a public entity.
External Debt as Percent of Gross National Income	Total external debt as a percentage of gross national income (GNI). GNI is the sum of value added by all resident producers plus any product taxes (less subsidies) not included in the valuation of output plus net receipts of primary income (compensation of employees and property income) from abroad.
External Debt as Percent of Exports of Goods and Services and Primary Income	Total external debt as a percentage of exports of goods, services, and income. Exports of goods, services, and primary income constitute the total value of exports of goods and services, receipts of compensation of nonresident workers, and investment income from abroad.
Total Debt Service Paid	The sum of principal repayments and interest actually paid in currency, goods, or services on long-term debt, interest paid on short-term debt, and repayments (repurchases and charges) to the IMF.
Total Debt Service Paid as Percent of Exports of Goods and Services and Primary Income	Total debt service as a percentage of exports of goods, services, and primary income.
Tourism	
International Tourist Arrivals	The number of tourists (overnight visitors) who travel to a country other than in which they usually reside, and outside their usual environment, for a period not exceeding 12 months and whose main purpose of visit is other than the activity remunerated from within the country visited. In some cases, data may also include same-day visitors when data on overnight visitors are not available separately. Data refer to the number of arrivals and not to the number of persons.
International Tourism, Receipts	The receipts earned by a destination country from inbound tourism and covering all tourism receipts resulting from expenditures made by visitors from abroad. These include lodging, food and drinks, fuel, transport in the country, entertainment, shopping, etc. This concept includes receipts generated by overnight as well as by same-day trips. It excludes, however, the receipts related to international transport contracted by residents of the other countries (for instance ticket receipts from foreigners travelling with a national company).

(continued on next page)

Indicator	Definition
TRANSPORT AND COMMUNICATIONS	
Transport	
Road Traffic Deaths	Death caused by a road traffic crash within 24 hours (Azerbaijan, the Federated States of Micronesia, Solomon Islands, Timor-Leste, Vanuatu); 7 days (Afghanistan, the People's Republic of China, Kiribati, Tajikistan, Viet Nam); 30 days (Australia, Bhutan, Brunei Darussalam, Cambodia, Georgia, Indonesia, Kazakhstan, the Republic of Korea, Malaysia, Maldives, the Marshall Islands, Myanmar, New Zealand, Pakistan, Singapore, Sri Lanka); 35 days in Nepal; 1 year (Japan, the Kyrgyz Republic, the Lao People's Democratic Republic, Mongolia, Tonga); unlimited time period (Armenia, Bangladesh, the Cook Islands, India, Palau, the Philippines, Thailand); no definition for other countries.
Road Network	The road network refers to the Asian Highway that consists of highway routes of international importance within Asia, including highway routes substantially crossing more than one subregion; highway routes within subregions that connect neighboring subregions; and highway routes located within member states that provide access to (i) capital cities; (ii) main industrial and agricultural centers; (iii) major air, sea, and river ports; (iv) major container terminals and depots; and (v) major tourist attractions.
Motor Vehicles	Include cars, buses, freight vehicles, and two- and three-wheeled vehicles.
Container Port Traffic	Port container traffic measures the flow of containers from land to sea transport modes, and vice versa, in twenty-foot equivalent units, or a standard-size container. Data refer to coastal shipping as well as international journeys. Transshipment traffic is counted as two lifts at the intermediate port (once to off-load and again as an outbound lift) and includes empty units.
Air Transport, Passengers Carried	Air passengers carried include both domestic and international aircraft passengers of air carriers registered in the country.
Air Transport, Carrier Departures Worldwide	Registered carrier departures worldwide are domestic takeoffs and takeoffs abroad of air carriers registered in the country.
Air Transport, Freight	Air freight is the volume of freight, express, and diplomatic bags carried on each flight stage (operation of an aircraft from takeoff to its next landing), measured in metric tons times kilometers traveled.
Rail Lines	Rail lines are the length of railway route available for train service, irrespective of the number of parallel tracks.
Rail Network	Length of rail lines divided by the land area (in square kilometers).
Railways, Passengers Carried	Passengers carried by railway are the number of passengers transported by rail times kilometers traveled.
Railways, Goods Transported	Goods transported by railway are the volume of goods transported by railway, measured in metric tons times kilometers traveled.
Communications	
Telephone Subscribers	Fixed telephone subscriptions refer to the sum of active number of analogue fixed telephone lines, voice over internet protocol subscriptions, fixed wireless local loop subscriptions, Integrated Services Digital Network voice-channel equivalents, and fixed public payphones.
Mobile Phone Subscribers	Proportion of individuals who used a mobile telephone in the last 3 months. A mobile (cellular) telephone refers to a portable telephone subscribing to a public mobile telephone service using cellular technology, which provides access to the public switched telephone network. This includes analogue and digital cellular systems and technologies such as IMT-2000 (3G) and IMT- Advanced. Users of both postpaid subscriptions and prepaid accounts are included.
Fixed-broadband Subscribers	Fixed broadband subscriptions refer to fixed subscriptions to high-speed access to the public internet (a TCP/IP connection), at downstream speeds equal to, or greater than, 256 kbit/s. This includes cable modem, DSL, fiber-to-the-home/building, other fixed (wired)-broadband subscriptions, satellite broadband and terrestrial fixed wireless broadband. This total is measured irrespective of the method of payment. It excludes subscriptions that have access to data communications (including the Internet) via mobile cellular networks. It should include fixed WiMAX and any other fixed wireless technologies. It includes both residential subscriptions and subscriptions for organizations.

(continued on next page)

Indicator	Definition
Internet Users	This is the frequency of internet use by individuals who used the internet from any location in the last 3 months. The internet is a worldwide public computer network. It provides access to a number of communication services including the World Wide Web and carries e-mail, news, entertainment and data files, irrespective of the device used (not assumed to be only via a computer—it may also be by mobile telephone, tablet, PDA, games machine, digital TV etc.). Access can be via a fixed or mobile network.
ENERGY AND ELECTRICITY	
Energy	
GDP per Unit of Energy Use	The ratio of GDP to total energy use (measured in terms of per kilogram of oil equivalent) with GDP converted to 2011 constant international dollars using PPP rates. An international dollar has the same purchasing power over GDP as a US dollar has in the United States.
Energy Production	Forms of primary energy—petroleum (crude oil, natural gas liquids, and oil from nonconventional sources); natural gas; solid fuels (coal, lignite, and other derived fuels); and combustible renewables and waste—and primary electricity, all converted into oil equivalents. Primary electricity is electricity generated by nuclear, hydroelectric, wind, and solar power.
Energy Use	Usage of primary energy before its transformation to other end-use fuels, which is equal to indigenous production plus imports and stock changes, minus exports and fuels supplied to ships and aircraft engaged in international transport.
Energy Imports, Net	Energy imports, net estimated as energy use less production, both measured in oil equivalents.
Electricity	
Electricity Production	Total amount of electricity generated by a power plant. It includes own-use electricity, as well as transmission and distribution losses.
Sources of Electricity	Electricity is produced as primary as well as secondary energy. Primary electricity is obtained from natural sources such as hydroelectric, wind, solar, tide, and wave power. Secondary electricity is produced from the heat of nuclear fission of nuclear fuels, from geothermal heat and solar thermal heat, and by burning primary combustible fuels such as coal, natural gas, oil and renewables and wastes. After electricity is produced, it is distributed to final consumers through national or international transmission and distribution grids.
Electric Power Consumption Per Capita	Measure of the production of power plants and combined heat and power plants less transmission, distribution, and transformation losses and own use by heat and power plants, divided by midyear population.
Household Electrification Rate	Percentage of households with an electricity connection.
ENVIRONMENT	
Land	
Agricultural Land or Area	Land area that is arable, under permanent crops, and under permanent meadows and pastures.
Arable Land	Land under temporary agricultural crops (multiple-cropped areas are counted only once), temporary meadows for mowing or pasture, land under market and kitchen gardens and land temporarily fallow (less than 5 years). The abandoned land resulting from shifting cultivation is not included. Data for arable land are not meant to indicate the amount of land that are potentially cultivable.
Permanent Cropland	Land cultivated with long-term crops that do not have to be replanted for several years (such as cocoa and coffee); land under trees and shrubs producing flowers, such as roses and jasmine; and nurseries (except those for forest trees, which should be classified under "forest"). Permanent meadows and pastures are excluded from land under permanent crops.
Deforestation Rate	Rate of permanent conversion of natural forest area into other uses, including shifting cultivation, permanent agriculture, ranching, settlements, and infrastructure development. Deforested areas do not include areas logged but intended for regeneration or areas degraded by fuel wood gathering, acid precipitation, or forest fires. A negative rate indicates reforestation or increase in forest area.

(continued on next page)

Indicator	Definition
Pollution	
Carbon Dioxide Emissions	Carbon dioxide emissions, largely by-products of energy production and use, account for the largest share of greenhouse gases, which are associated with global warming. Anthropogenic carbon dioxide emissions result primarily from fossil fuel combustion and cement manufacturing. In combustion, different fossil fuels release different amounts of carbon dioxide for the same level of energy use: oil releases about 50% more carbon dioxide than natural gas, and coal releases about twice as much. Cement manufacturing releases about half a metric ton of carbon dioxide for each metric ton of cement produced. Data for carbon dioxide emissions include gases from the burning of fossil fuels and cement manufacture, but excludes emissions from land use such as deforestation.
Nitrous Oxide Emissions	Nitrous oxide emissions are mainly from fossil fuel combustion, fertilizers, rainforest fires, and animal waste. Nitrous oxide is a powerful greenhouse gas, with an estimated atmospheric lifetime of 114 years, compared with 12 years for methane. The per kilogram global warming potential of nitrous oxide is nearly 310 times that of carbon dioxide within 100 years.
Methane Emissions	Methane omissions are those stemming from human activities such as agriculture and from industrial methane production. A kilogram of methane is 21 times as effective at trapping heat in the earth's atmosphere as a kilogram of carbon dioxide within 100 years.
Other Greenhouse Gases	By-product emissions of hydrofluorocarbons, perfluorocarbons, and sulfur hexafluoride.
Freshwater	
Internal Renewable Water Resources	Internal renewable water resources (IRWR) refer to long-term average annual flow of rivers and recharge of aquifers generated from endogenous precipitation. Double counting of surface water and groundwater resources is avoided by deducting the overlap from the sum of the surface water and groundwater resources. IRWR in billion cubic meters per year refers to surface water produced internally plus groundwater produced internally deducted by the overlap between surface water and groundwater. IRWR in cubic meter per inhabitant per year is calculated as total annual internal renewable water resources divided by total population.
Annual Freshwater Withdrawals	Sum of surface water withdrawal and groundwater withdrawal. Total water withdrawal summed by sector deducted by: desalinated water produced, direct use of treated wastewater, and direct use of agricultural drainage water.
Water Productivity	Water productivity is the ratio of the net benefits from crop, forestry, fishery, livestock, and mixed agricultural systems to the amount of water used to produce those benefits. It is calculated as GDP in constant US dollar prices divided by annual total water withdrawal.
GOVERNMENT AND GOVERNANCE	
Government Finance	
Fiscal Balance	Difference between total revenue (including grants) and total expenditure (including net lending). This provides a picture of the overall financial position of the government. When the difference is positive, then the fiscal position is in surplus; otherwise, it is in deficit.
Tax Revenue	Compulsory transfers to the central government for public purposes. Certain compulsory transfers such as fines, penalties, and most social security contributions are excluded. Refunds and corrections of erroneously collected tax revenue are treated as negative revenue.
Total Government Revenue	Includes current and capital revenues. Current revenue is the revenue accruing from taxes, as well as all current nontax revenues except transfers received from foreign governments and international institutions. Major items of nontax revenue include receipts from government enterprises, rents and royalties, fees and fines, forfeits, private donations, and repayments of loans properly defined as components of net lending. Capital revenue constitutes the proceeds from the sale of nonfinancial capital assets.
Total Government Expenditure	Sum of current and capital expenditures. Current expenditure comprises purchases of goods and services by the central government, transfers to noncentral government units and to households, subsidies to producers, and interest on public debt. Capital expenditure, on the other hand, covers outlays for the acquisition or construction of capital assets and for the purchase of intangible assets, as well as capital transfers to domestic and foreign recipients. Loans and advances for capital purposes are also included.

(continued on next page)

Indicator	Definition
Government Expenditure on Education	Consists of expenditure by government to provide education services at all levels.
Government Expenditure on Health	Consists of expenditure by government to provide medical products, appliances, and equipment; outpatient services; hospital services; public health services; among others.
Government Expenditure on Social Security and Welfare	Consists of expenditure by government to provide benefits in cash or in kind to persons who are sick, fully or partially disabled, of old age, survivors, or unemployed, among others.
Governance	
Cost of Business Start-Up Procedure	Cost to register a business normalized by presenting it as a percentage of GNI per capita. It includes all official fees and fees for legal or professional services if such services are required by law. Fees for purchasing and legalizing company books are included if these transactions are required by law. Although value added tax registration can be counted as a separate procedure, value added tax is not part of the incorporation cost. The company law, the commercial code, and specific regulations and fee schedules are used as sources for calculating costs. In the absence of fee schedules, a government officer's estimate is taken as an official source. In the absence of a government officer's estimate, estimates of incorporation lawyers are used. If several incorporation lawyers provide different estimates, the median reported value is applied. In all cases, the cost excludes bribes.
Time Required to Start a Business	Number of calendar days needed to complete the procedures to legally operate a business. If a procedure can be speeded up at additional cost, the fastest procedure, independent of cost, is chosen.
Corruption Perceptions Index	The Corruption Perceptions Index ranks countries and territories based on how corrupt their public sector is perceived to be. It is a composite index—a combination of polls—drawing on corruption-related data collected by a variety of reputable institutions. The index reflects the views of observers from around the world, including experts living and working in the countries and territories evaluated. From 2000 to 2011, score ranges from 10 (highly clean) to 0 (highly corrupt). Starting 2012, computation of the score used an updated methodology and is now presented on a 100 (very clean) to 0 (highly corrupt) scale. Scores from 2011 and previous years should not be compared with scores from 2012 onward due to differences in methodology. A country's rank indicates its position relative to the other countries or territories included in the index. It is important to keep in mind that a country's rank can change simply because new countries enter the index or others drop out.